Expert One-on-One™ Visual Basic® 2005 Database Programming

Expert One-on-One™ Visual Basic® 2005 Database Programming

Roger Jennings

Wiley Publishing, Inc.

Expert One-on-One™ Visual Basic® 2005 Database Programming

Published by
Wiley Publishing, Inc.
10475 Crosspoint Boulevard
Indianapolis, IN 46256
www.wiley.com

Copyright © 2006 by Wiley Publishing, Inc., Indianapolis, Indiana

Published simultaneously in Canada

ISBN-13: 978-0-7645-7678-2
ISBN-10: 0-7645-7678-X

Printed in the United States of America

Manufactured in the United States of America

10 9 8 7 6 5 4 3 2 1

1B/TQ/RR/QV/IN

About the Author

Roger Jennings

Roger Jennings is an author and consultant specializing in Microsoft Visual Basic .NET n-tier and client/server database applications, and data-intensive ASP.NET Web services. He's been a member of the beta test team for all versions of Visual Basic starting with the Professional Extensions for Visual Basic 2.0 (code-named Rawhide) and Visual Studio, all releases of Microsoft SQL Server starting with version 4.2 for OS/2, every version of Microsoft Access, and all Windows client and server operating systems beginning with the Windows 3.0 Multimedia Extensions.

Roger's 25 computer-oriented books have more than 1.25 million English copies in print and have been translated into more than 20 languages. He's the author of three editions of Database Developer's Guide to Visual Basic (SAMS Publishing), two editions of Access Developer's Guide (SAMS), nine editions of Special Edition Using Microsoft Access (QUE Publishing), and two editions of Special Edition Using Windows NT 4.0 Server (QUE). He has also written developer-oriented books about Windows 3.1 multimedia, Windows 95, Windows 2000 Server, Active Directory Group Policy, Visual Basic .NET Web services, and Microsoft Office InfoPath 2003 SP-1. Roger is a contributing editor of Fawcette Technical Publications' Visual Studio Magazine and a columnist for Fawcette's .NETInsight and XML & Web Services Insight newsletters.

Roger has more than 25 years of computer-related experience, beginning with real-time medical data acquisition and chemical process control systems driven by Wang 700 calculators/computers. He is a principal of OakLeaf Systems, a Northern California software consulting firm, the developer of the OakLeaf XML Web Services site (www.oakleaf.ws/), and author of the OakLeaf Systems weblog (oakleafblog.blogspot.com). His OakLeaf Code of Federal Regulations (CFR) ASP.NET Web service and client (www.oakleaf.ws/cfr/) projects won the charter Microsoft .NET Best Award for Horizontal Solutions (www.microsoft.com/presspass/features/2002/aug02/08-07netwinners.mspx). You can reach Roger at Roger_Jennings@compuserve.com.

Credits

Executive Editor
Robert Elliott

Development Editor
Adaobi Obi Tulton

Technical Editor
Thomas Rizzo

Production Editor
Pamela Hanley

Copy Editor
Nancy Rapoport

Editorial Manager
Mary Beth Wakefield

Production Manager
Tim Tate

Vice President & Executive Group Publisher
Richard Swadley

Vice President and Publisher
Joseph B. Wikert

Quality Control Technicians
Leeann Harney
Jessica Kramer
Joe Niesen

Project Coordinator
Michael Kruzil

Graphics and Production Specialists
Carrie Foster
Denny Hager
Barbara Moore
Alicia B. South

Proofreading and Indexing
TECHBOOKS Production Services

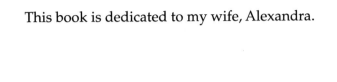

This book is dedicated to my wife, Alexandra.

Contents

Contents

Contents

Part III: Data Binding in ASP.NET 2.0   263

Chapter 7: Working with ASP.NET 2.0 DataSources and Bound Controls   265

Contents

Contents

Contents

Acknowledgments

Many thanks to Tom Rizzo, this book's technical editor, for corrections and suggestions as the chapters progressed through alpha, beta, and Community Technical Preview releases of VS 2005 and SQL Server 2005. Tom is Microsoft's Director for SQL Server Product Management, and he's a regular speaker on SQL Server topics at Microsoft Tech*Ed and Professional Developer Conferences, as well as Fawcette's VSLive! and SQLLive! conferences. Any technical gaffes, errors, or omissions that remain rest squarely on my shoulders.

Joe Wikert, Wiley Technical Publishing's Vice President and Publisher, and Executive Editor Bob Elliott convinced me to take on this challenging project. Adaobi Obi Tulton, Senior Development Editor, made sure that chapters didn't slip too far behind schedules that changed as estimated release-to-manufacturing (RTM) dates for VS 2005 and SQL Server 2005 came and went. Pamela Hanley, Production Editor, fixed many grammatical lapses. I appreciate their contributions, as well as those of all others in the production process, to the book's completion.

Introduction

It's a reasonably safe bet that more than 80% of Visual Basic 6.0 projects written since Microsoft released the product on June 15, 1998 involve connections to one or more relational databases. Access 1.0 introduced the Joint Engine Technology (Jet) indexed sequential access method (ISAM) database and Embedded Basic, the forerunner of Visual Basic for Applications (VBA), in 1992. Access 1.0 and 1.1 enabled rapid application development (RAD) for Jet, as well as SQL Server 4.2 and other client/server database front ends that had Open Database Connectivity (ODBC) drivers. Visual Basic 3.0 introduced databinding and the first databound grid control in 1993, which resulted in a flood of books and magazine articles devoted to VB database programming with SQL and ODBC. Visual Basic 4.0 introduced 32-bit projects but wasn't a robust development platform. 1995's Visual Basic 5.0 added ActiveX Data Objects (ADO) 1.0 and OLE DB. VB and VBA became the world's most popular programming languages with an estimated three million users. By 1998 most professional VB6 developers were writing production-grade Windows front ends for client/server databases and began to adopt Microsoft Transaction Server 1.0 for three-tier, distributed data access architectures. Developers wrote billions of lines of data-intensive VB code during the following four years.

The arrival of Visual Studio .NET in 2002 sounded the death knell for upgrades to COM-based VB and VBA. Visual Basic 6.0 has migrated to the maintenance-mode purgatory reserved for legacy development platforms. Microsoft announced that mainstream support for VB6 would end on March 31, 2005 and extended (paid) support will terminate in 2008. In early March 2005, a group of Microsoft Most-Valued Professionals (MVPs) organized a petition drive ". . . to include an updated version of VB6 inside the Visual Studio IDE." By mid-March, more than 200 past and present MVPs had endorsed the petition. Computer press coverage of the petition evoked innumerable blog entries that supported or opposed VB or VBA's reincarnation as unmanaged "VB.COM." The probability that Microsoft will ultimately adopt the petitioners' recommendations is miniscule, at best, and probably zero. "Managed code" is the Microsoft mantra for the foreseeable future. VB programmers who don't upgrade their skill set will be marginalized to the application lifecycle maintenance phase—or worse. If you haven't yet adopted the .NET Framework and managed VB code for new data-intensive projects, this book and its sample code and project examples are what you need to become a proficient VB 2005 database programmer.

Another issue facing VB developers is the perception of "second-class citizen" status compared to that of (Visual) C# developers. Rumors of VB's decreasing usage as a result of developer defections to C# or Java have been greatly exaggerated. VB 2005 is a remarkably complete and compatible implementation of the traditional, easily readable VB syntax. VS 2002/2003's VB dialects lacked many of C#'s language features, and the majority of managed code examples emanating from Redmond have been written in C#. Microsoft developers' preference for C# is understandable because most have years of C++ and JScript programming experience. VB 2005 gains increasing parity with C# by adding partial classes, operator overloading, generics, mathematical operations and type converters for unsigned `Integer` and `Long` data types, the `Using` keyword for intrinsic object disposal, and XML comments. There are few C# programming constructs that aren't available to VB 2005 programmers, and C# lacks the convenience of VB 2005's new `My` namespace and historical `With. . .End With` structures. This book contains detailed examples of new VB 2005 language constructs and features that pertain to data-intensive applications.

Visual Studio and Visual Basic Express Edition 2005 (VBX) enhance drag-and-drop generation of typed `DataSet` objects as partial classes with the Data Sources window, the `TableAdapter` wrapper for `DataAdapter` objects, and the TableAdapter Configuration Wizard. Dragging a table icon from the Data Sources window to a Windows form automatically adds your choice of bound text boxes or a DataGridView control, which replaces the much-maligned GridView. The `BindingSource` object connects the DataSource to bound controls, and the BindingNavigator—a pre-built ToolStrip control—handles row navigation. Web forms enable dragging table icons from Server explorer to generate new GridView and other databound controls. A new DataSet designer replaces VS 2002/2003's XML schema editor. Chapters 1, 2, and 7 show you how to build usable master-child Windows and Web forms from a sample database in less than five minutes without writing a line of code. The remaining chapters show you how to customize and extend the capabilities of bound and unbound controls with event-handling code.

Online help for Visual Studio 2005 suffers from a shortfall of non-trivial Windows and Web forms code examples for data-intensive projects. Most sample code in the help files generates console projects, which are ill suited to data-intensive applications. You won't find a single console project in the more than 100MB—20MB zipped—of downloadable data-centric sample projects for this book. The project examples emulate simple to moderately complex, real-world database front-end applications with Windows and Web forms.

Who This Book Is For

This book is intended for experienced VB programmers who are upgrading from VB6 or VS 2002/2003 to VB 2005. Basic familiarity with the VS 2005 integrated development environment (IDE) is assumed. However, no prior VB6, VBA, or VBScript database programming experience is necessary, except for Chapter 1, "Migrating from ADO to ADO.NET." Some experience with writing Microsoft Transact-SQL (T-SQL) statements and authoring simple stored procedures is expected. Familiarity with XML 1.0 and XML schemas will aid your understanding of DataSets and SQL Server 2005's new `xml` datatype. Some experience with writing XPath 1.0 expressions will be helpful to get the most benefit from Chapter 12, "Exploring the xml Datatype."

What This Book Covers

One-on-One Expert Visual Basic 2005 Database Programming concentrates on programming the .NET Framework 2.0's `System.Data` namespace, which implements ADO.NET 2.0 and related namespaces, such as `System.Transactions` and `System.Xml`. The book isn't a new user's guide to the .NET Framework, VS 2005, VBX, or VB 2005; it's devoted entirely to data-related topics.

Many code and project examples in the early chapters retrieve and update table data directly with customized `SqlConnection`, `SqlCommand`, and `SqlDataReader` objects. Later chapters' examples use strongly typed DataSets that are filled by TableAdapters and display data in bound text boxes, DataGridViews, and dropdown lists.

SQL Server 2000, MSDE 2000, SQL Server 2005, or SQL Server 2005 Express (SQLX) can serve as the data source for the code and sample projects of the book's Parts I through III. Most examples in these parts can be modified to run with Access 2000 or later .mdb files with the native OleDbproviders. Part IV covers important new features of SQL Server 2005 and SQLX. Thus, the T-SQL and VB 2005 code of Part IV's chapters requires SQL Server 2005 or SQLX. SQLX is missing some new SQL Server 2005 functions, so you'll need SQL Server 2005 Developer Edition or higher to get the most out of Part IV.

How This Book Is Structured

This book is divided into four parts of three chapters each. Most chapters build on the knowledge you've gained from preceding chapters. Thus, it's recommended that you work your way through the chapters sequentially. Following is a brief description of the parts and their chapters' contents.

Part I: ADO.NET 2.0 Basics

The chapters in Part I serve as an introduction to ADO.NET 2.0 for VB6 developers moving to VS 2005 or VBX and VS 2003/2004 developers adopting new VS 2005 data-related features.

❑ **Chapter 1**, Migrating from ADO to ADO.NET, introduces you to the members of the .NET Framework 2.0's System.Data namespace. The chapter then explains the similarities and differences between COM-based ADO programming with VB6 and VB 2005 code for ADO.NET 2.0 data objects. The chapter ends with an example of drag-and-drop generation of a master-details form whose data source is a typed `DataSet` object.

❑ **Chapter 2**, Introducing New ADO.NET 2.0 Features, shows you how to program new ADO.NET 2.0 runtime objects, such as `DbProviderFactories` and asynchronous `SqlCommand` objects. The chapter also shows you how to create more complex forms based on typed DataSets that update data in related tables.

❑ **Chapter 3**, Adopting Best Practices for Data-Centric Projects, starts with an overview of Microsoft's recommendations for architectural best practices, *patterns & practices* whitepapers, Design Guides, and Application Block Libraries for data-intensive and service-oriented .NET projects. The chapter concludes with specific recommendations for ADO.NET 2.0 projects with implementation examples.

Part II: Data Binding in Windows Forms and Controls

VS 2005's new ClickOnce deployment features let you deploy self-updating Windows form applications that users can install, update, and run from a Web site. ClickOnce deployment enables developers to replace Web-based applications with smart Windows form clients. Smart clients provide users with more versatile and responsive UIs, deliver offline operation, and increase data security. Part II's chapters show you how to design and program smart clients with typed DataSets as their data sources.

❑ **Chapter 4**, Programming TableAdapters, BindingSources, and DataGridViews, shows you how to parameterize master-details-subdetails forms with the `FillBy` method, format and add computed columns to DataGridViews, supply default values, add lookup combo boxes to DataGridView columns, and update data in three related tables.

- ❑ **Chapter 5**, Adding Data Validation and Concurrency Management, explains how to write data validation code for bound text boxes and DataGridViews, manage concurrency violations gracefully, and accommodate disconnected users with locally persisted typed DataSets.

- ❑ **Chapter 6**, Applying Advanced DataSet Techniques, shows you how to take advantage of DataSet partial classes, write partial-class code for transaction management, display and manipulate images in DataGridViews, generate DataSets from XML documents and their schema, use serialized objects as data sources, and bind DataGridViews to generic BindingList collections.

Part III: Data Binding in ASP.NET 2.0

ASP.NET 2.0 is a radical departure from its ASP.NET 1.*x* predecessors. Grid-based, fixed-position layout is gone; there's a new Visual Web Developer, and a lightweight Web server speeds development. Databound GridView controls replace DataGrids, and new FormView and DetailsView controls simplify creation of data-intensive Web applications.

- ❑ **Chapter 7**, Working with ASP.NET 2.0 DataSources and Bound Controls, introduces you to the new ASP.NET 2.0 designer, and the XHTML code for flow-based layouts. The chapter shows you how to generate SqlDataSources for bound controls, create templates for databound controls, and add DataList, DropDownList, FormView, GridView, and DetailsView controls.

- ❑ **Chapter 8**, Applying Advanced ASP.NET 2.0 Data Techniques, covers data validation, object and xml data sources, page-level and application-level performance tracing, and deployment to IIS Web sites with copied files or precompiled DLLS.

- ❑ **Chapter 9**, Publishing Data-Driven Web Services, leads you through initial generation of the default "Hello World" Web service and its client proxy, and then adds client credentials for Web service authentication. A data-intensive Web service shows you how to return a typed DataSet as a SOAP response message to a Windows form Web service client and update the service's tables. The chapter's final example is a Web service that returns a custom business object to a Web form client. The Web form client's bound data controls update the Web service's object data source.

Part IV: SQL Server 2005 and ADO.NET 2.0

SQL Server 2005 is a major upgrade to SQL Server 2000, as evidenced by its five-year gestation period. Part IV's chapters highlight new and improved SQL Server 2005 and SQLX features, T-SQL enhancements, VB 2005 SQL Server (SQLCLR) projects, and the new xml data type.

- ❑ **Chapter 10**, Upgrading from SQL Server 2000 to 2005, describes the differences between SQL Server 2005 editions, and shows you how to use the new management tools and Reporting Services. The chapter includes detailed examples of new database engine features, such as Service Broker, DatabaseMail, query notifications, and native SOAP Web services. The chapter covers new T-SQL keywords, such as PIVOT/UNPIVOT and FOR XML RAW, PATH, and TYPE modifiers.

- ❑ **Chapter 11**, Creating SQL Server Projects, leads you through the process of creating and deploying VB 2005 SQLCLR projects for managed stored procedures and triggers, and user-defined data types, functions, aggregates, and triggers.

SQL Server 2005 Developer Edition or higher provides the SQL Server Project template that's required to automate deployment of SQLCLR projects. Visual Basic Express Edition doesn't include an SQL Server Project template.

❑ **Chapter 12**, Exploring the xml Datatype, introduces the native xml data type and shows you how to create strongly typed xml columns with XML schemas, add XML indexes, write XQuery expressions to return scalar values or node-sets, and update elements or attributes of document instances in xml columns.

What You Need to Use This Book

You must have a computer that meets at least the minimum system requirements for your VS 2005 edition or VBX, *and* SQL Server 2005 or SQLX. Microsoft's minimum hardware requirements for SQL Server 2005 are an Intel or compatible Pentium 3 processor, minimum 550 MHz or higher, and 256MB RAM. 1 GHz or higher and 1GB RAM are recommended.

Don't expect a rewarding development experience if you run VS 2005 or VBX with less than an 833 MHz processor and 512MB RAM.

A full installation of SQL Server 2005 Developer Edition or higher requires about 1.6GB of free disk space, including 200MB for .NET Framework 2.0. A typical VS 2005 Developer Edition installation (without Visual J#, Visual C++, and Crystal Reports) requires about 1GB disk space, including documentation. Adding Visual J#, Visual C++, Crystal Reports, and SQL Express increases disk space to 2.5GB, without added documentation. Installing the complete documentation consumes another 1GB of disk space. You should have a minimum of 10GB of free disk space before you install SQL Server 2005 and VS 2005 Developer Edition or higher on a single partition.

VB Express 2005's minimum processor speed is 600MHz (1 GHz recommended); minimum RAM is 128MB (256MB recommended.) VBX, SQLX, MSDN Online Help, and XM require about 900MB of free disk space. The Northwind and AdventureWorks sample databases, which you must download from the Microsoft Web site, consume another 125MB. The free disk space of the partition on which you install VBX and SQLX should be at least 2GB.

Conventions

This book uses VB typographical conventions that are similar to those that appear in most offline help files. Three-letter Hungarian-notation prefixes identify most variables' data type, as in *strString*, int*Integer*, dat*DateTime*, and obj*Object*; some two-letter prefixes identity some classes, such as cn*SqlConnection*, cm*SqlCommand*, sb*StringBuilder*, xr*XmlReader*, and xw*XmlWriter*. Two-letter and three-letter prefixes identify Windows and Web form control types, as in gb*GroupBox*, btn*Button*, cbo*ComboBox*, and dgv*DataGridView*. Exceptions to the preceding conventions are autogenerated variable, object, and control names, such as *Database*ConnectionString, *Table*TableAdapter, and *Database*DataSet. Italics indicate replaceable elements.

T-SQL statements use uppercase keywords, and mixed-case object and variable names. Most XML element and attribute names are mixed-case, rather than camel-case, to correspond with SQL Server table and column name conventions.

Source Code and Sample Databases

As you work through the examples in this book, you may choose to implement simpler projects by creating the required Windows form or Web page and its data source, and adding brief VB 2005 code examples manually. More complex sample projects often depend on a "starter" project from the code files that accompany the book. All source code used in this book is available in a single 20MB archive file (VB2005DB.zip) for download at http://www.wrox.com. Once at the site, simply locate *One-on-One Visual Basic 2005 Database Programming* (either by using the Search box or by using one of the title lists) and click the Download Code link on the book's detail page to obtain all the source code for the book.

> *Because many books have similar titles, you might find it easiest to search by ISBN; for this book the ISBN is 0-7645-7678-X. Alternately, you can go to the main Wrox code download page at* http://www.wrox.com/dynamic/books/download.aspx *to see the code available for this book and all other Wrox books.*

> **The sample projects' connection strings for the Northwind and AdventureWorks sample databases specify `localhost` as the Data Source or Server parameter. The parameter assumes SQL Server 2000/2005 Developer Edition or higher, or MSDE 2000 is installed as the default instance on your system. Unless you perform a custom installation of SQL Server 2005 Express as the default instance, you must change `localhost` to `.\SQLEXPRESS` or `ServerName\SQLEXPRESS` to connect to SQLX**

Install the Source Code for the Sample Projects

The VB2005DB.zip file's archive structure consists of 12 archive files—one for each chapter—named Chapter01.zip to Chapter12.zip, which contain subfolders named for the project. There's also a ReadMe.txt file that describes how to extract the files and contains late-breaking information on the sample projects. Some projects have location-dependent files, so each Chapter##.zip file specifies full path names for its projects. These files extract to %SystemDrive%\VB2005DB\Chapter##*ProjectName* folders. If you're using WinZip or a similar archiving application to extract the files, be sure the Use Folder Names check box is marked before extracting them.

Install the Sample Databases

Most sample projects in this book use the SQL Server 2000 Northwind sample database; a few projects require the SQL Server 2005 version of the AdventureWorks sample database. SQL Server 2005 doesn't install the AdventureWorks OLTP database by default, and SQLX doesn't include sample databases. Following are the instructions for downloading and installing both sample databases on SQL Server 2005 Developer Edition or higher and SQLX.

Download the Sample Databases

The following download links for the Northwind, pubs, and AdventureWorks OLTP sample databases were valid when this book was written:

❏ Download SQL2000SampleDb.msi from the Northwind and pubs Sample Databases page at `http://go.microsoft.com/fwlink/?LinkId=30196`. Run the installer to create the inst-nwind.sql and instpubs.sql T-SQL scripts in the \Program Files\Microsoft SQL Server 2000 Sample Database Scripts folder. Installation adds a Microsoft SQL Server 2000 Sample Database item to the Programs menu.

❏ Download AdventureWorksDb.msi from the Microsoft Web site by searching for "SQL Server 2005 Express Documentation" (include the quotes). Run the installer to create the \Program Files\Microsoft SQL Server 2005 AdventureWorks Sample Database Scripts folder and add the OLTP (awdb), Analysis Services (awasdb), and data warehouse (awdwdb) folders, which contain T-SQL scripts to install each AdventureWorks version. Installation adds a Microsoft SQL Server 2005 AdventureWorks Sample Databases item to the Programs menu.

If you install the AdventureWorks sample databases from the SQL Server 2005 Developer Edition or higher setup program, you don't need to download them.

Install the Sample Databases to SQL Server 2005 Developer Edition or Higher

The following instructions require prior installation of SQL Server Management Studio (SSMS). If you have the post-RTM version of SMSS for SQL Server 2005 Express, you can use it to install the sample databases under SQLX. If you don't have a graphical management program for SQLX, skip to the "Install Sample Databases to SQL Server 2005 Express" section.

You can install Developer Edition under Windows XP SP2 or later. SQL Server 2005 Standard Edition and higher require Windows 2000 Server or Windows Server 2003. You also can use the full SMSS version to install the sample databases to SQLX.

Northwind and pubs

To install the Northwind database and, optionally, pubs, do this:

1. Open SSMS, and connect to your SQL Server 2005 instance.

2. Choose File ⇨ Open ⇨ File,navigate to the \Program Files\Microsoft SQL Server 2000 Sample Database Scripts folder, and double-click instnwind.sql.

3. Connect to your SQL Server 2005 instance to load the script into a new query window.

4. Click Execute to run the script.

5. Optionally, repeat Steps 2 through 4, but select instpubs.sql in Step 2.

This book doesn't include examples that require the pubs database.

AdventureWorks

Installation of the AdventureWorks OLTP database is system drive–dependent. To install the database, do the following:

1. Open SSMS, and connect to your SQL Server 2005 instance.

2. Choose File ⇨ Open ⇨ File, navigate to the \Program Files\Microsoft SQL Server 2005 AdventureWorks Sample Database Scripts\awdb folder, and double-click instawdb.sql.

3. Connect to your SQL Server 2005 instance to load the script into a new query window.

4. If your system drive isn't C:\, search for `@data_path = 'C:\` and replace C with the system drive letter.

5. Click Execute to run the script.

6. Expand Object Explorer's Databases\AdventureWorks node, right-click one of the Tables nodes, and choose Open table to verify that the table is populated.

> **If your system drive isn't C:\ and you don't edit the script in Step 4, the database installs but doesn't populate the tables.**

Install Sample Databases to SQL Server 2005 Express

Paul Flessner, then Microsoft's Senior VP of Server Applications, announced on September 15, 2005 that SQL Server 2005 Express Manager—a simplified management application for SQLX—would not be available for the SQLS RTM version or included with VS 2005 RTM editions. Paul promised "a scaled-down version of our SQL Server 2005 Management Studio for SQL Server 2005 Express Edition" to "be delivered in the first half of 2006." In the interim, SQLX users must use the SqlCmd utility to run the T-SQL scripts that install the Northwind and AdventureWorks databases on your SQLX instance. Attaching the database files permanently, rather than on-demand as a user database, simplifies modifications to the sample projects' SqlCommand.ConnectionStrings when changing between SQL Server 2005 (the default) and SQLX.

Northwind and pubs

To install the Northwind database and, optionally, pubs, do this:

1. Open a command prompt and navigate to the folder containing the instnwnd.sql script, usually C:\SQL Server Sample Databases.

2. Type **sqlcmd –S localhost\SQLEXPRESS –i instnwnd.sql**, and press Enter to execute the query, which creates the Northwind database and adds the sample data.

3. Type **sqlcmd –S localhost\SQLEXPRESS**, and press Enter to enter SqlCmd interactive mode.

4. Type **select * from northwind.dbo.customers**, press Enter, type **go**, and press Enter to verify in the window that sample data is present.

5. Optionally, repeat Steps 2 through 4, but substitute **instpubs.sql** for **instnwnd.sql** in Step 2. Then type **exit** and press Enter to return to the command prompt.

AdventureWorks

Installation of the AdventureWorks OLTP database is drive–dependent. If you didn't install the Microsoft SQL Server 2005 AdventureWorks Sample Database Scripts folder to C:\, copy the folder to C:\ before proceeding.

To install the database and its sample data, do the following:

1. Open a command prompt and navigate to the folder containing instawdb.sql, C:\Microsoft SQL Server 2005 AdventureWorks Sample Database Scripts\awdb.

2. Type **sqlcmd –S localhost\SQLEXPRESS –i instawdb.sql**, and press Enter to execute the query, which creates the AdventureWorks database and adds the sample data.

3. Type **sqlcmd –S localhost\SQLEXPRESS**, and press Enter to enter SqlCmd interactive mode.

4. Type **select * from adventureworks.person.contacttype**, press Enter, type **go**, and press Enter to verify in the window that sample data is present.

5. Type **exit**, and press enter to return to the command prompt.

AdventureWorks tables use SQL Server 2005's new user-schema separation feature, which lets you substitute an arbitrary prefix for the traditional database owner's name (dbo by default). AdventureWorks has five schemas: HumanResources, Person, Production, Purchasing, and Sales. You must include the schema prefix in the FROM clause's table name(s). If you omit the schema, you receive an "Invalid object name" error message.

Hardware Used to Create and Run the Sample Projects

Many of this book's sample projects include text boxes that report execution times. Sample project execution time depends on your test machine's processor, amount of available RAM, fixed-disk performance, and, to a lesser degree, operating system configuration.

The computer used to write this book is a Dell PowerEdge 400SC server with a single 2.261 GHz Pentium 4 processor (512KB cache), 1GB RAM, and a single 80GB ATA100 disk drive. The computer dual-boots the following operating systems and SQL Server instances:

❑ Windows Server 2003 Standard Edition with SQL Server 2005 Developer Edition, SQLX, and MSDE 2000 Release A instances

❑ Windows XP SP2 with SQLX and MSDE 2000 Release A

Examples that access networked SQL Server instances and components connect to an 866 MHz Pentium III box with 1GB RAM over a switched 100 Mbps network with relatively light traffic. The remote server runs Windows Server 2003 Standard Edition.

Errata

Every effort is made to ensure that there are no errors in the text or in the downloadable projects. However, no one is perfect, and mistakes do occur. If you find an error in this book, like a spelling mistake or faulty piece of code, we would be very grateful for your feedback. By sending in errata you may save another reader hours of frustration and at the same time you will be helping us provide even higher quality information.

This book's code examples and sample projects are based on VS 2005 Beta 2 and post-Beta 2 Community Technical Preview versions of SQL Server 2005/SQLX. Minor changes to these products might have occurred in the release-to-manufacturing (RTM) versions and those used in the book. The sample projects have been updated to the RTM versions. You might encounter unexpected results if you run the sample projects with pre-RTM versions of VS 2005 and SQL Server 2005.

To find the errata page for this book, go to http://www.wrox.com and locate the title using the Search box or one of the title lists. Then, on the book details page, click the Book Errata link. On this page you can view all errata that has been submitted for this book and posted by Wrox editors. A complete book list including links to each book's errata is also available at www.wrox.com/misc-pages/booklist .shtml.

If you don't spot "your" error on the Book Errata page, go to www.wrox.com/contact/techsupport .shtml and complete the form there to send us the error you have found. We'll check the information and, if appropriate, post a message to the book's errata page and fix the problem in subsequent editions of the book.

p2p.wrox.com

For author and peer discussion, join the P2P forums at p2p.wrox.com. The forums are a Web-based system for you to post messages related to Wrox books and related technologies and interact with other readers and technology users. The forums offer a subscription feature to e-mail you topics of interest of your choosing when new posts are made to the forums. Wrox authors, editors, other industry experts, and your fellow readers are present on these forums.

At http://p2p.wrox.com you will find a number of different forums that will help you not only as you read this book, but also as you develop your own applications. To join the forums, just follow these steps:

1. Go to p2p.wrox.com and click the Register link.
2. Read the terms of use and click Agree.
3. Complete the required information to join as well as any optional information you wish to provide and click Submit.
4. You will receive an e-mail with information describing how to verify your account and complete the joining process.

You can read messages in the forums without joining P2P but in order to post your own messages, you must join.

Once you join, you can post new messages and respond to messages other users post. You can read messages at any time on the Web. If you would like to have new messages from a particular forum e-mailed to you, click the Subscribe to this Forum icon by the forum name in the forum listing.

For more information about how to use the Wrox P2P, be sure to read the P2P FAQs for answers to questions about how the forum software works as well as many common questions specific to P2P and Wrox books. To read the FAQs, click the FAQ link on any P2P page.

Part I
ADO.Net 2.0 Basics

Migrating from ADO to ADO.NET

This chapter is an introduction to ADO.NET 2.0 for Visual Basic 6 developers who've decided to bite the bullet and move to Microsoft .NET Framework 2.0, Visual Studio 2005 (VS 2005) or Visual Basic Express (VBX), and Visual Basic 2005 (VB 2005) as their programming language. The ADO.NET 2.0 code examples and sample projects described in the chapter have the following prerequisites:

❑ Experience with VB6 database programming, using the Data Environment Designer, and writing code to create and manipulate ADODB `Connection`, `Command`, and `Recordset` objects, including disconnected `Recordset`s and databound controls.

❑ A basic understanding of the organization and use of .NET Framework namespaces and classes.

❑ Sufficient familiarity with using the VS 2005 IDE and writing VB 2005 code to create simple Windows Form projects.

❑ Microsoft SQL Server 2000 or 2005 Developer edition or higher, MSDE 2000, or SQL Server Express (SQLX) installed on your development computer or accessible from a network location. Access 2000 or later for Jet 4.0 examples is optional.

❑ The Northwind sample database installed on an accessible SQL Server instance.

❑ A working knowledge of XML document standards, including some familiarity with XML schemas.

> If you have experience with ADO.NET 1.*x*, consider scanning this chapter for new ADO.NET 2.0 features and then continue with Chapter 2, "Introducing New ADO.NET 2.0 Features," for more detailed coverage.

One of Microsoft's objectives for VS 2005 is to minimize the trauma that developers experience when moving from VB6 and VBA to the .NET Framework 2.0 and VB 2005. Whether VS .NET 2005's VB-specific My namespace and its accouterments will increase the rate of VB6 developer migration to VB 2005 remains to be seen. What's needed to bring professional VB6 database developers to the third iteration of the .NET Framework and Visual Studio's .NET implementation is increased programming productivity, application or component scalability and performance, and code reusability.

This chapter begins by demonstrating the similarities of VB6 and VBA code to create ADODB objects and VB 2005 code to generate basic ADO.NET 2.0 objects—database connections, commands, and read-only resultsets for Windows form projects. Native ADO.NET data provider classes—especially SqlClient for SQL Server—provide substantially better data access performance than ADODB and its OLE DB data providers. The remaining sections show you multiple approaches for creating ADO.NET DataSets by using new VS 2005 features and wizards to generate the underlying read-write data objects for you automatically. DataSets demonstrate VS 2005's improved data access programming productivity and ADO.NET 2.0's contribution to application scalability.

A New Approach to Data Access

Microsoft designed ADO.NET to maximize the scalability of data-intensive Windows and Web form applications and .NET components. Scalability isn't a critical factor when your project involves a few Windows form clients retrieving and updating tables in a single database. High-traffic Web sites, however, require the ability to *scale up* by adding more processors and RAM to a single server or to *scale out* by adding more application servers to handle the data processing load. Managed ADO.NET code that minimizes the duration and number of concurrent database server connections and uses optimistic concurrency tests for updating tables is the key to achieving a scalable data-intensive .NET project.

The sections that follow explain the role of ADO.NET 2.0 namespaces and managed data providers, which form the foundation of .NET 2.0 data access operations.

The System.Data Namespace

The .NET Framework 2.0 System.Data namespace contains all ADO.NET 2.0 namespaces, classes, interfaces, enumerations, and delegates. Figure 1-1 shows Object Browser displaying the System.Data namespaces.

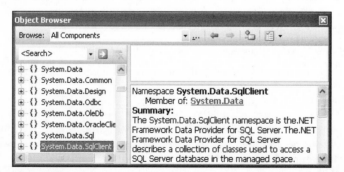

Figure 1-1

VS 2005 doesn't add a reference to the System.Data.dll assembly automatically when you start a new Windows form project. Creating a new data source with the Data Source Configuration Wizard adds references to the `System.Data` *and* `System.Xml` *namespaces. The section "Add a Typed DataSet from an SQL Server Data Source," later in this chapter, describes how to use the Data Source Configuration Wizard.*

ADO.NET `SqlConnection` and `SqlCommand` objects correspond to `ADODB.Connection` and `ADODB.Command` objects, but are restricted to use with SQL Server databases. Following are the ADO.NET namespace hierarchies for `SqlConnection`- and `SqlCommand`-managed data provider objects; namespaces new in ADO.NET 2.0 are emphasized:

```
System.Object
   System.MarshalByRefObject
      System.ComponentModel.Component
         System.Data.Common.DbConnection
            System.Data.SqlClient.SqlConnection

   System.Object
      System.MarshalByRefObject
         System.ComponentModel.Component
            System.Data.Common.DbCommand
               System.Data.SqlClient.SqlCommand
```

The following table provides brief descriptions of the `System.Data` namespaces shown in Figure 1-1 with the namespaces in the preceding hierarchy listed in order.

Namespace	Description
System.Object	The root of the .NET Framework 2.0 type hierarchy (member of System).
System.MarshalByRefObject	Enables remoting of data objects across application domain boundaries (member of System).
System.ComponentModel	Supports object sharing between components and enables runtime and design-time implementations of components.
System.Data	Provides the base classes, interfaces, enumerations, and event handlers for all supported data sources — primarily relational data and XML files or streams.
System.Data.Common	Provides classes that all managed data providers share, such as DbConnection and DbCommand in the preceding hierarchy list.
System.Data.Common.DbConnection	Provides inheritable classes for technology-specific and vendor-specific data providers (new in ADO.NET 2.0).

Table continued on following page

Namespace	Description
`System.Data.Odbc, System.Data .OleDb, System.Data.OracleClient, System.Data.SqlClient,` and `System.Data.SqlCeClient`	Namespaces for the five managed data providers included in ADO.NET 2.0; the next section describes these namespaces.
`System.Data.SqlTypes`	Provides a class for each SQL Server data type, including SQL Server 2005's new `xml` data type; these classes substitute for the generic `DbType` enumeration that supports all data providers.
`System.XML`	Adds the `System.Xml.XmlDataDocument` class, which supports processing of structured XML documents by `DataSet` objects.

After you add a project reference to System.Data.dll, you can eliminate typing `System.Data` namespace qualifiers and ensure strict type checking by adding the following lines to the top of your class code:

```
Option Explicit On
Option Strict On
Imports System.Data
Imports System.Data.SqlClient
```

Specifying Option Explicit On and Option Strict On in the Options dialog's Projects and Solutions, VB Defaults page doesn't ensure that other developers who work with your code have these defaults set. Substitute `Imports System.Data.OleDb` *for* `Imports System.Data.SqlClient` *if you're using the OleDb data provider.*

ADO.NET Data Providers

ADO.NET-managed data providers and their underlying data objects form the backbone of .NET data access. The data providers are an abstraction layer for data services and are similar in concept to ActiveX Data Objects' `ADODB` class, which supports only OLE DB data providers. ADO.NET supports multiple data provider types by the following data provider namespaces:

❑ `SqlClient` members provide high performance connectivity to SQL Server 7.0, 2000, and 2005. The performance gain comes from bypassing the OLE DB layer and communicating with SQL Server's native Tabular Data Stream (TDS) protocol. Most of this book's examples use classes in the `SqlClient` namespace.

❑ `SqlClientCe` provides features similar to `SqlClient` for SQL Server CE 3.0 and SQL Server 2005 Mobile Edition. This book doesn't cover SQL Server CE or Mobile versions.

❑ `OracleClient` members deliver functionality similar to `SqlClient` for Oracle 8i and 9i databases. Oracle offers Oracle Data Provider for .NET (ODP .NET) as a substitute for `OracleClient`; ODP .NET also supports Oracle 10g and later. You can learn more about ODP .NET at `http://otn.oracle.com/tech/windows/odpnet/`.

❑ OleDb members provide a direct connection to COM-based OLE DB data providers for databases and data sources other than SQL Server, SQL Server CE, and Oracle. You can select from 19 built-in OLE DB data providers when creating a new OleDbConnection object. A few of this book's examples use the Microsoft Jet 4.0 OLE DB Data Provider with the Access 2000 or later Northwind.mdb file. ADO.NET 2.0 doesn't provide access to the Microsoft OLE DB Provider for ODBC Drivers.

❑ Odbc members provide connectivity to legacy data sources that don't have OLE DB data providers. The Odbc namespace is present in .NET Framework 2.0 for backward compatibility with .NET Framework 1.x applications.

Each data provider namespace has its own set of data object classes. The provider you choose determines the prefix of data object names — such as SqlConnection, SqlCeConnection, OracleConnection, or OleDbConnection.

Basic ADO.NET Data Objects

This chapter defines *basic data objects* as runtime data-access types that have ADODB counterparts. ADO.NET 2.0 provides the following basic data objects for data retrieval, updates, or both:

❑ Connection objects define the data provider, database manager instance, database, security credentials, and other connection-related properties. The VB 2005 code to create a .NET Connection is quite similar to the VB6 code to create an ADODB.Connection object. You also can create a new, persistent (design-time) Connection object by right-clicking Server Explorer's Data Connections node and choosing Add Connection to open the Connection Properties dialog. Alternatively, choose Tools ➪ Connect to Database to open the dialog.

❑ Command objects execute SQL batch statements or stored procedures over an open Connection. Command objects can return one or more resultsets, subsets of a resultset, a single row, a single scalar value, an XmlDataReader object, or the RowsAffected value for table updates. Unlike opening ADODB.Recordset objects from an ADODB.Connection, the ADO.NET Command object isn't optional. Command objects support an optional collection of Parameter objects to execute parameterized queries or stored procedures. The relationship of ADODB and ADO.NET parameters to commands is identical.

❑ DataReader objects retrieve one or more forward-only, read-only resultsets by executing SQL batch statements or stored procedures. VB .NET code for creating and executing a DataReader from a Command object on a Connection object is similar to that for creating the default, cursorless ADODB Recordset object from an ADODB.Command object. Unlike the default forward-only ADODB.Recordset, you can't save a DataReader's resultset to a local file and reopen it with a client-side cursor by Save and Open methods.

❑ XmlReader objects consume streams that contain well-formed XML documents, such as those produced by SQL Server FOR XML AUTO queries or stored procedures, or native xml columns of SQL Server 2005. XmlReaders are the equivalent of a read-only, forward-only cursor over the XML document. An XmlReader object corresponds to the ADODB.Stream object returned by the SQLXML 3.0 and later SQLXMLOLEDB provider.

SqlClient doesn't support bidirectional (navigable) cursors. Microsoft added an `SqlResultset` *object, which emulated an updatable server-side cursor, to an early VS 2005 beta version. The VS 2005 team quickly removed the* `SqlResultset` *object after concluding that it encouraged "bad programming habits," such as holding a connection open during data editing operations. An* `ExecutePageReader` *method, which relied on the* `SqlResultset` *object, was removed at the same time and for the same reason.*

Figure 1-2 illustrates the relationships between ADO.NET `Connection`, `Command`, `Parameter`, `DataReader`, and `XmlReader` objects. Parameters are optional for ADODB and basic ADO.NET commands. The SqlClient types can be replaced by OleDb or Odbc types. Using the OleDb provider to return an `XmlDataReader` object from SQL Server 2000 requires installing SQLXML 3.0 SP-2 or later; the Odbc provider doesn't support XMLReaders. SQL Server 2005's setup program installs SQLXML 4.0.

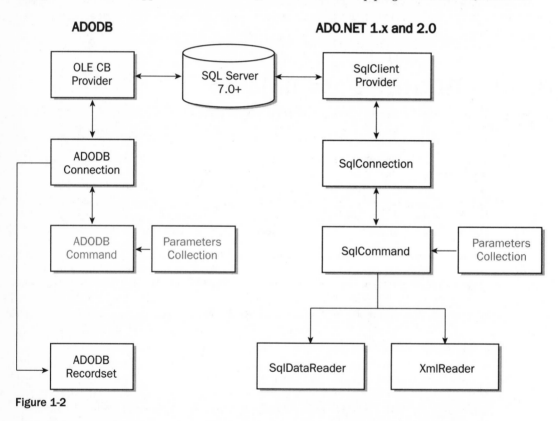

Figure 1-2

Creating Basic ADO.NET Data Objects with SqlClient

The following sections illustrate typical VB 2005 code for defining and opening an `SqlConnection` object, specifying an `SqlCommand` object, and invoking the command's `ExecuteReader` and `ExecuteXmlReader` methods. The procedures include code to display `SqlDataReader` column and `XmlReader` element values. All examples use a local SQL Server 2000 or 2005 Northwind sample database as their data source.

If you're using the default named instance of SQLX on your test machine, change `localhost` *to* `.\SQLEXPRESS` *in the* `strConn` *connection string. If you're using Access's MSDE 2000 instance as the local server, change* `Northwind` *to* `NorthwindCS`. *If you're using a remote SQL Server instance, replace* `localhost` *with the remote server's network name.*

> **The \VB2005DB\Chapter01\BasicDataObjects folder, which you create by expanding the Chapter01.zip file from the Wrox Web site for the book, contains complete source code for the following procedures. However, you must install the Northwind sample database before running the sample projects. See the Introduction's "Source Code and Sample Databases" section for details.**

SqlDataReaders with Multiple Resultsets

One of the most common uses of `SqlDataReader` objects is filling dropdown lists or list boxes with lookup data. You can use multiple resultsets from a single SQL batch query or stored procedure to fill multiple lists in the `FormName_Load` event handler. The following `OpenDataReader` procedure opens a connection to the Northwind sample database, specifies an `SqlCommand` object that returns two resultsets, and invokes its `ExecuteReader` method to generate the `SqlDataReader` instance. The `CommandBehavior` `.CloseConnection` argument closes the connection when you close the DataReader. All basic ADO.NET data objects follow this pattern; only the `ExecuteObject` method and DataReader iteration methods differ. The `SqlDataReader.Read` method, which replaces the often-forgotten `RecordSet.MoveNext` instruction, returns `True` while rows remain to be read. Similarly, the `SqlDataReader.NextResult` method is `True` if unprocessed resultsets remain after the initial iteration.

Only one resultset is open as you iterate multiple resultsets, which differs from SQL Server 2005's Multiple Active Resultsets (MARS) feature. Chapter 10, "Upgrading from SQL Server 2000 to 2005," describes how to enable the MARS feature.

```
Private Sub OpenDataReader()
    'Define and open the SqlConnection object
    Dim strConn As String = "Server=localhost;Database=Northwind;" + _
        "Integrated Security=SSPI"
    Dim cnnNwind As SqlConnection = New SqlConnection(strConn)
    cnnNwind.Open()

    'Define the SqlCommand to return two resultsets
    Dim strSQL As String = "SELECT * FROM Shippers"
    strSQL += ";SELECT EmployeeID, FirstName, LastName FROM Employees"
    Dim cmdReader As SqlCommand = New SqlCommand(strSQL, cnnNwind)
    cmdReader.CommandType = CommandType.Text

    'Define, create, and traverse the SqlDataReader
    'Close the connection when closing the SqlDataReader
    Dim sdrReader As SqlDataReader = _
        cmdReader.ExecuteReader(CommandBehavior.CloseConnection)
    sdrReader = cmdReader.ExecuteReader
    With sdrReader
        If .HasRows Then
            While .Read
                'Fill a Shippers list box
```

```
                      lstShippers.Items.Add(.Item(0).ToString + " - " + .Item(1).ToString)
            End While
            While .NextResult
                'Process additional resultset(s)
                While .Read
                    'Fill an Employees list box
                    lstEmployees.Items.Add(.Item(0).ToString + " - " + _
                        .Item(1).ToString + " " + .Item(2).ToString)
                End While
            End While
        End If
        'Close the SqlDataReader and SqlConnection
        .Close()
    End With
End Sub
```

Use of the HasRows *property is optional because initial invocation of the* Read *method returns* False *if the query returns no rows. The* SqlDataReader.Item(ColumnIndex) *property returns an* Object *variable that you must convert to a string for concatenation. Structured error handling code is removed for improved readability.*

XmlReaders with FOR XML AUTO Queries

Adding a FOR XML AUTO clause to an SQL Server SELECT query or stored procedure returns the resultset as an XML stream. The default XML document format is attribute-centric; add the Elements modifier to return an element-syntax document. Here's the XML document returned by a SELECT * FROM Shippers FOR XML AUTO, Elements query:

```xml
<?xml version="1.0" encoding="utf-8" ?>
<root>
  <Shippers>
    <ShipperID>1</ShipperID>
    <CompanyName>Speedy Express</CompanyName>
    <Phone>(503) 555-9831</Phone>
  </Shippers>
  <Shippers>
    <ShipperID>2</ShipperID>
    <CompanyName>United Package</CompanyName>
    <Phone>(503) 555-3199</Phone>
  </Shippers>
  <Shippers>
    <ShipperID>3</ShipperID>
    <CompanyName>Federal Shipping</CompanyName>
    <Phone>(503) 555-9931</Phone>
  </Shippers>
</root>
```

ADO.NET 2.0's new SqlCommand.ExecuteXmlReader method loads a System.Xml.XmlReader object with the stream, as shown in the following OpenXmlReader procedure listing. XmlReader is an abstract class with concrete XmlTextReader, XmlNodeReader, and XmlValidatingReader implementations. ADO.NET 2.0's ExecuteXmlReader method returns a concrete implementation.

```
Private Sub OpenXmlReader()
    'Define and open the SqlConnection object
    Dim strConn As String = "Server=localhost;Database=Northwind;" + _
        "Integrated Security=SSPI"
    Dim cnnNwind As SqlConnection = New SqlConnection(strConn)
    Dim xrShippers As System.Xml.XmlReader
    Try
        cnnNwind.Open()

        'Define the SqlCommand
        Dim strSQL As String = "SELECT * FROM Shippers FOR XML AUTO, Elements"
        Dim cmdXml As SqlCommand = New SqlCommand(strSQL, cnnNwind)
        xrShippers = cmdXml.ExecuteXmlReader
        With xrShippers
            .Read()
            Do While .ReadState <> Xml.ReadState.EndOfFile
                txtXML.Text += .ReadOuterXml
            Loop
            'Format the result
            txtXML.Text = Replace(txtXML.Text, "><", ">" + vbCrLf + "<")
        End With
    Catch exc As Exception
        MsgBox(exc.Message + exc.StackTrace)
    Finally
        xrShippers.Close
        cnnNwind.Close()
    End Try
End Sub
```

Substituting xrShippers.MoveToContent *followed by* xrShippers.ReadOuterXML *(without the loop) returns only the first* <Shippers> *element group.*

You must execute the XmlReader.Read method to move to the first element group, followed by a ReadOuterXml invocation for each element group, which represents a row of the resultset. The ExecuteXmlReader method doesn't support the CommandBehavior enumeration, so you must close the SqlConnection object explicitly. OleDbCommand doesn't support the ExecuteXmlReader method; Microsoft wants you to use SqlClient classes for *all* SQL Server data access applications, including SQLCLR code running in the SQL Server 2005 process.

Figure 1-3 shows the BasicDataObjects project's form after executing from the frmMain_Load event handler, which executes the preceding OpenDataReader and OpenXmlReader procedures, and the following LoadDataGridView procedure.

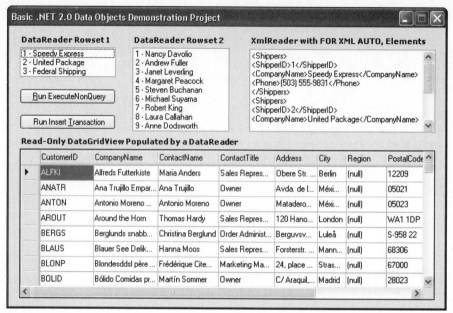

Figure 1-3

> FOR XML AUTO queries or stored procedures in production applications cause a
> substantial performance hit compared with traditional data-access methods. The
> server must generate the XML stream, many more data bytes travel over the network,
> and the client or component must transform the XML stream to a usable format.

Fill a DataGridView with a DataReader

If your application needs to display only tabular data , a read-only grid control that's populated by code
consumes the fewest resources. The DataGridView control replaces VS 2002 and VS 2003's DataGrid
control, and is easy to fill programmatically. A read-only DataGridView populated by a DataReader
behaves similarly to VB6's standard (unbound) Grid control, except that DataGridViews have sortable
columns by default.

The following code defines the dgvCusts DataGridView control's columns and then populates each row
with an instance of an objCells() Object array that contains cell values:

```
Private Sub LoadDataGridView()
    'Populate a read-only DataGridView control with an SqlDataReader
    Dim cnnNwind As SqlConnection = New SqlConnection(strConn)
    Try
        Dim strSql As String = "SELECT * FROM Customers"
        Dim cmdGrid As New SqlCommand(strSql, cnnNwind)
        cmdGrid.CommandType = CommandType.Text
        cnnNwind.Open()
        Dim sdrGrid As SqlDataReader = cmdGrid.ExecuteReader
        Dim intCol As Integer
```

```
                With sdrGrid
                    If .HasRows Then
                        dgvCusts.Rows.Clear()
                        'Add column definition: FieldName, and ColumnName
                        For intCol = 0 To .FieldCount - 1
                            dgvCusts.Columns.Add(.GetName(intCol), .GetName(intCol))
                        Next
                        'Base column width on header text width
                        dgvCusts.AutoSizeColumnsMode = _
                            DataGridViewAutoSizeColumnsMode.ColumnHeader
                        While .Read
                            'Get row data as an Object array
                            Dim objCells(intCol) As Object
                            .GetValues(objCells)
                            'Add an entire row at a time
                            dgvCusts.Rows.Add(objCells)
                        End While
                        .Close()
                    End If
                End With
            Catch exc As Exception
                MsgBox(exc.Message)
            Finally
                cnnNwind.Close()
            End Try
        End Sub
```

To sort the DataGridView control on column values, click the column header. Alternate clicks perform ascending and descending sorts.

Return a Single Data Row

Adding a CommandBehavior.SingleRow flag to the SqlDataReader object returns the first row of a resultset specified by an SQL query or stored procedure. The following code returns the first row of Northwind's Customers table, if you don't specify a WHERE clause. Otherwise the code returns the first row specified by WHERE criteria. Adding a CommandBehavior.CloseConnection flag closes the connection automatically when you close the SqlDataReader object.

```
        Private Sub OpenExecuteRow()
            Dim cnnNwind As SqlConnection = New SqlConnection(strConn)
            Try
                cnnNwind.Open()
                'Define the SqlCommand
                Dim strSQL As String = "SELECT * FROM Customers"
                'Following is optional for the first record
                'strSQL += " WHERE CustomerID = 'ALFKI'"
                Dim cmdRow As SqlCommand = New SqlCommand(strSQL, cnnNwind)
                cmdRow.CommandType = CommandType.Text
                Dim sdrRow As SqlDataReader = _
                    cmdRow.ExecuteReader(CommandBehavior.SingleRow Or _
                    CommandBehavior.CloseConnection)
                With sdrRow
                    If .HasRows Then
                        .Read()
```

```
                Dim intFields As Integer = .FieldCount
                Dim strCustID As String = .GetString(0)
                Dim strCompany As String = .GetString(1)
            End If
            'Closes the DataReader and Connection
            .Close()
        End With
        Catch exc As Exception
            MsgBox(exc.Message + exc.StackTrace)
        Finally
        'Close the SqlConnection, if still open
        cnnNwind.Close()
    End Try
End Sub
```

Return a Scalar Value

The `SqlCommand.ExecuteScalar` method returns the value of the first column of the first row of a resultset. The most common use of `ExecuteScalar` is to return a single SQL aggregate value, such as `COUNT`, `MIN`, or `MAX`. The following `OpenExecuteScalar` procedure listing returns the number of Customers table records:

```
Private Sub OpenExecuteScalar()
    'Return a single SQL aggregate value
    Dim strConn As String = "Server=localhost;Database=Northwind;" + _
     "Integrated Security=SSPI"
    Dim cnnNwind As SqlConnection = New SqlConnection(strConn)
    cnnNwind.Open()

    'Define the SqlCommand
    Dim strSQL As String = "SELECT COUNT(*) FROM Customers"
    Dim cmdScalar As SqlCommand = New SqlCommand(strSQL, cnnNwind)
    cmdScalar.CommandType = CommandType.Text
    Dim intCount As Integer = CInt(cmdScalar.ExecuteScalar)
    'Close the SqlConnection
    cnnNwind.Close()
End Sub
```

Execute Queries That Don't Return Data

You use the `SqlCommand.ExecuteNonQuery` method to execute SQL queries or stored procedures that update base table data — INSERT, UPDATE, and DELETE operations. As the following `OpenExecuteNonQuery` code demonstrates, `ExecuteNonQuery` rivals the simplicity of `ExecuteScalar`:

```
Private Sub RunExecuteNonQuery()
    'Add and delete a bogus Customers record
    Dim strConn As String = "Server=localhost;Database=Northwind;" + _
     "Integrated Security=SSPI"
    Dim cnnNwind As SqlConnection = New SqlConnection(strConn)
    Dim intRecordsAffected As Integer
    Try
        cnnNwind.Open()

        'Define and execute the INSERT SqlCommand
```

```
            Dim strSQL As String = "INSERT Customers (CustomerID, CompanyName) " + _
                "VALUES ('BOGUS', 'Bogus Company')"
            Dim cmdUpdates As SqlCommand = New SqlCommand(strSQL, cnnNwind)
            cmdUpdates.CommandType = CommandType.Text
            intRecordsAffected = cmdUpdates.ExecuteNonQuery

            'Update and execute the UPDATE SqlCommand
            strSQL = "UPDATE Customers SET CompanyName = 'Wrong Company' " + _
             "WHERE CustomerID = 'BOGUS'"
            cmdUpdates.CommandText = strSQL
            intRecordsAffected += cmdUpdates.ExecuteNonQuery

            'Define and execute the DELETE SqlCommand
            strSQL = "DELETE FROM Customers WHERE CustomerID = 'BOGUS'"
            cmdUpdates.CommandText = strSQL
            intRecordsAffected += cmdUpdates.ExecuteNonQuery
        Catch exc As Exception
            MsgBox(exc.Message + exc.StackTrace)
        Finally
            'Close the SqlConnection
            cnnNwind.Close()
            If intRecordsAffected <> 3 Then
                MsgBox("INSERT, UPDATE, DELETE, or all failed. " + _
                    "Check your Customers table.")
            End If
        End Try
    End Sub
```

Executing SQL update queries against production databases isn't a recommended practice and most DBAs won't permit direct updates to server base tables. The purpose of the preceding example is to provide a simple illustration of how the ExecuteNonQuery *method works. In the real world, parameterized stored procedures usually perform table updates.*

Applying Transactions to Multi-Table Updates

All updates within a single procedure to more than one table should run under the control of a transaction. The SqlTransaction object provides clients with the ability to commit or, in the event of an exception, roll back updates to SQL Server base tables. Managing transactions in ADO.NET is similar to that for ADODB.Connection objects, which have BeginTrans, CommitTrans, and RollbackTrans methods. SqlTransaction objects have corresponding BeginTransaction, CommitTransaction, and RollbackTransaction methods. Unlike ADODB connections, ADO.NET lets you selectively enlist commands in an active transaction.

Following are the steps to execute ADO.NET transacted updates:

❑   Define a local transaction as an SqlTransaction, OleDbTransaction, or OdbcTransaction object.

❑   Invoke the transaction's BeginTransaction method with an optional IsolationLevel enumeration argument. The default IsolationLevel property value is ReadCommitted.

❑   Enlist commands in the transaction by their Transaction property.

❑   Invoke the `ExecuteNonQuery` method for each command.

❑   Invoke the transaction's `Commit` method.

❑   If an exception occurs, invoke the transaction's `Rollback` method.

ADO.NET's `IsolationLevel` and ADODB's `IsolationLevelEnum` enumerations share many common members, as shown in the following table.

ADO.NET Member	ADODB Member	ADO.NET IsolationLevel Description
Chaos	adXactChaos	Prevents pending changes from more highly isolated transactions from being overwritten
ReadCommitted	AdXactReadCommitted adXactCursorStability	Avoids dirty reads but permits non-repeatable reads and phantom data (default)
ReadUncommitted	AdXactReadUncommitted adXactBrowse	Allows dirty reads, non-repeatable rows, and phantom rows
RepeatableRead	adXactRepeatableRead	Prevents non-repeatable reads but allows phantom rows
Serializable	AdXactSerializable adXactIsolated	Prevents dirty reads, non-repeatable reads, and phantom rows by placing a range lock on the data being updated
Snapshot	None	Stores a version of SQL Server 2005 data that clients can read while another client modifies the same data
Unspecified	adXactUnspecified	Indicates that the provider is using a different and unknown isolation level

`Snapshot` is a new ADO.NET 2.0 isolation level for SQL Server 2005 only. Snapshot isolation eliminates read locks by providing other clients a copy (snapshot) of the unmodified data until the transaction commits. You must enable Snapshot isolation in SQL Server Management Studio (SSMS) or by issuing a T-SQL `ALTER DATABASE DatabaseName SET ALLOW_SNAPSHOT_ISOLATION ON` command to take advantage of the transaction scalability improvement that this new isolation level offers.

The following `RunInsertTransaction` listing illustrates reuse of a single `SqlTransaction` and `SqlCommand` object for sets of update transactions on the Northwind Customers and Orders tables. Running this transaction makes non-reversible changes to the OrderID column of the Orders table, so it's a good idea to back up the Northwind database before running this type of code. Notice that you must re-enlist the `SqlCommand` object in the `SqlTransaction` after a previous transaction commits.

```
Public Sub RunInsertTransaction()
    'Add and delete new Customers and Orders records
    Dim strConn As String = "Server=localhost;Database=Northwind;" + _
    "Integrated Security=SSPI"
    Dim cnnNwind As SqlConnection = New SqlConnection(strConn)

    'Specify a local transaction object
    Dim trnCustOrder As SqlTransaction
```

```
Dim intRecordsAffected As Integer
Dim strTitle As String
Try
   cnnNwind.Open()
   Try
      trnCustOrder = cnnNwind.BeginTransaction(IsolationLevel.RepeatableRead)
      'Define and execute the INSERT SqlCommand for a new customer
      strTitle = "INSERT "
      Dim strSQL As String = "INSERT Customers (CustomerID, CompanyName) " + _
        "VALUES ('BOGUS', 'Bogus Company')"
      Dim cmdTrans As SqlCommand = New SqlCommand(strSQL, cnnNwind)
      cmdTrans.CommandType = CommandType.Text

      'Enlist the command in the transaction
      cmdTrans.Transaction = trnCustOrder
      intRecordsAffected = cmdTrans.ExecuteNonQuery

      'INSERT an Order record for the new customer
      strSQL = "INSERT Orders (CustomerID, EmployeeID, OrderDate, ShipVia) " + _
        "VALUES ('BOGUS', 1, '" + Today.ToShortDateString + "', 1)"
      cmdTrans.CommandText = strSQL
      intRecordsAffected += cmdTrans.ExecuteNonQuery
      'Commit the INSERT transaction
      trnCustOrder.Commit()

      'Delete the Orders and Customers records
      strTitle = "DELETE "
      trnCustOrder = cnnNwind.BeginTransaction(IsolationLevel.RepeatableRead)
      strSQL = "DELETE FROM Orders WHERE CustomerID = 'BOGUS'"
      cmdTrans.CommandText = strSQL

      'The previous transaction has terminated, so re-enlist
      cmdTrans.Transaction = trnCustOrder
      intRecordsAffected += cmdTrans.ExecuteNonQuery

      strSQL = "DELETE FROM Customers WHERE CustomerID = 'BOGUS'"
      cmdTrans.CommandText = strSQL
      intRecordsAffected += cmdTrans.ExecuteNonQuery

      'Commit the DELETE transaction
      trnCustOrder.Commit()

   Catch excTrans As SqlException
      MsgBox(excTrans.Message + excTrans.StackTrace, , _
        strTitle + "Transaction Failed")
      Try
         trnCustOrder.Rollback()
      Catch excRollback As SqlException
         MsgBox(excTrans.Message + excTrans.StackTrace, , _
           strTitle + "Rollback Failed")
      End Try
   End Try
Catch exc As Exception
   MsgBox(exc.Message + exc.StackTrace)
Finally
   'Close the SqlConnection
```

```
        cnnNwind.Close()
        Dim strMsg As String
        If intRecordsAffected = 4 Then
            strMsg = "INSERT and DELETE transactions succeeded."
        Else
            strMsg = "INSERT, DELETE, or both transactions failed. " + _
              "Check your Customers and Orders tables."
        End If
        MsgBox(strMsg, , "RunInsertTransaction")
    End Try
End Sub
```

This is another example of client operations that most DBAs won't permit. In production applications, stored procedures with T-SQL BEGIN TRAN[SACTION], COMMIT TRAN[SACTION], *and* ROLLBACK TRAN[SACTION] *statements handle multi-table updates.*

Using OleDb, SqlXml, and Odbc Member Classes

Most data-centric VB 2005 demonstration projects connect to an SQL Server instance with SqlClient objects while developers gain familiarity with .NET's panoply of System.Data classes. Thus, the preceding examples use the SqlClient data provider. You should, however, give the other managed providers — System.Data.OleDb, System.Data.Odbc, and Microsoft.Data.SqlXml — a test drive with the OleDbDataProjects.sln project in your \VB2005DB\Chapter01\ OleDbDataProjects folder. Figure 1-4 shows OleDbDataProject's form with list boxes and a text box that display data generated by each of the three providers. Marking the Use OdbcDataReader checkbox substitutes the Odbc for the OleDb data provider to fill the Rowset 1 (Shippers) list box.

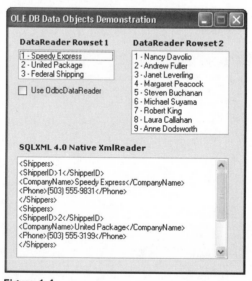

Figure 1-4

You can take advantage of ADO.NET 2.0's new `DbProviderFactories.GetFactory ("System.Data.Provider")` method and the `DbProviderFactory.CreateConnection` and `CreateCommand` methods to generate a connection to and commands for any available managed data provider. Chapter 2's "Use the DbProviderFactories to Create Database-Agnostic Projects" section shows you how to write applications that accommodate multiple relational database management systems.

Each sample procedure has its own connection string. You must modify each connection string to point to your Microsoft Access, SQL Server, or SQL Express instance.

The SQLXML Managed Classes (Microsoft.Data.SqlXml) native data provider for SQL Server 2000 isn't a member of the .NET Framework 2.0. It's a component of Microsoft SQLXML 4.0, which VS 2005 and VB Express install as Microsoft.Data.SqlXml.dll.

Substitute OleDb for SqlClient Objects

The OleDb data provider is your best bet for connecting to Access (Jet 4.0) database files or database servers for which you don't have a native .NET data provider. The OleDb provider also lets you create applications that *might* work with the user's choice of database servers. In most cases, you can replace `Imports System.Data.SqlServer` with `Imports System.Data.OleDb`, substitute the appropriate OLE DB connection string, and replace the prefix of data objects from `Sql` to `OleDb`. In some cases, you might need to alter the SQL statement for a specific database back end's SQL dialect. For example, the Jet query engine recognizes the semicolon as an SQL statement terminator but won't return additional resultsets from another SQL statement that follows the semicolon. Thus, the code for Northwind.mdb in the following `OpenOleDbDataReader` listing reuses the `OleDbCommand` with a second SQL statement:

```
Private Sub OpenOleDbDataReader()
    'Define and open the OleDbConnection object
    Dim strConn As String = "Provider=Microsoft.Jet.OLEDB.4.0;" + _
     "Data Source=C:\Program Files\Microsoft Office\OFFICE11" + _
     "\SAMPLES\Northwind.mdb;Persist Security Info=False"
    'Substitute the following if you don't have Northwind.mdb available
    'Dim strConn As String = "Provider=SQLOLEDB;" + _
    ' "Data Source=localhost;Initial Catalog=Northwind;Integrated Security=SSPI"

    Dim cnnNwind As OleDbConnection = New OleDbConnection(strConn)
    cnnNwind.Open()

    'Define the OleDbCommand
    Dim strSQL As String = "SELECT * FROM Shippers"
    'strSQL += ";SELECT EmployeeID, FirstName, LastName FROM Employees"
    Dim cmdReader As OleDbCommand = New OleDbCommand(strSQL, cnnNwind)
    cmdReader.CommandType = CommandType.Text

    'Define, create, and traverse the OleDbDataReader
    'Don't close the connection when closing the OleDbDataReader
    Dim odbReader As OleDbDataReader = _
        cmdReader.ExecuteReader(CommandBehavior.Default)
    lstShippers.Items.Clear()
    With odbReader
        If .HasRows Then
            While .Read
                'Process the rows
                lstShippers.Items.Add(.Item(0).ToString + _
                    " - " + .Item(1).ToString)
```

```
              End While
            .Close()
        End If
    End With
    lstEmployees.Items.Clear()
    cmdReader.CommandText = "SELECT EmployeeID, FirstName, LastName FROM Employees"
    odbReader = cmdReader.ExecuteReader(CommandBehavior.CloseConnection)
    'Process additional resultsets
    With odbReader
        If .HasRows Then
            While .Read
                'Process additional rows
                lstEmployees.Items.Add(.Item(0).ToString + " - " + _
                    .Item(1).ToString + " " + .Item(2).ToString)
            End While
        End If
        'Close the OleDbDataReader and the OleDbConnection
        .Close()
    End With
End Sub
```

You must close the first `DataReader` *before you change the* `CommandText` *property to reuse the* `OleDbCommand` *object.*

Replace SqlConnection and SqlCommand with SqlXmlCommand

Returning `XmlReader` objects with the OleDb data provider requires adding a project reference to `Microsoft.Data.SqlXml`. Adding an `Imports Microsoft.Data.SqlXml` statement to your form's class file simplifies references to its classes. An interesting feature of the `SqlXmlCommand` object is that it doesn't require an `SqlConnection` object, as illustrated by the following listing for the `OpenSqlXmlReader` procedure:

```
Private Sub OpenSqlXmlReader()
    'This procedure requires installing SQLXML 3.0 SP-2 or later
    'and a project reference to Microsoft.Data.SqlXml

    'Define OleDb connection string
    Dim strConn As String = "Provider=SQLOLEDB;Data Source=localhost;" + _
        "Initial Catalog=Northwind;Integrated Security=SSPI"

    'Define the SqlXmlCommand
    Dim strSQL As String = "SELECT * FROM Shippers FOR XML AUTO, Elements"
    Dim cmdXml As SqlXmlCommand = New SqlXmlCommand(strConn)
    cmdXml.CommandText = strSQL
    Dim xrShippers As System.Xml.XmlReader = cmdXml.ExecuteXmlReader
    With xrShippers
        .Read()
        Do While .ReadState <> Xml.ReadState.EndOfFile
            txtXML.Text += .ReadOuterXml
        Loop
        'Format the result
        txtXML.Text = Replace(txtXML.Text, "><", ">" + vbCrLf + "<")
        .Close()
    End With
End Sub
```

Test the Odbc Data Provider

You're not likely to use an Odbc data provider unless you're working with a legacy database server for which an OLE DB data provider isn't available. The following `OpenOdbcDataReader` procedure listing is present for completeness only:

```vb
Private Sub OpenOdbcDataReader()
    'Define and open the OdbcConnection object
    Dim strConn As String = "DRIVER={SQL Server};SERVER=localhost;" + _
        "Trusted_connection=yes;DATABASE=Northwind;"

    Dim cnnNwind As OdbcConnection = New OdbcConnection(strConn)
    cnnNwind.Open()

    'Define the OdbcCommand
    Dim strSQL As String = "SELECT * FROM Shippers"
    Dim cmdReader As OdbcCommand = New OdbcCommand(strSQL, cnnNwind)
    cmdReader.CommandType = CommandType.Text

    'Define, create, and traverse the OdbcDataReader
    'Close the connection when closing the OdbcDataReader
    Dim sdrReader As OdbcDataReader = _
     cmdReader.ExecuteReader(CommandBehavior.CloseConnection)
    If chkUseOdbc.Checked Then
        lstShippers.Items.Clear()
    End If
    With sdrReader
        If .HasRows Then
            While .Read
                'Process the rows
                Dim intShipperID As Integer = .GetInt32(0)
                Dim strCompany As String = .GetString(1)
                Dim strPhone As String = .GetString(2)
                If chkUseOdbc.Checked Then
                    lstShippers.Items.Add(.Item(0).ToString + _
                        " - " + .Item(1).ToString)
                End If
            End While
        End If
        'Close the OdbcDataReader and the OdbcConnection
        .Close()
    End With
End Sub
```

Working with Typed DataReader and SqlResultSet Data

The preceding code examples use `Reader.Item(ColumnIndex).ToString`, `Reader.GetString(ColumnIndex)`, and `Reader.GetInt32(ColumnIndex)` methods to extract column values to native .NET data types, which the `System` namespace defines. ADO.NET 2.0 provides the following data-specific enumerations:

❑   System.Data.DbType is a generic enumeration for setting the data types of OleDb and Odbc parameters, fields, and properties.

❑   System.Data.SqlDbType is an enumeration for use with SqlParameter objects only. VS 2005 automatically adds SqlParameters when you create typed DataSets from SQL Server tables in the following sections.

❑   System.Data.SqlTypes is a namespace that contains structures for all SQL Server 2000 and 2005 data types, except timestamp, and related classes and enumerations. Using SqlTypes structures improves data-access performance by eliminating conversion to native .NET types, and assures that column values aren't truncated.

VS 2005's online help provides adequate documentation for DbType and SqlDbType enumerations, and SqlTypes structures, so this chapter doesn't provide a table to relate these enumerations and types.

The following OpenDataReaderSqlTypes listing shows examples of the use of typical GetSql*DataType*(ColumnIndex) methods:

```
Private Sub OpenDataReaderSqlTypes()
    'Define and open the SqlConnection object
    Dim strConn As String = "Server=localhost;Database=Northwind;" + _
     "Integrated Security=SSPI"
    Dim cnnNwind As SqlConnection = New SqlConnection(strConn)
    Dim sdrReader As SqlDataReader
    Try
        cnnNwind.Open()

        'Define the SqlCommand
        Dim strSQL As String = "SELECT Orders.*, " + _
         "ProductID, UnitPrice, Quantity, Discount " + _
         "FROM Orders INNER JOIN [Order Details] ON " + _
         "Orders.OrderID = [Order Details].OrderID WHERE CustomerID = 'ALFKI'"
        Dim cmdReader As SqlCommand = New SqlCommand(strSQL, cnnNwind)

        'Create, and traverse the SqlDataReader, assigning SqlTypes to variables
        sdrReader = cmdReader.ExecuteReader(CommandBehavior.CloseConnection)
        With sdrReader
            If .HasRows Then
                While .Read
                    'Get typical SqlTypes
                    Dim s_intOrderID As SqlInt32 = .GetSqlInt32(0)
                    Dim s_strCustomerID As SqlString = .GetSqlString(1)
                    Dim s_datOrderDate As SqlDateTime = .GetSqlDateTime(3)
                    Dim s_curUnitPrice As SqlMoney = .GetSqlMoney(15)
                    Dim s_sngDiscount As SqlSingle = .GetSqlSingle(17)
                End While
            End If
        End With
    Catch exc As Exception
        MsgBox(exc.Message + exc.StackTrace)
    Finally
        'Close the SqlDataReader and the SqlConnection
        sdrReader.Close()
    End Try
End Sub
```

You can update `SqlResultSet` object column values with strongly typed variables by invoking the `SqlResultSet.SetSqlDataType(ColumnIndex)` method. You'll see more examples of strongly typed SQL Server data retrieval and update operations that use these methods in later chapters.

ADO.NET Typed DataSet Objects

The `DataSet` object is unique to ADO.NET and typed DataSets are the preferred method for retrieving and updating relational tables, although DataSets aren't limited to processing relational data. You create typed DataSets, which are defined by an XML schema and implemented by a very large amount of auto-generated VB 2005 code, with VS 2005 designers. Untyped DataSets are runtime objects that you create with code. DataSets have no corresponding ADODB object, but both classes of DataSets *behave* similarly to disconnected Recordsets in the following ways:

❑ They open a connection, retrieve and cache the data to edit, and then close the connection.

❑ They bind to simple and complex Windows form controls for editing.

❑ They permit editing locally cached data while the connection is closed.

❑ They can be saved to local files and reopened for editing.

❑ They let you reopen the connection and apply updates to base tables in batches.

❑ They implement optimistic concurrency for base table updates. You must write code to handle concurrency violations gracefully.

Following are the most important differences between DataSets and disconnected Recordsets:

❑ A DataSet consists of cached copies of one or more sets of records — called `DataTable` objects — selected from one or more individual base tables. A Recordset is a single set of records that can represent a view of one or two or more related tables.

❑ Persisting a DataSet serializes the DataTables' records to a hierarchical, element-centric XML Infoset document and saves it to the local file system. Disconnected Recordsets store data locally as a flat, attribute-centric XML file.

❑ DataTables usually are — but need not be — related by primary-key/foreign-key relationships.

❑ Primary-key and foreign-key constraints, and table relationships, must be manually defined, unless you create the DataSet automatically with VS 2005's Data Source Configuration Wizard.

❑ You can create DataTables from base tables of any accessible database server instance.

❑ You can create DataTables from structured (tabular) XML Infoset documents.

❑ TableAdapters fill and update DataTables through a managed connection. TableAdapters are wrappers over DataAdapter objects.

❑ The Data Source Configuration Wizard lets you choose an existing data connection that's defined in the Server Explorer, or create a new connection object. The wizard then generates parameterized SQL queries or stored procedures for performing UPDATE, INSERT, and DELETE operations. These queries are based on the SELECT query or stored procedure that you specify for filling each DataTable.

❑ DataSets cache copies of original and modified table data in XML format. Thus, DataSets that have a large number of rows consume much more client RAM resources than Recordsets that have the same number of rows.

❑ You can write code to create runtime data connections, DataAdapters, and basic DataSets, but it's much easier to take advantage of VS 2005 automated processes for generating the code to create typed DataSets, which are defined by an XML schema.

❑ DataSet updates occur row-by-row if you don't specify a value greater than 1 for the new `DataAdapter.BatchSize` property, which sets the maximum number of updated rows per batch.

Figure 1-5 compares the objects required by updatable ADODB Recordsets and ADO.NET 1.*x* and 2.0 typed DataSets. Components that are new in ADO.NET 2.0 are shaded. Parameters are optional for ADODB commands, but not for updatable TableAdapters, which have four standard commands — `SelectCommand`, `InsertCommand`, `UpdateCommand`, and `DeleteCommand`. Use of the new ADO.NET 2.0 BindingNavigator components is optional. The section "Add a DataGridView and DataNavigator Controls," later in this chapter, describes how the BindingSource fits into ADO.NET 2.0's data access architecture.

The following sections show you alternative methods for generating Figure 1-5's ADO.NET objects with VS 2005 and SQL Server 2000 or 2005.

> *VS 2005 materializes TableAdapters, DataSets, BindingSources, and BindingNavigators as named objects in the form design tray. TableAdapters and DataSets also appear in the Toolbox's ProjectName Components section; the Data section has DataSet, BindingSource, and BindingNavigator controls. During the early part of VS 2005's long gestation period, these design-time objects collectively were called Data Components, BindingSource was called a DataConnector, and BindingNavigator was DataNavigator. This book uses the term data component to refer to named design-time data objects that reside in the form design tray.*

Add a Typed DataSet from an SQL Server Data Source

ADO.NET uses the term *data source* as a synonym for a typed DataSet with a predefined, persistent database connection. The process of creating an ADO.NET data source is similar to using VB6's Data Environment Designer to specify an OLE DB data provider from one or more tables. Unlike the Data Environment Designer, multi-table DataSets don't have the hierarchical structure that the OLE DB Shape provider creates for display in VB6's Hierarchical FlexGrid control.

> *Web services and object instances also can act as ADO.NET data sources, as you'll see in later chapters.*

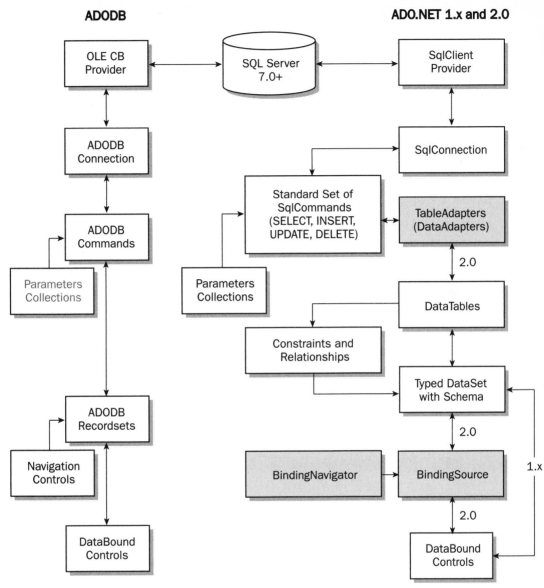

Figure 1-5

Here's how to add a new SQL Server Northwind data source for a new Windows form project and automatically generate a typed DataSet and its components from the Customers table:

1. Choose Data ⇨ Show Data Sources to open the Data Sources window, if necessary, and click Add New Data Source to start the Data Source Configuration Wizard.

2. On the Choose a Data Source Type page, accept the default Database type, and click Next to open the Choose Your Database Connection page, which displays existing data connections, if any, in a dropdown list.

3. Click the New Connection button to open a simplified Add Connection dialog, which usually defaults to Microsoft SQL Server Database File. This option requires attaching a copy of northwnd.mdb to your SQL Server or SQLX instance, so click the Change button to open the Change Data Source dialog, select Microsoft SQL Server in the Data Source list, and click Continue to open the full version of the Add Connection dialog.

4. Type **localhost** or **.\SQLEXPRESS** in the Select or Enter a Server Name combo box. Alternatively, select a local or networked SQL Server or MSDE instance that has a Northwind or NorthwindCS database.

5. Accept the default Use Windows NT Integrated Security option, and open the Select or Enter a Database Name list and select Northwind. Click Test Connection to verify the SqlConnection object, as shown in Figure 1-6.

Figure 1-6

6. Click OK to close the dialog and return to the Choose Your Data Connection page, which displays *ServerName*.Northwind.dbo as the new connection name, System.Data.SqlClient as the Provider, and `Data Source=localhost;Integrated Security=True;Database=Northwind` as the Connection String.

7. Click Next to display the Save the Connection String to the Application Configuration File page. Mark the Yes, Save the Connection As checkbox and accept the default NorthwindConnectionString as the connection string name.

8. Click Next to open the Choose Your Database Objects page, which displays treeview Tables, Views, Stored Procedures, and table-returning Functions. Expand the Tables node and mark the Customers table. Accept NorthwindDataSet as the DataSet Name, as shown in Figure 1-7.

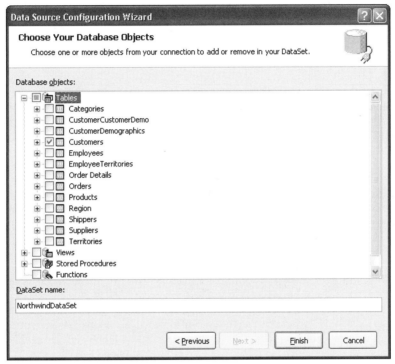

Figure 1-7

Selecting a table automatically generates the SelectCommand that retrieves all table rows, and an UpdateCommand, InsertCommand, and DeleteCommand for base table updates.

9. Click Finish to generate the NorthwindDataSet typed DataSet and display it in the Data Sources window. Expand the Customers node to display the Customers table's columns, as shown in Figure 1-8.

Figure 1-8

The new `SqlConnection` object you created in preceding Steps 3 through 5 appears under Server Explorer's DataConnections node as *ServerName*.Northwind.dbo. You can rename the node in Server Explorer to a simpler name, such as **localhost.Northwind**; doing this doesn't affect dependent objects in your project.

Adding a typed DataSet generates an XSD schema, NorthwindDataSet.xsd for this example, and adds 1,197 lines of VB 2005 code to the NorthwindDataSet.Designer.vb partial class file, which weighs in at 73KB. Partial classes are a new VB 2005 and C# feature that enable extending a class, such as NorthwindDataSet, with additional class files. VB 2005 uses the `Public Partial Class className` statement to identify a partial class file. You must choose Project ➪ Show All Files to see NorthwindDataSet.Designer.vb and two empty NorthwindDataSet.xsc and NorthwindDataSet.xss files.

Double-click the NorthwindDataSet.xsd node in Project Explorer to display the Customers DataTable and its associated Customers TableAdapter, as shown in Figure 1-9, in the Schema Designer window. The VB 2005 code in *DataSetName*.Designer.vb provides IntelliSense for DataSet objects and lets you early-bind DataTable and DataSet objects. The code also provides direct access to named classes, methods, and events for the DataSet and its TableAdapter(s) — Customers TableAdapter for this example — in the NorthwindDataSet.Designer.vb code window's Classes and Methods lists.

Figure 1-10 shows Internet Explorer displaying the first few lines of the 352-line schema .

> *If you've worked with typed DataSets in VS 2003, you'll notice that the schema for ADO 2.0 DataSets is much more verbose than the ADO 1.x version, which has only 30 lines that define the Customers DataSet. ADO.NET 2.0 prefixes the design-time schema with 258 lines of* `<xs:annotation>` *information, which provide a full definition of the DataSet and its connection string, commands and their parameters, and column mapping data. The part of the schema that defines the elements for the table fields grows from 30 to 94 lines because element definitions now contain* `maxLength` *attribute values and use* `restrictionBase` *attributes to specify XSD data types.*

Figure 1-9

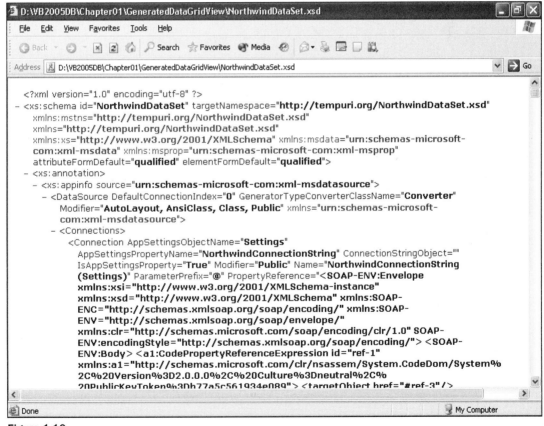

Figure 1-10

Using the `DataSet.WriteXml` and `DataSet.WriteXmlSchema` *methods to persist DataSets to local files shows that the Customers DataSet schema, which differs greatly from the design-time version, is 9.31KB and the XML data document is 37.3KB. The section "Create a Complete Data Entry Form in One Step," later in this chapter, includes code to save the schema for the Northwind Customers DataSet. You can't open the saved schema in the project's Schema Designer.*

Add a DataGridView and BindingNavigator Controls

Opening Form1 and the Data Sources window changes the appearance of the DataSource nodes. By default, the Customers DataTable icon now represents a DataGridView control. Dragging the Customers table node from the Data Sources window to your project's default Form1 autogenerates four components in the tray below the form designer and adds DataGridView and DataNavigator controls to a dramatically expanded form, as shown in Figure 1-11.

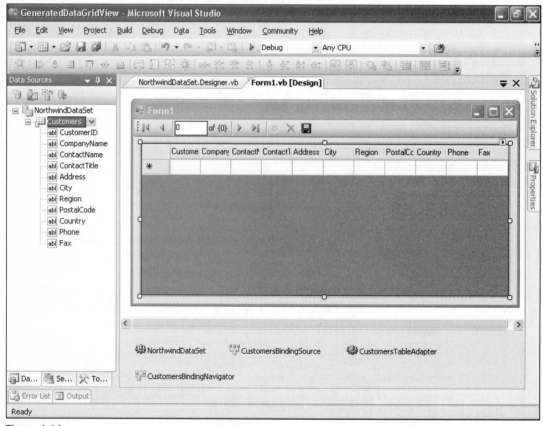

Figure 1-11

"Surfacing" is a common term for adding data and other components to the tray.

Here are descriptions of the four tray components shown in Figure 1-11:

❑ `NorthwindDataSet` is the form's reference to the data source for the form, NorthwindDataSource.xsd.

❑ `CustomersTableAdapter` is the form's wrapper for an `SqlDataAdapter` object, which fills the `NorthwindDataSet`'s `Customers` DataTable by invoking the `CustomersTableAdapter.Fill` method. `Update`, `Insert`, and `Delete` methods send DataSet changes to the database server. The `CustomersTableAdapter.Adapter` property lets you access the underlying `SqlDataAdapter`.

❑ `CustomersBindingSource` is a form-based `BindingSource` object that unifies control data binding and row data navigation for the `Customers` DataTable by providing direct access to the `BindingManager` object. To make it easier for VB6 developers to adapt to ADO.NET 2.0, BindingSources have properties and methods that emulate `ADODB.Recordset` objects. Examples are `AllowEdit`, `AllowAddNew`, and `AllowRemove` (delete) properties, and corresponding `AddNew`, `CancelNew`, `EndNew`, `Edit`, `CancelEdit`, and `EndEdit` methods. Familiar `MoveFirst`, `MoveLast`, `MoveNext`, and `MovePrevious` methods handle row navigation. Enabling navigation requires binding a DataGridView or adding other controls to manipulate the BindingSource.

❑ `CustomersBindingNavigator` is a custom ToolStrip control that emulates the VCR and other buttons of an `ADODB.DataControl`. Binding the `CustomersBindingNavigator` to the `CustomersBindingSource` enables the buttons to invoke the `Move...`, `AddNew`, and `Cancel...` methods. By default, BindingNavigators dock to the top of the form. When you run the form, you can drag a BindingNavigator to a more natural position at the bottom of the form; alternatively, you can set a DataNavigator's `Dock` property value to `Bottom` in the designer.

DataComponents, DataConnectors, and DataNavigators are new ADO.NET 2.0 components and controls that replace ADO.NET 1.x's form-based DataConnections and DataAdapters. VS 2005 data sources automatically create DataSet Relationships between tables, which previously required manual intervention. DataConnectors simplify code for navigating data tables. The DataSet.vb file contains the classes, interfaces, and event handlers for the data components.

The final step in the VS 2005 data form autogeneration process is adding the `CustomersComponent.Fill` method to the `Form1_Load` event handler, and code to save DataSet changes isn't added to the `bindingNavigatorSaveItem_Click` handler automatically, because of code complexity when the DataSet contains multiple DataTables. Saving multiple changes to parent and child tables requires sequencing inserts, updates, and deletions to maintain referential integrity.

```
Private Sub Form1_Load(ByVal sender As System.Object, _
    ByVal e As System.EventArgs) Handles MyBase.Load
    'TODO: This line of code loads data into the 'NorthwindDataSet.Customers' table.
    'You can move, or remove it, as needed.
    Me.CustomersTableAdapter.Fill(Me.NorthwindDataSet.Customers)
End Sub

Private Sub dataNavigatorSaveItem_Click(ByVal sender As System.Object, _
    ByVal e As System.EventArgs) Handles dataNavigatorSaveItem.Click
    Me.CustomersBindingSource.EndEdit()
    Me.CustomersTableAdapter.Update(Me.NorthwindDataSet.Customers)
End Sub
```

Figure 1-12 shows the final form after reducing the form's size, expanding the DataGridView control to fill the available space, and pressing F5 to build, debug, and run the project.

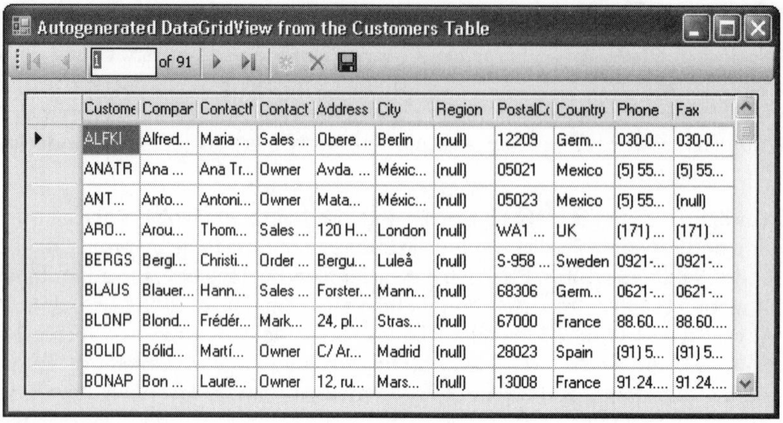

Figure 1-12

The CustomersDataGridView *is bound to the Northwind Customers table, and editing is enabled by default. Changes you make to the DataGridView don't propagate to the table until you click the Save Data button. To make editing easier, you can automate increasing the column widths to match the content by setting the DataGridView's* AutoSizeColumnsMode *property value to* AllCells *or* DisplayedCells, *which adds a horizontal scrollbar to the control.*

Persist and Reopen the DataSet

The project's frmDataGridView_Load event handler includes the following code to save the NorthwindDataSet's XML data document — with and without an embedded schema — and the schema only. You can add similar code after the last DataComponent.Fill or DataAdapter.Fill invocation of any data project to persist its DataSet.

```
Private Sub frmDataGridView_Load(ByVal sender As System.Object, _
    ByVal e As System.EventArgs) Handles MyBase.Load
    Me.CustomersTableAdapter.Fill(Me.NorthwindDataSet.Customers)
    Dim strPath As String = Application.StartupPath
    With Me.NorthwindDataSet
        .WriteXml(strPath + "CustsNoSchema.xml", XmlWriteMode.IgnoreSchema)
        .WriteXml(strPath + "CustsWithSchema.xml", XmlWriteMode.WriteSchema)
        .WriteXmlSchema(strPath + "CustsSchema.xsd")
    End With
End Sub
```

Persisting the DataSet as an XML document without the embedded schema lets you support disconnected users by reloading the DataSet from the file. You can substitute the following statement for Me.CustomersTableAdapter.Fill(Me.NorthwindDataSet.Customers) when the user is disconnected:

```
Me.NorthwindDataSet.ReadXml(strPath + "CustsNoSchema.xml", XmlReadMode.Auto)
```

The real-world scenario for persisting and reloading DataSets is more complex than that shown here. Later chapters describe how to save and reload pending DataSet changes that haven't been committed to the base tables. The XmlReadMode.Auto argument is the default, so including it is optional.

The sample project at this point is GeneratedDataGridView.sln in your \VB2005DB\Chapter01\ GeneratedDataGridView folder.

Change from a DataViewGrid to a Details Form

The default combination of DataViewGrid and DataNavigator controls speeds the creation of a usable form. However, a DataNavigator is much more useful for a details form that displays column values in text boxes or other bound controls, such as date pickers for `DateTime` and checkboxes for `Boolean` values. The Data Sources window makes it easy to change a DataGridView to a details form. Delete the DataGridView control, display the Data Sources window, open the dropdown list for the DataTable, and select Details, as shown in Figure 1-13.

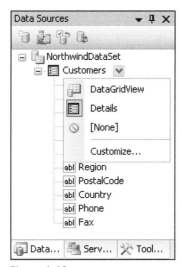

Figure 1-13

Drag the DataTable icon to the form to automatically add a column of labels with associated data-bound controls — text boxes for this example — to the form. Figure 1-14, which is a modified version of the GeneratedDataGridView project, shows the labels and text boxes rearranged to reduce form height.

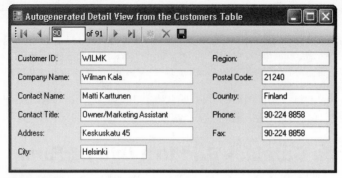

Figure 1-14

*The completed GeneratedDetailView.sln project is in the \VB2005DB\Chapter01\
GeneratedDetailView folder.*

Add a Related DataBound Control

You can add a related table to the Data Sources window and then add a control, such as a DataGridView, that you bind to the related BindingAdapter. To add a related OrdersDataGridView control to a copy of the GeneratedDetailView.sln project, do the following:

1. Copy and paste the GeneratedDetailView folder, and rename the new folder **OrdersDetailView**. Don't rename the solution or project.

2. Press F5 to build and compile the project. Correct any object name errors that the debugger reports.

3. Open the Data Source window, and click the Configure DataSet with Wizard button to open the Choose Your Database Objects page.

4. Expand the Tables node, mark the Orders table checkbox, and click Finish, which adds in the Data Sources window a related Orders node to the Customers table and a standalone Orders node (see Figure 1-15).

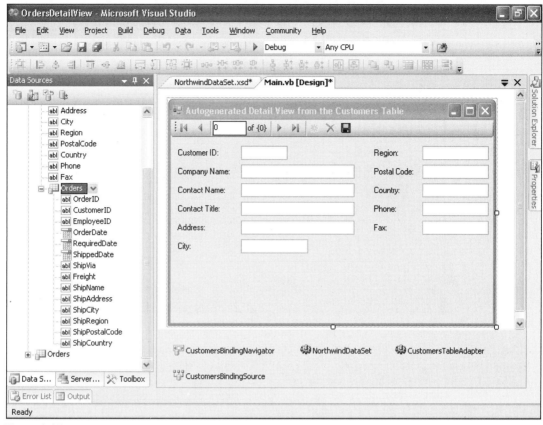

Figure 1-15

5. With DataGridView selected in the dropdown list, drag the related Orders node below the bound text boxes of the form to autogenerate an OrdersDataGridView control.

6. Adjust the size and location of the controls, and set the OrdersDataGridView
.AutoSizeRowsMode property value to DisplayedCells. Optionally, alter the form's Text property to reflect the design change.

7. Press F5 to build and run the project. The form appears as shown in Figure 1-16.

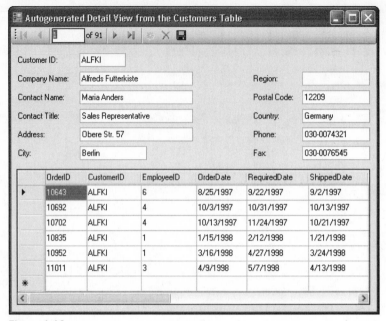

Figure 1-16

Dragging the related Orders table node to the form adds an `OrdersTableAdapter` and `OrdersBindingSource` to the tray and the `OrdersDataGridView` control to the form. The `OrdersDataGridView` control's `DataSource` property value is the `OrdersBindingSource`. The `OrdersBindingSource`'s `DataSource` property value is `CustomersBindingSource` and the `DataMember` property value is `FK_Orders_Customers`, which is the foreign-key relationship on the CustomerID field between the Customers and Orders tables. To verify the properties of `FK_Orders_Customers`, open NorthwindDataSet.xsd in the DataSet Designer, right-click the relation line between the Orders and Customers tables, and choose Edit Relation to open the Relation dialog (see Figure 1-17).

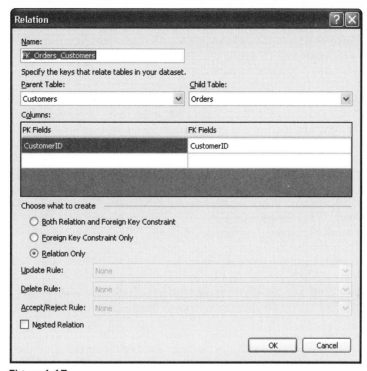

Figure 1-17

Relations you define by adding related tables to the Data Sources window don't enforce referential integrity by default. You must change the default Relation Only property value to one of the other options to maintain referential integrity. You also can specify cascade or other options for Update, Delete, and Accept/Reject Rules.

Summary

Microsoft designed the basic ADO.NET feature set to resemble that of ADO. The code to create a database connection with ADO.NET's SqlClient, OleDb, or Odbc managed providers is quite similar to that for ADODB.Connection objects. The same is true for ADO.NET's connection-specific commands and parameters. The primary differences between ADO and ADO.NET involve processing resultsets. DataReaders correspond to ADO's default forward-only, read-only Recordsets. The SqlClient data provider provides a substantial performance boost by eliminating the COM-based OLE DB layer and communicating with SQL Server 7.0 and later using SQL Server's native TDS protocol.

ADO.NET data binding to typed DataSet objects and data-related event handling differ radically from ADO. Many experienced VB6 database developers discovered that migrating from ADODB Recordsets to ADO.NET 1.*x* DataAdapters, typed DataSets, and databound controls wasn't a walk in the park. Creating an ordinary data entry form with ADO.NET 1.*x*'s DataGrid or other controls bound to a DataSet's DataTable and adding record navigation buttons involved writing much more code than that required for a corresponding VB6 project. To ease the pain of the transition from VS 6 to VS 2005, ADO.NET 2.0 provides drag-and-drop methods for autogenerating the components and controls to create a basic, single-table form with the new DataGridView and DataNavigator controls, plus DataComponent and DataContainer components. Changing the DataGridView to a details view with individual databound controls takes only a minute or two.

The new drag-and-drop methods and component configuration wizards are useful for product demos by Microsoft's .NET evangelists, which elicit "oohs" and "aahs" from conference and user-group attendees. Autogenerated data entry forms can help programmers gain a basic understanding of ADO.NET data binding and flatten the ADO.NET learning curve. But you'll probably find that autogenerated forms aren't useful in real-world production applications. A major shortcoming is the default to parameterized SQL statements for data retrieval and update operations; most DBAs require stored procedures for *all* operations on base tables. Fortunately, you can intervene in the autogeneration process to specify and create the required stored procedures. Another issue is the BindingNavigator's lack of shortcut keys, which are a necessity for heads-down data entry. You'll discover other limitations of autogenerated forms and their workarounds as you progress through the book.

> *The preceding comments on databound control autogeneration doesn't apply to generating typed DataSets. Writing VB 2005 code for typed DataSets isn't a practical alternative. You can, however, create lightweight, untyped DataSets with only a few lines of code. Later chapters provide code examples to create untyped DataSets at runtime.*

The following chapters of Parts I and II show you how to create production-quality Windows data entry forms by combining some of the techniques you learned in this chapter with DataSets, TableAdapters, and VB 2005 code to manage data retrieval, DataTable navigation, and multiple base table updates.

2

Introducing New
ADO.NET 2.0 Features

This chapter describes new ADO.NET 2.0 objects and their commonly used methods, properties, and events. Like Chapter 1, "Migrating from ADO to ADO.NET," the chapter begins with descriptions of new runtime objects, such as `DbProviderFactory` and `SqlBulkCopy`, and VB.NET code examples for creating and manipulating the new objects in Windows forms. The chapter continues with more advanced examples of ADO.NET 2.0's components and controls for Windows forms that you add with designers—DataTables, BindingSources, BindingNavigators, and DataGridViews.

You'll learn more from this chapter's examples if you have experience developing non-trivial Windows or Web forms with ADO.NET 1.*x* or have downloaded the sample files and worked through Chapter 1's sample projects. You'll need to download sample files and expand the Chapter02 sample code from the book's Web page to get the most from this chapter. See the Introduction's "Install the Source Code for the Sample Projects" section for details.

> *All SQL Server code examples in this chapter run with SQL Server 2000, SQL Server 2005, or SQL Server 2005 Express Edition (SQLX) and require system administrator (sa) privileges. If you're running SQLX, you must change each project's connection string from* `localhost` *to* `.\SQLEXPRESS`. *Several project examples make changes to the Northwind sample database, so you should make a backup of the original Northwind database if you haven't done so previously.*

Working with New ADO.NET 2.0 Runtime Windows Form Objects

This book defines a *runtime object* as a non-visual, data-related type that you can't—or don't want to—persist (surface) on a Windows form in design mode. You create ADO.NET 2.0 runtime objects by writing VB.NET 2005 code without the aid of VS 2005's design-time wizards or autogenerated code. Microsoft has devoted a substantial share of the VS 2005 and ADO.NET 2.0

development effort to simplifying drag-and-drop generation of basic databound Windows and Web forms. Additional developer investment went into supporting new SQL Server 2005 features with `System.Data` and `System.Xml` objects. Thus, ADO.NET 2.0 includes only a few new and upgraded runtime objects and features that are compatible with SQL Server 2000 data sources. The chapters of Part IV, "SQL Server 2005 and ADO.NET 2.0," cover ADO.NET 2.0 and VB.NET 2005 features that are specific to SQL Server 2005.

Following are the most important new and upgraded runtime objects, methods, and language features for Windows form projects:

❑ `DbProviderFactory` objects let you write common code for alternative data providers and database servers.

❑ `SqlBulkCopy` objects provide high-performance SQL Server batched inserts from relational and XML data sources.

❑ The `SqlConnection.RetrieveStatistics` method delivers detailed information about the open SQL Server connection.

❑ Asynchronous `SqlCommand` execution enables interleaving multiple long-running queries or updates.

❑ Upgraded `DataTable` objects now support common DataSet features, such as the `ReadXml` and `WriteXml` methods, return values from Web services, remoting, and streaming interfaces.

❑ DataTables can be assigned namespaces and namespace prefixes.

❑ Nullable types let you define strongly typed objects with members whose values can be set to `DbNull`.

The following sections explain how to use the preceding ADO.NET 2.0 features with code examples derived from sample Windows form projects.

Use the DbProviderFactories to Create Database-Agnostic Projects

The new `System.Data.Common.DbProviderFactories` class provides database developers the opportunity to attempt creation of data source–agnostic applications. Creating non-trivial data entry applications that can seamlessly interoperate with all relational database managers for which managed data providers are available isn't a piece of cake. Minor differences in SQL syntax, data types, stored procedure dialects, error handling, and other database-dependent features undoubtedly will require custom workarounds. If you're currently using the .NET Framework's OleDb managed data provider or ADODB with OLE DB providers to deliver database interoperability, you'll probably find that Microsoft and third-party ADO.NET managed providers offer improved performance and, as a result, greater scalability. On the other hand, the implementation latitude that .NET grants to managed data providers makes it difficult to write code that's totally provider-transparent.

> *Third-party suites of managed .NET data providers can reduce interoperability issues at the expense of added licensing cost. For example, DataDirect Technologies offers managed data providers for IBM DB2 and DB2 UDB; Oracle 8i, 9i, and 10g; SQL Server 7 and 2000; Sybase Adaptive Server 11.5 and 11.9; and Sybase Adaptive Server Enterprise 12.0 and 12.5. All DataDirect providers use escapes to minimize SQL syntax differences and communicate with servers by the database vendors' wire*

protocols. For more information on current .NET data provider interoperability issues, visit
`http://www.datadirect.com/products/dotnet/docs/dotnet-interop/`.

Creating a `DataReader` object from the `DbProviderFactories` class is a seven-step process:

1. Create a `DbProviderFactory` object by passing the full class name of the data provider, such as `System.Data.SqlClient`, as the argument of a `Dim FactoryName As DbProviderFactory = DbProviderFactories.GetFactory(strProvider)` statement.

2. Create an `IDbConnection` object by invoking the `Dim ConnectionName As IDbConnection = FactoryName.CreateConnection()` method.

3. Set the `ConnectionName.Connection.String` property value.

4. Create an `IDbCommand` object by invoking the `Dim CommandName As IDbCommand = ConnectionName.CreateCommand()` method.

5. Set the `CommandName.CommandType` (optional) and `CommandName.CommandText` property values that are appropriate for the provider.

6. Invoke the `ConnectionName.Open()` method.

7. Create an `IDataReader` object by invoking the `Dim ReaderName As IDataReader = CommandName.ExecuteReader` method.

The `IDataReader` object has the same members as the ADO.NET 1.*x* and 2.0 provider-specific DataReaders, plus a new `GetSchemaTable` method that the next section describes.

The sample DbFactoryTest.sln project displays data from one of three Northwind tables by creating and traversing SqlClient, OleDb, or Odbc `IDataReader` objects that you specify by selecting the appropriate option button. The form also includes a DataGridView control to display the table's schema DataTable, the subject of the next section, as shown in Figure 2-1.

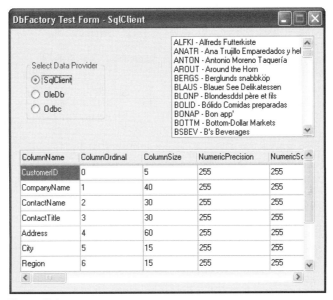

Figure 2-1

The following listing contains the code for the variable declarations and the option button event-handler for the OleDb DbProviderFactory:

```
'OleDb provider settings - Products table
Private strOleDbProvider As String = "System.Data.OleDb"
Private strOleDbConn As String = "Provider=SQLOLEDB;Data Source=localhost;" + _
    "Initial Catalog=Northwind;Integrated Security=SSPI"
Private strOleDbTable As String = "Products"

Private Sub optOleDb_CheckedChanged(ByVal sender As System.Object, _
 ByVal e As System.EventArgs) Handles optOleDb.CheckedChanged
    If optOleDb.Checked = True Then
       PopulateList(strOleDbProvider, strOleDbConn, strOleDbTable)
       Me.Text = "DbFactory Test Form - OleDb"
    End If
End Sub
```

The optOleDB_CheckedChanged event handler passes the required OleDb parameter values to the PopulateList procedure, which is implemented by the following code:

```
Private Sub PopulateList(ByVal strProvider As String, _
    ByVal strConn As String, ByVal strTable As String)
    'Create a DbProviderFactory, IDbConnection, IDbCommand, and IDataReader
    'for the specified data provider
    Dim cnFactory As IDbConnection
    Dim drCusts As IDataReader
    Try
       'Specify the DataProvider
       Dim dpFactory As DbProviderFactory = _
        DbProviderFactories.GetFactory(strProvider)
       'Create a connection
       cnFactory = dpFactory.CreateConnection()
       cnFactory.ConnectionString = strConn
       'Create a command and open the connection
       Dim cmFactory As IDbCommand = cnFactory.CreateCommand
       cmFactory.CommandType = CommandType.Text
       cmFactory.CommandText = "SELECT * FROM " + strTable
       cnFactory.Open()
       'Create and traverse a DataReader
       drData = cmFactory.ExecuteReader(CommandBehavior.KeyInfo)
       lstData.Items.Clear()
       Dim dtSchema As DataTable
       With drData
           While drData.Read
              'Must use Object because datatypes change
              lstData.Items.Add(.GetValue(0).ToString + _
              " - " + .GetValue(1).ToString)
           End While
           '...
       End With
    Catch exc As Exception
       MsgBox(exc.Message + exc.StackTrace)
    Finally
```

```
            drData.Close()
            cnFactory.Close()
        End Try
    End Sub
```

You must specify `CommandBehavior.KeyInfo` *as the* `ExecuteReader` *argument to return correct primary key and related field properties.*

If your projects must implement data-provider independence and you're willing to write workarounds for subtle or not-so-subtle differences between data provider implementations, give the DbProviderFactories a try. Bear in mind that vendor-independent code must use .NET native data types, rather than the provider-specific data types for SQL Server, Oracle, and other database servers supported by third-party add-ins.

DbProviderFactories implement database late binding, which defeats many features of the ADO.NET programming model. Vendor-specific SQL and stored procedure execution syntax make writing vendor-transparent code with ADO.NET 2.0 data providers difficult — if not impossible.

Retrieve Base Table Schemas

ADO.NET 1.*x* and 2.0 DataReaders and ADO.NET 2.0 DataTableReaders have a `GetSchemaTable` method that returns the corresponding object's metadata (schema) in a `DataTable` object. You use schema DataTable property values to provide data type information for projects that substitute code for bound controls to display and update base tables. Schema DataTables supply `ColumnLength` values to set the `MaxLength` property of text boxes and `IsReadOnly` values that you can apply to the `ReadOnly` property of common data-entry controls. These DataTables also return primary key information, such as column index(es) and autoincrement details.

The System.Data.ObjectSpaces.ObjectDataReader, which was included with early alpha and Community Technical Preview versions of VS 2005, provided members similar to those of other DataReaders, including the `GetSchemaTable` *method. In May 2004, Microsoft announced that ObjectSpaces will be released as a component of the WinFS file system enhancements.*

You create a DataReader's schema DataTable and populate a DataGridView to display column properties with code similar to the following:

```
Dim dtSchema as DataTable
dtSchema = drData.GetSchemaTable()
With dgvSchema
    .RowHeadersVisible = False
    .DataSource = dtSchema
    .AutoGenerateColumns = True
    .Columns(0).Frozen = True
    'Adjust column widths
    .Columns("BaseSchemaName").Width = 110
    If .Columns.Count = 24 Then
        'SqlClient only
        .Columns(23).Width = 200
    End If
End With
```

The sample DbFactoryTest.sln sample project's PopulateList *procedure contains the full version of the preceding code.*

The schema DataTable contains a row for each base table column, and 27 fields of SqlDataReader column properties. OleDbDataReaders and OdbcDataReaders return 18 properties; DataTableReaders have 25 property fields. The DataTableReader object is new in ADO.NET 2.0, so the following table compares the schema DataTable's field index and property names for the three classes of DataReaders.

Index	SqlDataReader	OleDb and Odbc DateReaders	DataTableReader
0	ColumnName	ColumnName	ColumnName
1	ColumnOrdinal	ColumnOrdinal	ColumnOrdinal
2	ColumnSize	ColumnSize	ColumnSize
3	NumericPrecision	NumericPrecision	NumericPrecision
4	NumericScale	NumericScale	NumericScale
5	IsUnique	DataType	DataType
6	IsKey	ProviderType	ProviderType
7	BaseServerName	IsLong	IsLong
8	BaseCatalogName	AllowDBNull	AllowDBNull
9	BaseColumnName	IsReadOnly	IsReadOnly
10	BaseSchemaName	IsRowVersion	IsRowVersion
11	BaseTableName	IsUnique	IsUnique
12	DataType	IsKey	IsKey
13	AllowDBNull	IsAutoIncrement	IsAutoIncrement
14	ProviderType	BaseSchemaName	BaseCatalogName
15	IsAliased	BaseCatalogName	BaseSchemaName
16	IsExpression	BaseTableName	BaseTableName
17	IsIdentity	BaseColumnName	BaseColumnName
18	IsAutoIncrement		AutoIncrementSeed
19	IsRowVersion		AutoIncrementStep
20	IsHidden		DefaultValue
21	IsLong		Expression
22	IsReadOnly		ColumnMapping
23	ProviderSpecific DataType		BaseTableNamespace
24	DataTypeName		BaseColumnNamespace

Index	SqlDataReader	OleDb and Odbc DateReaders	DataTableReader
25	XmlSchema CollectionDatabase		
26	XmlSchema CollectionOwningSchema		
27	XmlSchema CollectionName		

Field properties shown in bold are members of ADO.NET 2.0's new `System.Data.Common` `.SchemaTableColumn` *class and are required. The remainder are optional members of the* `SystemData.Common.SchemaOptionalTableColumn` *class.* `XmlSchemaCollection...` *fields appear for SQL Server 2005 tables only, and specify the schema, if present, for fields of the* `xml` *datatype.*

Database developers can translate most property names listed in the preceding table, so the following table lists only those properties whose meanings aren't evident or that return unexpected values.

Property Name	Description
ColumnSize	Returns –1 if data isn't available; otherwise, the column size in bytes
DataType	The native .NET data type that corresponds to the column datatype, such as `System.Int32` or `System.String`
ProviderType	The integer value of a data type enumeration that's specific to the data provider
IsLong	True indicates an SQL `text`, `ntext`, or `image` data type and a Jet Memo or OLE Object field.
ProviderSpecificDataType	One of the Sql*Types*, such as `SqlString` or `SqlInt32` (SqlClient only)
Expression	The expression for a calculated DataTable column (DataTable only)
ColumnMapping	A `string` value that specifies the column of a destination table or 1 if the column isn't mapped (DataTable only)
BaseTableNamespace	The XML namespace assigned to the table; inherited from the DataSet namespace if empty, such as `http://tempuri.org/DataSetName` (DataTable only)
BaseColumnNamespace	The XML namespace assigned to the table; inherited from the DataSet namespace if empty (DataTable only)

Table continued on following page

Property Name	Description
XmlSchema CollectionDatabase	The name of the SQL Server 2005 database containing the schema collection for a column of the xml datatype (null if the xml column doesn't have a schema)
XmlSchema CollectionOwningSchema	The SQL Server 2005 relational schema where the XmlSchema collection is located (null if the xml column doesn't have a schema)
XmlSchema CollectionName	The name of the schema collection for a column of the xml datatype (null if the xml column doesn't have a schema)

The section "Create Standalone DataTables," later in this chapter, describes how to load and persist DataTables from databases and XML files, and display schema information for DataTable objects.

Check Available SQL Server Instances and ADO.NET 2.0 Data Providers

The System.Data.Common.SqlDataSourceEnumerator.Instance.GetDataSources method returns a DataTable that has a row for each accessible SQL Server 2000 and 2005 instance. Columns display ServerName, InstanceName, IsClustered, and Version properties.

Invoking the DbProviderFactories.GetFactoryClasses() method returns a similar DataTable containing one row for each Microsoft .NET managed data provider installed, with columns for the provider's Name, Description, InvariantName, and AssemblyQualifiedName properties and the number of SupportedClasses. Third-party data providers, such as Oracle ODP .NET for Oracle 10g (Oracle.DataAccess.dll), don't appear in the table.

> *The machine.config file contains an element for each of the four ADO.NET 2.0 data provider namespaces, and a system.data section that adds these providers to DbProviderFactories. The* GetFactoryClasses *method reads the machine.config file to deliver the list of installed providers.*

The following code from the DataEnums.sln sample project populates two DataGridView controls with an SQL Server instance and an installed Microsoft .NET provider data:

```
Private Sub frmDataEnums_Load(ByVal sender As System.Object, _
    ByVal e As System.EventArgs) Handles MyBase.Load
  'Get and load list of SQL Server instances
  Dim dtServers As DataTable = SqlDataSourceEnumerator.Instance.GetDataSources
  With dgvServers
    .DataSource = dtServers
    .AutoGenerateColumns = True
    .RowHeadersVisible = False
    .BorderStyle = BorderStyle.None
  End With
  'Get and load list of .NET data providers installed
  Dim dtProviders As DataTable = DbProviderFactories.GetFactoryClasses()
  With dgvProviders
```

```
            .DataSource = dtProviders
            .AutoGenerateColumns = True
            .RowHeadersVisible = False
            'Increase the row height
            .RowTemplate.Height = 22
            .BorderStyle = BorderStyle.None
        End With
    End Sub
```

Running the DataEnums project enumerates your SQL Server instances and data providers. Figure 2-2 shows an SQL Server 2000 default instance (OAKLEAF-W2K3), an MSDE named instance (OAKLEAF-W2K3\SHAREPOINT), an SQL Server 2005 instance (OAKLEAF-MS18), an SQL Express (SQLX) named instance (OAKLEAF-MS18\SQLEXPRESS), and data providers that are accessible to or installed on the development computer used to write this book.

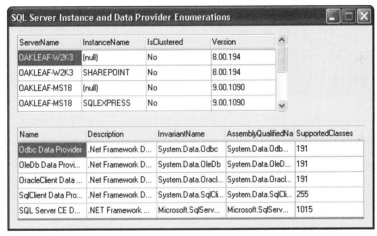

Figure 2-2

Batch Inserts to SQL Server Tables with the SqlBulkCopy Object

SQL Server's bcp utility and BULK INSERT statement are the traditional methods for high-speed addition of rows to SQL Server tables. ADO.NET 2.0 gives you another option — programming the new SqlBulkCopy object. A DataReader for a relational table is the most common row source. Alternatively, you can insert rows from tabular XML documents by creating a runtime DataSet with one or more DataTables to copy.

Bulk copying XML documents to SQL Server tables — a process called shredding — is much simpler with SqlBulkCopy than SQLXML 3.0's bulk loading feature. Bulk loading requires an annotated XML schema to map elements or attributes to base table columns. SqlBulkCopy has a ColumnMappings *collection that lets you define the relationship between source DataTable and destination base-table columns.*

Here are the steps to insert rows from a DataReader into an existing destination base table:

1. Create a Connection and Command for the source data. You can use any .NET data provider to connect to the data source and create the DataReader.

2. Apply the `Command.ExecuteReader` method to create the DataReader.

3. Create a New `SqlBulkCopy` object with the connection string and appropriate `SqlBulkCopyOptions` enumeration members as its two arguments.

4. Set the `SqlBulkCopy.DestinationTableName` property value.

5. Add `ColumnMapping` members to the `ColumnMappings` collection if the schema of the destination table differs from the source table or query.

6. Set other optional SqlBulkCopy property values, such as `BatchSize` and `BulkCopyTimeout`.

7. If your copy operation involves a very large number of records or runs over a slow network connection, add a handler for the `SqlBulkCopy.SqlRowsCopied` event to display the number or percentage of records copied.

8. Invoke the `SqlBulkCopy.WriteToServer` method to perform the copy operation.

9. Apply the `SqlBulkCopy.Close()` method and, if you're done, close the Connection. Otherwise reuse the `SqlBulkCopy` object to perform another operation.

The following table describes members of the `SqlBulkCopyOptions` enumeration.

Member Name	Description
CheckConstraints	Applies constraint checking during the copy process
Default	Uses no options (defaults) for the bulk copy operation
FireTriggers	Allows INSERT triggers to fire during the copy process
KeepIdentity	Uses identity values from the source table instead of generating new identity values based on the destination table's seed and increment values
KeepNulls	Retains source null values in spite of destination table default values
TableLock	Applies a table lock for the duration of the copy process, instead of default row locks
UseInternalTransaction	Causes each bulk-copy batch to execute within a transaction

KeepIdentity is the most important member of the SqlBulkCopyOptions enumeration for tables that use an identity column as the primary key. If you don't specify this option, the destination table keys might differ from the source table values. It's also a good practice to add the UseInternalTransaction option to prevent partial copies if the process throws an exception.

The simplest example of an SqlBulkCopy operation creates copies of tables in the same database. The following code from the BulkCopySameSchema.sln project copies the Northwind Products tables as ProductsCopy:

```
Private Sub btnCopyProds_Click(ByVal sender As System.Object, ByVal e As
System.EventArgs) Handles btnCopyProds.Click
    'Copy Products table to ProductsCopy
    Dim sdrProds As SqlDataReader
    Dim sbcProds As SqlBulkCopy
    Try
        cnnNwind.Open()
        'Delete records, if present
        cmdProds.CommandText = "DELETE FROM ProductsCopy"
        Dim intRecs As Integer = cmdProds.ExecuteNonQuery

        'Create and execute the source reader
        cmdProds.CommandText = "SELECT * FROM Products"
        sdrProds = cmdProds.ExecuteReader()

        'Create a bulk copy object with an associated connection
        'Specify KeepIdentity to retain ProductId values
        sbcProds = New SqlBulkCopy(strConn, _
          SqlBulkCopyOptions.UseInternalTransaction Or _
          SqlBulkCopyOptions.KeepIdentity)
        'Add a handler
        AddHandler sbcProds.SqlRowsCopied, _
            New SqlRowsCopiedEventHandler(AddressOf ProdRowAdded)
        With sbcProds
            .DestinationTableName = "ProductsCopy"
            'Use a single batch, if possible
            .BatchSize = 0
            .BulkCopyTimeout = 30
            .NotifyAfter = 1
            .WriteToServer(sdrProds)
            .Close()
        End With
        sdrProds.Close()
    Catch excCopy As Exception
        MsgBox(excCopy.Message + excCopy.StackTrace, , _
            "Products Bulk Copy Exception")
    Finally
        sbcProds.Close()
        sdrProds.Close()
        cnnNwind.Close()
        btnCopyProds.Enabled = True
    End Try
End Sub
```

The SqlBulkCopy.NotifyAfter property determines the number of rows added before the SqlRowsCopied event fires. Here's the code for an SqlRowsCopied event handler that displays the Products table copy progress in a text box:

```
Sub ProdRowAdded(ByVal oSource As Object, ByVal oArgs As SqlRowsCopiedEventArgs)
    'Display number of rows added
    txtProdRows.Text = oArgs.RowsCopied.ToString
    Application.DoEvents()
End Sub
```

> **Displaying copy progress causes a substantial reduction in bulk copy performance. In production applications that must provide user feedback, set the** NotifyAfter **property value to no less than 10 percent of the total number of records added.**

Figure 2-3 shows the BulkCopySameSchema.sln project's form after copying both tables. Transact-SQL scripts recreate the table in the `frmBulkCopy_Load` event handler. The list boxes display source table primary key and second-column values when the form loads and destination table values after copying. The Batch Size spin (numeric up-down) button determines the number of rows per batch; 0 (the default) attempts to send all rows to the server in a single batch. Setting the batch size to 1 and recopying the tables lets you compare performance of bulk versus row-by-row operations.

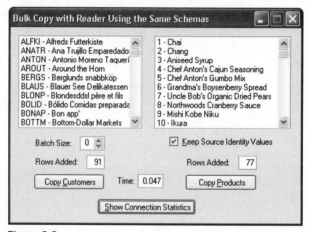

Figure 2-3

Data and code caching results in a substantial execution time difference between initial and subsequent bulk copy operations. Thus, you should compare execution times for varying batch sizes after one or two tests with the batch size set to 0.

Clearing the Keep Source Identity Values checkbox removes the `KeepIdentity` option from the Products table's SqlBulkCopy constructor. In this case, the primary key values increment by 77 for each copy operation. The next section describes the event handler for the Show Connection Statistics button.

Get SQL Server Connection Statistics

The new `SqlConnection.RetrieveStatistics` method queries the target SQL Server instance for current connection data and returns an `IDictionary` object that contains the 18 name/value pairs shown in Figure 2-4.

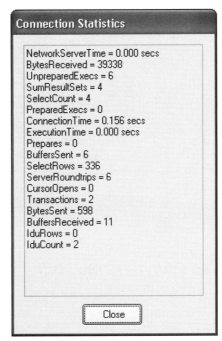

Figure 2-4

You must explicitly enable this feature by executing an `SqlConnection.EnableStatistics = True` instruction prior to invoking the `RetrieveStatistics` method. The simplest method for handling the name/value pairs is to cast the `IDictionary` object to a `HashTable` type, and then iterate the HashTable in a `For Each ... Next` loop. The following code from the BulkCopySameSchema.sln project displays the statistics in the text box of a simple frmConnStats form:

```
Private Sub btnShowStats_Click(ByVal sender As System.Object, _
  ByVal e As System.EventArgs) Handles btnShowStats.Click
    'Display connection statistics
    Try
        htStats = CType(cnnNwind.RetrieveStatistics(), Hashtable)
        Dim txtStats As Control = frmConnStats.Controls.Item("txtStats")
        txtStats.Text = ""
        Dim oStat As Object
        Dim strStat As String
        For Each oStat In htStats.Keys
```

```
            strStat = oStat.ToString
            If InStr(strStat, "Time") > 0 Then
               txtStats.Text += strStat + " = " + _
                  Microsoft.VisualBasic.Format(CLng(htStats(strStat)) / 1000, _
                  "#,##0.000") + " secs" + vbCrLf
            Else
               txtStats.Text += strStat + " = " + htStats(strStat).ToString + vbCrLf
            End If
         Next
         frmConnStats.Show()
         frmConnStats.Controls.Item("btnClose").Focus()
      Catch excStats As Exception
         MsgBox(excStats.Message + excStats.StackTrace, , _
         "Exception Displaying Connection Statistics")
      End Try
   End Sub
End Sub
```

You can add the preceding code and the `frmConnStats` form to any project that uses an `SqlConnection`. Invoke the `SqlConnection.ResetStatistics` method to initialize the data, except `ConnectionTime`.

Retrieving connection statistics requires a server round-trip, so reserve use of the feature to diagnosing connection problems.

Execute SqlCommands Asynchronously

ADO.NET 2.0 adds `BeginExecuteReader`, `BeginExecuteXmlReader`, and `BeginExecuteNonQuery` methods — together with the corresponding `End...` methods — to the `SqlCommand` classes. These methods let you execute code while waiting for a command to complete execution. To execute an asynchronous SqlCommand, you must add `;Async=True` to the command string that you pass to the SqlConnection's constructor. The following sections provide descriptions and code examples for the three asynchronous SqlCommand execution models that the `IAsyncResult` interface's overloads support. Figure 2-5 illustrates the databases, connections, and commands used with the three models. You'll get more interesting results from the AsyncDataOperations.sln sample project if you have two or three instances of SQL Server 2000 or 2005 with the Northwind sample database available from each instance.

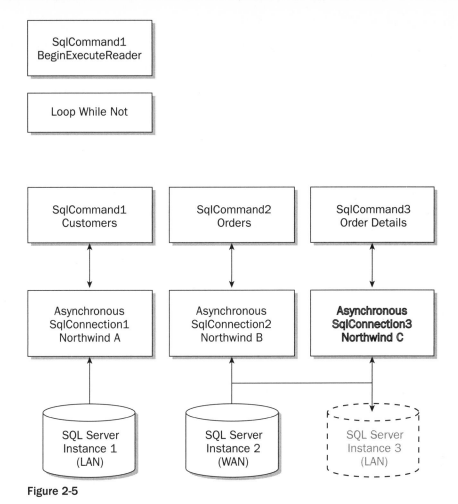

Figure 2-5

The default shared memory provider for SQL Server 2000 doesn't support asynchronous commands. Thus, you must use localhost, *not* (local), *as the Server or Data Source value of the connection string for a local instance of SQL Server 2000.*

The asynchronous SqlCommand examples assume that you're familiar with use of the IAsyncResult *interface, which monitors the progress of an asynchronous method invocation. For more information on asynchronous method operation, see VS 2005's "Asynchronous Programming Overview" help topic.*

The Polling Model

The polling model is the simplest of the three models. Figure 2-6 illustrates program flow for three asynchronous connections.

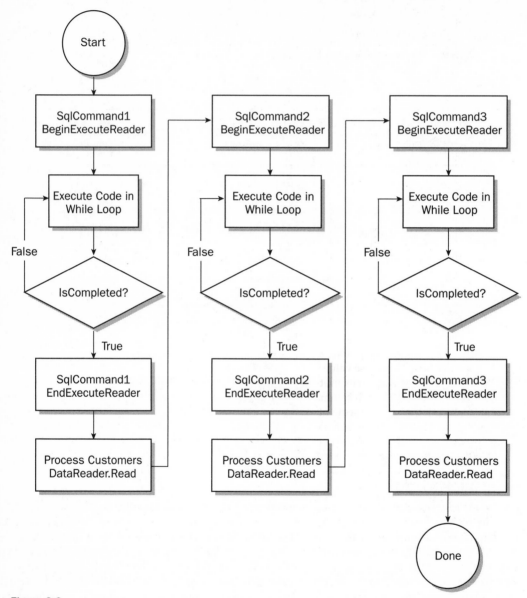

Figure 2-6

The following code opens an asynchronous command to the Northwind database on a local SQL Server instance and uses a `While` loop that polls for completion of the `BeginExecuteReader` method:

```
Private Sub PollingAsyncCommand()
    'Execute an SqlCommand asynchronously with polling for completion
    Try
        Dim strConn As String = "Data Source=localhost;" + _
            "Initial Catalog=Northwind;Integrated Security=SSPI;Async=True"
        Dim cnnCusts As SqlConnection = New SqlConnection(strConn)
        Dim cmdCusts As SqlCommand = cnnCusts.CreateCommand
        With cmdCusts
            .CommandType = CommandType.Text
            .CommandTimeout = 60
            .CommandText = "SELECT * FROM Customers"
        End With

        Dim asrCustsReader As IAsyncResult = _
            cmdCusts.BeginExecuteReader(CommandBehavior.CloseConnection)
        While Not asrCusts.IsCompleted
            'Do something while waiting
        End While
        Dim sdrCusts As SqlDataReader = cmdCusts.EndExecuteReader(asrCustsReader)
        'Do something with the data
        sdrCusts.Close()
        sdrCusts.Dispose()
    Catch excAsync As Exception
        MsgBox(excAsync.Message + excAsync.StackTrace, , "Async Operation Exception")
    End Try
End Sub
```

Asynchronous execution with polling is practical for simple operations within the `While` loop, such as displaying a progress bar whose value is set by counting timer ticks. You also can include code that lets the user cancel a command prior to expiration of its `CommandTimeout` property value. When you exit the loop, code execution blocks until each command completes or times out. All code executes on the form's thread, so multiple commands execute sequentially on separate connections. If multiple `DataReader.Read` operations are complex, you can run them on a dedicated thread with the new `BackgroundWorker` object. Doing this permits invoking the next `BeginExecuteReader` method immediately after the `IAsyncResult.IsComplete` property changes to `True`.

The Callback Model

The asynchronous callback model is more flexible than the polling model because it uses a callback handler that runs on its own thread that's drawn from the thread pool. The callback model permits interleaving commands to multiple databases that run on the same or different servers. In this case, you specify the callback handler and pass the Command as an Object to the second parameter of the overloaded `BeginExecuteReader` method. Passing the Command provides access to the `EndExecuteReader` method with the `IAsyncResult.AsyncState` property in the callback handler. Figure 2-7 shows program flow for the callback mode. Dashed lines indicate direct execution of `Read` methods without the need to wait for all rowsets to become available.

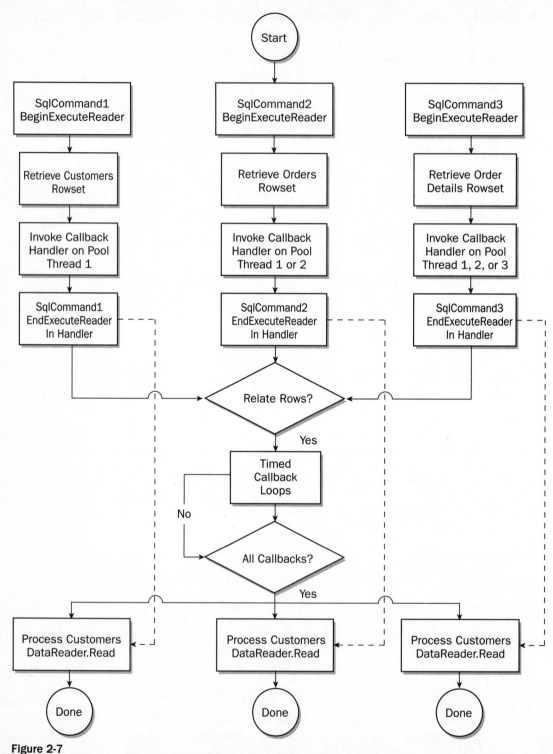

Figure 2-7

Following is an example of code for a simple asynchronous SqlCommand that uses the callback approach:

```
Private Sub CallbackAsyncCommand()
    'Execute commands asynchronously with a callback
    Try
        Dim strConn As String = "Data Source=localhost;" + _
         "Initial Catalog=Northwind;Integrated Security=SSPI;Async=True"
        Dim cnnCusts As SqlConnection = New SqlConnection(strConn)
        cnnCusts = New SqlConnection(strCusts)
        Dim cmdCusts As SqlCommand = cnnCusts.CreateCommand
        With cmdCusts
            .CommandType = CommandType.Text
            .CommandTimeout = 60
            .CommandText = "SELECT * FROM Customers"
        End With
        cnnCusts.Open()
        'Provide the SqlCommand as the stateObject
        Dim objCmdCusts As Object = CType(cmdCusts, Object)
        Dim asrCustsReader As IAsyncResult = _
         cmdCusts.BeginExecuteReader(New AsyncCallback(AddressOf CustsHandler), _
            objCmdCusts, CommandBehavior.CloseConnection)
    Catch excAsync As Exception
        MsgBox(excAsync.Message + excAsync.StackTrace, , "Async Operation Exception")
    End Try
End Sub
```

Here's the callback handler code for the preceding procedure:

```
Private Sub CustsHandler(ByVal iarResult As IAsyncResult)
    Try
        Dim sdrData As SqlDataReader = _
            CType(iarResult.AsyncState, SqlCommand).EndExecuteReader(iarResult)
        With sdrData
            Dim intCtr As Integer
            Dim objValue As Object
            While .Read
                For intCtr = 0 To .FieldCount - 1
                    objValue = .GetValue(intCtr)
                Next intCtr
            End While
            .Close()
            .Dispose()
        End With
    Catch excHandler As Exception
        MsgBox(excHandler.Message + excHandler.StackTrace, , _
            "Customers Handler Exception")
    End Try
End Sub
```

Most of this book's client examples connect to back ends on the same machine as the client, so synchronous execution of DataReaders completes quickly or throws an immediate exception. Asynchronous execution is best suited for projects with multiple DataReaders that connect to remote databases on individual connections, especially if one or more connections run on a WAN.

The AsyncDataOperations.sln sample project emulates a production application that connects to multiple networked databases by establishing individual SqlConnections to Northwind Customers, Orders, and Order Details tables. If you have access to three SQL Server instances, you can alter the connection strings by changing the second and third server names (OAKLEAF-W2K3 and OAKLEAF-MS2K3) to RemoteServerName, and mark the Use Multiple Instances text box to display the sequence of Connection.Open, BeginExecuteReader, and EndExecuteReader method invocations. Figure 2-8 shows two instances of AsyncDataOperations' form.

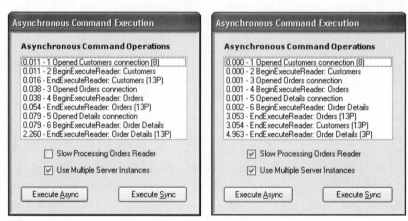

Figure 2-8

A VB.NET timer class, written by Alastair Dallas, provides the resolution required to obtain meaningful timing data. The numbers in parentheses of list box items are the System.Threading.Thread .CurrentThread.ManagedThreadId *values of the form instance and the three callback handlers. The P suffix indicates that the handler threads are from the thread pool. Timing data is for a second (cached) execution.*

The sample code executes Customers objects from localhost, and Orders and Order Details objects from networked servers. (The Orders Details table has about 500,000 rows, so reading the entire table takes about 2 seconds.) Execution speed on a LAN with low traffic usually is sufficiently fast to return the data in the BeginExecuteReader calling sequence, as shown in Figure 2-8 (left). All data retrieval operations run on a single pooled thread (13P.) To simulate a WAN connection to the Orders table, code in OrdersHandler induces a few-second delay by making multiple operations on each DataReader row in a nested loop. In this case, the Orders DataReader completes execution before the Customers DataReader, which finishes execution before the Order Details DataReader, as shown in Figure 2-8 (right). In this case, Order Details retrieval runs on one pooled thread (3P), and Customers and Orders run on a second pooled thread (13P).

Use of the callback model in Windows forms applications is a controversial topic. Members of Microsoft's VS 2005 data team recommend that you avoid applying the callback model to Windows forms projects. ADO.NET objects aren't thread-safe and threading problems are difficult to debug.

The WaitAll Model

An alternative to the callback model is to use a `WaitHandle` array and assign it an element for each `BeginExecuteReader` method call. A `WaitHandle.WaitAll(whArray)` suspends code execution until all DataReaders are ready for their `EndExecuteReader` calls. This behavior makes the WaitAll model especially suited for clients that process related rowsets because you don't need the timing loop shown in Figure 2-7. Figure 2-9 shows the program flow for the WaitAll model.

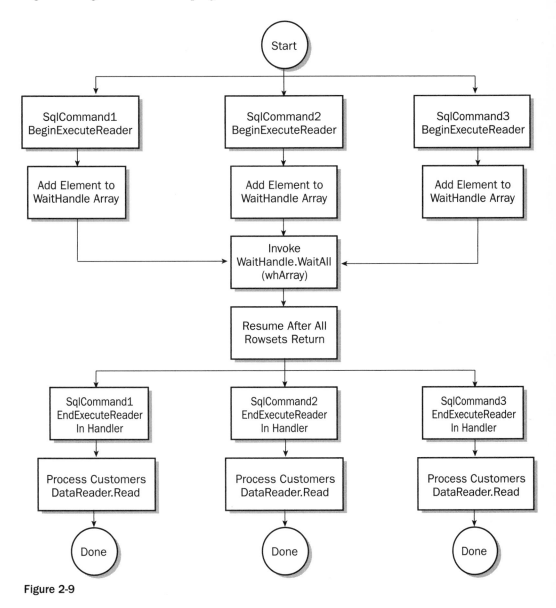

Figure 2-9

The simplest method for displaying the WaitAll model's performance data in a Windows form environment is to create a multi-threaded apartment (MTA) version of a custom Sub Main procedure. By default, VB.NET procedures use the single-threaded apartment (STA) model that's required for Win32-based forms. Calling `WaitAll` with multiple `WaitHandles` throws an exception within STA procedures, so you must add an `<MTAThreadAttribute()>` prefix to the `Shared Sub Main` statement. The following listing is an adaptation of the callback model's code to implement a multi-element `WaitHandle` array:

```vb
<MTAThreadAttribute()> _
Shared Sub Main()
'Set true for multi-server operation
Dim blnIsMultiServer As Boolean
Try
    cnnCusts = New SqlConnection(strCusts)
    Dim cmdCusts As SqlCommand = cnnCusts.CreateCommand
    With cmdCusts
        .CommandType = CommandType.Text
        .CommandTimeout = 10
        .CommandText = "SELECT * FROM Customers"
    End With

    If blnIsMultiServer Then
        cnnOrders = New SqlConnection(strOrders)
    Else
        cnnOrders = New SqlConnection(strCusts)
    End If
    Dim cmdOrders As SqlCommand = cnnOrders.CreateCommand
    With cmdOrders
        .CommandType = CommandType.Text
        .CommandTimeout = 10
        .CommandText = "SELECT * FROM Orders"
    End With

    If blnIsMultiServer Then
        cnnDetails = New SqlConnection(strDetails)
    Else
        cnnDetails = New SqlConnection(strCusts)
    End If
    Dim cmdDetails As SqlCommand = cnnDetails.CreateCommand
    With cmdDetails
        .CommandType = CommandType.Text
        .CommandTimeout = 10
        .CommandText = "SELECT * FROM [Order Details]"
    End With

    'Create the WaitHandle array with an element for each DataReader
    Dim awhHandle(2) As WaitHandle

    'Open the Customers connection
    cnnCusts.Open()

    Dim asrCustomersReader As IAsyncResult
    asrCustomersReader = _
        cmdCusts.BeginExecuteReader(CommandBehavior.CloseConnection)
```

```vb
            awhHandle(0) = asrCustomersReader.AsyncWaitHandle

            'Open the Orders connection
            cnnOrders.Open()

            Dim asrOrdersReader As IAsyncResult
            asrOrdersReader = _
                cmdOrders.BeginExecuteReader(CommandBehavior.CloseConnection)
            awhHandle(1) = asrOrdersReader.AsyncWaitHandle

            'Open the Details connection
            cnnDetails.Open()

            Dim asrDetailsReader As IAsyncResult
            asrDetailsReader = _
                cmdDetails.BeginExecuteReader(CommandBehavior.CloseConnection)
            awhHandle(2) = asrDetailsReader.AsyncWaitHandle

            'Wait for all DataReaders to execute
            WaitHandle.WaitAll(awhHandle)

            Dim sdrCustomers As SqlDataReader = _
                cmdCusts.EndExecuteReader(asrCustomersReader)
            'Do something with the data
            sdrCustomers.Close()
            sdrCustomers.Dispose()

            Dim sdrOrders As SqlDataReader = _
                cmdOrders.EndExecuteReader(asrOrdersReader)
            'Do something with the data
            sdrOrders.Close()
            sdrOrders.Dispose()

            Dim sdrDetails As SqlDataReader = _
                cmdDetails.EndExecuteReader(asrDetailsReader)
            'Do something with the data
            sdrDetails.Close()
            sdrDetails.Dispose()
            frmAsync.ShowDialog()
        Catch excAsync As Exception
            MsgBox(excAsync.Message + excAsync.StackTrace, , "Async Operation Exception")
        End Try
    End Sub
```

The first step is to create a `WaitHandle` array with the number of elements equal to the number of asynchronous commands. As with the callback model, you open the connections, execute the `SqlCommand` `.BeginExecuteReader` instructions, and add the corresponding `SqlDataReader.AsyncWaitHandle` objects to the `WaitHandle` array in any order. Execution suspends at the `WaitHandle.WaitAll` `(awhHandle)` instruction until all `DataReaders` are filled. When execution resumes, you process related rowsets in the desired order — in this case parent, child, and grandchild.

You can run the AsyncDataOperations.sln sample project's Shared Sub Main code, by opening the project's Properties window, selecting the Application page, marking the Startup with Custom Sub Main checkbox, and pressing Ctrl+S to save the changes. Figure 2-10 shows the form with the blnIsMultiServer flag set to True.

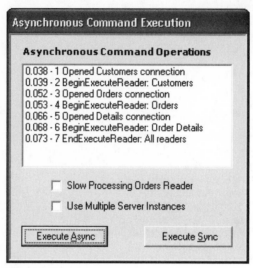

Figure 2-10

Create Standalone DataTables

ADO.NET 1.x DataTables ordinarily are members of DataSet objects. ADO.NET 2.0 lets you create lightweight, standalone DataTables that share many DataSet methods, such as ReadXml, ReadXmlSchema, WriteXml, and WriteXmlSchema. DataTables also support streaming DataReader interfaces with the Load(DataReader) method and DataTableReader object. You also can assign a namespace and namespace prefix to the DataTable. This chapter's earlier sections "Retrieve Base Table Schemas" and "Check Available SQL Server Instances and ADO.NET 2.0 Data Providers" introduced you to DataTables and DataGridView controls populated by the GetSchemaTable, GetDataSources, and GetFactoryClasses methods.

The StandaloneDataTables.sln project demonstrates the following DataTable features:

- ❑ Creating a DataTable with an SqlDataReader, executing a DataTableReader, and binding the DataTable to an editable DataGridView

- ❑ Persisting the content of a DataTable to XML files for data and schema only, in DataSet format, and with DataTable edits in diffgram format

- ❑ Setting the Namespace and optional Prefix property values

- ❑ Using the ReadXml method to load a DataTable from the saved DataSet.xml file

- ❑ Displaying the schema DataTable with the DataTable.GetSchemaTable method

Figure 2-11 shows the StandaloneDataTables.sln project's form after making a minor edit to the ContactName column of the first row. The Show... buttons open saved XML documents in Internet Explorer. The lower grid displays the schema DataTable for the SqlDataReader or, after clicking the Reload from XML Files button, the schema for the primary DataTable.

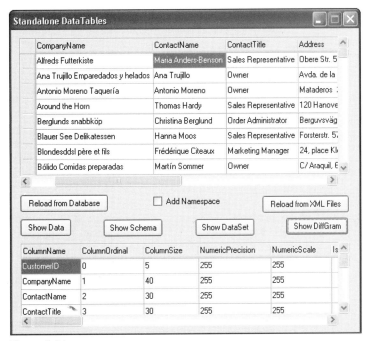

Figure 2-11

The following procedure loads a DataTable from the Northwind Customers file, adds an optional namespace and prefix, designates the primary key column (if it's missing), creates a schema DataTable, iterates the primary DataTable with a DataTableReader, and calls the `LoadDataGridViews` procedure to display the table contents and schema:

```
Private Sub LoadFromDatabase(ByVal blnWithNamespace As Boolean)
    'Load and display the DataTable with or without a table namespace
    Dim strConn As String = _
      "Server=localhost;Integrated Security=True;Database=Northwind"
    Dim cnnNwind As SqlConnection = New SqlConnection(strConn)
    Try
        Dim cmdCusts As SqlCommand = cnnNwind.CreateCommand
        With cmdCusts
            .CommandType = CommandType.Text
            .CommandText = "SELECT * FROM Customers"
        End With
        cnnNwind.Open()
        Dim drCusts As SqlDataReader = _
            cmdCusts.ExecuteReader(CommandBehavior.KeyInfo)
        dtCusts = New DataTable
        dtSchema = drCusts.GetSchemaTable
```

```
            With dtCusts
                .TableName = "Customers"
                If blnWithNamespace Then
                    'Uncomment the following line to view effect on data and schemas
                    '.Prefix = "custs"
                    .Namespace = "http://www.oakleaf.ws/schemas/northwind/customers"
                End If

                'Load the data and accept changes
                .Load(drCusts)
                .AcceptChanges()

                If .PrimaryKey.Length = 0 Then
                    'Set the primary key constraint
                    Dim acolKeys(1) As DataColumn
                    acolKeys(0) = .Columns(0)
                    .PrimaryKey = acolKeys
                End If

                'Test the DataSet property
                If Not .DataSet Is Nothing Then
                    Dim strName As String = .DataSet.DataSetName
                    MsgBox(strName)
                End If
            End With
            drCusts.Close()

            'Test the DataTableReader
            Dim dtrCusts As New DataTableReader(dtCusts)
            intRows = 0
            While dtrCusts.Read
                intRows += 1
            End While
            dtrCusts.Close()

            LoadDataGridViews()
        Catch excDT As Exception
            MsgBox(excDT.Message + excDT.StackTrace, , "DataTable Load Exception")
        Finally
            cnnNwind.Close()
        End Try
    End Sub
```

Remove the ExecuteReader *method's* CommandBehavior.KeyInfo *argument to add the primary key with code. The DataSet test instructions prove that DataTables don't generate a DataSet under the covers.*

DataTables that you load from DataReaders are updatable, and you can persist them as XML document files in data-only, schema-only DataSet or diffGram formats. The SaveXmlFiles procedure generates data and schema XML documents and persists the DataTable's content in DataSet format. The procedure saves all edits you make in the DataGridView as a diffgram file.

```
Private Sub SaveXmlFiles(ByVal blnShowMessage As Boolean)
    'Delete and resave data, schema, and (if changes) diffgram files
    DeleteXmlFiles()
    With dtCusts
        .WriteXml(strPath + "Data.xml", System.Data.XmlWriteMode.IgnoreSchema)
        .WriteXml(strPath + "DataSet.xml", System.Data.XmlWriteMode.WriteSchema)
        .WriteXmlSchema(strPath + "Schema.xsd")
    End With
    If chkAddNS.Checked Then
        btnShowImportSchema.Enabled = True
    End If
    'HasChanges property is missing
    Dim dtChanges As New DataTable
    dtChanges = dtCusts.GetChanges
    Dim strMsg As String
    If dtChanges Is Nothing Then
        strMsg = "Data and schema for " + intRows.ToString + " rows written to '" _
            + strPath + "' folder."
        btnShowDiffGram.Enabled = False
    Else
        dtChanges.WriteXml(strPath + "Diffgram.xml", _
            System.Data.XmlWriteMode.DiffGram)
        strMsg = "Data for " + intRows.ToString + " rows, schema, and changes " _
            + diffgram written to '" + strPath + "' folder and changes accepted."
        dtCusts.AcceptChanges()
        btnShowDiffGram.Enabled = True
    End If
    If blnShowMessage Then
        MsgBox(strMsg, , "XML Files Saved")
    End If
    btnReadXML.Enabled = True
End Sub
```

The `btnReadXML_Click` event handler loads the DataTable from the saved DataSet.xml file, applies previous edits saved as a diffgram file, and displays the schema DataTable.

Adding a namespace to the DataTable when importing values from the database table causes a schema validation failure when you save the XML data file.

```
Private Sub btnReadXML_Click(ByVal sender As System.Object, _
        ByVal e As System.EventArgs) Handles btnReadXML.Click
    'Load or attempt to load DataTable from saved DataSet
    btnShowDiffGram.Enabled = False
    Try
        dtCusts = New DataTable
        With dtCusts
            .ReadXml(strPath + "DataSet.xml")
            If File.Exists(strPath + "Diffgram.xml") Then
                'Apply the changes
                .ReadXml(strPath + "Diffgram.xml")
            End If
            .AcceptChanges()
```

```
          End With

          'Get the schema and test the DataTableReader
          Dim dtrCusts As New DataTableReader(dtCusts)
          dtSchema = dtrCusts.GetSchemaTable
          intRows = 0
          While dtrCusts.Read
              intRows += 1
          End While
          dtrCusts.Close()

          LoadDataGridView()
      Catch excXML As Exception
          MsgBox(excXML.Message + excXML.StackTrace, , "DataTable ReadXml Exception")
      End Try
End Sub
```

DataTables have `ChildRelations` *and* `ParentRelations` *collections that let you add code to define the relationships between multiple DataTable objects. In most cases, however, creating a typed DataSet is the better approach for projects that have more than one related DataTable.*

Use Nullable Types to Support DBNull Values

.NET Framework 2.0 adds generic types to VB.NET 2005 by adding the `(Of Type)` type parameter to variable declarations. Nullable variables are an extension of generic types that enable value types — Integer, Int16, Decimal, Date, DateTime, and the like — to support null values. Assigning `Nothing` to a value type returns the default value for the type — 0 for numeric types and `01/01/0001 12:00:00 AM` for dates.

You enable the null values by replacing value type data type identifiers with `Nullable(Of Type)`. Reference types, such as `String`, support null values intrinsically, so adding `Nullable(Of String)` isn't appropriate. The most useful application for nullable variables is in method signatures where nullable value types eliminate the need for overloading. For example, inserting a new row in the Northwind Orders table from a typed DataSet ordinarily requires the two `Insert` method signatures shown here and two corresponding `Overloads` functions:

```
Function Insert(ByVal CustomerID As String,
              ByVal EmployeeID As Integer, _
              ByVal OrderDate As Date, _
              ByVal RequiredDate As Date, _
              ByVal ShippedDate As Date, _
              ByVal ShipVia As Integer,
              ByVal Freight As Decimal,
              ByVal ShipName As String, _
              ByVal ShipAddress As String,
              ByVal ShipCity As String, _
              ByVal ShipRegion As String,
              ByVal ShipPostalCode As String, _
              ByVal ShipCountry As String) As Integer

Function Insert(ByVal CustomerID As Object,
```

```
             ByVal EmployeeID As Object, _
             ByVal OrderDate As Object,
             ByVal RequiredDate As Object, _
             ByVal ShippedDate As Object, _
             ByVal ShipVia As Object, _
             ByVal Freight As Object, _
             ByVal ShipName As Object, _
             ByVal ShipAddress As Object, _
             ByVal ShipCity As Object, _
             ByVal ShipRegion As Object, _
             ByVal ShipPostalCode As Object, _
             ByVal ShipCountry As Object) As Integer
```

The first method signature is valid if all values are present. If any value type passed to the function is null, the second, untyped signature is required. In this case, your code could supply a `String` in place of an `Integer` or `Decimal` value, an error that the compiler wouldn't catch. Adding `Nullable(Of Type)` to value types, as shown here, lets a single function handle null value types:

```
Function Insert(ByVal CustomerID As String, _
               ByVal EmployeeID As Nullable(Of Integer), _
               ByVal OrderDate As Nullable(Of Date), _
               ByVal RequiredDate As Nullable(Of Date), _
               ByVal ShippedDate As Nullable(Of Date), _
               ByVal ShipVia As Nullable(Of Integer), _
               ByVal Freight As Nullable(Of Decimal), _
               ByVal ShipName As String, _
               ByVal ShipAddress As String, _
               ByVal ShipCity As String, _
               ByVal ShipRegion As String, _
               ByVal ShipPostalCode As String, _
               ByVal ShipCountry As String) As Integer
```

Setting INSERT or UPDATE parameter values associated with nullable types requires testing for the presence of an assigned value with the `HasValue` property and, if `HasValue` is `True`, passing the `Value` property, as shown in the following snippet for an INSERT command that has required parameters added:

```
...
Me.InsertCommandParameters(0).Value = CustomerID
If EmployeeID.HasValue Then
   Me.InsertCommandParameters(1).Value = EmployeeID.Value
Else
   Me.InsertCommandParameters(1).Value = DBNull.Convert
End If
If OrderDate.HasValue Then
   Me.InsertCommandParameters(2).Value = OrderDate.Value
Else
   Me.InsertCommandParameters(2).Value = DBNull.Convert
End If
If RequiredDate.HasValue Then
   Me.InsertCommandParameters(3).Value = RequiredDate.Value
Else
```

```
        Me.InsertCommandParameters(3).Value = DBNull.Convert
    End If
    If ShippedDate.HasValue Then
        Me.InsertCommandParameters(4).Value = ShippedDate.Value
    Else
        Me.InsertCommandParameters(4).Value = DBNull.Convert
    End If
    ...
```

It's not necessary to specify a nullable type for variables that can't be null because of base table foreign key constraints, such as EmployeeID in the preceding example. The same is true for variables that are subject to business rules, such as requiring an OrderDate value for every order.

You also can apply `Nullable(Of Type)` to `Public` or `Private` class members. Following is an example of a simple business object with `Public` properties that map to the Northwind Orders table's fields. Business rules and foreign key constraints determine which fields are nullable—RequiredDate, ShippedDate, Freight, ShipRegion, and ShipPostalCode for this example. ShipRegion and ShipPostalCode are reference types, which are nullable by definition.

```
Public Class Orders
    Public OrderID As Integer
    Public CustomerID As String
    Public EmployeeID As Integer
    Public OrderDate As Date
    Public RequiredDate As Nullable(Of Date)
    Public ShippedDate As Nullable(Of Date)
    Public ShipVia As Integer
    Public Freight As Nullable(Of Decimal)
    ...
    Public ShipCountry As String
End Class
```

Here's an abbreviated version of the preceding class that uses private members with `Get` and `Set` accessors:

```
Public Class Orders
    Private m_OrderID As Integer
    Public Property OrderID() As Integer
        Get
            Return m_OrderID
        End Get
        Set(ByVal value As Integer)
            m_OrderID = value
        End Set
    End Property

    ...

    Private m_RequiredDate As Nullable(Of Date)
    Public Property RequiredDate() As Nullable(Of Date)
        Get
            Return m_RequiredDate
        End Get
        Set(ByVal value As Nullable(Of Date))
```

```
                m_RequiredDate = value
            End Set
        End Property

        Private m_ShippedDate As Nullable(Of Date)
        Public Property ShippedDate() As Nullable(Of Date)
            Get
                Return m_ShippedDate
            End Get
            Set(ByVal value As Nullable(Of Date))
                m_ShippedDate = value
            End Set
        End Property

    . . .

        Private m_Freight As Nullable(Of Decimal)
        Public Property Freight() As Nullable(Of Decimal)
            Get
                Return m_Freight
            End Get
            Set(ByVal value As Nullable(Of Decimal))
                m_Freight = value
            End Set
        End Property

    . . .

        Private m_ShipCountry As String
        Public Property ShipCountry() As String
            Get
                Return m_ShipCountry
            End Get
            Set(ByVal value As String)
                m_ShipCountry = value
            End Set
        End Property
    End Class
```

Specifying nullable class members and using `HasValue` and `Value` properties is equivalent to using `If ReferenceType Is Nothing Then . . .` or `If ValueType = Nothing Then . . .` tests for assigned property values. The sample NullableTypes.sln project tests both approaches with objects populated from an SqlDataReader for the Orders table.

Using New ADO.NET 2.0 Persistent Windows Form Objects

This book defines *persistent objects* as elements that are visible (surfaced) on Windows forms or in the forms designer tray and whose property values you can set in design mode. You add persistent data objects from the toolbox's Data category or with code-generation tools (designers) that you invoke by dragging table or field nodes from the new Data Sources window. VS 2005's Data Sources window replaces Server Explorer as the starting point for adding DataSets and DataTables to projects.

VS 2005 replaces earlier versions' Windows form Toolbox Data controls — except DataSet — with the following new objects and wrappers:

❑ **TableAdapters** replace provider-specific Connections and DataAdapters, such as `SqlConnection` and `SqlDataAdapter` objects. Provider-specific Connections and DataAdapters no longer appear in the toolbox's Data category.

❑ **BindingSources** are wrappers for the project's data sources, which usually — but not necessarily — are DataTables that are members of a typed DataSet. BindingSources provide code-based data record or list item navigation and editing capabilities. BindingSources also serve as the binding source for the DataGridView or other bound editing controls.

❑ **BindingNavigators** are special-purpose ToolStrip controls that you associate with a BindingSource to provide toolbar-style record or list navigation and related operations, such as adding new items, deleting items, and saving data edits.

❑ **DataGridView** controls replace the DataGrid control. You can bind DataGridViews to DataConnectors, DataTables, and ArrayLists. Unlike the DataGrid, DataGridViews can't display hierarchical data.

Provider-specific Connections and DataAdapters no longer appear in the form designer tray. Private members of the DataSet's `Partial Public Class TableNameTableAdapter` class define runtime SqlConnections, SqlDataAdapters, and SqlTransactions for SQL Server–based projects. Partial classes for designer-generated code, stored in *ClassName*.Designer.vb files, let you add code to DataSet classes that isn't overwritten by the designer when you reconfigure DataSets.

The following sections introduce you to ADO.NET 2.0's new or upgraded controls, as well as autogenerated parameterized data display and editing forms, and the new batch update feature for data tables.

Compare ADO.NET 1.x and 2.0 Data Designers

As mentioned early in the chapter, one of the Visual Studio development team's primary objectives for VS 2005 is to flatten the learning curve for developers — especially VB developers — migrating from VS 6.0 to VS 2005. Adding the `My` namespace and its classes to VB.NET projects is an example of simplifying access to local computer properties and resources at the expense of increased source code file structure complexity.

Fortunately, the new VS 2005 wizards and designers for creating basic data entry forms streamline initial generation of DataSets without adding code complexity. The following two sections compare the process for generating a grid-based data entry and editing form with ADO.NET 1.x and ADO.NET 2.0 wizards and designers.

ADO.NET 1.x

Here's the conventional ADO.NET 1.x method for creating a typed DataSet with a single table specified by an SQL statement, and displaying records in a DataGrid control:

1. Add an SqlDataAdapter from the toolbox to the form's tray, which opens the Data Adapter Configuration Wizard.

2. Select an existing SQL Server connection or create a new one, specify SQL statements, and generate the SQL `SELECT`, `INSERT`, `UPDATE`, and `DELETE` statements. The designer adds SqlConnection1 and SqlDataAdapter1 to the tray.

3. Choose Data ➪ Generate Dataset to create a typed DataSet with the DataTable specified in the SELECT query. The designer adds *DataSetName*1 to the tray.

4. Add a DataGrid control to the form, set its `DataSource` property value to `DataSetName1`, and set the `DataMember` property to the table name you specified in the SELECT query.

5. Add a Fill button and `SqlDataAdapter1.Fill(DataSetName1)` instruction to the `btnFill_Click` event handler.

6. Add an Update button and `SqlDataAdapter1.Update(DataSetName1)` instruction to the `btnUpdate_Click` event handler.

Dragging a table node from an existing connection in Server Explorer combines preceding Steps 1 and 2, but you don't have the opportunity to select new or existing stored procedures for the queries.

ADO.NET 2.0

VS 2005's ADO.NET 2.0 designers simplify creating classic single-table forms by changing the sequence of DataSet and related data component generation. Here's the drill for the ADO.NET 2.0 process:

1. Open the Data Sources window, if necessary, by choosing Data ➪ Show Data Sources, and click the Add New Data Source link to start the Data Source Configuration Wizard.

2. Select Database as the data source type, and select an existing database connection or create a new connection with the Connection Properties dialog. Optionally, save the connection string to the application configuration file. Completing the wizard's steps adds a *TableName* node under the Data Sources window's top-level *DataSetName* node.

3. Drag the TableName node to the form. The designer adds *DatabaseName*DataSet, *TableName*TableAdapter, *TableName*BindingSource, and *TableName*BindingNavigator items to the tray, and *TableName*DataGridView and *TableName*BindingNavigator controls to the form.

Step 3 also adds a `TableNameTableAdapter.Fill(DatabaseNameDataSet)` instruction to the `Form1_Load` event handler and a `bindingNavigatorSaveItem_Click` event handler to the form.

You can substitute a set of bound text boxes for the DataGridView control by selecting Details from the Data Source window's TableName node's dropdown list before dragging the node to the form in preceding Step 3.

Unlike the ADO.NET 1.*x* process, you don't have the opportunity to create or select stored procedures to fill or update DataTables that the wizard creates. However, you can reconfigure DataTableAdapters to create new or use existing stored procedures by opening the *DataSetName*.xsd file in the schema designer, right-clicking the *TableName*TableAdapter header, and choosing Configure to start the Data Component Configuration Wizard. Click Back to display the Choose a Command Type dialog, select the Create New Stored Procedures or Use Existing Stored Procedures option, and complete the wizard's steps.

ADO.NET 2.0 designers make it much easier to create master data editing forms with synchronized single-level or multiple-level DataGridView subforms, which VS 2005 calls *Master Detail* forms. Chapter 1's "Add a Related DataBound Control" section describes the process for creating a Northwind Customers-Orders form. The later "Add Multi-Level Subforms" section shows you how to add a related second-level subform with a Customers-Orders-Order Details example. It's also much easier to create a parameterized data entry form, as you'll discover in the section "Parameterize the MasterDetailsForm," later in this chapter.

Add Missing ADO.NET Controls to the Toolbox

If you want to use the ADO.NET 1.*x* components to create provider-specific DataAdapter objects, you must add the appropriate Connection and DataAdapter controls to the toolbox. If you have other vendor-specific data providers, such as the Oracle ODP .NET provider for Oracle 10g or earlier, you might add the ODP .NET OracleConnection and OracleDataAdapter to the toolbox. You also can add the ADO.NET 1.*x* Windows form DataGrid control to create new projects with the look and feel of pre–VS 2005 projects.

To add non-standard data controls to the toolbox, right-click in the Data section, and select Choose Items to open the Choose Toolbox Items dialog. Type the first few letters of the component or control in the Filter text box to simplify selection. Figure 2-12 shows the dialog with three Oracle.DataAccess.Client providers selected. Mark the checkboxes of the items you want to install, and click OK to add them to the toolbox and close the dialog.

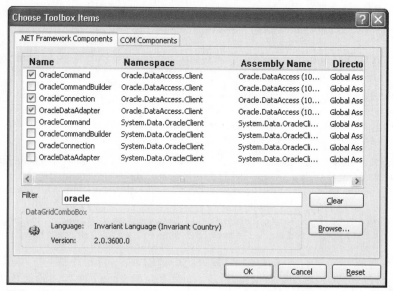

Figure 2-12

> *Adding non-standard data controls to the toolbox might take a minute or two, depending on your test machine's CPU speed and available RAM.*

You can remove all non-standard toolbox items you added by right-clicking the toolbox and choosing Reset Toolbox.

> *Using legacy DataAdapters and the Generate DataSet command creates the ADO.NET 1.x version of DataSetName.xsd, which is much smaller than the ADO.NET 2.0 schema.*

Upgrade 1.x Projects to ADO.NET 2.0 Components

Opening a VS 2002 or VS 2003 project in VS 2005 starts the Visual Studio Upgrade Wizard, which converts the project to VS 2005 format and, optionally, saves a backup of the original project in the folder you specify. With simple projects, the only changes you'll notice are references that are updated to .NET

Framework 2.0 versions and the data source(s) for your form that automatically appear in the Data Sources window. Upgrading the project doesn't add code files to implement the My namespace or make ADO.NET 2.0–specific additions to the DataSet code.

Adding the data source as a Data Sources windows node lets you quickly replace a DataGrid with a DataGridView and automatically add BindingSource and BindingNavigator controls for navigation and editing. Delete the DataGrid and drag the *TableName* node to the form to add the two ADO.NET 2.0 controls. You won't see a *TableName*DataAdapter component in the tray or the schema designer window because *DataSourceName*.xsd isn't upgraded to the new DataSet schema format.

The AdapterGridView2003.sln project, shown in Figure 2-13, was upgraded from the VS 2003 project in the ...Chapter02\AdapterGridView2003\AdapterGridView2003_Backup folder. You can test the upgrade process by opening the backup project copy in VS 2005.

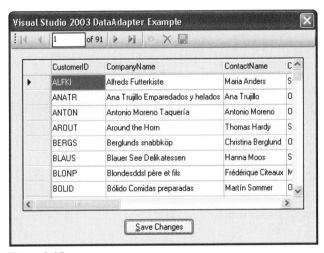

Figure 2-13

Add Multi-Level Subforms

VS 2005 and VB Express automate the generation of multi-level data entry and editing forms for related tables. When you add multiple related tables to the Data Sources window, the VS 2005 schema designer automatically determines foreign-key constraints and establishes relations between the tables based on pre-established base table constraints. The Schema Designer names the relations FK_*ManySideTable_OneSideTable*, as shown for the Northwind Customers, Orders, and Order Details tables in Figure 2-14.

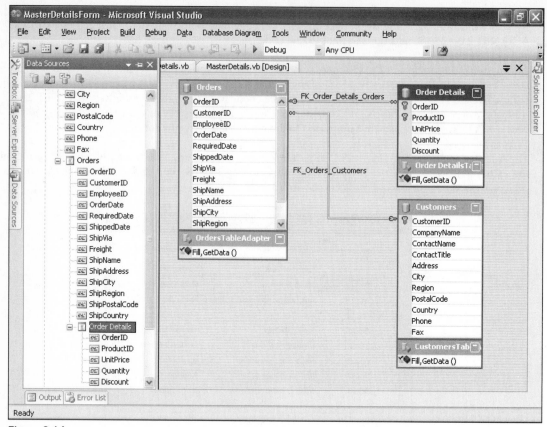

Figure 2-14

VS 2002 and VS 2003 required you to manually establish *all* relations in the Relation dialog. By default, VS 2005 doesn't cascade key value changes for update and delete operations, but you can alter this behavior and set other relation properties in the Relation dialog.

First, add a DataGridView or, preferably, bound text boxes and a DataNavigator for the form's master data source. Next, add the first detail level by dragging the Data Sources window's related table node — Orders for this example — to the form to display related records in a DataGridView. Then drag more deeply nested table nodes — Order Details in this case — to display additional levels of related records.

> *Be sure to drag the node for the related tables, which are the last entry in the column list of the parent tables. If you drag nodes that are at the same hierarchical level as the parent, the related table records won't synchronize when you select a parent table record.*

Finally, verify that the designer has added these three `DataTableTableAdapter.Fill` instructions to the `FormName_Load` event handler:

```
Private Sub frmMasterDetails_Load(ByVal sender As System.Object, _
  ByVal e As System.EventArgs) Handles MyBase.Load
    'TODO: This line of code loads data into the 'NorthwindDataSet.Order_Details'
    'table. You can move, or remove it, as needed.
    Me.Order_DetailsTableAdapter.Fill(Me.NorthwindDataSet.Order_Details)
    'TODO: This line of code loads data into the 'NorthwindDataSet.Orders' table.
    'You can move, or remove it, as needed.
    Me.OrdersTableAdapter.Fill(Me.NorthwindDataSet.Orders)
    'TODO: This line of code loads data into the 'NorthwindDataSet.Customers' table.
    'You can move, or remove it, as needed.
    Me.CustomersTableAdapter.Fill(Me.NorthwindDataSet.Customers)
End Sub
```

Then press F5 to build and run the project, which appears as shown in Figure 2-15.

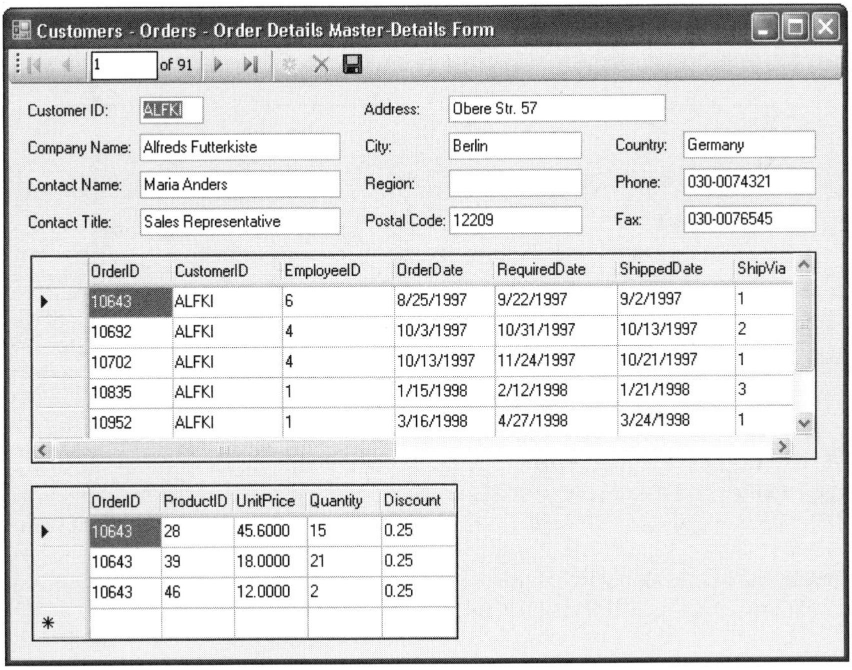

Figure 2-15

Parameterize the MasterDetailsForm

ADO.NET 2.0 TableAdapters support collections of SELECT queries or stored procedures, which can include parameterized queries. The default SELECT query name is Fill, as illustrated by the preceding event-handling code; parameterized queries default to FillBy. Selecting a bound text box or DataGridView enables the Data menu's Add Query choice, which opens a Search Criteria Builder dialog. You write — or use the Query Builder to create — a parameterized SELECT query that specifies a subset of the master table records for the DataTableTableAdapter.FillBy method, as shown in Figure 2-16.

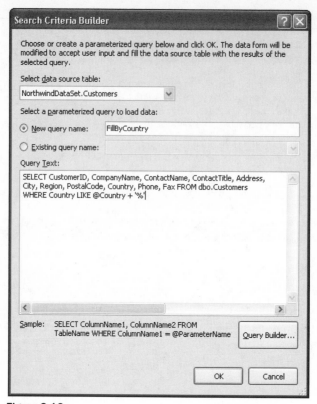

Figure 2-16

Click OK to add the `FillBy` query to the collection, a new FillBy ToolStrip to the form's topRaftingContainer, and a `FillByTooStripButton_Click` event handler to the form's class. The added FillBy member appears in the *TableName*DataConnector element of the schema designer.

As an example, the MasterDetailsParam.sln sample project adds a parameterized search of the Customers TableAdapter's CustomerID column, so the `FillBy` query statement is:

```
SELECT CustomerID, CompanyName, ContactName, ContactTitle, Address,
    City, Region, PostalCode, Country, Phone, Fax
FROM dbo.Customers WHERE CustomerID LIKE @CustomerID + '%'
```

The `LIKE` predicate returns Customers records that begin with the first characters supplied; an empty `@CustomerID` value returns all Customers records. The parameter ToolStrip's left label text defaults to the parameter name plus a colon (`CustomerID:`), and button text is the query name (`FillByCountry`), as shown in Figure 2-17.

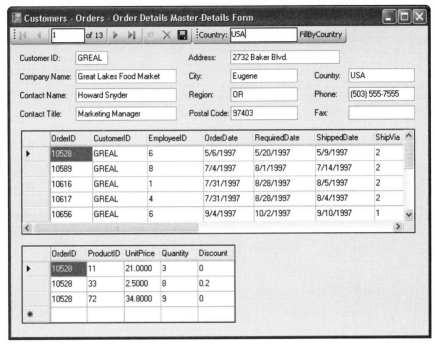

Figure 2-17

The Search Criteria Builder adds the following event handler to the main form's class:

```
Private Sub FillByToolStripButton_Click(ByVal sender As System.Object, _
  ByVal e As System.EventArgs) Handles FillByToolStripButton.Click
  Try
      Me.CustomersTableAdapter.FillBy(Me.NorthwindDataSet.Customers, _
          CustomerIDToolStripTextBox.Text)
  Catch ex As System.Exception
      System.Windows.Forms.MessageBox.Show(ex.Message)
  End Try
End Sub
```

You can add multiple parameterized `FillBy` queries and their ToolStrip controls; the second and later `FillBy` query names have a default incremental integer suffix. Later chapters show you how to customize `FillBy` queries and substitute form-based controls for ToolStrip parameter controls.

Batch Multiple Updates

ADO.NET 1.x DataSets that contain many updates or inserts create a serious performance hit when updating base tables. Each new, modified, or deleted row for every table requires a database server round-trip to execute parameterized SQL statements or stored procedures. ADO.NET 2.0 adds a new batched update feature that lets you specify the value of the `UpdateBatchSize` property of `SqlDataAdapter` and `OracleDataAdapter` objects. The behavior of batched DataTable updates is similar to the SqlBulkCopy operations described earlier in this chapter. Setting `SqlDataAdapter` `.UpdateBatchSize = 0` attempts to perform all updates to the corresponding base table in a single batch operation, which seldom is the optimum choice. The default value is 1, which turns off batched updates. As is the case with SqlBulkCopy operations, you might find that setting the batch size to a specific value can improve update performance.

The BatchedUpdates.sln project in the \VB2005DB\Chapter02\BatchedUpdates folder lets you compare performance of individual and batched updates of the OrderDate value of Northwind Orders records. Figure 2-18 shows the project executing an update operation with 51 OrderDate updates per batch. In this case, a batch consists of 2,040 parameter values for optimistic concurrency tests and has a total length of 85,527 characters (approximately 160,000 bytes). Running tests on a networked server provides more realistic timing comparisons than using a local server. As an example, non-batched updates to all 830 Orders records require about 7.2 seconds, while tests of 51 updates per batch execute in about 3.6 seconds on the network used to write this book. Setting updates per batch to 11 results in an execution time of about 4.3 seconds.

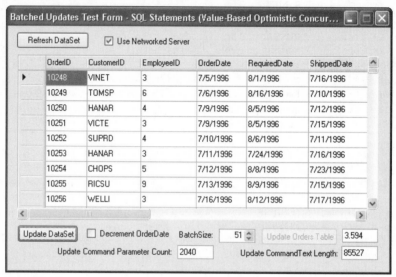

Figure 2-18

To run batch execution timing tests with the sample project, do the following:

1. Edit the connection strings in the `btnRefresh_Click` event handler to point to your local instance of Northwind and, if available, a network instance of Northwind or NorthwindCS.

2. If you have a networked instance of Northwind, mark the Use Networked Server checkbox and click Refresh DataSet.

3. Click the Update DataSet button to add or subtract one day from the DataSet's OrderDate value for all Orders records.

4. Set the BatchSize value to 1 to obtain the baseline time for unbatched updates, and click Update Orders Table.

5. Repeat Steps 3 and 4 with different BatchSize values to determine the performance improvement gained from batching updates.

You'll receive an error when executing a batched update operation if you don't set `SqlDataAdapter` `.UpdateCommand.UpdatedRowSource = UpdateRowSource.None.` *You also must do the same for the* `InsertCommand` *and* `Delete` *command.*

ADO 2.0 batched updates to SQL Server tables occur "under the covers," which means that SQL Profiler doesn't display the parameterized T-SQL statements for batched updates. Only Network Monitor or a network sniffer lets you observe the T-SQL instructions required for batched updates.

Design and Display Reports with the ReportViewer Control

VB and VS releases prior to VS .NET have relied on Crystal Reports add-ins to design, display, and publish tabular reports, graphs, or both from a specified data source. Several other independent software vendors (ISVs) offer report writers and chart designers for VS 2002 and later versions. To eliminate reliance on third-party report writers and charting applications, Microsoft introduced SQL Server Reporting Services as a no-charge add-on to SQL Server 2000. All editions of SQL Server 2005, except SQLX, integrate Reporting Services, which include Report Server and Report Builder, into the setup program. These editions use the VS IDE's Business Intelligence project's Report Server Project, Report Server Project Wizard, or Report Model Project templates to design and deploy server-based (also called *remote*) reports that are independent of .NET Windows or Web forms projects.

The ReportViewer control for Windows forms is a container for a pre-configured toolbar, which is similar to a BindingNavigator control, and a report viewing area to display conventional (table) or crosstab (matrix) reports, or charts bound to ADO.NET 2.0 data sources. Charts are quite similar to Excel PivotCharts or those created with the Office Web Components (OWC) 12 Chart control. The toolbar has Page Setup, Page Layout, and Print buttons for printing, and an Export button that lets you save reports in Excel worksheet or Adobe PDF file format. Reports that you create with the ReportViewer control consume far fewer client resources than corresponding Crystal Reports versions.

ReportViewer enables designing reports with a client (local) designer derived from ReportBuilder. You use the local designer within VS 2005 or VBX to create a local client report definition file_*ReportName*.rdlc_in the project folder. Online help's "Walkthrough: Using a Database Data Source with the ReportViewer Windows Forms Control in Local Processing Mode" topic leads you through the process of creating a simple report from AdventureWorks tables. The \VB2005DB\Chapter02\ReportViewerDemo.sln sample project has two tabular reports based on Northwind and AdventureWorks data sources, a crosstab report that uses the Northwind Orders, Order Details, and Products tables, and a chart generated from data that's similar to that for the crosstab report. Figure 2-19 shows the ReportViewerDemo application displaying a stacked-area chart of orders received by product category in each quarter of 1997.

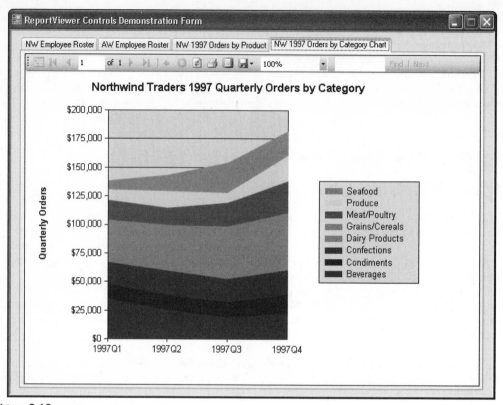

Figure 2-19

Following are generic steps for creating a new Windows form project with a ReportViewer control:

1. Create a new Windows form project, and add a ReportViewer control from the toolbox's Data section.

2. Open the ReportViewer's smart tag, select Dock in Parent Container, and then select Design a New Report to open a local client report definition file_Report1.rdlc_in the report designer.

3. Drag a Table, Matrix, or Chart control from the toolbox to the designer. This example uses a Matrix control to create a crosstab report. Unless you added a Chart control, position the Table or Matrix control, and add a text box with a report heading.

4. Open the Data Sources window, click Add New Data Source to start the Data Source Configuration Wizard, and create a DataSet with a DataTable to provide the report's data. This example uses the NWOrders1997 DataTable that's filled by the following SQL statement:

```
SELECT Products.ProductName, Categories.CategoryName,
    '1997Q' + CONVERT(varchar, DATEPART(quarter, Orders.OrderDate)) AS Quarter,
    CONVERT(money, SUM((([Order Details].UnitPrice * [Order Details].Quantity) *
    (1 - [Order Details].Discount))) AS ProductOrders
FROM Categories INNER JOIN Products INNER JOIN Orders INNER JOIN [Order Details]
    ON Orders.OrderID = [Order Details].OrderID ON Products.ProductID =
    [Order Details].ProductID ON Categories.CategoryID = Products.CategoryID
WHERE (Orders.OrderDate BETWEEN '1/1/1997' AND '12/31/1997')
GROUP BY Products.ProductName, Categories.CategoryName,
    DATEPART(quarter, Orders.OrderDate)
ORDER BY Categories.CategoryName, Products.ProductName, Quarter
```

5. Drag column icons to the appropriate report designer cells. For this example, drag the Quarter column to the Columns cell, the ProductName column to the Rows cell, and the ProductOrders column to the Data cell. Figure 2-20 shows the designer with an added grouping and subtotal by CategoryName.

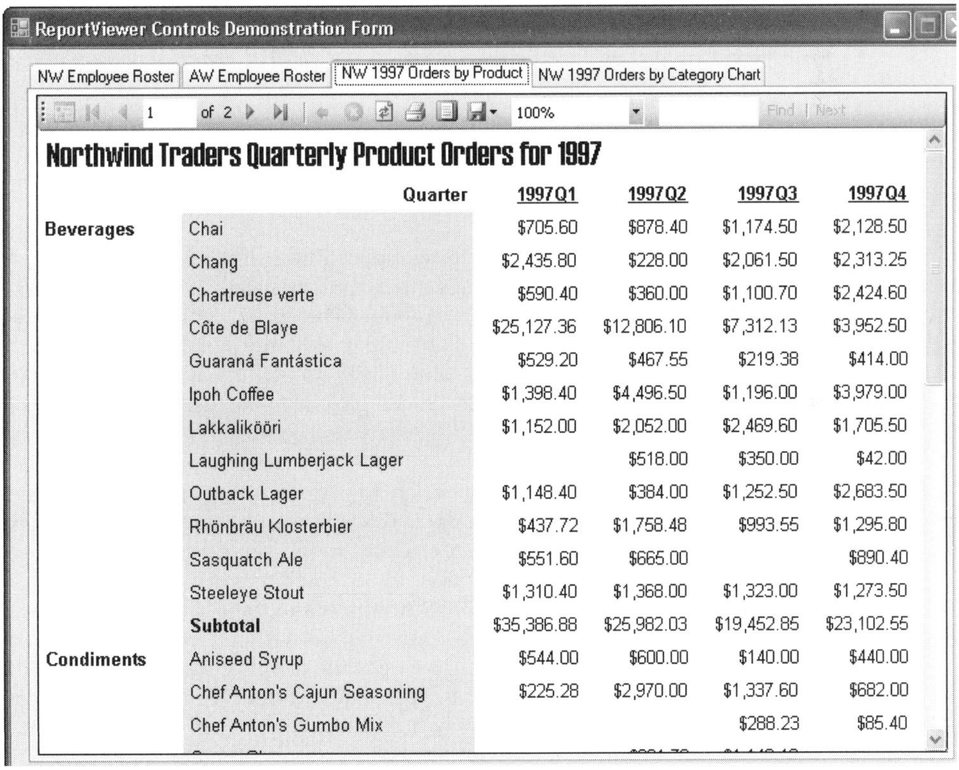

Figure 2-20

6. Run the form to display the initial report, and then format the cells to suit the data.

Figure 2-21 shows the ReportViewerDemo project displaying the finished NWOrders1997.rdlc report.

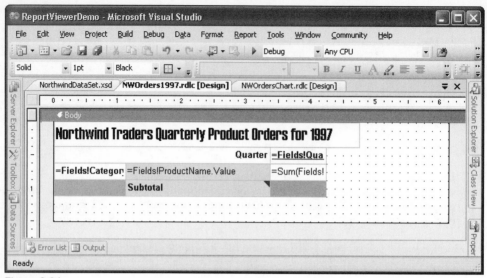

Figure 2-21

Summary

ADO 2.0 adds a few runtime features for Windows form applications — DbProviderFactories for vendor-agnostic data projects, SQLBulkCopy operations that simplify bulk transfers of data between tables, the `RetrieveStatistics` method for obtaining details about a current SqlConnection, asynchronous command execution, standalone DataTables, and nullable types. With the possible exception of nullable types and standalone DataTables, these new features aren't likely to play a major role in new data-intensive VS 2005 projects. The runtime code examples and sample projects in the first half of this chapter should provide enough evidence to arrive at your own conclusion about the usefulness of these new features.

New ADO.NET 2.0 persistent objects are much more likely to gain popularity in new and upgraded Windows form data projects. You can create a basic data editing form with graphical record navigation controls in less than five minutes. A BindingNavigator docked to the top of a form might not be what you want for record navigation in a production project, but the combination is a welcome quick-start enhancement, especially for parameterized forms. TableAdapters and, especially, BindingSource components reduce coding requirements dramatically. The master-details designer makes cloning Access form-subform projects a quick and easy process. Adding multiple details grids for tables at the third or lower level of the relation hierarchy is equally simple. The DataGridView is a considerably improved version of the DataGrid, despite its inability to display hierarchical data. Later chapters in Part II show you how to customize these new controls and components for production-grade data projects.

3

Adopting Best Practices for Data-Centric Projects

Today's business processes require real-time access to a wide variety of public and proprietary data. Almost all business-oriented applications connect to one or more networked data stores. Relational database tables are the most common data stores, but messaging systems, worksheets, word-processing files, and, increasingly, XML documents also serve as data sources. ADO.NET requires tabular data sources, so this chapter concentrates on best practices for processing data contained in relational databases, structured XML Infosets, and SOAP messages.

Microsoft Access 2.0 and Visual Basic 3.0 applications delivered desktop data connectivity to millions of Windows users. Both platforms enabled quick and relatively easy access to local and networked databases. Access enabled Office power users to create database front ends and set up multi-user Jet databases for departmental projects. Visual Basic let amateur and professional developers with a wide range of skill sets create client applications for corporate database servers. Much of this early development activity was prompted by the inability—or unwillingness—of IT departments to deliver officially sanctioned applications on a timely basis (or at all). Unsanctioned ad hoc projects often fell under IT management's radar and weren't discovered until data contamination became evident or improperly managed connections impacted database performance.

> *A recent survey by a large U.S. government agency found more than 150,000 Access 97 .mdf files on employees' workstations and agency file servers. Most files turned out to be obsolete or backups, but more than 10,000 Jet databases were in active use.*

Year 2000 compliance audits and subsequent database upgrades uncovered most unsanctioned or defective database front ends. SQL Server back ends with sa accounts having empty or easy-to-guess passwords were secured. IT departments of most organizations gained full control over internal connections to centralized corporate or government databases. Centralized administration of and establishment of best practices for database front-end development became the norm. Ubiquitous Internet connectivity and the prevalence of external attacks resulted in an increased emphasis on establishing best practices for data security and integrity. However, many small and medium-sized organizations continue to operate with informal, ad hoc database application development practices.

The SQL Snake/Spida exploit, which occurred in May 2002, proved that many Internet-accessible SQL Server databases had empty or easy-to-guess passwords. January 2003's Slammer/Sapphire worm demonstrated that thousands of unsanctioned MSDE 2000 instances, as well as unpatched SQL Servers under IT department control, were accessible to TCP port 1433 exploits.

The U.S. General Accounting Office defines best practices as "processes, practices, and systems identified in public and private organizations that performed exceptionally well and are widely recognized as improving an organization's performance and efficiency in specific areas. Successfully identifying and applying best practices can reduce business expenses and improve organizational efficiency." Regardless of the size of your employer or consulting clients, adopting and enforcing a set of application architecture and development best practices delivers very high short-term and long-term returns on investment. Even if your development duties aren't guided by an official set of best practices, take the time to become familiar with Microsoft's current architecture and implementation recommendations for .NET projects.

This chapter discusses best practices for .NET application development in top-down sequence — from overall architecture to specific recommendations for increased scalability, interoperability, performance, security, and code reusability in all tiers of data-centric .NET projects.

Establish Architectural Best Practices

Keeping up with Microsoft's successive application architectures and frameworks can become a full-time occupation. Conventional client-server projects gave way to COM-based three-tier designs and then to *n*-tier architectures with components under the control of Microsoft Transaction Server. Windows Distributed interNet Architecture (WinDNA) and Universal Data Access (UDA), which Microsoft introduced in 1997, formalized the design of three-tier Web applications. In 1999, Windows DNA 2000 framework added XML and Web services to the data access mix. Bill Gates announced in July 2002 the short-lived ".NET platform," which incorporated all Microsoft server-side systems, Visual Studio .NET, and the ill-fated .NET My Services project. At the time of this writing, the latest architecture incarnation is the Microsoft Enterprise Application Platform that, as of 2004, combined Windows 2003 Server, Visual Studio .NET 2003, and *patterns & practices* (P&P) architectural guidance.

P&P are developed by Microsoft's Platform Architectural Guidance (PAG) team, which has established a three-day International Patterns and Practices Summit conference and provides weekly Webcasts on .NET architectural and application development topics.

The PAG group's home page is http://www.microsoft.com/practices/.

Following are brief descriptions of the four P&P elements:

❏ **Reference architectures** identify design decisions and make overall recommendations for implementing solutions with interconnected components. The Data Services implementation guide of *Windows Server System Reference Architecture* (WSSRA) and *Application Architecture for .NET: Designing Applications and Services* are the most useful reference architecture documents for ADO.NET developers.

❏ **Patterns** are models of common operations performed by applications that are presented as a problem/solution pair. A typical example, taken from the 196-page *Data Patterns* book is the Master/Slave Snapshot Replication pattern for copying slowly changing information, such as customer and product lists, from database tables to frequently disconnected users' laptop computers.

❏ **Application blocks** are VB and C# components that provide a framework for specific elements of applications or components. An example is the Data Access Application Block for .NET. Several design guides provide documentation for application blocks.

❏ **Design guides** provide detailed architectural and implementation recommendations for specific application, component, and service types. The *.NET Data Access Architecture Guide* (2003) and *Designing Data Tier Components and Accessing Data Through Tiers* (2002) are the two most important members of this group for ADO.NET programmers.

> *The original P&P aren't affected significantly by the VS 2005 and ADO.NET 2.0 upgrades or migration to SQL Server 2005. The design principles are consistent for all .NET versions.*

The following sections provide more detailed information on members of the preceding list with emphasis on elements that are of the most interest to database developers.

Reference Architectures

Reference architectures provide .NET architects and developers with system-level guidance for typical business scenarios, such as distributed systems for Web-based retail and banking applications. Reference architectures attempt to model typical IT structures and operations of medium to large enterprises. The following sections describe the primary reference architectures for multi-tier, data-driven projects.

> *The home page for Microsoft reference architectures is* `http://msdn.microsoft.com/`
> `architecture/`. *This page has links to the Microsoft Architects JOURNAL (PDF files), related sites, and Weblogs.*

Windows Server System Reference Architecture

WSSRA is the March 2005 Windows Server 2003 update of *Microsoft Systems Architecture 1.5* for Windows 2000 Server. WSSRA provides recommendations for hardware and operating system configurations for enterprise-level systems. The Data Services implementation guide is based on SQL Server 2000, but the recommendations also apply to SQL Server 2005.

Links to all WSSRA implementation guides are at `http://www.microsoft.com/technet/`
`itsolutions/wssra/raguide/`.

Designing Applications and Services

Application Architecture for .NET: Designing Applications and Services (2002) is a 169-page book that describes the recommended architecture for distributed systems constructed with multiple tiers. Individual chapters cover the reference implementation and goals; component design and interaction; security and management; and deployment. This publication provides the foundation for all other .NET reference architectures. All developers of non-trivial .NET applications should read this book.

The reference implementation is a relatively simple Web-based retail sales application that demonstrates the following component types:

User interface	Service agent
User process components	Service interface
Business workflows	Security
Business components and entities	Management
Data access logic	Communication

The sections "Data Patterns," "Designing Data Tier Components and Passing Data Through Tiers," and "The .NET Data Access Architecture Guide," later in this chapter, describe data access logic components (DALCs). Service agent and service interface components connect to XML Web services.

Search http://msdn.microsoft.com *with ".NET: Designing Applications" to obtain the most recent version of this book as a PDF file.*

Microsoft released in early 2003 the PAG Enterprise Template: Application Architecture for .NET 2002 and 2003. PAG is an acronym for Prescriptive Architecture Guidance. The installer adds an Application Architecture for the .NET Wizard node to your VS 2003 templates folder. Subnode templates create project stubs for 11 of the component types that the book describes. Most stubs have references to the .NET namespaces that are required for the component's project, but don't include any code.

You can download this PAG from http://gotdotnet.com/team/architecture/patterns/ templates.aspx.

Enterprise Development Reference Architecture

The Microsoft Enterprise Development Reference Architecture (ERDA) v1.0 (originally codenamed Shadowfax) is a framework for developing service-oriented applications with SQL Server, ASP.NET Web services, Microsoft Message Queue (MSMQ), and other back-end systems. The reference implementation, called GlobalBank, is the starting point for an online banking portal that lets customers access their personal banking information. The section "Integration Patterns," later in this chapter, describes the new *Integration Patterns* book, which uses GlobalBank as its reference implementation.

You can download version 1.1 of GlobalBank at http://workspaces.gotdotnet .com/shadowfx. *Background information from members of the PAG is available at* http:// channel9.msdn.com/wiki/default.aspx/Channel9.GlobalBankInformation. *Search the GotDotNet site for "Global Bank" to find the latest version of the Global Bank Implementation (GBI) project. When this book was written, the latest GBI build was for VS 2003.*

Find Patterns for Projects

A software pattern defines a common solution for specific recurring IT tasks, such as retrieving data from and updating database tables by applications that frequently lack network database connectivity for an extended period — the classic *disconnected client* scenario. The general rule is that a particular pattern must be applicable to at least three instances of the task. The AntiPatterns Web site's What Is a Pattern page (http://www.antipatterns.com/whatisapattern/) describes the first instance as an *event*, the second as a *coincidence*, and the third as a possible *pattern*. Additional instances lend increasing credence to the pattern.

A pattern that gains widespread use within an organization or software community is likely to be transformed into a template. A common definition of a pattern template is structured documentation for a pattern that can be added to pattern or template catalog. The following sections describe patterns that apply to all .NET applications in general and data-driven applications in particular.

> *The Microsoft Patterns home page is* `http://msdn.microsoft.com/architecture/` `patterns/`. *You can download all patterns for the following sections from links on this page. The discussion group for patterns, and VS 2005 and earlier templates, is at* `http://gotdotnet.com/team/architecture/patterns/`.

Enterprise Solution Patterns Using Microsoft .NET

Enterprise Solution Patterns Using Microsoft .NET (2003, version 2.0) is the mother of all .NET patterns. This 367-page book is a catalog of 32 patterns in five clusters — Web Presentation, Data Access, Performance and Reliability, Services, and Deployment. The "Data Transfer Object," "Implementing Data Transfer Object in .NET with a Data Set," and "Implementing Data Transfer Object in .NET with a Typed Data Set," topics of Chapter 5, "Distributed Systems Patterns," are the members of the Data Access cluster.

> *You can read or download a PDF version of the book at* `http://msdn.microsoft.com/library/` `en-us/dnpatterns/html/Esp.asp`.

The book defines the Data Transfer Object (DTO) as "a simple container for a set of aggregated data that needs to be transferred across a process or network boundary" and then goes on to spend a few pages discussing "chunky versus chatty" issues with remote data calls. The often-referenced "Implementing Data Transfer Object in .NET with Serialized Objects," topic is missing from the second edition. Its source is identified in Appendix A, "Pattlets," as Microsoft P&P, but a full search on the term returns only the DataSet-related items. The two implementations provide C# sample code for unit testing with the `NUnit.Framework` namespace. The later "Automate Test-Driven Development" section provides more detail on unit testing patterns with NUnit.

> *It's a stretch to describe DTOs as "simple containers" and then recommend implementation with ADO.NET untyped or, especially, typed ADO.NET 2.0 DataSets. The implementation patterns recognize the non-interoperability liability of DataSets, but the book doesn't discuss the XML overhead added by typed DataSets when marshaled by .NET remoting in XML or binary format, or serialized to Web service messages. Unlike Application Architecture for .NET: Designing Applications and Services, you can safely skip the data-related topics of this pattern collection.*

Data Patterns

Data Patterns (2003) is a 196-page book that identifies a cluster of data movement patterns. A *cluster* is a group of related patterns with a root pattern for the set — Moving Copy of Data is the cluster for the first *Data Patterns* edition. Pattern clusters have varying levels of abstraction — architecture, design, and implementation; only implementation is platform-dependent and database vendor-specific. Database, application, deployment, and infrastructure viewpoints represent members of typical IT departments: DBAs, developers, network administrators, and system architects.

> *You can read or download the book's PDF version at* `http://msdn.microsoft.com/library/` `en-us/dnpatterns/html/dp.asp`.

The Moving Copy of Data cluster branches to extract-transform-load (ETL) operations and various types of server-based replication, such as master-master and master-slave, with transactional and snapshot designs. Implementations, of course, use Microsoft SQL Server 2000 or later. Each pattern has a template with Context, Problem, Forces, and Solution topics.

Data Patterns doesn't directly address one of the most common ADO.NET approaches to moving data—caching frequently used but slowly changing data on client workstations as persistent DataSets.

Distributed Systems Patterns

The Distributed Systems Patterns (Version 1.1.0) white paper outlines a cluster of patterns for object collaboration across process and network boundaries. The cluster includes remote object invocation patterns with Singleton and Broker patterns for .NET remoting, and the Data Transfer Object (DTO), which creates a local instance copy of a remote object. This is one of the few patterns books and white papers that doesn't deal with service-oriented architecture and Web services.

You can read this white paper and follow links to C# implementation at http://msdn.microsoft.com/library/en-us/dnpatterns/html/EspDistributedSystemsPatternsCluster.asp.

Integration Patterns

Integration Patterns (2004) is a catalog of enterprise application integration (EAI) patterns. The Electronic Commerce Dictionary (http://www.tedhaynes.com/haynes1/atol.html) defines EAI as:

The linking and sharing of multiple business applications and data, including extensions to business partners, through the use of application-to-application modules, object middleware and message broker-ing, or multi-tier application server platforms. Motivations for EAI include the need to rapidly implement Web-based projects, the need to link to legacy data, and the need to forge links to different systems acquired through corporate mergers and acquisitions.

Integration Patterns traces the steps that the fictitious Global Bank's IT development group follow in development of a Web-based, self-service customer payments portal. The portal connects to a diverse set of data sources and implements payment operations with these ten EAI patterns:

Entity Aggregation	Function Integration
Process Integration	Service-Oriented Integration
Implementing Process Integration with BizTalk Server 2004	Implementing Service-Oriented Integration with ASP.NET
Portal Integration	Implementing Service-Oriented Integration with BizTalk Server 2004
Data Integration	Presentation Integration

Search microsoft.com for "Integration Patterns," and click the "Download details: Integration Patterns" link to download IntPatt.pdf (2.4MB).

Integration Patterns' "Data Integration" chapter discusses three approaches to data retrieval and updates:

❑ **Shared database** gives multiple applications direct access to a single database; this approach minimizes data latency.

❑ **Maintain data copies** provides each application with its own database, which replicates data to and from a master database. Replication type and scheduling determine data synchronization and latency.

❑ **File transfer** involves moving logical files between the data store and independent applications. Sending serialized DataSets to persistent storage on a client as XML files is an example of the file transfer approach.

Like most other P&P, *Integration Patterns* emphasizes the use of Web services and messaging in EAI projects. The section "Prepare for Service-Oriented Architecture," later in this chapter, discusses the pros and cons of using Web services for data access.

Try Application Block Libraries

Application blocks are class libraries of reusable subsystem-level components for implementing common application services, such as data access, encryption, and event logging. Each application block comes with a quick-start example, documentation, and source code. Providing the source code lets you modify and extend the blocks to suit your application development environment and requirements. Microsoft released the original application blocks for VS 2002 (then called Visual Studio .NET) and .NET 1.0 in 2002 as version 1.0. The blocks were upgraded to VS 2003 and .NET 1.1 as version 2.0 in 2004. Most original application block libraries were rewritten as members of the patterns & practices Enterprise Library, which Microsoft released in January 2005. Enterprise Library incorporates parts of the Avenade Connected Architecture for .NET (ACA.NET). Avenade, Inc., is a joint-venture software consulting company formed by Accenture and Microsoft in 2000.

> *You can download the current set of application blocks from the Enterprise Library page at* `http://msdn.microsoft.com/library/en-us/dnpag2/html/entlib.asp`.

Following are the application blocks available in .NET 1.*x* versions at the time of this writing:

Aggregation Application Block	Data Access Application Block*
Asynchronous Invocation Application Block	Exception Handling Application Block*
Authorization and Profile Application Block	Logging and Instrumentation Application Block*
Caching Application Block*	Security Application Block*
Configuration Application Block*	Smart Client Offline Application Block
Cryptography Application Block*	Updater Application Block
	User Interface Process Application Block - V2

> *Application blocks in the preceding table that are marked with an asterisk (*) are included in the Enterprise Library application blocks download of January 2005.*

Enterprise Library application blocks require you to build the .NET 1.1 source code with batch files or VS 2003 to create .NET 1.1 Microsoft.Practices.EnterpriseLibrary.*BlockName*.dlls. You then add references to the appropriate assemblies in your VS 2005 project. QuickStart clients require building solutions from multiple projects that have many files. Most block assemblies have dependencies on core assemblies, such as Microsoft.Practices.EnterpriseLibrary.Common.dll and Microsoft.Practices.EnterpriseLibrary .Configuration.dll. Earlier application block versions included VB and C# libraries; Enterprise Library has only C# libraries. However, QuickStart clients include VB and C# source code.

The following two sections describe the Data Access Application Block (DAAB) and its QuickStart test client, a sample Windows form project that uses the Data Application block to retrieve and update SQL Server 2000 or 2005 data. Using the VS 2005 Upgrade Wizard isn't practical with VS 2005 and the January 2005 Enterprise Library source code because the automated upgrade fails. Thus, the DataAccessQuickStart.sln VB 2005 sample project includes the manually upgraded components necessary to create DAB objects and execute their methods in VS 2005.

The Data Access Application Block

The original DAAB's primary objective was to minimize the number of lines of custom code needed to create and manipulate runtime ADO.NET 1.*x* SQL Server data access components. The Enterprise Library version enables integrating other application blocks that provide standardized configuration, instrumentation, and security features with data retrieval and update operations. The upgraded DAAB manipulates DataSets, DataReaders, XmlReaders, and scalar values of SQL Server, Oracle, and DB2 database tables. The Enterprise Library's DAAB is totally incompatible with earlier versions. The only commonality between the two versions is use of the `SqlCommandBuilder` class for autogenerating `SqlCommand` objects.

To install the sample database, stored procedures, and triggers, and test the upgraded DataAccessQuickStart.sln project, do the following:

1. Navigate to the \VB2005DB\Chapter03\DataAccessQuickStart folder, which contains the upgraded QuickStart and DAB files.

2. If you're running SQL Server 2000 or 2005, open the DataAccessQuickStart.sql script in SQL Server Management Studio (SSMS), and execute it to create the EntLibQuickStarts SQL Server sample database on `localhost` with Customers, Products, Credits, and Debits tables, eight stored procedures, and two triggers on the Products table.

    If you're running SQL Server Express, execute the DataAccessQuickStart.sql script with SqlCmd.exe. In this case, you must change the dataConfiguration.config file's `server` parameter's `value` attribute from `localhost` to `.\SQLEXPRESS` or `\localhost\SQLEXPRESS`, as illustrated in the following listing.

3. Open DataAccessQuickStart.sln in VS 2005 or VBX, and press F5 to build and run the project.

4. If you receive build errors related to missing namespaces, delete the references to the three Microsoft.Practices... assemblies, and re-create them from the assembly DLL copies in the ...\DataAccessQuickStart\Assemblies folder.

5. Test database connectivity and updated sample code by clicking each of the seven buttons, which invokes the applicable data application block method.

The Data Configuration File

A dataConfiguration.config file contains the settings for the database-specific connection string. The Configuration application block's assembly deserializes the config file. Following is the dataConfiguration.config file for the DataAccessQuickStart's EntLibQuickStarts SQL Server sample database with the databaseType and connectionString elements emphasized:

```xml
<?xml version="1.0" encoding="utf-8"?>
<dataConfiguration>
  <xmlSerializerSection type=
    "Microsoft.Practices.EnterpriseLibrary.Data.Configuration.DatabaseSettings,
    Microsoft.Practices.EnterpriseLibrary.Data">
    <enterpriseLibrary.databaseSettings
      xmlns:xsd="http://www.w3.org/2001/XMLSchema"
      xmlns:xsi="http://www.w3.org/2001/XMLSchema-instance"
      defaultInstance="DataAccessQuickStart"
      xmlns="http://www.microsoft.com/practices/enterpriselibrary/08-31-2004/data">
      <databaseTypes>
        <databaseType name="Sql Server"
         type="Microsoft.Practices.EnterpriseLibrary.Data.Sql.SqlDatabase,
         Microsoft.Practices.EnterpriseLibrary.Data" />
      </databaseTypes>
      <instances>
        <instance name="DataAccessQuickStart" type="Sql Server"
          connectionString="LocalQuickStart" />
      </instances>
      <connectionStrings>
        <connectionString name="LocalQuickStart">
          <parameters>
            <!-- For SQL Express value=".\SQLEXPRESS" or "localhost\SQLEXPRESS" -->
            <parameter name="server" value="localhost" isSensitive="false" />
            <parameter name="database" value="EntLibQuickStarts"
             isSensitive="false" />
            <parameter name="Integrated Security" value="True"
             isSensitive="false" />
          </parameters>
        </connectionString>
      </connectionStrings>
    </enterpriseLibrary.databaseSettings>
  </xmlSerializerSection>
</dataConfiguration>
```

Theoretically, only a modification to the dataConfiguration.config file is required to change between one of the three supported database types. Specifying the databaseType determines the connection, command, and operator class — Sql..., Oracle..., or DB2....

Data Retrieval Code

After you define a connection to a database with the configuration file and a Dim db As Database = DatabaseFactory.CreateDatabase() instruction, you can retrieve or update data with db.DBCommandWrapper method overloads and one of the following instructions:

```
db.ExecuteReader(dbCommandWrapper)
db.ExecuteXmlReader(dbCommandWrapper)
db.ExecuteScalar(dbCommandWrapper)
```

```
db.ExecuteDataSet(dbCommandWrapper)
db.UpdateDataSet(dbCommandWrapper)
db.ExecuteNonQuery(dbCommandWrapper)
```

As an example, the following snippet returns an untyped `DataSet` object that can serve as a `DataGridView.DataSource` property value:

```
Dim dbSQL as Database = DatabaseFactory.CreateDatabase()
Dim strSQL as String = "SELECT * FROM Products WHERE CategoryID = 2"
Dim cwSQL as DBCommandWrapper = dbSQL.GetSqlStringCommandWrapper(strSQL)
Dim dsProducts As DataSet = dbSQL.ExecuteDataSet(cwSQL)
```

`DBCommandWrapper.AddInParameteter()` and `DBCommandWrapper.AddOutParameteter()` overloads handle parameterized queries and stored procedures. The following skeleton code assumes that the GetProductDetails stored procedure has a `@ProductID` input parameter, and `@ProductName` and `@UnitPrice` output parameters:

```
Dim dbSQL as Database = DatabaseFactory.CreateDatabase()
Dim cwSP as DBCommandWrapper = _
  dbSQL.GetStoredProcCommandWrapper("GetProductDetails")
cwSP.AddInParameter("@ProductID", DbType.Int32, 2)
cwSP.AddOutParameter("@ProductName", DbType.String, 50)
cwSP.AddOutParameter("@UnitPrice", DbType.Currency, 8)
dbSQL.ExecuteNonQuery(cwSP)
Dim strReturn As String = cwSP.GetParameterValue("@ProductID").ToString + ", " + _
  cwSP.GetParameterValue("@ProductName").ToString + ", " + _
  Format(cwSP.GetParameterValue("@UnitPrice"), "$#,##0.00")
```

The third argument of the `AddInParameter` *method is the value supplied to the stored procedure parameter. The third argument of the* `AddOutParameter` *method is the data length.*

Retrieving parameter metadata for the `GetStoredProceCommandWrapper(strProcName)` method ordinarily requires a roundtrip to the server for each execution of a parameterized stored procedure. The data application block eliminates repetitive retrievals by caching parameter metadata in a hashtable. The method retrieves the parameters for a specified stored procedure only if they're not present in the cache. Support for cached parameters is automatic.

Data Update Code

The `Database.UpdateDataSet(dsDataSet, strTableName, cwInsert, cwUpdate, cwDelete, intUpdateBehavior)` method performs multiple update operations on a DataTable specified by the `strTableName` argument. The `UpdateBehavior` enumeration determines how the method responds to an update error: `Standard` (0, the default) stops execution, `Continue` (1) updates remaining rows, and `Transactional` (2) rolls back all updates.

The DAAB's sample database incorporates AddProduct, UpdateProduct, and DeleteProduct stored procedures. The following snippet, which derives from the DataAccessQuickStart sample project, creates a new untyped DataSet, adds and populates a Products DataTable, adds a new row to the Products base table, updates an existing row, and claims to delete the added row:

```
Dim dbSQL As Database = DatabaseFactory.CreateDatabase()
'Create an untyped DataSet; add and populate the Products table
Dim dsProducts As DataSet = New DataSet
```

```
Dim cwSelect As DBCommandWrapper = _
  dbSQL.GetSqlStringCommandWrapper("SELECT * FROM Products")
dbSQL.LoadDataSet(cwSelect, dsProducts, "Products")
Dim dtProducts As DataTable = dsProducts.Tables("Products")

'Add a new row to the Products table
Dim objRow(3) As Object
objRow(0) = DBNull.Value              'ProductID int identity
objRow(1) = "Added Row Product Name"  'ProductName
objRow(2) = 11                        'CategoryID
objRow(3) = 12.5                      'UnitPrice
dtProducts.Rows.Add(objRow)
'Create the InsertCommand for the added row
Dim cwInsert As DBCommandWrapper = dbSQL.GetStoredProcCommandWrapper("AddProduct")
cwInsert.AddInParameter("@ProductName", DbType.String, "ProductName", _
 DataRowVersion.Current)
cwInsert.AddInParameter("@CategoryID", DbType.Int32, "CategoryID", _
 DataRowVersion.Current)
cwInsert.AddInParameter("@UnitPrice", DbType.Currency, "UnitPrice", _
 DataRowVersion.Current)

'This delete command doesn't work because the parameter value is DbNull
Dim cwDelete As DBCommandWrapper = _
  dbSQL.GetStoredProcCommandWrapper("DeleteProduct")
cwDelete.AddInParameter("@ProductID", DbType.Int32, "ProductID", _
 DataRowVersion.Current)

'Modify the first Products table Row and create the UpdateCommand
dtProducts.Rows(0).Item(1) = "Modified Row Product Name"
Dim cwUpdate As DBCommandWrapper = _
  dbSQL.GetStoredProcCommandWrapper("UpdateProduct")
cwUpdate.AddInParameter("@ProductID", DbType.Int32, "ProductID", _
 DataRowVersion.Current)
cwUpdate.AddInParameter("@ProductName", DbType.String, "ProductName", _
 DataRowVersion.Current)
cwUpdate.AddInParameter("@LastUpdate", DbType.DateTime, "LastUpdate", _
 DataRowVersion.Current)

'Execute the three commands
Dim intRowsUpdated = dbSQL.UpdateDataSet(dsProducts, "Products", cwInsert, _
 cwUpdate, cwDelete, UpdateBehavior.Transactional)
```

The `AddInParameter()` *method overload for update operations on* `DataTable` *objects is*
`AddInParameter(strParamName, intDbType, strDataTableColumnName,`
`intDataRowVersion).` *The* `strDataTableColumnName` *parameter is specific to DataSet updates.*

Invoking the `dbSQL.UpdateDataSet()` method executes the `cwDelete` command but doesn't delete the Products table row that the `cwInsert` command adds. The `DataRowVersion.Current` value for the added row is `DbNull.Value`, so the command deletes no row(s) from the base table. You can verify the failure to delete the added "New product" row by running the DataAccessQuickStart.sln project, clicking the Update a Database Using a DataSet button, and opening the EntLibQuickStarts.Products table in VS 2005 Standard Edition or higher, SSMS, or XM.

To solve the preceding problem, you can add the following code to return the Products table to its original condition (except the current identity seed value) after the changes made by the preceding snippet or the DataAccessQuickStartClient:

93

```
'Create a DeleteCommand for the added row
Dim dbSQL As Database = DatabaseFactory.CreateDatabase()
Dim strDeleteSQL As String = _
 "DELETE FROM Products WHERE ProductName = 'Added Row Product Name'"
Dim intCtr As Integer = dbSQL.ExecuteNonQuery(CommandType.Text, strDeleteSQL)
strDeleteSQL = "DELETE FROM Products WHERE ProductName = 'New product'"
intCtr += dbSQL.ExecuteNonQuery(CommandType.Text, strDeleteSQL)
'Create a UpdateCommand for the modified first ProductName
Dim strUpdateSQL As String = _
 "UPDATE Products SET ProductName = 'Chai' WHERE ProductID = 1"
intCtr += dbSQL.ExecuteNonQuery(CommandType.Text, strUpdateSQL)
```

The Enterprise Library developers expended a substantial amount of effort on test-driven development of the C# application blocks and adding NUnit test cases, but short-changed testing of the first Enterprise Library DataAccessQuickStartClient implementation.

The preceding oversight should be corrected and a VB 2005 version of the blocks' source code included in the Enterprise Library version promised for VS 2005.

The DataAccessQuickStart Client

The DataAccessQuickStart client includes a `salesData` VB class that emulates a simple database-specific DALC for SQL Server and the EntLibQuickStarts sample database. Seven button event handlers invoke `salesData` methods, such as `GetCustomerList()`, `GetProductsInCategory(intCategory)`, and `UpdateProducts()`. Figure 3-1 shows the QuickStartForm after clicking the top button (Retrieve multiple rows using a DataReader), which invokes the `SalesData.GetCustomerList()` method.

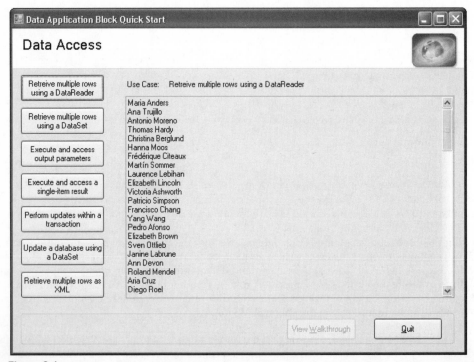

Figure 3-1

Following is commented code for the `SalesData.GetCustomerList()` method:

```
Public Function GetCustomerList() As String
    'Create a Microsoft.Practices.EnterpriseLibrary.Data.Database instance
    Dim db As Database = DatabaseFactory.CreateDatabase()
    'Define the query string
    Dim sqlCommand As String = "SELECT CustomerID, Name, Address, City, " + _
    "Country, PostalCode FROM Customers"
    'Wrap the query string with a dbCommandWrapper
    Dim dbCommandWrapper As DBCommandWrapper = _
    db.GetSqlStringCommandWrapper(sqlCommand)
    Dim dataReader As IDataReader = db.ExecuteReader(dbCommandWrapper)
    Dim readerData As StringBuilder = New StringBuilder
    While dataReader.Read()
        ' Get the value of the 'Name' column in the DataReader
        readerData.Append(dataReader("Name"))
        readerData.Append(Environment.NewLine)
    End While
    dataReader.Close()
    Return readerData.ToString()
End Function
```

Following is conventional ADO.NET 2.0 code that accesses the `SqlClient` objects directly from the QuickStartForm.vb class file with the connection string saved in the app.config file:

```
Private Sub compareUsingReaderButton()
    'Added alternative (conventional) code (15 lines)
    strConn = My.Settings.QuickStartConnection
    Dim cnQS As New SqlClient.SqlConnection(strConn)
    Dim strSQL As String = "SELECT CustomerID, Name, Address, City, " + _
    "Country, PostalCode FROM Customers"
    Dim cmQS As New SqlClient.SqlCommand(strSQL, cnQS)
    cnQS.Open()
    Dim sdrData As SqlClient.SqlDataReader = cmQS.ExecuteReader
    Dim sbData As New System.Text.StringBuilder
    With sdrData
        While .Read
            sbData.Append(sdrData(1).ToString + vbCrLf)
        End While
        .Close()
    End With
    cnQS.Close()
    Me.DisplayResults("Alternative Data Reader", sbData.ToString)
End Sub
```

A comparison of the preceding two code examples, which have about the same number of active lines, indicates that there's no appreciable reduction in the amount of code required to implement a DataReader scenario with the DAAB. DataSet updates with the DAAB reduce the requirement for hand-written code but don't implement typed DataSets or sequenced groups of updates, inserts, and deletions for updating related base tables.

Chapter 4's "Save Changes to the Base Tables" section explains why sequenced groups of updates are required to maintain referential integrity of related tables.

The market research firm Gartner cited Avenade as one of its four "Cool Vendors in IT Services and Outsourcing 2005" because of ACA.NET 4.0. ACA.NET 4.0 adds aspect-oriented programming (AOP) features to the ACA.NET-based Enterprise Library application blocks. One of the principles of AOP is "separation of concerns." Concerns about a software application might be issues such as performance, accuracy, auditability, optimization, security, data structures, and data flow. If the application's programmers can rely on the availability of reliable, standardized methods for managing data structures and data flow, programmers need not be concerned about writing code to implement such methods. The question is whether the additional level of data management abstraction provided by the DAAB beyond that inherent in ADO.NET 2.0 and VS 2005's data toolset justifies the DAAB's learning curve, potential limitations, or both.

Adhere to Design Guides

Design guides predate formation of the P&P group and don't share a common structure or writing style with reference architectures and patterns. The guides don't cover the new ADO.NET 2.0 objects and features described in the preceding two chapters, but most of their recommendations apply to .NET 2.0 projects.

> You can read all current design guides by following the Guides link on the P&P page at http://www .microsoft.com/resources/practices/.

The .NET Data Access Architecture Guide

".NET Data Access Architecture Guide" (2001, updated 2003) is an 86-page primer that's directed to developers new to ADO.NET. The updated guide makes specific recommendations for the following ADO.NET 1.1 topics:

Managing Database Connections	Performing Database Updates with DataSets
Error Handling	Using Strongly Typed DataSet Objects
Performance	Working with Null Data Fields
Connecting Through Firewalls	Transactions
Handling BLOBs	Data Paging

The guide emphasizes use of DataSets, which isn't surprising when you consider that DataSets are one of ADO.NET's primary distinguishing features and that Microsoft has made a very large investment in automating typed DataSet creation in all VS versions. This book's two preceding chapters and Parts II and III, which follow, provide detailed coverage of many of the guide's topics.

Improving .NET Application Performance and Scalability

"Improving .NET Application Performance and Scalability" (2004) is the largest of all P&P publications — 1,124 pages. This guide, which is targeted specifically at .NET 1.1 application developers, incorporates and updates performance recommendations from earlier architectural best practice and design pattern books. Most chapters have a related checklist that summarizes the detailed performance recommendations.

Database application developers will find the following four chapters to be the most useful:

- ❑ Chapter 12, "Improving ADO.NET Performance"
- ❑ Chapter 14, "Improving SQL Server Performance"
- ❑ Chapter 10, "Improving Web Service Performance"
- ❑ Chapter 11, "Improving Remoting Performance"

Chapter 12, which was released in May 2004, includes a few references to performance improvements delivered by pre-beta versions of ADO.NET 2.0 objects.

Designing Data Tier Components and Passing Data Through Tiers

"Designing Data Tier Components and Passing Data Through Tiers" (2002) is a 65-page white paper that makes recommendations for adding new layers to the three conventional tiers—presentation, business rules, and data. The paper defines business entities (BEs), data access logic components (DALCs), and business process components (BPCs), and discusses the relationships of BEs, DALCs, and BPCs with the presentation tier and the physical data store. This is the most widely quoted of all data-related .NET white papers.

Here are brief descriptions of the three layers defined by the paper:

- ❑ **BE**s represent typical elements in a business's operation—such as a customer, order, invoice, product, or supplier—as business objects. BEs usually map to relational tables, in which case the BE can contain data from related tables. For example, Order and Invoice BEs contain line item members because orders and invoices aren't valid without at least one line item. If a Customers table has related tables that store contact, billing address, or shipping address information, the Customer BE includes these members. Retailers and distributors might include related supplier data with a Product BE.

- ❑ **DALC**s deliver BEs by abstracting create, retrieve, update, and delete (CRUD) operations from the underlying data store. DALCs are stateless classes that hide data store implementation details, such as schema metadata and stored procedure properties, from objects that invoke their methods. DALCs also are responsible for managing data consistency and handling concurrency conflicts when executing SQL statements rather than stored procedures for updates. A properly designed DALC should be able to deliver a BE to Windows or Web forms, handheld devices, or Web services.

- ❑ **BPC**s implement business rules and aggregate data and handle transaction management when operations involve more than one BE. BPCs are responsible for implementing many-to-many relationships, such as that between Customer and Product BEs. If the BEs map to tables in multiple databases or depend on Web services, distributed transactions are required for updates. BPCs can incorporate workflow management for long-running transactions, which might require compensating transactions to reverse previously committed changes to the data stores.

Like many other .NET design and implementation guides, code examples are C#-only, which lends additional credence to the assertion that VB.NET suffers "second-class citizen" status among Microsoft developers. On the other hand, this paper grants equal time to implementing BEs with custom data objects and DataSets. However, the custom data object implementation of the `OrderEntity` class specifies an `OrderDetails` member of the `DataSet` type, which defeats cross-platform interoperability.

Following is a simple example of a typed, hierarchical BE Order object:

```
Public Class Order
    Public OrderID As Int32
    Public CustomerID As String
    Public EmployeeID As Int32
    Public OrderDate As Date
    Public RequiredDate As Date
    Public ShippedDate As Date
    Public ShipVia As Int32
    Public Freight As Decimal
    Public ShipName As String
    Public ShipAddress As String
    Public ShipCity As String
    Public ShipRegion As String
    Public ShipPostalCode As String
    Public ShipCountry As String
    Public OrderDetails(24) As OrderDetail
End Class

Public Class OrderDetail
    Public OrderID As Int32
    Public ProductID As Int32
    Public UnitPrice As Decimal
    Public Quantity As Int16
    Public Discount As Decimal
End Class
```

The Order class's design emphasizes versatility and interoperability, so it exposes public fields and represents line items as a simple array of OrderDetail items with a maximum initial length, rather than an ArrayList or generic List(Of OrderDetail) object. (A Redim Preserve statement removes empty OrderDetail elements after populating the array.) This design ensures platform and language independence, and enables VS 2002 and 2003 Web methods to serialize Order BEs to SOAP messages. .NET 2.0 Web services also handle objects with Get and Set accessors for private field properties.

Chapter 9, "Publishing Data-Driven XML Web Services," provides the details of new VS 2005 Web service features.

Following is an example of a serialized Order BE:

```
<?xml version="1.0" encoding="utf-8"?>
<Order>
  <OrderID>1617968</OrderID>
  <CustomerID>QUICK</CustomerID>
  <EmployeeID>9</EmployeeID>
  <OrderDate>1996-08-15T00:00:00.0000000-07:00</OrderDate>
  <RequiredDate>1996-09-02T00:00:00.0000000-07:00</RequiredDate>
  <ShippedDate>1996-09-02T00:00:00.0000000-07:00</ShippedDate>
  <ShipVia>3</ShipVia>
  <Freight>76.07</Freight>
  <ShipName>QUICK-Stop</ShipName>
  <ShipAddress>Taucherstraße 10</ShipAddress>
  <ShipCity>Cunewalde</ShipCity>
```

```
        <ShipRegion />
        <ShipPostalCode>01307</ShipPostalCode>
        <ShipCountry>Germany</ShipCountry>
        <OrderDetails>
          <OrderDetail>
            <OrderID>1617968</OrderID>
            <ProductID>5</ProductID>
            <UnitPrice>21.35</UnitPrice>
            <Quantity>13</Quantity>
            <Discount>0.18</Discount>
          </OrderDetail>
          <OrderDetail>
            <OrderID>1617968</OrderID>
            <ProductID>17</ProductID>
            <UnitPrice>39</UnitPrice>
            <Quantity>11</Quantity>
            <Discount>0.12</Discount>
          </OrderDetail>
        </OrderDetails>
      </Order>
```

Here's a simple XML schema for the serialized BE with attributes to support referential integrity constraints, a maximum of 25 line items per order, and optional (`nillable`) `dateTime`, `decimal`, and `string` values:

```
<?xml version="1.0" encoding="utf-8"?>
<xs:schema attributeFormDefault="unqualified" elementFormDefault="qualified"
    xmlns:xs="http://www.w3.org/2001/XMLSchema">
  <xs:element name="Order">
    <xs:complexType>
      <xs:sequence>
        <xs:element name="OrderID" type="xs:int" />
        <xs:element name="CustomerID" minOccurs="1" >
          <xs:simpleType>
            <xs:restriction base="xs:string">
              <xs:length value="5" fixed = "true"/>
            </xs:restriction>
          </xs:simpleType>
        </xs:element>
        <xs:element name="EmployeeID" type="xs:int" />
        <xs:element name="OrderDate" type="xs:dateTime" />
        <xs:element name="RequiredDate" type="xs:dateTime" nillable="true" />
        <xs:element name="ShippedDate" type="xs:dateTime" nillable="true" />
        <xs:element name="ShipVia" type="xs:int" />
        <xs:element name="Freight" type="xs:decimal" nillable="true" />
        <xs:element name="ShipName" type="xs:string" minOccurs="1" />
        <xs:element name="ShipAddress" type="xs:string" minOccurs="1" />
        <xs:element name="ShipCity" type="xs:string"  minOccurs="1" />
        <xs:element name="ShipRegion" type="xs:string" nillable="true" />
        <xs:element name="ShipPostalCode" type="xs:string" nillable="true" />
        <xs:element name="ShipCountry" type="xs:string" minOccurs="1" />
        <xs:element name="OrderDetails">
          <xs:complexType>
            <xs:sequence>
```

```
        <xs:element minOccurs = "1" maxOccurs="25" name="OrderDetail">
          <xs:complexType>
            <xs:sequence>
              <xs:element name="OrderID" type="xs:int" />
              <xs:element name="ProductID" type="xs:int" />
              <xs:element name="UnitPrice" type="xs:decimal" />
              <xs:element name="Quantity" type="xs:short" />
              <xs:element name="Discount" type="xs:decimal" />
            </xs:sequence>
          </xs:complexType>
        </xs:element>
      </xs:sequence>
    </xs:complexType>
  </xs:element>
      </xs:sequence>
    </xs:complexType>
  </xs:element>
</xs:schema>
```

Adding the `nillable="true"` *attribute to string values ensures that the element is present in the XML document if it doesn't have a value.*

A public ASP.NET 1.1 Web service at `http://www.oakleaf.ws/nwordersws/nwordersws.asmx` emulates real-world use of the Order BE. The `GetOrderSP` Web method returns the order specified by an `intOrderID` parameter. The `UpdateOrInsertOrderSP` method updates an individual order; an `intOrderID` value of 0 inserts a new order. The Web service is compatible with Java, Perl, and other Web service client toolkits. Unlike Web services that deliver and update DataSets, the XML schema for custom BE objects contains no implementation details.

VS 2005 makes Web services that publish custom BEs the data source equivalent of typed DataSets. When you add a Web reference to a Web service that publishes a strongly typed, serialized BE object, the Data Sources window displays field icons that are almost identical to those of a corresponding pair of related records. As an example, the Order BE data source representation is almost identical to that of the data source for the Northwind Orders and Order Details tables; only the fields' sequences differ (see Figure 3-2). Like a pair of related DataTables, you can drag the Order node to a Windows form and generate an `OrderBindingSource`, an `OrderDetailsBindingSource`, and a set of bound master-details text box and DataGridView controls.

The NWOrdersWSClient.sln project in the \VB2005DB\Chapter03\NWOrderWSClient folder demonstrates the simplicity of a Windows form editing application for a sales order BE (see Figure 3-3). Clicking the BoundClient.vb form's Connect to Web Service button fills the combo box with a list of the last ten sales orders. Clicking the Get Selected Order button retrieves a single sales order and its line items with four lines of code. You can edit the sales order header and line item data, and then update the database by clicking the Update Order button, which executes a single line of code. Line items are a simple array, so you can't add or delete line items in a DataGridView without additional code.

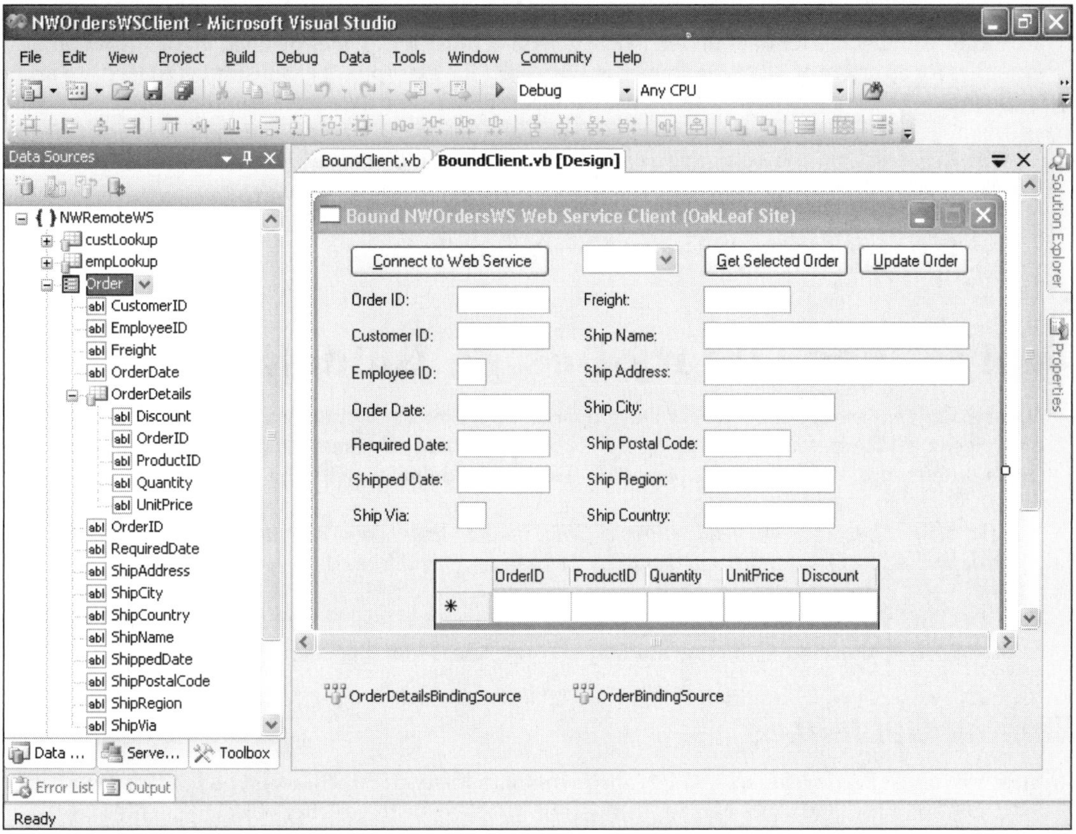

Figure 3-2

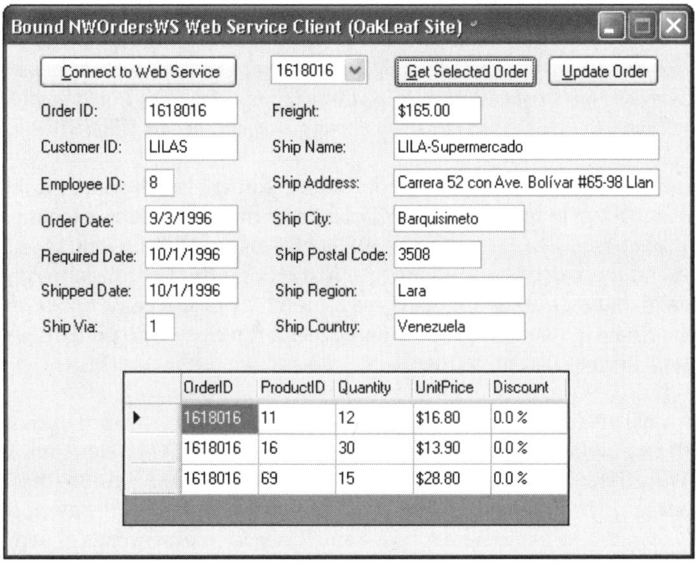

Figure 3-3

"Designing Data Tier Components and Passing Data Through Tiers" is one of the most useful application architecture guidelines for data-driven .NET projects because it provides detailed implementation examples for a variety of BE usage scenarios. Disregard the examples that substitute DataSets for arrays or collections of child objects if your BEs must interoperate with non-Windows applications.

> *The Web service client code to display and update an Order BE is minimal, but the Web service code isn't. The \VB2005DB\Chapter03\NWOrdersWS Web site folder has the code for the Web service and the T-SQL script (NWOrdersWSStoredProcs.sql) for the stored procedures you must add to the Northwind sample database to run the Web service on localhost.*

Apply Class Library Design Guidelines

"Design Guidelines for Class Library Developers" is a reference document that provides detailed, prescriptive guidance for programming .NET classes. To read this member of the .NET Framework General Reference, search the MSDN site for "Design Guidelines" (with the quotes).

> *The section "Use FxCop to Validate Project Code," later in this chapter, describes VS 2005's built-in code analysis tool for testing conformance to the class design guidelines.*

The class library guidelines consist of 14 primary topics, which lead to numerous subtopics. Two of the most important topics are "Naming Guidelines" and "Class Member Usage Guidelines."

Naming Guidelines

Most VB6 and VBA developers apply Hungarian notation-style (camelCase) type prefixes to variables, form, control, class, and class member names. This practice for three-letter object name prefixes originated with Microsoft's "Visual Basic Programmers Guide" in the VB3 era. Microsoft Consulting Services extended the recommended practice with two-letter and three-letter prefixes for Jet database objects. Most of this book's examples and some Microsoft sample VB code use similar prefixes for VB.NET variable and type instance names.

> *See Microsoft Knowledge Base article Q110264 for Microsoft Consulting Services naming conventions. Search the MSDN site for "Visual Basic Coding Conventions" for VB6; use "Visual Basic .NET Coding Conventions" to find a very brief set of naming conventions for VB.NET.*

The "Naming Guidelines" topic contains subtopics for naming classes and their members, but not instance names. PascalCase is *de rigeur* for .NET class and member names except parameters, which use camelCase, as in typeName. The earlier Orders BE conforms to .NET PascalCase naming practices, but not to the recommendation against use of Public instance fields. The guidelines also recommend not using underscores in names, but use of _ or m_ as a prefix for Private or Protected instance fields is — and probably will remain — commonplace. Finally, using the class type prefix (C as in CTypeName) is out, but always use the I prefix to identify interfaces.

Some developers have a tendency to use camelCase for class and member names so that serialized instances conform to a de-facto camelCase naming convention for XML elements and attributes. All examples in the W3C Extensible Markup Language (XML) 1.0 (Third Edition) recommendation use camelCase element and attribute names. The W3C XML Schema Part 0: Primer recommendation at http://www.w3.org/TR/xmlschema-0/ uses camelCase for element tags of sample XML Infosets such as po.xml, which has a structure that's similar to the Order BE. You'll also see examples of camelCase type names in some NWOrdersWS Web service methods; these names were formatted to comply with InfoPath 2003's XML naming conventions. XHTML tag names require lowercase, but XML Infosets don't. Follow the "Naming Guidelines" for public classes *and* their members, and use your choice of camelCase or PascalCase for XML element and attribute names.

Class Member Usage Guidelines

The "Class Member Usage Guidelines" topic has subtopics for all class members. The "Field Usage Guidelines" subtopic recommends avoiding exposing `Public` or `Protected` instance fields to developers because changing a public field to a property doesn't maintain binary compatibility. Instead, use `Get` and `Set` accessors. The guide also recommends the use of constants for fields that don't change value, because the compiler stores constants directly in the code that calls the object. This topic recommends camelCase to distinguish private field names from public property names, which works in C# but not in case-insensitive VB.

> *Visual Studio Team Services adds a Class Diagram template to the Add New Item dialog. If you have any edition of Team Services installed, open the VB2005DB\Chapter03\ClassDesigner.sln project to display examples of classes with varying levels of conformance to the guidelines. For more information on Team Services, see the section "Automate Test-Driven Development," later in this chapter.*

The "Property Usage Guidelines" subtopic provides useful advice on determining when to use a property or method and, if you decide on a property, how to avoid pitfalls with indexed properties, such as properties that get and set arrays. Use a single indexed property per class, and make it the default indexed property. These recommendations apply to the `OrderDetails` member of the Orders BE, if you change the member from a public to a private field and add an `OrderDetails` public property.

Prepare for Service-Oriented Architecture

Service-oriented architecture (SOA) is today's "Next Big Thing" for IT. A Google search on "service-oriented architecture" returns close to a million hits as of this writing. Computer business analyst, marketing, and public relations types are the major contributors of fuel for the SOA hype machine, which they began assembling in the late stages of the dot-com bust. The rise of interest in SOA occurred as the bloom was fading fast from an earlier hype-cycle for SOAP-based (XML) Web services.

Not surprisingly, Microsoft has climbed on the SOA bandwagon. Nearly half of Tech*Ed 2004's architecture track sessions (9 out of 19) included "Service" and "Oriented" in their titles. The MSDN site returns more than 200 hits on SOA articles, white papers, Web casts, and MSDN TV episodes. The www.microsoft.com site has about four times as many SOA references. One of Microsoft's primary incentives for encouraging developers to buy into SOA is to promote the sale of VS 2005 licenses and adoption of .NET Framework 2.0. VS 2002 and 2003 greatly simplified the process of writing and publishing basic ASP.NET Web services; the jury is still out on whether VS 2005's new approach simplifies or complicates coding and testing Web services.

> *The .NET Architecture Center: Service Oriented Architecture page at* http://msdn.microsoft.com/architecture/soa/ *has links to articles and presentations that relate to Microsoft's SOA strategies.*

The Road to Service-Oriented Architecture

Over the past half-century, data processing application architecture evolved in these three stages:

❑ **Monolithic architecture** encapsulated the user interface, business logic, data access, and data storage operations in a single component. Early monolithic applications consisted of alphanumeric terminals connected to mainframe databases and transaction managers. PCs let users and developers take advantage of desktop database management software, such as dBASE, Fox Pro, and Access, to create monolithic applications with data stored in local or networked files. Business logic incorporated in the application can't be used by other applications.

❑ **Client-server architecture** moved data management and storage to a networked application server but retained the UI, business logic, and data access elements in a single program — typically a Visual Basic or other executable, or an Access .adp file. Client-server architecture allowed centralized data management and offloaded CRUD query processing operations from PC client applications to the database server. Each client maintained a dedicated connection to the database server, which limited application scalability. Client business logic and data access code couldn't be shared with other applications.

❑ *N*-tier architecture encapsulates business logic and data access into individual layered components. Client UIs access the business logic component, which connects to one or more data access components. Stateless data access layers share database connections with multiple business logic components, which share state management responsibilities with the client. DCOM, CORBA, and other distributed component technologies allow business logic and data access components to reside on multiple application servers, which contributes to scalability, robustness, and maintainability.

Client-server architecture lets clients interoperate with database back ends that provide .NET, ODBC, JDBC, or OLE DB drivers and run under Windows, UNIX, Linux, and mainframe operating systems. It's much more difficult to achieve interoperability between distributed *n*-tier components that are written in different programming languages, run on multiple operating systems, or both. Overcoming distributed component interoperability problems has spawned a very large market for combinations of component software and consulting services called enterprise application integration (EAI). The EAI market remained relatively robust during the dot-com meltdown and regained its momentum faster that any other IT market segment during the economy's recovery.

Adding a dedicated EAI layer between otherwise-incompatible components increases application *brittleness*. Applications become brittle when a minor change to a single component results in a catastrophic system failure. This phenomenon is similar to a stress crack in an aircraft structure that ultimately leads to a crash, but the crash is much quicker in *n*-tier computer systems. Brittleness is responsible for many large-scale telecommunication network outages.

Another *n*-tier architecture problem is *tightly coupled* networked components that communicate by remote procedure calls (RPCs) implemented by DCOM, CORBA, Java RMI, or J2EE Enterprise Beans. Traditional middle-tier components use synchronous RPCs, which require an immediate response to each request; failure to receive a timely response from any component blocks the entire process. Asynchronous RPCs and messaging systems — such a Microsoft Message Queue Server (MSMQ) or IBM QSeries — mitigate this problem, but don't necessarily provide an interoperable solution.

None of the preceding RPC-based approaches can communicate through today's network firewalls, which usually restrict traffic to TCP ports 80 and 443. This limitation makes Internet access by business partners to special-purpose business logic components difficult or impossible.

Implement SOA with Web Services

Service-oriented architecture can overcome most *n*-tier interoperability problems described in the preceding section. Following are the basic requirements of SOA:

❑ Interfaces that present standards-based access points to business logic components

❑ Encapsulation of business logic components and their functions to hide implementation details from callers

❑ Loose-coupling provided by semi-synchronous or asynchronous, stateless access methods implemented by text-based (usually Unicode) messages

❑ Standards-based interface descriptions and message formats

❑ Standards-based protocols for communicating with interfaces and functions, including the capability to pass messages through firewalls, if present

❑ Standards-based security and error-handling features

❑ Contract-based interoperation between the interface provider and its callers

Implementing SOA doesn't require the use of SOAP-based Web services, but only industry-wide Web service standards — SOAP, Web Services Description Language (WSDL), and WS-Security — combined with other W3C, IETF, and OASIS standards can fulfill the preceding SOA requirements today.

> *SOAP 1.1 and WSDL 1.1 are W3C notes — not recommendations — but have become de-facto industry standards for Web services. VS 2005 supports SOAP 1.1 and the W3C SOAP 1.2 recommendations. WSDL 2.0 is a W3C working draft as of this writing. WS-Security became an OASIS standard in April 2004.*

XML 1.0 documents and Infosets form the foundation of Web services. WSDL documents define Web service interfaces (`port` and `operations`) and access points (`address`), and include an XML schema for SOAP request and response message documents. The schema lets Web service client programmers use a local copy of a WSDL document to enable design-time IDE features, such as IntelliSense. The schema and messages don't include service implementation details.

The most common transport protocols for SOAP-based Web services are HTTP and HTTPS, but TCP, email (SMTP, POP3, and others), and FTP are potential alternatives. Regardless of the transport type, Web services are stateless and autonomous. State must be maintained by the Web service client or by one of the pending standards for implementing Web service transactions (WS-Coordination, WS-AtomicTransaction) or business processes (WS-BusinessActivity, Business Process Execution Language for Web Services [BPEL4WS], WS-Choreography).

Web service security issues are the primary impediment to widespread adoption of SOA. HTTPS encrypts SOAP messages between two access points (often called *end points*), and HTTPS with client certificates can authenticate individual callers. More sophisticated security implementations require digital signatures and customized message encryption provided by the WS-Security specification. Implementing WS-Security with ASP.NET 2.0 Web services requires installing Web Services Extensions (WSE) 2.0 SP3 or later on Web service server and client machines.

The MSDN Web Services Developer Center home page at `http://msdn.microsoft.com/` `webservices/` *has links to WSE 2.0 documentation and download points. You can access other Microsoft-supported WS-* specifications from this page.*

Ensure Fully Interoperable Web Services

Best practices for SOA architecture dictate that services be operating system–independent and programming language–agnostic. As an example, a Java Web service client running under FreeBSD or Linux must be able to interoperate with a VB.NET or C# ASP.NET Web service delivered by a Windows 2000 or 2003 server.

VS 2005 attempts to ensure that the ASP.NET Web services you create conform to the Web Services Interoperability (WS-I) Organization's Basic Profile (BP) 1.0. BP 1.0 achieved "Final Specification" status in April 2004, more than two years after WS-I's formation by Microsoft, IBM, and 53 other members of the Web services community. BP 1.0 explicitly forbids use of SOAP Section 5 encoding, which precludes rpc/encoded and document/encoded message formats because of interoperability issues. BP 1.0 supports both document/literal (doc/lit) and rpc/literal formats, but rpc/literal services are very uncommon. ASP.NET's standard SOAP message format is doc/lit.

As of August 24, 2004, WS-I's Basic Profile Version 1.1 (BP 1.1) and Simple SOAP Binding Profile 1.0 supersede BP 1.0. Changes in version 1.1 are minor. ASP.NET 2.0 Web services claim conformance to BP 1.1 in their `WebServiceBinding` *attribute.*

The first of BP 1.1's "Guiding Principles" in section 1.3 states: "No guarantee of interoperability. It is impossible to completely guarantee the interoperability of a particular service. However, the Profile does address the most common problems that implementation experience has revealed to date." If this clause wasn't present, unsuspecting developers might assume that ASP.NET 2.0 Web services that deliver and update serialized DataSet objects, and claim to meet BP 1.1's requirements, would interoperate with clients written in Java, Perl, Python, or any other language (including VB6 or VBA) that has a BP-1.0-compliant SOAP 1.1 or 1.2 toolkit. Web service toolkits map SOAP messages to objects by referring to the schema included in the WSDL document for doc/lit Web services.

Microsoft deprecated the SOAP Toolkit 3.0 in favor of the .NET Framework in early 2004 and standard support discontinued as of April 2005. (Extended support continues until April 2008.) The native message format for the Toolkit is rpc/encoded, which doesn't comply with BP 1.0, and writing d ocument/literal (doc/lit) services with the Toolkit's low-level API is an agonizing process, to be charitable. Another reason for the Toolkit's retirement is that Windows Server 2003 doesn't support the Toolkit's server components or ISAPI Listener.

VB6 and VBA developers can use Simon Fell's PocketSOAP and the PocketSOAP WSDL Wizard to replace SOAP Tookit 1.0. You can download these and other PocketSOAP utilities from `http://www.pocketsoap.com.`

ASP.NET 2.0 Web services that deliver or update generic DataSets *will not* interoperate with current versions of any Web service toolkit except Microsoft's. The culprits are the reference to `s:schema` and the `<s:any />` wildcard element in Web method nodes. This combination is a flag that tells .NET's WSDL processor that the schema is embedded in the SOAP response message. Here's an excerpt from a typical WSDL document for a typed or untyped DataSet:

```
<s:element name="GetAllCustomersResponse">
  <s:complexType>
    <s:sequence>
      <s:element minOccurs="0" maxOccurs="1" name="GetAllCustomersResult">
        <s:complexType>
          <s:sequence>
            <s:element ref="s:schema" />
            <s:any />
          </s:sequence>
        </s:complexType>
      </s:element>
    </s:sequence>
  </s:complexType>
</s:element>
```

Generic DataSets are presumed to be dynamic, so they expose their schema at runtime by embedding it in the SOAP message rather than in the WSDL document. However, static typed DataSets produce WSDL schema nodes that are identical to those for untyped DataSets. This means that non-Microsoft toolkits must use a low-level API to process the SOAP response message as an XML NodeList, which isn't a trivial programming project. Writing Java code to deliver a diffgram with DataSet updates in a SOAP request message would be a Herculean — and probably Sisyphean — task.

> *Aaron Skonnard's article "Web Services and DataSets" at* `http://msdn.microsoft.com/msdnmag/issues/03/04/XMLFiles/` *provides a detailed analysis of DataSet-based Web service compatibility with Java toolkits in general and Apache Axis in particular.*

Embedding XML schemas in SOAP messages doesn't violate the SOAP 1.1 or 1.2 specification, but it's a very unconventional (and controversial) practice. DataSet schemas incorporate numerous Microsoft (proprietary) namespaces, such as `xmlns:msdata="urn:schemas-microsoft-com:xml-msdata"` and `xmlns:diffgr="urn:schemas-microsoft-com:xml-diffgram-v1"`. Messages are decorated with `xmlns:diffgr="urn:schemas-microsoft-com:xml-diffgram-v1"` also. DataSets add proprietary attributes to schemas and messages — `msdata:IsDataSet="true"`, `msdata:PrimaryKey="true"`, `diffgr:id="Customers1"`, and `msdata:rowOrder="0"` are examples.

Schemas for ADO.NET 2.0 typed DataSets contain much more detailed information than ADO.NET 1.*x* versions, which are almost identical to untyped DataSet schemas. As an example, ADO.NET 2.0 adds nine `msprop:PropertyName` attributes to each `<xs:element ... >` tag. These added elements expose Web service operational details to Web service clients, which contravenes SOA's dictum that services hide implementation details from callers.

The following sections preview Chapter 9's Web services and test clients to demonstrate interoperability issues with Web services that process both types of DataSets.

Install and Publish the DataSetWS Web Service

The sample DataSetWS.sln ASP.NET 2.0 Web service project exposes four Web methods that operate on an untyped dsNwind DataSet: `GetAllCustomers`, `GetOrdersByCustomerID`, `UpdateCustomersDataSet`, and `UpdateOrdersDataSet`. To install, test, and publish the Web service to your local instance of IIS, do the following:

1. Open VS 2005, choose File ⇨ Open ⇨ Web Site, navigate to the \VB2005DB\Chapter03\ DataSetWS Web site, click Open, and open the DataSetWS.vb code file from Solution Explorer. Change the strConn connection string value to conform to your SQL Server security settings. (This book's sample Web services use SQL Server security with sa as the UserID and whidbey as the Password.)

2. Press F5 to start the DataSetWS service, click the GetAllCustomers link, and click Invoke to return a response message that contains a diffgram with all Customers records.

3. Return to the main Web service help page, click the GetOrdersByCustomerID link, type **RATTC** in the Customer ID Parameter Value text box, and click Invoke to return a diffgram with Orders records for Rattlesnake Canyon Grocery.

4. Close the DataSetWS.asmx page or press Shift+F5 to terminate the Web service instance.

5. Choose Build ⇨ Publish *SitePath* to open the Publish Web dialog, type **http://localhost/ DataSetWS** in the text box, mark the Allow This Pre-Compiled Site to be Updatable checkbox, and click OK to create the IIS virtual directory and add the precompiled files to the \Inetpub\DataSetWS folder.

6. Test the deployment to IIS by opening IE and navigating to http://localhost/ datasetws/datasetws.asmx and invoking the GetAllCustomers and GetOrdersByCustomerID Web methods.

If you encounter an error related to the Web service's configuration file, launch Internet Services Manager, right-click the Default Web Site\DataSetWS node, and choose properties to open the properties dialog. Click the ASP.NET tab and select ASP.NET Version 2.0.BuildNumber in the dropdrown list.

The primary incentive for taking the DataSet shortcut on the server side is the minimal code required to add Web methods. As an example, here's the code that implements the GetAllCustomers Web method:

```
<WebMethod(Description:=strGetCustomers)> _
Public Function GetAllCustomers() As DataSet
    Dim dsNwind As New DataSet
    Dim daCusts As SqlDataAdapter = Nothing
    Try
        'Create an SqlDataAdapter and fill the DataSet
        daCusts = New SqlDataAdapter("SELECT * FROM Customers", strConn)
        daCusts.Fill(dsNwind)

        'Replace "NewDataSet" with "Customers" and assign namespace
        dsNwind.DataSetName = "Northwind"
        'dsNwind.Namespace = "http://oakleaf.ws/webservices/datasetws/northwind"
        With dsNwind.Tables(0)
            'Assign the table name
            .TableName = "Customers"
            'Specify the primary key
            .PrimaryKey = New DataColumn() {.Columns(0)}
            'Require a CompanyName value (table constraint)
            .Columns(1).AllowDBNull = False
        End With
        Return dsNwind
    Catch excSys As Exception
        Dim excSoap As New SoapException(excSys.Message, _
            SoapException.ClientFaultCode, Context.Request.Url.AbsoluteUri)
```

```
        Throw excSoap
    Finally
        dsNwind.Dispose()
        daCusts.Dispose()
    End Try
End Function
```

The code to update an untyped DataSet is equally simple. The ADO.NET 2.0 `SqlCommandBuilder` object automatically generates the SQL statements and, if specified, `Parameters` collections needed to support optimistic concurrency for updates and deletions when you specify `cbCusts.ConflictOption = ConflictOption.CompareAllSearchableValues`, as emphasized in the following code:

```
<WebMethod(Description:=strUpdateOrdersDataSet)> _
Public Function UpdateOrdersDataSet(ByVal dsNwind As DataSet) As Boolean
    Dim cnNwind As New SqlConnection(strConn)
    Dim daOrders As SqlDataAdapter = Nothing
    Dim cbOrders As SqlCommandBuilder = Nothing
    Try
        daOrders = New SqlDataAdapter("SELECT * FROM Orders", cnNwind)
        cbOrders = New SqlCommandBuilder(daOrders)
        cbCusts.ConflictOption = ConflictOption.CompareAllSearchableValues
        daOrders.Update(dsNwind, "Orders")
        Return True
    Catch excSys As Exception
        Dim excSoap As New SoapException(excSys.Message, _
            SoapException.ClientFaultCode, Context.Request.Url.AbsoluteUri)
        Throw excSoap
        Return False
    Finally
        cbOrders.Dispose()
        daOrders.Dispose()
        dsNwind.Dispose()
    End Try
End Function
```

Compare the preceding code with that required to update the Orders and Order Details tables in the earlier NWOrdersWS example. Creating a `CommandBuilder` instance at runtime to generate `DeleteCommand`, `InsertCommand`, and `UpdateCommand` objects degrades performance and, thus, isn't a best practice. The section "Avoid Adding Runtime CommandBuilder Instances," later in this chapter, discusses this issue and its solution.

Test the DataSetWS Web Service

The DataSetWSClient.sln project is a simple Web service test client that has a Web reference to the WSDL document at `http://localhost/datasetws/datasetws.asmx`. Figure 3-4 shows the project's form after adding a new Order record to the DataSet. A value is required in the OrderID field, but the DataSet disregards the value when you click the Update DataSet button to invoke the `UpdateOrdersDataSet` Web method. Typing a character in the CustomerID column of a new Order DataTable row fills the required columns with sample data. The primary key field is read-only except when entering a new grid row. You must type a character in the CompanyName column for the Customers DataTable to enable adding the CustomerID key value.

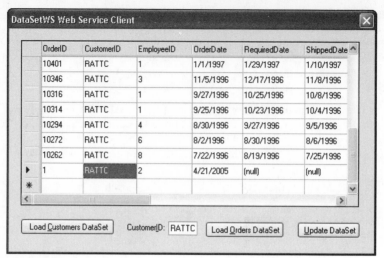

Figure 3-4

Loading the grid saves a DataSet diffgram, schema, and data as XML files in the project's ...\bin folder.

If Web service client data binding and minimizing development time are your primary project criteria, consider DataSet-based Web services as a substitute for .NET remoting behind your organization's firewall. If you intend to provide Internet access to your Web services, expend the effort required to implement full interoperability with all current Web service toolkits that support WS-I BP 1.0 or later.

Use FxCop to Validate Project Code

FxCop is a Microsoft code analysis tool that tests managed code assemblies for conformance to the .NET Framework Design Guidelines and code correctness standards. About half the approximately 200 tests check for Design Guidelines conformance. FxCop originated in standalone Windows and command-line versions as a member of the GotDotNet Tools collection, and the .NET Framework 2.0 includes FxCop classes. VS 2005 Team System (VSTS) integrates optional FxCop analysis for all projects. You turn on FxCop by opening the Project Properties window, clicking the Code Analysis tab, and marking the Enable Code Analysis checkbox. You can disable rules in nine categories and expand the category nodes to read rule descriptions and disable individual rules.

> *John Robbins' article "Bad Code? FxCop to the Rescue" at* http://msdn.microsoft.com/msdnmag/issues/04/06/Bugslayer/ *provides a detailed description of standalone FxCop 1.30. Version 1.312 for .NET 1.1 and beta versions of .NET 2.0 are current and available from* http://www.gotdotnet.com/team/fxcop/ *as of this writing.*

Running a relatively simple project—DataAccessQuickStart.sln for this example—with VSTS's Code Analysis enabled—throws 1 error and 38 warnings (see Figure 3-5); FxCop v.1.312 displays 49 errors and messages.

To display Code Analysis warnings in the sample projects, rebuild them. If the Errors window isn't visible, choose View ⇨ Errors List to open it.

A simple typed DataSet project—Chapter 1's GeneratedDetailView.sln—generates 90 FxCop 1.312 errors and warnings with Office 2003 installed on the machine running VS 2005. FxCop uses the standard spell-checker dictionary and current user's custom dictionaries, if present. All but a few of the messages originate from autogenerated VB 2005 code. It's apparent that the Microsoft developers who wrote the DataSet code generator didn't adhere to FxCop rules for autogenerated classes.

The current Code Analysis and FxCop rule sets clearly are overkill for most Windows form projects. You can customize the rule set applied to a specific project, which FxCop or VSTS persists when you close the project. It takes a major effort, however, to establish a custom rule set that applies to all your projects. The Options dialog doesn't enable specifying a default FxCop rule set for all projects.

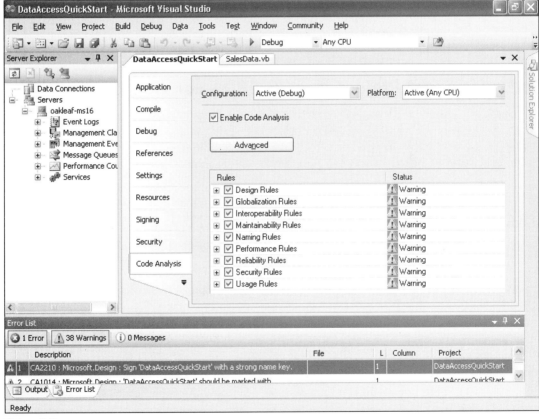

Figure 3-5

Automate Test-Driven Development

Test-driven development (TDD) is a programming methodology that emphasizes testing code in small chunks (units) and writing automated tests regimens (unit tests) before writing application code. You base unit tests on the application's specifications and write code to determine whether units meet or fail specification requirements. You add special instructions to your code to define each unit test. As you develop the application, the unit tests you define become a member of a complete test suite that runs when you build the project. One of the primary advantages of unit testing is that the process detects the regression bugs that often occur in large projects that involve many development teams.

VSTS is a suite of add-on tools for VS 2005 with five editions targeted at architects, project managers, individual developers, team developers, and testers. VSTS for Developers and VSTS for Testers editions include fully integrated, automated unit test generation and execution capabilities. Installing VSTS for Developers or Testers adds Test Project and Empty Test Project templates to the Add New Project dialog.

> *For additional information on all VSTS editions, go to* `http://msdn.microsoft.com/vstudio` `/teamsystem/`. *This page has links to a description page for each edition. The Developer edition page is at* `http://msdn.microsoft.com/vstudio/teamsystem/developer/`.

Add a Unit Test Project to a VS 2005 Solution

If you have the VSTS for Developers or VSTS for Testers edition, you can create a new test solution with a unit test project, and then add a new project to contain new forms or pages. This approach is faithful to the test-first, code-later principle of test-driven development. To gain insight into VSTS's approach to TDD, it's simpler to add unit tests to an existing solution.

> *Most Microsoft unit test examples and demonstration videos test trivial methods, such as functions to add two integers. The following example uses a small — but non-trivial — example to demonstrate the effect of method latency on unit test results. You must publish the DataSetWS Web service to your test machine, as described in the section "Install and Publish the DataSetWS Web Service," earlier in this chapter, to run the following example. The completed solution file is UnitTestProject.sln in the ...\Chapter03\UnitTestWSClient folder.*

To wrap an existing project, DataSetWSClient.sln for this example, with a unit test harness, do the following:

1. Right-click the solution node, choose Add ⇨ New Project, select the Test Projects\Test Documents node's Test Project template, specify a folder (\VB2005DB\Chapter03 for this example), give the project a name (UnitTestProject or the like), and click OK. Creating a test project adds a default Test Run Configuration template (LocalTestRun.testrunconfig) file and metadata file (UnitTestProject.vsmdi) to the solution, and ManualTest1.mht and UnitTest1.vb stub files to the project.

2. Right click the UnitTestProject.sln node, choose Add ⇨ Existing Project, navigate to the \VB2005DB \Chapter03\DataSetWSClient folder, and double-click DataSetWSClient.vbproj to link the project to UnitTestProject.sln.

3.   Choose Test ⇨ New Test to open the Add New Test dialog, and double-click the Unit Test Wizard icon to open the Generate Unit Tests dialog.

4.   Expand the nodes for the form file (WSClient.vb) and mark the members you want to test — the GetAllCustomers and GetOrdersByCustomerID functions of the DataSetWSClient project for this example — as shown in Figure 3-6.

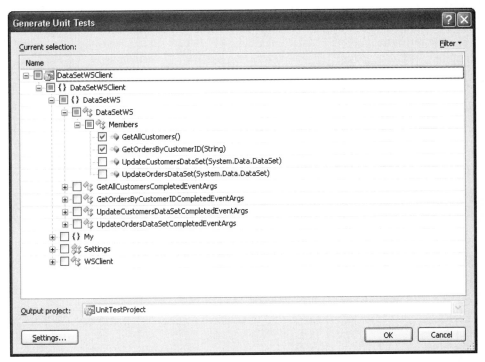

Figure 3-6

5.   Click OK twice to add a DataSetWSTest.vb class file to the UnitTestProject, and open the file in the IDE.

You can test your work so far by pressing F5 to build and run the test project, which activates the Test Results pane and runs the test wrapper. The default manualtest1 and UnitTest1 tests report Pending and Passed status, respectively. The added GetAllCustomers and GetOrdersByCustomerID tests report Failed status, as shown in Figure 3-7. You must edit the code added by the Unit Test Wizard to obtain the correct status.

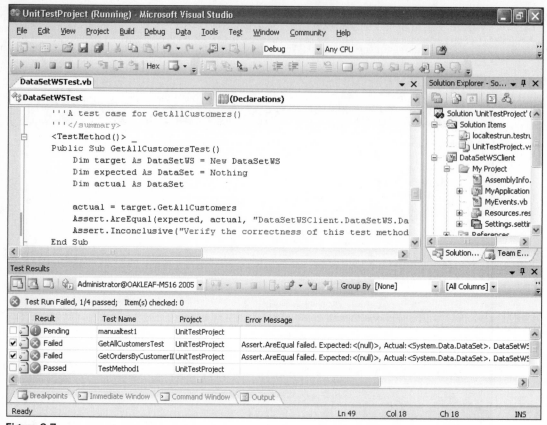

Figure 3-7

Edit and Run the Wizard-Generated Tests

The WSClientTest.vb file contains a `<TestClass()>` with `<TestInitialize()>`, `<TestCleanup()>` methods, and two `<TestMethod()>` members for the procedures you specified in the preceding section. Each `<TestMethod()>` method has default `Assert.AreEqual(expected, actual, message)` and `Assert.Inconclusive(message)` instructions.

The default code assigns an empty DataSet instance to the `expected` object and the DataSet returned by the DataSetWS Web service's Web method to the `actual` object. Thus, the more appropriate `Assert` method is `AreNotEqual` because successful execution of the Web method returns a DataSet that has a DataTable with one row or more. You must supply an appropriate CustomerID value to return Orders table rows with the `GetOrdersByCustomerIDTest` method. If you include the default `Assert`. `Inconclusive(message)` instructions in your tests, successful tests display Inconclusive results and "Assert.Inconclusive failed . . ." error messages instead of Passed results.

The changes shown emphasized in the following two procedures deliver the result shown in the Test Results pane of Figure 3-8. (The unused ManualTest1.mht and UnitTest1.vb files were removed from the UnitTestProject before running this test.)

```
<TestMethod()> _
Public Sub GetAllCustomersTest()
    Dim target As DataSetWS = New DataSetWS
    Dim expected As DataSet = Nothing
    Dim actual As DataSet

    actual = target.GetAllCustomers
    Assert.AreNotEqual(expected, actual,
        "DataSetWSClient.DataSetWS.DataSetWS.GetAllCustomers " + _
        "did not return the expected value.")
    'Assert.Inconclusive("Verify the correctness of this test method.")
End Sub

<TestMethod()> _
Public Sub GetOrdersByCustomerIDTest()
    Dim target As DataSetWS = New DataSetWS
    Dim CustomerID As String = "RATTC" 'Nothing
        'TODO: Initialize to an appropriate value
    Dim expected As DataSet = Nothing
    Dim actual As DataSet

    actual = target.GetOrdersByCustomerID(CustomerID)
    Assert.NotAreEqual(expected, actual,
        "DataSetWSClient.DataSetWS.DataSetWS.GetOrdersByCustomerID " + _
        "did not return the expected value.")
    'Assert.Inconclusive("Verify the correctness of this test method.")
End Sub
```

The preceding examples aren't intended to represent production unit test best practices. Production tests, which are beyond the scope of this book, require more thorough comparison of actual and expected results than simple `AreNotEqual` tests.

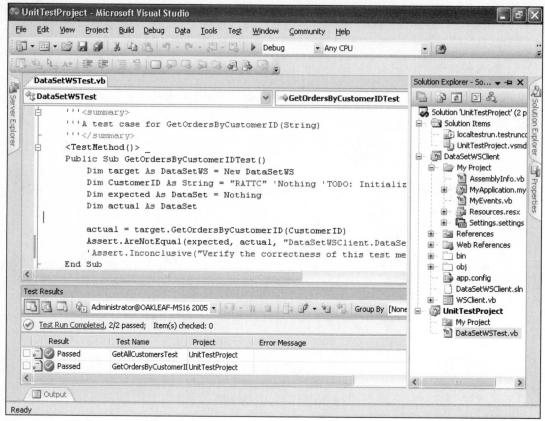

Figure 3-8

Run the SQL Server 2000 Best Practices Analyzer

The Best Practices Analyzer (BPA) Tool for Microsoft SQL Server 2000 is a .NET 1.1 application that tests SQL Server and MSDE 2000 instances for security and administrative best practices. This application is directed primarily to DBAs and IT administrators, but database developers can — and should — run periodic analyses on their test and development servers. After you've set up BPA, you can schedule the tests to run at night or other periods of relatively low database activity.

> You can download BPA from the SQL Server Tool and Utility Downloads page at http://msdn .microsoft.com/sql/downloads/tools/default.aspx. You can't install the BPA database on SQL Server 2005 or SQL Server Express.

Analysis categories include Backup and Recovery, Configuration Options, Database Administration, Database Design, Deprecation, Full-Text, General Administration, SQL Server 2005 Readiness, and T-SQL. Surprisingly, BPA doesn't have a security test category that verifies the existence and strength of sa passwords for instances that implement mixed-mode authentication.

Installing BPA creates an sqlbpa repository database on the designated BPA server. You then specify the SQL Server, MSDE, or SQL Express instances to test, set up Best Practices Groups (BPGs) for each instance, and specify the groups for execution, as shown in Figure 3-9.

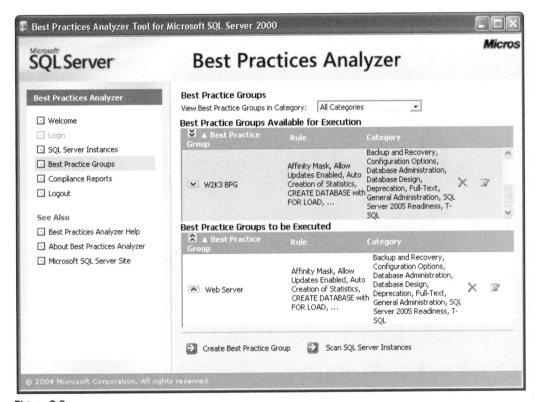

Figure 3-9

Clicking the Scan SQL Server Instances link displays a list of the servers for which you've specified BPGs and selected for execution. Clicking the Next link starts the server scans, whose duration depends on server/network performance and load, and the number of objects on the server. When the analysis completes, you can filter the results by non-compliance to highlight issues that need correction, as illustrated by Figure 3-10.

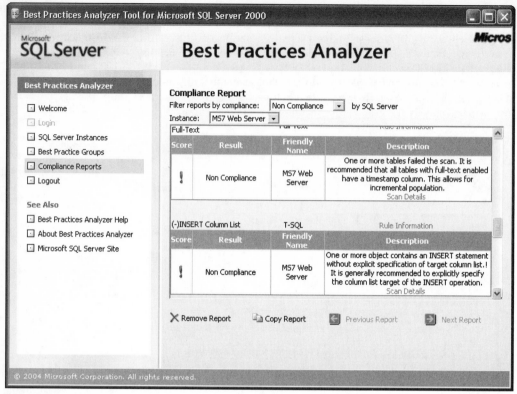

Figure 3-10

Apply Specific Best Practices to ADO.NET 2.0 Projects

If you've taken the time to read the Microsoft P&P publications that pertain to ADO.NET, you'll probably be aware of most—if not all—of the following recommendations for ADO.NET 2.0 best practices.

Use Identical Connection Strings to Pool Database Connections

All Microsoft and third-party ADO.NET data providers support database connection pooling. The first client to connect to the database automatically adds a connection to the pool, if the pool hasn't been created. All other clients that use *identical* ConnectionString values share pooled connections. A minor change to a ConnectionString value for a specific server and database—such as changing Integrated Security=SSPI to Integrated Security=True or adding/removing a space— generates a new connection pool.

Creating a new connection in Server Explorer generates a standardized connection string for Windows or SQL Server authentication. However, you don't have direct access to the text of the connection string at this point. Ensuring an exact match between connection strings that you add to your code and those generated by Server Explorer requires maintaining reference copies. Save the Server Explorer version to a ConnectionStrings.txt file the first time you use it in a project. You can copy the connection string to the text file from the disabled Connection String text box in the first Choose Your Data Connection page of the Data Source Configuration Wizard.

Setting Connection Pool Size

The default minimum pool size is 0 and default maximum pool size is 100. You can maximize performance of widely deployed clients by increasing the minimum pool size to 10 or more, and increasing the maximum pool size to the expected number of simultaneously connected clients. For example, the following connection string establishes a minimum pool size of 10 and a maximum of 200:

```
Dim strConn As String = "Server=OAKLEAF-MS16;Database=Northwind;" + _
    "Integrated Security=True;Min Pool Size=10;Max Pool Size=200"
```

Creating the ten-connection pool causes a performance hit to the first client that opens a connection, but improves performance of the next nine clients that connect simultaneously. Setting a `Min Pool Size` value for Web services is a common practice, because the initial call to an uncached ASP.NET Web service involves an instantiation delay that's much longer than the time required to create the ten connections.

Storing Connection Strings in Configuration Files

It's a common practice to include a `ConnectionString` or similarly named `key` attribute to App.config or Web.config files. When you mark the Yes, Save the Connection As checkbox in the Data Component Configuration Wizard's Save Connection String . . . dialog, the DataSet designer saves the connection string in the App.config file, as emphasized here:

```
<configuration>
  <connectionStrings>
    <add name="ProjectName.MySettings.ConnectionName"
      value="ClientConnectionString"/>
  </connectionStrings>
</configuration>
```

The DataSet designer adds the entry to the MyProject.MySettings property page's list, and code to the *DataSetName*.Designer.vb file's `InitConnection` procedure to retrieve the `ClientConnectionString` value from App.config. This approach eliminates the need to alter source code and rebuild projects when changing server or database names.

You can't reverse the decision to store the connection string in the App.config file. The Save Connection String . . . dialog no longer appears when you reconfigure a data connector.

Encrypting Connection Strings That Contain User Names and Passwords

It's reasonably safe to expose the connection string for Windows authentication; the Web.config file for ASP.NET pages or Web services isn't accessible to Internet or intranet users. In this case, the .config file discloses only the server and database names. Any connection string that contains user ID and values should be encrypted, regardless of whether it's contained in the project's source code, or in the Web.config or App.config file. ASP.NET 2.0 provides two new encryption providers—`DataProtectionConfigurationProvider` and `RSAProtectedConfigurationProvider`—that are specifically intended to simplify protecting designated sections of Web.config files. However, after you've protected the `<connectionStrings>` section by encryption, you must decrypt and re-encrypt any changes you make to the application's connection string.

> *For more information on encrypting connection strings, open the "Walkthrough: Encrypting Configuration Information Using Protected Configuration" VS 2005 help topic.*

Run SQL Server Profiler to Inspect SQL and RPC Queries

SQL Server Profiler is your friend. You can use Profiler to inspect SQL batch statements sent for direct execution or `exec sp_executesql` RPC calls with parameterized SQL statements. Profiler also can display the time required for SQL Server to execute queries and stored procedures. Profiler generates traces based on a set of standard templates designed for specific tasks. You can modify the standard template or design custom templates to create traces with the information that's most important for performance or other analyses.

> *To eliminate Profiler noise from Reporting Services' notifications, open SQL Server Configuration Manager, select SQL Server 2005 Services, and temporarily stop the Reporting Server service.*

Figure 3-11 shows Profiler displaying in the T-SQL_Duration trace template event captures that result from DataSetWSClient executing DataSetWS Web methods.

Profiler traces also are useful in comparing performance of batched updates with conventional updates that require a roundtrip for each change made to a DataSet, which is the subject of the section "Batch Updates to Minimize Server Roundtrips," later in this chapter.

> *You'll find the Profiler trace that's generated during the Data Component Configuration Wizard's command-building operation to be interesting. The process runs `EXEC sp_MShelpcolumns N'dbo.TableName', null` for each table and several complex select queries. You can copy the TextData column values to SQL Server Management Studio's query window and run the queries to view the information that the Wizard uses to build the DataAdapter update queries.*

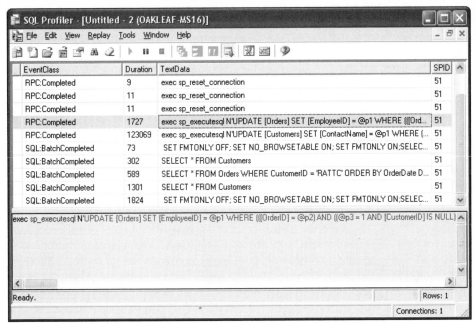

Figure 3-11

Avoid Adding Runtime CommandBuilder Instances

Microsoft recommends not instantiating `CommandBuilder` objects at runtime, and most ADO.NET gurus and trainers agree. As mentioned in the section "Install and Publish the DataSetWS Web Service," earlier in this chapter, `CommandBuilder` objects generate `DeleteCommand`, `InsertCommand`, and `UpdateCommand` instances from the SQL statement of the `SelectCommand`. Regenerating these commands at runtime causes a performance hit. Best practices dictate writing code to define a static `SqlParameter` collection at design time for custom CRUD operations. An alternative is to cache the parameters with the technique used by the DAAB.

> *If you instantiate an* `SqlCommandBuilder` *object and your* `SelectCommand` *calls a stored procedure, you must execute the* `CommandBuilder.DeriveParameters` *method to retrieve the stored procedure's SELECT statement, which requires a server roundtrip.*

VS 2005's upgraded `SqlCommandBuilder` lets you overcome some of the runtime performance hit by specifying the `CompareRowVersion` or `OverwriteChanges` member of the `ConflictOption` enumeration. Later sections describe the conditions required to gain the performance benefit.

Substitute Stored Procedures for SQL Batch Queries

This best practice states the obvious, but you'll find that most DataReader and DataSet code examples, including many in this book, execute SQL statements for CRUD operations rather than stored procedures. Dragging SQL Server tables from the Data Sources window to a Windows form generates SQL statements for all four operations. Substituting new or existing stored procedures for SQL statements requires reconfiguring the DataSet in the designer. You must click Back in the Generate SQL Statements page of the TableAdapter Configuration Wizard to open the Choose a Command Type page, which enables selecting stored procedures for `SqlCommand` objects.

> *The prevalence of SQL statement usage in the VS 2005 IDE is apt to lead developers who are new to database programming—or those whose experience is limited to working with Access (Jet) databases— to omit SQL Server stored procedures from consideration. Many users of the Visual Basic 2005 Express Edition are likely to fall into one of these categories.*

SQL statements executed by applications that connect to database back ends that support stored procedures or their equivalents might be justified for application prototypes and simple code examples, or situations in which managing a large number of stored procedures isn't practical. Otherwise, best practices dictate that all database front ends return views or execute stored procedures and not access base tables directly.

You won't find dramatic differences in performance between parameterized stored procedures and parameterized SQL batch statements executed with `exec sp_executesql` RPC calls. Large-scale performance tests with SQL Server 2000 indicate that parameterized, transacted SQL batch queries update typical sets of related records (Northwind Orders and Order Details) about 13 percent faster than executing multiple stored procedures within an explicit transaction. SELECT and INSERT operations, however, are faster with stored procedures.

> *For more information about the test regimen used to compare SQL statement and stored procedure execution times, and the detailed tabular and graphical results, read "Optimize SQL Server Data Access" at* http://www.ftponline.com/vsm/2003_11/magazine/features/jennings/.

Add Default Values for Parameters That Aren't Required

If you roll your own `SqlParameter` collections, you can minimize the size of `exec` statements for stored procedures if you assign default values to parameters for fields that don't need values in specific cases. For example, the Order BE's RequiredDate, ShippedDate, Freight, Region, and PostalCode are nullable. If you assign NULL as the default parameter values for these fields, you can omit the corresponding members of the named parameters collection when updating or inserting records. This practice offers the added benefit of not inserting January 1, 0001 as `System.Xml`'s `nil` value (`0001-01-01T00:00:00.0000000-07:00` for Pacific Standard Time) of dates serialized in XML documents.

Use sp_executesql and Named Parameters to Reuse Cached Query Plans

If you *must* use parameterized SQL statements to update base tables, take advantage of sp_executesql to prevent regenerating a new query plan with each SQL statement execution. This advice applies if you roll your own client update code instead of using the DataAdapter's autogenerated `DeleteCommand`, `InsertCommand`, and `UpdateCommand` instances.

Tests similar to those in the section "Substitute Stored Procedures for SQL Batch Queries," earlier in this chapter, show that taking advantage of sp_executesql with a random-valued named parameter to return an Order object delivers a 37 percent performance increase over executing the same statement with the OrderID value as a raw (unnamed) parameter. The performance hit occurs as a result of SQL Server regenerating the SELECT query plan for each execution with a different OrderID value.

Add timestamp Columns for Optimistic Concurrency Control

SqlDataAdapters use optimistic concurrency control for base table updates and deletions by default. Optimistic concurrency control requires comparing original values of each cell at the time of a proposed update or deletion with those when the DataSet was filled. Following is the 3,878-character (7,756-byte) SQL batch statement that updates a single row of the Northwind Orders table with value-based optimistic concurrency control:

```
exec sp_executesql N'UPDATE [dbo].[Orders] SET [CustomerID] = @CustomerID,
[EmployeeID] = @EmployeeID, [OrderDate] = @OrderDate,
[RequiredDate] = @RequiredDate, [ShippedDate] = @ShippedDate,
[ShipVia] = @ShipVia, [Freight] = @Freight, [ShipName] = @ShipName,
[ShipAddress] = @ShipAddress, [ShipCity] = @ShipCity,
[ShipRegion] = @ShipRegion, [ShipPostalCode] = @ShipPostalCode,
[ShipCountry] = @ShipCountry WHERE ((([OrderID] = @Original_OrderID) AND
((@IsNull_CustomerID = 1 AND [CustomerID] IS NULL) OR
([CustomerID] = @Original_CustomerID)) AND ((@IsNull_EmployeeID = 1
AND [EmployeeID] IS NULL) OR ([EmployeeID] = @Original_EmployeeID)) AND
((@IsNull_OrderDate = 1 AND [OrderDate] IS NULL) OR
([OrderDate] = @Original_OrderDate)) AND ((@IsNull_RequiredDate = 1 AND
[RequiredDate] IS NULL) OR ([RequiredDate] = @Original_RequiredDate)) AND
((@IsNull_ShippedDate = 1 AND [ShippedDate] IS NULL) OR
([ShippedDate] = @Original_ShippedDate)) AND ((@IsNull_ShipVia = 1 AND
[ShipVia] IS NULL) OR ([ShipVia] = @Original_ShipVia)) AND
((@IsNull_Freight = 1 AND [Freight] IS NULL) OR ([Freight] = @Original_Freight))
AND ((@IsNull_ShipName = 1 AND [ShipName] IS NULL) OR
([ShipName] = @Original_ShipName)) AND ((@IsNull_ShipAddress = 1 AND
[ShipAddress] IS NULL) OR ([ShipAddress] = @Original_ShipAddress)) AND
((@IsNull_ShipCity = 1 AND [ShipCity] IS NULL) OR
([ShipCity] = @Original_ShipCity)) AND ((@IsNull_ShipRegion = 1 AND
[ShipRegion] IS NULL) OR ([ShipRegion] = @Original_ShipRegion)) AND
((@IsNull_ShipPostalCode = 1 AND [ShipPostalCode] IS NULL) OR
([ShipPostalCode] = @Original_ShipPostalCode)) AND ((@IsNull_ShipCountry = 1 AND
[ShipCountry] IS NULL) OR ([ShipCountry] = @Original_ShipCountry)))',
N'@CustomerID nchar(5),@EmployeeID int,@OrderDate datetime,
@RequiredDate datetime,@ShippedDate datetime,@ShipVia int,@Freight money,
@ShipName nvarchar(26),@ShipAddress nvarchar(15),@ShipCity nvarchar(11),
@ShipRegion nvarchar(2),@ShipPostalCode nvarchar(5),@ShipCountry nvarchar(3),
@Original_OrderID int,@IsNull_CustomerID int,
@Original_CustomerID nchar(5),@IsNull_EmployeeID int,
@Original_EmployeeID int,@IsNull_OrderDate int,
@Original_OrderDate datetime,@IsNull_RequiredDate int,
@Original_RequiredDate datetime,@IsNull_ShippedDate int,
@Original_ShippedDate datetime,@IsNull_ShipVia int,
@Original_ShipVia int,@IsNull_Freight int,@Original_Freight money,
@IsNull_ShipName int,@Original_ShipName nvarchar(26),
```

123

```
@IsNull_ShipAddress int,@Original_ShipAddress nvarchar(15),
@IsNull_ShipCity int,@Original_ShipCity nvarchar(11),
@IsNull_ShipRegion int,@Original_ShipRegion nvarchar(2),
@IsNull_ShipPostalCode int,@Original_ShipPostalCode nvarchar(5),
@IsNull_ShipCountry int,@Original_ShipCountry nvarchar(3)',
@CustomerID = N'RATTC', @EmployeeID = 1, @OrderDate = 'May  6 1998 12:00:00:000AM',
@RequiredDate = 'Jun  3 1998 12:00:00:000AM', @ShippedDate = NULL, @ShipVia = 2,
@Freight = $8.5300, @ShipName = N'Rattlesnake Canyon Grocery',
@ShipAddress = N'2817 Milton Dr.', @ShipCity = N'Albuquerque', @ShipRegion = N'NM',
@ShipPostalCode = N'87110', @ShipCountry = N'USA', @Original_OrderID = 11077,
@IsNull_CustomerID = 0, @Original_CustomerID = N'RATTC', @IsNull_EmployeeID = 0,
@Original_EmployeeID = 1, @IsNull_OrderDate = 0,
@Original_OrderDate = 'May  7 1998 12:00:00:000AM', @IsNull_RequiredDate = 0,
@Original_RequiredDate = 'Jun  3 1998 12:00:00:000AM', @IsNull_ShippedDate = 1,
@Original_ShippedDate = NULL, @IsNull_ShipVia = 0, @Original_ShipVia = 2,
@IsNull_Freight = 0, @Original_Freight = $8.5300, @IsNull_ShipName = 0,
@Original_ShipName = N'Rattlesnake Canyon Grocery', @IsNull_ShipAddress = 0,
@Original_ShipAddress = N'2817 Milton Dr.', @IsNull_ShipCity = 0,
@Original_ShipCity = N'Albuquerque', @IsNull_ShipRegion = 0,
@Original_ShipRegion = N'NM', @IsNull_ShipPostalCode = 0,
@Original_ShipPostalCode = N'87110', @IsNull_ShipCountry = 0,
@Original_ShipCountry = N'USA'
```

ADO.NET 2.0's upgraded `SqlCommandBuilder` object has a `ConflictOption` property that provides the following three enumeration members to specify how DataSet updates deal with changes to base table data that occur after populating the DataSet:

❑ `ConflictOption.CompareAllSearchableValues` (the default) generates parameterized SQL batch statements or EXECUTE commands for stored procedures that require value-based optimistic concurrency control.

❑ `ConflictOption.CompareRowVersion` generates shorter parameterized SQL batch statements or EXECUTE commands for stored procedures against tables with a column of the `timestamp` (also called a `rowversion`) data type that's provided specifically for optimistic concurrency control.

❑ `ConflictOption.OverwriteChanges` generates even shorter parameterized SQL batch statements or EXECUTE commands for stored procedures that don't enforce concurrency control. Updates or deletions occur regardless of whether another user had made changes to the row's column values.

Selecting `ConflictOption.CompareRowVersion` requires the table to include a column of SQL Server's `timestamp` data type. A timestamp value corresponds to a .NET array of type `Byte` with a `Length` value of 8. A change to any row value updates the timestamp value, which is guaranteed to be unique within the table. Comparing the original timestamp value with that when performing the update is the fastest and most accurate method to prevent overwriting data that changed after populating a DataSet or caching original data with custom code.

> *Displaying a DataTable that has a timestamp column in a DataGridView throws an exception for each row. By default, the DataGridView interprets an array of type Byte as an image. Use the DataGridView.Columns.Remove("timestamp") method to prevent the exceptions.*

Following is a typical 262-character update statement for timestamp-based optimistic concurrency control:

```
exec sp_executesql N'UPDATE [OrdersTS] SET [OrderDate] = @p1
WHERE (([OrderID] = @p2) AND ([timestamp] = @p3))',
N'@p1 datetime,@p2 int,@p3 timestamp', @p1 = 'May  6 1998 12:00:00:000AM',
@p2 = 11077, @p3 = 0x0000000000004CB3
```

The Original_ColumnName and IsNull_ColumnName parameters and their values are missing, and only the changed value (OrderDate for this example) is included. Thus, substituting timestamp-based for value-based optimistic concurrency saves a substantial amount of network traffic and reduces resource consumption by the database engine's query processor.

Figure 3-12 shows the sample TimeStampTest.sln project's form with a 5-row batch size specified after a purposely induced concurrency error. Notice the error indicators in the first five row headers of the DataGridView control.

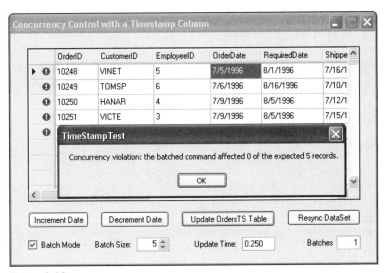

Figure 3-12

Running the TimeStampTest project requires adding a timestamp *column to the Northwind Orders table with the AddTimeStamp.sql script in theVB2005DB\Chapter03\TimeStampTest folder. If you don't add the timestamp column, you receive a message "Dynamic SQL generation for the UpdateCommand is not supported against a SelectCommand that does not contain a row version column" when you build and run the project. To generate a concurrency error, click Increment Date, Update OrdersTS Table, Decrement Date, and Update OrdersTS Table. To eliminate the concurrency error, click Resync DataSet.*

An alternative to a timestamp column is to add and populate a datetime column named LastModified or the like to all tables. LastModified values can be serialized to the readable XML dateTime datatype. Fields of the datetime data type have an inherent uncertainty of 3.33 milliseconds. VB's Now method, which is based on system time, claims a resolution of 10 milliseconds. Tests show the resolution is closer to 16 milliseconds with most system timers, so you should assume a potential uncertainty of up to 20 milliseconds. If you add a LastModified column, you must provide insert and update triggers to maintain the value and write custom code for concurrency tests.

Check All Related Records in Concurrency Tests

Data currency issues with DataSets can lead to unexpected results. If user A adds a record to a related table—for example, Order Details—and user B alters or deletes a record in the same table, conventional optimistic concurrency tests fail for user B with either the timestamp or original values method. The same problem occurs if user A deletes a record that user B doesn't attempt to update. This problem, which occurs if user B doesn't update her DataSet immediately before updating it, can have serious consequences in databases that store critical information, such as medicinal prescriptions for individual patients. If a physician A adds a new prescription for a patient, the consequences of physician B substituting or updating another drug's dosage might be life-threatening.

Including a count of related records in the DataSet is a partial solution, but doesn't solve the problem that occurs if user A adds a new related record and deletes a related record that user B doesn't test. A true solution requires comparing the row count and each related record's original timestamp or column values to those of the base table. You can use ADO.NET 2.0's new `RowState.SetModified` method to mark all related DataTable rows as modified and include them in the comparison.

> The "Optimize Update-Concurrency Tests" article at `http://www.fawcette.com/vsm/2003_10/magazine/columns/databasedesign/` provides a detailed analysis of the preceding problem and performance comparisons of original column values versus timestamp approaches to concurrency control.

Batch Updates to Minimize Server Roundtrips

Chapter 2's "Batch Multiple Updates" section describes the improved performance you gain by setting the `SqlDataAdapter.UpdateBatchSize` property value to 0 or a number that is significantly greater than 1. The default value (1) requires a server roundtrip for each modified row. Update operations that affect a large number of rows are more common with ADO.NET's disconnected DataSet operating mode than with the conventional, real-time online transaction processing (OLTP) approach.

Your application won't gain a major performance improvement by batching multi-row updates, but minimizing roundtrips conserves database server resources. The TimeStampTest.sln project includes a `BatchUpdated` handler for the `SqlDataAdapter.RowUpdated` event, which fires for each row or batch processed. The `SqlRowUpdatedEventArgs` type provides detailed status information on the row being processed.

Avoid SqlExceptions with Client-Side Validation

DataSets handle primary key uniqueness and foreign key constraints of related DataTables, but many data-entry operations require testing foreign key constraints with tables that aren't included in the DataSet. The most common reason for not including related source tables is excessive resource consumption by the DataSet and the load on the database server when populating the tables. You can minimize resource consumption and validate foreign key values by doing the following:

❑ Get MIN and MAX values of `int identity` primary key columns with an SqlDataReader that returns a single rowset for each table, and store the values in `Private Integer` variables. Your application will throw server-side exceptions for deleted items, but missing values should be rare.

- ❏ Get individual values of char, nchar, varchar, or nvarchar primary key columns and store them in an ArrayList object.

- ❏ Alternatively, create an untyped DataSet, add character-based columns to DataTables, and set the primary key so you can use the Find method with an index. The Select method doesn't use indexes.

Use the ErrorProvider control to indicate an out-of-range numeric value or a not-found character set. Substitute the new MaskedTextBox control for a conventional TextBox to eliminate testing entries with invalid character sets.

> Chapter 5, "Adding Data Validation and Concurrency Management," provides additional examples of client-side data validation methods.

For reference data that changes infrequently, such as employee rosters, customer and product lists, and shipping firm selections, consider creating an untyped DataSet that contains basic lookup data—for example, employee ID and name—in DataTables. You can use lookup data to populate dropdown list boxes that make foreign key value selection easier. If you choose this approach, add a DataTable to hold a row of minimum and maximum values for primary key values that you don't want to store as individual rows in its own DataTable. You can populate all DataTables in one server roundtrip by executing a single compound stored procedure or, if you must, an SQL query.

> If your applications must support frequently disconnected users, consider storing lookup or full copies of partitioned tables in DataSets and persisting them as XML files for offline use. The article "Store Large Lookup Tables in DataSets" at http://www.ftponline.com/vsm/2004_07/magazine/ features/rjennings/ demonstrates that persisting data sets as XML files with a size of 10MB or more is practical for applications running on high-performance laptops.

Summary

This chapter demonstrates that there's no shortage of prescriptive architecture and application design advice for .NET developers. The abundance of P&P publications, many of which have overlapping content, can lead to a choice crisis—read "how to do it" guides or write and test code. Best practices, however, dictate that you should be familiar with the .NET architectural guides in general and their data-related content in particular.

Developers will find that software patterns, class design and naming guidelines, and application blocks are most relevant to writing performant, scalable, and secure code. "Design Guidelines for Class Library Developers" is a must-read for all .NET developers. "Improving .NET Application Performance and Scalability" is an especially useful guide that offers concrete advice and includes code examples. The Data Application Block is a useful, generic tool for minimizing the amount of code required to create useful data-centric applications, but it's probably overkill for production projects. New VS 2005 design-time features and run-time improvements reduce DAB's importance, but you might find that parts of its source code—such as that for parameter caching—are worth incorporating in your applications.

The architectural model described by the "Designing Data Tier Components and Passing Data Through Tiers" white paper and its DALC, BE, and BPC tiers is a useful model for layered applications and SOA. BE objects aren't a new concept and there is considerable controversy about Web service toolkits that expose programming objects in SOAP messages. VS 2005's capability to use Get and Set accessors for private fields might quell some concern among Web service developers. Regardless of your stance on this issue, Web services that process typed BEs are far more efficient than those that send and receive DataSets.

If you've used NUnit for test-driven development, the new VSTS unit-testing features dramatically reduce the time required to implement TDD. Hopefully, an enterprising .NET developer will provide an NUnit-to-VSTS conversion utility for VB 2005 Test Projects.

Most developers don't have production DBA responsibilities, but that doesn't mean you should ignore the SQL Server 2000 Best Practices Analyzer for development databases. BPA points out issues, such as SELECT * FROM TableName and INSERT statements without field lists in stored procedures, which are shortcuts that no longer meet best practices standards. You also receive warnings if you don't back up your databases on a reasonable schedule. Future BPA versions will support SQL Server 2005.

Finally, any list of specific best practices for .NET database applications is arbitrary and bound to be incomplete. All developers have their own opinions about the relative importance of best practices topics, and it's certain that many new recommendations will arise as VS 2005 users upgrade and write new data-centric projects. The section "Apply Specific Best Practices to ADO.NET 2.0 Projects" only scratches the surface. You'll find many more best-practice notes in the chapters that follow.

Part II

Data Binding in Windows Forms and Controls

Programming TableAdapters, BindingSources, and DataGridViews

The preceding chapters introduced you to VS 2005's new data components — BindingSources, BindingNavigators, and TableAdapters — and the DataGridView control. This chapter shows you how to take maximum advantage of these design-time components in a traditional client/server configuration.

This chapter's examples depart from several best practices that Chapter 3 describes. The Windows form UI contains the data access logic component (DALC) and business process component (BCP) layers. The business entities (BEs) are DataTables of a typed DataSet. This architecture represents the classic two-tier client/server model — not the *n*-tier, Web services–based structure of Microsoft's "connected solutions" strategy.

> *According to a mid-2004 Jupiter Research report, many IT organizations are migrating from Web-based clients to Windows "Smart Client" applications, which includes Microsoft Office 2003 and Business Solutions members, and VS 2005 Windows forms projects. You can expect this trend to accelerate when Microsoft releases Windows Vista.*

The data-entry front ends you create in this chapter start with a designer-generated order-entry form, which you convert to the more typical tabbed window format. The first tab displays the customer data and a grid for orders; the second tab displays text boxes for order data and a grid for line items. The final steps add DataGridViewComboBox columns for making numeric foreign-key selections. Completing this chapter's examples qualifies you as an apprentice-level data components and DataGridView programmer.

Design a Basic Customer-Orders-Order Details Form

The most common — and essential — business processes are handling customer orders, issuing invoices, and ensuring that invoices are paid. These activities require forms that display a specified customer's billing information, order/invoice history, and line items. This three-level structure is also typical for professional services: Attorneys might use a client/case/activity structure and physicians can employ a patient/visit/prescription or similar model.

The simplest presentation scenario for a customers/orders/line items or similar database schema is a details view (bound TextBox controls) for a specified customer, and the most recent orders and their line items in bound DataGridView controls. VS 2005's new Data Sources window, data components, and the DataGridView control let you create a three-level UI by dragging the top-level table and its descendants from the Data Sources window to your form.

Reduce DataSet Size with Parameterized Queries

VS 2005's data tools let you create a basic data entry form without writing a single line of code. When you drag a table from the Data Sources window, the designer adds a `Me.TableNameTableAdapter` `.Fill(Me.DataSetName.TableName)` statement to the `FormName_Load` event handler. The price you pay for this convenience is generating gargantuan DataSets when the base tables contain a large number of records. Opening the form generates an extremely heavy load on the database server and network, and users experience a prolonged delay before the form appears.

> *The NorthwindCS database, which serves as the data source for Chapter 3's public NWOrdersWS Web service, has about 173,000 Orders and 470,000 Order Details records for the original 91 Customers records. Loading these records creates a 250MB in-memory DataSet and a 30-second delay when opening a test form. The autogenerated* `TableAdapter.Fill` *instructions aid novices in creating a sample data entry form with the Northwind or Pubs databases. Never use the default* `Fill` *code in a production application.*

Parameterized queries' `FillBy` methods make it easy to display a specific customer record and its related orders and line items records. You add `FillBy` queries with a Search Criteria Builder dialog that generates a ToolStrip text box to supply parameter values, a button to execute `FillBy` methods for each DataTable, and event handlers for the buttons. Here's a typical `FillBy` method call with the default query name changed to `FillOrders`:

```
Me.OrdersTableAdapter.FillOrders(Me.NorthwindDataSet.Orders, _
    CustomerIDToolStripTextBox.Text)
```

Retrieving line items for a specific order requires a sub-select query as the `CommandText` value for the `FillBy` method, if the line items table doesn't contain a foreign key value for the customer. Following is a sub-select query for the Order Details table:

```
SELECT OrderID, ProductID, UnitPrice, Quantity, Discount FROM dbo.[Order Details]
    WHERE OrderID IN (SELECT OrderID FROM Orders WHERE CustomerID = @CustomerID)
```

The following four sections show you how to design—and modify autogenerated code for—a basic order entry and editing form for the Northwind sample database. The instructions are more detailed than those in the preceding chapters because the process is far from intuitive and is more complex than creating an equivalent Access or InfoPath data entry form. On the other hand, databound forms generated by VS 2005 offer disconnected data entry and editing, increased programming flexibility, and improved error handling.

> *Most of this book's project examples use the Northwind sample database because its design (schema definition) is simpler than that of SQL Server 2005's AdventureWorks sample database. Creating an equivalent AdventureWorks version of the Customer-Orders-Order Details data entry form requires at least 12 related tables: Sales.Customer, Sales.CustomerAddress, Sales.Individual, Sales.Store, Person.Contact, Person.Address, Person.StateProvince, Person.CountryRegion, Sales.SalesOrderHeader, Sales.SalesOrderDetail, Sales.SpecialOffer, and Sales.SpecialOfferProduct. Most VS 2005 data-related help file topics use Northwind or similar tables; most SQL Server 2005 Books Online's examples use AdventureWorks.*
>
> *If you haven't installed the Northwind sample database, see the section "Install the Sample Databases" of the book's Introduction. If you're using SQL Server Express, open app.config, and change* `Server=localhost` *to* `Server=.\SQLEXPRESS`*.*

Create the Data Source and Add the Controls

The first steps in the design process add a details view for customer data, a parent (master) DataGridView to display Orders records, and a child (details) DataGridView for Order Details records. Look ahead to Figure 4-1 for the form's layout.

Do the following to generate a form that loads and displays all Customers, Orders, and Order Details records:

1. Create a new Windows Application project named OrdersByCustomer, and choose Data ➪ Add New Data Source to start the Data Source Configuration Wizard. Select Database, and click Next to open the Choose Your Data Connection page.

2. If you've created a connection to the Northwind database previously, select it from the dropdown list. Otherwise, click New Connection to open the Add Connection dialog and type the connection's server name—**localhost** for SQL Server or **.\SQLEXPRESS** for SQL Express—in the Server name text box.

3. Select Northwind from the Select or Enter a Database Name list, click Test Connection to verify the connection string, and click OK to close the dialog. Click Next, save the connection string with the default name—NorthwindConnectionString—and click Next to open the Choose Your Database Objects dialog.

4. Expand the Tables node and mark the tables to include in the project—Customers, Orders, and Order Details for this example.

5. Accept the default DataSet name (NorthwindDataSet), and complete the wizard to add the new DataSet and its tables to the Data Sources window.

6. In the Data Sources window, which you display by choosing Data ⇨ Show Data Sources, select the Customers table, change DataGridView to Details by clicking the arrow on the table name, and drag the table icon to Form1. The designer adds labels, databound text boxes, and a BindingNavigator control to the form, and NorthwindDataSet, CustomersBindingSource, CustomersTableAdapter, and CustomersBindingNavigator icons to the tray. Rearrange the bound text boxes in two columns to conserve form area.

7. Expand the Customers table icon, and drag its related Orders table icon (below the Fax field icon) to the form to add an OrdersDataGridView control to Form1, and an OrdersBindingSource and OrdersTableAdapter to the tray.

8. Expand the Orders table icon, and drag its related Orders Details table icon (below the ShipCountry field icon) to the form to add an Order_DetailsDataGridView control to Form1, and an Order_DetailsBindingSource and Order_DetailsTableAdapter to the tray.

9. Press F5 to build and run the project, which appears as shown in Figure 4-1. Display a few Customers records to verify that the two DataGridViews display related records, and then close the form to return to design mode.

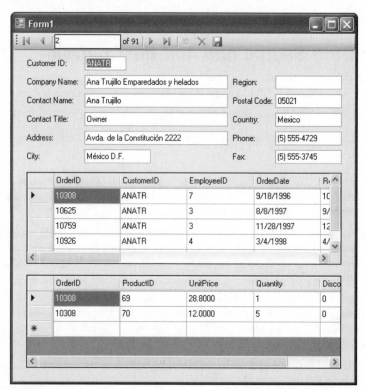

Figure 4-1

At this point, autogenerated `Fill` method code in the `Form1_Load` event handler loads all records from the three base tables into the NorthwindDataSet.

Only special circumstances, such as frequently disconnected users, warrant loading all or a substantial part of a large database and saving the DataSet for offline use.

134

Add FillBy Methods for Each Data Table

You must add a `FillBy` method to populate each table with a SELECT query that includes an `@CustomerID` parameter. Renaming the default `FillBy` query to a more descriptive method name improves code readability.

Follow this drill to add and test renamed `FillBy` queries to each DataTable:

1. Right-click the CustomersTableAdapter icon, and choose Add Query to open the Search Criteria Builder dialog.

2. Accept the default NorthwindDataSet.Customers as the source table and change the name of the new query to FillByCustomerID. In the Query Text box, add a `WHERE CustomerID = @CustomerID` criterion after `FROM dbo.Customers`, as shown in Figure 4-2. Click OK to add a ToolStrip with a text box to enter the CustomerID parameter value and a FillByCustomerID button to execute the query.

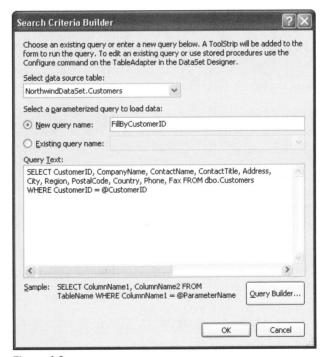

Figure 4-2

3. Right-click the ToolStrip's CustomerID text box at the top of the form, and choose Convert To ⇨ ComboBox. Open the combo box's Properties window, change the `Name` property to `cboCustomerID`, change the `DropDownStyle` property value to `DropDownList`, add a few sample CustomerID values to the `Items` collection, and change the `Width` property value to `75`.

4. Select the FillByCustomerID button and change its `Text` property value to `Get Orders` and the `ToolTipText` value to `Select a Customer ID`. Delete the CustomerIDLabel and CustomerIDTextBox from the form.

5. Select the CustomersBindingNavigator's separator bar and the Save Data button, press Ctrl+C, select the top ToolStrip, and press Ctrl+V to add the objects. Then select the CustomersBindingNavigator and delete it.

6. Build and run the project, select RATTC from the combo box, and click the Get Orders button to display the RATTC Customers record, and return to design mode.

7. Right-click the OrdersTableAdapter, and choose Add Query.

8. Select NorthwindDataSet.Orders as the source table and change the name of the new query to `FillByCustomerID`. In the Query Text box, add `WHERE CustomerID = @CustomerID ORDER BY OrderID DESC` after `FROM dbo.Orders`. Click OK to add another ToolStrip with a text box to enter the CustomerID parameter value.

9. Right-click the Order_DetailsTableAdapter, and choose Add Query.

10. Select NorthwindDataSet.Order Details as the source table and change the name of the new query to `FillByCustomerID`. In the Query Text box, add a `WHERE OrderID IN (SELECT OrderID FROM Orders WHERE CustomerID = @CustomerID)` criterion after `FROM [dbo.Order Details]`. Click OK to add a third ToolStrip with a text box to enter the CustomerID parameter value.

11. Build and run the project, type RATTC in the two empty ToolStrip text boxes, and click the three buttons to populate the controls.

12. Select a different order row in the Orders grid to verify that the relationship with the Order Details grid works correctly. Your form should appear as shown in Figure 4-3.

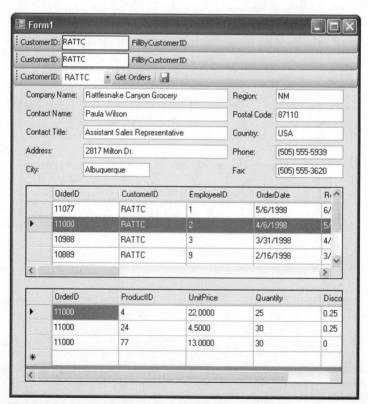

Figure 4-3

Alter the Autogenerated Code to Fill the Controls

The preceding steps added autogenerated code to the Form1_Load event handler, and Click event handlers for the three ToolStrip buttons. Code to load the DataTables is present, but you must move instructions to fill the Orders and Order_Details DataTables into the GetCustomerOrdersStripButton_Click event handler.

Here's the procedure for eliminating the default Fill methods and moving the two new FillByCustomerID instructions to their correct location:

1. Open Form1.vb and delete the Form1_Load event handler, which contains the autogenerated instructions for filling the DataSet with the entire contents of the base tables.

2. Copy the Me.OrdersTableAdapter.FillByCustomerID... instruction from the FillByCustomerIDToolStripButton1_Click event handler below the FillByCustomerIDToolStripButton_Click event handler's Me.CustomersTableAdapter .FillByCustomerID instruction.

3. Repeat step 2 to for the Me.Order_DetailsTableAdapter.FillByCustomerID... instruction.

4. Change CustomerIDToolStripTextBox and CustomerIDToolStripTextBox1 to cboCustomerID so the combo box supplies the @CustomerID parameter value to the three instructions in the FillByCustomerIDToolStripButton_Click event handler.

Following is the final FillByCustomerIDToolStripButton_Click event handler code:

```
Private Sub FillByCustomerIDToolStripButton_Click(ByVal sender As System.Object, _
  ByVal e As System.EventArgs) Handles FillByCustomerIDToolStripButton.Click
    Try
        Me.CustomersTableAdapter.FillByCustomerID(_
        Me.NorthwindDataSet.Customers, cboCustomerID.Text)
        Me.OrdersTableAdapter.FillByCustomerID(_
        Me.NorthwindDataSet.Orders, cboCustomerID.Text)
        Me.Order_DetailsTableAdapter.FillByCustomerID(_
        Me.NorthwindDataSet.Order_Details, cboCustomerID.Text)
    Catch ex As System.Exception
        System.Windows.Forms.MessageBox.Show(ex.Message)
    End Try
End Sub
```

Fill the ComboBox with CustomerID Values

At this point, the cboCustomerID combo box's Items collection contains only a few sample values for testing. The fastest and lowest-overhead method to fill semi-static lists is to use an SqlDataReader object, so add Imports System.Data and Imports System.Data.SqlClient to Form1.vb. Double-click the form to regenerate the Form1_Load event handler, and add the following code to populate the cboCustomerID combo box's list:

```
Private Sub Form1_Load(ByVal sender As System.Object, ByVal e As System.EventArgs)
  Handles MyBase.Load
    Dim cnNwind As New SqlConnection(My.Settings.NorthwindConnectionString)
    Dim strSQL As String = "SELECT CustomerID FROM dbo.Customers"
    Dim cmNwind As New SqlCommand(strSQL, cnNwind)
```

```
    Try
        cnNwind.Open()
        Dim sdrCustID As SqlDataReader = cmNwind.ExecuteReader
        With sdrCustID
            If .HasRows Then
                cboCustomerID.Items.Clear()
                While .Read
                    cboCustomerID.Items.Add(sdrCustID(0).ToString)
                End While
                cboCustomerID.Text = cboCustomerID.Items(0).ToString
            End If
            .Close()
        End With
    Catch exc As Exception
        MsgBox("Error loading CustomerID combo box.")
    Finally
        cnNwind.Close()
    End Try
End Sub
```

Clean Up the UI and Code

These final steps verify the preceding changes and remove the unneeded ToolStrips:

1. Build and run the project, which opens with all controls except the combo box empty, and click the Get Orders button to verify that the code you added and modified populates the controls.

2. Close the form and delete the FillByCustomerIDToolStripButton1_Click and FillByCustomerIDToolStripButton1_Click event handlers.

3. Select and delete the two added FillByCustomerID ToolStrips.

4. Build and run the project again, and click the Get Orders button to verify operability. Figure 4-4 shows the form with the preceding modifications.

The completed version of the data-entry project, OrdersByCustomerV1, is in the \VB2005\Chapter04 sample files folder. This project stores the connection string in the app.config file's <connectionStrings> element. Using app.config to store the connection string lets you change the database connection to another SQL Server 2000 or 2005, MSDE, or SQL Express instance without modifying the NorthwindDataSet .Designer.vb code.

This relatively simple data-entry form generates large, complex DataSet schema and designer-generated code files. The NorthwindDataSet.xsd file weighs in at 129KB and NorthwindDataSet.Designer.vb contains about 3,300 instructions. You can locate the schema annotations for the FillBy queries by opening the schema in IE and searching for @CustomerID.

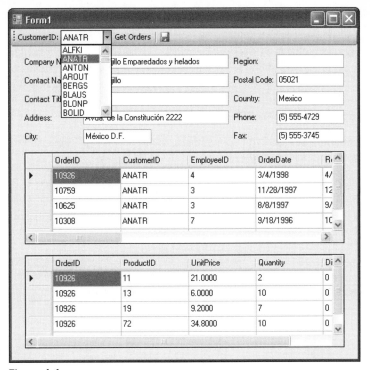

Figure 4-4

Format and Add DataGridView Columns

To make editing and adding new Orders and, especially, Order Details records in DataGridView controls easier for data entry operators requires turning off word-wrap, adjusting column widths, and formatting currency and percentage values. Preceding chapters' examples use code to make these formatting changes. The DataGridView's Edit Columns dialog simplifies column-management tasks. The Edit Columns dialog lets you specify column width, re-order columns, and add unbound computed columns. You use the CellStyle Builder dialog to set columns' Format and WrapMode property values.

The following sections' examples require the project that you completed in the preceding sections or \VB2005DB\Chapter04\OrdersByCustomerV1.sln.

Format the OrdersDataGridView Columns

Right-clicking a DataGridView and choosing Edit Columns opens the Edit Columns dialog, which displays a list of bound columns in the Selected Columns list and a Bound Column Properties sheet. The fastest and most effective method for setting column widths is to specify the `AutoSizeCriteria` property value. Auto-sizing columns is faster with `ColumnHeader` because no examination of row values for maximum width is required. Thus, you should specify `AllCells` or `DisplayedCells` only where the row value's width exceeds or is likely to exceed the column header width.

Alternatively, you can open the Edit Columns dialog from the DataGridView's Actions menu or the Columns item in the Properties menu.

For the OrdersDataGridView, `HeadersOnly` is the appropriate value of the `AutoSizeCriteria` property for all but the OrderDate and Freight through ShipCountry columns, which require `AllCells`. Figure 4-5 shows the property settings for the OrderID column with `Frozen` specified as `True` to display the column when scrolling horizontally.

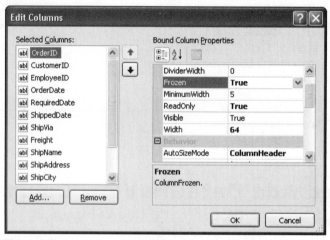

Figure 4-5

The Freight column requires currency formatting. To format column values, select the column and the `DefaultCellStyle` property, and open the CellStyle Builder dialog. Select the `Format` property, open the Format String Dialog, and select Currency with two decimal places and an empty cell for the `DbNull` value, as shown in Figure 4-6.

The CellStyle Builder and Format String Dialog have many other property settings that aren't discussed here. The effect of most property settings is obvious from their names.

Consider setting the `SortMode` property value of all columns — except, perhaps, OrderID — to `NotSortable` or `Programmatic`. Users might accidentally sort columns and not know how to return to the original order. The same advice applies to the `Resizable` property value; set it to `False` unless you have a good reason to do otherwise. Setting the `SortMode` property to `NotSortable` removes the right padding of column headers that's needed to accommodate the sort direction arrows. You might need to set the Width property in pixels, which requires setting the `AutoSizeCriteria` property value to `None`.

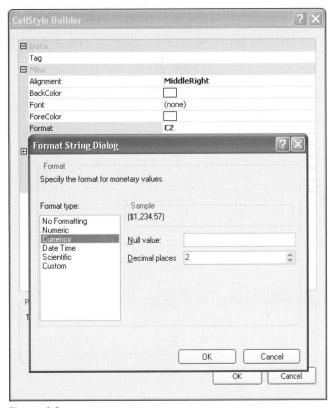

Figure 4-6

Format and Add a Computed Column to the Order_DetailsDataGridView

Order Details records have numeric values, so HeadersOnly is appropriate for the AutoSizeCriteria property value of all columns, unless you disable sorting by column. It's a common practice for Quantity to precede product information in sales order and invoice forms, so move the Quantity column after OrderID with the Edit Columns dialog's up-arrow button. Format the UnitPrice column with the C2 format string. Format the Discount column as a percentage with one decimal place (P1).

Add an Computed Extended Amount Column

An unbound Extended amount column to display the product of Quantity and UnitPrice less Discount values is a useful addition to the Order Details grid. To add an unbound column, select the Discount column in the Edit Columns dialog, and click the Add Column button to open the Add Column dialog. Select the Unbound Column option, and type **Extended** as the value in the Name and Header Text text boxes, and mark the Read-Only checkbox, as shown in Figure 4-7. Click Add and Close to create the new column, and then set the SortMode and AutoSizeCriteria or Width property values. Finally, format the column with the C2 currency format string.

Figure 4-7

Compute and Display the Extended Value

You add the computed value to the Extended column by setting the Order_DetailsDataGridView's VirtualMode property value to True in the Properties window and handling the DataGridView_CellValueNeeded event. Virtual mode is required when a bound DataGridView includes unbound columns. You also use virtual mode and the CellValueNeeded event to page additional rows into a row-limited DataGridView bound to a very large DataTable.

The CellValueNeeded event's DataGridViewCellValueEventArgs argument returns ColumnIndex and RowIndex property values that specify the current cell whose value is needed, and a Value property to set it. The formula for the Value property is Quantity * UnitPrice * (1 – Discount); you obtain these values from cells 1, 3, and 4 in the current row. If any of theses cell types is DBNull, assignment to a numeric variable throws an exception. Thus you must test for the DBNull type before assigning values.

Here's the code for the Order_DetailsDataGridView_CellValueNeeded event handler:

```
Private Sub Order_DetailsDataGridView_CellValueNeeded(ByVal sender As Object, _
    ByVal e As System.Windows.Forms.DataGridViewCellValueEventArgs) _
    Handles Order_DetailsDataGridView.CellValueNeeded
    'Calculate and display the unbound Extended column values
    With Order_DetailsDataGridView
        'Test for correct column and DBNull values, which throw exceptions
        If e.ColumnIndex = 5 And _
        Not (TypeOf (.Rows(e.RowIndex).Cells(1).Value) Is DBNull _
        OrElse TypeOf (.Rows(e.RowIndex).Cells(3).Value) Is DBNull _
        OrElse TypeOf (.Rows(e.RowIndex).Cells(4).Value) Is DBNull) Then
            'Variables are declared for readability
            Dim intQuan As Integer
            Dim decPrice As Decimal
            Dim decDisc As Decimal

            intQuan = CInt(.Rows(e.RowIndex).Cells(1).Value)
            decPrice = CDec(.Rows(e.RowIndex).Cells(3).Value)
```

```
        decDisc = CDec(.Rows(e.RowIndex).Cells(4).Value)
        e.Value = intQuan * decPrice * (1 - decDisc)
      End If
   End With
End Sub
```

You can substitute the column name for the numeric Cells(ColumnIndex) *value, but doing this causes a small performance hit.*

Figure 4-8 shows the order-entry form with formatted DataGridViews and the Extended column populated.

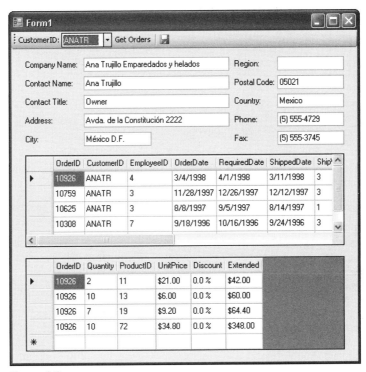

Figure 4-8

This example is specific to the Order_DetailsDataTable, but the process is basically the same for any computed column. You're not limited to cell values for computing unbound column values.

Provide Default Values for New Records

Previous chapters have code examples for setting default values when adding a new record to a DataGridView. The DataGridView has a DefaultValuesNeeded event that's similar to the CellValuesNeeded event, but DefaultValuesNeeded fires when the user adds a new row in virtual or non-virtual mode. Writing a `DefaultValuesNeeded` event handler can simplify data entry for a new order and minimize potential errors caused by missing values when adding new Order Details records. The `DataGridViewRowEventArgs` argument has a `Row` property that returns the new `DataGridViewRow` instance.

Add Default Orders Record Values

Default values for all Orders columns except OrderID and ShippedDate are appropriate, but users must enter at least one value. Thus, EmployeeID retains the default `DBNull` value. The Freight value isn't known until on or near the shipping date, but a `DBNull` value for Freight isn't allowed. Following is the code to populate a new Orders row:

```
Private Sub OrdersDataGridView_DefaultValuesNeeded(ByVal sender As Object, _
    ByVal e As System.Windows.Forms.DataGridViewRowEventArgs) _
    Handles OrdersDataGridView.DefaultValuesNeeded
    'Add default values to a new Orders row
    With e.Row
        .Cells(1).Value = Me.CustomerIDTextBox.Text
        'Andrew Fuller gets default credit because he's the sales VP
        .Cells(2).Value = 2
        .Cells(3).Value = Today.ToShortDateString
        'Two weeks is the default shipment arrival time
        .Cells(4).Value = Today.AddDays(14).ToShortDateString
        'United Package is the preferred shipper
        .Cells(6).Value = 2
        'Freight requires a 0 value, null throws an exception
        .Cells(7).Value = 0
        'Default shipping address is the billing address
        .Cells(8).Value = Me.CompanyNameTextBox.Text
        .Cells(9).Value = Me.AddressTextBox.Text
        .Cells(10).Value = Me.CityTextBox.Text
        .Cells(11).Value = Me.RegionTextBox.Text
        .Cells(12).Value = Me.PostalCodeTextBox.Text
        .Cells(13).Value = Me.CountryTextBox.Text
        'Deselect any selected cells
        Dim intCtr As Integer
        For intCtr = 0 To 13
            .Cells(intCtr).Selected = False
        Next
        'Select EmployeeID
        .Cells(2).Selected = True
    End With
End Sub
```

The user must change at least one value—ordinarily EmployeeID—to fire the UserAddedRows event and add an empty new row to the OrdersDataGridView. Thus the code sets EmployeeID as the selected cell.

The preceding code sets the CustomerID value, which is constant for all Orders rows. It's a good practice to set such columns' `ReadOnly` *property value to* `True`.

Add Default Order Details Record Values

Providing defaults for Order Details columns is problematic because ProductID is a member of the table's composite primary key. Thus ProductID default values set by, for example, the `Rows.Count` value might conflict with previous selections. At this point, the ProductID value is set without testing prior values. Following is the code for the `Order_DetailsDataGridView_DefaultValuesNeeded` event handler:

```
Private Sub Order_DetailsDataGridView_DefaultValuesNeeded(ByVal sender _
    As Object, ByVal e As System.Windows.Forms.DataGridViewRowEventArgs) _
    Handles Order_DetailsDataGridView.DefaultValuesNeeded
    'Add temporary default values
    With e.Row
        .Cells(1).Value = 1
        .Cells(2).Value = 17
        .Cells(3).Value = 0
        .Cells(4).Value = 0
    End With
End Sub
```

ProductID 17 is Alice Mutton, the first product in alphabetic order. An alternative to hard-coding a selection is a UNION *query that adds* 0 *as the ProductID and UnitPrice values,* (Product Not Selected) *as the Product name, and* None *as the QuantityPerUnit value. A parenthesis causes the added record to appear first in an alphabetically sorted combo box.*

Figure 4-9 shows the order entry form with added Orders and Order Details rows with the default values.

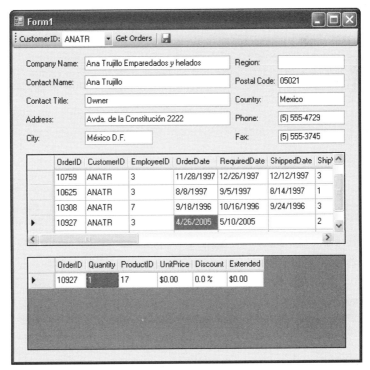

Figure 4-9

Handle the DataErrors Event

When a DataGridView throws an exception, the default error message contains more information than most users want to know about the problem. Adding a delegated `DataGridView.DataErrors` event handler lets you substitute a more meaningful message for the default "The following exception occurred in the DataGridView" message, followed by the `StackTrace` string. The message returned by `e.Exception.Message` is "Exception has been thrown by the target of an invocation." Thus, you must provide your own message; adding the column and row numbers can assist users in finding their transgression(s).

Here's an example of a simple `DataErrors` event handler:

```
Private Sub OrdersDataGridView_DataError(ByVal sender As Object, _
    ByVal e As System.Windows.Forms.DataGridViewDataErrorEventArgs) _
    Handles OrdersDataGridView.DataError
    'Handle data entry errors (delegate)
    Dim strMsg As String = "Invalid data in column " + e.ColumnIndex.ToString + _
        " of row " + e.RowIndex.ToString + " of the Orders grid. " + _
        "Press Esc to cancel the edit or enter an appropriate value."
    MsgBox(strMsg, MsgBoxStyle.Exclamation, "Data Entry Error")
End Sub
```

Later chapters provide examples of more sophisticated error handlers that convey more specific error information to the user.

Streamline Heads-Down Data Entry

Heads-down data entry implies that an application's users spend most or all of their working hours retrieving and updating data. Typical heads-down applications are telephone order entry, customer service, insurance claims processing, help-desk requests, and software technical assistance. The primary requisites of these projects are high-speed data retrieval and efficient data entry. Thus, Windows forms—rather than Web forms—are the most common UI for heads-down data entry.

Following are a few best practices for the design of heads-down data-entry forms:

❑ Provide accelerator keys (Alt+*Key*) for all buttons and those labels that are adjacent to commonly used text and combo boxes. Moving a hand from the keyboard to the mouse and back to the keyboard reduces data-entry productivity and leads to operator fatigue. Select accelerator keys that minimize contorted fingering, such as Alt+*NumberKey*. If you run out of related letter keys, you can specify other combinations, such as Ctrl+Shift+*Key* with a `KeyDown` event handler.

❑ Avoid flashy graphics, company logos, and other elements that aren't relevant to data entry tasks.

❑ Design for 800 × 600 resolution to maximize form readability. Data-entry operators usually are the last to receive PC hardware and operating system upgrades.

❑ Don't enable editing as the default data-entry mode. Bound text box and DataGridView controls should open in read-only mode and require an operator action to edit data. This practice prevents inadvertent data edits.

❑ Hide or disable controls that aren't appropriate to the current task or user role. The `My.User` namespace provides the `IsInRole` method to determine the current user's authorization to, for example, edit data based on domain security group membership.

❑ Substitute dropdown combo lists for text boxes to set primary key values. Populate the combo lists from lookup tables, which can be standalone DataTables or members of an untyped DataSet. Minimize the size of the DataTables and server load by specifying only the columns you need to populate the list. For this chapter's examples, CustomerID, EmployeeID, ShipperID, and ProductID values should be set by combo lists.

❑ Add tooltips to provide instructions for buttons and important text boxes and other controls. New operators are willing to use the mouse to review the purpose of mysterious controls. Tooltips suffice until you complete the online or printed help files for your project.

❑ Don't add menus unless you need them for printing or saving local files. Most heads-down data-entry applications are single-purpose.

❑ Consider substituting controls on the main form body for ToolStrip controls. ToolStrips have a limited control repertoire and must reside in one of the four rafting containers. It's a better practice to locate text boxes, combo lists, and buttons adjacent to other associated controls.

❑ Use the MaskedTextBox control for text boxes that require a specific data format, such as telephone and social security numbers, and alphabetic or alphanumeric primary keys. DataGridView and ToolStrip controls don't support MaskedTextBox controls.

❑ Choose the `DataGridView.EditMode` property value to suit operator preference. Consider replacing the default `EditOnKeystrokeOrF2` mode with `EditOnEnter`. If you select `EditOnEnter`, it's easier to replace the default column selection you set in the `DefaultValuesNeeded` event handler.

❑ Don't force users to view or edit complex, multi-column data in a DataGridView row. Some data-entry operators are accustomed to scrolling horizontally while editing, but you should provide the option to edit the row with text boxes. Form area limitations might require a tabbed form to provide room for text boxes.

❑ Use a single tabbed form — instead of multiple forms — to provide alternate editing methods. Tabbed forms with tabs that follow the workflow sequence are preferable to MDI forms for most data-entry applications. Another advantage of tabbed forms is that navigating between tabbed pages is similar to moving between Web pages.

> **Bound controls, including DataGridViews, might lose their DataBinding properties when moved from the form's surface to the tab page. Rebinding DataGridView controls resets all column properties to default values. You must rebind the controls, as described in the following section.**

Figure 4-10 shows version 2 of the order entry form, which implements many of the preceding best practices and includes the code described in the earlier "Format and Add DataGridView Columns," "Provide Default Values for New Records," and "Handle the DataErrors Event" sections.

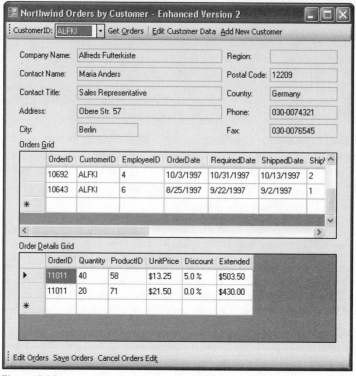

Figure 4-10

The OrdersByCustomerV2 project is in the ...\Chapter04\OrdersByCustomerV2 folder. The following sections describe modifications to this project.

Here are a few of OrderByCustomerV2's added features:

- ❑ All ToolStrip buttons and the two DataGridViews have accelerator keys.

- ❑ The form opens with empty, read-only text box controls and disabled, read-only DataGridViews.

- ❑ Clicking the Get Orders button enables the DataGridViews for scrolling.

- ❑ You must click Edit Customer Data to enable editing text boxes — except CustomerID — and display the OrdersToolStrip at the bottom of the form.

- ❑ Clicking Edit Orders enables the two DataGrid views.

- ❑ Clicking New Customer clears the text boxes, enables them for editing, and sets the focus to the CompanyName text box.

- ❑ Typing a CompanyName and pressing tab generates a five-character CustomerID value and enables the OrdersDataGridView.

- ❑ Adding a new record to the OrdersDataGridView enables the Order_DetailsDataGridView.

The Cancel ToolStrip buttons don't have event handlers at this point.

Migrate the UI to a Tabbed Form

Tabbed forms support workflow applications, such as adding and editing customer data, orders, line items, backorders, and invoices. One of the primary advantages of tabbed forms is your ability to specify tab page visibility by user role.

Most problems with databound controls on tab pages that ADO.NET 1.x users encountered appear to be corrected in ADO.NET 2.0.

You can convert a conventional data-entry form to a tabbed version that provides multiple pages for data-entry chores, but it's more efficient to start with a tabbed form. Moving controls from the form to a tab page requires the following steps:

1. Resize the form to accommodate the tabs.

2. Cut the form body controls to the Clipboard.

3. Add a Tab control with two or more pages.

4. Select the first tab page, and paste the controls to it.

5. If your form has DataNavigator or ToolStrip controls, delete them and replace their controls with buttons and, where necessary, text boxes on the appropriate tab page — usually the first page. This step requires changes to the associated button event-handling code.

6. Change the BackColor property of all labels to Transparent to match the fixed BackColor property of tab pages.

To save you the effort of converting the OrdersByCustomerV2 project, the initial version of OrdersByCustomersV3 is in the \VB2005DB\Chapter04\OrdersByCustomerV3 – Initial folder. This project includes the modifications described in the following sections, which require about 800 instructions.

Test Drive the OrdersByCustomersV3 Project

The initial version of the OrdersByCustomersV3 project includes the following modifications to the OrdersByCustomersV2 project:

❑ Conventional Button and TextBox controls replace ToolStrip controls.

❑ Individual Save and Cancel buttons enable customer and order additions and edits, and order/line-item deletions. Updating base tables isn't implemented in the initial version.

❑ Sample items populate the cboCustomerID dropdown list and text boxes when adding a new customer.

❑ An empty help text box is visible when the form opens and when adding a new customer. The text box can be populated from a constant string or a text file that you include as a project resource.

❑ Business logic prevents editing or deleting orders that have shipped by setting the ReadOnly property of rows with ShippedDate values to True.

❑ Clicking the Add New Order button positions OrdersDataGridView to the new record row and adds a new record to the OrdersBindingSource and Order_DetailsBindingSource.

❑   An Edit on Tab Page checkbox enables editing Orders and Order Details data on a second tab page, which reduces the height of the form and provides text boxes for editing the selected order.

❑   Business logic prevents adding more than one order for a customer without saving the new order and its line items.

❑   Clicking the Edit Orders button selects the last order in the grid. The down arrow selects earlier orders. If Edit on Tab Page is checked, pressing F2 with an unshipped order selected opens the second tab page for editing, which preserves mouseless data entry.

Figure 4-11 shows the form in single-page format.

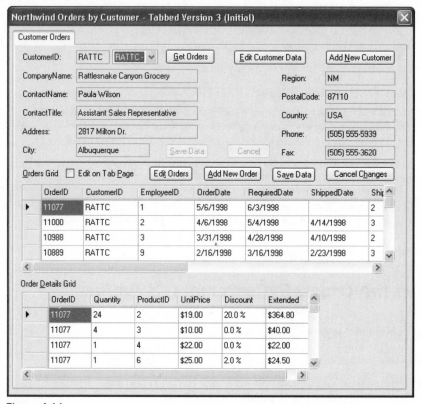

Figure 4-11

Fix Missing Default Values When Adding Rows with Code

Adding rows to a BindingSource and its bound DataGridView in code doesn't fire the DefaultValuesNeeded event. These events are UI-driven. Thus, you must modify the OrdersDataGridView_DefaultValuesNeeded event handler by moving its code to another procedure, SetDefaultValues for this example, and call the procedure as shown here:

```
Private Sub OrdersDataGridView_DefaultValuesNeeded(ByVal sender As Object, _
    ByVal e As System.Windows.Forms.DataGridViewRowEventArgs) _
    Handles OrdersDataGridView.DefaultValuesNeeded
    'Add default values to a new Orders row
    SetDefaultOrderValues(e.Row)
End Sub
```

You must modify the `Order_DetailsDataGridView_DefaultValuesNeeded` event handler similarly. Once you've made these modifications, you can add rows with default values programmatically, as shown here:

```
Private Sub btnNewOrder_Click(ByVal sender As System.Object, _
 ByVal e As System.EventArgs) Handles btnNewOrder.Click
    'Add new Orders and Order Details rows programmatically
    EnableOrdersGrid(True, False)
    With OrdersBindingSource
        .AddNew()
        .MoveLast()
    End With
    With OrdersDataGridView
        .Focus()
        'Rows.Count includes the default new row
        Dim rowAdded As DataGridViewRow = .Rows(.Rows.Count - 2)
        'Add the default values
        SetDefaultOrderValues(rowAdded)
    End With
    blnIsNewOrderRow = True
    btnCancelOrderEdits.Enabled = True
    btnSaveOrders.Enabled = False
    'Add a new OrderDetails row
    EnableOrder_DetailsGrid(True, False)
    With FK_Order_Details_OrdersBindingSource
        .AddNew()
        .MoveLast()
    End With
    With Order_DetailsDataGridView
        Dim rowAdded As DataGridViewRow = .Rows(.Rows.Count - 2)
        'Add the default values
        SetDefaultDetailsValues(rowAdded)
    End With
    btnNewOrder.Enabled = False
    If blnUseTabs Then
        If tabOrders.TabPages.Count = 1 Then
            tabOrders.TabPages.Add(pagEditOrder)
        End If
        tabOrders.SelectedTab = pagEditOrder
        blnIsNewOrderRow = False
        EmployeeIDTextBox.Focus()
    End If
    pagEditOrder.Text = "Edit New Order"
End Sub
```

Edit a Selected DataGridView Record on the Second Tab Page

Tab controls have two default tab pages. VS 2005's Data Sources window and the BindingSources make it easy to add databound text boxes and a cloned `Order_DetailsDataGridView` to the second tab page. The BindingSource synchronizes the two bound DataGridViews automatically. Add the text boxes by setting the Data Sources window's node for the data source—Orders for this example—to Details, dragging the controls to the page, and rearranging the layout. `Date` and `DateTime` fields appear as DateTimePicker controls. Set the `ReadOnly` property value for primary-key and foreign-key text boxes to `True`.

> *Microsoft still hasn't solved the DateTimePicker's null-valued date problem. If your data source permits fields with null date values, you must replace DateTimePickers with TextBox controls, which you bind to the appropriate data source field.*

Clone the first page's DataGridView by dragging its node to the page. You must add unbound fields and format numeric fields, as is required when cutting and pasting DataGridViews from a form to a tab page. A single `CellValueNeeded` event handler serves all cloned DataGridView instances.

The following code prevents the user from editing orders that have non-null ShippedDate values when the user presses F2:

```
Private Sub tabOrders_KeyDown(ByVal sender As Object, _
  ByVal e As System.Windows.Forms.KeyEventArgs) Handles tabOrders.KeyDown
    'Only allow editing of order with null ShippedDate fields
    If blnUseTabs And e.KeyCode = Keys.F2 And OrdersDataGridView.Enabled Then
        Try
            With OrdersDataGridView
                If .SelectedCells(0).ColumnIndex = 0 Then
                    If .Rows(.SelectedCells(0).RowIndex).Cells("ShippedDate").Value _
                        Is DBNull.Value Then
                        If tabOrders.TabPages.Count = 1 Then
                            tabOrders.TabPages.Add(pagEditOrder)
                        End If
                        tabOrders.SelectedTab = pagEditOrder
                    End If
                End If
            End With
        Catch excSys As Exception
            'Ignore the exception
        End Try
    End If
End Sub
```

Figure 4-12 shows the Edit Selected Order page with the last order for CustomerID RATTC open for editing.

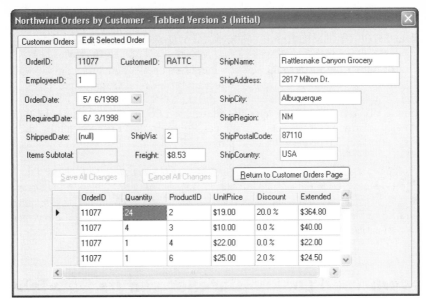

Figure 4-12

Create and Bind Lookup Lists for Primary Key Values

Data-entry operators can't be expected to remember name fields associated with primary-key or foreign-key values. Thus, DataGridView columns and text boxes bound to primary-key or foreign-key values need combo boxes that are populated by lookup lists and bound to the key field.

You create the data source for a combo box's lookup list with one of the following methods:

❑ If the project's typed DataSet contains the DataTable to populate a lookup list in a DataGridView, in the Edit Columns dialog, set the `DataSource` property value to the DataTable, set `ValueMember` to the primary-key value, and set `DisplayMember` to the field to populate the Items collection.

❑ If the project's typed DataSet contains the DataTable to populate a lookup list in a combo box on the form, in the Properties window, expand the (DataBindings) node, set the `(Advanced)` property value to the DataTable, set `SelectedValue` to the primary-key value, and set `SelectedItem` to the field to populate the Items collections.

❑ Otherwise, create an untyped DataSet, add DataAdapters for the lookup tables, and set the `DataSource`, `ValueMember`, and `DisplayMember` property values with code. If the combo box is on a form — not in a DataGridView column — you must invoke the `DataBindings.Add` method with a `New Binding` object to bind the combo box to the appropriate field of the typed DataSet's DataTable.

The advantage of adding lookup DataTables to the typed DataSet is your ability to set the required property values at design time and maintain referential integrity automatically. The downside of this approach is the inability to customize the combo box's `DisplayMember` (Items) values. In either case, you can save the lookup tables for reuse as a DataSet XML file. Loading the lookup tables from a local file eliminates one or more roundtrips to the server when users open a new project session. If you create and load an untyped lookup DataSet, you can fill all lookup tables in one roundtrip.

The following sections show you how to create an untyped DataSet that includes lookup DataTables created from the Northwind Customers, Employees, Shippers, and Products tables, and then populate unbound and bound combo boxes with lookup items.

All sections that follow add code to the OrdersByCustomersV3 project in the \VB2005DB\Chapter04\ OrdersByCustomersV3 – Initial folder. Most of the code you add in the following sections is in the \VB2005DB \Chapter04\OrdersByCustomerV3 – Final\OrdersByCustomerV3.sln project's OrderFormV3.vb file. This file contains `Partial Public Class OrdersForm` *as a demonstration of the use of custom partial classes. Comments that begin with* `'V3Final` *identify final code changes to OrdersForm.vb.*

Create an Untyped Lookup DataSet and Its DataTables

Runtime (untyped) DataSets and their DataTables are much lighter objects than DataTables added to typed DataSets. As mentioned in the preceding section, you can fill all untyped DataTables with a single server roundtrip. To minimize server load, you should save the lookup DataSet locally as an XML file; in subsequent sessions, you can load the tables from the file.

Add the following procedure to create the four DataTables that populate multiple combo boxes on the initial version of the form's two tab pages and saves the DataSet as LookupsDataSet.xml:

```
Private Sub LoadLookupLists()
    'Use runtime DataSet and DataAdapters to load combo boxes
    Me.Cursor = Cursors.WaitCursor
    'Customers
    Dim strSQL As String = "SELECT CustomerID, CustomerID + ' - ' + " + _
        CompanyName AS IDName FROM dbo.Customers;"
    'Employees
    strSQL += "SELECT EmployeeID, LastName + ', ' + FirstName AS EmployeeName " + _
        "FROM dbo.Employees;"
    'Shippers
    strSQL += "SELECT ShipperID, CompanyName FROM dbo.Shippers;"
    'Products
    strSQL += "SELECT ProductID, ProductName, UnitPrice, QuantityPerUnit " + _
        "FROM dbo.Products"
    'An example of use of My.Settings to retrieve connection strings
    Dim strConn As String = My.Settings.NorthwindConnection.ToString
    Dim daLookups As New SqlDataAdapter(strSQL, strConn)
    Try
        daLookups.Fill(dsLookups)
        With dsLookups
            .Tables(0).TableName = "CustsLookup"
            .Tables(1).TableName = "EmplsLookup"
            .Tables(2).TableName = "ShipsLookup"
```

```
               .Tables(3).TableName = "ProdsLookup"
          End With
          'Save dsLookups as a file with the embedded schema
          Dim strFile As String = Application.StartupPath + "\LookupsDataSet.xml"
          dsLookups.WriteXml(strFile, XmlWriteMode.WriteSchema)
      Catch excFill As Exception
          MsgBox(excFill.Message + excFill.StackTrace, , "Error Filling Lookup Tables")
      Finally
          If daLookups.SelectCommand.Connection.State = ConnectionState.Open Then
              'Shouldn't happen
              daLookups.SelectCommand.Connection.Close()
          End If
      End Try
  End Sub
```

Delete the following code, which adds sample data to the list, from the end of the OrderForm_Load
event handler:

```
If blnUseSampleData Then
    With cboCustomerID
        'Emulate final version
        .Items.Add("QUEDE - Que Delícia")
        .Items.Add("QUEEN - Queen Cozinha")
        ...
        .Items.Add("SPECD - Spécialités du monde")
        .SelectedIndex = 4
    End With
End If
```

Replace the deleted code with the following to call the LoadLookupLists procedures when needed and
provide a default CustomerID value for testing convenience:

```
Dim strFile As String = Application.StartupPath + "\LookupsDataSet.xml"
If File.Exists(strFile) Then
    'Load dsLookups from the file
    dsLookups.ReadXml(strFile)
Else
    LoadLookupLists()
End If
'Bind all combo box lists to their DataSources
LoadAndBindComboBoxes()

'Following is optional
'Set the combo box to RATTC which has an unshipped order
With dsLookups.Tables(0)
    Dim intRow As Integer
    For intRow = 0 To .Rows.Count - 1
        If Mid(.Rows(intRow).Item(0).ToString, 1, 5) = "RATTC" Then
            cboCustomerID.SelectedIndex = intRow
            Exit For
        End If
    Next intRow
End With
```

Populate the cboCustomerID Combo Box

Add the following code to populate the combo box with CustomerID values and CustomerID/
CustomerName items from the `CustsLookup` DataTable:

```
Private Sub LoadAndBindComboBoxes()
    With cboCustomerID
        .DataSource = dsLookups.Tables("CustsLookup")
        .DisplayMember = "CustIDName"
        .ValueMember = "CustomerID"
    End With
    ...
End Sub
```

The `cboCustomerID` *combo box isn't bound to a BindingSource, so you don't need to add a member to
the* `DataBindings` *collection.*

Replace DataGridView Text Boxes with Combo Boxes

The `OrdersDataGridView's` EmployeeID and ShipVia text boxes are logical candidates to replace
with combo boxes. To replace a text box column with a combo box column, open the DataGridView's
Edit Column dialog, select the appropriate column, set the `ColumnType` property value to
`DataGridViewComboBoxColumn`, change the `HeaderName` property value, if necessary, and set the
`Width` value to accommodate the items list.

> *Set the* `AutoSizeCriteria` *property value to* `None` *to enable changing the* `Width` *property.*

For this example, change the `EmployeeID` column header to `Employee`, and set the width to `120` pixels.
Change the ShipVia column's `Width` to `110` pixels. Figure 4-13 shows two changes for the EmployeeID
column; `Width` is scrolled out of sight.

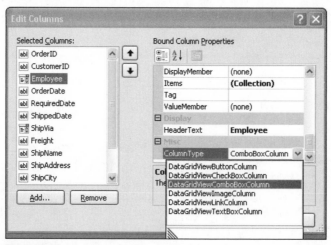

Figure 4-13

Add Code to Populate the Employees and ShipVia Combo Boxes

Before you run the program, you must add code to populate the two new combo boxes; if you don't, you'll throw many DataErrors when navigating the DataGridView. To find the new combo box names — DataGridViewComboBoxColumn followed by an arbitrary integer — search OrdersForm.Designer.vb for 'DataGridViewComboBox (include the single quote) to find these two combo box definition groups, which are emphasized in the following snippets:

```
'DataGridViewComboBoxColumn2
'
Me.DataGridViewComboBoxColumn2.DataPropertyName = "EmployeeID"
Me.DataGridViewComboBoxColumn2.DefaultCellStyle = DataGridViewCellStyle1
Me.DataGridViewComboBoxColumn2.HeaderText = "Employee"
Me.DataGridViewComboBoxColumn2.MaxDropDownItems = 8
Me.DataGridViewComboBoxColumn2.Name = "EmployeeID"
Me.DataGridViewComboBoxColumn2.Resizable = _
    System.Windows.Forms.DataGridViewTriState.[True]
Me.DataGridViewComboBoxColumn2.SortMode = _
    System.Windows.Forms.DataGridViewColumnSortMode.Automatic
Me.DataGridViewComboBoxColumn2.ValueType = GetType(Integer)
Me.DataGridViewComboBoxColumn2.Width = 120

'DataGridViewComboBoxColumn3
'
Me.DataGridViewComboBoxColumn3.DataPropertyName = "ShipVia"
Me.DataGridViewComboBoxColumn3.DefaultCellStyle = DataGridViewCellStyle1
Me.DataGridViewComboBoxColumn3.HeaderText = "ShipVia"
Me.DataGridViewComboBoxColumn3.MaxDropDownItems = 8
Me.DataGridViewComboBoxColumn3.Name = "ShipVia"
Me.DataGridViewComboBoxColumn3.Resizable = _
    System.Windows.Forms.DataGridViewTriState.[True]
Me.DataGridViewComboBoxColumn3.SortMode = _
    System.Windows.Forms.DataGridViewColumnSortMode.Automatic
Me.DataGridViewComboBoxColumn3.ValueType = GetType(Integer)
Me.DataGridViewComboBoxColumn3.Width = 110
```

Using the names you discovered, whose numeric suffixes are likely to differ from those in the preceding code, add the following code to the LoadAndBindComboBoxes procedure:

```
Private Sub LoadAndBindComboBoxes()
   ...
   With DataGridViewComboBoxColumn2
      .DataSource = dsLookups.Tables("EmplsLookup")
      .DisplayMember = "EmployeeName"
      .ValueMember = "EmployeeID"
   End With
   ...
   With DataGridViewComboBoxColumn3
      .DataSource = dsLookups.Tables("ShipsLookup")
      .DisplayMember = "CompanyName"
      .ValueMember = "ShipperID"
   End With
End Sub
```

Replace Null Default Values in New Rows

The Combo boxes can't handle null values without throwing an error so you must assign a valid default EmployeeID value in the initial version's `SetDefaultOrderValues` event handler. The logical value would be 0 for EmployeeID with Unassigned as the LastName value but would require modifying the Employees table. An alternative is to specify a `UNION` query to populate the combo box with the added item. If you choose this approach, change the `SELECT` statement for the EmplsLookup table to:

```
SELECT 0, 'Unassigned' UNION SELECT EmployeeID, LastName + ', ' +
FirstName AS EmployeeName FROM dbo.Employees;.
```

If your code synchronizes combo box selection values with other objects, such as a BindingSource's `Position` *property value, you must account for the added combo box item.*

The simplest alternative is to default all orders to the Sales Vice-President, Andrew Fuller (2), as shown here in bold text:

```
Private Sub SetDefaultOrderValues(ByVal rowAdded As DataGridViewRow)
   With rowAdded
      'Default values
      .Cells(1).Value = Me.CustomerIDTextBox.Text
      .Cells(2).Value = 2
      .Cells(3).Value = Today.ToShortDateString
      'Two weeks is the default shipment arrival time
      .Cells(4).Value = Today.AddDays(14).ToShortDateString
      ...
   End With
End Sub
```

When you build and run the form, the orders DataGridView with a new order added appears as shown in Figure 4-14.

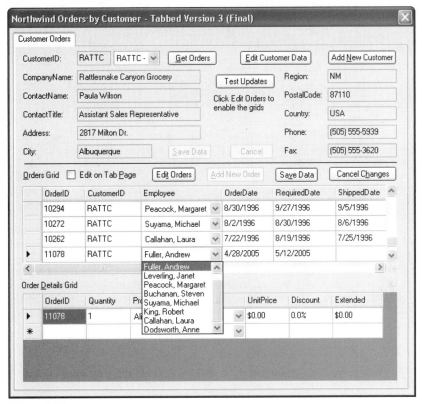

Figure 4-14

Associate Combo Boxes with Text Boxes

The Edit Selected Orders tab page needs similar lookup combo boxes, but retaining the original EmployeeID and ShipVia text boxes verifies that the bound column values change when selecting different values from the combo boxes.

For this example, add combo boxes named cboEmployeeID and cboShipVia to the Edit Selected Orders page, and change their DropDownStyle property value to DropDownList. Add the following code to populate and bind the combo boxes to the OrdersDataTable's EmployeeID and ShipVia fields:

```
Private Sub LoadAndBindComboBoxes()
   ...
   With cboEmployeeID
      .DataSource = dsLookups.Tables("EmplsLookup")
      .DisplayMember = "EmployeeName"
      .ValueMember = "EmployeeID"
      .DataBindings.Clear()
      'Any of these bindings work; BindingSource is the preferred data source
      '.DataBindings.Add("SelectedValue", NorthwindDataSet.Orders, "EmployeeID")
      '.DataBindings.Add(New Binding("SelectedValue", NorthwindDataSet, _
```

```
         '"Orders.EmployeeID"))
      .DataBindings.Add(New Binding("SelectedValue", OrdersBindingSource, _
         "EmployeeID", True))
   End With
   ...
   With cboShipVia
      .DataSource = dsLookups.Tables("ShipsLookup")
      .DisplayMember = "CompanyName"
      .ValueMember = "ShipperID"
      .DataBindings.Clear()
      .DataBindings.Add(New Binding("SelectedValue", OrdersBindingSource, _
         "ShipVia", True))
   End With
   ...
End Sub
```

A quirk in the synchronization of text and combo boxes bound to the same field prevents bidirectional text box updates. To update the text boxes with combo box changes, add the following event handlers:

```
Private Sub cboEmployeeID_SelectionChangeCommitted(ByVal sender As Object, _
      ByVal e As System.EventArgs) Handles cboEmployeeID.SelectionChangeCommitted
   'Update the associated text box
   EmployeeIDTextBox.Text = cboEmployeeID.SelectedValue.ToString
End Sub

Private Sub cboShipVia_SelectionChangeCommitted(ByVal sender As Object, _
      ByVal e As System.EventArgs) Handles cboShipVia.SelectionChangeCommitted
   'Update the associated text box
   ShipViaTextBox.Text = cboShipVia.SelectedValue.ToString
End Sub
```

You must handle the `SelectionChangeCommitted` *event — not the* `Click` *event, which occurs before the selection change is valid.*

To update the combo box selection with text box changes, add the code modification shown in bold to the initial version, and an event handler for the `ShipViaTextBox`'s `TextChanged` event:

```
Private Sub EmployeeIDTextBox_TextChanged(ByVal sender As System.Object, _
   ByVal e As System.EventArgs) Handles EmployeeIDTextBox.TextChanged
   With EmployeeIDTextBox
      'Test for value within range
      If Val(.Text) > 0 And CInt(Val(.Text)) <= cboEmployeeID.Items.Count Then
         btnCancelPage1Changes.Enabled = True
         btnSavePage1Changes.Enabled = True
         'Sync combo box with changes
         cboEmployeeID.SelectedIndex = CInt(Val(.Text)) - 1
      End If
   End With
End Sub

Private Sub ShipViaTextBox_TextChanged(ByVal sender As System.Object, _
      ByVal e As System.EventArgs) Handles ShipViaTextBox.TextChanged
```

```
                'Synchronize combo box with text box
            With ShipViaTextBox
                'Test for value within range
                If Val(.Text) > 0 And CInt(Val(.Text)) <= cboShipVia.Items.Count Then
                    cboShipVia.SelectedIndex = CInt(Val(.Text)) - 1
                    btnCancelPage1Changes.Enabled = True
                    btnSavePage1Changes.Enabled = True
                End If
            End With
        End Sub
```

You should add `TextChanged` *event handlers with code to enable the* `btnCancelPage1Changes` *and* `btnSavePage1Changes` *buttons for all text boxes.*

Figure 4-15 shows the Edit Selected Order page with the two combo boxes added.

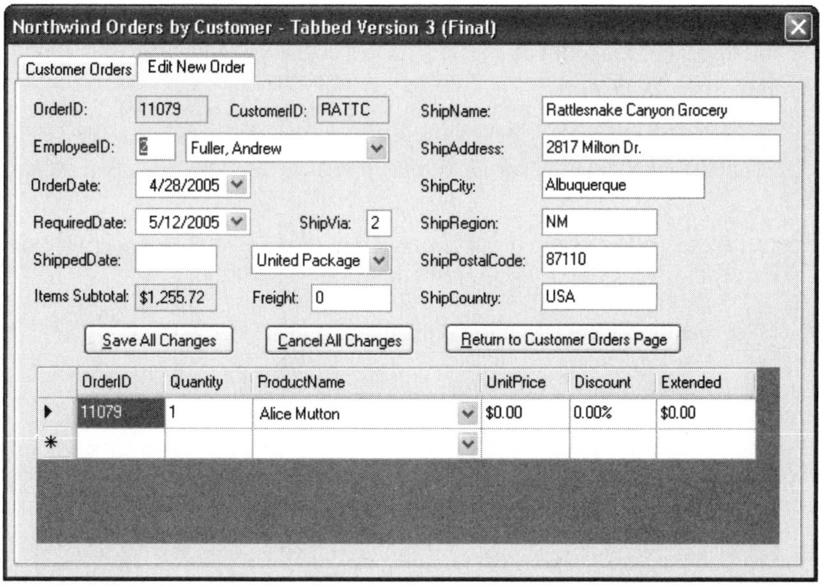

Figure 4-15

After adding combo boxes to a page, it's a good practice to review and, if necessary, change the tab order.

> **Beware of using the Tab Order view because you can confuse the Remove Tab action with removing a control from the tab order. The Remove Tab action is fatal unless you perform an immediate undo operation.**

Add a Combo Box That Sets Additional Values

Changing the value of a bound text or combo box often has side effects that you must handle with code. As an example, the Order_DetailsDataGridView's UnitPrice column value must be updated when making changes to the ProductID column. The OrdersByCustomerV3 initial version requires the data-entry operator to refer to a list to correlate ProductID, ProductName, and UnitPrice values. Thus, the ProductID column needs a combo box to display ProductName values, and selecting an item must supply the correct UnitPrice value. The ProdsLookup DataTable includes the UnitPrice data, as well as a QuantityPerUnit column. Displaying QuantityPerUnit in an unbound column is optional.

Create and Bind a DataView Sorted by ProductName

Replacing the ProductID column's text box with a combo box in the two DataGridViews follows the same process as that for the EmployeeID and ShipVia columns of the Orders grid. EmployeeID and ShipVia list items appear in the order of the DataTable's bound column. This isn't a problem for combo boxes with a few list items, but the ProductID combo box should be sorted alphabetically by ProductName. Sorting items requires creating a sorted DataView over the DataTable.

Setting ComboBoxName.Sort = True *throws a runtime error when the* DataSource *property is assigned.*

Adding ORDER BY ProductName *to the* ProdsLookup *DataTable's* SELECT *query is a simpler approach. The objective of this section is to demonstrate use of sorted DataViews.*

First, add the following form-level variables to the OrdersForm.vb class:

```
Private dvProdsLookup As DataView
Private blnHasLoaded As Boolean
```

Add the following code to the LoadAndBindComboBoxes procedure to create a dvProdsLookup DataView sorted by ProductName, and populate the combo lists from dvProdsLookup:

```
Private Sub LoadAndBindComboBoxes()
    ...
    'ProductID combo boxes
    'Create a
    dvProdsLookup = New DataView(.Tables(3))
    dvProdsLookup.Sort = "ProductName"

    With DataGridViewComboBoxColumn4
        .DataSource = dvProdsLookup
        .DisplayMember = "ProductName"
        .ValueMember = "ProductID"
    End With

    With DataGridViewComboBoxColumn5
        .DataSource = dvProdsLookup
        .DisplayMember = "ProductName"
        .ValueMember = "ProductID"
```

```
    End With

    'Set the loaded flag
    blnHasLoaded = True
End Sub
```

You can specify filter criteria and sort order in the third overload of the DataView *constructor, but applying the* Sort *method is simpler.*

The combo box control names don't indicate association with a specific DataGridView. The code for both Order Details grids is the same, so this ambiguity isn't an important issue.

The next section's code uses the blnHasLoaded *flag.*

Test for Duplicates and Update the UnitPrice Column

The Order Details table has a composite primary key—OrderID and ProductID—to prevent duplicating an existing line item. To prevent server roundtrips that return key violation error messages, you should test new or altered ProductID values for duplication and inform the operator of the error.

Duplicate ProductID entries will throw a DataError exception when the operator completes the edit and moves to the next row. However, it's a better practice to capture the error immediately after it occurs.

If the new ProductID value is acceptable, you must scan the ProdsLookup table for the matching row and update the unit price with the following procedure, which applies to both Order Details grids. You pass dgvDetails by reference to obtain a pointer to the active DataGridView instance.

```
Private Sub GetUnitPrice(ByVal intRow As Integer, ByVal intCol As Integer, _
    ByRef dgvDetails As DataGridView)
    'Test the ProductID value for duplication
    'Update the unit price, if not a duplicate
    Try
        If intCol = 2 Then
            'ProductID combo box change
            Dim intProdID As Integer = CInt(dgvDetails.Rows(intRow).Cells(2).Value)
            Dim decPrice As Decimal
            Dim intRowCtr As Integer
            Dim rowProd As DataRow
            Dim strName As String = Nothing

            'Test for duplicate ProductID (primary key violation)
            Dim intDups As Integer
            With dgvDetails
                For intRowCtr = 0 To .Rows.Count - 1
                    If CInt(.Rows(intRow).Cells(2).Value) = intProdID Then
                        intDups += 1
                        If intDups > 1 Then
                            Exit For
                        End If
                    End If
                Next intRowCtr
            End With
            If intDups > 1 Then
```

```
            Dim strMsg As String = "ProductID " + intProdID.ToString + _
                " has been added previously to this order. " + vbCrLf + vbCrLf + _
                "Please select a different product or press Esc to cancel the edit."
            MsgBox(strMsg, MsgBoxStyle.Exclamation, strTitle)
            Return
        End If

        'Search the DataTable for the ProductID and update UnitPrice
        With dsLookups.Tables(3)
            For intRowCtr = 0 To .Rows.Count - 1
                rowProd = .Rows(intRowCtr)
                If CInt(rowProd.Item(0)) = intProdID Then
                    decPrice = CDec(rowProd.Item(2))
                    'Change UnitPrice value
                    With Order_DetailsDataGridView1
                        .Rows(intRow).Cells(3).Value = decPrice
                        Exit For
                    End With
                End If
            Next intRowCtr
        End With
    End If
Catch exc As Exception
    MsgBox(exc.Message + exc.StackTrace, , exc.Source)
End Try
End Sub
```

An alternative to scanning is creating a DataView with its `Filter` *property value set to* `ProductID`
`= intProdID`*. Filter expressions use SQL* WHERE *clause syntax (without* WHERE*), so literal string arguments must be enclosed by single quotes.*

You must pass the appropriate `intRow` and `intCol` values and a `DataGridView` pointer to the procedure in these added `CellValueChanged` event handlers.

```
Private Sub Order_DetailsDataGridView_CellValueChanged(ByVal sender As Object, _
    ByVal e As System.Windows.Forms.DataGridViewCellEventArgs) _
    Handles Order_DetailsDataGridView.CellValueChanged
    'Get the UnitPrice value
    If blnHasLoaded Then
        GetUnitPrice(e.RowIndex, e.ColumnIndex, Order_DetailsDataGridView)
    End If
End Sub

Private Sub Order_DetailsDataGridView1_CellValueChanged(ByVal sender As Object, _
    ByVal e As System.Windows.Forms.DataGridViewCellEventArgs) _
    Handles Order_DetailsDataGridView1.CellValueChanged
    'Get the UnitPrice value
    If blnHasLoaded Then
        'Run only after loading the combo boxes
        GetUnitPrice(e.RowIndex, e.ColumnIndex, Order_DetailsDataGridView1)

        'The following applies only to the Edit Selected Orders page
        If Not (e.ColumnIndex = 0 Or e.ColumnIndex = 5) Then
            'Update the items subtotal for Quantity, ProductID,
```

```
            'UnitPrice, and Discount changes
            GetOrderSubtotal()
            btnCancelPage1Changes.Enabled = True
            btnSavePage1Changes.Enabled = True
        End If
    End If
End Sub
```

Following is the code for the `GetOrderSubtotal` procedure, which updates the `txtSubtotal` text box:

```
Private Sub GetOrderSubtotal()
    'Calculate and display order subtotal on F2 and CellValueChanged
    With Order_DetailsDataGridView1
        Dim decSubtotal As Decimal
        Dim intCtr As Integer
        For intCtr = 0 To .Rows.Count - 1
            decSubtotal += CDec(.Rows(intCtr).Cells(5).Value)
        Next
        txtSubtotal.Text = Format(decSubtotal, "$#,##0.00")
    End With
End Sub
```

Figure 4-16 shows the Edit Selected Order tab page with the ProductID DataGridView column converted from a text box to a combo box, multiple line items added to a new order, and the Items Subtotal value updated.

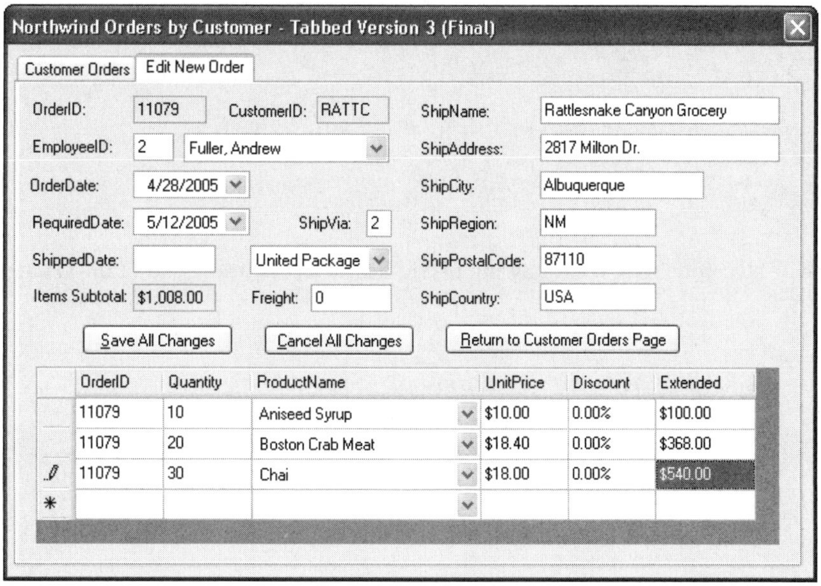

Figure 4-16

The UnitPrice and Extended column values don't change until you move the focus to the column. The Items Subtotal value doesn't update until you update the Extended column value.

Add Lookup Table Rows for New Customer Entries

The OrdersByCustomersV3 – Initial project adds the computed CustomerID item to the `cboCustomerID` combo box when completing the CompanyName entry for a new customer. You can't add items to combo boxes whose `DataSource` is a DataTable, so you must add a new row to the `CustsLookup` DataTable. The easiest way to manage runtime DataTables is to add a BindingSource to the form and use its methods to add a row for the new CustomerID value. You use the BindingSource's `AddNew`, `EndEdit`, `CancelNew`, and `CancelEdit` methods to handle editing chores.

Add and Bind a CustomerID BindingSource

Add a `BindingConnector1` component from the toolbox and rename it `bsCustsLookup`. Then add the following binding code after the `LoadAndBindComboBoxes` procedure's `blnHasLoaded = True` statement:

```
bsCustsLookup.DataSource = dsLookups
bsCustsLookup.DataMember = "CustsLookup"
'Test the BindingSource (optional)
Dim intRows As Integer = bsCustsLookup.Count
```

In the `ContactNameTextBox_GotFocus` event handler, remove this code that adds a combo box list item, which throws a runtime exception, and searches for the new item:

```
.Items.Add(strCustID + " - " + CompanyNameTextBox.Text)
'List is sorted, so need to find the new entry
'(Lists can't be sorted when they use a DataSource)
For intCtr = 0 To .Items.Count - 1
    If Mid(.Items(intCtr).ToString, 1, 5) = strCustID Then
        .SelectedIndex = intCtr
        Exit For
    End If
Next
```

Replace the deleted code with the following to add a new record at the end of the DataTable and set its values:

```
'Add new table row
Dim objNewRow As Object = bsCustsLookup.AddNew()
Dim drvNewRow As DataRowView = CType(objNewRow, DataRowView)
With drvNewRow
    .Item(0) = strCustID
    .Item(1) = strCustID + " - " + CompanyNameTextBox.Text
    .EndEdit()
End With
.SelectedIndex = .Items.Count - 1
```

*You can determine the object type (`DataRowView`) by typing **? objNewRow** in the Immediate window.*

If you don't invoke the EndEdit method, the record doesn't appear as the last item in the combo box list.

Applying `drvNewRow.EndEdit` requires deleting the added row — instead of invoking `CancelEdit` — in the `btnCancelCustEdit_Click` event handler. Add the following line shown in bold text:

```
Private Sub btnCancelCustEdit_Click(ByVal sender As System.Object, _
    ByVal e As System.EventArgs) Handles btnCancelCustEdit.Click
    'Undo the customer edits
    'For testing
    Dim intCtr As Integer = CustomersBindingSource.Count
    If blnIsNewCustomer Then
        'Remove the added (last) record
        dcCustsLookup.RemoveAt(dcCustsLookup.Count - 1)
        ClearCustomerTextBoxes()
        CustomersBindingSource.CancelEdit()
        blnIsNewCustomer = False
    Else
        CustomersBindingSource.CancelEdit()
    End If
    ...
End Sub
```

Test for Duplicates with a DataRowView

Changing the combo box's data source to a DataTable also requires modifications to the duplicate CustomerID test. The `.Items(intCtr).ToString` expression in the following code block returns `System.Windows.Forms.ComboBox, Items.Count = 94`, not the expected `CustomerID – CustomerName` string:

```
For intCtr = 0 To .Items.Count - 1
    If Mid(.Items(intCtr).ToString, 1, 5) = strCustID Then
        CompanyNameTextBox.Focus()
        Dim strMsg As String = "CustomerID '" + strCustID + _
            "' duplicates existing entry '" + .Items(intCtr).ToString + "." + strHelp
        MsgBox(strMsg, MsgBoxStyle.Exclamation, strTitle)
        blnIsDup = True
        Exit For
    End If
Next intCtr
```

You must cast the combo box item to a DataRowView object and test the `DataRowView.Row.Item(0)` value, so make the following emphasized changes to the preceding block:

```
For intCtr = 0 To .Items.Count - 1
    Dim drvCustID As DataRowView = CType(.Items(intCtr), DataRowView)
    With drvCustID.Row
        If .Item(0).ToString = strCustID Then
            CompanyNameTextBox.Focus()
            Dim strMsg As String = "CustomerID '" + strCustID + _
                "' duplicates existing entry '" + .Item(1).ToString + "." + strHelp
            MsgBox(strMsg, MsgBoxStyle.Exclamation, strTitle)
            blnIsDup = True
            Exit For
        End If
    End With
Next intCtr
```

The objective of the preceding two sections is to demonstrate how to program combo boxes populated by a DataTable. A less-involved alternative is to change the method of populating an unbound cboCustomerID *combo box's list by adding items with an* SqlDataReader *object and setting* cboCustomerID.Sort = True. *Adopting this approach provides the added benefit of placing new customer items in alphabetic order.*

Apply Business Rules to Edits

As mentioned at the beginning of the chapter, business rules are enforced by the client application in this chapter's examples. Enforcing business rules in the presentation tier violates best practices because a change to the rules requires that a new version of the application be deployed to all users' PCs. If you enforce business rules with SQL Server triggers or stored procedures, each data-entry error requires a server roundtrip. There are two business rules, however, that aren't likely to change—prohibiting orders without line items and $0.00 as the UnitPrice value.

Add the following code to the beginning of the btnSaveOrders_Click event handler to enforce the two rules:

```
'Test for at least one line item
Dim strMsg As String
If Order_DetailsBindingSource.Count < 1 Then
    strMsg = "An new order must have at least one line item. " + _
     "Please add a line item or click Cancel All Changes."
    MsgBox(strMsg, MsgBoxStyle.Exclamation, strTitle)
    Return
End If
'Test for $0.00 as UnitPrice
Dim intRow As Integer
strMsg = "A UnitPrice of $0.00 isn't permitted. Please edit line "
With Order_DetailsDataGridView1
    For intRow = 0 To .Rows.Count - 2
        If CDec(.Rows(intRow).Cells(3).Value) = 0D Then
            strMsg += (intRow + 1).ToString + "."
            MsgBox(strMsg, MsgBoxStyle.Exclamation, strTitle)
            Return
        End If
    Next
End With
```

Most data-entry operators aren't permitted to give customers arbitrary discounts; nor can operators be expected to memorize quantity discount tables. For this example, it's assumed that a single quantity discount schedule applies to all products and customers and that changing a discount for existing items that have a Discount value other than 0.0% is prohibited.

Discount schedules and sales or value-added tax tables are examples of business rules that should be implemented by a mid-tier BPC. Discounts that vary by purchase quantity, customer type, location, and other parameters or taxes require a database lookup.

To establish a fixed quantity discount schedule, add the following code to the beginning of the GetUnitPrice procedure:

```
If intCol = 1 Then
    'Calculate fixed discounts for default 0.0%
    With dgvDetails
        If CInt(.Rows(intRow).Cells(4).Value) = 0D Then
            Dim intQuan As Integer = CInt(.Rows(intRow).Cells(intCol).Value)
            Dim decDisc As Decimal
            Select Case intQuan
                Case Is >= 100
                    decDisc = 0.25D
                Case Is >= 50
                    decDisc = 0.15D
                Case Is >= 25
                    decDisc = 0.1D
                Case Is >= 10
                    decDisc = 0.075D
                Case Is >= 5
                    decDisc = 0.05D
            End Select
            Update the Discount value
            .Rows(intRow).Cells(4).Value = decDisc
        End If
    End With
End If
```

Quantity and ProductID are now the only Order Details field values that aren't autogenerated for the user, so you should set the ReadOnly property value of the UnitPrice and Discount columns to True.

Save Changes to the Base Tables

Up to this point, the Save... buttons on the two tab pages update only the typed DataSet. Before you make changes to the Northwind base tables, you should decide on an update strategy. You can accumulate changes in the DataSet and add a button to send all changes to the server as a batch or send incremental changes as the user makes edits. Either alternative results in the same number of server roundtrips unless you enable DataAdapter batch updates. Enabling batch updates requires adding Me.m_adapter.UpdateBatchSize = n statements to the *DataSetName*.designer.vb file and doesn't provide a substantial performance improvement in a LAN environment.

The better policy for well-connected (LAN) clients is to save changes to the base tables when the operator clicks any Save... button. This approach minimizes the likelihood of concurrency conflicts and reduces the amount of data lost as the result of a client application crash, hardware failure, or power loss.

Maintain Referential Integrity

Maintaining referential integrity requires executing DELETE, UPDATE, and INSERT SQL statements or stored procedures for related tables in a specific order. Deletions require a bottom-up sequence in the relationship hierarchy, and updates and additions must occur in top-down order, unless cascading updates and deletions are specified for tables below the topmost table. The Northwind FK_Order_Details_Orders and FK_Orders_Customers relationships don't have cascading updates or deletions specified.

> *Cascading updates and — especially — deletions are an anathema to most DBAs. It's possible to accidentally delete a customer record, but you can reconstruct it from multiple types of backup data sources. (However, recreating a customer record with an* int identity *primary key is an involved process.) If cascading deletions are in effect, the deletion also deletes all associated order, invoice, and line item records. In this case, you must rely on the most recent database backup and transaction logs to repair the damage.*

You change the update and deletion rules in the DataSet designer window by right-clicking the relationship line between parent and child tables, and choosing Edit Relation to open the Relation dialog. The DataSet designer creates a relationship between its DataTables by default. You can specify Relation Only, Foreign Key Constraint Only, or Both Relation and Foreign Key Constraint. If you specify a foreign-key constraint, you have the following choices for the ForeignKeyConstraint.UpdateRule, DeleteRule, and AcceptChangesRule property values:

- ❑ **Cascade** (the default) deletes child records when the parent-table record is deleted and updates the foreign-key value of child records to that of the parent table's new primary-key value.

- ❑ **None** makes no changes to child records when deleting the parent table or changing the primary key value, which throws exceptions automatically. The result is orphaned child records, unless you manage changes to child records with code in the Catch block.

- ❑ **SetNull** sets the child table's foreign-key value to DBNull and orphans the records.

- ❑ **Set Default** sets the child table's foreign-key value to the column's default value, which depends on the column data type.

This chapter's examples don't permit deleting Customers records or altering the CustomerID value, so specifying Both Relation and Foreign Key Constraint and accepting the FK_Orders_Customers foreign-key constraint default of None is valid for all three Rule values. Figure 4-17 shows the Relation dialog with the change applied.

> *With the preceding change made, DataSet cascading updates and deletions affect only the current order's OrderDetails values. You can't change the primary key value of an existing order. Thus, only cascading deletions occur; these are required to delete an order that doesn't have a ShippedDate value if your code doesn't delete line items before deleting the order.*

Create and Test the UpdateBaseTables Function

Regardless of whether cascading updates, deletions, or both are specified for DataSets or base tables, the general rule is to apply updates to base tables in the following sequence:

1. Deletions of child-table records

2. Insertions, modifications, and deletions of parent-table records

3. Insertions and modifications of child-table records

Figure 4-17

Playing by these rules requires that your base-table update code create a new `ChangeTypeDataTable` for each update type of each base table, and execute the `TableNameTableAdapter.Update (ChangeTypeDataTable)` for all DataTables that have changes. You generate each table by copying updated DataRows that are identified by their `DataRowState` enumeration value: `Added`, `Modified`, or `Deleted`.

Understand Change Table Generation and Base Table Update Instructions

ADO.NET 1.*x* DataAdapters require the following expression to generate a *ChangeType*DataTable and update the corresponding base table:

```
Dim ChangeTypeDataTable As DataSet.DataTable = _
    DataSet.DataTable.GetChanges(DataRowState.Type)
If Not ChangeTypeDataTable Is Nothing Then
    OrdersDataAdapter.Update(ChangeTypeDataTable)
End If
```

TableAdapters require casting the *ChangeType*DataTable to the *DataSet.DataTable* type. You populate an ADO.NET 2.0 `ChangeTypeDataTable` and update the base table with the following generic instruction:

```
Dim ChangeTypeDataTable As DataSet.DataTable = _
    CType(DataSet.DataTable.GetChanges(DataRowState.Type), DataSet.DataTable)
If Not ChangeTypeDataTable Is Nothing Then
    OrdersTableAdapter.Update(ChangeTypeDataTable)
End If
```

The type cast is a very small price to pay for the added versatility of TableAdapters.

Here's the code to obtain modified rows of the OrdersDataTable and update the Orders base table:

```
Dim ModOrders As NorthwindDataSet.OrdersDataTable = _
    CType(NorthwindDataSet.Orders.GetChanges(DataRowState.Modified), _
    NorthwindDataSet.OrdersDataTable)
If Not ModOrders Is Nothing Then
    OrdersTableAdapter.Update(ModOrders)
End If
```

Updating the three Northwind tables requires eight variations of the preceding theme, as illustrated by Figure 4-18. If you include the very dangerous capability to delete a Customer record, you need nine versions. Use copy, paste, edit, and replace operations to minimize typing.

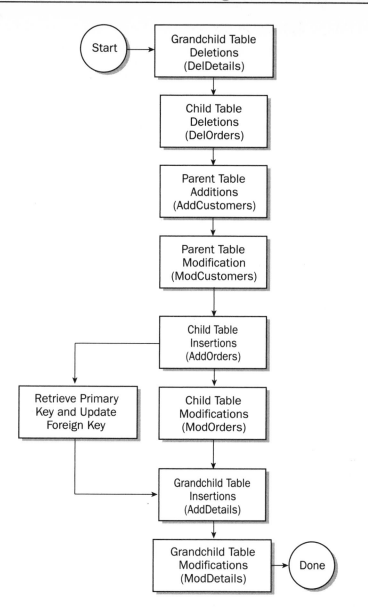

Figure 4-18

Add the UpdateBaseTables Function

It's a good practice to test your update code before making changes to the base tables. One way to validate your update procedure is to save the proposed changes as an XML file in diffgram format and then review the file for typical update operations. It's another good practice to let users know if they have changes pending—preferably how many changes—before closing the application. The following code for the `UpdateBaseTables` function accomplishes these goals:

```
Private Function UpdateBaseTables(ByVal blnTest As Boolean) As Boolean
    'Returns True if updates succeed or customer cancels form close
    'Returns False if updates fail or DataSet has no updates

    If NorthwindDataSet.HasChanges Then
        'Customers is the parent table and Deletions aren't allowed
        'Thus it's not necessary to insert or update by DataRowState
        'However, test mode needs to detect the number of changes made
        Dim NewCustomers As NorthwindDataSet.CustomersDataTable = _
            CType(NorthwindDataSet.Customers.GetChanges(DataRowState.Added), _
            NorthwindDataSet.CustomersDataTable)

        Dim ModCustomers As NorthwindDataSet.CustomersDataTable = _
            CType(NorthwindDataSet.Customers.GetChanges(DataRowState.Modified), _
            NorthwindDataSet.CustomersDataTable)

        'Orders (inserts, updates, and Deletions)
        Dim DelOrders As NorthwindDataSet.OrdersDataTable = _
            CType(NorthwindDataSet.Orders.GetChanges(DataRowState.Deleted), _
            NorthwindDataSet.OrdersDataTable)

        Dim NewOrders As NorthwindDataSet.OrdersDataTable = _
            CType(NorthwindDataSet.Orders.GetChanges(DataRowState.Added), _
            NorthwindDataSet.OrdersDataTable)

        Dim ModOrders As NorthwindDataSet.OrdersDataTable = _
            CType(NorthwindDataSet.Orders.GetChanges(DataRowState.Modified), _
            NorthwindDataSet.OrdersDataTable)

        'Order Details (inserts, updates, and Deletions)
        Dim DelDetails As NorthwindDataSet.Order_DetailsDataTable = _
            CType(NorthwindDataSet.Order_Details.GetChanges(DataRowState.Deleted), _
            NorthwindDataSet.Order_DetailsDataTable)

        Dim NewDetails As NorthwindDataSet.Order_DetailsDataTable = _
            CType(NorthwindDataSet.Order_Details.GetChanges(DataRowState.Added), _
            NorthwindDataSet.Order_DetailsDataTable)

        Dim ModDetails As NorthwindDataSet.Order_DetailsDataTable = _
            CType(NorthwindDataSet.Order_Details.GetChanges(DataRowState.Modified), _
            NorthwindDataSet.Order_DetailsDataTable)

        Dim dsChanges As DataSet = Nothing
        Dim intChanges As Integer
        If blnTest Then
            'Create a dataset of the changes
            dsChanges = New DataSet
```

```
            dsChanges.DataSetName = "dsChanges"
End If
Try
    '1. Delete Order Details records
    If Not DelDetails Is Nothing Then
        If blnTest Then
            DelDetails.TableName = "DelDetails"
            dsChanges.Tables.Add(DelDetails)
        Else
            Order_DetailsTableAdapter.Update(DelDetails)
        End If
        intChanges += DelDetails.Count
    End If

    '2. Delete Orders records
    If Not DelOrders Is Nothing Then
        DelOrders.TableName = "DelOrders"
        If blnTest Then
            dsChanges.Tables.Add(DelOrders)
            intChanges += DelOrders.Count
        Else
            OrdersTableAdapter.Update(DelOrders)
        End If
        intChanges += 1
    End If

    '3. Insert New Customers records
    If Not NewCustomers Is Nothing Then
        If blnTest Then
            NewCustomers.TableName = "NewCustomers"
            dsChanges.Tables.Add(NewCustomers)
        Else
            CustomersTableAdapter.Update(NewCustomers)
        End If
        intChanges += NewCustomers.Count
    End If

    '4. Update Modified Customers records
    If Not ModCustomers Is Nothing Then
        If blnTest Then
            ModCustomers.TableName = "ModCustomers"
            dsChanges.Tables.Add(ModCustomers)
        Else
            CustomersTableAdapter.Update(ModCustomers)
        End If
        intChanges += ModCustomers.Count
    End If

    '5. Insert New Orders records
    If Not NewOrders Is Nothing Then
        If blnTest Then
            dsChanges.Tables.Add(NewOrders)
            NewOrders.TableName = "NewOrders"
        Else
            OrdersTableAdapter.Update(NewOrders)
        End If
```

```
            intChanges += NewOrders.Count
        End If

        '6. Update Modified Orders records
        If Not ModOrders Is Nothing Then
            If blnTest Then
                dsChanges.Tables.Add(ModOrders)
                ModOrders.TableName = "ModOrders"
            Else
                OrdersTableAdapter.Update(ModOrders)
            End If
            intChanges += ModOrders.Count
        End If

        '7. Insert New Order Details records
        If Not NewDetails Is Nothing Then
            If blnTest Then
                dsChanges.Tables.Add(NewDetails)
                NewDetails.TableName = "NewDetails"
            Else
                Order_DetailsTableAdapter.Update(NewDetails)
            End If
            intChanges += NewDetails.Count
        End If

            '8. Update Modified Order Details records
        If Not ModDetails Is Nothing Then
            If blnTest Then
                dsChanges.Tables.Add(ModDetails)
                ModDetails.TableName = "ModDetails"
            Else
                Order_DetailsTableAdapter.Update(ModDetails)
            End If
            intChanges += ModDetails.Count
        End If
        If blnTest Then
            'Warn the user if changes are pending
            Dim strFile As String = Application.StartupPath + _
              "\DataSetUpdategram.xml"
            If intChanges > 0 Then
                'Save the updates as a DiffGram
                dsChanges.WriteXml(strFile, XmlWriteMode.DiffGram)
                Dim strMsg As String = "You have update(s) pending to " + _
                intChanges.ToString + " records(s)." + vbCrLf + vbCrLf + _
                "Are you sure you want to quit without " + _
                " saving these updates to the Northwind database?"
                If MsgBox(strMsg, MsgBoxStyle.Question Or MsgBoxStyle.YesNo, _
                "Pending Updates Not Saved") = MsgBoxResult.Yes Then
                    Return False
                Else
                    Return True
                End If
            Else
                If File.Exists(strFile) Then
                    File.Delete(strFile)
```

```
                End If
             End If
          End If
          Return True
       Catch exc As Exception
          MsgBox(exc.Message + exc.StackTrace, MsgBoxStyle.Exclamation, _
             "Database Updates Failed")
          Return False
       Finally
          'Dispose the new objects now
          If Not dsChanges Is Nothing Then
             dsChanges.Dispose()
          End If
          If Not NewCustomers Is Nothing Then
             NewCustomers.Dispose()
          End If
          If Not ModCustomers Is Nothing Then
             ModCustomers.Dispose()
          End If
          If Not DelOrders Is Nothing Then
             DelOrders.Dispose()
          End If
          If Not NewOrders Is Nothing Then
             NewOrders.Dispose()
          End If
          If Not ModOrders Is Nothing Then
             ModOrders.Dispose()
          End If
          If Not DelDetails Is Nothing Then
             DelDetails.Dispose()
          End If
          If Not NewDetails Is Nothing Then
             NewDetails.Dispose()
          End If
          If Not ModDetails Is Nothing Then
             ModDetails.Dispose()
          End If
       End Try
   Else
       If Not blnTest Then
          MsgBox("There are no data updates to save.", MsgBoxStyle.Information, _
             "Save Requested Without Updates")
       End If
       Return False
   End If
End Function
```

The "Database Updates Failed" error message doesn't provide users with the information they need to solve the problem. The section "Handle Concurrency Errors Gracefully" in Chapter 5 shows you how to determine the cause of the error and tell the user how to overcome the problem, if possible.

Preview Update Operations

The easiest way to generate initial DataSetUpdategram.xml test files is to add a temporary Test Updates button to the Customer Orders tab page, and add the following Click event handler:

```
Private Sub btnTestUpdates_Click(ByVal sender As Object, _
    ByVal e As System.EventArgs) Handles btnTestUpdates.Click
    'Temporary button for testing
    Dim blnQuit As Boolean = UpdateBaseTables(True)
End Sub
```

Make a few changes to Customers, Orders, and Order Details records, click Test Updates, and inspect the DataSetUpdategram.xml file in Internet Explorer. Verify that the changes you made are reflected in the <dsChanges> group.

Invoke the Update Base Tables Function

After you've completed testing the UpdateBaseTables function with the NorthwindDataSet, remove the temporary test button and invoke the function by adding the lines in bold text after the btnSaveCustData_Click event handler's EndEdit method call, as shown here:

```
CustomersBindingSource.EndEdit()
If UpdateBaseTables(False) Then
    NorthwindDataSet.Customers.AcceptChanges()
Else
    Return
End If
```

Invoke the function in the btnSaveOrders_Click event handler to update the Orders and Order Details tables with this added code:

```
Order_DetailsBindingSource.EndEdit()
OrdersBindingSource.EndEdit()
If UpdateBaseTables(False) Then
    NorthwindDataSet.Orders.AcceptChanges()
    NorthwindDataSet.Order_Details.AcceptChanges()
Else
    Return
End If
```

Now add an Imports System.IO statement to OrdersForm.vb and then add this code near the end of the ContactNameTextBox_GotFocus event handler to repopulate the cboCustomerID with new CustomerID values when restarting the project:

```
.SelectedIndex = .Items.Count - 1
Dim strFile As String = Application.StartupPath + _
 "\LookupsDataSet.xml"
If File.Exists(strFile) Then
    File.Delete(strFile)
End If
```

Check the Server for Duplicate CustomerID Values

Adding a new customer and an initial order fails if another user has added a customer with the same CustomerID value after the last refresh of the dsLookups DataSet. Unless you save the failed updategram and add code to retry it with a different CustomerID value, the entire entry is lost. To prevent data loss, you should test the new CustomerID for a duplicate in the server's Customers table.

Add the following `CheckServerForCustID` function, which uses the `SqlCommand.ExecuteScalar` method to perform a fast test for server duplicates:

```
Private Function CheckServerForCustID(ByVal strCustID As String) As Boolean
    'Run a fast duplicate check on the server
    'Called by ContactNameTextBox_GotFocus in OrdersForm.vb
    Dim cnNwind As SqlConnection = Nothing
    Try
        Dim strConn As String = My.Settings.NorthwindConnection.ToString
        cnNwind = New SqlConnection(strConn)
        Dim strSQL As String = "SELECT COUNT(CustomerID) FROM Customers " + _
            "WHERE CustomerID = '" + strCustID + "'"
        Dim cmCustID As New SqlCommand(strSQL, cnNwind)
        cnNwind.Open()
        Dim intCount As Integer = CInt(cmCustID.ExecuteScalar)
        cnNwind.Close()
        If intCount > 0 Then
            'Duplicate found
            Return True
        Else
            Return False
        End If
    Catch exc As Exception
        MsgBox(exc.Message + exc.StackTrace, MsgBoxStyle.Exclamation, _
            "Test Duplicates Error")
        Return False
    Finally
        If Not cnNwind Is Nothing Then
            If Not cnNwind.State = ConnectionState.Closed Then
                cnNwind.Close()
            End If
            cnNwind.Dispose()
        End If
    End Try
End Function
```

To execute the `CheckServerForCustID` function, add the lines shown in bold text to the `ContactNameTextBox_GotFocus` procedure prior to the `Exit Sub` test:

```
If Not blnIsDup Then
    'Function is in OrderFormV3.vb
    blnIsDup = CheckServerForCustID(strCustID)
    If blnIsDup Then
        CompanyNameTextBox.Focus()
        Dim strMsg As String = "CustomerID '" + strCustID + _
            "' duplicates existing entry in Customers table." + strHelp
        MsgBox(strMsg, MsgBoxStyle.Exclamation, strTitle)
    End If
End If
If blnIsDup Then
    Exit Sub
End If
```

The final version of the project in the. \VB2005DB\Chapter04\OrdersByCustomer – Final folder has a few housekeeping procedures that aren't included in the preceding sections' descriptions.

At this point, you have a reasonably complete data-entry front end, but it's not ready for deployment without wrapping the order-entry process in a transaction and generating error messages that enable users to recover from errors, when possible. You add transaction management and other features to this and related data-management projects in the examples of the following two chapters, which advance you to journeyman status as a data components and DataGridView programmer.

Summary

VS 2005's new data components let you drag table and relationship icons from the Data Sources window to quickly create basic data-entry forms. The autogenerated form requires substantial modification to qualify for production data-entry operations.

The default code that the designer adds to the FormName_Load event handler populates the typed DataSet's DataTables with every row of the server's base tables. Opening the form and filling tables from a large database generate a massive load on the server and a large spike in network traffic. You must add parameterized SELECT queries to limit the load on the database server and generate a local DataSet of reasonable size.

BindingNavigator controls docked at the top and bottom of a data-entry form are suitable for testing, but require users to move between the mouse and keyboard for data-entry operations. Adding accelerator key definitions to ToolStripButtons and ToolStripLabels helps minimize these transitions, which reduce data-entry efficiency greatly. A better approach is to replace BindingNavigators with accelerator key–enabled buttons that are located adjacent to the controls that they affect. It's much easier to navigate a DataGridView with the arrow keys than with a mouse.

DataGridViews require column formatting to optimize data-entry operations and display currency and percentage values correctly. You can set column formatting properties with code, but using the Edit Columns dialog and its CellStyleBuilder to set properties in design mode is more efficient. Use these two dialogs to add and format unbound columns, which you populate with code in the CellValueNeeded event handler. Add default values for new DataGridView rows with code in the DefaultValuesNeeded event handler.

A form with a Tab control minimizes the screen space required for complex, multi-level data-entry projects and can establish a workflow sequence for editing and adding new items. Adding a tab page and substituting text boxes for wide DataGridView columns increases data-entry efficiency and minimizes typographical errors. BindingSources let you bind multiple controls to a single data source. Binding combo boxes with lookup lists to controls that set foreign-key values is crucial for production-grade forms.

Optimizing the form design for heads-down data entry requires a substantial amount of code to enable and disable controls, automate tab page movement, enforce business rules, and maintain referential integrity when updating the base tables. The final version of this chapter's example form has about 1,500 lines of code. The effort you invest in optimizing data-entry operations pays long-term dividends and gains you the respect of the application's users.

5

Adding Data Validation and Concurrency Management

Validating data entries in text boxes, other simply bound Windows form controls, and DataGridViews is a relatively simple task. Simply bound Windows form controls require defining an `ErrorProvider` object to specify the location and other attributes of the error icon, which is a white exclamation mark within a red circle by default. DataGridViews have a built-in error provider, which makes validating cell values even easier. Data validation usually is sufficient for simple single-user database front ends, although you might need to query the server within the validation event handler to prevent data updates from failing—for example, when adding a new row to a table with a value-based primary key, such as the Northwind Customers table. If your proposed primary-key value is present, you incur an `SqlException` and must resubmit your updates. The first few sections of this chapter cover data entry validation techniques for bound text boxes and DataGridViews.

Multi-user front ends, which are much more common than the single-user variety, require concurrency management. Performing server-side base-table `UPDATE` or `DELETE` operations with DataTableAdapters executes value-based concurrency tests by default. If any base-table value on the server doesn't match a DataRow's original values, the `DataTableAdapter.Update` method fails and you receive a `DBConcurrencyException`. Overcoming concurrency errors with a process that's reasonably easy for users is *not* simple, as you'll discover shortly. Most of this chapter is devoted to concurrency management.

This chapter demonstrates VB 2005 code for data validation and concurrency management with a sample Windows form project—OrdersByCustomerTx.sln. Figure 5-1 shows the OrdersByCustomerTx .sln project's main form, which is based on Chapter 4's OrdersByCustomerV2 form and the OrdersByCustomerV3.sln (Final) project's UpdateBaseTables function and related event handlers for update operations. Although you can emulate concurrency errors by running two instances of OrdersByCustomerTx.sln, it's more convenient to develop and test concurrency management strategies by emulating conflicts in a single project instance. Thus, the main form has three buttons that induce concurrency errors by writing updates directly to the server.

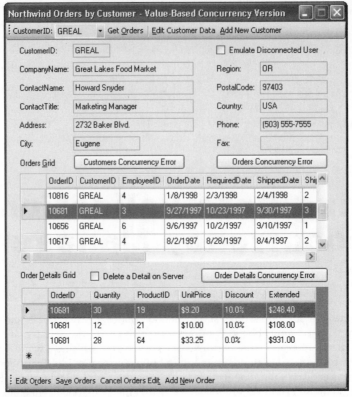

Figure 5-1

This chapter demonstrates two concurrency management techniques that you won't find in Visual Studio 2005's online help or ADO.NET best practices white papers — comparing the number of child records on the server with those in the client's DataTable and restoring an order that's been deleted on the server by another user.

All sample projects in the preceding chapters assume that you or the client's user has an always-on local or network connection to the database server. This chapter shows you how to design applications that support disconnected users who make offline updates to the client's DataSet and then update the server tables when they reconnect to the network. Marking the sample project's Emulate Disconnected User checkbox simulates offline status. If you make offline updates and clear the checkbox, update processing begins automatically. Concurrency management techniques are similar for connected users and reconnecting mobile users, but you must add a substantial amount of code to create and manage the disconnected user's local DataSet.

The OrdersByCustomerTx.sln sample project's source code is in the \VB2005DB\Chapter05\ OrdersByCustomerTx folder. App.config's default connection string requires the Northwind sample database to be installed on a local instance (localhost) of SQL Server 2000, MSDE 2000, or SQL Server 2005. If you're using SQL Express, change localhost to .\SQLEXPRESS.

You'll find illustrated online help files for entering data and testing the project at http://www
.oakleaf.ws/concurrency/. *Abridged HTML copies of the online help files — Connected.htm and
Disconnected.htm — are in the \VB2005DB\Chapter05\OrdersByCustomerTx\bin\Debug\Help
folder. Right-click the form to display Connected.htm. If you mark the Emulate Disconnected User
checkbox, right-clicking the form displays Disconnected.htm.*

The sample project adds more than 2,500 lines of Visual Basic code to its predecessor. Most of the added
code implements concurrency management. Developing and testing production-grade ADO.NET 2.0
concurrency management techniques require a database with at least a three-level hierarchy, a variety
of field data types, and representative sample data, including DBNull values. Simple master-details
tables with a few columns and rows won't disclose the many concurrency management design and
implementation issues that this chapter describes.

*To make finding this chapter's code examples in the OrdersForm.vb editor easier, each example includes
a reference to a numbered 'HACK ##: Description Task List comment, such as* 'HACK 1: Text Box
Data Validation. *Choose View ⇨ Other Windows ⇨ Task List to open the Task List window, and
select Comments from the dropdown list.*

*Some code listings are abridged to remove code that isn't applicable to the topic of the section where the
listing appears.*

Validate Data Entries

Most Windows form controls fire a Validating event when the user edits a control's value and a
Validated event after the edited value commits. Validation events for keyboard operations — such as
Tab or Shift+Tab — occur within the following event sequence: Enter, GotFocus, Leave, Validating,
Validated, and LostFocus. Mouse operations and the Focus method generate a slightly different
sequence: Enter, GotFocus, LostFocus, Leave, Validating, and Validated. To validate the edited
value of an unbound or simply bound control, you add a ControlName_Validating event handler
with expressions to test the edited value and generate an error icon and tooltip with an ErrorProvider
object.

*Error icons and tooltips are much less intrusive than message boxes, which users must acknowledge by
clicking OK or pressing Enter.*

Validate Text Boxes

Following is a simple example of a TextBox_Validating event handler (Task List comment 01) to
ensure that the CompanyName text box contains at least five characters:

```
Private Sub CompanyNameTextBox_Validating(ByVal sender As Object, _
    ByVal e As System.ComponentModel.CancelEventArgs) _
    Handles CompanyNameTextBox.Validating
    'Require CompanyName to have at least five characters
    If CompanyNameTextBox.Text.Length < 5 Then
        Dim strError As String = "CompanyName requires at least five characters"
        e.Cancel = True
```

```
            epCompanyName.SetError(CompanyNameTextBox, strError)
        Else
            epCompanyName.SetError(CompanyNameTextBox, String.Empty)
        End With
    End Sub
```

This chapter's sample OrdersByCustomerTx.sln project includes the text box and DataGridView validation examples. Build and run the project, click New Customer, and press Tab to generate a CustomerID. Then clear the CompanyName text box to display the error icon. Type at least five characters in the text box, and click Cancel Edit to abandon the Customers record addition.

Setting `e.Cancel = True` prevents the user from leaving the control without correcting the error. The `epCompanyName.SetError(CompanyNameTextBox, strError)` expression requires defining an `ErrorProvider` object in the `FormName_Load` event handler or the form's constructor with code such as the following (Task List comment 02):

```
    Private epCompanyName As ErrorProvider()
    ...
        epCompanyName = New ErrorProvider()
        With epCompanyName
            .SetIconAlignment(CompanyNameTextBox, ErrorIconAlignment.MiddleRight)
            .SetIconPadding(CompanyNameTextBox, 2)
            .BlinkRate = 500    'half-second
            .BlinkStyle = System.Windows.Forms.ErrorBlinkStyle.AlwaysBlink
        End With
```

If you provide a Cancel button or the like to abandon the entry without correcting the validation error, you must add a `ControlName.SetError(CompanyNameTextBox, String.Empty)` instruction to remove the icon and permit the user to regain focus control. A control with an active `ErrorProvider` object also prevents the user from closing the form, unless you add a `FormName_Closing` event handler and set `e.Cancel = False`.

Validate DataGridViews

DataGridViews have a built-in error provider, so you don't need to add an `ErrorProvider` object for this control. In addition to the common `Validating` and `Validated` events, which apply to the entire contents of the control, DataGridViews fire `CellValidating`, `CellValidated`, `RowValidating`, and `RowValidated` events. `Cell...` events fire when the user attempts to leave or leaves the current cell, and `Row...` events occur when the user tries to leave or leaves the current row. The `CellValidating` event is the most useful of the six validation events. The `e.ColumnIndex` and `e.RowIndex` properties return the coordinates of the cell with the error. Adding an error message to the `DataGridView.Row.ErrorText` property displays an icon in the corresponding `RowHeader` and adds a tooltip to the row. You clear the icon and tooltip by setting the `DataGridView.Row.ErrorText` property to an empty string in the `DataGridView_CellValidating` or `DataGridView_CellEndEdit` event.

The default values added for the EmployeeID column of new Orders rows and ProductID for new Order Details rows cause a foreign-key constraint `SqlException` if the user attempts to save changes without changing 0 to a valid value. Setting foreign-key values with a dropdown list solves this problem; for simplicity, this chapter's sample project requires the user to enter numeric values. The following event-handling code for DataGridView_CellValidating and DataGridView_CellValidating or DataGridView_CellEndEdit is typical of simple validation expressions (Task List comments 03 and 04).

```
Private Sub OrdersDataGridView_CellValidating(ByVal sender As Object, _
 ByVal e As System.Windows.Forms.DataGridViewCellValidatingEventArgs) _
 Handles OrdersDataGridView.CellValidating
    'Validate the EmployeeID column value
    Try
       With OrdersDataGridView
          If e.ColumnIndex = 2 Then
             If CInt(e.FormattedValue) < 1 Or CInt(e.FormattedValue) > 9 Then
                Dim strError As String = "EmployeeID value must be a number " + _
                "between 1 and 9"
                .Rows(e.RowIndex).ErrorText = strError
                e.Cancel = True
             End If
          End If
       End With
    Catch exc As Exception
       MsgBox(exc.Message, MsgBoxStyle.Information, "Invalid EmployeeID Entry")
    End Try
End Sub

Private Sub OrdersDataGridView_CellEndEdit(ByVal sender As Object, _
 ByVal e As System.Windows.Forms.DataGridViewCellEventArgs) _
 Handles OrdersDataGridView.CellEndEdit
    'Clear row error tooltip
    With OrdersDataGridView
       If e.ColumnIndex = 2 Then
          .Rows(e.RowIndex).ErrorText = ""
       End If
    End With
End Sub

Private Sub Order_DetailsDataGridView_CellValidating(ByVal sender As Object, _
 ByVal e As System.Windows.Forms.DataGridViewCellValidatingEventArgs) _
 Handles Order_DetailsDataGridView.CellValidating
    'Validate ProductID column value
    Try
       With Order_DetailsDataGridView
          If e.ColumnIndex = 2 Then
             If CInt(e.FormattedValue) < 1 Or CInt(e.FormattedValue) > 77 Then
                Dim strError As String = "ProductID value must be a number " _
                   "between 1 and 77"
                .Rows(e.RowIndex).ErrorText = strError
                e.Cancel = True
             End If
          End If
       End With
    Catch exc As Exception
       MsgBox(exc.Message, MsgBoxStyle.Information, "Invalid ProductID Entry")
    End Try
```

```
   End Sub

Private Sub Order_DetailsDataGridView_CellEndEdit(ByVal sender As Object, _
 ByVal e As System.Windows.Forms.DataGridViewCellEventArgs) _
 Handles Order_DetailsDataGridView.CellEndEdit
    'Clear row error tooltip
   With Order_DetailsDataGridView
      If e.ColumnIndex = 2 Then
         .Rows(e.RowIndex).ErrorText = ""
      End If
   End With
End Sub
```

Run the sample project, and click the Add New Order ToolStrip button to display the error icons and tooltips. Type valid EmployeeID and ProductID values to clear the error icons. Click Cancel Orders Edit to abandon the new order entry.

Catch Primary Key Constraint Violations on Entry

The Order Details table has a composite primary key — OrderID and ProductID — so duplicate ProductID values cause a primary-key constraint exception in the local Order_Details table. Thus, the preceding validation code for the ProductID column should test for duplicates also. A simple and lightweight method for detecting duplicate values is to create a HashTable instance and populate its key/value pairs with the DataGridView's formatted ProductID value and row number. If you add a duplicate ProductID key, the HashTable throws an exception that you process with the following listing's emphasized code (Task List comment 04):

```
Private Sub Order_DetailsDataGridView_CellValidating(ByVal sender As Object, _
  ByVal e As System.Windows.Forms.DataGridViewCellValidatingEventArgs) _
    Handles Order_DetailsDataGridView.CellValidating
    'Validate ProductID column value and test for duplication
    Try
       With Order_DetailsDataGridView
          Dim strError As String = Nothing
          If e.ColumnIndex = 2 Then
             If CInt(e.FormattedValue) < 1 Or CInt(e.FormattedValue) > 77 Then
                strError = "ProductID value must be a number between  1 and 77"
                .Rows(e.RowIndex).ErrorText = strError
                e.Cancel = True
                SaveOrdersToolStripButton.Enabled = False
             Else
                'Create a hashtable of ProductID values
                'Adding a duplicate key value throws an exception
                Dim htDupes As Hashtable = New Hashtable
                Dim intRow As Integer
                Try
                   'Remove previous error text
                   .Rows(intRow).ErrorText = ""
                   For intRow = 0 To .Rows.Count - 2
                      'Use the EditedFormattedValue property for proposed value
                      Dim objID As Object = _
                         .Rows(intRow).Cells(2).EditedFormattedValue
                   htDupes.Add(.Rows(intRow).Cells(2).EditedFormattedValue, intRow)
```

```
                    Next intRow
                Catch exc As Exception
                    If intRow = e.RowIndex Then
                        strError = "ProductID duplicates entry in another row"
                    Else
                        strError = "ProductID duplicates entry in row " + _
                            intRow.ToString
                    End If
                    SaveOrdersToolStripButton.Enabled = False
                    .Rows(e.RowIndex).ErrorText = strError
                    e.Cancel = True
                End Try
            End If
        End If
    End With
    Catch exc As Exception
        MsgBox(exc.Message, MsgBoxStyle.Information, "Invalid ProductID Entry")
    End Try
End Sub
```

Build and run the sample project, and click the New Order button. Type a valid EmployeeID to clear the OrderDataGridView error icon. Change the default row's ProductID to 1 or some other valid value and then add a new Order Detail record with the same value to display the primary-key error icon and tooltip. Correct the violation, and click Cancel Orders Edit.

Validate Default Values

When adding default values that contain deliberately erroneous values, such as a dropdown list with a default No Value Selected item or the like, it's a good practice to flag the new row with an error icon to indicate an editing requirement. The `NewOrderToolStripButton_Click` event handler simplifies adding a new order by inserting and selecting a new row in both grids. The following code highlights instructions to add the error icons and tooltips (Task List comment 05):

```
Private Sub NewOrderToolStripButton_Click(ByVal sender As Object, _
    ByVal e As System.EventArgs) Handles NewOrderToolStripButton.Click
    'Add a new order programmatically
    OrdersDataGridView.EndEdit(DataGridViewDataErrorContext.Commit)
    Order_DetailsDataGridView.EndEdit(DataGridViewDataErrorContext.Commit)

    EditOrdersToolStripButton.PerformClick()
    OrdersBindingSource.AddNew()
    OrdersBindingSource.MoveLast()
    Dim dgvRow As DataGridViewRow = Nothing
    With OrdersDataGridView
        dgvRow = .Rows(.Rows.Count - 2)
        .CurrentCell = .Rows(.Rows.Count - 2).Cells(2)
        Dim strError As String = "EmployeeID value must be a number " + _
        "between 1 and 9"
        dgvRow.ErrorText = strError
    End With
    AddDefaultOrderValues(dgvRow)
    FK_Order_Details_OrdersBindingSource.AddNew()
    FK_Order_Details_OrdersBindingSource.MoveLast()
```

```
    With Order_DetailsDataGridView
        dgvRow = .Rows(0)
        .CurrentCell = .Rows(0).Cells(2)
        Dim strError As String = "ProductID value must be a number " + _
        "between 1 and 77"
        dgvRow.ErrorText = strError
    End With
    AddDefaultDetailsValues(dgvRow)
    OrdersDataGridView.Focus()
    blnIsNewOrder = True

    SaveOrdersToolStripButton.Visible = True
    CancelOrdersEditToolStripButton.Visible = True
End Sub
```

Adding a new row with code doesn't fire the `DataGridView_DefaultValuesNeeded` event, so you should add the highlighted instructions to those event handlers for testing new rows that the user adds manually. Alternatively, add the instructions to the `AddDefaultOrderValues` and `AddDefaultDetailsValues` procedures, which supply the default values.

Figure 5-2 illustrates the OrdersByCustomerTx form with error icons for the CompanyName text box and the two DataGridViews. (The Customers section of the form is an overlay; you can't add a new customer while editing Orders or Order Details rows.)

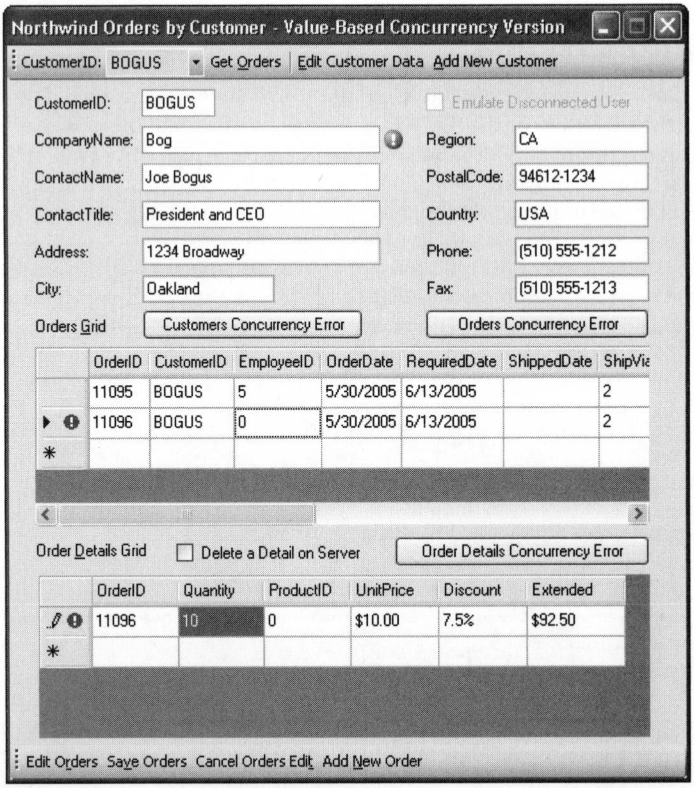

Figure 5-2

Manage Concurrency Violations

Concurrency control prevents a user from overwriting other users' modifications to the same base table record. As the number of concurrent users of an ADO.NET 2.0 data-editing application increases, the type of concurrency control that the data-editing application employs plays an increasingly important role in determining data availability. Data availability is the primary determinant of data-intensive application scalability.

Following are the two common approaches to concurrency control:

❑ **Pessimistic concurrency control** places locks on all rows undergoing modification by a user. The locks prevent other users from reading or modifying the rows until the first user commits the modifications to the database. It's a common pessimistic-concurrency practice to place locks on all child records when a user updates a parent record. In this case, a user that suspends the update operation can prevent access to a potentially large number of records by all other users.

❑ **Optimistic concurrency control** places locks on rows only while updating the rows, which ordinarily requires about 5 to 50 milliseconds. The application tests rows for updates by other users prior to committing data changes. If another user updates a row after the current user reads it, a concurrency violation occurs. Unless the front-end application contains business logic to control which update has precedence, the later update doesn't commit.

The "last user wins" approach, which overwrites previous row changes with the current user's values, isn't a concurrency control method. In this case, the front end doesn't implement concurrency control. Concurrency control is essential for almost all multi-user database front ends or middle tiers.

The data components' disconnected architecture requires optimistic concurrency control in multi-user environments. Users receive a snapshot of data to display and edit. DataTables store snapshot data as `Original` values; `Current` values store edited and unaltered data. As the amount of editing activity (*volatility*) in the database and age (*latency*) of the snapshot increase, the probability of concurrency violations increases. You can minimize potential concurrency violations by refreshing the snapshot immediately before updating records with, for example, an Edit Records button that also removes read-only restrictions. However, this approach increases the load on the database server and network, which reduces scalability, and won't work for frequently or usually disconnected mobile users. Unless you implement a timeout test, the user can refresh the snapshot, go to lunch or on break, and then commence editing with a stale snapshot.

ADO.NET 2.0 Concurrency Control and Transaction Changes

ADO.NET 2.0 TableAdapters and typed DataSets require a new approach to writing optimistic concurrency control code. ADODB disconnected Recordsets provide an elaborate mechanism for handling concurrency violations when applying the `Recordset.UpdateBatch` method. Concurrency violations add members to the `Errors` collection, and applying the `Recordset.Filter = adFilterConflictingRecords` returns the set of records having concurrency errors. Disconnected Recordsets let you invoke the `Recordset.Resync` method to undo the set of offending updates. ADO.NET 1.*x* and 2.0 don't have a built-in equivalent to the `Resync` method, so you must add code to retrieve current base-table data if you want to let users choose whether to overwrite server data or undo their pending updates.

ADO.NET 1.*x* DataAdapters and ADO.NET 2.0 TableAdapters detect concurrency errors for UPDATE and DELETE operations by including the original values from DataTable.Fill operations in the WHERE clause. Updating the ProductID value of an Order Details record from 2 to 3 generates the following SQL UPDATE statement:

```
exec sp_executesql N'UPDATE [dbo].[Order Details]
SET [OrderID] = @OrderID,[ProductID] = @ProductID, [UnitPrice] = @UnitPrice,
   [Quantity] = @Quantity, [Discount] = @Discount
WHERE (([OrderID] = @Original_OrderID) AND ([ProductID] = @Original_ProductID) AND
   ([UnitPrice] = @Original_UnitPrice) AND ([Quantity] = @Original_Quantity) AND
   ([Discount] = @Original_Discount))',

N'@OrderID int,@ProductID int,@UnitPrice money,@Quantity smallint,@Discount real,
@Original_OrderID int,@Original_ProductID int,@Original_UnitPrice money,
   @Original_Quantity smallint,@Original_Discount real',

@OrderID = 11094, @ProductID = 3, @UnitPrice = $12.0000, @Quantity = 10,
   @Discount = 7.500000298023224e-002,
@Original_OrderID = 11094, @Original_ProductID = 2, @Original_UnitPrice = $12.0000,
   @Original_Quantity = 10, @Original_Discount = 7.500000298023224e-002
```

The preceding SQL statement was captured by SQL Server 2005 Profiler. The trailing decimal values in the mantissa for Discount values are the result of using the real *(single-precision floating point) value, instead of decimal(4,2) or double as the datatype. This rounding-error issue originated in the Microsoft Access 1.0 Northwind.mdb sample database, which the SQL Server team adopted without changing the datatype.*

Moving from ADO.NET 1.*x* Connections, DataAdapters, and CurrencyManagers to ADO.NET 2.0's new TableAdapters and BindingSources complicates concurrency violation management. The typed DataSet absorbs database connection management and doesn't expose important DataAdapter properties.

Hidden Connection and Transaction Properties

Most DBAs don't permit front-end applications to access tables directly or update related tables without wrapping multiple update operations within a transaction. Substituting stored procedures for SQL statements with the Data Component Configuration Wizard satisfies the first requirement but not the second. It's easy to implement client-side transactions with SqlConnection and SqlDataAdapter objects but not with ADO.NET 2.0 data components.

VS 2005 Beta 1 typed DataSets exposed TableAdapter.Transaction and TransactionConnection properties as Friend Property Transaction() As System.Data.SqlClient.SqlTransaction and Friend ReadOnly Property Connection() As System.Data.SqlClient.SqlConnection. Subsequently, these properties became private, so you can't implement transactions directly with ADO.NET 2.0 typed DataSets. TableAdapters open and close the connection for each command, which precludes creating a usable SqlTransaction object. (Transactions are dedicated to a single connection that must remain open until you invoke the Commit or Rollback method.) Writing Partial Class DataSetName code to enable a single SqlConnection and create its SqlTransaction object isn't easy, as demonstrated by the examples of Chapter 6.

Some DBAs might not accept ADO.NET client-side transactions as a substitute for T-SQL transactions that wrap stored procedures. Before you expend time implementing a partial class, verify that the DBA(s) in charge of the affected database(s) are amenable to client-side transactions.

The ContinueUpdateOnError Property

ADO.NET 1.x DataAdapters and ADO.NET 2.0 TableAdapters provide a `ContinueUpdateOnError` property, which you can set to `True` to prevent throwing `DBConcurrencyExceptions` when concurrency violations occur upon executing `DataAdapter.Update` commands. Eliminating these exceptions permits multiple updates — some of which have concurrency violations — to proceed without user intervention. When a violation occurs, the DataAdapter sets the `DataRow.RowError` property value of its source DataTable to "Concurrency violation: the UpdateCommand affected 0 of 1 records" or the like. Rows with errors in DataGridViews display a red exclamation mark icon. You must write a substantial amount of business logic code to resolve the errors *ex post facto*.

The `ContinueUpdateOnError` property is useful primarily with simple update scenarios for a single DataTable. Updating related tables requires creating three temporary DataTables for each `DataSet.DataTable`, as described in Chapter 4's "Maintain Referential Integrity" section and later in this chapter. Setting the `ContinueUpdateOnError` property to `True` for more than one related table isn't a good database programming practice because it's very difficult to resolve concurrency violations for related tables.

Concurrency Control Strategies

Before you begin writing concurrency-control code, you and your consulting client or the application's owner must agree on the concurrency-control specification. The following questions cover the most important specification elements for handling concurrency violations:

❑ Should updates be permitted to more than one data entity, such as a customer record or sales order, without saving the data for individual entities to the server? In an always-connected LAN environment, it's a good practice to save changes to one data entity before creating or editing another. Frequently disconnected mobile users, however, need to make updates to multiple entities before reconnecting to the network and saving their changes. Multiple entity updates require row-by-row update processing to accommodate concurrency control, as described in the section "Accommodate Disconnected Users," later in this chapter. Processing temporary update files as a batch complicates concurrency tests for child records. Adding multiple new entities doesn't require concurrency control.

❑ Will all users be permitted to decide whether to overwrite other users' changes? If overwriting specific users' changes is restricted to particular user roles, all tables must include a column to identify the user who added or last modified the row.

❑ What information must be presented to the user to make an informed overwrite decision? In most cases, the user needs to see the changes others made to the row; obtaining this data requires a roundtrip to the server. Displaying original values, in addition to the user's current modifications, is useful but not usually essential.

❑ Are message boxes with the preceding information sufficient for resolving conflicts or is a more complex UI, such as a DataGridView or another form, required? Message boxes usually suffice, but you might need a pop-up dialog or a tab page to handle violations that occur with complex data structures.

❑ Should a single concurrency violation prevent or roll back all changes associated with an update? Rolling back all changes requires a client-side transaction, which isn't easy to implement with data components, as you see in Chapter 6's "Apply Transactions to DataSet Updates" section. It's even more challenging to assign a specific transaction to a particular data entity when you permit updating multiple data entities in a single update operation.

❑   Do users need the choice of regenerating a new order if another user has deleted the entire order from the server? The process of re-creating the order is reasonably easy, but you must test for a deleted order prior to attempting an order update operation or modification to child records. Code to compare the number of child records will detect the deleted order, but that code doesn't provide the ability to regenerate the order.

The specifications that you agree upon will have a profound effect on the number of hours that you'll spend writing and debugging concurrency-management code, as you'll see in the sections that follow and by exploring the OrdersByCustomerTx project.

The "Missing Links" of Concurrency Management

In related-table scenarios, multiple users can insert or delete child rows of parent tables. Newly inserted child rows aren't visible to users with stale snapshots. Deleted child rows aren't detected unless the updating user modifies them and later applies the `ChildTableAdapter.Update` method. Prior to detecting the child-table deletion, the updating user might have modified the parent row, or added or deleted child rows during the update operation.

Altering base table records before detecting child-record additions or deletions can be dangerous. For example, a physician with a laptop or Pocket PC that's disconnected from the network might alter a patient's prescriptions or dosages without knowing that another health worker has added or deleted a prescription. When the physician reconnects to the network and updates the base tables, undetected additions or deletions might ultimately threaten the patient's health or, potentially, her life.

Very few concurrency-control articles and code examples, including those in VS 2005's online help, include tests for child-record count mismatches. This omission is surprising when you consider the potential impact of another user's undetected modifications.

Detect Child-Record Count Mismatches

Detecting child-record additions or deletions by other users requires comparing the number of child records on the server with that in the updating user's local DataTable prior to executing any updates to the master or child rows. Autogenerated TableAdapter UPDATE commands don't include this test, so you must add code to detect the difference between the number of child rows.

The following sample function obtains the current Order Details count from the server, adjusts the local count for rows to be added or deleted in later update operations, when applicable, and returns True if the count values match (Task List comment 06):

```
Private Function TestNumberOfDetails(ByVal intOrderID As Integer, _
   ByVal intAdded As Integer) As Boolean
   'Returns True if number of Order Details records are the same as on the server
   'or it's a new order and has no details records yet
   'Returns False if other users have changed the number on the server.
   'Takes into account pending new records during the test

   Dim strConn As String = My.Settings.NorthwindConnection
   Dim cnNwind As New SqlConnection(strConn)
   Dim cmCurrent As New SqlCommand("", cnNwind)
   Dim intCurrent As Integer
```

```vbnet
    Try
        'Get the first OrderID from the first row
        cnNwind.Open()

        Dim strSQL As String = "SELECT COUNT(*) FROM [Order Details] WHERE " + _
         "OrderID = " + intOrderID.ToString
        With cmCurrent
            .CommandType = CommandType.Text
            .CommandText = strSQL
            intCurrent = CInt(.ExecuteScalar)
        End With
        cnNwind.Close()

        If intCurrent = 0 Then
            'New order; don't perform further tests
            Return True
        End If

        'Get the filtered value from the Order_Details table
        'Dim dvDetails As New DataView(NorthwindDataSet.Order_Details, _
        ' "OrderID = " + intOrderID.ToString, "OrderID", _
        ' DataViewRowState.CurrentRows)
        'Dim intCount As Integer = dvDetails.Count

        'Following is claimed to be a faster method than the preceding
        Dim dvDetails As New DataView
        Dim intCount As Integer
        With dvDetails
            .Table = NorthwindDataSet.Order_Details
            .Sort = "OrderID"
            Dim drvDetails As DataRowView()
            drvDetails = .FindRows(intOrderID)
            intCount = drvDetails.Length
            .Dispose()
        End With

        If intCurrent = intCount - intAdded Then
            'No change in number of Order Details
            Return True
        Else
            Return False
        End If
    Catch exc As Exception
        MsgBox(exc.Message, MsgBoxStyle.Exclamation, _
        "Can't Retrieve Current Server Data")
        Return False
    Finally
        If Not cnNwind.State = ConnectionState.Closed Then
            cnNwind.Close()
        End If
        cmCurrent.Dispose()
        cnNwind.Dispose()
    End Try
End Function
```

The "Sorting and Filtering Data Using a DataView" online help topic suggests that creating a DataView of the table and applying the DataView.FindRows method to return an array of DataRowView objects is faster than returning a set of DataRows from a filtered DataView object. You must set the DataView.Sort property value to the appropriate column name to apply the DataView.FindRows method. The performance differences between the two methods isn't likely to be significant with a small number of rows.

> You apply the preceding test prior to invoking the TableAdapter.Update methods for the parent and child tables — Orders and Order Details for this example. The sample project uses an SQL query, but you can substitute a stored procedure easily.

Uncover Other Potential Concurrency Conflicts

It's another good practice to test all child rows for concurrency errors, not just rows modified by the user in a DataGridView. Doing this requires applying the SetModified method to all rows when the user changes a value in the DataGridView. As an example, the following DataGridView_CellValueChanged event handler sets all Order_Details rows for the current Orders row to Modified when the user changes a single cell value (Task List comment 07):

```
Private Sub Order_DetailsDataGridView_CellValueChanged(ByVal sender As Object, _
  ByVal e As System.Windows.Forms.DataGridViewCellEventArgs) _
  Handles Order_DetailsDataGridView.CellValueChanged
    If Order_DetailsDataGridView.Enabled Then
        SaveOrdersToolStripButton.Visible = True
        CancelOrdersEditToolStripButton.Visible = True
        Dim blnMarkAllRows As Boolean = True 'For testing
        Dim intRow As Integer
        If blnMarkAllRows Then
            Try
                Dim objCurrent As Object = _
                FK_Order_Details_OrdersBindingSource.Current
            If Not objCurrent Is Nothing Then
                'Get the OrderID
                Dim drvCurrent As DataRowView = CType(objCurrent, DataRowView)
                Dim strOrderID As String = drvCurrent.Item(0).ToString
                With NorthwindDataSet.Order_Details
                    Dim drDetails As DataRow() = .Select("OrderID = " + strOrderID)
                    'If the table has a DateTime modified field, sort ascending
                    '(oldest first) to throw concurrency violation errors before
                    'reaching the user-updated value
                    If drDetails.Length > 0 Then
                        For intRow = 0 To drDetails.Length - 1
                            If drDetails(intRow).RowState = DataRowState.Unchanged Then
                                Try
                                    'Required to ignore non-fatal exception
                                    drDetails(intRow).SetModified()
                                Catch exc as Exception
                                End Try
                            End If
                        Next
                    End If
                End With
            End If
        Catch exc As Exception
```

```
                MsgBox(exc.Message + exc.StackTrace)
            End Try
        End If
    End If
End Sub
```

The `DataTable.Select` method returns an array of `DataRow` objects, which you iterate to apply the new `DataRow.SetModified` method. You must test each row with the `DataRow.DataRowState` method because you can apply the `SetModified` method to unchanged rows only.

Enable Users to Recreate Deleted Orders

Data-entry personnel might delete an active order unknowingly or maliciously. If an updating user's DataSet includes a copy of the deleted order, you can add code to provide the choice of accepting the deletion or generating a new order with current updates. The following `IsOrderModifiedOrDeleted` function returns a member of the `OrderServerStatus` enumeration (Task List comment 08).

> *This version doesn't test for modified Order Details records on the server because concurrency errors detect these modifications. In a production version, this function could include the concurrency management code that's described in the section "Handle Concurrency Errors Gracefully," later in this chapter.*

The initial set of tests prevents testing Orders and Order Details records that the user has added to the local DataSet before saving the updates to the server. In this case, the `DataRowState` is `Added`. Notice that you must use the temporary new OrderID value assigned by the DataTable (`intOrigID`), not the OrderID value of the new Orders record (`intOrderID`) to test Order Details records because the update sequence inserts Orders records before Order Details records.

```
Private Function IsOrderModifiedOrDeleted(ByVal intOrderID As Integer, _
    ByVal intProductID As Integer, ByVal intOrigID As Integer) As OrderServerStatus
    'Called by most UpdateBaseTables operations
    'Returns one of the OrderServerStatus enums
    Dim eStatus As OrderServerStatus

    'Don't test server status for added Orders
    'Added or modified Order Details records for existing orders must be tested
    Dim drAdded As DataRow
    If intProductID = 0 Then
        'It's an Orders record
        drAdded = NorthwindDataSet.Orders.FindByOrderID(intOrderID)
        If Not drAdded Is Nothing Then
            If drAdded.RowState = DataRowState.Added Then
                'It's an added Orders record
                Return OrderServerStatus.NewRow
            End If
        End If
    Else
        If intOrigID <> intOrderID Then
            'It's a added Order Details record for a new Orders record
            'Must use the original, not the new OrderID
            drAdded = _
                NorthwindDataSet.Order_Details.FindByOrderIDProductID(intOrigID, _
                intProductID)
            If drAdded Is Nothing Then
```

```
                    Return OrderServerStatus.Unmodified
                Else
                    If drAdded.RowState = DataRowState.Added Then
                        'It's an added Orders record
                        Return OrderServerStatus.NewRow
                    End If
                End If
            End If
        End If

        'Test for order on server
        Dim dtModified As DataTable = NorthwindDataSet.Orders.Clone
        Dim strSQL As String = "SELECT * FROM Orders " + _
         "WHERE OrderID = " + intOrderID.ToString
        Dim strMsg As String = Nothing
        Dim strConn As String = My.Settings.NorthwindConnection
        Dim cnNwind As New SqlConnection(strConn)
        Dim cmCurrent As New SqlCommand(strSQL, cnNwind)
        Try
            cnNwind.Open()
            Dim sdrCurrent As SqlDataReader = cmCurrent.ExecuteReader
            With sdrCurrent
                If .HasRows Then
                    'For modified on server test, if implemented
                    dtModified.Load(sdrCurrent, LoadOption.OverwriteRow)
                Else
                    'Order is deleted on server
                    eStatus = OrderServerStatus.DeletedOnServer
                End If
                .Close()
                .Dispose()
            End With
            cnNwind.Close()
        Catch exc As Exception
            MsgBox(exc.Message, MsgBoxStyle.Exclamation, _
            "Can't Retrieve Current Server Data")
            eStatus = OrderServerStatus.ServerInaccessible
        Finally
            If Not cnNwind.State = ConnectionState.Closed Then
                cnNwind.Close()
            End If
            cnNwind.Dispose()
            cmCurrent.Dispose()
        End Try

        'Test the local DataSet
        Try
            Dim drCurrent As DataRow = NorthwindDataSet.Orders.FindByOrderID(intOrderID)
            If drCurrent Is Nothing Then
                'Row is deleted locally
                eStatus = OrderServerStatus.DeletedLocally
            ElseIf eStatus <> OrderServerStatus.DeletedOnServer Then
                If intProductID > 0 Then
                    'Order Details record
                    drAdded = _
```

```
              NorthwindDataSet.Order_Details.FindByOrderIDProductID(intOrderID, _
                intProductID)
        If drAdded Is Nothing Then
            eStatus = OrderServerStatus.DeletedLocally
        Else
            If drAdded.RowState = DataRowState.Added Then
                'It's an added Orders record
                eStatus = OrderServerStatus.NewRow
            Else
                eStatus = OrderServerStatus.Unmodified
            End If
        End If
    End If
End If
If eStatus = OrderServerStatus.DeletedOnServer Then
    strMsg = "Another user has deleted order " + intOrderID.ToString + _
      " from the server." + vbCrLf + vbCrLf + "Click Yes if you agree " _
      "that the order should be deleted." + vbCrLf + vbCrLf + _
      "Click No to create a new order with your current order data " + _
      "and notify the customer of the OrderID change."
    If MsgBox(strMsg, MsgBoxStyle.Exclamation Or MsgBoxStyle.YesNo, _
      "Order " + intOrderID.ToString + " Deleted from Database") = _
      MsgBoxResult.Yes Then
        'Remove the order and details records
        Dim drRows As DataRow()
        Dim drRow As DataRow

        'Delete all Order Details rows
        drRows = NorthwindDataSet.Order_Details.Select("OrderID = " + _
          intOrderID.ToString)
        If drRows.Length > 0 Then
            For Each drRow In drRows
                If drRow.RowState = DataRowState.Added Then
                    drRow.AcceptChanges()
                End If
                drRow.Delete()
                drRow.AcceptChanges()
            Next
        End If

        'Delete the Order row
        drRows = NorthwindDataSet.Orders.Select("OrderID = " + _
          intOrderID.ToString)
        If drRows.Length > 0 Then
            drRows(0).Delete()
            drRows(0).AcceptChanges()
        End If
        eStatus = OrderServerStatus.DeletedLocally
    Else
        'Add as a new Orders row by changing RowState to Added
        Dim drRows As DataRow()
        drRows = NorthwindDataSet.Orders.Select("OrderID = " + _
          intOrderID.ToString)
        If drRows.Length > 0 Then
            drRows(0).AcceptChanges()
```

```
                    drRows(0).SetAdded()
            End If

            'Add Order Details rows if not deleted
            Dim drRow As DataRow
            drRows = NorthwindDataSet.Order_Details.Select("OrderID = " + _
             intOrderID.ToString)
            If drRows.Length > 0 Then
                For Each drRow In drRows
                    drRow.AcceptChanges()
                    If drRow.RowState = DataRowState.Deleted Then
                        Stop
                    Else
                        drRow.SetAdded()
                    End If
                Next
            End If
            eStatus = OrderServerStatus.AddedLocally
        End If
    End If
    Catch exc As Exception
        MsgBox(exc.Message + exc.StackTrace)
    End Try
    Return eStatus
End Function

Private Enum OrderServerStatus As Integer
    Unmodified = 0
    NewRow = 1
    DeletedLocally = 2
    DeletedOnServer = 3
    ModifiedOnServer = 4
    ServerInaccessible = 5
    AddedLocally = 6
    DeletedFromAddedOrder = 7
End Enum
```

Clicking Yes in the message box deletes local rows for the order and its child records by setting the `DataRowState` to `Deleted` and applying the `AcceptChanges` method. Clicking No generates a new order by setting `DataRowState` to `Added` and applying the `AcceptChanges` method.

If you don't apply `AcceptChanges` to all rows you delete, the temporary DelOrders and DelDetails update tables will contain the rows and the corresponding `Update` operations will throw exceptions.

Anticipate Value-Based Primary-Key Constraint Violations

Using an `int identity` or `uniqueidentifier` (GUID) column as the base table's primary key eliminates potential primary-key violations. If the base table's primary key is a character field, such as the Customers table's five-character CustomerID column, adding a new customer with an existing CustomerID value throws an `SqlException` for a primary-key violation. In this case, the user must make a choice between canceling the addition or editing the primary-key value and retrying the update. Making this choice requires code to provide the user with the conflicting data from the server, such as that shown emphasized in the following listing.

If you specify Cascade as the Update Rule for the FK_Orders_Customers relation and the user edits the CustomerID primary key, the change cascades to the child table's related foreign-key column.

Code in the `UpdateBaseTables` function's `SqlException` event handler calls the following `ResolveDuplicateCustomerID` function if the exception's message contains `PK_Customers` (Task List comment 09):

```
Private Function ResolveDuplicateCustomerID(ByVal strCustomerID As String) _
   As Boolean
   'Process duplicate new CustomerID

   'Retrieve the existing customer data
   Dim strSQL As String = "SELECT * FROM Customers " + _
   "WHERE CustomerID = '" + strCustomerID + "'"
   Dim strConn As String = My.Settings.NorthwindConnection
   Dim cnNwind As New SqlConnection(strConn)
   Dim cmCurrent As New SqlCommand(strSQL, cnNwind)
   Dim objCurrent(10) As Object
   Try
       cnNwind.Open()
       Dim sdrCurrent As SqlDataReader = cmCurrent.ExecuteReader
       With sdrCurrent
          .Read()
          .GetValues(objCurrent)
          .Close()
          .Dispose()
       End With
       cnNwind.Close()
   Catch exc As Exception
       MsgBox(exc.Message, MsgBoxStyle.Exclamation, _
       "Can't Retrieve Current Server Data")
   Finally
       If Not cnNwind.State = ConnectionState.Closed Then
          cnNwind.Close()
       End If
       cnNwind.Dispose()
       cmCurrent.Dispose()
   End Try
   Dim intOrders As Integer
   With NorthwindDataSet.Orders
       Dim drRows As DataRow()
       drRows = .Select("CustomerID = '" + strCustomerID + "'")
       intOrders = drRows.Length
   End With
   'Create the details string
   Dim strDetails As String = Nothing
   Dim intCol As Integer
   Dim strColName As String = Nothing
   With NorthwindDataSet.Customers
       For intCol = 0 To objCurrent.Length - 1
          If intCol = 0 Then
             frmCustomer.Text = "Current Customers Record for CustomerID '" + _
             objCurrent(0).ToString + "'"
          End If
          'Pad right for readability
```

```vb
            strColName = .Columns(intCol).ColumnName
            Dim strPad As New String(" "c, 13 - Len(strColName))
            strDetails += strColName + ":" + strPad + _
             objCurrent(intCol).ToString + vbCrLf
        Next intCol
    End With
    frmCustomer.txtDetails.Text = strDetails
    Dim strMsg As String = "CustomerID '" + strCustomerID + _
     "' exists on the server. Review the customer information " + _
     "below to determine if it duplicates your new customer entry. " + _
     "If so, click Cancel New Customer. Otherwise click Edit New " + _
     "Customer, modify the CustomerID value, and click Save again."
    If intOrders > 0 Then
        'New orders with bad CustomerIDs only occur from offline entries
        strMsg += vbCrLf + vbCrLf + "You have " + intOrders.ToString + _
        " order(s) pending for '" + strCustomerID + "'. New orders will " + _
        "be preserved in either case."
        blnSaveNewOrders = True
    Else
        strMsg += vbCrLf + vbCrLf + "There are no " + _
        "orders pending for '" + strCustomerID + "'."
    End If
    frmCustomer.lblMessage.Text = strMsg
    If frmCustomer.ShowDialog = Windows.Forms.DialogResult.Cancel Then
        frmCustomer.Dispose()
        'Remove the new order
        CustomerIDToolStripComboBox.Items.Remove(strCustomerID)
        With OrdersBindingSource
            'Accept changes so removal doesn't attempt to remove the record
            'being duplicated from the database when rerunning save changes
            With NorthwindDataSet.Customers
                Dim rowDup As DataRow
                rowDup = .FindByCustomerID(strCustomerID)
                If Not rowDup Is Nothing Then
                    'Will not appear in temporary update tables
                    rowDup.AcceptChanges()
                End If
            End With
            With CustomerIDToolStripComboBox
                .Text = .Items(0).ToString
            End With
            GetCustomerOrdersToolStripButton.PerformClick()
            SaveCurrentDiffGram()
            Return False
        End With
    Else
        'Fix the new order
        frmCustomer.Dispose()
        NewCustomerControlState(True)
        'Enable entering a new order
        EnableOrdersGrid(True, False)
        EnableOrder_DetailsGrid(True, False)
        blnSyncCustomerID = True
        blnAutoContinue = False
        'Enable editing when returning from offline
```

```
            LockTextBoxes(False, False)
            Return False
        End If
    End Function
```

The `SqlDataReader.GetValues` method returns an `Object` array of field values. Figure 5-3 shows the dialog after populating the text box with existing server data by the highlighted code in the `ResolveDuplicateCustomerID` function.

Figure 5-3

Handle Concurrency Errors Gracefully

The easiest method for handling `DBConcurrencyException`s and mismatched numbers of child records is to display a simple warning message. The user or code must update the DataSet with the base-table values of the offending row and its child rows to eliminate the concurrency violation. The update overwrites the user's changes, which you can't retrieve from the DataTables' original values. At this point, the DataTable's original and current values are identical because the `TableAdapter.AcceptChangesDuringFill` property is `True`. It's possible to store original values prior to the update and let the user retrieve them for comparison, but the code required for this approach is cumbersome. Stale original values also can produce subsequent concurrency violations.

The better approach is to query the server for current data as conflicts occur during the online update process. This means that you must process user updates row by row, rather than as a batch. For reference, this code from Chapter 4's "Add the UpdateBaseTables Function" section processes each temporary update table as a batch, without handling `DBConcurrencyException`s:

```
'1. Delete Order Details records
If Not DelDetails Is Nothing Then
    Order_DetailsTableAdapter.Update(DelDetails)
    Order_DetailsTableAdapter.FillOrder_Details(NorthwindDataSet.Order_Details, _
```

```
        strCustomerID)
    intChanges += DelDetails.Count
End If


'2. Delete Orders records
If Not DelOrders Is Nothing Then
    DelOrders.TableName = "DelOrders"
    OrdersTableAdapter.Update(DelOrders)
    OrdersTableAdapter.FillOrders(NorthwindDataSet.Orders, _
        strCustomerID)
    intChanges += 1
End If


'3. Insert New Customers records
If Not NewCustomers Is Nothing Then
    CustomersTableAdapter.Update(NewCustomers)
    CustomersTableAdapter.GetCustomerOrders(NorthwindDataSet.Customers, _
        strCustomerID)
    intChanges += NewCustomers.Count
End If
```

If a `DBConcurrencyException` occurs during an update, you can examine the errant DataRow for its original and current values, but the DataRow contains the original value that caused the error, not the server's value. The DataRow for exceptions thrown during deletions isn't readable; attempting to read the DataRow throws a `DeletedRowInaccessibleException`.

Obtain Current Data from the Server

Both updates and deletions need the current data from the server to find the conflicting field values, which requires the OrderID value of the Orders row or OrderID and ProductID values of the Order Details row being processed. As an example, the following excerpt from the `UpdateBaseTables` function retrieves the OrderID and ProductID values from a DataView of the current row of the DelDetails temporary table that's created with a `DataViewRowState.Deleted` parameter (Task List comment 10). You must create a `DataView` object to obtain values from rows marked `Deleted`.

```
'7. Delete Order Details records
If Not DelDetails Is Nothing Then
    strTableErr = "Order Details"
    Dim intPreviousID As Integer
    intChanges += DelDetails.Count
    While DelDetails.Count > 0
        'Deletion ultimately removes all rows from DelDetails,
        'so use the first row when deleting
        'Get the OrderID (a DataView is the only way possible with a deleted row)
        Dim dvDeleted As New DataView(DelDetails, Nothing, Nothing, _
            DataViewRowState.Deleted)
        intOrderID = CInt(dvDeleted.Item(0).Item(0))
        Dim intProductID As Integer = CInt(dvDeleted.Item(0).Item(1))
        dvDeleted.Dispose()
        Dim eStatus As OrderServerStatus = _
         IsOrderModifiedOrDeleted(intOrderID, intProductID, intOrigID)
        Dim drUpdate As DataRow = DelDetails.Rows(0)
        If eStatus = OrderServerStatus.DeletedOnServer Then
```

```
                'Don't attempt to delete orders added by others
        Else
            If intOrderID = intPreviousID Or eStatus = _
                OrderServerStatus.DeletedLocally Then
                'Don't test number of Order details
                Order_DetailsTableAdapter.Update(drUpdate)
            Else
                'Only test the first deletion for an OrderID, subsequent tests mismatch
                If TestNumberOfDetails(intOrderID, 0, False) Then
                    Order_DetailsTableAdapter.Update(drUpdate)
                Else
                    Return False
                End If
            End If
            intPreviousID = intOrderID
        End If
    End While
    blnSkipCount = False
End If
```

A `False` *return value causes a loop to the beginning of the* `UpdateBaseTables` *function when the user clicks Yes to continue updates in the message box that opens after processing an exception.*

Finding the server values doesn't solve the concurrency error. You must add code to reset the DataSet's DataTable row's original values to the server values, which isn't an easy task. You can update the DataRow with the server values and apply the `AcceptChanges` method for updates, which overwrites the user's update, but you can't change values of a deleted DataRow because it isn't accessible.

The `DataRow` *property of a* `DataViewRow` *is read-only, so this approach doesn't let you alter the values or* `DataRowState` *of a deleted row.*

Figure 5-4 is a flow diagram for updating base tables with tests for orders deleted on the server, child-table count mismatches, and concurrency errors. Moving deletions from the first to the last step of the `UpdateBaseTables` function (Task List comments 10 and 11) permits testing rows prior to their potential deletion on the server. Successfully resolving concurrency exceptions is the subject of the next section.

Shaded boxes in Figure 5-4 represent `UpdateBaseTables` *operations; boxes with rounded corners represent the* `IsOrderModifiedOrDeleted` *function. The remaining boxes include the function name in parentheses.*

Retrieve and Compare Server and Client Cell Values

The `DBConcurrencyException` handler calls the `ResolveConcurrencyErrors` function (Task List comment 12), which compares the server and DataTable row values. `ResolveConcurrencyErrors` and its related functions and procedures have more than 500 lines of code, so it's not practical to provide a complete listing here. Figure 5-5 is a simplified flow diagram of the `ResolveConcurrencyErrors` function.

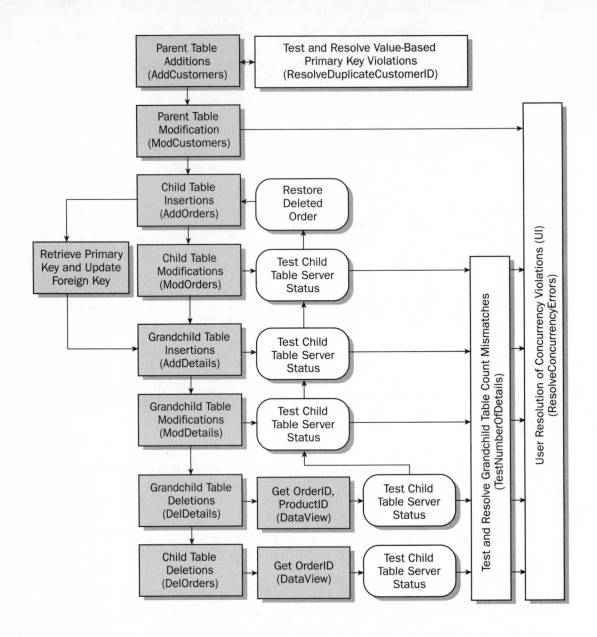

Figure 5-4

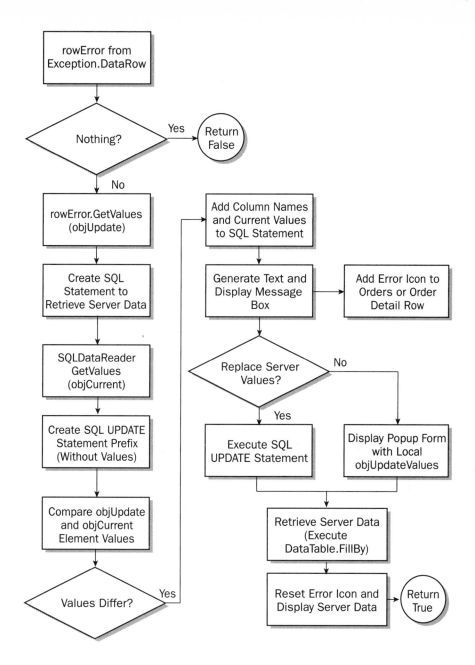

Figure 5-5

The most important element of the `ResolveConcurrencyErrors` function is the code that compares the server and client values to generate the SQL `UPDATE` statement's column name and values list, shown in the following listing (Task List comment 13). The comparison requires handling potential `DBNull` values and insignificant differences of `System.Decimal` and `System.DateTime` data type values.

```
'Create the error message and complete the UPDATE statement
Dim intErrors As Integer
Dim strMsg As String = Nothing
Dim blnHasError As Boolean
For intCtr = 0 To objCurrent.Length - 1
    If objCurrent(intCtr) Is Nothing Then
        'No more columns
        Exit For
    End If
    'Compare non-string data types and handle nulls
    If strColTypes(intCtr) = "System.Decimal" Then
        'Decimal values mismatch on money types, which are 0.0000 on the server
        'and nulls might occur
        If objCurrent(intCtr) Is DBNull.Value Then
            objCurrent(intCtr) = 0
        End If
        If objUpdate(intCtr) Is DBNull.Value Then
            objUpdate(intCtr) = 0
        End If
        If CType(objCurrent(intCtr).ToString, Decimal) <> _
        CType(objUpdate(intCtr).ToString, Decimal) Then
            blnHasError = True
        Else
            blnHasError = False
        End If
    ElseIf strColTypes(intCtr) = "System.DateTime" Then
        'Orders have null ShippedDates
        If objCurrent(intCtr) Is DBNull.Value Then
            objCurrent(intCtr) = "1/1/0001"
        End If
        If objUpdate(intCtr) Is DBNull.Value Then
            objUpdate(intCtr) = "1/1/0001"
        End If
        If CType(objCurrent(intCtr).ToString, Date) <> _
        CType(objUpdate(intCtr).ToString, Date) Then
            blnHasError = True
        Else
            blnHasError = False
        End If
    ElseIf objCurrent(intCtr).ToString <> objUpdate(intCtr).ToString Then
        'Also works for integer values
        blnHasError = True
    Else
        blnHasError = False
    End If
    If blnHasError Then
        'Fill in the SQL UPDATE statement
        strSQL += strColNames(intCtr) + " = "
        If strColTypes(intCtr) = "System.String" Or strColTypes(intCtr) = _
```

```
                "System.DateTime" Then
                    strSQL += "'" + objUpdate(intCtr).ToString + "', "
            Else
                    strSQL += objUpdate(intCtr).ToString + ", "
            End If
            'Create the message string
            strMsg += strColNames(intCtr) + " in database is '" + _
                objCurrent(intCtr).ToString + "' and your current entry is '" + _
                objUpdate(intCtr).ToString + "'." + vbCrLf
            intErrors += 1
        End If
    Next

    'Handle null date values and remove 12:00:00 AM
    strMsg = Replace(strMsg, "1/1/0001", "(null)")
    strMsg = Replace(strMsg, " 12:00:00 AM", "")

    'Fix null values in SQL UPDATE statement
    strSQL = Replace(strSQL, "'1/1/0001'", "NULL")
```

Following is the SQL UPDATE statement for a client update with four locally modified fields, including setting the RequiredDate value to DBNull.Value by typing (null) in the cell:

```
UPDATE Orders SET EmployeeID = 1, OrderDate = '9/3/2004 12:00:00 AM',
RequiredDate = NULL, Freight = 15.50 WHERE OrderID = 11207
```

Figure 5-6 shows the two message boxes that open for concurrency errors that don't involve differences in child-record counts. If the child-record count differs, all pending user updates are overwritten.

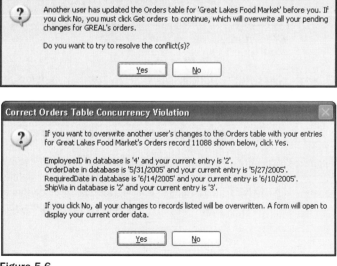

Figure 5-6

To emulate an Orders table concurrency error, select an order that has a (null) shipped date, click the Orders Concurrency Error button to change the EmployeeID value, and click No in the message box that asks if you want to delete the order. Make a few edits to the same order, click Save Orders, and click Yes when asked if you want to try to resolve the changes. Right-click the form to open Connected.htm from the ...\Debug\Help folder and scroll to the "Emulate Other Users Base-Table Modifications" for more detailed instructions.

Clicking Yes executes the UPDATE statement and shows a success message box. Clicking No displays a pop-up OrderDetailsForm that contains the user's data for reference while redoing the update (see Figure 5-7). The same form opens if a child-record count mismatch occurs.

Figure 5-7

The GetCurrentOrderData subprocedure populates the text box shown in Figure 5-7.

Accommodate Disconnected Users

In an always-connected user scenario, you can apply business logic code that requires the user to persist current data entity changes to the database server before adding, editing, or deleting another entity. One of the primary objectives of ADO.NET DataSets is to enable frequently disconnected users to accumulate entity additions, modifications, and deletions to a DataSet that the project persists in diffgram format as a local XML file. The mobile user downloads the appropriate set of current data from the server, and then disconnects from the network. The user later connects to the network, saves the accumulated changes to the server, and refreshes the local DataSet by downloading and merging data that was modified since the last snapshot.

> *The XML files of locally persisted DataSets can become very large, but performance with laptop computers that have up-to-date processors and 500MB RAM or more is adequate to handle diffgram files of 20MB or more. Multi-megabyte diffgram XML files load in a few seconds or less. The "Store Large Lookup Tables in DataSets" article at* www.ftponline.com/vsm/2004_07/magazine/features/rjennings/ *describes a downloadable VS.NET 2003 project that loads and searches large lookup DataTables. (This project upgrades to VS.NET 2005 with no errors.) A 202KB products table loads in 0.3 seconds and an 11MB customers table loads in 1.8 seconds on a 2.6 GHz Pentium 4 machine with 1GB RAM.*

Data latency is a much more serious problem for disconnected users who might have a hundred or more updates pending when offline for a day or two. In this case, reconnecting and processing updates inevitably incurs concurrency conflicts with moderately volatile database tables. Best practices dictate implementing concurrency management for all projects that support offline DataSet updates. You might choose to skip child-record count mismatches and deleted data regeneration, but implementing features similar to those of the `ResolveConcurrencyErrors` function is an *absolute requirement* for production applications.

Create and Manage Offline DataSets

Disconnected users must be provided with and maintain up-to-date offline datasets. Following are the basic actions required to maintain currency of offline DataSets:

- ❑ New disconnected users must obtain an initial DataSet from the server and save it to a local diffgram XML file. The following section describes how to establish the set of base-table records required for initial and subsequent DataSet load operations.

- ❑ During offline data entry, saving parent record changes or descendant record updates must resave the local diffgram file. Saving every change set ensures that updates don't disappear as a result of application crashes or power failures.

- ❑ Closing the application's main form must save the local diffgram file.

- ❑ When reconnecting, updating the base tables with offline changes should be automatic.

- ❑ After update operations complete, the offline user must retrieve a snapshot of the base-table contents to repopulate the local DataSet and save the diffgram file. Otherwise, only those records that the user has updated reflect current values.

Figure 5-8 is a simplified flow diagram that compares data-entry and update processing for connected-only and disconnected users while online. Procedure and function names are enclosed by parentheses.

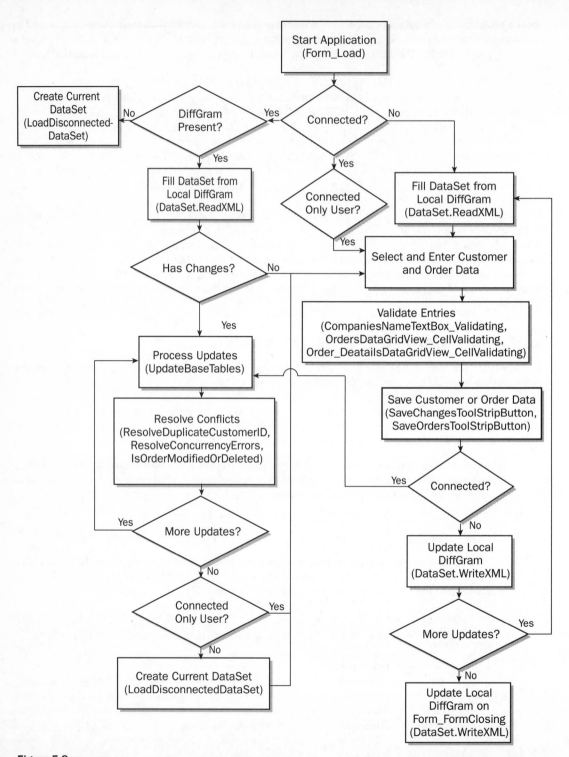

Figure 5-8

Right-click the form and click the Disconnected link to open Disconnected.htm in the ...\Help folder for detailed instructions on running the sample project in disconnected mode.

Enable Handling Multiple Parent Records

Connected users usually open a single parent record and retrieve its related descendant records from the server. Most disconnected users need to update more than a single parent and descendant record; a salesperson or caseworker might need offline records for a hundred or more clients. Following are the most important design considerations when altering an always-connected client front end to support disconnected users:

- ❑ Disconnected users' parent record choices are limited to those available in their offline DataSet. The sample project relies on a comma-separated list of CustomerID values — stored in User .config — to load the CustomerID dropdown list. (Connected users have a combo box that permits them to type any valid CustomerID in the list's text box.)

- ❑ If parent records are self-assigned, a simple form with a checked list box of parent records lets the user specify the records to include. (The sample project doesn't include this form.)

- ❑ If a supervisor assigns the parent-table list, the database must include an assignment table that the client application reads to create the initial DataSet and after completing the offline update process to handle assignment changes.

- ❑ Unless the application requires a complete history of a client's transactions, descendant records can be limited to a specific number of records, a time span, or a special field. Chapter 6 covers the use of SELECT TOP n FillBy queries or stored procedures to limit the number of descendant records.

Following is a summary of the most important sample application code changes required to accommodate updates by disconnected users:

- ❑ The CustomersTableAdapter.Count value can determine if a disconnected user has reconnected to the network. Disconnected users can operate in connected mode after applying their offline updates, so this isn't a reliable test for updating the local DataSet after offline updates complete. In the production version, you can test for online-only users by the absence of a local diffgram file.

- ❑ The Get Orders ToolStrip button isn't visible in disconnected mode. Changing the CustomerID list's SelectedIndex property calls the GetCustomerOrdersToolStripButton_Click event handler, which filters the CustomersBindingSource to include the appropriate row only (Task List comment 14).

- ❑ Changing the DataSource property value of the OrdersDataGridView from OrdersDataConnector to FK_Customers_OrdersDataConnector doesn't work. This issue requires applying the same filter to the OrdersBindingSource to include only the rows for the selected customer in the OrdersDataGridView.

- ❑ Adding a new customer requires setting the CustomersBindingSource.Filter value to Nothing or applying the RemoveFilter method, and supplying an invalid filter string to the OrdersBindingSource (Task List comment 15). These filters return no Orders or Order Details rows in the DataGridViews until the user saves the changes. Canceling the new customer entry displays the default Customers record and its related records.

❑   Processing offline updates requires synchronizing the form's contents with the current customer record by calling the SynchronizeOfflineOrders procedure (Task List comment 16).

Most changes to online-only code required to support disconnected users have a 'Flag: chkDisconnected modification *comment. The group of four procedures that are required to emulate disconnected users (and aren't applicable to connected-only users) is located at the end of the OrdersForm.vb file (Task List comment 17).*

Summary

Data validation is a basic requirement for all production database front ends. Validating data locally before sending updates to the back-end server saves roundtrips and minimizes the amount of code required to handle SqlExceptions for invalid entries. The OrdersByCustomerTx.sln sample project validates a single critical text box and a column value in the two DataGridViews. A production application would perform basic validation operations for most or all data entries before attempting an update. Best practices dictate that validation of data for conformance to business rules, such as quantity discounts, occurs in a middle tier.

Multi-user front ends require concurrency conflict detection and management. DBConcurrencyExceptions detect concurrency conflicts, but enabling users to decide whether to update their local DataSet to the server values or overwrite the server data requires a substantial amount of code. DBConcurrencyExceptions don't detect other users' additions or deletions of child records on the server, which is an important element of concurrency management. Attempts to add, modify, or delete child records that aren't present on the server throw SqlExceptions. Production-quality concurrency management requires handling child-record count mismatches. The capability to regenerate deleted orders is a useful adjunct to your data concurrency management strategy.

Users who have LAN access to the database server ordinarily update a single parent record or set of child and grandchild records during a session. Frequently or usually disconnected users often require multiple parent records and sets of related descendant records. Accommodating disconnected users, who work with DataSets that are persisted in a local diffgram file, requires additional code to manage the diffgram file and the server update process when the user reconnects to the network. Refreshing the reconnected user's diffgram file after processing offline updates is necessary to maintain DataSet currency.

6

Applying Advanced DataSet Techniques

DataSets and bound DataGridViews are the centerpieces of ADO.NET 2.0 data access and Visual Studio 2005 data tools. The preceding two chapters covered DataSet and bound Windows form control basics. This chapter extends the coverage of DataSet and DataGridView programming techniques with the following topics:

- ❑ Enabling lightweight, promotable transactions for updating base tables
- ❑ Adding columns to DataTables and DataGridViews from SELECT queries with an INNER JOIN
- ❑ Displaying and manipulating images in DataGridViews
- ❑ Generating DataSets from existing or inferred XML schemas
- ❑ Editing XML data documents with DataGridViews
- ❑ Creating and working with serializable object classes
- ❑ Binding DataGridViews to generic DataList collections

All but one of this chapter's project examples rely on the Northwind sample database to provide a sufficient number of records and variety of data types to demonstrate relative performance of the data access and editing techniques described. Examples that use simple base tables with a few rows and columns, and trivial XML source documents or schemas won't uncover the performance problems and other code design issues that this chapter demonstrates.

The SystemTransactions.sln and DataGridViewImages.sln examples require SQL Server 2005 or SQL Server Express with the Northwind and AdventureWorks sample databases installed. All other sample projects work with SQL Server 2000, MSDE, SQL Server 2005, or SQL Express and the Northwind database.

Apply Transactions to DataSet Updates

Almost all DBAs require update, insert, and delete operations on "their" production tables to be conducted with stored procedures that are wrapped in a transaction. The transaction ensures that all updates to each table in a batch operation succeed (commit) or fail (roll back) as a group. ADO.NET 1.0 introduced the IDbCommand.Transaction property and IDbTransaction interface to enable transacted updates to multiple tables, as described in Chapter 1's "Applying Transactions to Multi-Table Updates" section. SqlTransaction and OracleTransaction are native CLR objects; OleDbTransaction and OdbcTransaction are managed wrappers for OLE DB and ODBC COM–based transaction components.

Chapter 1's SqlTransaction example is relatively simple because a pair of SqlCommand.ExecuteNonQuery methods update the tables within a local transaction. However, ADO.NET 1.x DataSets require substantially more code to assign a single SqlTransaction object to the UpdateCommand.Transaction, InsertCommand.Transaction, and DeleteCommand.Transaction properties of multiple SqlDataAdapters. A typical ADO.NET 1.x procedure that performs base table updates from emulated user modifications to disconnected DataTables requires code to perform the following actions:

1. Create an untyped DataSet with an SqlDataAdapter for each table in the transaction.

2. Create a CommandBuilder to set each DataAdapter's ...Command property from the SelectCommand statement or stored procedure.

3. Open an SqlConnection, populate the DataTables with the DataAdapter.Fill method, and close the database connection.

4. Modify a few rows of each DataTable for test purposes.

5. Declare and initiate an SqlTransaction object.

6. Open the database connection and assign the SqlTransaction to the three data management language (DML) ...Command.Transaction properties of each DataAdapter.

7. Invoke the Update method on each DataAdapter, which executes the appropriate ...Command for the modified row's DataRowState property value—Added, Modified, or Deleted.

8. Commit the transaction if no exceptions are encountered; otherwise roll back the transaction, and close the database connection.

The following listing, which implements the preceding operations, emphasizes instructions that relate directly to SqlTransaction processing:

```
'Typical code to implement ADO.NET 1.x SqlTransactions for SqlDataAdapters
Dim trnUpdate As SqlTransaction = Nothing
Dim cnNwind As New SqlConnection(My.Settings.NorthwindConnectionString)
Dim dsNwind As New DataSet("dsNwind")
Try
    'Create DataAdapter, CommandBuilder, and generate/assign Commands
    Dim daOrders As New SqlDataAdapter("SELECT * FROM Orders " + _
        "WHERE OrderID > 11077;", cnNwind)
    Dim cbOrders As SqlCommandBuilder = New SqlCommandBuilder(daOrders)
    daOrders.UpdateCommand = cbOrders.GetUpdateCommand
    daOrders.InsertCommand = cbOrders.GetInsertCommand
    daOrders.DeleteCommand = cbOrders.GetDeleteCommand

    Dim daDetails As New SqlDataAdapter("SELECT * FROM [Order Details] " + _
```

```
                "WHERE OrderID > 11077;", cnNwind)
        Dim cbDetails As New SqlCommandBuilder(daDetails)
        daDetails.UpdateCommand = cbDetails.GetUpdateCommand
        daDetails.InsertCommand = cbDetails.GetInsertCommand
        daDetails.DeleteCommand = cbDetails.GetDeleteCommand

        'Fill the DataTables with DataAdapters
        cnNwind.Open()
        daOrders.Fill(dsNwind, "Orders")
        daDetails.Fill(dsNwind, "OrderDetails")
        cnNwind.Close()

        'Update the DataSet's Orders and OrderDetails DataTables (offline)
        Dim dtOrders As DataTable = dsNwind.Tables("Orders")
        Dim intRow As Integer
        For intRow = 0 To dtOrders.Rows.Count - 1
            If blnReset Then
                dtOrders.Rows(intRow).Item("ShippedDate") = DBNull.Value
            Else
                dtOrders.Rows(intRow).Item("ShippedDate") = Today.ToShortDateString
            End If
        Next intRow

        Dim dtDetails As DataTable = dsNwind.Tables("OrderDetails")
        For intRow = 0 To dtDetails.Rows.Count - 1
            If blnReset Then
                dtDetails.Rows(intRow).Item("Quantity") = _
                    dtDetails.Rows(intRow).Item("Quantity") - 1
            Else
                dtDetails.Rows(intRow).Item("Quantity") = _
                    dtDetails.Rows(intRow).Item("Quantity") + 1
            End If
        Next intRow

        If chkViolateConstraint.Checked Then
            'Create a foreign-key constraint to force a rollback
            dtDetails.Rows(intRow - 1).Item("OrderID") = 100
        End If

        cnNwind.Open()
        'Start a new Transaction and assign it to each Command
        trnUpdate = cnNwind.BeginTransaction
        daOrders.UpdateCommand.Transaction = trnUpdate
        daOrders.InsertCommand.Transaction = trnUpdate
        daOrders.DeleteCommand.Transaction = trnUpdate
        daOrders.Update(dsNwind, "Orders")

        daDetails.UpdateCommand.Transaction = trnUpdate
        daDetails.InsertCommand.Transaction = trnUpdate
        daDetails.DeleteCommand.Transaction = trnUpdate
        daDetails.Update(dsNwind, "OrderDetails")

        trnUpdate.Commit()
    Catch exc As Exception
        If trnUpdate IsNot Nothing Then
```

```
        trnUpdate.Rollback()
    End If
Finally
    cnNwind.Close()
End Try
```

If you don't explicitly set the `DataAdapter.TypeCommand` *property value with the* `CommandBuilder.GetTypeCommand` *method, enlisting the command in the transaction with the* `SQLDataAdapter.TypeCommand.Transaction` *property value fails.*

The SystemTransactions.sln project in the \VB2005DB\Chapter06\SystemTransactions folder contains the sample code for this and the following two sections. The Transactions.vb's `DataAdapterTransactions` procedure contains the preceding example. To execute the procedure, open, build, and run the project, and then click the Update button with the Show Updates in Grid checkbox marked. Code updates the Orders table's ShippedDate values to the current system date and adds one to the Order Details table's Quantity value for records that have an OrderID value greater than 11077 (see Figure 6-1). Click Reset to set updated ShippedDate values to Null and deduct one from Quantity values.

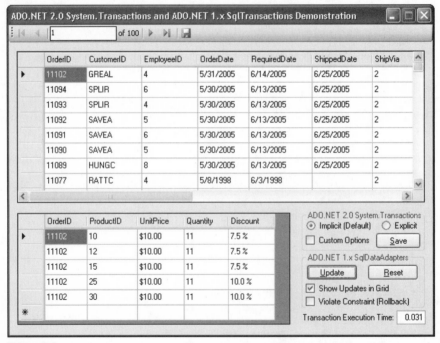

Figure 6-1

If you haven't added Orders and Order Details records to the Northwind sample database in earlier chapters, you must do this now to enable updates with SqlDataAdapters.

`IDbTransaction` implementations by ADO 1.*x* native data providers limit you to local transactions in a single database. Distributed transactions that the Distributed Transaction Coordinator (MSDTC) manages rely on the `System.EnterpriseServices` namespace and inheritance from `ServicedComponent`.

Simplify Enlistment with System.Transactions

The .NET Framework 2.0 adds the `System.Transactions` namespace, which defines several key classes that enhance ADO.NET 2.0 transaction capabilities and simplify programming. The most commonly used classes are `TransactionScope`, `Transaction`, and `CommittableTransaction`. The primary benefit that `System.Transactions` classes bring to transaction management is automatic enlistment of a local resource manager (RM), such as SQL Server 2005, in a transaction managed by a default Lightweight Transaction Manager (LTM). Subsequent enlistment of a remote RM automatically promotes the local transaction to a distributed transaction with an OleTx Transaction Manager (OTM). Enlistment of a local RM that doesn't support promotable transactions, such as SQL Server 2000, also promotes a lightweight transaction. The LTM offers high performance with minimal resource consumption; promotion to OTM and DTC exacts performance and resource penalties similar to those of ServicedComponents.

Autoenlist SqlDataAdapters in an Implicit Transaction

Taking advantage of .NET 2.0's new transaction model requires adding a project reference to the `System.Transactions` namespace and an `Imports System.Transactions` statement to your class file. You provide an enlistable ambient transaction by creating a `TransactionScope` object and assigning it to a `Using . . . End Using` block that encloses a `Try . . . End Try` block. (*Implicit transaction* is a synonym for ambient transaction.) Transactable methods—such as `SqlDataAdapter.Update` or `SqlTableAdapter.Update`—that you execute within the `Using` block automatically enlist in the transaction. If the methods succeed, executing the `TransactionScope.Complete` method and disposing the `TransactionScope` object by exiting the `Using` block commits the transaction. If a method throws an exception, exiting the `Using` block without executing the `TransactionScope.Complete` method rolls back the transaction.

The following procedure replaces the ten lines of code in the preceding listing (starting at `cnNwind.Open()`) that create the `SqlTransaction` object and enlists the `DataAdapter.TypeCommand` objects in the transaction:

```
'cnNwind.Open() 'Opening the connection here disables enlistment (no transaction)
Dim tsExplicit As New TransactionScope
Using tsExplicit
    Try
        'cnNwind.Open() 'Opening here uses one connection for the transaction
        daOrders.Update(dsNwind, "Orders")
        daDetails.Update(dsNwind, "OrderDetails")
        tsExplicit.Complete()
    Catch exc As Exception
        MsgBox(exc.Message)
    Finally
        cnNwind.Close()
    End Try
End Using
```

If you rely on the DataAdapters to open (and close) their connections automatically, the preceding `Using` block opens two SQL Server 2005 connections (usually SPID 51 and SPID 53) and promotes the transaction, which exacts a minor performance toll. Opening a single connection (cnNwind) explicitly before creating the ambient transaction with the `TransactionScope` constructor disables transactions for the `Update` methods. Opening the connection explicitly after creating the ambient transaction executes both `Update` operations on the same connection (usually SPID 51), which maximizes execution speed.

> *To execute the preceding example with the sample SystemTransactions.sln project, set* `blnSysTran = True` *in the* `DataAdapterTransactions` *procedure and click the Update or Reset buttons. You can verify that the Update operations are transacted by marking the Violate Constraint (Rollback) checkbox, clicking Update, and verifying that a single Order Details table foreign-key constraint violation rolls back all changes to the Orders and Order Details table.*

Autoenlist SqlTableAdapters in an Implicit Transaction

This snippet performs a transacted update of two ADO.NET 2.0 SqlTableAdapters by autoenlisting their `Update` methods within an LTM:

```
Dim tsImplicit As New TransactionScope
Using tsImplicit
   Try
       'Adapter opens connections automatically
       Me.Order_DetailsTableAdapter.Update(Me.NorthwindDataSet.Order_Details)
       Me.OrdersTableAdapter.Update(Me.NorthwindDataSet.Orders)
       tsImplicit.Complete()
   Catch exc As Exception
       'Error handling
   Finally
       'Adapter closes connections automatically
   End Try
End Using
```

As is the case for ADO.NET 1.*x* SqlDataAdapters, ADO.NET 2.0 SqlTableAdapters automatically open two connections, which promotes the ambient transaction. The following snippet opens a single connection and assigns it to both SqlTableAdapters to prevent promoting the transaction:

```
Dim tsImplicit As New TransactionScope
Using tsImplicit
   Try
       'Open a single connection and assign it to both SqlTableAdapters
       Dim cnNwind As New SqlConnection(My.Settings.NorthwindConnectionString)
       cnNwind.Open()
       Me.Order_DetailsTableAdapter.Connection = cnNwind
       Me.OrdersTableAdapter.Connection = cnNwind
       Me.Order_DetailsTableAdapter.Update(Me.NorthwindDataSet.Order_Details)
       Me.OrdersTableAdapter.Update(Me.NorthwindDataSet.Orders)
       tsImplicit.Complete()
   Catch exc As Exception
       'Error handling
   Finally
       cnNwind.Close()
   End Try
End Using
```

To open a single connection for implicit transactions, set `blnOpenConnection = True` *in the* `bindingNavigatorSaveData` *event handler, modify an Orders record and at least one of its Order Details records, and click the Save button or the Save Data toolbar button.*

Use SQL Profiler to Trace Transactions

SQL Server 2005's Profiler tool has been updated for new features, such as promotable transactions. To trace `BEGIN TRAN`, `PROMOTE TRAN`, `COMMIT TRAN`, and `ROLLBACK TRAN` events, you must add these events from the Transactions category to the default T-SQL or a similar customized trace template. Figure 6-2 shows an SQL Profiler trace of a transacted SqlTableAdapter update with autogenerated connections that result in promoting the transaction. Figure 6-3 illustrates the same transaction with a single, explicit transaction assigned as the Connection property value of the two SqlTableAdapters.

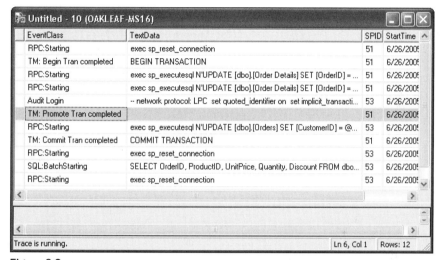

Figure 6-2

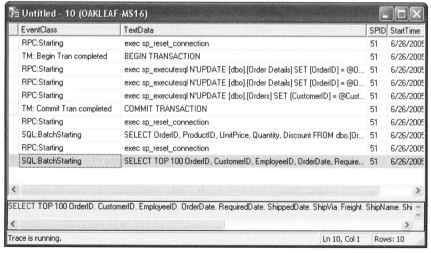

Figure 6-3

SQL Server Express Edition doesn't include or support the use of SQL Profiler. You can, however, use the Component Services Manager to count instances of the distributed transactions that result from promoting implicit transactions or executing explicit transactions, which are the subject of the next section. Figure 6-4 shows the Component Services Manager displaying statistics for 94 promoted transactions generated by the sample project. Notice that the average response time for the distributed transactions is about 4 seconds. Transaction items appear in the Transaction List window only while they are active.

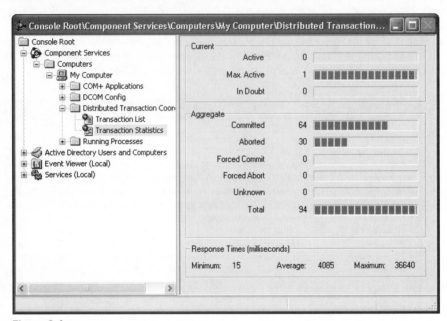

Figure 6-4

You can open the Component Services Manager from the Programs\Administrative Tools menu or from Control Panel's Administrative Tools list.

Manually Enlist SqlTableAdapters in an Explicit Transaction

If you prefer the "traditional" transaction model with explicit enlistment of transacted objects and granular control of `Commit` or `Rollback` method invocations, you can employ the `CommittableTransaction` object, as shown in the following snippet:

```
'Open and enlist connection(s) in an explicit transaction
Dim tsExplicit As New CommittableTransaction
Try
    Me.Order_DetailsTableAdapter.Connection.Open()
    Me.OrdersTableAdapter.Connection.Open()
    Me.Order_DetailsTableAdapter.Connection.EnlistTransaction(tsExplicit)
    Me.OrdersTableAdapter.Connection.EnlistTransaction(tsExplicit)
    Me.Order_DetailsTableAdapter.Update(Me.NorthwindDataSet.Order_Details)
```

```
        Me.OrdersTableAdapter.Update(Me.NorthwindDataSet.Orders)
        tsExplicit.Commit()
    Catch exc As Exception
        tsExplicit.Rollback()
    Finally
        Me.OrdersTableAdapter.Connection.Close()
        Me.Order_DetailsTableAdapter.Connection.Close()
    End Try
```

Explicit (committable) transaction wrappers for SqlTableAdapter updates default to distributed transactions. Promotion occurs when your code enlists a second `SqlTableAdapter.Connection` object in the transaction.

Set TransactionScope and Transaction Options

The `TransactionScope` constructor has seven overloads, but the following two overloads are the most useful for database transactions:

```
Public Sub New(ByVal scopeOption As System.Transactions.TransactionScopeOption,
    ByVal scopeTimeout As System.TimeSpan)
Public Sub New(ByVal scopeOption As System.Transactions.TransactionScopeOption,
    ByVal transactionOptions As System.Transactions.TransactionOptions)
```

The `TransactionScopeOption` enum has the following three members:

```
TransactionScopeOption.Requires
TransactionScopeOption.RequiresNew
TransactionScopeOption.Suppress
```

The default is `Requires` (a transaction). Specify `Suppress` if you don't want the `TransactionScope` to use the ambient transaction.

Following are the two `TransactionScopeOption` members:

```
TransactionOption.IsolationLevel
TransactionOption.Timeout
```

`IsolationLevel` defaults to `Serializable`, but can be any of the seven members listed in the table of Chapter 1's "Applying Transactions to Multi-Table Updates" section. Only SQL Server 2005 supports `Snapshot` isolation. The default `Timeout` value is 1 minute.

Marking the sample application's Custom Options checkbox changes the `TransactionScopeOption` *to* `RequiresNew`, `IsolationLevel` *to* `RepeatableRead`, *and* `Timeout` *to a* `TimeSpan` *of 15 seconds.*

Add Joins to DataTable Select Commands

DataSets make updates to individual tables, but that doesn't mean you can't add joins to the `SelectCommand` for a table. Joins let you improve users' editing experiences by adding read-only columns from a many-to-one join with a related table. As an example, adding ProductName, QuantityPerUnit, and UnitPrice columns of the Northwind Products table to a DataGridView of Order Details items improves readability and minimizes data entry errors. You can use the UnitPrice column of the Products table to provide default values for new records and update the UnitPrice column of the Order Details table for ProductID changes.

> *Adding columns from many-to-one joins isn't a full-fledged substitute for combo box columns populated by lookup lists. The technique described in Chapter 4's "Add a Combo Box That Sets Additional Values" section usually is a better approach for data entry forms if the number of items in the combo box's list is less than 100.*

This section's sample project — SelectCommandJoins.sln — demonstrates how to add joins to SelectCommands and take advantage of the many-to-one relationship to simplify updating the Order Details base table. The project starts with a data source from the Northwind database that includes the Orders, Order Details, and Products tables. Data components include autogenerated Orders and Order_Details DataGridViews, TableAdapters, and BindingSources. The Products table provides the ProductName and UnitPrice data that's required for new and edited Order Details records.

> *The SelectCommandJoins.sln example is in the VB2005DB \Chapter06\SelectCommandJoins folder and assumes that the Northwind database is accessible from the* localhost *server.*

Add the ProductsTableAdapter and ProductsBindingSource to the tray by dragging the Products table icon from the Data Sources window to the Join.vb form, and then delete the ProductsDataGridView that's added to the form.

Add a Join to the SelectCommand

Following are the steps to add an INNER JOIN between the Order Details and Products tables for the Fill operation:

1. In the DataSet Editor window, right-click the Order Details TableAdapter header and choose Properties.

2. In the Properties tool window, expand the SelectCommand node, click the CommandText node, and click the builder button to open the QueryBuilder dialog.

3. Right-click the tables pane, choose Add Table, and add the Products table.

4. Select the Product table's ProductName, QuantityPerUnit, and UnitPrice columns.

5. Change `dbo.Products.UnitPrice AS Expr1` to `dbo.Products.UnitPrice AS ListPrice` (see Figure 6-5).

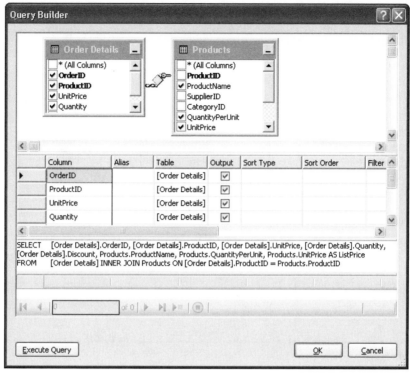

Figure 6-5

6. Click Execute Query to display the resultset in the grid.

7. Click OK to close the QueryBuilder dialog, and click No when asked if you want to regenerate the update commands based on the new select command.

8. Right-click the [Order Details] header and choose AutoSize to display the ProductName, ListPrice, and QuantityPerUnit columns (see Figure 6-6).

9. Open the Properties tool window and verify that the CommandText SQL statement for the DeleteCommand, InsertCommand, and UpdateCommand nodes includes columns of the Order Details table only.

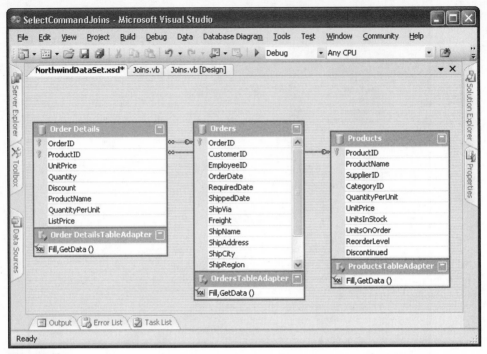

Figure 6-6

> Don't run the Data Component Configuration Wizard for the Order Details table
> after changing the SelectCommand. Doing this might remove the DeleteCommand,
> InsertCommand, and UpdateCommand of the Order_DetailsTableAdapter.

Following is the SelectCommand's CommandText property value:

```
SELECT dbo.[Order Details].OrderID, dbo.[Order Details].ProductID,
    dbo.[Order Details].UnitPrice, dbo.[Order Details].Quantity,
    dbo.[Order Details].Discount, dbo.Products.ProductName,
    dbo.Products.UnitPrice AS ListPrice, dbo.Products.QuantityPerUnit
FROM dbo.[Order Details] INNER JOIN
    dbo.Products ON dbo.[Order Details].ProductID = dbo.Products.ProductID
```

Add the Joined Columns to the DataGridView

You must add the Products table's columns manually by right-clicking the Order_DetailsDataGridView
and choosing Edit Columns to open the same-named dialog. Click Add Columns and add the
ProductName column after ProductID. Add the QuantityPerUnit and List Price columns, and format
the columns using the techniques described in Chapter 4's "Format the OrdersDataGridView Columns"
section. Set the ReadOnly property for these three columns to True and change the column order to
OrderID, Quantity, ProductID, ProductName, QuantityPerUnit, ListPrice, UnitPrice, and Discount.

Provide Default Values and Update Read-Only Columns

Navigating the Products DataTable to supply ProductName, QuantityPerUnit, and UnitPrice values, and—optionally—to test the Discontinued field value requires the ProductsBindingSource you added in the section "Add Joins to DataTable Select Commands," earlier in this chapter. Set the ProductsBindingSource's AllowNew property value to False, and verify that the DataSource is NorthwindDataSet, and DataMember is Products.

The following event handler supplies intentionally invalid default values and displays an error icon when you add a new Order Details item:

```
Private Sub Order_DetailsDataGridView_DefaultValuesNeeded(ByVal sender As Object, _
    ByVal e As System.Windows.Forms.DataGridViewRowEventArgs) _
    Handles Order_DetailsDataGridView.DefaultValuesNeeded
    'Set invalid default values
    With e.Row
        'Illegal Quantity
        .Cells(1).Value = 0
        'Illegal ProductID
        .Cells(2).Value = 0
        'ProductName
        .Cells(3).Value = "ProductID not selected"
        'Quantity per Unit
        .Cells(4).Value = "Not applicable"
        'ListPrice
        .Cells(5).Value = 0D
        'UnitPrice
        .Cells(6).Value = 0D
        'Discount
        .Cells(7).Value = 0D
        .ErrorText = "Default values: You must enter ProductID and Quantity."
    End With
End Sub
```

If the Products table doesn't have a uniform correspondence between the ProductID value and row number, you can apply a ProductID = intProductID.ToString *filter to the ProductsBindingSource and obtain* drvItems *from the single row.*

This handler for the CellValueChanged event displays error icons for invalid ProductID, Quantity, or both values, and discontinued products:

```
Private Sub Order_DetailsDataGridView_CellValueChanged(ByVal sender As Object, _
    ByVal e As System.Windows.Forms.DataGridViewCellEventArgs) _
    Handles Order_DetailsDataGridView.CellValueChanged
    If blnIsLoaded AndAlso e.ColumnIndex = 2 Then
        'User edited ProductID value
        With Order_DetailsDataGridView
            'Clear error icon
            .Rows(e.RowIndex).ErrorText = ""
            'Get the new ProductID value
            Dim intProductID As Integer = _
```

```
                   CType(.Rows(e.RowIndex).Cells(2).Value, Integer)
            Dim srtQuantity As Short = CType(.Rows(e.RowIndex).Cells(1).Value, Short)
            If intProductID = 0 OrElse intProductID > ProductsBindingSource.Count Then
                'Bad ProductID value
                .Rows(e.RowIndex).ErrorText = "ProductID value must be between " + _
                "1 and " + ProductsBindingSource.Count.ToString
                Return
            End If
            'Get the required data from the ProductsBindingSource
            Dim drvItem As DataRowView
            drvItem = CType(ProductsBindingSource(intProductID - 1), DataRowView)
            If CBool(drvItem.Item(9)) Then
                'Discontinued products (5, 9, 17, 24, 28, 29, 42, 53)
                .Rows(e.RowIndex).ErrorText = "ProductID " + intProductID.ToString + _
                " (" + drvItem.Item(1).ToString + ") is discontinued."
            Else
                'ProductName
                .Rows(e.RowIndex).Cells(3).Value = drvItem.Item(1)
                'Quantity per Unit
                .Rows(e.RowIndex).Cells(4).Value = drvItem.Item(4)
                'ListPrice
                .Rows(e.RowIndex).Cells(5).Value = drvItem.Item(5)
                'UnitPrice
                .Rows(e.RowIndex).Cells(6).Value = drvItem.Item(5)
                'Discount
                .Rows(e.RowIndex).Cells(7).Value = 0D
                If srtQuantity = 0 Then
                    .Rows(e.RowIndex).ErrorText = "Quantity of 0 is not permitted."
                End If
            End If
        End With
    End If
End Sub
```

Figure 6-7 shows the SelectCommandJoins.sln sample project's Joins.vb form in the process of adding a new Order Details line item. The next sections describe the purpose of the controls above the Orders DataGridView.

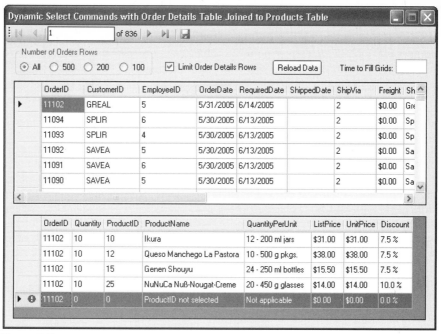

Figure 6-7

Improve Performance by Reducing DataSet Size

Loading DataSets and populating DataGridViews with unneeded records can cause a substantial performance hit on servers and clients, especially when recreating large persisted DataSets for disconnected users. The following sections describe how to reduce server load and local resource consumption, and improve data-editing performance by limiting the number of rows returned by `DataTableAdapter` `.Fill` operations. Conventional `TOP` n queries based on descending sorts of `int identity` and `datetime` column values are suitable for most connected and disconnected clients. Paging techniques further minimize resource consumption and provide access to older data for connected users.

Limit Rows Returned with TOP n Queries

The most obvious approach to limiting the number of records returned by Fill operations is to add a TOP n or TOP n PERCENT modifier and appropriate ORDER BY clause to the TableAdapter's SQL query for the SelectCommand. For example, the following SQL query loads the last 100 rows of the Orders table to populate the SelectCommandJoins.sln sample project's Orders DataGridView:

```
SELECT TOP 100 OrderID, CustomerID, EmployeeID, OrderDate, RequiredDate,
    ShippedDate, ShipVia, Freight, ShipName, ShipAddress, ShipCity, ShipRegion,
    ShipPostalCode, ShipCountry
FROM dbo.Orders ORDER BY OrderID DESC
```

When you apply TOP n queries to a parent table, you should do the same to TableAdapter.Fill operations for child tables. The Order Details SelectCommand query of the earlier "Add a Join to the SelectCommand" section loads all extended Order Details rows into the Order_DetailsDataTable, which consumes much more resources than necessary. You add an IN predicate with a *subselect* — also called a *subquery* — to return only those child rows that depend on the Orders rows, as emphasized in the following query:

```
SELECT dbo.[Order Details].OrderID, dbo.[Order Details].ProductID,
    dbo.[Order Details].UnitPrice, dbo.[Order Details].Quantity,
    dbo.[Order Details].Discount, dbo.Products.ProductName,
    dbo.Products.QuantityPerUnit, dbo.Products.UnitPrice AS ListPrice
FROM dbo.[Order Details] INNER JOIN
    dbo.Products ON dbo.[Order Details].ProductID = dbo.Products.ProductID
WHERE dbo.[Order Details].OrderID IN (SELECT TOP 100 dbo.Orders.OrderID
    FROM dbo.Orders ORDER BY dbo.Orders.OrderID DESC)
```

SQL Server 2005 and SQL Express let you substitute bigint *or* float *variables for literal TOP n [PERCENT] queries. This chapter's examples use literal values to ensure compatibility with SQL Server or MSDE 2000.*

Add Partial Classes for TableAdapters

TableAdapter classes aren't nested in ADO.NET 2.0 DataSets. Instead, TableAdapters have their own namespace to prevent collision of duplicate autogenerated class names. Autogenerated namespace names are DataSetNameTableAdapters — such as NorthwindDataSetTableAdapters, which contains Partial Public Class OrdersTableAdapter, Public Class Order_DetailsTableAdapter, and Public Class ProductsTableAdapter. Substituting dynamic SQL SELECT statements for the SelectCommand that you add in the query designer requires overloading the Fill method and passing the variable CommandText property value as a second argument. If you add the overload signature to the DataSet's partial classes you lose the additions when regenerating the DataSet. Thus, you must add a partial class file to the project — TableAdapters.vb for this example — that contains code similar to the following:

```
Namespace NorthwindDataSetTableAdapters
    Partial Class OrdersTableAdapter
        Public Overloads Function Fill(ByVal DataTable As
                NorthwindDataSet.OrdersDataTable, _
            ByVal strSelect As String) As Integer
            Me.Adapter.SelectCommand = Me.CommandCollection(0)
            'Replace the CommandText
```

```
                    Me.Adapter.SelectCommand.CommandText = strSelect
                    If (Me.m_clearBeforeFill = True) Then
                        DataTable.Clear()
                    End If
                    Dim returnValue As Integer = Me.Adapter.Fill(DataTable)
                    Return returnValue
                End Function
            End Class


        Partial Class Order_DetailsTableAdapter
            Public Overloads Function Fill(ByVal DataTable As
        _           NorthwindDataSet.Order_DetailsDataTable, _
                    ByVal strSelect As String) As Integer
                Me.Adapter.SelectCommand = Me.CommandCollection(0)
                'Replace the CommandText
                Me.Adapter.SelectCommand.CommandText = strSelect
                If (Me.m_clearBeforeFill = True) Then
                    DataTable.Clear()
                End If
                Dim returnValue As Integer = Me.Adapter.Fill(DataTable)
                Return returnValue
            End Function
        End Class
    End Namespace
```

Marking the sample project's Limit Order Details Rows checkbox and clicking Reload Data adds the subselect predicate to the `Order_DetailsDataTable.SelectCommand`. You probably won't notice a substantial load time difference between the two query types because the `IN` predicate increases query execution time. However, the IN predicate decreases the persisted DataSet's size from about 824KB for all to 182KB for 100 Orders rows.

Clicking the DataNavigator's Save Data button saves the DataSet to AllDetails.xml with the checkbox cleared, and Subselect.xml with the checkbox marked.

Work with Images in DataGridViews

DataGridViews require a `DataGridViewImageColumn` to display images returned from tables that contain graphics stored as binary data, such as in SQL Server `image` or `varbinary` columns. `DataGridViewImageColumns` contain a `DataGridViewImageCell` for each row. By default, cells without images (null values) display Internet Explorer's graphic for an HTML link to a missing image file. `DataGridViewImageColumns` share most properties and methods of other data types, but add two properties, `Image` and `ImageLayout`, which are specific to graphics. The `Image` property lets you specify a default image from MyResources.resx or another resource file. The `ImageLayout` property lets you select a member of the `DataGridViewImageCellLayout` enumeration—`NotSet`, `Normal`, `Stretch`, or `Zoom`. The members correspond approximately to the PictureBox's `SizeMode` enumeration. As you would expect, `Normal` is the default that centers the image with its native resolution.

Like PictureBoxes, `DataGridViewImageColumns` support BMP, GIF, JPEG, PNG, and WMF image formats.

Add Image Columns to DataGridViews

When you create a data source from a table with an `image` or `varbinary` column, the data sources window displays the column's node as disabled. When you drag the table node onto the form to autogenerate a DataGridView, DataSet, and other data components, the DataGridView doesn't display a `DataGridViewImageColumn` for the bitmap.

To add the missing image column to the DataGridView, right-click the DataGridView and choose Edit Columns to open the dialog of the same name. Click Add Column to open the dialog, and, with the Databound Column option button selected, select the column and click Add (see Figure 6-8). Then specify a `Width` property value that's appropriate to your DataGridView design. Alternatively, select `Rows` as the `AutoSizeCriteria` property value. Set the DataGridView's `AutoSizeRowsMode` property value to `AllCellsExceptHeaders` initially. After an initial test, you can set the `RowTemplate.Height` property to a value that maintains the image aspect ratio with the column's `Width` value.

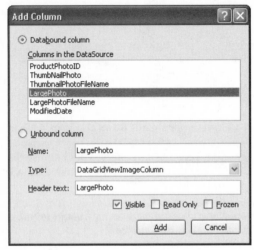

Figure 6-8

The SQL Server 2005 AdventureWorks sample database's ProductPhoto table provides the data source for this section's project example—DataGridViewImagesAW.sln. The ProductPhoto table has ThumbNailPhoto and LargePhoto `varbinary` columns that contain 101 GIF bitmaps; the size of the LargePhoto bitmaps for the DataGridView is 240 pixels by 149 pixels. Figure 6-9 shows three columns of the first two rows of the table in `Normal ImageLayout`.

The connection string of the DataGridViewImagesAW.sln in the VB2005DB\Chapter06\ DataGridViewImagesAW folder points to a specific instance of SQL Server 2005. If you have the AdventureWorks sample database installed, change the connection string on the Settings page of the DataGridViewImagesAW Properties dialog. If not, open ProductPhoto.vb in the editor, and change the value of `blnLoadFromFile` *to* `True` *to load the AdventureWorksDataSet from ProductPhoto.xml.*

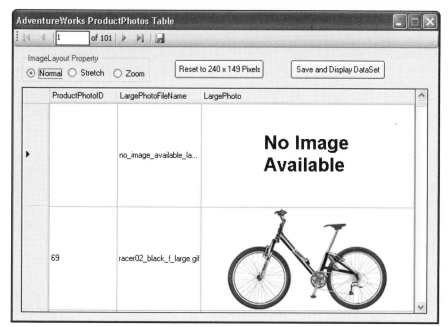

Figure 6-9

Manipulate DataGridView Images

Code added to the ProductPhoto class lets you test the effect of ImageLayout changes to the appearance of the images, save a selected DataGridViewImageCell's contents to its corresponding LargePhotoFileName (.gif) file, display an image in a PictureBox, and replace the selected image with a copy from the saved file.

Change ImageLayout

By default, the LargePhoto column's width and the rows' height match the dimensions of the images. To test the three image modes, drag the right edge of the column headers to the right border of the DataGridView, and then select the Stretch radio button to distort the image by changing its aspect ratio. Selecting Zoom sets the AutoSizeRowsMode property value to DataGridViewAutoSizeRowsMode.None, which lets you manipulate the row height and column width to demonstrate image resizing while retaining the bitmaps' common aspect ratio. The following handlers respond to the radio buttons' CheckChanged event:

```
Private Sub rbNormal_CheckedChanged(ByVal sender As System.Object, _
    ByVal e As System.EventArgs) Handles rbNormal.CheckedChanged
    'Normal layout
    If blnLoaded And rbNormal.Checked Then
        With ProductPhotoDataGridView
            Dim colImage As DataGridViewImageColumn = _
                CType(.Columns(2), DataGridViewImageColumn)
            colImage.ImageLayout = DataGridViewImageCellLayout.Normal
            .AutoSizeRowsMode = DataGridViewAutoSizeRowsMode.ColumnsAllRows
        End With
```

```
        End If
    End Sub

    Private Sub rbStretch_CheckedChanged(ByVal sender As System.Object, _
        ByVal e As System.EventArgs) Handles rbStretch.CheckedChanged
        'Stretch layout
        If blnLoaded And rbStretch.Checked Then
            With ProductPhotoDataGridView
                Dim colImage As DataGridViewImageColumn = _
                    CType(.Columns(2), DataGridViewImageColumn)
                colImage.ImageLayout = DataGridViewImageCellLayout.Stretch
                .AutoSizeRowsMode = DataGridViewAutoSizeRowsMode.ColumnsAllRows
            End With
        End If
    End Sub

    Private Sub rbZoom_CheckedChanged(ByVal sender As System.Object, _
        ByVal e As System.EventArgs) Handles rbZoom.CheckedChanged
        'Zoom layout
        If blnLoaded And rbZoom.Checked Then
            With ProductPhotoDataGridView
                Dim colImage As DataGridViewImageColumn = _
                    CType(.Columns(2), DataGridViewImageColumn)
                colImage.ImageLayout = DataGridViewImageCellLayout.Zoom
                .AutoSizeRowsMode = DataGridViewAutoSizeRowsMode.None
            End With
        End If
    End Sub
```

Save a Selected Image to a File, Display It in a PictureBox, and Replace It from a File

Manipulating image data in DataGridViews isn't an intuitive process. The `Value` property of a `DataGridViewImageCell` has an underlying data type of `Byte()`, not the expected `Image` data type. You must cast `Value` to `Byte()` and then create a `FileStream` instance to save the `Byte` array to a corresponding *LargePhotoFileName*.gif file. Creating a `MemoryStream` instance to supply the `Image` property of the `frmPictureBox` form's PictureBox is more efficient than loading the PictureBox from the saved file. Replacing the original image with a copy from the saved file takes advantage of the `File.ReadAllBytes` method to simplify reading a file of unknown length. These operations are emphasized in the following `SaveGifFile` procedure that's called by the `bindingNavigatorSaveItem_Click` event handler:

```
    Private Sub SaveGifFile()
        'Save the selected file
        Dim strFile As String = Nothing
        Try
            With ProductPhotoDataGridView
                If .CurrentCell.ColumnIndex = 2 Then
                    If Not frmPictureBox Is Nothing Then
                        frmPictureBox.Close()
                    End If
                    'Create a Byte array from the value
                    Dim bytImage() As Byte = CType(.CurrentCell.Value, Byte())
                    'Specify the image file name
                    Dim intRow As Integer = .CurrentCell.RowIndex
```

```
                    strFile = .Rows(intRow).Cells(1).Value.ToString
                    'Save the image as a GIF file
                    Dim fsImage As New FileStream("..\" + strFile, FileMode.Create)
                    fsImage.Write(bytImage, 0, bytImage.Length)
                    fsImage.Close()

                    'Create a MemoryStream and assign it as the image of a PictureBox
                    Dim msImage As New MemoryStream(bytImage)
                    frmPictureBox.pbBitmap.Image = Image.FromStream(msImage)

                    If frmPictureBox.ShowDialog = Windows.Forms.DialogResult.Yes Then
                        'Replace the CurrentCell's image from the saved version, if possible
                        If File.Exists("..\" + strFile) Then
                            'The easy was to obtain a Byte array
                            Dim bytReplace() As Byte = File.ReadAllBytes("..\" + strFile)
                            .CurrentCell.Value = bytReplace
                            If AdventureWorksDataSet.HasChanges Then
                                AdventureWorksDataSet.AcceptChanges()
                                Dim strMsg As String = "File '" + strFile + _
                                    " has replaced the image in row " + intRow.ToString + _
                                    " cell 2 (" + Format(bytReplace.Length, "#,##0") + _
                                    " bytes). " + vbCrLf + vbCrLf + _
                                    "AcceptChanges has been applied to the DataSet."
                                MsgBox(strMsg, MsgBoxStyle.Information, _
                                    "Image Replaced from File")
                            Else
                                Dim strMsg As String = "Unable to replace image " + _
                                    "with file '" + strFile + "'. DataSet does not have changes."
                                MsgBox(strMsg, MsgBoxStyle.Exclamation, "Image Not Replaced")
                            End If
                        End If
                    End If
                Else
                    MsgBox("Please select the image to save.", MsgBoxStyle.Exclamation, _
                        "No Image Selected")
                End If
            End With
        Catch exc As Exception
            With ProductPhotoDataGridView
                If strFile = Nothing Then
                    Dim intRow As Integer = .CurrentCell.RowIndex
                    strFile = .Rows(intRow).Cells(1).Value.ToString
                End If
            End With
            Dim strExc As String = "File '" + strFile + "' threw the following " + _
                "exception: " + exc.Message
            MsgBox(strExc, MsgBoxStyle.Exclamation, "Exception with Image")
        End Try
    End Sub
```

Some images, such as ProductPhotoID 77, appear in the PictureBox but won't replace the original image.

Figure 6-10 shows the ProductPhotoColumn displaying three images zoomed to approximately 25 percent, 50 percent, and 125 percent, and frmPictureBox open with the topmost image selected. In this case, the row height determines the size of the zoomed image.

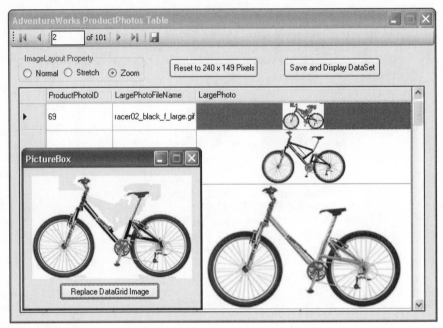

Figure 6-10

The transparency RGB value doesn't correspond to the white background, so the selected image shows shaded areas as transparent.

Avoid Creating Images from Access OLE Object Fields

The SQL Server 2000 Northwind sample database contains Categories and Employees tables that were imported from an earlier Access version. The Categories table's Picture column and Employees table's Photo column have the image data type, but the BMP-format bitmaps have an OLE Object wrapper. The images appear in the DataGridView, but the wrapper makes it impossible to display the images in a PictureBox or save the file in BMP format.

The DataGridViewImagesNW.sln project in the VB2005DB\Chapter06\DataGridViewImagesNW folder connects to SQL Server 2000's Northwind sample database with localhost as the server name. You receive an "Invalid parameter used" exception message when attempting to save the image to a CategoryName.bmp file.

Edit XML Documents with DataSets and DataGridViews

The emergence of XML documents as the newly predominate data interchange format has created a requirement for client applications that enable users to review, edit, and create XML Infosets. Business documents that use XML Infosets to represent tabular data with a hierarchy of one or more one-to-many relationships are common in customer relationship management (CRM), supply chain management (SCM), and other business applications or platforms, such as BizTalk Server 2004. These applications seek to minimize human intervention in their automated workflow processes, but manual document processing is inevitable in most business activities.

Microsoft Word, Excel, and InfoPath 2003 provide XML document editing capability, but hierarchical documents with multiple one-to-many relationships are difficult to edit in Word or Excel. Access 2003 lets you import an XML schema to create tables with designated data types, establish keys and relationships, append and edit data, and then export the tables or a query to an XML file. However, an exported hierarchical XML document's structure bears no relationship whatsoever to the source document's structure. Writing an XML transform to regenerate the original document structure is likely to involve more trouble than it's worth. InfoPath 2003 handles hierarchical document editing and preserves document structure, but its HTML-based forms have a limited control repertoire and, like other Office 2003 members, InfoPath 2003 requires a client license for each user.

Users accustomed to editing database tables with Windows forms created with any version of Visual Studio undoubtedly will prefer a similar — or identical — UI for editing tabular XML Infosets with DataGridView controls and, where applicable, bound text boxes or other Windows form controls. You can't bind DataGridView controls to XML documents directly, so you should try to generate a DataSet from the document's schema. If you don't have the schema or the schema won't generate a DataSet, you can use VS 2005's XML Editor to attempt to infer a schema from the document's contents.

Adapt an Existing XML Schema to Generate a DataSet

Microsoft designed DataSets to store relational data in DataTables; the XML representation of DataSets and their DataTables is intended primarily as a persistence or remoting mechanism. Thus, XML documents that serve as the source data for DataSets must have a schema that DataSets can accommodate. Following are the most important considerations for using existing schemas to generate typed DataSets:

❑ The DataSet designer assigns the top-level (root or document) element name as the DataSet name. If the schema contains a global namespace declaration, it becomes the DataSet's namespace.

❑ Subsequent elements that have child elements or child elements with attributes generate DataTables. This feature accommodates attribute-centric documents, such as the XML representation of ADO Recordsets, but can result in generating a DataTable for an attribute instead of a column.

❑ Child elements that represent DataTable columns must have simple XSD datatypes that correspond to .NET System data types.

❑ DataSets are element-centric; if your schema specifies attributes at the DataTable level, the DataSet designer adds the attributes as DataTable columns.

❏ Schemas with nested child-element groups establish one-to-many relationships between DataTables automatically and add a *TableName*_Id primary-key and foreign-key column for each relationship to the DataTable. The primary-key *TableName*_Id is an Int32 AutoIncrement column; reading an XML document into the DataSet generates the *TableName*_Id values.

❏ If the child-element groups aren't nested, you must specify the relationships between DataTables in the DataSet Editor.

❏ If you need to load the DataTables from individual, related XML source documents, your schema must not specify a nested DataTable relationship.

❏ The DataSet designer has problems importing secondary schemas to support multiple namespaces and namespace-qualified elements. The DataSet designer uses the XML Schema Definition Tool (Xsd.exe) to generate typed DataSets. Xsd.exe doesn't use the `<xs:import>` `schemaLocation` attribute to load secondary schemas automatically.

The preceding restrictions make it difficult or impossible to generate typed DataSets from complex XML schemas for standardized business documents, such as Universal Business Language (UBL) 1.0 or Human Resources XML (HR-XML). UBL 1.0 schemas make extensive use of `<xs:import>` directives and specify complex types for elements that represent DataTable columns.

> *You can learn more about UBL 1.0 at* `http://www.oasis-open.org/committees/tc_home` `.php?wg_abbrev=ubl`*. Click the Documents link to download the current draft of the UBL 1.0 specification, schemas, and sample source document instances.*

> *The HR-XML Consortium at* `http://www.hr-xml.org/` *offers all current HR-XML schemas and sample source document instances in a single download (registration required).*

Most XML editing applications must produce an output document with the same structure as the source document, which implies that the edits affect only the elements' contents. The tabular structure of DataSets enables exporting the entire content or selected rows of individual tables to XML streams or files. You also can generate DataSets from individual related source documents with structures that are defined by a single schema.

If your application must restructure the output document, you can apply an XSLT transform to the final edited version of the document. Alternatively, you can synchronize the DataSet with an `XmlDataDocument` instance and apply the transform to the instance.

Schemas for Nested Hierarchical XML Data Documents

The ideal structure for a DataSet's source document is an XML Infoset that has a nested hierarchy of related elements. The DataSet designer automatically generates DataSets from compatible schemas for nested documents. The following abbreviated XML document is typical of XML files generated by serializing a set of business-related objects into a three-level hierarchy:

```
<rootElement>
  <parentGroup>
    <parentField1>String</parentField1>
    ...
    <parentFieldN>1000</parentFieldN>
```

```
      <childGroup>
        <childField1>String</childField1>
        ...
        <childFieldN>15.50</childFieldN>
        <grandchildGroup>
          <grandchildField1>String</grandchildField1>
          ...
          <grandchildFieldN>15</grandchildFieldN>
        </grandchildGroup>
      </childGroup>
    </parentGroup>
</rootElement>
```

Many — but by no means all — XML-enabled programming languages are capable of serializing business objects to nested XML documents.

Following is the generic schema for the preceding document, which has a root `<xs:complexType>` element with `<xs:complexType>` elements that contain an `<xs:sequence>` grouping of field elements and nested `<xs:complexType>` descendant elements:

```
<?xml version="1.0" encoding="utf-8"?>
<xs:schema attributeFormDefault="unqualified" elementFormDefault="qualified"
xmlns:xs="http://www.w3.org/2001/XMLSchema">
  <xs:element name="rootElement">
    <xs:complexType>
      <xs:sequence>
        <xs:element maxOccurs="unbounded" name="parentGroup">
          <xs:complexType>
            <xs:sequence>
              <xs:element name="parentField1" type="xs:string" />
              ...
              <xs:element name="parentFieldN" type="xs:int" />
              <xs:element maxOccurs="unbounded" name="childGroup">
                <xs:complexType>
                  <xs:sequence>
                    <xs:element name="childField1" type="xs:string" />
                    ...
                    <xs:element name="childFieldN" type="xs:decimal" />
                    <xs:element maxOccurs="unbounded" name="grandChildGroup">
                      <xs:complexType>
                        <xs:sequence>
                          <xs:element name="grandChildField1" type="xs:string" />
                          ...
                          <xs:element name="grandChildFieldN" type="xs:short" />
                        </xs:sequence>
                      </xs:complexType>
                    </xs:element>
                  </xs:sequence>
                </xs:complexType>
              </xs:element>
            </xs:sequence>
          </xs:complexType>
        </xs:element>
```

```
            </xs:sequence>
          </xs:complexType>
        </xs:element>
      </xs:sequence>
    </xs:complexType>
  </xs:element>
</xs:schema>
```

The DataSet designer interprets non-root <xs:complexType> groups that have field elements, nested <xsd:complexType> elements, or both as DataTables. Thus, field elements must have simple datatypes — such as xs:string, xs:int, or xs:decimal — or <xs:complexType> groups that represent related tables.

A source XML document that specifies a default namespace attribute with <rootElement xmlns= "documentNamespace"> requires schema to include a targetNamespace="documentNamespace" attribute for the top-level <xs:schema> element. If your schema has the preceding example's basic structure and has only a targetNamespace or no document namespace, you're in luck. Make the changes highlighted in the code that follows to the first two schema elements to indicate that the schema represents a typed DataSet:

```
<xs:schema attributeFormDefault="unqualified" elementFormDefault="qualified"
xmlns:xs="http://www.w3.org/2001/XMLSchema"
xmlns:msdata="urn:schemas-microsoft-com:xml-msdata">
  <xs:element name="rootElement" msdata:IsDataSet="true">
```

Copy the *Schema*.xsd file to your project folder, right-click the file icon in Project Explorer, and choose Add to Project, which generates *Schema*.Designer.vb, *Schema*.xsc, and *Schema*.xss files. Double-click the *Schema*.xsd icon to open it in the DataSet Editor and display the Data Sources window. You can add the DataSet to the form designer's tray by dragging the *DataSetName* tool from the *ProjectName* Components section to the form, or choose the DataSet tool from the Data section and select *ProjectName.DataSet* name from the Typed DataSet list.

> *VS 2005 adds the msdata namespace and attribute automatically when you double-click the schema file to display it in the DataSet Editor.*

At this point, you can drag the *parentGroup* DataTable from the Data Sources window to add a BindingNavigator and text boxes or a DataGridView for editing the parentGroup, and then add DataGridViews for the childGroup and grandchildGroup DataTables.

A nested schema example

Figure 6-11 shows a typed DataSet generated from a schema (NorthwindDS.xsd) for a nested XML document (NorthwindDS.xml), which contains a small subset of data from the Northwind Customers, Orders, and Order_Details tables.

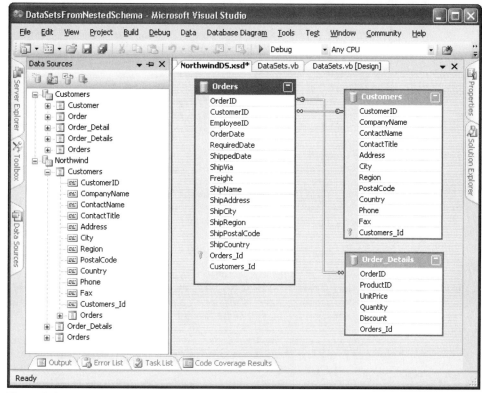

Figure 6-11

The DataSetsFromNestedSchema.sln project in the VB2005DB\Chapter06\DataSetsFromNestedSchema folder includes the NorthwindDS.xml and NorthwindDS.xsd files in the ...\bin\debug folder.

Generating the DataSet adds the Customers_Id primary key column to the Customers table, and a corresponding Customers_Id foreign key column to the Orders table to create the Customers_Orders relationship. The Orders table gains an Orders_Id primary key for the Orders_Order_Details relationship with the Orders_Id foreign key of the Order_Details table.

Following is the NorthwindDS.xsd schema for the nested data document:

```xml
<?xml version="1.0" encoding="utf-8"?>
<xs:schema id="Northwind" xmlns="" xmlns:xs="http://www.w3.org/2001/XMLSchema"
xmlns:msdata="urn:schemas-microsoft-com:xml-msdata">
  <xs:element name="Northwind" msdata:IsDataSet="true">
    <xs:complexType>
      <xs:choice minOccurs="0" maxOccurs="unbounded">
        <xs:element name="Customers">
          <xs:complexType>
            <xs:sequence>
              <xs:element name="CustomerID" type="xs:string" />
              <xs:element name="CompanyName" type="xs:string" />
```

```
            <xs:element name="ContactName" type="xs:string" minOccurs="0" />
            <xs:element name="ContactTitle" type="xs:string" minOccurs="0" />
            <xs:element name="Address" type="xs:string" />
            <xs:element name="City" type="xs:string" />
            <xs:element name="Region" type="xs:string" minOccurs="0" />
            <xs:element name="PostalCode" type="xs:string" minOccurs="0" />
            <xs:element name="Country" type="xs:string" />
            <xs:element name="Phone" type="xs:string" />
            <xs:element name="Fax" type="xs:string" minOccurs="0" />
            <xs:element name="Orders" minOccurs="0" maxOccurs="unbounded">
              <xs:complexType>
                <xs:sequence>
                  <xs:element name="OrderID" type="xs:int" />
                  <xs:element name="CustomerID" type="xs:string" />
                  <xs:element name="EmployeeID" type="xs:int"   />
                  <xs:element name="OrderDate" type="xs:dateTime" />
                  <xs:element name="RequiredDate" type="xs:dateTime"
                    minOccurs="0" />
                  <xs:element name="ShippedDate" type="xs:dateTime"
                    minOccurs="0" />
                  <xs:element name="ShipVia" type="xs:int" />
                  <xs:element name="Freight" type="xs:decimal" minOccurs="0" />
                  <xs:element name="ShipName" type="xs:string" />
                  <xs:element name="ShipAddress" type="xs:string"/>
                  <xs:element name="ShipCity" type="xs:string" />
                  <xs:element name="ShipRegion" type="xs:string" minOccurs="0" />
                  <xs:element name="ShipPostalCode" type="xs:string"
                    minOccurs="0" />
                  <xs:element name="ShipCountry" type="xs:string" />
                  <xs:element name="Order_Details" minOccurs="0"
                    maxOccurs="unbounded">
                    <xs:complexType>
                      <xs:sequence>
                        <xs:element name="OrderID" type="xs:int" />
                        <xs:element name="ProductID" type="xs:int" />
                        <xs:element name="UnitPrice" type="xs:decimal" />
                        <xs:element name="Quantity" type="xs:short" />
                        <xs:element name="Discount" type="xs:decimal" />
                      </xs:sequence>
                    </xs:complexType>
                  </xs:element>
                </xs:sequence>
              </xs:complexType>
            </xs:element>
          </xs:choice>
        </xs:complexType>
      </xs:element>
</xs:schema>
```

The `minOccurs="0"` attributes of the ContactName, ContactTitle, Region, PostalCode, Fax, RequiredDate, ShipDate, ShipRegion, and ShipPostalCode elements enable displaying and entering (null) values when editing the data.

Notice that the NorthwindDS.xsd schema doesn't contain references to the added primary-key and foreign-key columns. Generating a DataSet from a schema for a nested source document doesn't modify the schema. The NorthwindDS.Designer.vb file's `Northwind.InitClass` method adds these DataColumns to the DataTables when specifying ForeignKeyConstraints, and then adds the DataRelations with their `Nested` property value set to `True`.

> **Save a copy of your source schema before creating the DataSet. Editing any member of the DataSet modifies the schema file.**

The Column Properties window

To examine the properties of the added columns, select the column and right-click it to display the Properties tool window. Figure 6-12 shows the Properties window for the Orders table's Orders_Id primary-key column (left) and the Order_Details table's Orders_Id foreign-key column (right).

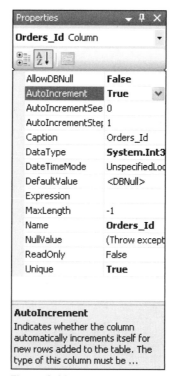

Figure 6-12

You can edit the data type, column name, and other properties of any table column in the Properties window. Right-click the window and choose Add to add a new column to the DataTable. You can specify a calculated column by typing an expression in the Expression text box. As an example, you can add an Extended column to the Order_Details table that you compute by the expression `Quantity * UnitPrice * (1 - Discount)`.

Altering a single property value in the Properties window causes a dramatic change to the schema file. The schema gains an `<xs:annotation>` group to specify the data source, most elements acquire a panoply of `msprop` attributes, and the schema file size grows by almost an order of magnitude—NorthwindDS.xsd increases from 4KB to 35KB. If you need to edit the schema and retain its original structure, right-click the schema file in Solution Explorer, choose Open With, and select XML Editor—not the default DataSet Editor or XML Schema Editor—in the Open With dialog.

A nested schema with attributes

Adding attributes to elements that generate DataTables adds a column named for the attribute to the table. For example, an attribute of the Order_Details field defined by `<xs:attribute name="totalAmount" type="xs:decimal" use="required" />` adds a totalAmount column to the Order_Details table. Figure 6-13 shows the NWAttributes.xsd schema open in the DataSet Editor. Each table's first column is generated from an attribute that's defined by the schema and included in the NWAttributes.xsd source document. An attribute added to a table adds a consecutively numbered `msdata:Ordinal="n"` attribute to each child node that represents a table column.

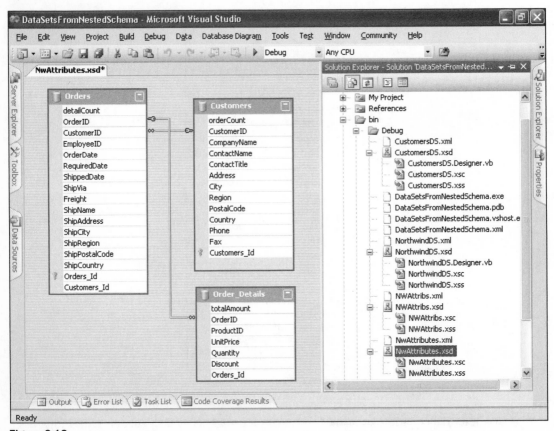

Figure 6-13

If you add a custom attribute to a table child element, such as ProductID, the designer creates a ProductID table, which is probably not what you want.

The DataSetsFromNestedSchema.sln project includes the NWAttributes.xml and NWAttributes.xsd files.

A wrapped nested schema example

It's a common XML document design practice to enclose sets of elements within outer groups. An example is wrapping Customer and its child elements with a Customers group, Order with an Orders Group, and Order_Detail with an Order_Details group to create the following abbreviated structure:

```
<Customers>
  <Customer>
    <CustomerID>GREAL</CustomerID>
    ...
    <Fax></Fax>
    <Orders>
      <Order>
        <OrderID>11061</OrderID>
        ...
        <ShipCountry>USA</ShipCountry>
        <Order_Details>
          <Order_Detail>
            <OrderID>11061</OrderID>
            ...
            <Discount>0.075</Discount>
          </Order_Detail>
        </Order_Details>
      </Order>
    </Orders>
  </Customer>
<Customers>
```

Following is the abbreviated schema for the preceding source document with the wrapping elements highlighted:

```
<?xml version="1.0" encoding="utf-8"?>
<xs:schema id="Customers" xmlns="" xmlns:xs="http://www.w3.org/2001/XMLSchema"
xmlns:msdata="urn:schemas-microsoft-com:xml-msdata">
  <xs:element name="Customers" msdata:IsDataSet="true">
    <xs:complexType>
      <xs:choice minOccurs="0" maxOccurs="unbounded">
        <xs:element name="Customer">
          <xs:complexType>
            <xs:sequence>
              <xs:element name="CustomerID" type="xs:string" minOccurs="0" />
              ...
              <xs:element name="Fax" type="xs:string" minOccurs="0" />
              <xs:element name="Orders" minOccurs="0" />
                <xs:complexType>
                  <xs:sequence>
                    <xs:element name="Order" minOccurs="0" maxOccurs="unbounded">
```

```
                    <xs:complexType>
                      <xs:sequence>
                        <xs:element name="OrderID" type="xs:string"
                          minOccurs="0" />
                        ...
                        <xs:element name="ShipCountry" type="xs:string"
                          minOccurs="0" />
                        <xs:element name="Order_Details" minOccurs="0" />
                          <xs:complexType>
                            <xs:sequence>
                              <xs:element name="Order_Detail"
                                minOccurs="0" maxOccurs="unbounded">
                                <xs:complexType>
                                  <xs:sequence>
                                    <xs:element name="OrderID" type="xs:string"
                                      minOccurs="0" />
                                    ...
                                    <xs:element name="Discount" type="xs:string"
                                      minOccurs="0" />
                                  </xs:sequence>
                                </xs:complexType>
                              </xs:element>
                            </xs:sequence>
                          </xs:complexType>
                        </xs:element>
                      </xs:sequence>
                    </xs:complexType>
                  </xs:element>
                </xs:sequence>
              </xs:complexType>
            </xs:element>
          </xs:sequence>
        </xs:complexType>
      </xs:element>
    </xs:choice>
  </xs:complexType>
</xs:element>
</xs:schema>
```

The DataSetsFromNestedSchema.sln project in the VB2005DB\Chapter06\DataSetsFromNestedSchema folder includes the CustomersDS.xml and CustomersDS.xsd files.

The CustomersDS.xsd schema generates two additional tables to establish the relationships between Orders and Order elements, and Order_Details and Order_Detail elements. To make the DataSet suitable for editing with DataGridViews, you must add relationships between the CustomersID fields of the Customers and Orders tables, and the OrderID fields of the Orders and Order_Details table, as described in the section "The EditCustomersDS Sample Project," later in this chapter.

Figure 6-14 shows the Customers DataSet in the designer without the relationships between the Customers and Orders, and Orders and Order_Details tables added.

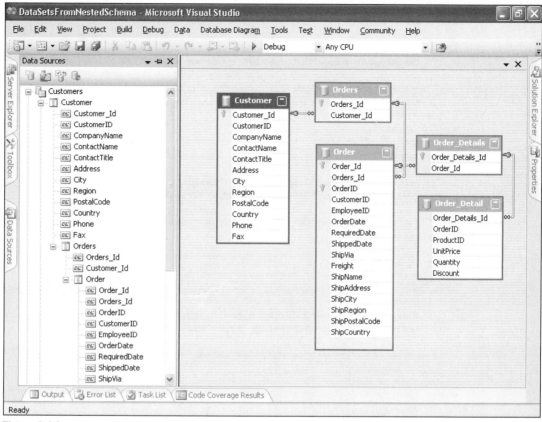

Figure 6-14

A Flat Schema Example

Nested schemas can export tables as XML documents by invoking the `DataTable.WriteXML` `(ExportFileName, XmlWriteMode.IgnoreSchema)` method. Flat schemas add the capability to import individual XML documents that conform to the DataSet schema for related tables. However, the DataSet designer doesn't add *TableName*_Id columns, ForeignKeyConstraints, or DataRelations.

Individual tables that you import must have a root element with the same name as the DataSet root element and, if specified, the same global namespace.

Following is the abbreviated Northwind.xsd schema for Northwind.xml, which is the flat version of NorthwindDS.xml, with primary and foreign keys emphasized:

```
<?xml version="1.0" encoding="utf-8"?>
<xs:schema id="Northwind" attributeFormDefault="unqualified"
    elementFormDefault="qualified" xmlns:xs="http://www.w3.org/2001/XMLSchema"
    xmlns:msdata="urn:schemas-microsoft-com:xml-msdata">
  <xs:element name="Northwind" msdata:IsDataSet="true">
    <xs:complexType>
```

```
        <xs:sequence>
          <xs:element maxOccurs="unbounded" name="Customers">
            <xs:complexType>
              <xs:sequence>
                <xs:element name="CustomerID" type="xs:string" />
                ...
                <xs:element minOccurs="0" name="Fax" type="xs:string" />
              </xs:sequence>
            </xs:complexType>
          </xs:element>
          <xs:element minOccurs="0" maxOccurs="unbounded" name="Orders">
            <xs:complexType>
              <xs:sequence>
                <xs:element name="OrderID" type="xs:int" />
                <xs:element name="CustomerID" type="xs:string" />
                ...
                <xs:element name="ShipCountry" type="xs:string" />
              </xs:sequence>
            </xs:complexType>
          </xs:element>
          <xs:element minOccurs="0" maxOccurs="unbounded" name="Order_Details">
            <xs:complexType>
              <xs:sequence>
                <xs:element name="OrderID" type="xs:int" />
                <xs:element name="ProductID" type="xs:int" />
                ...
                <xs:element name="Discount" type="xs:decimal" />
              </xs:sequence>
            </xs:complexType>
          </xs:element>
        </xs:sequence>
      </xs:complexType>
    </xs:element>
</xs:schema>
```

The `minOccurs="0"` *attribute for the Orders and Order_Details tables supports building the DataSet by reading individual Customers, Orders, and Order_Details documents in sequence.*

The Northwind.xml, Northwind.xsd, TableCustomers.xml, TableOrders.xml, and TableDetails.xml files are in the VB2005DB\Chapter06\DataSetsFromFlatSchema\DataSetsFromFlatSchema.sln project. This project's form lets you populate the Northwind DataSet from a single data document or from individual tables.

Creating an editable version of Northwind.xsd requires the following actions in the DataSet Editor window:

1. Add primary keys to each DataTable. Select and then right-click the primary-key column and choose Set Primary Key for the three tables. Optionally, choose Edit Key to open the Unique Constraint dialog and change the name to `PK_TableName` or the like.

2. The Order_Details table has a composite primary key, so right-click the OrderID column, choose Edit Key, and mark the ProductID checkbox.

3. Right-click the DataSet Editor's surface and choose Add ⇨ Relation to open the Relation dialog with the default values for a relationship between Customers and Orders named `FK_Customers_Orders`. Change the Foreign Key Columns list's OrderID entry to CustomerID.

4. Choose Add ➪ Relation again, change the name of the relation from `FK_Customers_Orders1` to `FK_Orders_Order_Details`, and select Orders from the Parent Table list and Order_Details from the Child Table list. The Key Columns and Foreign Key Columns lists display OrderID.

5. If you want users to be able to add new Orders and Order_Details records, select the OrderID primary-key column, choose Properties, and change the `AutoIncrement` property value from `False` to `True`.

Figure 6-15 shows the DataSet Editor with the preceding steps completed.

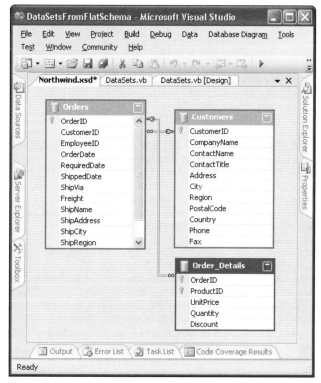

Figure 6-15

Adding new records to DataTables in a document-editing application isn't a common practice, but it's practical if the destination application can detect and handle added records properly. As an example, the editing application might receive XML order documents from customers or distributors, review and edit the documents as necessary, apply the DataRow.SetModified *or* DataRow.SetAdded *method, as applicable, send updates to a database, retrieve the updated data, and return individual XML documents as e-mail enclosures. Nested documents are better suited to this scenario than flat documents, as you'll see in the section "Create Editing Forms from XML Data Sources," later in this chapter.*

Adding the primary keys and relationships to the tables adds to the end of the schema the following `<xs:unique>` and `<xs:keyref>` elements of the Northwind element:

```
<xs:schema id="Northwind" xmlns="" xmlns:xs="http://www.w3.org/2001/XMLSchema"
    xmlns:msdata="urn:schemas-microsoft-com:xml-msdata"
    xmlns:msprop="urn:schemas-microsoft-com:xml-msprop">
  <xs:element name="Northwind" msdata:IsDataSet="true"
      msprop:User_DataSetName="Northwind"
      msprop:DSGenerator_DataSetName="Northwind">
    ...
    <xs:unique name="PK_Customers" msdata:PrimaryKey="true">
      <xs:selector xpath=".//Customers" />
      <xs:field xpath="CustomerID" />
    </xs:unique>
    <xs:unique name="PK_Orders" msdata:PrimaryKey="true">
      <xs:selector xpath=".//Orders" />
      <xs:field xpath="OrderID" />
    </xs:unique>
    <xs:unique name="PK_Order_Details" msdata:PrimaryKey="true">
      <xs:selector xpath=".//Order_Details" />
      <xs:field xpath="OrderID" />
      <xs:field xpath="ProductID" />
    </xs:unique>
    <xs:keyref name="FK_Orders_Order_Details" refer="PK_Orders"
        msprop:rel_Generator_RelationVarName="relationFK_Orders_Order_Details"
        msprop:rel_User_ParentTable="Orders"
        msprop:rel_User_ChildTable="Order_Details"
        msprop:rel_User_RelationName="FK_Orders_Order_Details"
        msprop:rel_Generator_ParentPropName="OrdersRow"
        msprop:rel_Generator_ChildPropName="GetOrder_DetailsRows">
      <xs:selector xpath=".//Order_Details" />
      <xs:field xpath="OrderID" />
    </xs:keyref>
    <xs:keyref name="FK_Customers_Orders" refer="PK_Customers"
        msprop:rel_Generator_RelationVarName="relationFK_Customers_Orders"
        msprop:rel_User_ParentTable="Customers" msprop:rel_User_ChildTable="Orders"
        msprop:rel_User_RelationName="FK_Customers_Orders"
        msprop:rel_Generator_ParentPropName="CustomersRow"
        msprop:rel_Generator_ChildPropName="GetOrdersRows">
      <xs:selector xpath=".//Orders" />
      <xs:field xpath="CustomerID" />
    </xs:keyref>
  </xs:element>
</xs:schema>
```

The `<xs:unique>` elements define primary keys, and `<xs:keyref>` elements specify foreign-key constraints. The `msprop` attributes are references to DataRelations added by the Northwind.Designer.vb file's partial Northwind class.

Infer an XML Schema to Generate a DataSet

If you don't have a schema for your XML source document, you have the following five choices for generating the schema with VS 2005:

❑ Open a representative XML source document in the XML Editor, choose XML ➪ Create Schema to infer a schema, and save it in your project folder as `SchemaName.xsd`. The XML Editor's schema generator attempts to infer XSD datatypes by examining the text values of the source document's fields. Unfortunately, the inference process rarely succeeds with unsigned numeric values that don't have decimal fractions; it assigns them the smallest possible XSD numeric datatype. For example, values 0 through 255 become xs:unsignedByte, 256 through 65,535 become xs:unsignedShort, and larger numbers become xs:unsignedInt or xs:unsignedLong. Unless you have a reason for doing otherwise, assign xs:int to all numeric values without decimal fractions.

❑ Create an empty runtime DataSet, invoke the DataSet.ReadXml(DocumentFileName) method, and save the schema file by invoking DataSet.WriteXmlSchema(SchemaFileName). This method generates an untyped schema — all elements are assigned the xs:string datatype and a minOccurs="0" attribute. Open *SchemaFileName*.xsd in the XML Editor, change the datatypes of numeric and date or date/time values to the appropriate xs:datatype, and remove inappropriate minOccurs="0" attributes.

❑ Generate a typed schema by the preceding process, but invoke the DataSet.ReadXml (DocumentFileName, XmlReadMode.InferTypedSchema) method to generate a schema that's identical to the schema generated by the XML Editor.

❑ Open a VS 2005 Command Prompt, navigate to your project folder, and type **xsd.exe** *DocumentFileName***.xml** to generate *DocumentFileName*.xsd. The schema is identical to that generated by the preceding method.

❑ If you don't have a single XML document that's representative of all possible XML document instances — or don't want to manually create one — you can use the Microsoft XSD Inference 1.0 Tool at http://apps.gotdotnet.com/xmltools/xsdinference/ to generate and refine a typed schema. You specify an initial source document to infer the initial schema, and then process additional source documents to refine the schema.

The "Xsd.exe Workarounds for Complex Documents" article at http://www.fawcette.com/ xmlmag/2002_07/online/webservices_rjennings_07_29_02/ *explains how to overcome problems you might encounter when using Xsd.exe to generate schemas. You can learn more about the Microsoft XSD Inference 1.0 Tool in the "Generate XSD Schemas by Inference" article at* http:// www.fawcette.com/xmlmag/2002_11/online/xml_rjennings_11_11_02/.

If you must infer and refine schemas routinely, you can use the System.Xml.Schema.InferSchema method to emulate the Microsoft XSD Inference 1.0 Tool. The following code infers a schema for an initial document instance (Initial.xml), refines the schema with three additional document instances, and writes the refined schema as Initial.xsd:

```
Private Sub InferAndRefineSchema
    'Use System.Xml.Schema.InferSchema to infer and refine a schema
    Dim alFiles As New ArrayList
    alFiles.Add("Initial.xml")
    alFiles.Add("Refine2.xml")
    alFiles.Add("Refine3.xml")
    alFiles.Add("Refine4.xml")

    Dim intCtr As Integer
    Dim xss As XmlSchemaSet = Nothing
    Dim xsi As Inference = Nothing
    For intCtr = 0 To alFiles.Count - 1
       Dim xr As XmlReader = XmlReader.Create(alFiles(intCtr).ToString)
       If intCtr = 0 Then
```

```
            'Infer schema
            xss = New XmlSchemaSet()
            xsi = New Inference()
        End If
        xss = xsi.InferSchema(xr)
        xr.Close()
    Next
    Dim strXsdFile As String = Replace(alFiles(0).ToString, ".xml", ".xsd")
    Dim xsd As XmlSchema
    For Each xsd In xss.Schemas()
        Dim sw As StreamWriter = Nothing
        sw = My.Computer.FileSystem.OpenTextFileWriter(strXsdFile, False)
        xsd.Write(sw)
        sw.Close()
        'Only one schema is generated
        Exit For
    Next
End Sub
```

Create Editing Forms from XML Data Sources

The process of creating editing forms for XML data documents is similar to that for editing database tables. After you've generated a typed DataSet from your existing schema, drag the top-level table from the Data Sources window to the form to add a DataNavigator and DataGridView or details text boxes. Repeat the process with DataGridViews for the related tables and specify the appropriate DataRelation to generate a *DataRelation*BindingSource for the `DataSource` property value. Unlike binding DataGridViews to FK_*ParentTable_ChildTable*BindingSources generated from database tables, you create the BindingSource when you specify a related list in the `DataSource` property pop-up list.

The following two project examples illustrate the changes required to create *DataRelation*BindingSource, enable adding new document elements, and accommodate wrapped nested DataSets.

The EditNorthwindDS Sample Project

The EditNorthwindDS.sln project in the VB2005DB\Chapter06\EditNorthwindDS folder is based on the NorthwindDS.xml source document and NorthwindDS.xsd schema. The form has DataGridViews populated from the Customers, Orders, and Order_Details DataTables, as shown in Figure 6-16.

The following processes are completed in the sample project. If you want to give the following operations a test drive, create a new project, add the NorthwindDS.xml and NorthwindDS.xsd files to it, and drag the Customers, Orders, and Order_Details tables as DataGridViews to Form1. Add a `Me.Northwind` `.ReadXml("\Path\NorthwindDS.xml")` *instruction to the* `Form1_Load` *event handler to populate the DataTables.*

Open the Data Sources window and drag the Customers parent group icon, its Orders subgroup icon, and the Orders group's Order Details subgroup icon to the form to add the three DataGridViews. Add code to the `Form_Load` event handler to populate the DataSet with the NorthwindDS.xml document.

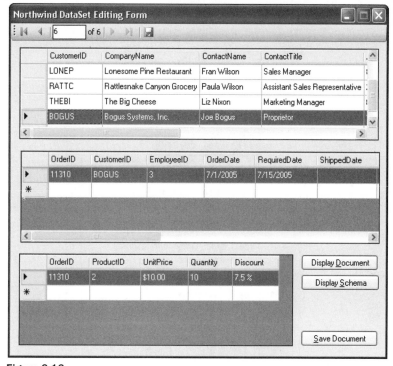

Figure 6-16

You might need to change the Order_DetailsDataGridView's DataSource *property value to* Customers_OrdersBindingSource *and the* DataMember *property value to the* Orders_Order_Details *relation to track Orders DataGridView selection changes.*

You can safely delete the OrdersBindingSource and Order_DetailsBindingSource at this point because they no longer bind to any controls.

Figure 6-17 shows the DataSource list after completing the preceding operations and loading the NorthwindDS.xml document. An OrdersDataGridView..Sort(.Columns(0), System .ComponentModel.ListSortDirection.Descending) instruction in the Form_Load event handler applies the descending sort order by OrderID.

If you want to enable users to add new Orders and Order_Details records with appropriate OrderID column values, you must edit the schema and set the OrderID and Order_Id columns' AutoIncrement property to True in the *ColumnName* Properties dialog. Otherwise, set the DataGridViews' AllowUserToAddRows property value to False.

Figure 6-17

You can add the autogenerated Customers_Id, Orders_Id, and Order_Details_Id attributes as columns of the DataGridViews. While you're customizing the DataGridViews' Columns collections in the Edit Columns dialog, move the autogenerated columns to the end of the Selected Columns list, and set their ReadOnly property value to True. If you don't allow users to add new rows, you can delete these columns from the DataGridView.

Add a button to save DataSet changes and invoke the NorthwindDS..WriteXml(strFile, Data .XmlWriteMode.IgnoreSchema) method to save the edited data document. The sample project saves a diffgram (NorthwindDS.xsd) before saving changes and has buttons to display the saved XML document and the schema in Internet Explorer.

Adding new rows requires an OrdersDefaultValues procedure that the OrdersDataGridView _DefaultValuesNeeded event handler calls. The procedure's code is similar to that for Chapter 5's DefaultValuesNeeded event handler, but you must add the Customers_Id value to maintain the relationship, as shown highlighted in the following listing:

```
Private Sub OrdersDefaultValues(ByVal rowNew As DataGridViewRow)
    Try
        With CustomersDataGridView
            Dim intRow As Integer = .CurrentCell.RowIndex
            rowNew.Cells(1).Value = .Rows(intRow).Cells(0).Value
```

```
                rowNew.Cells(2).Value = 0
                rowNew.Cells(3).Value = Today
                rowNew.Cells(4).Value = Today.AddDays(14)
                'Leave ShippedDate empty
                rowNew.Cells(6).Value = 3
                'Freight defaults to 0
                'CompanyName
                rowNew.Cells(8).Value = .Rows(intRow).Cells(1).Value
                'Address to Country fields
                Dim intCol As Integer
                For intCol = 9 To 13
                    rowNew.Cells(intCol).Value = .Rows(intRow).Cells(intCol - 5).Value
                Next
                'Add the current Customers_Id value
                rowNew.Cells(15).Value = .Rows(intRow).Cells(11).Value
                OrdersDataGridView.EndEdit(DataGridViewDataErrorContexts.Commit)
                'Store the autoincremented Orders_Id for Order_Details default values
                intNewOrder_ID = CInt(rowNew.Cells(14).Value)
                'Store the autoincremented OrderID value
                intOrderID = CInt(rowNew.Cells(0).Value)
            End With
        Catch exc As Exception
            MsgBox(exc.Message + exc.StackTrace, , )
        End Try
    End Sub
```

The `DetailsDefaultValues` procedure requires a similar modification for the OrdersID and Orders_Id values:

```
    Private Sub DetailsDefaultValues(ByVal rowNew As DataGridViewRow)
        'Default values for Order_Details
        Try
            With OrdersDataGridView
                Dim intRow As Integer = .CurrentCell.RowIndex
                'Add OrderID
                rowNew.Cells(0).Value = .Rows(intRow).Cells(0).Value
                'Add Orders_Id
                rowNew.Cells(5).Value = .Rows(intRow).Cells(14).Value
            End With
            With Order_DetailsDataGridView
                rowNew.Cells(1).Value = 0
                rowNew.Cells(2).Value = .Rows.Count * 10
                rowNew.Cells(3).Value = .Rows.Count * 5
                rowNew.Cells(4).Value = .Rows.Count * 0.01
            End With
        Catch exc As Exception
            rowNew.Cells(5).Value = intNewOrder_ID
        Finally
            Order_DetailsDataGridView.EndEdit(DataGridViewDataErrorContexts.Commit)
        End Try
    End Sub
```

The EditCustomersDS Sample Project

The EditCustomersDS.sln project in the VB2005DB\Chapter06\EditCustomersDS folder is based on the CustomersDS.xml source document and CustomersDS.xsd schema. The project's form appears identical to that of the EditNorthwindDS.sln project, but you can't use the default indirect relationships between the Customer and Order or Order and Order_Detail tables to bind the Order and Order_Detail DataGridViews.

Wrapped nested documents require adding direct relationships between the tables manually. Thus, you must add DataRelations and, optionally, foreign-key constraints between Customer.CustomerID and Order.CustomerID, and Order.OrderID and Order_Details.OrderID. Figure 6-18 shows the DataSet Editor with the added relationships—FK_Customer_Order and FK_Order_Order_Detail. You don't need to change the `OrdersDefaultValue` or `DetailsDefaultValue` code because updates to the `Orders` and `Order_Details` connecting tables are automatic.

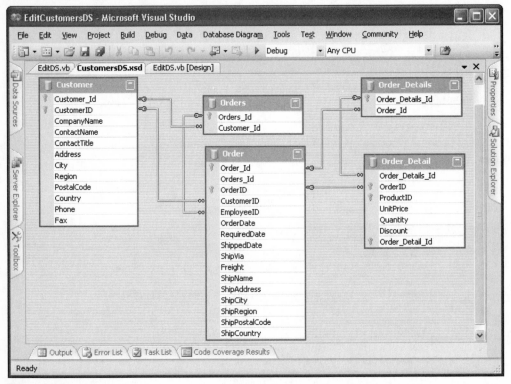

Figure 6-18

Generate Serializable Classes from Schemas

Xsd.exe's /c and /l:vb command-line switches let you generate serializable VB classes from schemas that don't have the msdata namespace declaration and msdata:IsDataSet="True" attribute. NET Framework 1.x's Xsd.exe generates classes with public fields; the 2.0 version generates public properties and private fields, which is considered a best practice. XML serialization — the process of persisting an object as an XML document stream — enables you to save DataSets as XML files, publish and consume ASP.NET Web services, and remote objects across application domains in XML format.

If the msdata namespace declaration and attribute are present, Xsd.exe generates a typed DataSet from the schema, which is the equivalent of setting the /d and /l:vb switches for non-DataSet schemas.

Remoting XML streams doesn't maintain type fidelity; remoting with binary serialization lets you pass the object By Value to other application domains. .NET Framework 2.0 adds a binary serialization option for DataSets, which is much more efficient than XML encoding.

Designating a class as serializable with XML encoding requires adding attributes from the System .Xml.Serialization namespace to the root object and its elements. Following is the code for the top-level Northwind class generated by typing Xsd.exe /c /l:vb Northwind.xsd at the Visual Studio 2005 Command Prompt:

```vb
<System.SerializableAttribute(), _
    System.Xml.Serialization.XmlRootAttribute([Namespace]:="", IsNullable:=False)> _
Public Class Northwind

    Private customersField() As NorthwindCustomers
    Private ordersField() As NorthwindOrders
    Private order_DetailsField() As NorthwindOrder_Details

    <System.Xml.Serialization.XmlElementAttribute("Customers")> _
    Public Property Customers() As NorthwindCustomers()
        Get
            Return Me.customersField
        End Get
        Set(ByVal value As NorthwindCustomers())
            Me.customersField = value
        End Set
    End Property

    <System.Xml.Serialization.XmlElementAttribute("Orders")> _
    Public Property Orders() As NorthwindOrders()
        Get
            Return Me.ordersField
        End Get
        Set(ByVal value As NorthwindOrders())
            Me.ordersField = value
        End Set
    End Property

    <System.Xml.Serialization.XmlElementAttribute("Order_Details")> _
    Public Property Order_Details() As NorthwindOrder_Details()
```

```
      Get
          Return Me.order_DetailsField
      End Get
      Set(ByVal value As NorthwindOrder_Details())
          Me.order_DetailsField = value
      End Set
    End Property
End Class
```

The Customers(), Orders(), and Order_Details() fields are arrays. The complete code for the Northwind *class is in the clsNorthwind.vb file of the ClassesFromSchemas.sln sample project in the VB2005DB\Chapter06\ClassesFromSchemas folder.*

You can instantiate a serializable class with its default constructor and set property values — a process called *deserializing, hydrating,* or *re-hydrating* an object — by loading an XML source document stream with an XMLSerializer instance. Serializing or *dehydrating* an object gets its property values and generates the corresponding XML stream.

The following code snippet is from the ClassesFromSchemas.sln project's Classes.vb file. The highlighted code deserializes the Northwind object from the Northwind.xml file, updates the contents of the CompanyName, ShipName, and Discount fields, serializes the object, and saves the resulting XML document as Output.xml.

```
Private Sub btnNorthwind_Click(ByVal sender As System.Object, _
      ByVal e As System.EventArgs) Handles btnNorthwind.Click
    'Prove no cheating is going on
    File.Delete("..\Output.xml")

    'Hydrate the Northwind object instance by deserializing it
    Dim objNwind As New Northwind
    Dim xsInput As New XmlSerializer(objNwind.GetType)
    Dim srInput As New StreamReader("..\Northwind.xml")
    objNwind = CType(xsInput.Deserialize(srInput), Northwind)
    srInput.Close()

    'Change field values to prove the procedure works
    Dim intCtr As Integer
    For intCtr = 0 To objNwind.Customers.Length - 1
       objNwind.Customers(intCtr).CompanyName += " (Edited)"
    Next
    'Same change to Orders
    For intCtr = 0 To objNwind.Orders.Length - 1
       objNwind.Orders(intCtr).ShipName += " (Edited)"
    Next
    'Give everyone a 25% discount
    For intCtr = 0 To objNwind.Order_Details.Length - 1
       objNwind.Order_Details(intCtr).Discount = 0.25D
    Next

    'Dehydrate the Northwind object by serializing it to Output.xml
    Dim xsOutput As New XmlSerializer(objNwind.GetType)
    Dim srOutput As New StreamWriter("..\Output.xml")
    xsOutput.Serialize(srOutput, objNwind)
    srOutput.Close()
End Sub
```

The preceding code uses StreamReader *and* StreamWriter *instances to generate and consume the XML streams.* XmlSerializer *can accommodate other stream-based objects, such as* FileStream, *as demonstrated by the project's* btnNorthwindDS_Click *and* btnCustomersDS_Click *event handlers.*

Create Data Sources from Serializable Classes

Adding a serialized class file to a project lets you add its classes to the Data Sources window. Click the window's Add New Data Source button or choose Data ⮑ Add New Data Source to start the Data Sources Configuration Wizard, select Object on the Choose a Data Source Type page, and click Next. In the Select an Object You Wish To Bind To page, expand the project node, and select the serializable class to add. Figure 6-19 illustrates how the NorthwindCustomers class was added to the ClassesFromSchemas.sln project.

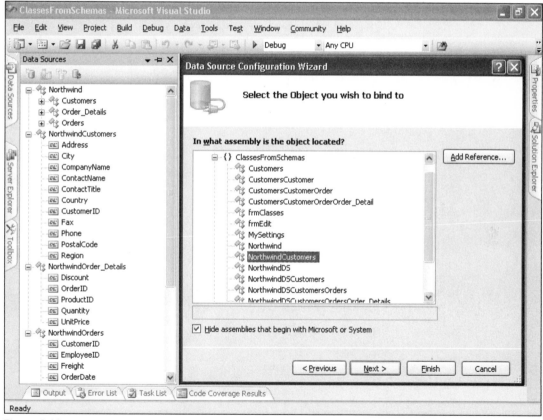

Figure 6-19

Creating a data source from the top-level element of the class doesn't enable generating editing controls for child elements. The top-level element's subnodes are inactive, as shown for the Northwind *class in Figure 6-16. This limitation also applies to classes created from schemas for nested source documents, such as NorthwindDS.xml and CustomersDS.xml.*

Dragging active class nodes to a form generates a DataNavigator and DataGridView or text boxes for the first node, DataGridViews for the remaining nodes, and a BindingSource for each node. Users can't add or delete rows bound to arrays of classes. Adding and deleting element groups requires substituting `BindingLists` for class arrays, which is the subject of the next section. BindingSources don't support `Filter` and `Sort` properties for object arrays, so you can't apply a filter to display rows based on a selection made with the DataNavigator or in DataGridViews. Filtering and sorting require the data source to implement the `System.ComponentModel.IBindingListView` interface. Another limitation of object arrays as data sources is handling null (missing) date values. The DataGridView doesn't respect the `NullValue` property value — usually (null) — that you set in the CellStyle Builder dialog for date columns; instead the column displays 1/1/0001 for null date values.

The following abbreviated version of the `btnLoadData_Click` event handler in the sample project's EditForm.vb file tests the loading of three DataGridViews with data from the three `Northwind...` classes:

```
Private Sub btnLoadData_Click(ByVal sender As System.Object, _
    ByVal e As System.EventArgs) Handles btnLoadData.Click
  blnIsLoaded = False
  Me.Cursor = Cursors.WaitCursor
  'Hydrate the NorthwindDS object by deserializing it
  objNwind = New Northwind
  Dim xsInput As New XmlSerializer(objNwind.GetType)
  Dim fsInput As New FileStream("..\Northwind.xml", FileMode.Open)
  objNwind = CType(xsInput.Deserialize(fsInput), Northwind)
  fsInput.Close()

    With NorthwindCustomersBindingSource
      .Clear()
      DoEvents()
      .DataSource = objNwind
      .DataMember = "Customers"
    End With

    DoEvents()
    With NorthwindOrdersBindingSource
      .Clear()
      DoEvents()
      .DataSource = objNwind
      .DataMember = "Orders"
    End With

    DoEvents()
    With NorthwindOrder_DetailsBindingSource
      .Clear()
      DoEvents()
      .DataSource = objNwind
      .DataMember = "Order_Details"
    End With
  Me.Cursor = Cursors.Default
  blnIsLoaded = True
End Sub
```

Code to bypass the BindingSources and load the DataGridViews directly is identical to the preceding example; just change ...BindingSource *to* ...DataGridView *and* .Clear() *to* .Rows.Clear().

Loading DataGridViews with data contained in class arrays isn't a speedy process. Populating three DataGridViews with 106 records requires about 10 seconds initially; successive trials take about 5 seconds on a machine with a 2.3 GHz Pentium 4 processor. Reading and deserializing the Northwind.xml source document file consumes only about 0.25 second.

Enhance Editing with Generic BindingList Collections

The .NET Framework 2.0's new `System.Collections.Generics` namespace provides generic implementations for type-safe `List(Of T)`, `LinkedList(Of T)`, `Stack(Of T)`, `Queue(Of T)`, `Dictionary(Of T)`, and other more specialized collections. `T` is a placeholder for a type, such as `String` or `Integer`, that the instantiating code provides to the collection's constructor. Generics substitute compile-time for runtime type-checking, and avoid the boxing and unboxing operations required for type casts between references and values. Thus, generic collections can deliver substantial performance benefits.

The `System.ComponentModel` namespace provides the `BindingList(Of T)` collection, which reduces DataGridView loading time by a factor of about 10. `BindingList(Of T)` collections support `AddNew` and `Remove` methods — but not `Filter` and `Sort` properties — on classes generated from schemas. The following code substitutes `BindingList(Of Northwind...)` for the preceding example's arrays:

```
Imports System.Xml.Serialization
Imports System.ComponentModel.Collections.Generic

<System.SerializableAttribute(), _
 System.Xml.Serialization.XmlTypeAttribute(AnonymousType:=True), _
 System.Xml.Serialization.XmlRootAttribute([Namespace]:="", IsNullable:=False)> _
Public Class Northwind
    Private customersField As BindingList(Of NorthwindCustomers)
    Private ordersField As BindingList(Of NorthwindOrders)
    Private order_DetailsField As BindingList(Of NorthwindOrder_Details)

    <System.Xml.Serialization.XmlElementAttribute("Customers")> _
    Public Property Customers() As BindingList(Of NorthwindCustomers)
        Get
            Return Me.customersField
        End Get
        Set(ByVal value As BindingList(Of NorthwindCustomers))
            Me.customersField = value
        End Set
    End Property

    <System.Xml.Serialization.XmlElementAttribute("Orders")> _
    Public Property Orders() As BindingList(Of NorthwindOrders)
        Get
            Return Me.ordersField
        End Get
        Set(ByVal value As BindingList(Of NorthwindOrders))
            Me.ordersField = value
        End Set
```

```
        End Property

    <System.Xml.Serialization.XmlElementAttribute("Order_Details")> _
    Public Property Order_Details() As BindingList(Of NorthwindOrder_Details)
        Get
            Return Me.order_DetailsField
        End Get
        Set(ByVal value As BindingList(Of NorthwindOrder_Details))
            Me.order_DetailsField = value
        End Set
    End Property
End Class
```

The GenericClassesFromSchemas.sln project in the VB2005DB\Chapter06\GenericClassesFromSchema folder provides an editing form that's identical to that of the ClassesFromSchemas.sln project, but lets you add and delete rows from the DataGridView.

Figure 6-20 shows the sample project's EditForm.vb with an added customer, order, and line item. No changes are required to the previous example's code that sets and gets the three `BindingList` field values, because both examples' field types—`NorthwindCustomers`, `NorthwindOrders`, and `NorthwindOrder_Details`—are defined by the schema for Northwind.xml. However, a substantial amount of validation code and several schema modifications are needed to deliver a production-quality document editing or generation form.

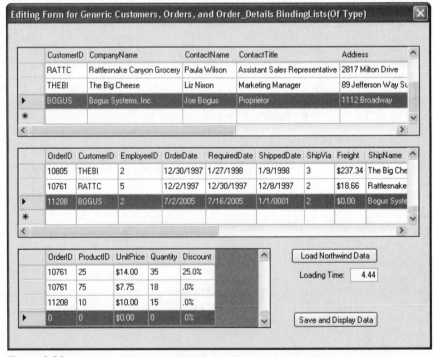

Figure 6-20

You must devote much of the added code to work around the lack of direct support for filtering `BindingList(Of T)` *collections or* `BindingSource` *objects whose* `DataSource` *property specifies a* `BindingList(Of T)` *collection. A built-in filterable, sortable* `BindingListView(Of T)` *collection would simplify development greatly, but developers must create their own or adopt third-party classes. Andrew Davey posted a C# implementation of a* `BindingListView<T>` *collection in September 2005; search Google for* **BindingListView<T>** *or* **BindingListView(Of T)** *for third-party C# 2.0 or VB 8.0 implementations.*

Microsoft's Language Integrated Query (LINQ) project for the next .NET, C#, and VB versions_scheduled for the Visual Studio "Orcas" release_promises to simplify business-object filtering, sorting, databinding, and editing. LINQ also eases relational-to-object and XML-to-object mapping with DLinq and XLinq APIs. You can learn more about LINQ at `http://msdn.microsoft.com/netframework/future/linq/` and the VB 9.0 implementations of LINQ, DLinq, and XLinq at `http://msdn.microsoft.com/vbasic/future/`. The VB 9.0 page has links to download the latest version of the Visual Basic 9.0 Technology Preview, which runs under VS 2005 or VBX and enables developers to gain pre-release experience with LINQ, DLinq, and XLinq.

Summary

The .NET Framework 2.0's new partial classes enable dividing class files, such as *FormName*.vb, into a set of individual files that contain elements of the class definition. Partial classes let you make additions to or override methods of designer-generated files — such as *FormName*.Designer.vb and *DataSetName*.Designer.vb — without losing your added code when editing objects in the form design window or DataSet Editor.

Displaying images in DataGridView cells is a straightforward process that's similar to the techniques for adding graphics to ADO.NET 1.*x* DataGrid controls. A DataGridView that contains 101 GIF images of moderate — 240 pixels by 149 pixels — size loads in less than 2 seconds from the ProductPhotos table of SQL Server 2005's AdventureWorks sample database. You can add a new image to a DataGridView cell from a bitmap file, save a selected image to a file, or display an image in a PictureBox control with a few lines of code. You can display images from a Microsoft Access OLE Object field, such as those in the Northwind sample database's Categories table and early versions of the Employees table, in a DataGridView column. However, you can't save these images to usable bitmap files or display them in PictureBoxes because the images include an OLE header block that specifies the images' editing application.

Substituting XML Infoset source documents and their schema for database tables lets you edit documents with bound text boxes, DataGridViews, and other databound Windows form controls. You can use VS 2005's XML Editor to infer untyped schemas from source documents or use the .NET Framework's schema inference engine or the Xsd.exe command-line tool to infer typed schemas that guess the datatypes of the source documents' string representation of numeric values. Simple one-to-many hierarchical source documents with nested or wrapped-nested structures are the easiest to bind to DataGridViews.

Xsd.exe generates serializable classes from XML schemas. .NET Framework 2.0's Xsd.exe version creates classes with private fields and public properties, which you can use as object data sources to create typed DataSets and generate editing forms. Serialized classes generate instances from XML source documents and permit editing with DataGridViews and saving edited documents. Replacing the default object arrays with generic `BindindList(Of T)` collections speeds document loading, and lets you add and delete DataGridView rows and their corresponding elements, groups, or both.

Part III

Data Binding in ASP.Net 2.0

7

Working with ASP.NET 2.0 DataSources and Bound Controls

.NET Framework 2.0's Windows form data sources, data components, and bound controls evolved from their .NET Framework 1.0 counterparts. Visual Studio 2005's data tools and wizard simplify common tasks, such as generating typed DataSets and designing master/details forms, but the tools and wizards strongly resemble their forebears. Making the transition from earlier Visual Studio data tools and components requires a modest learning curve for seasoned .NET developers. Substituting DataGridViews for the obsolescent DataGrid takes a bit more effort, but the DataGridView's added features and improved performance justify its more complex object model.

ASP.NET 2.0 — on the other hand — represents a radical departure from ASP.NET 1.x. Microsoft's free Web Matrix ASP.NET development tool was an instant success; a major contributor to its popularity was the lack of VS 2002 or 2003 and Internet Information Services (IIS) prerequisites. Web Matrix combines a graphical Web page designer and code editor (codenamed *Venus*) for ASP.NET 1.1 with a built-in, lightweight Web server (*Cassini*). Venus and Cassini provide the foundation for VS 2005's Visual Web Developer UI and the Visual Web Developer Web Server. Visual Web Developer (VWD) 2005 Express Edition is the equivalent of Web Matrix upgraded to the VS 2005 UI and ASP.NET 2.0. Unlike the language-specific Express editions, VWD 2005 Express supports VB, C#, and J#.

This chapter assumes that you have some experience creating and deploying data-driven Web sites with Active Server Pages (ASP), ASP.NET 1.x, or Web Matrix. This book is devoted to data-related topics. Thus the chapters in Part III, "Data Binding in ASP.NET 2.0," don't cover ASP.NET 2.0 Web site architecture and page design, such as site navigation, master pages, themes, and skins.

The sample projects' connection strings assume that you're running an SQL Server 2000, MSDE 2000, or SQL Server 2005 as the default `localhost` instance with the Northwind sample database.

If you're using Visual Web Developer 2005 Express Edition or a named SQL Server 2005 instance, you must modify the following Web.config section to point to the named instance:

```
<connectionStrings>
  <add name="NorthwindConnection" connectionString="Server=localhost;Integrated
  Security=True;Database=Northwind" providerName="System.Data.SqlClient" />
</connectionStrings>
```

Change localhost to .\SQLExpress to use the Shared Memory provider with SQL Server 2005 Express.

Explore New ASP.NET 2.0 Features

The process of creating Web form applications with VS 2005 differs markedly from that of VS 2002 and 2003, which depend on a previously defined IIS virtual directory. VS 2005's New Project dialog no longer includes ASP.NET Web Project, ASP.NET Web Service, and other Web-related icons. The File ⇨ New menu offers a Web site choice that opens the New Web Site dialog with file system–based ASP.NET Web Site, ASP.NET Web Service, and other template icons. \WebSites is the default root folder for adding new Web site or Service subfolders. You can click the Browse button to open the Choose Location dialog, accept the default File System option, and navigate to or add a more appropriately named path to the Location text box (see Figure 7-1).

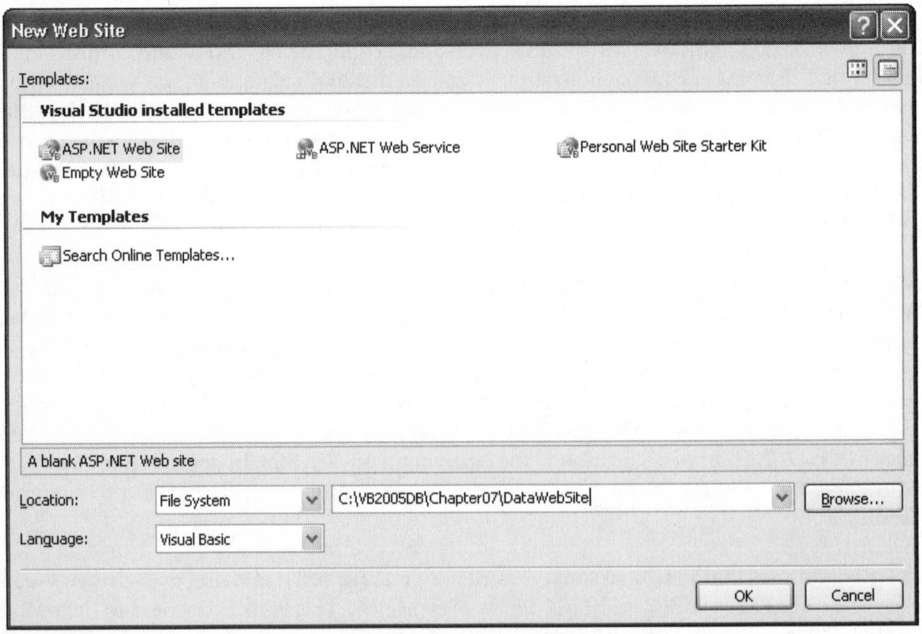

Figure 7-1

Click OK to generate a site folder with *FolderName* solution and project items, add an empty App_Data folder, a Default.aspx page file, and a Default.aspx.vb code-behind file. If Default.aspx.vb isn't present, right-click Default.aspx in Solution Explorer and choose View Code to generate the file. Default.aspx.vb contains empty `Partial Class Default_aspx` and `Inherits System.Web.UI.Page` declarations for code behind the Default.aspx page.

> *The Add New Item dialog has a Place Code in Separate File checkbox that's marked by default. Unless you clear the checkbox, all new ASP.NET Web forms, master pages, Web services, and user controls you add have an associated code-behind partial class file.*

Default.aspx opens in the inline XHTML 1.1 Source (markup) editor with the default page directive, `DOCTYPE` declaration, and `<html>`, `<head>`, `<body>`, `<form>`, and `<div>` elements, as shown reformatted in Figure 7-2.

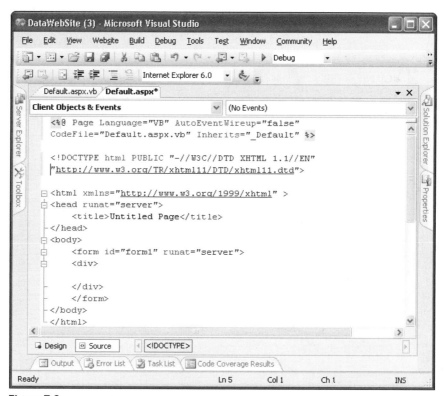

Figure 7-2

Replace `Untitled Page` with a more descriptive name, and click the View Designer button to display an empty page in the designer, which supports conventional HTML flow layout mode only. ASP.NET 2.0 doesn't support ASP.NET 1.*x*'s default grid-based fixed element positioning mode by default.

The explanation for the missing fixed-position design mode is that flow layout supports a wider range of browsers and devices. Place controls in table cells to control relative positioning; add cascading style sheets (CSS) for fixed positioning. To specify alternative positioning methods for Web controls, choose Tools ⇨ Options ⇨ HTML Designer ⇨ CSS Positioning, mark the Change Positioning . . . checkbox, and select the position method from the dropdown list.

Choose Layout ⇨ Insert Table to open the Insert Table dialog, select the Template option, accept the default Header style, and click OK to add a full-page table with a header and no borders. Type and format a title for the table, select the entire table by clicking in the upper-left corner, open the Properties window, and assign a table Id value (such as tblmain) and a Web color name (such as Gainsboro) to the BgColor property; the named color changes to its RGB value (see Figure 7-3).

Finally, press F5 to build and run your work so far. Click OK in the Debugging Not Enabled dialog to add a Web.config file to the project. The Visual Web Developer Web Server starts and displays Default.aspx in IE. Right-click the Web Server icon on the taskbar and select show details to open the server's properties dialog, which displays the randomly selected TCP port for the page (see Figure 7-4).

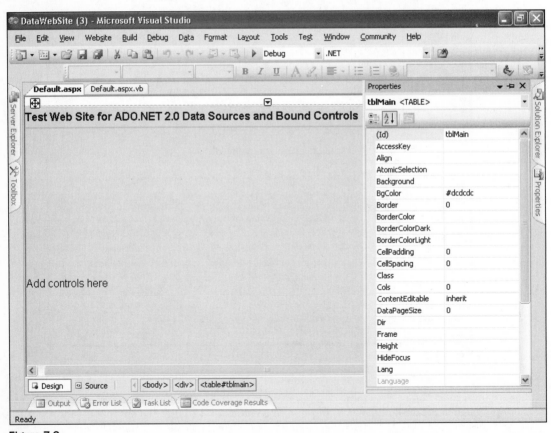

Figure 7-3

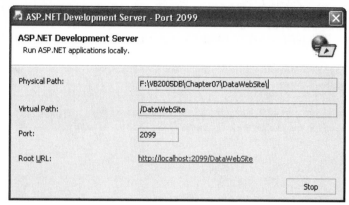

Figure 7-4

Web sites don't create solution files by default until you add another project to the solution. To add a *SiteName*.sln file to all Web site projects, open the Options dialog's Projects and Solutions\General page and verify that the Always Show Solution checkbox is marked. To ensure that the solution file is present in the correct folder, select the Solution item in Solution Explorer, choose File ➪ Save *SolutionName*.sln As, and navigate to the desired folder in the Save File As dialog.

The ASP.NET 2.0 Compilation Model

An ASP.NET 1.1 page directive specifies the name of the code-behind file and the form's base class name, as shown here:

```
<%@ Page Language="vb" AutoEventWireup="false" Codebehind="Default.aspx.vb"
    Inherits="DataWebSite.Form1"%>
```

ASP.NET 1.*x PageName*.aspx.vb files contain an initialization region and initialization code for each control on the page. The first time you open `http://www.company.com/datawebsite/default.aspx`, the ASP.NET 1.*x* runtime compiles the code behind the page and generates a set of temporary files, including a file for the `Public Class Default_aspx` definition that's derived from the `WebSiteName.Form1` base class.

Following is the ASP.NET 2.0 page directive for the Default.aspx page you added in the preceding section:

```
<%@ Page Language="VB" AutoEventWireup="false" CodeFile="Default.aspx.vb"
    Inherits="_Default" %>
```

Partial classes for HTML markup and code behind the page eliminate the need for a derived class. The `CodeFile` instruction specifies that markup and code in Default.aspx, and code in Default.aspx.vb, is to be compiled into a single `_Default` class.

The DataWebSite project folder doesn't include the traditional \bin subfolder. Building and running an ASP.NET 2.0 solution with the built-in Web server generates a collection of temporary files in a \WINDOWS\Microsoft.NET\Framework\v2.0. *BuildNumber*\Temporary ASP.NET Files*websitename*\ *random1**random2* folder; *websitename* is the lowercased folder name, datawebsite for this example, and *random1**random2* are two random eight-character folder names, such as *e7ae7f95**aa3fd637* (see Figure 7-5). ASP.NET 1.1 generates temporary files in a similar folder hierarchy.

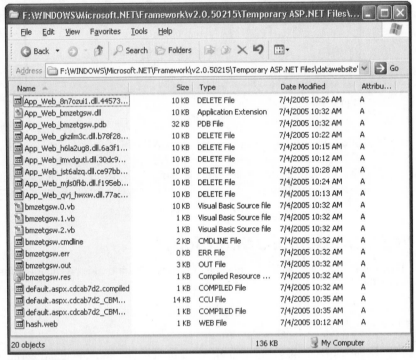

Figure 7-5

The last ' .NET ': Loaded . . . *entry in the Output window displays the full path to the current set of temporary files.*

Pressing F5 to build and run the project with the built-in Web server night not generate all temporary files. Copy the URL from the IE instance to the Clipboard, open another instance of IE, and paste the URL to generate the full set of temporary files. You can read most temporary files in Notepad.

The following table describes the temporary files shown in Figure 7-5. File names in boldface identify similar temporary files generated by ASP.NET 1.1.

Temporary File Name	Description
App_Web_bmzetgsw.dll	Compiled assembly of 0.vb, 1.vb, and 2.vb files
App_Web_bmzetgsw.pdb	Symbols (debugging) file for bmzetgsw.dll

Temporary File Name	Description
bmzetgsw.0.vb	`Partial Class Default_aspx` for the HTML, server controls, and inline code on the page (autogenerated from Default.aspx)
bmzetgsw.1.vb	`Partial Class Default_aspx` for code behind the page (copy of Default.aspx.vb)
bmzetgsw.2.vb	`Public Class FastObjectFactory` with an unused (dummy) `Shared Function Create_Default_aspx() As Object` function
bmzetgsw.cmdline	Vbc.exe compiler parameters for compiling the assembly
bmzetgsw.err	Compilation errors (empty if compilation is successful)
bmzetgsw.out	Full Vbc.exe compiler command (includes bmzetgsw.cmdline)
bmzetgsw.res	Compiled resource file, which contains the main table inline code
default.aspx.cdcab7d2 .compiled	File dependencies and hash values list for the page (XML)
default.aspx.cdcab7d2_ CBMResult.ccu	`CodeCompileUnit` (container for a CodeDOM program graph for the page)
default.aspx.cdcab7d2_ CBMResult.compiled	File dependencies list and hash values for the `CodeCompileUnit` (XML)
default.aspx.vb .cdcab7d2.compiled	File dependencies and hash values list for code behind the page (XML)
hash.web	16-byte hexadecimal hash value

ASP.NET 1.x doesn't add the Asp_Web_ prefix. ASP.NET 1.x temporary files include another set of random.0.vb ... random.pdb files for the Global_asax class. ASP.NET 2.0 projects don't include a default Global.asax file.

Compiling the HTML markup and code for each page improves productivity while you're developing individual pages or a complete site with the built-in Web server. Only modified pages recompile when you run the project. Chapter 8's "Publish Precompiled Web Sites" section describes how to deploy a completed Web form project to an IIS 5.0 or 6.0 virtual directory. Publishing a precompiled Web form project generates a single DLL in the \bin folder, removes the source code, and eliminates the compilation delay when the first user opens the project's Default.aspx or another designated startup page.

Special ASP.NET 2.0 Folders

ASP.NET 2.0 designates a set of "special directories" that the runtime recognizes when compiling the Web site. An Application_ prefix instructs the runtime to include the files in these folders during the compilation process. Prepending Application_ to folder names minimizes reserved folder name conflicts when upgrading ADO.NET 1.x Web projects to ADO.NET 2.0.

The following list briefly describes new ADO.NET 2.0 reserved folders:

❑ **App_Assemblies** replaces the \bin folder.

❑ **App_Data** stores a default SQL Express database file to support Web site login and personalization features, XML source documents and schemas, or other application-level data sources. App_Data is the only default reserved folder.

❑ **App_Code** is the location for class files and other code required for the project, except partial code-behind class files. The runtime generates references to classes defined in these files automatically; classes are accessible to code in any page in the project.

❑ **App_WebReferences** contains client proxy class files for projects that consume Web services.

❑ **App_Browsers** stores definition files for supported browsers.

❑ **App_GlobalResources** and **App_LocalResources** contain XML *Resource*.resx files that the runtime compiles into .res or .resource files.

❑ **App_Themes** stores page themes for the site or individual pages, default or named control skins, style sheets, and graphics for control icons.

You must add the special folders that you need as first-level subfolders of the project folder. The ASP.NET 2.0 runtime won't recognize special folder names in other locations.

New ASP.NET 2.0 Data Controls

ASP.NET 2.0 adds about 40 new Web controls to ASP.NET 1.1's repertoire. Many new server controls support declarative data connectivity and databinding with little or no inline code or code behind the page required. Databinding also automates optional update, insert, and delete operations for database tables and custom data access objects and components.

Following are brief descriptions of the new ASP.NET 2.0 server controls that support databinding and updates:

❑ **DataSource** controls connect to databases, data access objects, and tabular and hierarchical XML documents, including serialized typed DataSets. DataSource controls provide the binding source for two-way databound controls and other server controls, such as DropLists and ListBoxes, that support read-only databinding. DataSource controls replace the ADO.NET 1.1 data-related controls, such as ...Connections and ...DataAdapters.

❑ **DataList** controls display and edit tabular DataSource rows sequentially in one or more columns.

❑ **FormView** controls display and edit a single DataSource row in a conventional HTML form.

❑ **GridView** controls display and edit multiple DataSource rows in a grid that's similar to the Windows form DataGridView. GridView replaces ASP.NET 1.x's DataGrid.

❑ **DetailsView** controls display and edit a single DataSource row in a two-column table. DetailsView controls support master/child data editing pages.

The remainder of this chapter covers the preceding new data-related controls. Chapter 8 describes how to program the ASP.NET 2.0 version of the Repeater and TreeView controls.

DataSource Controls

The Data section of the VS 2005 toolbox replaces VS 2002 and 2003's ADO.NET 1.*x* DataSet, DataView, Connection, Command, and Adapter tools with a set of predefined DataSource tools. An ASP.NET 2.0 DataSource combines the required elements for the type of data source you specify into a named component that appears in page Design mode as a *DataSourceType – DataSourceName* placeholder. In Source mode, an `<asp:DataSourceType>` element stores the data source's definition.

You add a DataSource control to a page in Design view by dragging the control from the Toolbox's Data section to the page. VS 2005 provides the following built-in DataSource controls:

❑ **SqlDataSource** for client/server databases. The `<asp:SqlDataSource>` element includes `ConnectionString` and `SelectCommand` attributes that you add with the Configure Data Source dialogs. Updatable data sources let you add `DeleteCommand`, `InsertCommand`, and `UpdateCommand` attributes. Unlike Windows forms, which restrict `SqlConnection`, `SqlCommand`, and related objects to SQL Server databases, SqlDataSource lets you use any connection that you've defined in Server Explorer or define a new connection.

❑ **AccessDataSource** for Access .mdb files. The `<asp:AccessDataSource>` element substitutes a `datafile="~/App_Data/FileName.mdb"` relative path attribute for the SqlDataSource's `Connection` string attribute. You must use the Add Existing Item command to add the *FileName*.mdb file to the ...*ProjectName*\App_Data folder to make the file accessible to the Configure Data Source Wizard's Choose a Database dialog. AccessDataSources use the OLE DB Jet data provider, so you can specify a username and password for secure databases by modifying the Server Explorer connection.

❑ **ObjectDataSource** for custom business objects, Web services, data components, or DataSets that return and, optionally, update data. The object must support the `IEnumerable` interface and provide at least a public method to perform a select operation; delete, insert, and update methods are optional. You must add the object's class definition file to the App_Code folder or copy the object's assembly to the App_Assemblies folder. Alternatively, add a reference to the object's compiled class library with the Add Reference dialog or a Web Reference for the Web service with the Add Web Reference dialog.

❑ **XmlDataSource** for tabular or hierarchical XML source data. In this case, you store the XML source document file and its optional XML schema in the App_Data folder. XmlDataSource doesn't use the schema, but some bound controls can take advantage of the datatypes assigned to source document elements. You can update the XML source data by invoking the `GetXmlDocument` method to create an in-memory `XmlDataDocument` object, which exposes editable `XmlNode` objects. Alternatively, you can use XPath expressions to update the data.

❑ **SiteMapDataSource** connects to the project's site map tree, which you create with the XmlSiteMapProvider object.

This chapter's sample Web form projects use AsscessDataSource and SqlDataSource controls exclusively. Chapter 8, "Applying Advanced ASP.NET Data Techniques," covers the ObjectDataSource and XmlDataSource. The SiteMapDataSource is outside the scope of this book because its purpose is related to Web site design and navigation.

Built-in DataSource server controls extend the `DataSourceControl` base class, which provides the base `IDataSource` interface. DataSource controls contain named `DataSourceView` objects; databound Web controls connect to the default `DataSourceView`. You can create custom DataSource server controls by adding code to extend the `DataSourceControl` class.

The online help topic "About the DataSourceControlClass" includes the source code for a CsvDataSource server control that retrieves data from a comma-separated value file.

When you drag a server control that derives from the `DataBoundControl` abstract base class—such as a DataList, DetailsView, GridView, FormView, or TreeView—or a Repeater control to the page, the Common *ControlType* Tasks smart tag opens with the Choose Data Source dropdown list active. You can select (None), an existing DataSource for the page, or <New Data Source> to start the Data Source Configuration Wizard. Alternatively, drag one of the DataSource controls from the Toolbox and use this as your data source. You also can start the Data Source Configuration Wizard from the Data menu by choosing Add Data Source or by clicking the Data Sources window's Add Data Source button.

Multiple controls on a page can share the same DataSourceControl, but Microsoft recommends (strongly) that each control should have its own DataSourceControl. All SqlDataSources in a Web form project can share a common connection string, if you store the connection string in the Web.config file.

Other server controls that derive from the `ListControl` base class—such as the DropDownList, ListBox, RadioButtonList, and BulletedList—support simple (read-only) databinding. These controls' smart tags offer a Choose Data Source option, which opens a dialog of the same name. The Choose Data Source dialog has the same options as the `DataBoundControl`-based server control's smart tag, but the dialog also includes dropdown lists to select the data and value fields of the list.

The DataList Control

The DataList server control is the simplest of the built-in `DataBoundControl` derivatives. By default, the DataList displays column names and values for all rows returned by the `SelectCommand`'s SQL statement in a single column of labels. You can specify multiple columns and the order in which the columns display the rows, along with myriad other formatting options. Figure 7-6 shows the DataWebSite's DataList.aspx page, which displays orders for the country you select in a DropDownList in left-to-right, top-to-bottom descending sequence of OrderID values. The first list sets the ShipCountry WHERE clause criterion. The second list lets you select any order record in the current country list; selecting an order row displays the CustomerID value in an unbound text box.

The sample DataWebSite project in the VB2005DB\Chapter07\DataWebSite folder includes a completed version of the DataList.aspx page as FinalDataList.aspx. Right-click FinalDataList.aspx in the Solution Explorer, choose Set As Start Page, and press F5 to build the project and open the page in Internet Explorer (IE).

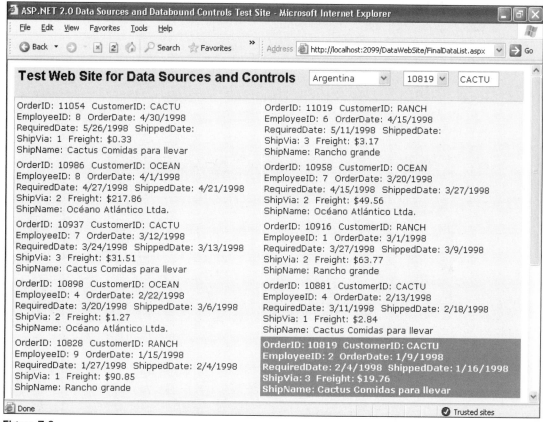

Figure 7-6

SqlDataSources for Bound Controls

You create an SqlDataSource for bound controls by dragging a DataList, FormView, GridView, DetailsView, or Repeater control from the Toolbox's Data section to a Web page. For this example, you start with the Default.aspx page that you added in the "Explore New ASP.NET 2.0 Features" section at the beginning of the chapter or the empty Default.aspx page in the VB2005DB\Chapter07\DataWebSite folder.

This and the remaining example projects assume the existence of a connection in the Data Connections to a local instance of SQL Server 2000 or 2005 with the Northwind database installed.

1. Copy and paste Default.aspx; rename the copy of Default.aspx to DataList.aspx. Open DataList.aspx in Source mode, and change `CodeFile="Default.aspx.vb"` `Inherits="_Default "` in the page directive to `CodeFile="DataList.aspx.vb"` `Inherits="DataList "`. Open DataList.aspx.vb and change `Partial Class _Default` to `Partial Class DataList`, and close the editor window.

2. Right-click DataList.aspx in Solution Explorer and choose Set as Start Page. Press F5 to verify your page addition and start page setting.

3. Close IE, change to DataList.aspx Design mode, and drag a DataList control from the Toolbox to DataList.aspx's empty table cell. A DataList – DataList1 placeholder is added to the form and the DataLists Tasks smart tag opens.

4. Select <New Data Source> in the Select Data Source list to start the Data Source Configuration Wizard. Select Database in the Select a Data Source list, and replace SqlDataSource1 with dsOrders (see Figure 7-7).

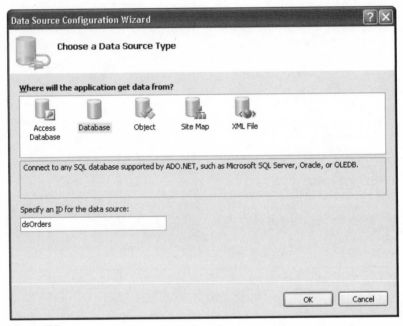

Figure 7-7

5. Click OK to open the Choose a Connection dialog, select an existing connection to the Northwind sample database, or create a new connection. If you want to be able to deploy the site to an IIS Web server that supports anonymous connections, select or add a connection that uses SQL Server security. Click Next.

6. Leave the Yes, Save This Connection As checkbox marked, and edit the connection string name as desired. Click Next to open the Configure Data Source dialog.

7. Select the Orders table in the Name list, and mark the first nine checkboxes—OrderID through ShipName (see Figure 7-8).

8. Click the ORDER BY button to open the Add ORDER BY Clause dialog, select OrderID in the Sort By list, and select the Descending option (see Figure 7-9). Click OK.

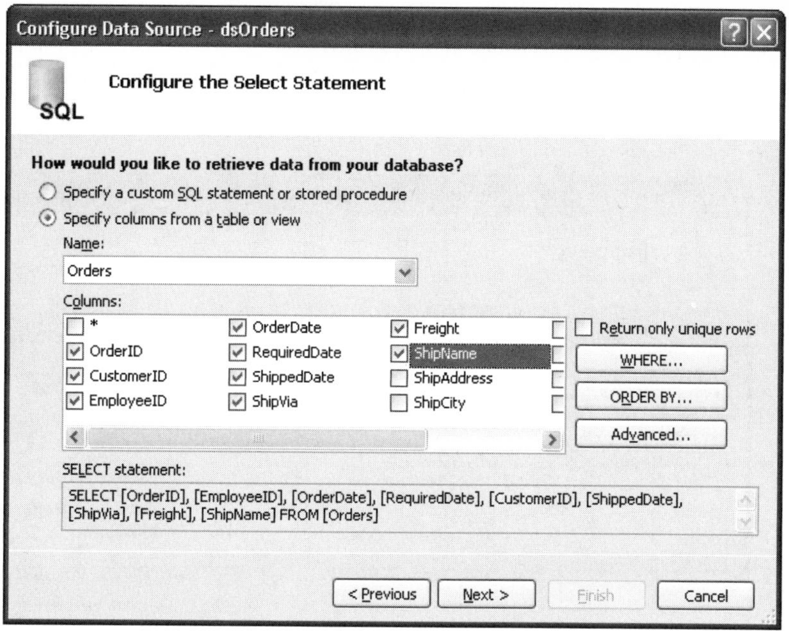

Figure 7-8

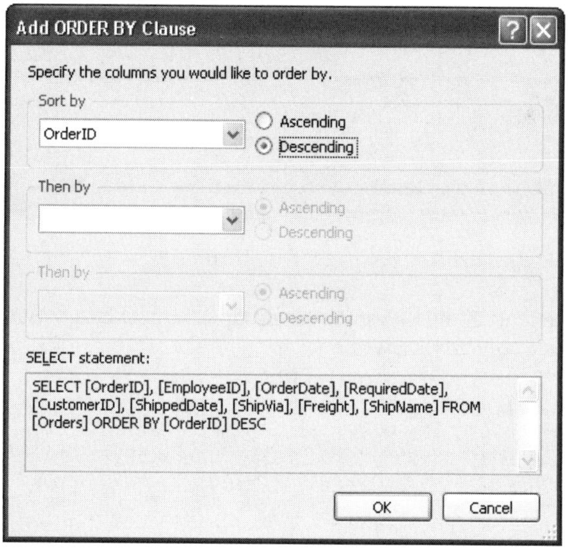

Figure 7-9

9.   Click the Advanced Options button to open the Advanced SQL Generation Options dialog; mark the Generate Insert, Update, and Delete Statements checkbox. For this example, don't mark the Use Optimistic Concurrency checkbox. Click OK and Next to open the Test Query dialog.

10.   Click Test Query to display the query resultset in a DataGridView (see Figure 7-10).

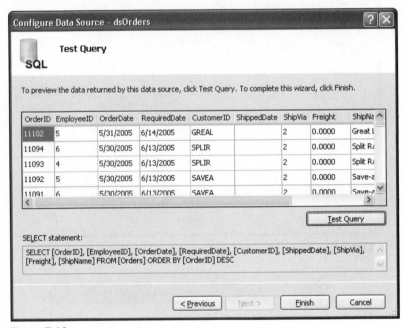

Figure 7-10

11.   Click Finish to display the default design format for a DataList, which consists of five simulated instances of the data for the columns you selected in Step 7.

12.   Press F5 to build and display the page, which appears as shown in Figure 7-11.

The dsOrders data source with the Generate Insert, Update, and Delete Statements checkbox marked adds the following source code to the page:

```
<asp:SqlDataSource ID="dsOrders" Runat="server"
    DeleteCommand="DELETE FROM [Orders] WHERE [OrderID] = @original_OrderID"
    InsertCommand="INSERT INTO [Orders] ([CustomerID], [EmployeeID], [OrderDate],
        [RequiredDate], [ShippedDate], [ShipVia], [Freight], [ShipName])
        VALUES (@CustomerID, @EmployeeID, @OrderDate, @RequiredDate, @ShippedDate,
        @ShipVia, @Freight, @ShipName)"
    SelectCommand="SELECT [OrderID], [CustomerID], [EmployeeID], [OrderDate],
        [RequiredDate], [ShippedDate], [ShipVia], [Freight], [ShipName]
        FROM [Orders] ORDER BY [OrderID] DESC"
    UpdateCommand="UPDATE [Orders] SET [CustomerID] = @CustomerID,
        [EmployeeID] = @EmployeeID, [OrderDate] = @OrderDate,
        [RequiredDate] = @RequiredDate, [ShippedDate] = @ShippedDate,
        [ShipVia] = @ShipVia, [Freight] = @Freight, [ShipName] = @ShipName
        WHERE [OrderID] = @original_OrderID"
```

```
          ConnectionString="<%$ ConnectionStrings:NorthwindConnection %>">
          <DeleteParameters>
              <asp:Parameter Type="Int32" Name="OrderID"></asp:Parameter>
          </DeleteParameters>
          <UpdateParameters>
              <asp:Parameter Type="String" Name="CustomerID"></asp:Parameter>
              <asp:Parameter Type="Int32" Name="EmployeeID"></asp:Parameter>
              <asp:Parameter Type="DateTime" Name="OrderDate"></asp:Parameter>
              <asp:Parameter Type="DateTime" Name="RequiredDate"></asp:Parameter>
              <asp:Parameter Type="DateTime" Name="ShippedDate"></asp:Parameter>
              <asp:Parameter Type="Int32" Name="ShipVia"></asp:Parameter>
              <asp:Parameter Type="Decimal" Name="Freight"></asp:Parameter>
              <asp:Parameter Type="String" Name="ShipName"></asp:Parameter>
              <asp:Parameter Type="Int32" Name="OrderID"></asp:Parameter>
          </UpdateParameters>
          <InsertParameters>
              <asp:Parameter Type="String" Name="CustomerID"></asp:Parameter>
              <asp:Parameter Type="Int32" Name="EmployeeID"></asp:Parameter>
              <asp:Parameter Type="DateTime" Name="OrderDate"></asp:Parameter>
              <asp:Parameter Type="DateTime" Name="RequiredDate"></asp:Parameter>
              <asp:Parameter Type="DateTime" Name="ShippedDate"></asp:Parameter>
              <asp:Parameter Type="Int32" Name="ShipVia"></asp:Parameter>
              <asp:Parameter Type="Decimal" Name="Freight"></asp:Parameter>
              <asp:Parameter Type="String" Name="ShipName"></asp:Parameter>
          </InsertParameters>
      </asp:SqlDataSource>
```

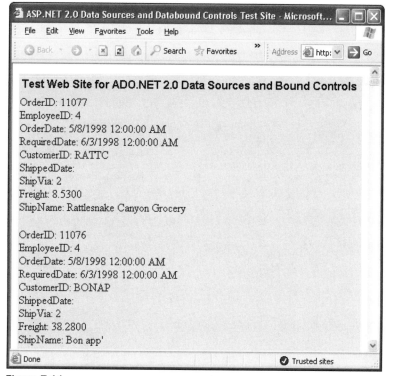

Figure 7-11

Control Properties

The Properties window for bound controls lets you specify the font and other properties that apply to the control. In addition to properties that apply to all server controls, the DataList has properties that specify the number of list columns and the flow of data in the columns. To emulate the design of FinalDataList.aspx, right-click the control and choose Properties to open the Properties window with DataList1 selected, and set the property values shown in the following table.

Property	Value
Id	dlOrders
Font\Name	Verdana
Font\Size	10pt
RepeatColumns	2
RepeatDirection	Horizontal

Then drag the right edge of the dlOrders DataList to the right border of the table. The preceding property values generate a page with data for orders in the left-to-right, top-to-bottom descending sequence shown in Figure 7-12.

> *Alternatively, open the DataList Tasks smart tag, and select Property Builder to open the DataList Properties sheet to set the preceding property values, except Id.*

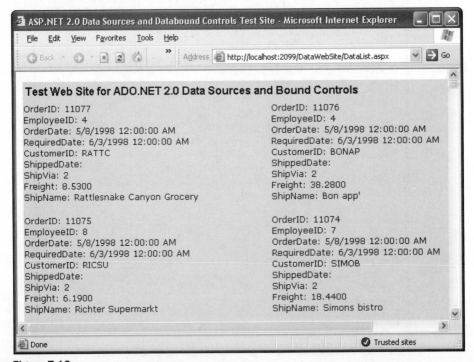

Figure 7-12

Databound Templates and Data Formatting

DataLists introduce the template concept for fields of DataBoundControls. Right-click the DataList control in Design mode, choose Show Smart Tag to open the smart tag panel for the control, and click the smart tag's Edit Templates verb to open an editing form for the default Item template. Item templates contain HTML text for the column names and *ColumnName*Label controls to display the column values.

Reformat the Item Template

To conserve vertical space, you can modify the template to show multiple column names and values on a single line. Widen the template to about 500 pixels, position the cursor after the OrderIDLabel item, press delete to remove the <br /> element, and replace it with two spaces ( ). Do the same for the EmployeeIDLabel, RequiredDateLabel, and ShipViaLabel. Your template now appears as shown in Figure 7-13.

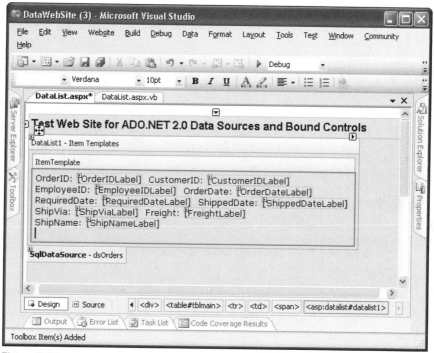

Figure 7-13

Format DateTime and Currency Data

When you run the redesigned form, datetime values include the default 12:00:00 AM time, and the Freight (money) value is formatted as a numeric value with four decimal places. To remove the time values from the dates, click the smart tag arrow of the OrderDateLabel to open the Label Tasks smart tag, and click the Edit DataBindings verb to open the OrderDateLable DataBindings dialog. With the default Text property selected in the Bindable Properties list, select Short Date {0:d} in the Format list, and click OK (see Figure 7-14).

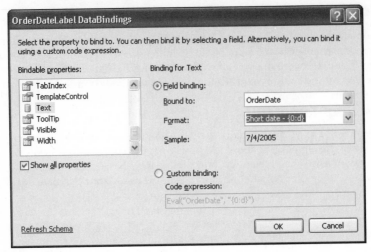

Figure 7-14

If the Field Binding radio button is disabled, click the Refresh Schema link to enable it and its associated controls.

Repeat the preceding process for the RequiredDateLabel and ShippedDateLabel. Then select the FreightLabel, but select Currency {0:C} as the format. Press F5 and scroll to orders that have a ShippedDate value to verify your formatting, which should conform to that of Figure 7-6. Finally, open the common DataList Tasks smart tag for the entire Datalist and click the End Template Editing verb.

Review the Generated XHTML Source Code

Each Item Template definition adds HTML *ColumnName* text followed by a Label server control instruction with the Label's Text property value specified by an `Eval("ColumnName")` or `Eval("ColumnName", "FormatString")` instruction that's enclosed by databinding tags (`<%# ... %>`). Selecting the template's End Editing verb or building the project adds the source code to the page.

Following is the source code — reformatted for readability — generated by the Item Template shown in Figure 7-13:

```
<ItemTemplate>
    OrderID: <asp:Label ID="OrderIDLabel" Runat="server"
        Text='<%# Eval("OrderID") %>'></asp:Label> 
    CustomerID: <asp:Label ID="CustomerIDLabel" Runat="server"
        Text='<%# Eval("CustomerID") %>'></asp:Label><br />
    EmployeeID: <asp:Label ID="EmployeeIDLabel" Runat="server"
        Text='<%# Eval("EmployeeID") %>'></asp:Label> 
    OrderDate: <asp:Label ID="OrderDateLabel" Runat="server"
        Text='<%# Eval("OrderDate", "{0:d}") %>'></asp:Label><br />
    RequiredDate: <asp:Label ID="RequiredDateLabel" Runat="server"
        Text='<%# Eval("RequiredDate", "{0:d}") %>'></asp:Label> 
    ShippedDate: <asp:Label ID="ShippedDateLabel" Runat="server"
```

```
        Text='<%# Eval("ShippedDate", "{0:d}") %>'></asp:Label><br />
    ShipVia: <asp:Label ID="ShipViaLabel" Runat="server"
        Text='<%# Eval("ShipVia") %>'></asp:Label> 
    Freight: <asp:Label ID="FreightLabel" Runat="server"
        Text='<%# Eval("Freight", "{0:C}") %>'></asp:Label><br />
    ShipName: <asp:Label ID="ShipNameLabel" Runat="server"
        Text='<%# Eval("ShipName") %>'></asp:Label> <br />
</ItemTemplate>
```

The {0:d} expression is a standard format string for short date; {0:C} specifies currency format. 0: represents the value; letters correspond to the numeric or DateTime formatting strings you apply as arguments to the ToString method, as in NumericValue.ToString("C") or DateTimeValue.ToString("d").

The online help topic "Standard Numeric Format Strings" contains a table that describes the set of format strings for numbers. The "Standard DateTime Format Strings" topic covers formatting DateTime data types.

DataSource WHERE Constraints from Bound Control Values

The dsOrders' SqlDataSource returns all Orders records, which isn't likely to be convenient for users, and opening the page consumes a substantial amount of database server and network resources. One approach to limiting the number of records returned by the server is to add a DropDownList that adds a WHERE clause constraint to the DataList's DataSource. For this example, the constraint is based on the Orders table's ShipCountry column; alternatives might be EmployeeID or ranges of OrderDate values, such as year and month.

Add a DropDownList Populated by a New DataSource

To add a DropDownList populated by unique values of the ShipCountry column, do the following:

1. Drag a DropDownList server control to the right of the title in the top table cell and add a few spaces between it and the title.

2. Click the smart tag arrow to open the DropDownList Tasks smart tag, mark the Enable AutoPostBack checkbox, and click the Choose Data Source link to open the same-named dialog.

3. Choose <New Data Source> in the Select a Data Source list to open the Data Source Configuration Wizard. Select Database, name the DataSource dsCountries, and click OK. In the Choose a Connection dialog, select the NorthwindConnectionString string you saved when creating the primary DataSource, and click Next.

4. In the Configure Select Statement dialog, select the Orders table, mark the ShipCountry column and Return Only Unique Rows checkboxes, click the ORDER BY button, apply an ascending sort on ShipCountry, and click OK.

5. Click Next, test your query, and click Finish to return to the Choose Data Source dialog, which displays ShipCountry as the display and value fields (see Figure 7-15). Click OK to close the dialog.

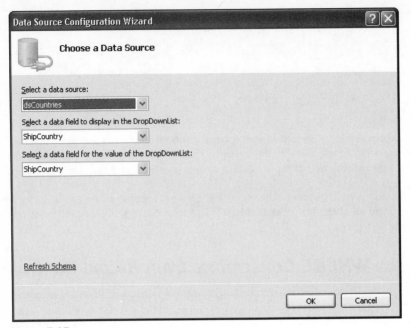

Figure 7-15

6. Open the Properties window for DropDownList1 and change its Id property value to ddlCountry or the like.

7. Press F5 and verify that the DropDownList displays the countries in alphabetic order. Selecting a country other than Argentina causes the server to refresh the page with the postback operation you specified in Step 2.

Add a WHERE Clause Constraint Based on the List's Selected Index

To hook the DropDownList selection to a WHERE clause constraint that you add to the dsOrders SqlDataSource, do the following:

1. Click the dsOrders placeholder's smart tag arrow to open the SqlDataSource Tasks smart tag, click the Configure Data Source verb to start the Data Source Configuration Wizard, and click Next.

2. Select the NorthwindConnectionString, click Next, and repeat the Orders table field selection and ORDER BY clause for the SelectCommand.

3. Click the WHERE button to open the Add WHERE Clause dialog, select ShipCountry in the Column list, accept the default = Operator, and select Control in the Source list, which displays the Parameter Properties group box.

4. Select ddlCountry in the Control ID list and, optionally, add a country as the Default Value (see Figure 7-16).

5. Click Add to add the [ShipCountry] = @ShipCountry criterion and ddlCountry.SelectedValue as the @ShipCountry value.

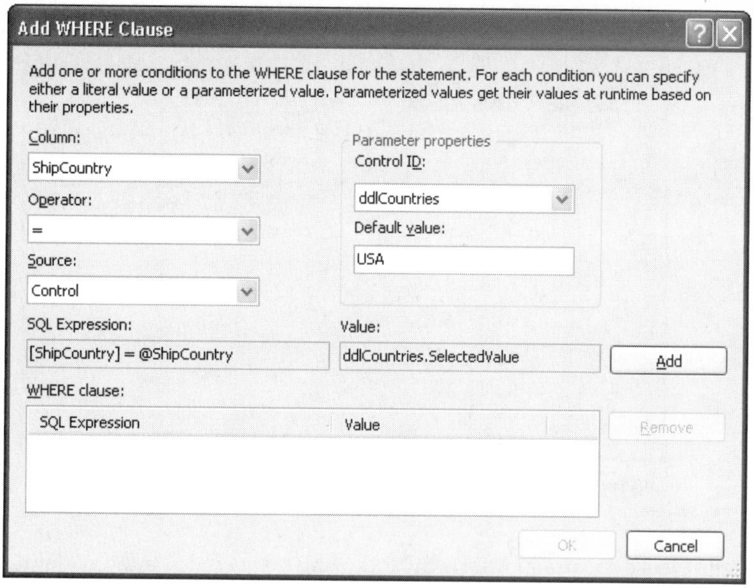

Figure 7-16

6. Click OK to close the dialog; then click Next, and then Test Query to open the Parameter Value Editors dialog. Click OK to accept the default value, if you added it in Step 4. Otherwise type USA as the parameter value. Click OK to close the dialog, review the query result set, and click Finish.

7. Press F5 and verify that selecting a country other than Argentina in ddlCountry refreshes the DataList with the appropriate records.

If you'd prefer to require users to select a country, rather than display records for the first country in the list, you can take advantage of a new ASP.NET 2.0 list property — AppendDataBoundItems. Open ddlCountry's Properties window, and set the AppendDataBoundItems property value to True. Click ddlCountries smart tag arrow. Select Edit Items to open the Items collection's ListItem Collection Editor dialog, click Add, and type **[Select a Country]** as the Text value, which also appears in the Value text box (see Figure 7-17). Click OK and reopen the page with an initially empty table cell.

If you substitute angle brackets (< >) for square brackets ([ ]), your page will throw a security exception when you select [Select a Country].

Following is the page source code for the ddlCountry and dsCountries:

```
<asp:DropDownList ID="ddlCountry" Runat="server" DataSourceID="dsCountries"
    Width="115px" Height="22px" AutoPostBack="True" DataTextField="ShipCountry"
    DataValueField="ShipCountry" AppendDataBoundItems="True">
    <asp:ListItem>[Select a Country]</asp:ListItem>
</asp:DropDownList>
<asp:SqlDataSource ID="dsCountries" Runat="server" SelectCommand="SELECT
    DISTINCT [ShipCountry] FROM [Orders] ORDER BY [ShipCountry]"
    ConnectionString="<%$ ConnectionStrings:NorthwindConnection %>">
</asp:SqlDataSource>
```

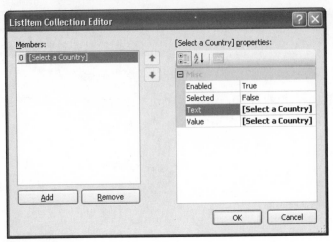

Figure 7-17

Adding the WHERE clause constraint inserts the following ControlParameter definition into the dsOrders <asp:SQLDataSource ...> source code:

```
<SelectParameters>
    <asp:ControlParameter Name="ShipCountry" DefaultValue="USA" Type="String"
    ControlID="ddlCountry" PropertyName="SelectedValue"></asp:ControlParameter>
</SelectParameters>
```

Edit Items in DataLists

It's cumbersome for users to edit items in a DataList, especially if it has a large number of items. Using a GridView or DetailsView control to edit data is a much faster and simpler approach because the designer creates the required edit, insert, and delete templates for you. Later sections describe the features of the new GridView and DetailsView controls. You also must write code to obtain original and updated values in the DataList_UpdateCommand event handler and assign them as values of DataSource.Command.Parameters collection members in the DataSource_Updating event handler. The following code behind the DataWebSite sample project's EditableDataList.aspx.vb file obtains and assigns the parameter values to update a selected item:

```
Public Sub dlOrders_UpdateCommand(ByVal source As Object,
  ByVal e As System.Web.UI.WebControls.DataListCommandEventArgs)
  Handles dlOrders.UpdateCommand
    'Read-only OrderID value
    Dim strOrderID As String = dlOrders.DataKeys(e.Item.ItemIndex).ToString
    Dim strCustomerID As String = Nothing
    Dim txtBox As TextBox
    Dim strTextBox As String = Nothing
    Dim intParam As Integer
    alParamValues = New ArrayList
    For intParam = 0 To dsOrders.UpdateParameters.Count - 1
        strTextBox = "TextBox" + (intParam + 2).ToString
        txtBox = CType(e.Item.FindControl(strTextBox), TextBox)
        If intParam = dsOrders.UpdateParameters.Count - 1 Then
```

```
                    '@original_OrderID
                    alParamValues.Add(strOrderID)
            Else
                If txtBox Is Nothing Then
                    alParamValues.Add(Nothing)
                Else
                    'Other parameter values
                    If txtBox.Text.Contains("$") Then
                        'Remove currency symbol for freight
                        alParamValues.Add(Mid(Trim(txtBox.Text), 2))
                    Else
                        alParamValues.Add(Trim(txtBox.Text))
                    End If
                End If
            End If
        Next
        'Execute the Update method
        dsOrders.Update()

        'Return to Item mode
        dlOrders.EditItemIndex = -1
        dlOrders.DataBind()
End Sub

Protected Sub dsOrders_Updating(ByVal sender As Object, _
  ByVal e As System.Web.UI.WebControls.SqlDataSourceCommandEventArgs) _
  Handles dsOrders.Updating
    Try
        Dim strUpdateCmd As String = e.Command.CommandText
        Dim intCtr As Integer
        For intCtr = 0 To e.Command.Parameters.Count - 1
            Dim strName As String = e.Command.Parameters(intCtr).ParameterName
            If alParamValues(intCtr).ToString = "" _
            Or alParamValues(intCtr) Is Nothing Then
                e.Command.Parameters(intCtr).Value = DBNull.Value
            Else
                e.Command.Parameters(intCtr).Value = alParamValues(intCtr)
            End If
        Next
    Catch exc As Exception
        'Ignore
    End Try
End Sub
```

The parameter value assignment instructions substitute NULL for empty strings or missing value types, which otherwise throw an "Invalid data format" exception.

If you decide to add editing capability to a DataList, you can add an EditItem template to the DataList by copying the Item template to the EditItems template and replacing the labels with text boxes. You must add buttons to activate the EditItem template, update the DataSource, or cancel the update operation. Unlike the buttons you add to FormView controls in the next section, you must add handlers for the EditCommand, UpdateCommand, and CancelCommand events to the page or in the code-behind file. Figure 7-18 shows the sample project's EditableDataList.aspx page with an item in edit mode. For this and most other examples in this chapter, the code-behind file contains all event handlers.

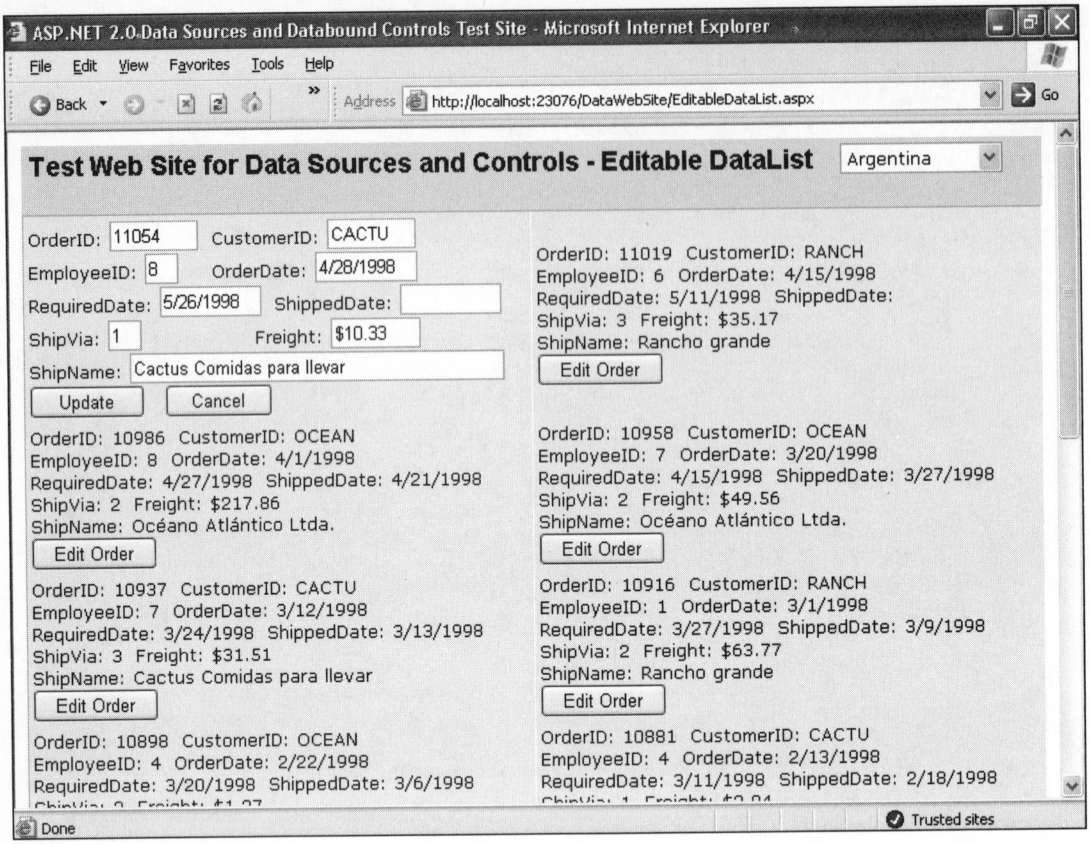

Figure 7-18

The FormView Control

The FormView control enables free-form design of the Item template. For example, you can add a multi-column table to the Item template, and then cut and paste the default *ColumnName* text and *ColumnName*Label controls into the table cells. You can specify table cell border style, width, and color, as well as background colors for labels. FormView is a more flexible alternative to GridView or DetailsView controls for updating and adding base-table records.

The process of adding a FormView and its SqlDataSource to a page is almost identical to that for a GridView. When you use a FormView to edit base table data, it's a good practice to add all table columns to the data source.

Page the DataSource

The FormView control supports paging, which enables you to select a specific record to display or edit. To enable paging, open the Properties window for the FormView and set the `AllowPaging` property value to True. PagerSettings default to a set of ten sequential item number values and ellipsis buttons to select the next or previous decade, but you can set the Pager's Mode property value to NumericFirstLast and then type First and Last as the values of the FirstPageText and LastPageText property values. Finally, expand the PagerStyle node and set the Font node's property values to emphasize the Pager at the bottom of the form (see Figure 7-19).

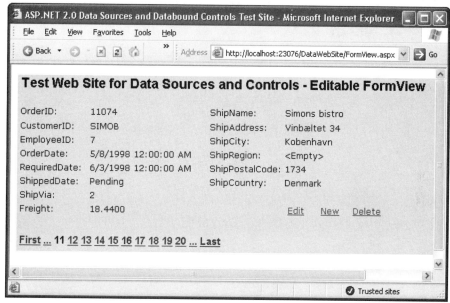

Figure 7-19

Paging is a very resource-intensive operation, especially for tables with a large number of records. Clicking any pager button executes the SelectCommand and retrieves all rows from the database server that meet the WHERE clause criterion, if present. Filtering records with a WHERE clause generated from the one or more dropdown lists usually is the most effective method to reduce the size of the SelectCommand's query resultset. For sequentially ordered records, you can minimize resource consumption by adding a TOP n modifier and ORDER BY clause to the SelectCommand's SQL statement.

Replace Null Values with Column-Specific Text

The following code behind the FormView.aspx page adds the Pending and <Empty> text elements that replace null values for missing ShippedDate, ShipRegion, and ShipPostalCode values in the Item template:

```
Partial Class FormView_aspx
    Protected Sub fvOrders_DataBound(ByVal sender As Object, _
    ByVal e As System.EventArgs) Handles fvOrders.DataBound
        'Add default values for null ShippedDate, ShipRegion, and ShipPostalCode
        'Disable deletion of shipped orders
        Try
            If IsDBNull(fvOrders.DataItem("ShippedDate")) Then
                Dim lblDate As Label = _
```

```
                    CType(fvOrders.FindControl("ShippedDateLabel"), Label)
                If Not lblDate Is Nothing Then
                   lblDate.Text = "Pending"
                End If
                'Enable deletion of orders not shipped
                Dim btnDelete As Button = _
                 CType(fvOrders.FindControl("btnDelete"), Button)
                If Not btnDelete Is Nothing Then
                   btnDelete.Enabled = True
                End If
            Else
                'Disable deletion of shipped orders
                Dim btnDelete As Button = _
                 CType(fvOrders.FindControl("btnDelete"), Button)
                If Not btnDelete Is Nothing Then
                   btnDelete.Enabled = False
                End If
            End If
            If IsDBNull(fvOrders.DataItem("ShipRegion")) Then
                Dim lblRegion As Label = _
                 CType(fvOrders.FindControl("ShipRegionLabel"), Label)
                If Not lblRegion Is Nothing Then
                   lblRegion.Text = "&lt;Empty&gt;"
                End If
            End If
            If IsDBNull(fvOrders.DataItem("ShipPostalCode")) Then
                'Applies to Ireland only
                Dim lblCode As Label = _
                 CType(fvOrders.FindControl("ShipPostalCodeLabel"), Label)
                If Not lblCode Is Nothing Then
                   lblCode.Text = "&lt;Empty&gt;"
                End If
            End If
        Catch exc As Exception
            'Ignore exceptions
        End Try
    End Sub
End Class
```

The `DataBound` event fires after all DataSource rows populate. The `FormView.DataItem("ColumnName")` method returns the late-bound value of the currently selected data row. `Dim varName As ControlType = CType(FormView.FindControl("ControlId"), ControlType)` statements return a reference to the control that enables you to set its property values—such as `Text` or `Enabled`. The event handler also disables the Delete button for orders that have been shipped.

You can add text to replace all empty column values as the FormView's `EmptyDataText` *property value, but specifying different text for specific elements requires adding code.*

Edit, Add, and Delete Records

The FormView control is a better choice than the DataList for editing records because it displays a single item. You can create an EditItem or InsertItem template quickly in the editor's Source mode by copying and pasting the `<ItemTemplate>` node and its child nodes. (Deleting a row doesn't require a template.) The designer automatically renames labels that have duplicate `Id` values to `LabelN`, where N is a sequential number.

Rename the copied `<ItemTemplate>` to `<EditItemTemplate>`, and replace all instances of `Label` in `<EditItemTemplate>` child nodes with `TextBox` to complete the new template. If your Items template table has borders, tweak the EditItem template's table cell border property to remove them. Alternatively, change the `BorderColor` property to the table's `BgColor` or the FormView's `BackColor` property value. Figure 7-20 shows the FormView of Figure 7-19 with the EditItem template active.

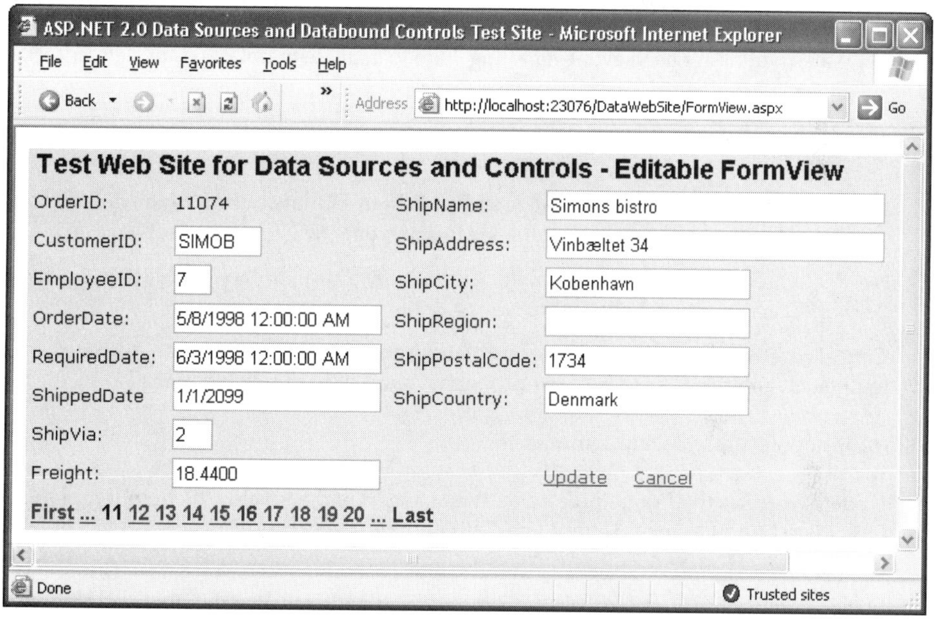

Figure 7-20

You can't insert arbitrary Text values for null date column values or apply special formatting to numeric values, such as currency symbols, in Edit mode. Your page will throw exceptions for values that don't correspond to `UpdateParameter` or `InsertParameter` data types. The 1/1/2099 value represents a NULL ShipDate value; the 1/1/0001 value that represents a null XML datetime value isn't a valid SQL Server date time value. Code in the `dsFormView_Updating` event handler translates the 1/1/2099 parameter value to NULL.

After you finalize the EditItem template's design, copy and paste in Source mode the `<EditItem Template>` and its child nodes, and rename the copy to `<InsertItemTemplate>` to enable adding new items.

DataWebSite.sln contains the completed version of the FormView.aspx page. Right-click FormView.aspx in the Solution Explorer and choose Set As Start Page to build and open the page. Clicking the Delete button throws an exception for orders with Order Details records. Eliminating the exception requires specifying cascading deletions for the FK_Order_Details_Orders relationship.

Add Command Buttons

FormView controls define a set of mode and action verbs for activating the EditItem or InsertItem template, canceling an edit or insert operation, and executing the DataSource's `UpdateCommand`, `InsertCommand`, or `DeleteCommand`. You add a Button, LinkButton, or ImageButton control to a template and assign a verb to the button by typing the verb name in the `CommandName` property's text box. Unlike similar buttons in DataList templates, you don't need event-handling code to activate templates or update, insert, or delete items.

Here's how you use the three mode verbs to activate templates:

❑ **Edit** activates the EditItem template. Add an Edit or Update button to the default Item template with its `CommandName` property value set to `edit` or `Edit`.

❑ **New** activates the InsertItem template. Add a New button to the default Item template with its `CommandName` property value set to `new` or `New`.

❑ **Cancel** reactivates the default Item template. Add Cancel buttons to the EditItem and InsertItem templates with their `CommandName` property value set to `cancel` or `Cancel`.

The following action verbs execute commands:

❑ **Update** executes the DataSource's `UpdateCommand` and activates the Item template. Add a Save or Update button to the EditItem template with its `CommandName` property value set to `update` or `Update`.

❑ **Insert** executes the DataSource's `InsertCommand` and activates the Item template. Add a Save, Add, or Insert button to the InsertItem template with its `CommandName` property value set to `insert` or `Insert`.

❑ **Delete** executes the DataSource's `DeleteCommand`. Add a Delete or Remove button to the default Item template with its `CommandName` property value set to `delete` or `Delete`.

Clicking any mode or action button executes the `SelectCommand` to refresh the page's data. For example, clicking the Edit button, followed by the Update button, executes the `SelectCommand` (to ensure current data), the `UpdateCommand`, and the `SelectCommand` a second time (to display the updated record).

Figure 7-21 shows the FormView.aspx page with the InsertItem template activated and data entry partly completed. Paging controls are hidden in Insert mode.

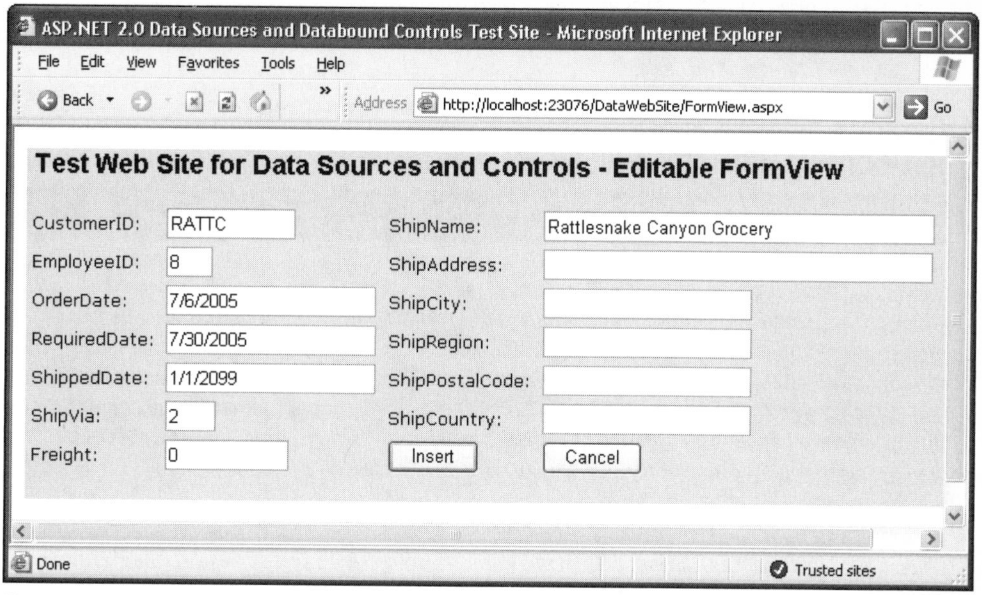

Figure 7-21

The GridView Control

The GridView control, which replaces ASP.NET 1.x's DataGrid, emulates the DataGridView Windows form control to a reasonable extent, when you consider the browser-based limitations of HTML server controls. The process of adding a GridView to a form is similar to that for a DataList or FormView. Drag a GridView control to a page, and select an existing or specify a new DataSource. Figure 7-22 shows a paged, read-only GridView control that's populated by the dsOrders SqlDataSource and has an auto-generated Select Command field.

The GridAndDetailsViews project in the ...\Chapter07\GridAndDetailsViews folder contains Default.aspx (shown in Figure 7-22), LinkedGridView.aspx, LinkedDetailsView.aspx, EditableGridView.aspx, and EditableDetailsView.aspx pages.

You add a Select Command field for read-only GridViews by marking the Enable Selection checkbox of the GridView Tasks smart tag. Marking the Enable Paging checkbox adds a default numeric paging section to the form. Marking the Enable Sorting checkbox adds underlines to and changes the color of the column headers to indicate sorting capability. You can disable sorting on selected fields by clearing their SortExpression property value in the Fields dialog. GridViews with updatable DataSources add Enable Editing and Enable Deleting checkboxes, as shown in Figure 7-23. A serious limitation of GridViews is the inability to add new items. To add items, use either a DetailsView or a FormView, which can be on the same or a different page. The "The DetailsView Control" section, later in this chapter, describes how to add items with a DetailsView control on another page.

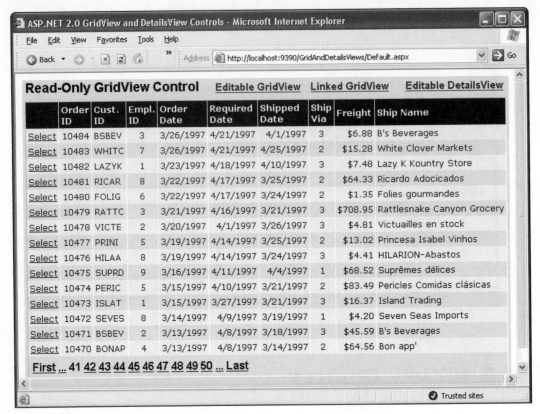

Figure 7-22

Figure 7-23

GridView controls support the following seven field types:

❑ CommandFields correspond to the FormView's mode verbs. Available CommandFields are Select, Edit, Cancel, Update, and Delete, which fire ItemCommand, SelectedIndexChanging, SelectedIndexChanged, RowEditing, RowCancelingEdit, RowUpdating, RowUpdated, RowDeleting, and RowDeleted events. The default control for CommandFields is a text Link button. You can substitute a conventional button or image by setting the field's ButtonType property value to Button or Image.

❑ BoundFields display values in Label controls by default. When you click a row's Edit button, the Label controls of editable columns change to TextBoxes. The width of the text boxes is fixed; you must change the BoundField to a TemplateField to change the TextBox widths.

❑ CheckBoxFields display and edit binary values, such as 0 and 1 or False and True.

❑ ButtonFields display a conventional Button control.

❑ HyperlinkFields display text and provide an additional hidden field for page navigation. You can replace Select command fields with hyperlink fields to load editing pages.

❑ ImageFields display graphics from SQL Server image or varbinary columns, or base64-encoded image data in XML files.

❑ TemplateFields let you customize the formatting of TextBoxes or substitute other controls — such as DropDownLists — for editing. You convert a BoundField to a TemplateField by clicking the Field dialog's Convert This Field Into a Template Field link.

Convert BoundFields to EditItemTemplate Fields

TextBoxes with autogenerated widths are satisfactory for initial tests but usually require adjustment to provide a GridView that's tailored for data editing. Figure 7-24 shows the EditableGridView.aspx page with a row in Edit mode. All columns of this page — other than Order ID, which is read-only — are TemplateFields. The Empl. ID and Ship Via templates specify bound DropDownLists to set the numeric column values. The Customer ID text box is read-only because it's an uncommon practice to reassign an order to a different customer.

To convert a BoundField to a TemplateField, open the GridView Tasks smart tag, and click the Edit Columns link to open the Fields dialog. Select the bound field to convert in the Selected Fields list, click the Convert This Field Into a Template Field link, and click OK. Click the smart tag's Edit Templates link to display the Template Editing Mode smart tag, which defaults to the ItemTemplate of the leftmost column you've converted. The conversion process adds an ItemTemplate with a Label control, an EditItemTemplate with a text box control, and empty AlternatingItemTemplate, HeaderTemplate, and FooterTemplate items under a Column[#] – *ColumnName* header for each converted column.

Open the Display list and select EditItemTemplate for the TemplateField to display the default editing TextBox control. Alternatively, right-click the GridView, select Edit Template, and the column to edit, which displays active and empty templates. Adjust the width of the TextBox or set the value of its Width property. If the Height property contains a value, delete it to use the default TextBox height. Optionally, assign a more informative Id property value for the control (see Figure 7-25).

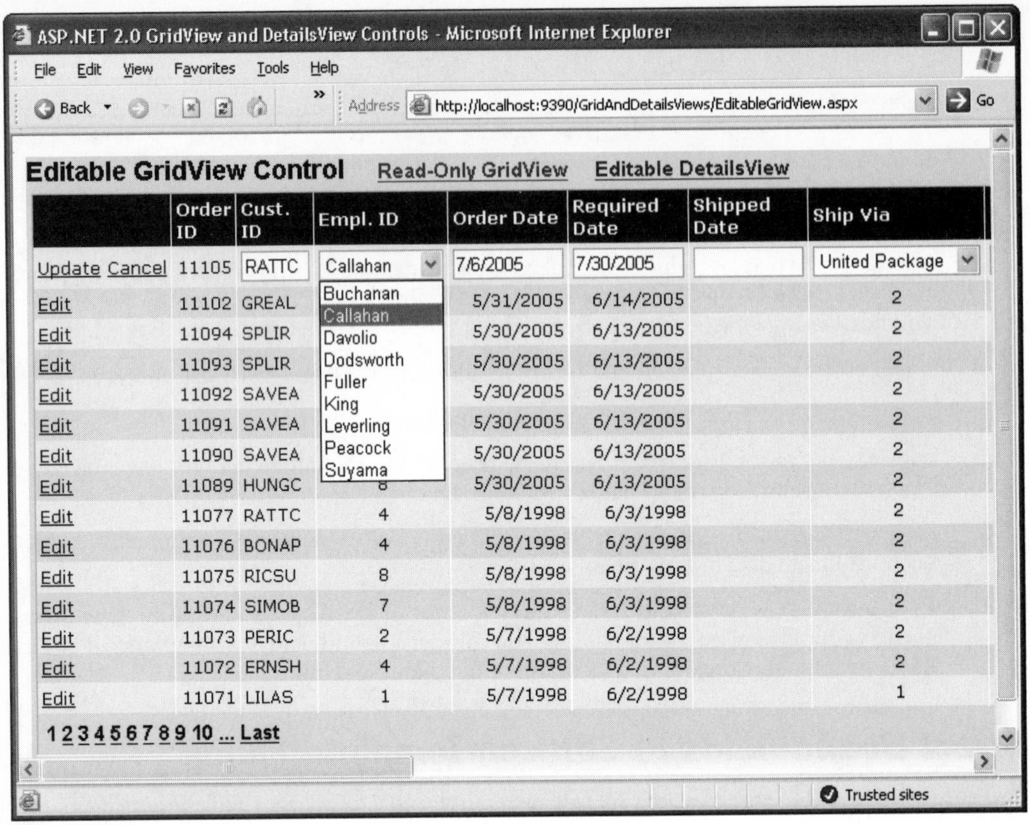

Figure 7-24

Following is the reformatted source code for the read-only Order ID Label and Customer ID TextBox columns:

```
<Columns>
    <asp:BoundField ReadOnly="True" HeaderText="Order ID" InsertVisible="False"
        DataField="OrderID" SortExpression="OrderID">
        <ItemStyle HorizontalAlign="Right"></ItemStyle>
    </asp:BoundField>
    <asp:TemplateField SortExpression="CustomerID" HeaderText="Cust. ID">
        <EditItemTemplate>
            <asp:TextBox ID="txtCustomerID" Runat="server" Width="52px"
                Text='<%# Bind("CustomerID") %>' ReadOnly="True"></asp:TextBox>
        </EditItemTemplate>
        <ItemStyle HorizontalAlign="Left"></ItemStyle>
        <ItemTemplate>
            <asp:Label Runat="server" Text='<%# Bind("CustomerID") %>'
                ID="Label3"></asp:Label>
        </ItemTemplate>
    </asp:TemplateField>
    ...
</Columns>
```

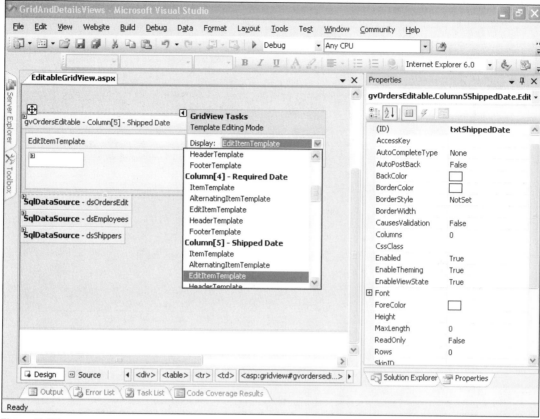

Figure 7-25

Replace TextBoxes with DropDownLists for Editing

It's a good design practice to provide databound DropDownLists to set foreign-key values that have a limited number of choices. To replace a TextBox with a DropDownList, create a DataSource for the list, and delete the TextBox. Drag a DropDownList from the Toolbox, set its DataSource, define its display and value fields, and then bind the `SelectedValue` property to the foreign-key column by typing `Bind("DataColumnName")` in the *ListName* DataBindings dialog's Code expression text box (see Figure 7-26). The GridView's `Bind` method replaces the `Eval` method of DataLists and FormViews.

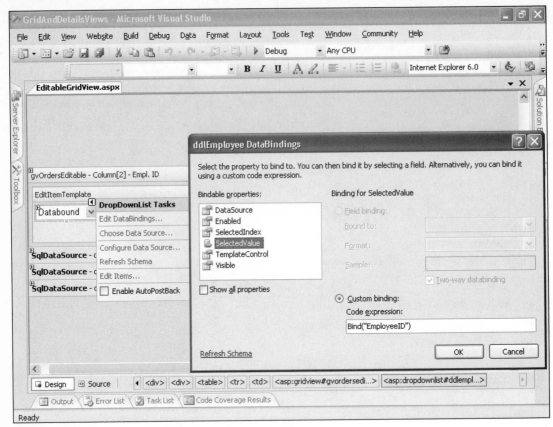

Figure 7-26

Following is the reformatted source code for the Empl. ID column template:

```
<Columns>
...
   <asp:TemplateField HeaderText="Empl. ID">
   <EditItemTemplate>
     <asp:DropDownList ID="ddlEmployee" Runat="server" Height="22px"
        Width="94px" DataSourceID="dsEmployees" DataValueField="EmployeeID"
        DataTextField="LastName" SelectedValue='<%# Bind("EmployeeID") %>'>
     </asp:DropDownList>
   </EditItemTemplate>
     <ItemStyle HorizontalAlign="Center"></ItemStyle>
     <ItemTemplate>
        <asp:Label Runat="server" Text='<%# Bind("EmployeeID") %>'
           ID="Label2"></asp:Label>
     </ItemTemplate>
   </asp:TemplateField>
...
</Columns>
```

Design a GridView with an ImageField

Following are the detailed steps to add a GridView that contains an ImageField column to a new page in the DataWebSite project. Unlike DataGridView controls, ImageField columns in GridViews and other ASP.NET 2.0 databound server controls require images to be stored as files in a supported graphics format. ImageField columns store the relative URL of the image file to display in the current row.

Microsoft removed the DynamicImage control as of VS 2005 Beta 2, so ASP.NET 2.0 doesn't support declarative rendering of images from database tables. Thus the following examples use image files (eight CATIDn.gif and nine EMPIDn.gif files) that are stored in the \VB2005\Chapter07\DataWebSite\Images folder.

ImageFields have a `DataImageUrlField` property that you typically set to the name of a text field that stores image URLs or a numeric primary-key field value. If you must add text to generate the image file name and, if necessary, its relative path, the `DataImageUrlFormatString` property value enables you to add the selected row's `DataImageUrlField` property value. For example, specifying `CategoryID` as the `DataImageUrlField` property value and Images/CATID{0}.gif as the `DataImageUrlFormatString` property value displays one of the ...\Images\CATIDn.gif images in a Picture ImageField that you add to the GridView in the following sections.

Configure a Categories GridView

To add an `ImageField` to a GridView based on the Northwind Categories table and CATIDn.gif image files, do the following:

1. Copy and paste Default.aspx; rename the copy of Default.aspx to GridViewCat.aspx, and set GridViewCat.aspx as the start page. Rename the class name to `CatGridView`.

2. Drag a GridView control from the Toolbox to GridView.aspx's empty table cell. Select New Data Source in the Select Data Source list to start the Data Source Configuration Wizard. Select Database in the Select a Data Source list, and replace SqlDataSource1 with **dsCategories**. Click OK.

3. In the Choose a Connection dialog, select an existing connection to the Northwind sample database or create a new connection. If you want to be able to deploy the site to an IIS Web server for anonymous access, select or add a connection that uses SQL Server security. Click Next.

4. Accept or replace the default connection string name, and click Next to open the Configure Data Source dialog.

5. Select the Categories table in the Name list, mark the four column checkboxes, and click Next.

6. Click Test Query to display the query result set in a DataGridView, which displays the eight bitmap images in the Pictures column.

7. Click Finish to add column names to the GridView, which displays numbers 0 through 4 in the CategoryID column and abc in the CategoryName and Description.

    The missing Picture column is an indication that the page isn't likely to render as expected when you build and run the project.

8. Open GridView1's Properties window, and change its `Id` property value to `gvCategories` or the like. To match the style of the completed examples, expand the Font node, select `Verdana` for the `Name` property value, and type **10pt** in the `Size` text box.

9. Press F5 to build and display the page with the built-in Web server.

Add and Configure an ImageField

Unlike the DataGridView control, the GridView doesn't add columns of data types that .NET data providers translate to arrays of System.Byte. Thus, you must add and bind the Categories table's Picture column manually. Here's the drill for displaying in GridView controls images from specially named image files:

1. Open the GridView Tasks smart tag and click the Add New Column link to open the Add Field dialog. Select the Picture field in the Selected Fields list and delete it.

2. In the Available Field list, select the Picture field under the Image Fields node, and click Add to add the field to the Selected Fields list. Set the ReadOnly property value to True (see Figure 7-27).

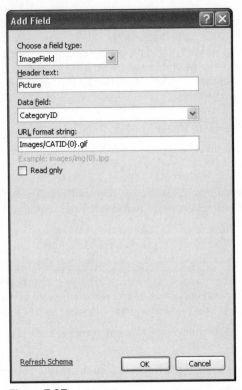

Figure 7-27

3. Click OK to close the dialog. The added Picture column displays Databound as the four default cell values.

4. Press F5 to build and display the page, which now appears as expected (see Figure 7-28).

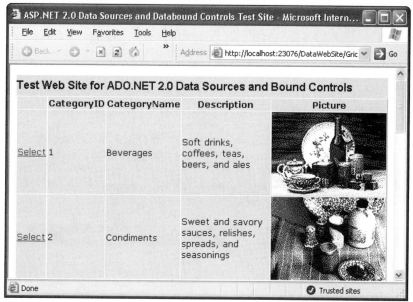

Figure 7-28

5. Choose View ➪ Source to open the XHTML page code in Notepad. Scroll to the Beverages cell and note the source of the image data, which appears similar to the highlighted elements in the following snippet:

```
<tr>
  <td><a href="javascript:__doPostBack('gvCategories$ctl02$ctl00','')">
  Select</a></td>
  <td>1</td>
  <td>Beverages</td>
  <td>Soft drinks, coffees, teas, beers, and ales</td>
  <td><img src="Images/CATID1.gif"
    alt="Picture of Beverages" style="border-width:0px;" /></td>
</tr>
```

Enabling selection adds the JavaScript postback function call. `CategoryName` as the `DataAlternateTextField` and `Picture of {0}` `DataAlternateTextFormatString` property values provide the `alt` attribute value, which appears if the image file is missing or the user has disabled the browser's image rendering feature.

> *The DataWebSite project contains a FinalGridViewCat.aspx page that's the result of the procedures described in this and the preceding section.*

Scale Image Rendering

The ImageField control renders images in their original size only; the control doesn't support scaling or cropping operations. The Image Web server control scales (zooms) rendered images to the Height and Width property values you specify. Creating thumbnail graphics is the most common use for Web-page image scaling.

Enabling image scaling requires converting the ImageField to a template field that contains an Image Web server control. To perform the conversion, activate the GridView's smart tag, click the Edit Columns link, select the ImageField column, and click the Convert This Field into a TemplateField link. This operation adds an Image control to the ItemTemplate for the column sets the ImageUrl property value to that specified for the former ImageField. Figure 7-29 shows the sample FinalGridViewEmp.aspx page rendering a 43px × 50px thumbnail and a 188px × 217px original image from the \VB2005DB\ Chapter07\DataWebSite\Images\EMPID1.gif file.

Figure 7-29

Following is XHTML source code for the sample project's TemplateField:

```
<asp:TemplateField HeaderText="Thumbnail">
  <ItemTemplate>
    <asp:Image ID="imgPhoto" runat="server" BorderStyle="None" Height="50px"
      ImageUrl='<%# Eval("EmployeeID", "Images/EMPID{0}.gif") %>' Width="43px" />
  </ItemTemplate>
  <EditItemTemplate>
    <asp:TextBox ID="TextBox1" runat="server"
      Text='<%# Eval("EmployeeID") %>'></asp:TextBox>
  </EditItemTemplate>
</asp:TemplateField>
```

The FinalGridViewEmp.aspx page's AccessDataSource (dsNwindJet) is four fields of the Employees table from a modified version of the Access 2003 Northwind.mdb sample database that's stored in the ...\App_Data folder and included in the sample project. The modification removes all database objects other than tables.

The DetailsView Control

The DetailsView control is a fixed-format variation on the FormView theme. DetailsViews display header text and data in two columns of a table that has a row for each column that's returned by the DataSource's `SelectCommand`. DetailsViews support the GridView's Command verbs and add `New` and `Insert` verbs, and fire `ItemInserting` and `ItemInserted` events. Figure 7-30 shows the GridAndDetailsViews project's EditableDetailsView.aspx page in Edit mode. The Order Details GridView and DetailsView controls are filtered by the pager selection you make in the Orders DetailsView.

The process of adding a DetailsView control to a page is identical to that for adding a GridView. The controls on the EditableDetailsView.aspx page use `BoundFields`; adding and adjusting EditItem and NewItem templates follows the process described in the section "Convert BoundFields to EditItemTemplate Fields," earlier in this chapter.

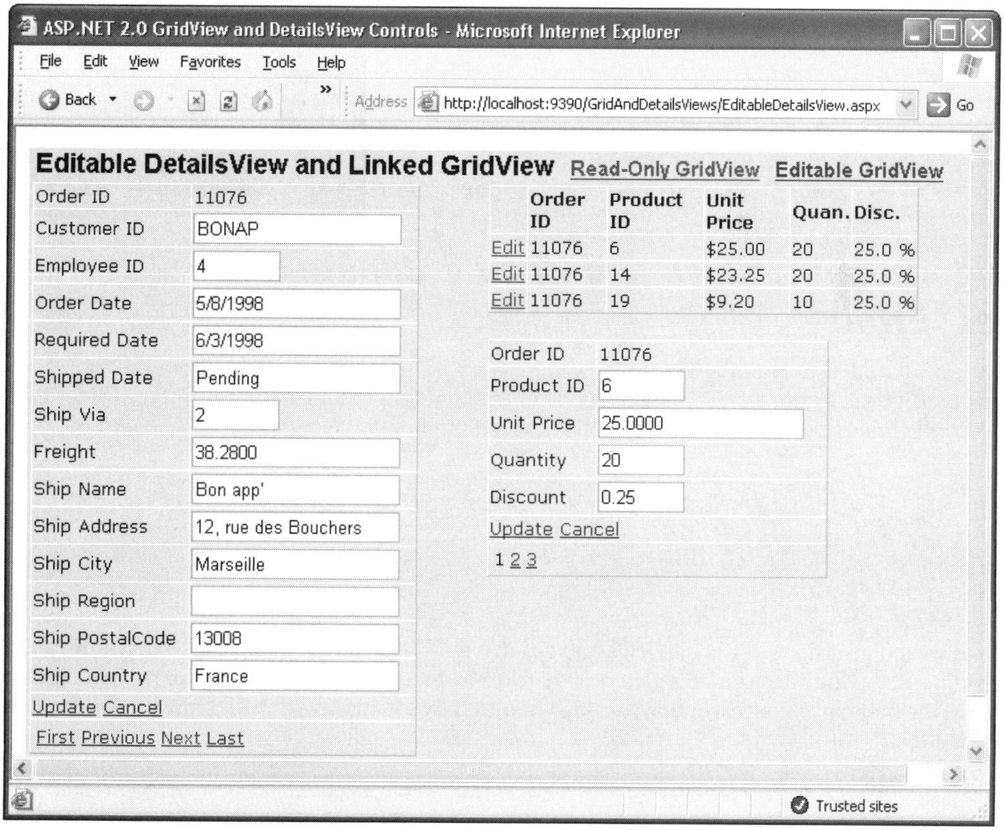

Figure 7-30

Synchronize a Child Table GridView and DetailsView

If you parameterize the SelectCommand for a child table's foreign key value, such as OrderID for the Order Details table, you can synchronize the contents of GridView, DetailsView, or both controls on a page with the selected value of the parent table's primary key in a paged DetailsView.

To synchronize the Order Details GridView and DetailsView with the SelectedValue property of the Orders DetailsView, create or re-create the DataSource for the child controls and, in the Configure Data Source Wizard's Add WHERE Clause dialog, specify OrderID as the Column, = as the Operator, and Control as the Source. Select the parent DetailsView — dvOrders for this example — as the ControlID and type an optional Default Value. Complete the remaining wizard steps to link the child controls to the parent control's SelectedValue property.

Make a Composite Primary Key Value Editable

The Order Details table's composite primary key causes the ProductID column to be read-only by default, which prevents changing a ProductID value in Edit mode. To make the ProductID column editable, change the UpdateCommand's SQL statement in the Source editor from:

```
UpdateCommand="UPDATE [Order Details] SET [UnitPrice] = @UnitPrice,
    [Quantity] = @Quantity, [Discount] = @Discount
    WHERE [OrderID] = @original_OrderID AND [ProductID] = @original_ProductID">
```

to:

```
UPDATE [Order Details] SET [ProductID] = @ProductID, [UnitPrice] = @UnitPrice,
    [Quantity] = @Quantity, [Discount] = @Discount
    WHERE [OrderID] = @original_OrderID AND [ProductID] = @original_ProductID">
```

Assign Default Values and Handle Update and Insert Errors

You can take advantage of the ItemInserting event to supply default values for items you add to a base table. As an example, the following code in UpdatableDetailsView.aspx inserts the selected OrderID value of the dvOrders DetailsView into the same column of the dvOrderDetails control:

```
Protected Sub dvOrderDetails_ItemInserting(ByVal sender As Object,
  ByVal e As System.Web.UI.WebControls.DetailsViewInsertEventArgs)
  Handles dvOrderDetails.ItemInserting
    e.Values(0) = dvOrders.SelectedValue
End Sub
```

Updates and insertions in DetailsViews and GridViews fail silently if the database server returns an error message. The page contains a txtError text box that's not visible if no errors occur. Figure 7-31 shows the first part of the exception message returned by attempting to add a row with a duplicated ProductID.

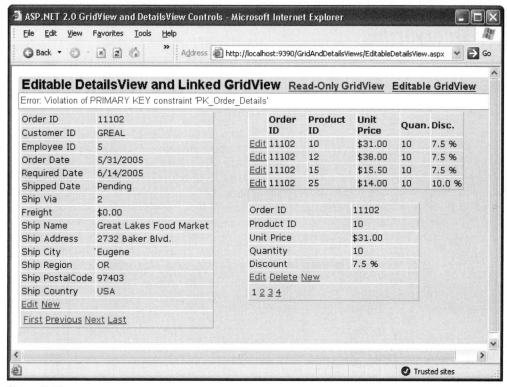

Figure 7-31

Here's the exception handler for the `ItemUpdated` event:

```
Protected Sub dvOrderDetails_ItemUpdated(ByVal sender As Object, _
 ByVal e As System.Web.UI.WebControls.DetailsViewUpdatedEventArgs) _
 Handles dvOrderDetails.ItemUpdated
    If e.Exception Is Nothing Then
       'Refresh the OrderDetails GridView
       txtError.Visible = False
       gvOrderDetails.DataBind()
    Else
       'Display first sentence of Exception.Message
       txtError.Visible = True
       txtError.Text = "Error: " + _
       Mid(e.Exception.Message, 1, e.Exception.Message.IndexOf("."))
       e.ExceptionHandled = True
    End If
End Sub
```

EditableDetailsView.aspx contains identical inline code to handle `ItemInserted` exceptions.

Link a DetailsView Page to a GridView Page with a QueryString

As mentioned in the section "The GridView Control," earlier in this chapter, you can replace the Select CommandField with a HyperlinkField to open a DetailsView page for editing a record selected in the GridView page. A query string added to the GridView page's URL provides the name/value pair to supply the parameter value for the DetailsView page's DataSource. The format of the URL and query string with the built-in Web server is:

```
http://localhost:TcpPort/ProjectName/PageName.aspx?ParamName=ParamValue
```

Set the HyperlinkField's DataNavigateUrl property value to the DataSource column name and the DataNavigateUrlFormatString property value to PageName.aspx?ParamName={0}. The LinkedGridView.aspx page has a HyperlinkField bound to the OrderID column value with Select as the Text property value and LinkedDetailsView.aspx?orderid={0} as the DataNavigate UrlFormatString property value (see Figure 7-32).

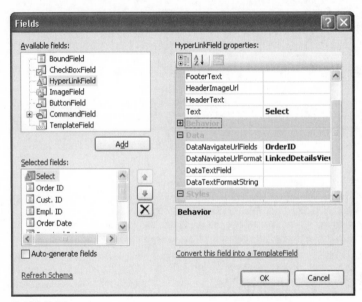

Figure 7-32

Create a parameterized DataSource for the DetailsView page. In the Add WHERE Clause dialog, select OrderID as the Column, = as the Operator, and QueryString as the Source. Type the ParamName value — **orderid** for this example — in the QueryString Field text box and add an optional Default Value.

Open the LinkedDataGrid.aspx page, and click the Select HyperlinkField for an order. The LinkedDetails View.aspx page opens with the Orders and Order Details DetailsView controls for the selected OrderID value (see Figure 7-33).

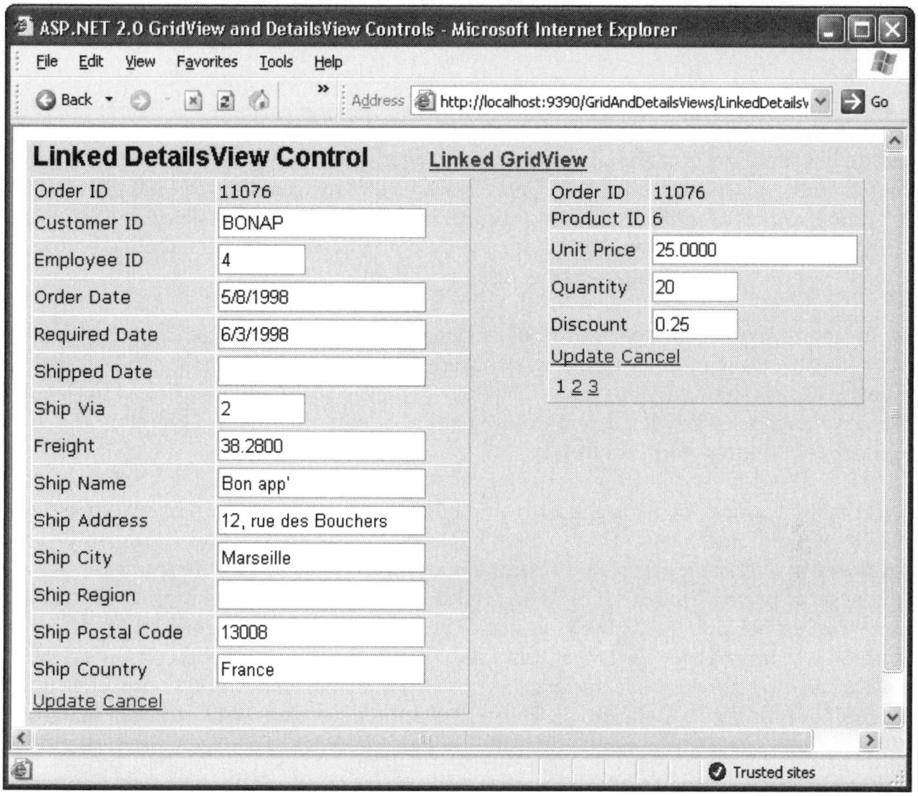

Figure 7-33

To return to the LinkedDataGrid.aspx page after clicking the Orders DetailsView's Cancel button, add the following event handler to LinkedDetailsView.aspx.vb:

```
Protected Sub dvOrdersLinked_ItemCommand(ByVal sender As Object,
 ByVal e As System.Web.UI.WebControls.DetailsViewCommandEventArgs)
 Handles dvOrdersLinked.ItemCommand
    'Redirect to the LinkedGridView page on cancel
    Response.Buffer = True
    If e.CommandName = "Cancel" Then
        Response.Redirect("LinkedGridView.aspx")
    End If
End Sub
```

Summary

Visual Studio 2005 and ASP.NET 2.0 simplify Web site development and page design with a new editor for XHTML 1.1 source code and inline event-handling code. Partial *PageName*.aspx.vb classes let you separate event-handling code from page-layout code. The new compilation model and built-in, lightweight Web server streamline the site development process. However, VS 2005's Web page Design mode is restricted to flow layout and doesn't support VS 2002 and 2003's grid-based fixed control positioning feature.

ASP.NET 2.0's new SqlDataSource, ObjectDataSource, and XmlDataSource server controls simplify databinding of DataList, FormView, GridView, and DetailsView controls to tabular data sources. The GridView control replaces ASP.NET 1.x's DataGrid control. The Data Source Configuration Wizard enables adding and configuring databound controls in a few steps, and generates usable data display and editing pages without adding any inline or code-behind event handlers. Only editable DataLists require event handlers for editing, deleting, or adding items.

The new databound server controls make extensive use of templates to customize page layouts for read-only and updatable DataSources. FormView controls offer the greatest design flexibility for data entry and editing pages; DetailsViews sacrifice custom layouts for simplicity. GridViews linked to DetailsViews by query strings emulate master/details Windows forms but don't offer the rich object model and fine-grained events of Windows form controls.

Improved paging features let users choose a single item to display in a FormView or DetailsView or a sequential group of items in a GridView control. Restricting the `SelectCommand`'s resultset to a selected group of paged records isn't practical, so paging operations return the entire resultset each time users select a new set of pages. Thus, limiting with WHERE clauses the number of records returned from large tables is critical for designing scalable Web sites. The SqlDataSource implements the client/server model, which is suitable for projects that don't require complex business logic. If site scalability requires you to place custom business logic or data components in a middle tier, one approach is to substitute an ObjectDataSource for the SqlDataSource. The next chapter covers use of ObjectDataSources with custom business objects and data components; Chapter 9 shows you how to use the ObjectDataSource with ASP.NET 2.0 Web services.

8

Applying Advanced ASP.NET 2.0 Data Techniques

This chapter expands your VB.NET development horizon beyond simple, data-intensive Web pages and databound Web controls. This chapter's advanced ASP.NET 2.0 topics show you how to take full advantage of the following new or updated Web controls and VS 2005 features:

❑ **Data validation** with RequiredFieldValidator, RangeValidator, RegularExpressionValidator, CompareValidator, CustomValidator, and ValidationSummary controls

❑ **ObjectDataSources** based on DataTables of typed DataSets defined by DataSet.xsd files or class library references, and custom business objects that have `Nullable(Of DataType)` fields

❑ **XmlDataSources** designed for use with read-only GridView, DetailsView, DataList, Repeater, and TreeView controls

❑ **Web page performance analysis** with page-level and application-level tracing data

❑ **Web Site deployment** to production Web servers by automated copying of files and publishing of precompiled site DLLs to IIS virtual directories

You won't gain the skills you need to design functional, scalable Web sites that have data source samples with a few text fields and five or ten rows or element groups. Using the Northwind Orders and Order Details tables as the data source for most of this chapter's sample projects exposes many potential issues you'll face when you develop production Web pages with VS 2005.

Validate Entries in Databound Controls

Validating user input before submitting edited values to the database server eliminates needless roundtrips, reduces server load, and increases application scalability. If your databound controls connect to a middle-tier data access logic component (DALC) that enforces business rules, client-side validation of required fields and data formats reduces network traffic and middle-tier resource consumption. All production Windows and Web forms should provide initial client-side validation of user input, regardless of the data access architecture you adopt.

ASP.NET enables two approaches to validating user input to bound controls—server validation controls or code added to the `ControlId_Updating` or `ControlId_Inserting` event handlers. Server validation controls display validation error messages when the user types or selects a value that doesn't pass the validation test and moves to another control. Event-handling code can display one or more validation error messages in a text box, but the error messages don't appear until the user completes the editing process and clicks an Update or Insert link button. Delaying validation until the submit operation will frustrate users, especially after a lengthy data entry session.

ASP.NET 2.0 Validation Controls

ASP.NET 2.0 provides the same server validation controls as ASP.NET 1.1. Validation controls aren't limited to databound fields; you can assign a validator to any server control that accepts user input. Validating GridView columns or DetailsView fields requires an EditItem template for each item you want to validate.

> *The ValidateBoundControls Web Site in the \VB2005DB\Chapter08\ValidateBoundControls folder demonstrates use of each validator with a modified version of Chapter 7's GridAndDetailsViews project. Both projects require a* `localhost` *instance of the SQL Server Northwind sample database or editing the connection string in the Web.config file.*

Following are brief descriptions of the six ASP.NET validation controls:

❑ **RequiredFieldValidator** tests a control specified by its `Id` property for a value that doesn't match the `InitialValue` property value, which defaults to an empty string. If you supply a value from a DropDownList with `[Select an Item]` as the first member of the Items collection and set `AppendDataBoundItems` to `True`, specify `[Select an Item]` as the `InitialValue`. If the value entered matches the `InitialValue`, the validator displays its `Text` or `ErrorMessage` property value in red type to the right of or under the control.

❑ **RangeValidator** tests a specified control for a value ranging from the `MinValue` to the `MaxValue` property values, whose type you specify as the `DataType` property. These two values can be `String`, `Integer`, `Double`, `Date`, or `Currency` constants. The error message appears when the entered or selected value falls outside the specified range. The RangeValidator control doesn't test empty controls, so you must add a RequiredFieldValidator to the specified control.

❑ **RegularExpressionValidator** tests the text of the specified control for conformance to a regular expression (regex) you type as the `ValidationExpression` property value. For example, the `[A-Z]{5}` regex validates a CustomerID entry if it contains five uppercase letters. Alternatively, click the `ValidationExpression`'s builder button to select from a few standard regexs, such as e-mail addresses, URLs, telephone numbers, postal codes, and Social Security or ID formats. You must add a RequiredFieldValidator to test for empty values.

❑ **CompareValidator** lets you test whether the value of the specified control is less than, less than or equal to, equal to, greater than or equal to, or greater than the value of another control whose `Id` value you specify as the `ControlToCompare` property value. The CompareValidator tests the same data types as the RangeValidator. You must add a RequiredFieldValidator to test for empty values.

❑ **CustomValidator** lets you test the specified control with a custom JScript or VBScript `ClientValidationFunction` and a similar VB.NET handler you write for the `OnServerValidate` event. The `ClientValidationFunction` provides client-side validation and the `OnServerValidate` event handler executes when the user submits the page.

❑ **ValidationSummary** provides a means of displaying all current validation control's `ErrorMessage` property values in a single text box or bulleted list. Alternatively or additionally, you can display the errors in a message box for users who run IE 4.0 or later. Summary error messages don't appear until the user submits the form.

The Edit and New LinkButton controls' `CausesValidation` *property value defaults to* `True`*, which enables all validator controls in the EditItem template and, for DetailsView, the InsertItem template.*

The New ValidationGroup Property

ASP.NET 2.0 adds a new `ValidationGroup` property to enable selective validation by groups of validator controls in data-entry forms that don't use the prebuilt databound controls. As an example, you might not want to apply all validators to a new Orders table entry. In this case, you assign a group name — such as `EditGroup1` — to the `ValidationGroup` property of an Edit Group 1 submit button and the validator controls of the form's text boxes and other databound controls. Other data-entry controls with validators in `EditGroup2` update the remaining fields.

Applying validation groups to bound GridView controls is problematic. Autoinserted CommandFields don't provide direct access to their properties, so you can't specify the required `ValidationGroup` name without adding a custom CommandField. If you add an InsertItem template to a FormView or DetailsView control, you add the required validator controls to both EditItem and InsertItem templates. This process emulates validation control grouping for edits and insertions.

Other Shared Validation Properties

Following are brief descriptions of the most important control properties that most validator controls have in common:

❑ `ControlToValidate` is a required control `ID` property value for all validator controls except the CustomValidator.

❑ `ErrorMessage` appears adjacent to the associated control if you don't specify a `Text` value. Always specify a `Text` value and add `ErrorMessage` text to display in SummaryValidator text or message boxes.

❑ DisplayMode specifies how the validator control displays its Text property. Static (the default) reserves room for the message under or beside the control, depending on space available. Dynamic occupies space on the form only when displaying a validation error and is the preferred setting in most cases. None prevents displaying the message, except in the associated ValidationSummary control, if present.

❑ ToolTip text aids the user by permitting a lengthy description of the validation error. For example, you can copy the ErrorMessage value to ToolTip and add additional information to aid users when correcting the error.

❑ EnableClientScript determines if client-side validation occurs; the default value is True. If you set the value to False, validation occurs only when the user submits the form.

Following is an example of the reformatted source code for a RequiredFieldValidator:

```
<asp:TemplateField SortExpression="OrderDate" HeaderText="Order Date">
   <EditItemTemplate>
      <asp:TextBox ID="txtOrderDate" Runat="server" Width="76px"
         Text='<%# Bind("OrderDate", "{0:d}") %>'></asp:TextBox>
      <asp:RequiredFieldValidator ID="rfvOrderDate" Runat="server"
         ControlToValidate="txtOrderDate" ErrorMessage="OrderDate is required."
         Display="Dynamic" ToolTip="OrderDate is a required field.">Required!
      </asp:RequiredFieldValidator>
   </EditItemTemplate>
   <ItemStyle HorizontalAlign="Right" VerticalAlign="Top"></ItemStyle>
   <ItemTemplate>
      <asp:Label Runat="server" Text='<%# Bind("OrderDate", "{0:d}") %>'
         ID="lblOrderDate"></asp:Label>
   </ItemTemplate>
</asp:TemplateField>
```

The RequiredFieldValidator's EnableClientScript *property doesn't appear in the preceding source code because its default value (*True*) is accepted. Assigning names to labels isn't necessary unless you encounter a duplicate value error. However, assigning meaningful names to all controls is a good programming practice and helps you find related controls in complex pages.*

Figure 8-1 shows the Text property value — Required! — under a missing OrderDate entry.

If you delete an entry and move to another field, return to the errant field, and then press Esc twice to restore the value, the error message remains. You must retype a valid entry to remove the Text *message.*

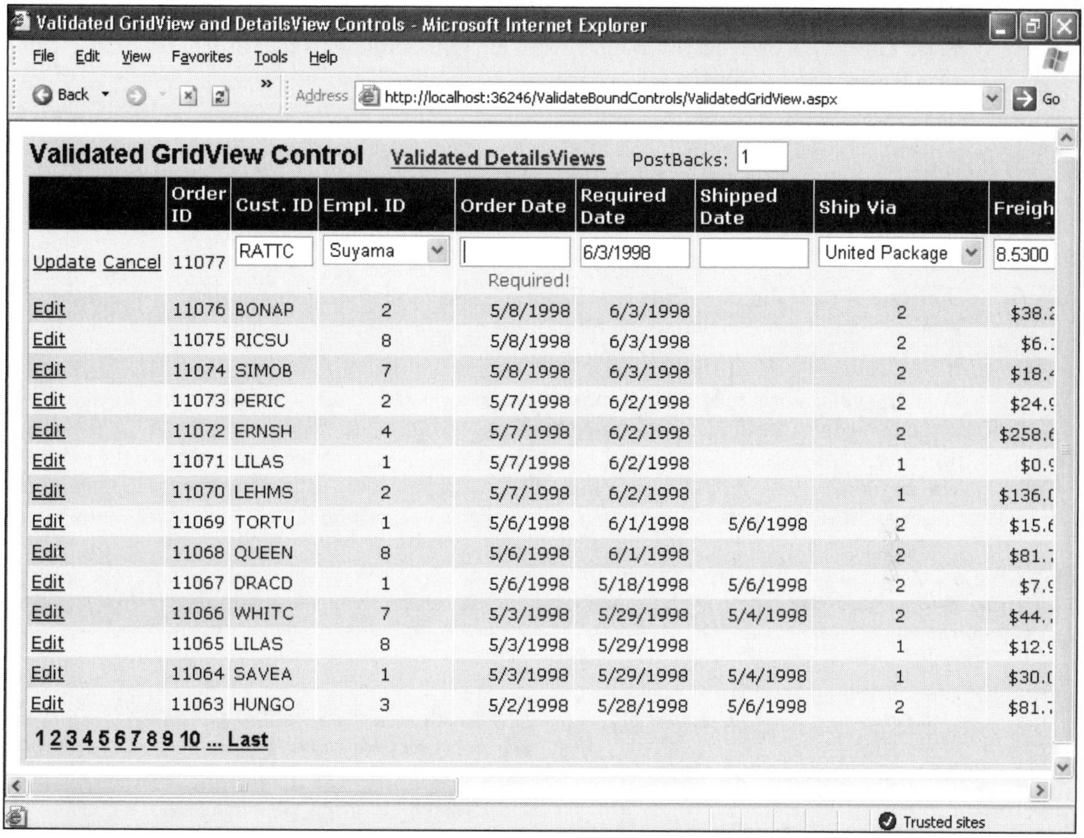

Figure 8-1

Validate GridView Edits

The following sections demonstrate how to require users to enter data in specific fields, apply regular expressions to verify data formatting, limit entries to a range of values, base data validity on comparison with another column or calculated value, and take advantage of the ValidationSummary control. Although a GridView bound to an SqlDataSource provides the validation control test fixture, the techniques you learn here apply to any editable control, regardless of its data source type.

The ValidatedGridView.aspx page has RequiredFieldValidators for all columns except OrderID, which is read-only, and ShippedDate, ShipRegion, and ShipPostalCode, which can be empty. You can use the ValidateBoundControls Web site's EditableGridView.aspx page as the starting point for adding your own validator controls.

Add Required Field Validation to a GridView Control

Following is the basic process for adding a validator control to a GridView's EditItem template in Design mode:

1. Use the Fields dialog to convert the bound fields you want to validate to template fields, if you haven't done this previously. Chapter 7's "Convert BoundFields to EditItemTemplate Fields" section describes the conversion process.

2. Open the GridView's smart tag, and click Edit Templates. Right-click the ItemTemplate smart tag, and choose Edit Templates and the column template for validation.

3. Adjust the width of the TextBox control in the EditItemTemplate pane to accommodate the entry text, delete the default `Height` property value, and change the `ID` property value to a descriptive name — `txtCustomerID` for this example.

4. Drag one of the validator controls — RequiredFieldValidator for this example — from the Toolbox's Validation section to the right of the text box; the control displays the default red `RequiredFieldValidator` error message.

5. Open the validator's properties window, assign a related name — such as `rfvCustomerID` — to the `ID` property value and the associated text box name to the `ControlToValidate` property. Change the `Display` property value from `Static` to `Dynamic`, replace the default `ErrorMessage` with a brief description of the validation rule, add a short message to appear under the text box as the `Text` property value, and add optional `ToolTip` text, as shown in Figure 8-2.

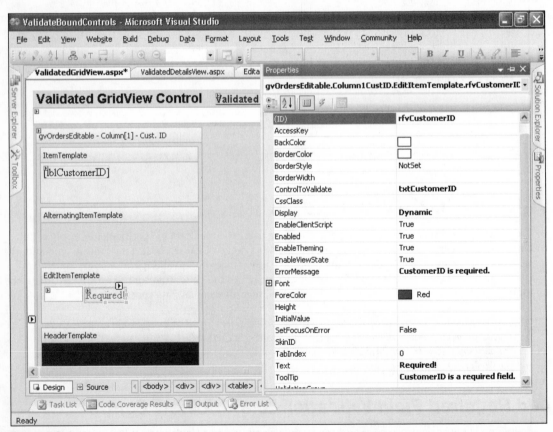

Figure 8-2

When validating GridViews, set the ItemStyle.VerticalAlign *property value to* Top *in the Fields dialog. This setting aligns all edit text boxes horizontally when a validation error message is present.*

Validate CustomerID Entries with a RegularExpressionValidator

The Order table's CustomerID field requires five uppercase letters, so it's a good candidate for testing validation by a regular expression. A simple [A-Z]{5} expression performs this test; [A-Z] specifies the capital letters A through Z and {5} specifies the number of occurrences of a letter in the matched text.

Writing regular expressions is beyond the scope of this book. The Regular Expressions Library site at http://www.regexlib.com/ *has about 800 indexed expressions for a wide range of standard and semi-standard text formats. The online help topic "About Regular Expressions" has sections that explain how regular expressions work and describe the classes of the* System.Text.RegularExpressions *namespace.*

To add a RegularExpressionValidator to the GridView's CustomerID EditItemTemplate, follow the procedure described in the preceding section, but drag a RegularExpressionValidator control to the right of the RequiredFieldValidator. Make the appropriate changes to the property values that apply to the RequiredFieldValidator, and type **[A-Z]{5}** as the ValidationExpression property value. Clicking the builder button in the ValidationExpression text box opens the Regular Expression Editor dialog, which offers a few prebuilt expressions for U.S., European, and Asian strings (see Figure 8-3).

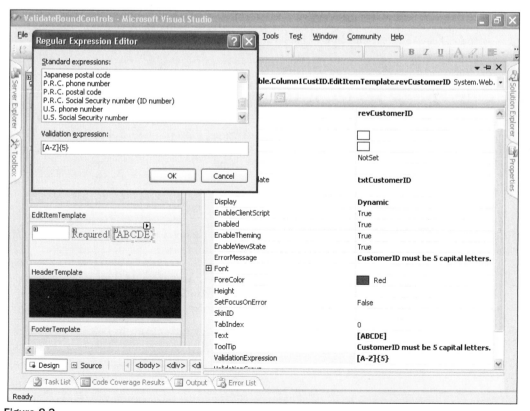

Figure 8-3

Following is the reformatted source code for the CustomerID `TemplateField` with the RequiredValueValidator and RegularExpressionValidator added:

```
<asp:TemplateField SortExpression="CustomerID" HeaderText="Cust. ID">
   <EditItemTemplate>
      <asp:TextBox ID="txtCustomerID" Runat="server" Width="52px"
         Text='<%# Bind("CustomerID") %>'></asp:TextBox>
      <asp:RequiredFieldValidator ID="rfvCustomerID" Runat="server"
         ErrorMessage="CustomerID is required." Display="Dynamic"
         ControlToValidate="txtCustomerID"
         ToolTip="CustomerID is a required field."> Required!
      </asp:RequiredFieldValidator> 
      <asp:RegularExpressionValidator ID="revCustomerID" Runat="server"
         ErrorMessage="CustomerID must be 5 capital letters."
         Display="Dynamic" ControlToValidate="txtCustomerID"
         ValidationExpression="[A-Z]{5}"
         ToolTip="CustomerID must be 5 capital letters.">[ABCDE]
      </asp:RegularExpressionValidator>
   </EditItemTemplate>
   <ItemStyle HorizontalAlign="Left" VerticalAlign="Top"></ItemStyle>
   <ItemTemplate>
      <asp:Label Runat="server" Text='<%# Bind("CustomerID") %>'
         ID="lblCustomerID"></asp:Label>
   </ItemTemplate>
</asp:TemplateField>
```

The preceding example is contrived to demonstrate regex validation. In a real-world application, CustomerID values would be set by a DropDownList (similar to that for the ValidatedGridView's EmployeeID or ShipVia column) or tested by a Custom Validator against a DataTable of valid CustomerID values.

Test EmployeeID Values with a RangeValidator

EmployeeID foreign-key values for the Employees table must range from 1 to 9. The original `ddlEmployee` dropdown list, which lets users select from a list of last names, prevents users from selecting an invalid EmployeeID value. For this example, the SQL query for the `dsEmployees` SqlDataSource has been modified as follows to include an invalid `[LastName]` item:

```
SELECT [EmployeeID], [LastName] FROM [Employees]
UNION SELECT 0, '[Last Name]' ORDER BY [LastName]
```

The RangeValidator requires selecting the appropriate `Type` property value (`Integer`) and specifying `MinimumValue` (1) and `MaximumValue` (9) property values for numeric and date data types.

You don't need a RequiredFieldValidator for this contrived example because the DropDownList limits the field value to a member of the list. Unless the MinimumValue and MaximumValue property values are immutable, a production application would need at least a CustomValidator control to obtain and use the current MaximumValue.

Apply a RangeValidator and RegularExpressionValidator to Date Entries

Avoiding server roundtrips that result from users entering improperly formatted or nonexistent dates requires verification that the entry is a valid date with a RangeValidator that accepts dates within a set of limits. The limits that you set depend on the data source for the field, but it's likely that 1/1/1980 as the MinimumValue through 12/31/2099 as the MaximumValue will accommodate most applications. When you specify Date as the Type property value, the .NET DateTime parser tests for a valid date. As an example, 2/29/2005 or 11/31/00 raises an error, but 2/29/2004 or 02/29/00 doesn't. Thus, it's a good programming practice to add a RangeValidator to all datetime columns of bound text boxes. By default, the DateTime parser accepts two-digit or four-digit years and virgules (forward slashes) or hyphens as separators.

If you want to enforce a specific short-date format, such as M/D/YYYY, you must add a RegularExpression validator. The following regex requires virgules and four-digit years:

```
^(((((0?[13578])|(1[02]))[\/]?((0?[1-9]|[0-2][0-9])|(3[01]))))|(((0?[469])|(11))[\/]
?((0?[1-9]|[0-2][0-9])|(30)))|(0?[2][\/]?(0?[1-9]|[0-2][0-9])))[\/]?\d{4}$
```

The preceding regex is a modification of an expression contributed by Cliff Schneide to the Regular Expressions Library site. The modifications prevent matching hyphen separators and require four-digit years.

Here's the reformatted source code for the OrderDate TemplateField with RequiredFieldValidator, RangeValidator, and RegularExpressionValidator controls:

```
<asp:TemplateField SortExpression="OrderDate" HeaderText="Order Date">
   <EditItemTemplate>
      <asp:TextBox ID="txtOrderDate" Runat="server" Width="76px"
         Text='<%# Bind("OrderDate", "{0:d}") %>'></asp:TextBox>
      <asp:RequiredFieldValidator ID="rfvOrderDate" Runat="server"
         ControlToValidate="txtOrderDate"
         ErrorMessage="OrderDate is required." Display="Dynamic"
         ToolTip="OrderDate is a required field.">Required!
      </asp:RequiredFieldValidator>
      <asp:RangeValidator ID="rvOrderDate" Runat="server"
         ToolTip="Dates must be in ShortDate format (MM/DD/YYYY)"
         ControlToValidate="txtOrderDate"
         ErrorMessage="Dates must be in M/D/YYYY format."
         MinimumValue="1/1/1980" MaximumValue="12/31/2099" Type="Date"
         Display="Dynamic">[M/D/YYYY]
      </asp:RangeValidator>
      <asp:RegularExpressionValidator ID="revOrderDate" Runat="server"
         ToolTip="Date format must be M/D/YYYY and date must be valid."
         Display="Dynamic" ErrorMessage="Date format must be M/D/YYYY."
         ControlToValidate="txtOrderDate"
         ValidationExpression="^(((((0?[13578])|(1[02]))[\/]?((0?[1-9]|[0-2]
            [0-9])|(3[01]))))|(((0?[469])|(11))[\/]?((0?[1-9]|[0-2][0-9])|
            (30)))|(0?[2]\/?(0?[1-9]|[0-2][0-9])))[\/]?\d{4}$">[M/D/YYYY]
      </asp:RegularExpressionValidator>
   </EditItemTemplate>
```

```
        <ItemStyle HorizontalAlign="Right" VerticalAlign="Top"></ItemStyle>
        <ItemTemplate>
            <asp:Label Runat="server" Text='<%# Bind("OrderDate", "{0:d}") %>'
                ID="lblOrderDate"></asp:Label>
        </ItemTemplate>
    </asp:TemplateField>
```

Prevent Unreasonable Entries with a CompareValidator

You can use the CompareValidator control to prevent numeric and date entries that violate simple business rules (or common sense), such as a RequiredDate that's equal to or less than the OrderDate. The CompareValidator control's `ControlToCompare` property requires that the ID of a control have a data type that's compatible with the datatype of the specified `ControlToValidate`. For example, to compare an `Integer` with a value that has a decimal fraction, you must specify `Double` as the `Type` property value.

For this example, you substitute a CompareValidator for the RangeValidator control. Specify `txtRequiredDate` as the `ControlToValidate` property value, `txtOrderDate` as the `ControlToCompare`, `GreaterThan` as the `Operator`, and `Date` as the `Type`.

Following is the reformatted source code for the RequiredDate `TemplateField`:

```
<asp:TemplateField SortExpression="RequiredDate" HeaderText="Required Date">
    <EditItemTemplate>
        <asp:TextBox ID="txtRequiredDate" Runat="server" Width="76px"
            Text='<%# Bind("RequiredDate", "{0:d}") %>'></asp:TextBox>
        <asp:RequiredFieldValidator ID="rfvRequiredDate" Runat="server"
            ToolTip="RequiredDate is required and must be later than OrderDate."
            Display="Dynamic" ErrorMessage="RequiredDate is required."
            ControlToValidate="txtRequiredDate">Required!
        </asp:RequiredFieldValidator>
        <asp:CompareValidator ID="cvRequiredDate" Runat="server"
            ToolTip="RequiredDate must be later than OrderDate." Display="Dynamic"
            ErrorMessage="RequiredDate must be later than OrderDate."
            ControlToValidate="txtRequiredDate" Operator="GreaterThan"
            ControlToCompare="txtOrderDate">Impossible!
        </asp:CompareValidator>
        <asp:RegularExpressionValidator ID="revRequiredDate" Runat="server"
            ToolTip="Date format must be M/D/YYYY and date must be valid."
            Display="Dynamic" ErrorMessage="Date format must be M/D/YYYY."
            ControlToValidate="txtRequiredDate"
            ValidationExpression="^(((((0?[13578])|(1[02]))[\/]?((0?[1-9]|[0-2]
                [0-9])|(3[01])))|(((0?[469])|(11))[\/]?((0?[1-9]|[0-2][0-9]))|
                (30)))|(0?[2]\/?(0?[1-9]|[0-2][0-9])))[\/]?\d{4}$">[M/D/YYYY]
        </asp:RegularExpressionValidator>
    </EditItemTemplate>
    <ItemStyle HorizontalAlign="Right" VerticalAlign="Top"></ItemStyle>
    <ItemTemplate>
        <asp:Label Runat="server" Text='<%# Bind("RequiredDate", "{0:d}") %>'
            ID="lblRequiredDate"></asp:Label>
    </ItemTemplate>
</asp:TemplateField>
```

Add a *CustomValidator* Control

CustomValidator controls require adding a server-side validation handler for the `ValidatorName_ServerValidate` event and an optional JScript or VBScript function for client-side validation. This example validates Freight column edits and requires an entry of 5 or greater if the ShippedDate column contains a date. The validator enforces Northwind Traders' policy of a $5.00 minimum shipping and handling charge.

Here's the reformatted source code for the Freight `TemplateField`, which specifies the `cvFreight_ServerValidate` server-side event handler and the client-side VBScript `ClientValidationFunction` property value:

```
<asp:TemplateField SortExpression="Freight" HeaderText="Freight">
   <EditItemTemplate>
      <asp:TextBox ID="txtFreight" Runat="server" Width="52px"
         Text='<%# Bind("Freight") %>'></asp:TextBox>
      <asp:RequiredFieldValidator ID="rfvFreight" Runat="server"
         ErrorMessage="Freight is required; enter 0 if not known."
         Display="Dynamic" ControlToValidate="txtFreight">Required!
      </asp:RequiredFieldValidator>
      <asp:CustomValidator ID="cvFreight" Runat="server"
         ToolTip="Freight for shipped order cannot be less than $5.00"
         ControlToValidate="txtFreight" Display="Dynamic"
         ErrorMessage="Freight for shipped order is less than $5.00"
         OnServerValidate="cvFreight_ServerValidate"
         ClientValidationFunction="ValidateFreight">
         <5=Bad!
      </asp:CustomValidator>
   </EditItemTemplate>
   <ItemStyle HorizontalAlign="Right" VerticalAlign="Top"></ItemStyle>
   <ItemTemplate>
      <asp:Label Runat="server" Text='<%# Bind("Freight", "{0:C2}") %>'
         ID="lblFreight"></asp:Label>
   </ItemTemplate>
</asp:TemplateField>
```

The following `cvFreight_ServerValidate` event handler demonstrates code to obtain the value of another GridView column of the edited row. The code also sets the `args.IsValid` property value to `False` if a date is present in the ShippedDate column and the Freight value is less than $5.00.

```
Sub cvFreight_ServerValidate(ByVal source As Object,
  ByVal args As System.Web.UI.WebControls.ServerValidateEventArgs)
     'Invalid if order has shipped and Freight < $5.00
     args.IsValid = True
     If Val(args.Value) < 5 Then
        With gvOrdersEditable
           'Get the edited GridViewRow from its EditIndex property
           Dim gvrRow As GridViewRow = .Rows(.EditIndex)
           'Obtain a TextBox control from the row's ShippedDate text box
           Dim txtShipped As TextBox = _
            CType(gvrRow.FindControl("txtShippedDate"), TextBox)
           If txtShipped IsNot Nothing Then
              If Len(txtShipped.Text) > 4 Then
                 'Order has been shipped
                 args.IsValid = False
```

```
                End If
            End If
        End With
    End If
End Sub
```

Writing the script for the client-side validation function is a bit more challenging. You must derive the name of the field to test from the `Document.activeElement.id` value, which returns `gvOrdersEditable_ctl14_txtFreight` from the following active `<input>` element:

```
<input name="gvOrdersEditable$ctl14$txtFreight" type="text" value="0"
    id="gvOrdersEditable_ctl14_txtFreight" style="width:52px;" />
```

Replace `txtFreight` with `txtShippedDate` to create the `id` attribute value for the same row and apply the `Document.getElementById(ShipDateId).outerHTML` method to return the ShippedDate `<input>` element:

```
<input name="gvOrdersEditable$ctl14$txtShippedDate" type="text" value="5/10/1998"
    id="gvOrdersEditable_ctl14_txtShippedDate" style="width:76px;" />
```

Finally, extract the `value` attribute's text to determine if a ShippedDate value is present.

Following is the VBScript function in the `<head>` section that implements the client-side validation:

```
<script language="vbscript">
    Function ValidateFreight(source, args)
        'Test for Freight value < $5.00 if order has shipped
        If args.Value < 5 Then
            FreightID = Document.activeElement.id
            'Format: gvOrdersEditable_ctl##_txtFreight (## is a sequential number)
            ShipDateID = Left(FreightID, InStrRev(FreightID, "_")) & _
                "txtShippedDate"
            ShipDate = Document.getElementById(ShipDateID).outerHTML
            ShipDate = Mid(ShipDate, Instr(ShipDate, "value=") + 6)
            ShipDate = Left(ShipDate, Instr(ShipDate, " name=") -1)
            If Len(ShipDate) > 4 Then
                args.IsValid = False
            Else
                args.IsValid = True
            End If
        End If
    End Function
</script>
```

You can write similar code to perform date validation calculations, such as replacing the CompareValidator for RequiredDate with a CustomValidator that requires a minimum of seven days between OrderDate and RequiredDate values. CustomValidators provide much more flexibility than prebuilt validators at the expense of writing and testing event handlers and script.

Client-side CustomValidators don't detect violations unless the user changes the associated value. For example, replacing an empty ShippedDate value doesn't display a validation error for a Freight field with an existing 0 value, nor does retyping 0. In this case, the user must type a valid value and then an invalid value to obtain an error message. However, server-side validation will detect an unedited value less than 5.

Provide a Validation Summary Message

The ValidatedGridView.aspx page inherits from EditableDataGridView.aspx a text box that displays error messages from the server. You can create a similar text box to display uncorrected validator `ErrorMessage` values by adding a ValidationSummary control to the top of the page. The ValidationSummary text box appears only when users submit a page that has uncorrected errors.

Add a validation summary text box to the page by dragging a ValidationSummary control above the GridView, set the `DisplayMode` property value to `SingleParagraph`, add optional `HeaderText`, and apply formatting as required.

```
<asp:ValidationSummary ID="vsOrderData" Runat="server" Font-Size="10pt"
    Font-Bold="False"Font-Names="Verdana" DisplayMode="SingleParagraph"
    ShowMessageBox="False" Width="802px" Height="18px" BorderColor="DimGray"
    BorderStyle="Solid" BackColor="White" BorderWidth="1px"
    HeaderText=" Validation summary:"
    ToolTip="This is a summary of all order data validation errors." />
```

If you want to display a message box instead of a text box, set `ShowMessageBox` *to* `True` *and change the* `DisplaySummary` *property value to* `False`.

Figure 8-4 shows a ValidationSummary control displaying several editing errors. The PostBacks text box shows the number of session postbacks, which lets you distinguish client-side from server-side validation when running the built-in Web server.

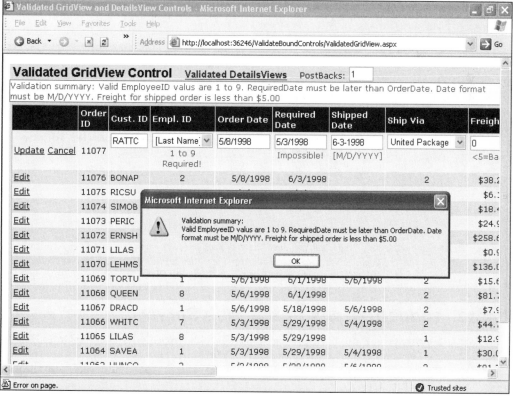

Figure 8-4

Validate DetailsView Controls

Adding validator controls to a DetailsView follows the procedure for a GridView. However, you must duplicate each EditItemTemplate validator control as an InsertItemTemplate control, if you allow inserting new items. In this case, you can copy and paste the EditItemTemplate validator control to the InsertItemTemplate, replace the default ID property value, and change the ControlToValidate property value to the associated inserting controls's ID. Figure 8-5 shows the Edit Templates smart tag for the CustomerID column with a RegularExpressionValidator control that was copied and pasted to the InsertItemTemplate.

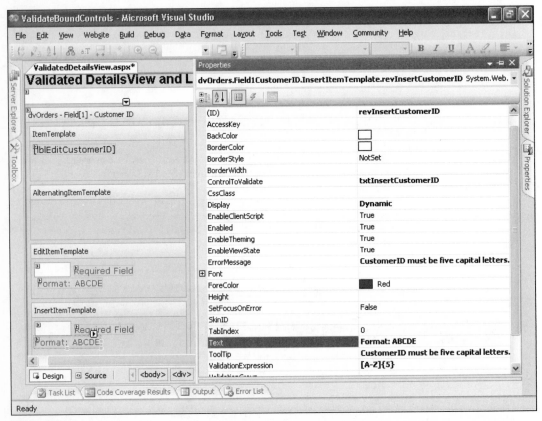

Figure 8-5

The ValidateBoundControls Web site's ValidatedDetailsView.aspx page includes DetailsView controls for the Orders and Order Details tables, and a GridView for the Order Details table. The Orders DetailsView has validator controls for most fields and the Order Details GridView has validators for all columns.

Validate ProductID Edits at the Web Server

Edits or insertions that create duplicate ProductID values for a single OrderID in the Order Details table throw a primary-key constraint exception. The Order Details GridView (gvOrderDetails) has a CustomValidator control (cvProductID) for the ProductID column that tests for duplicate values with the following event handler:

```
Sub cvProductID_ServerValidate(ByVal source As Object, _
  ByVal args As System.Web.UI.WebControls.ServerValidateEventArgs)
    Dim intRow As Integer
    Dim lblTest As Label = Nothing
    args.IsValid = True
    'Test edited value for duplicate ProductID
    With gvOrderDetails
        For intRow = 0 To .Rows.Count - 1
            lblTest = CType(.Rows(intRow).FindControl("lblProductID"), Label)
            If lblTest IsNot Nothing Then
                If args.Value = lblTest.Text Then
                    args.IsValid = False
                    Exit For
                End If
            End If
        Next
    End With
End Sub
```

The preceding event handler works correctly because there's no <span> element that contains a lblProductID control for the row being edited.

Test for Duplicate ProductID Values at the Client

Client-side script to invalidate edits that create duplicate ProductID values is more complex than the server-side code. The server-generated HTML assigns numeric values to the lblProductID's ID attribute value, as in this example for the first row of the gvOrderDetails control:

```
<span id="gvOrderDetails_ctl03_lblProductID">5</span>
```

Design modifications might change the initial 03 sequence value and Orders records have differing numbers of Order Details records. The safe method to test for duplicates is to start searching with 01 and end the search when a duplicate is encountered or all details rows for an order have been tested. The following VBScript function tests orders with fewer than 98 rows:

```
<script language="vbscript">
    Function ValidateProductID(source, args)
        args.IsValid = True
        Prefix = "gvOrderDetails_ctl"
        Suffix = "_lblProductID"
        LastRow = 99
        For Ctr = 1 To 99
            If Ctr < 10 Then
                CtlNum = "0" & Ctr
            Else
                CtlNum = Ctr
            End If
            CtlName = Prefix & CtlNum & Suffix
            Set objCtl = Document.getElementById(CtlName)
            If objCtl Is Nothing Then
                If Ctr > LastRow Then
                    'Last valid row
```

```
                    Exit For
            End If
        Else
            ProductID = objCtl.innerText
            LastRow = Ctr
            If ProductID = args.Value Then
                args.IsValid = False
                Exit For
            End If
        End If
    End If
  Next
End Function
</script>
```

Accommodating more than 97 rows doesn't affect performance because the `Exit For` statement executes when encountering a duplicated value or passing the last valid row. Figure 8-6 shows the ValidatedDetailsView.aspx page with multiple client-side editing violations, including a duplicate ProductID value.

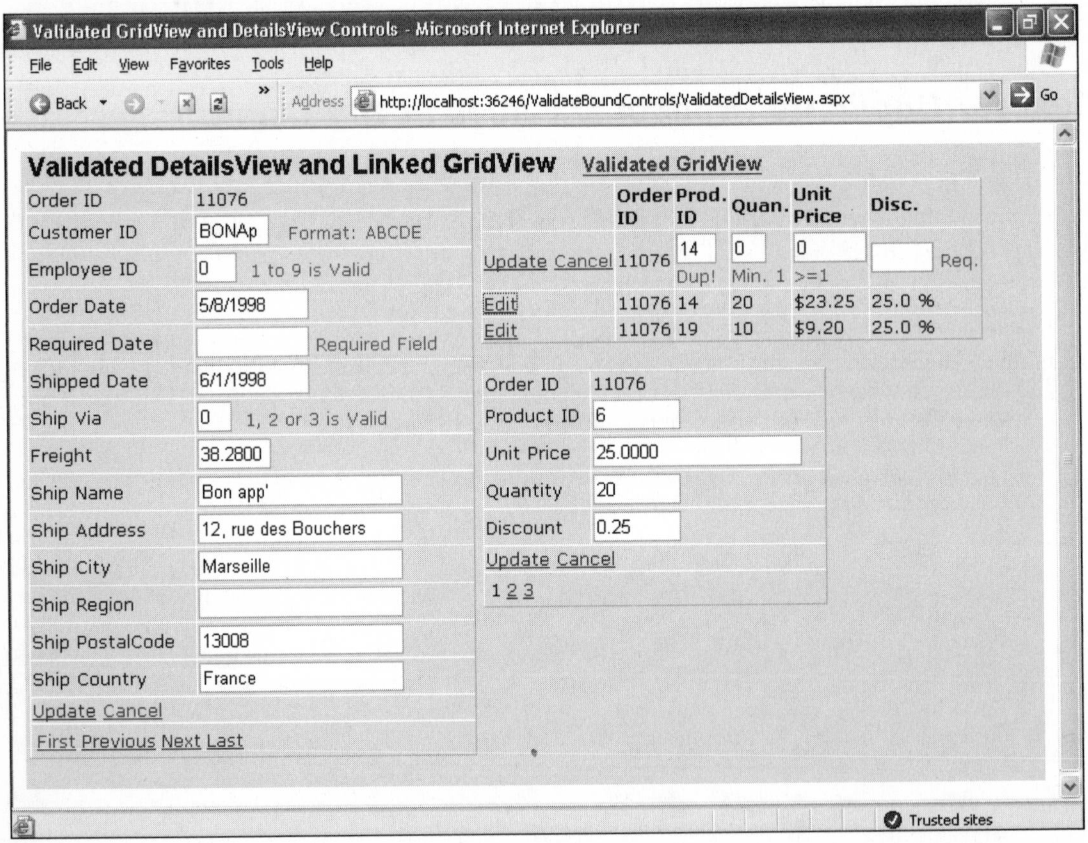

Figure 8-6

Replace SqlDataSources with ObjectDataSources

SqlDataSources implement a two-tier (client/server) architecture, which usually is satisfactory for a Web site that has a few hundred simultaneous users, simple or no business logic requirements, and stored procedures or SELECT queries with WHERE clauses to restrict the number of rows for populating DataLists or DataViews. The simplicity of two-tier data access minimizes application development and test time, but client/server architecture ties your Web applications to a specific relational data structure. Stored procedures can improve performance, and accommodate table and column name changes, as well as added columns. Stored procedures also provide increased database security by preventing direct client or middle-tier access to the underlying tables. However, stored procedures don't provide the level of data abstraction that ObjecDataSources deliver.

The sample Web site projects in Chapter 7 and many of the sample Web site projects in this chapter use SQL SELECT, UPDATE, INSERT, and DELETE queries without parameters for simplicity. Parameterized queries are recommended (strongly) for those production projects that execute SQL batch commands. Most DBAs of production sites that use SqlDataSources and two-tier or three-tier architecture require stored procedures for data retrieval and editing.

ObjectDataSources enable you to add a custom data access layer component (DALC) between the Web page that provides the UI and the stored procedures or SQL queries that access base tables. The logical DALC that implements the middle tier can — but isn't required to — be added as a physical tier. The following sections describe ObjectDataSources created from a typed DataSet's DataTables.

ObjectDataSources from DataTables

The ASP.NET 2.0 ObjectDataSource control enables binding business objects to data-enabled Web server controls. The simplest ObjectDataSource incarnation is a typed DataSet's DataTable object. An ObjectDataSource that you create from a DataTable doesn't enable abstracting the associated databound control from the metadata of the underlying base table or stored procedure. Generating at compile-time a typed DataSet class to support DataTables increases resource requirements and exacts a greater performance toll than invoking an SqlDataSource. The following sections' examples are intended to simplify your introduction to ObjectDataSources and do *not* constitute a recommendation to use typed DataSets as DALCs in production Web applications.

To add the schema for a typed DataSet to a Web site, right-click the site's App_Code folder, choose Add New Item, select DataSet in the Add New Item dialog's Visual Studio Installed Templates list, rename *DataSet*.xsd, and click Add. The XML Schema designer opens with a default, empty TableAdapter1 designer. Right-click the TableAdapter1 designer and choose Configure to start the DataTable Configuration Wizard.

If your Web site doesn't have an App_Code folder, you can add it from Solution Explorer or right-click the ProjectName node and add the DataSet's schema. Adding a DataSet to the Project folder opens a message box that suggests creating the App_Code folder and adding the DataSet.xsd file to it.

The process of configuring ASP.NET DataTables is identical to that for configuring a Windows form's typed DataSet's DataTables. Choosing to store the ConnectionString in an application configuration file adds the string to the Web.config file's <ConnectionStrings> group. Unlike the persistent DataSets you add to Windows form projects, ASP.NET data components don't add a *DataSetName*.designer.vb file to the project. Instead, compiling the *DataSet*.xsd file generates a temporary *Random*.2.cs file that defines the `Public Partial Class DataSetName`.

> *Generating the typed DataSet's C# code at runtime causes a performance hit the first time you build the project or when the first user opens a deployed Web Site. Another drawback of C# DataSet classes is that you can't add a VB.NET partial class to modify them. An alternative is to compile a Windows form typed DataSet to a class library and add a reference to the library to your page. The section "ObjectDataSources from Typed DataSet DALCs," later in this chapter, describes this approach, which also applies to Web services.*

Add Multiple DataTables to an Existing Web Site

The most convenient method of exploring ObjectDataSources is to add a DataSet and DataTables to an existing Web site that has GridView and DetailsView controls populated by SqlDataSources. Chapter 7's GridAndDetailsViews Web site is a good starting point for converting from two-tier SqlDataSources to three-tier ObjectDataSources.

> *The VB2005DB\Chapter08 folder includes a copy of the EditableGridAndDetailsView Web site that you can use for the following procedure.*

To add a DataSet with the Northwind Orders and Order Details DataTables and the SQL statements required for the sample Web site, do this:

1. Open the copy of the GridAndDetailsView Web site, right-click the App_Code folder or the project name, and choose Add New Item to open the dialog of the same name. Select DataSet, change DataSet.xsd to `OrdersDataSet.xsd`, and click Add. Click Yes to dismiss the message box, if it appears.

2. Right-click the empty DataTable1 editor to start the Table Adapter Configuration Wizard.

3. Accept the default connection name (`NorthwindConnectionString`), click Next, accept the default Use SQL Statements option, and click Next.

4. Click Query Builder, add the Orders table, and select each of the table's 13 original columns. In the OrderID row's Sort Type column, select Descending as the sort order. Click Execute Query to test the statement, click OK, and click Next.

5. Accept the default method names or change Fill to `FillOrders` and GetData to `GetOrders`, click Next to generate the SQL statements, and click Finish to dismiss the wizard.

> *ObjectDataSources require `GetData` methods. `Fill` methods aren't used, so you can omit them.*

6. Right-click the OrdersDataSet.xsd window's background and choose Add, and then Data Component to start another wizard instance.

7. Repeat Steps 2 through 4, but add the [Order Details] table in Step 4, and replace Fill with `FillDetails` and GetData with `GetDetails` in Step 5.

The `GetData` or `GetOrdersData` method populates the sample project's three GridViews. The following process adds parameterized queries to return a single Orders row or set of Order Details records:

1. Right-click the OrdersTableAdapter header and choose Add Query to start the Data Component Query Configuration Wizard. Accept the default Use SQL Statements option, and click Next. Then accept the default Select Which Returns Rows option, and click Next again.

2. In the What Data Should the Table Load? text box, replace ORDER BY OrderID DESC with WHERE OrderID = @OrderID, and click Next.

3. Replace FillBy with FillOrdersByOrderID and GetDataBy with GetOrdersByOrderID. Click Next and then click Finish to add the query.

4. Repeat Steps 1 through 3 for the [Order Details] TableAdapter, add WHERE OrderID = @OrderID in Step 2, and substitute Details for Orders in Step 3.

5. Press F5 to build and run the project.

Your OrdersDataSet.xsd window with the added parameterized queries appears as shown in Figure 8-7.

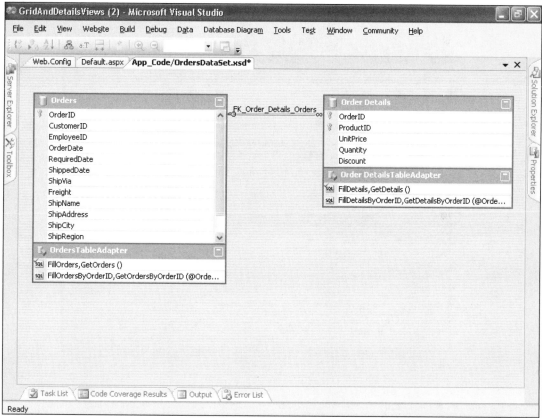

Figure 8-7

Create and Assign ObjectDataSources from the DataSet

The next process is to add ObjectDataSources for the GridViews and DetailsViews to pages of the sample project. The new ObjectDataSources duplicate the sample project's SqlDataSources, which enables you to use the existing templated GridViews and basic DetailsViews.

Add an ObjectDataSource to the EditableGridView Page

To add an ObjectDataSource for the EditableGridView page, do the following:

1. Open the EditableGridView.aspx page in Design mode and drag an ObjectDataSource from the Toolbox to under the dsOrdersEdit SqlDataSource, which adds an `ObjectDataSource1` place-holder and opens the Common DataSource Task smart tag.

2. Click the Configure DataSource link to open the dialog of the same name. Mark the Show Only Data Components checkbox, open the dropdown list, and select OrdersDataSetTableAdapters.OrdersTableAdapter. Click Next to open the Define Data Methods dialog (see Figure 8-8).

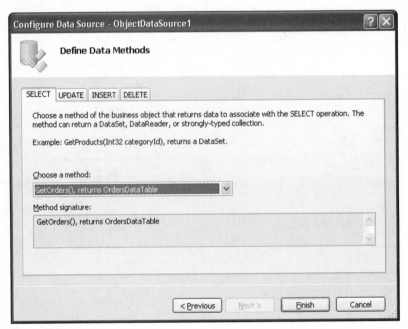

Figure 8-8

If you didn't build the project in Step 5 of the preceding section, the dropdown list is empty. In this case, click Cancel, build the Web site, and repeat this step.

3. Accept the SELECT tab's default `GetOrders()` method, which returns an `OrdersDataTable` object — not a DataSet.

4. Click the UPDATE tab to verify that the ObjectDataSource is updatable. Notice that the Method Signature text box prefixes each UPDATE parameter that has a value datatype with `Nullable` (see Figure 8-9).

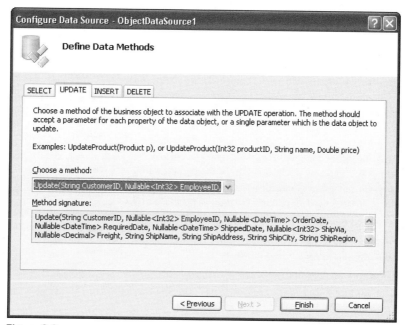

Figure 8-9

5. Click the INSERT and DELETE tabs to review the remaining method signatures, and click Finish to complete the process.

6. Open `ObjectDataSource1`'s Properties window and change the `ID` property value to `odsOrdersEdit` (see Figure 8-10).

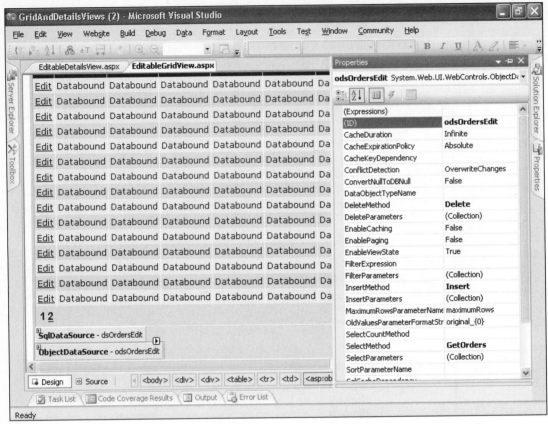

Figure 8-10

You can implement optimistic concurrency for edits and deletions by changing the ConflictDetection
property value from OverwriteChanges *to* CompareAllValues. *The* gvOrdersEditable
GridView *supports paging, but you don't need to set the* EnablePaging *property to* True. *For this
example, the GridView handles the paging process.*

Assign odsOrdersEdit to gvOrdersEditable and Verify Operability

The final step in the process replaces dsOrdersEdit with odsOrdersEdit. Open gvOrdersEditable's
smart tag, open the Choose Data Source list and select odsOrdersEdit, which opens a Refresh Fields and
Keys for 'gvOrdersEditable' message box (see Figure 8-11). Click No to leave the GridView intact.

> If you click Yes, you destroy and regenerate the GridView, which deletes all
> formatting and templates.

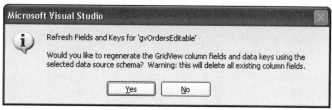

Figure 8-11

If you click Yes by mistake, press Ctrl+Z to undo the data source change. You might need to press Ctrl+Z several times to revert the GridView to its original state.

Press F5 to build and run the project, click the Edit button, and update one of the orders by changing the EmployeeID or ShipVia value. There's no detectable operational difference of the GridView with the ObjectDataSource substituted for the SqlDataSource.

Following is the source code for `odsOrdersEdit`:

```
<asp:ObjectDataSource ID="odsOrdersEdit" runat="server" DeleteMethod="Delete"
  InsertMethod="Insert" SelectMethod="GetOrders" UpdateMethod="Update">
  TypeName="OrdersDataSetTableAdapters.OrdersTableAdapter">
    <DeleteParameters>
        <asp:Parameter Name="Original_OrderID" Type="Int32" />
    </DeleteParameters>
    <UpdateParameters>
        <asp:Parameter Name="CustomerID" Type="String" />
        <asp:Parameter Name="EmployeeID" Type="Int32" />
        <asp:Parameter Name="OrderDate" Type="DateTime" />
        <asp:Parameter Name="RequiredDate" Type="DateTime" />
        <asp:Parameter Name="ShippedDate" Type="DateTime" />
        <asp:Parameter Name="ShipVia" Type="Int32" />
        <asp:Parameter Name="Freight" Type="Decimal" />
        <asp:Parameter Name="ShipName" Type="String" />
        <asp:Parameter Name="ShipAddress" Type="String" />
        <asp:Parameter Name="ShipCity" Type="String" />
        <asp:Parameter Name="ShipRegion" Type="String" />
        <asp:Parameter Name="ShipPostalCode" Type="String" />
        <asp:Parameter Name="ShipCountry" Type="String" />
        <asp:Parameter Name="Original_OrderID" Type="Int32" />
    </UpdateParameters>
    <InsertParameters>
        <asp:Parameter Name="CustomerID" Type="String" />
        <asp:Parameter Name="EmployeeID" Type="Int32" />
        <asp:Parameter Name="OrderDate" Type="DateTime" />
        <asp:Parameter Name="RequiredDate" Type="DateTime" />
        <asp:Parameter Name="ShippedDate" Type="DateTime" />
        <asp:Parameter Name="ShipVia" Type="Int32" />
        <asp:Parameter Name="Freight" Type="Decimal" />
        <asp:Parameter Name="ShipName" Type="String" />
```

```
            <asp:Parameter Name="ShipAddress" Type="String" />
            <asp:Parameter Name="ShipCity" Type="String" />
            <asp:Parameter Name="ShipRegion" Type="String" />
            <asp:Parameter Name="ShipPostalCode" Type="String" />
            <asp:Parameter Name="ShipCountry" Type="String" />
        </InsertParameters>
    </asp:ObjectDataSource>
```

The primary differences between the source code for the `odsOrdersEdit` ObjectDataSource and the corresponding `dsOrdersEdit` SqlDataSource are addition of a `TypeName="NameDataSetDataTableAdapters.NameDataTableAdapter"` attribute, and substitution of method names for SQL commands.

Add ObjectDataSources to the LinkedGridView and LinkedDetailsView Pages

The LinkedGridView.aspx page needs the same `odsOrdersEdit` ObjectDataSource as the EditableGridView.aspx page. Copy the `odsOrdersEdit` placeholder to the Clipboard, open the LinkedGridView.aspx page in Design mode, and paste the placeholder copy below the `dsOrders` placeholder. Open the Properties window, change the `ID` property value to `odsOrders` and, optionally, set the `DeleteMethod`, `InsertMethod`, and `UpdateMethod` property values to None because the `gvOrders` GridView is read-only. Change `gvOrders`' DataSource to `odsOrders`, press F5, and test the page's operation.

The LinkedDetailsView.aspx page requires two counterparts to the SqlDataSources for `gvOrdersLinked` and `dvOrderDetailsLinked`. To create the `odsOrderLinked` ObjectDataSource, do the following:

1. Drag an ObjectDataSource placeholder below the `dsOrdersLinked` placeholder, select Configure Data Source in the smart tag, select OrdersDataSetTableAdapters.OrdersTableAdapter in the drop-down list, and click Next.

2. In the Define Data Methods dialog, select the GetOrdersByOrderID parameterized query as the SELECT method, and click Next.

3. In the Define Parameters dialog, open the Parameter Source list and choose QueryString. Type **orderid** as the `QueryStringField` and **11077** as the `DefaultValue` property values (see Figure 8-12). Click Finish and press F5 to build and run the page.

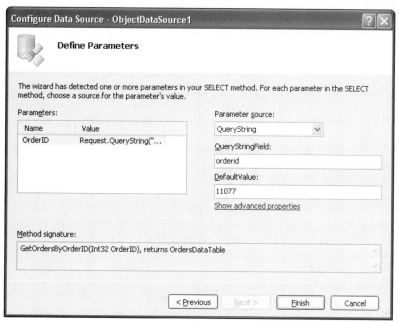

Figure 8-12

4. Change the ID to odsOrderLinked and the data source for gvOrdersLinked to odsOrderLinked. Don't refresh the keys when the message box opens.

5. Press F5, open the LinkedGridView.aspx page, and click an order other than 11077 to test the link to gvOrdersLinked. Verify that updates are operational by changing the EmployeeID, ShipVia, or both values.

Repeat the preceding procedure for the dvOrderDetailsLinked DetailsView, but select OrdersDataSetTableAdapters.Order_DetailsTableAdapter in Step 1 and GetDetailsByOrderID in Step 2. In Step 3, select the Update and Delete method from list on the UPDATE and DELETE tabs. Substitute odsOrderDetailsLinked for odsOrderLinked and dvOrderDetailsLinked for gvOrdersLinked in Step 4.

The Update method's signature is Update(Object OrderID, Object ProductID, Object UnitPrice, Object Quantity, Object Discount, Object Original_OrderID, Object Original_ProductID), returns Int32.

Work Around Problems with CompositePrimaryKeys

Attempting to edit an Order Details item throws an "ObjectDataSource 'odsOrderDetailsLinked' could not find a method 'Update' that has parameters: UnitPrice, Quantity, Discount, original_OrderID, original_ProductID" exception. Both OrderID and ProductID fields are read-only because these fields provide the composite primary key values of the Order Details table.

Enabling updates to a DetailsView whose data source is a table with a composite primary key requires a workaround. To conform the UPDATE parameters to the Update method's signature—shown in the note of the preceding section—you must supply the OrderID and ProductID parameter values in addition to the original_OrderID and original_ProductID values. By default, primary-key values are read-only in GridViews and DetailsViews; read-only fields don't provide parameter values. To supply the OrderID and ProductID parameter values, click the dvDetailsLinked's Fields property builder button to open the Fields dialog and change the ReadOnly property of the OrderID and ProductID fields to False.

To set the source of the UPDATE parameters, open odsOrderDetailsLinked's Properties window, select the UpdateParameters property's text box, and click its builder button to open the Parameter Collection Editor dialog. Set each parameter's Source to Control and set the ControlID value to the DetailsView, dvOrderDetails for this example.

You must add the required original_OrderID and original_ProductID parameters, if they're missing from the . Click the Add Parameter button, rename the default newparameter to original_OrderID, and repeat the process for original_ProductID. When you're finished editing the parameters, the Parameter Collection Editor appears as shown in Figure 8-13.

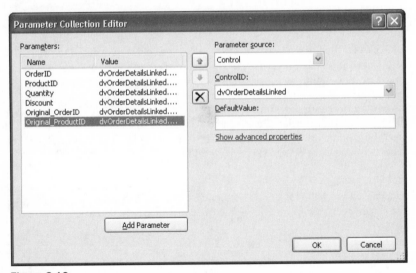

Figure 8-13

Click OK to save your UpdateParameters values, press F5, and edit an Order Details item to verify that your modifications behave as expected. Add a new Order Details item to test the Insert method parameters.

The \VB2005DB\Chapter08 folder's Web site is a complete implementation of the changes to the GridAndDetailsViews Web site described in the preceding sections.

ObjectDataSources from Typed DataSet DALCs

Data access layer components that you create as typed DataSets in Windows class libraries have the following advantages over DataSets created from data components:

- ❏ The VB.NET `Partial Class DataSetName` is accessible, so you can add a custom `Partial Class DataSetName` to customize the DataSet or add business logic.

- ❏ The ASP.NET runtime doesn't need to build the DataSet source code into a temporary file the first time a user opens the page.

- ❏ Multiple pages, Web Sites, or both can share the class library.

- ❏ The class library and an optional business-logic wrapper can be installed on a middle-tier server to enhance scalability.

If you intend to use typed DataSets with ASP.NET 2.0 Web Sites, class libraries are likely to be the most versatile and scalable approach.

Create the Class Library

Following are the basic steps to create an ObjectDataSource from a typed DataSet class library:

1. Create a new Visual Basic class library project. For this example, name the project `NwindDALC`.

2. Add a new data source to the project to start the Data Source Configuration Wizard and select Database as the data source type. For this example, select a connection to the Northwind sample database. A production application would use SQL Server security and a user account that has read-write permissions. In this case use your administrator account, save your password for SQL Server security, include sensitive information in the connection string, and do *not* save the configuration string in the App.config file.

3. Add the tables you need to the DataSet. For this example, add the Orders and Order Details tables, accept or change the default NorthwindDataSet DataSet name, and click Finish.

4. Use the TableAdapter Query Configuration Wizard to change the names of the `Fill` and `GetData` methods for the tables, and add `FillBy` and `GetDataBy` queries. For this example, duplicate the names and SQL statements in the section "Add Multiple DataTables to an Existing Web Site," earlier in this chapter.

5. Rename Class1.vb and change `Public Class1` to `Partial Public Class DataSetName`. Verify that the DataSet methods and properties are visible in the Declarations section.

6. Build the class library to create, for this example, NwindDALC.dll.

Create the Web Site

As was the case for the earlier ObjectDataSource DataSet example, it's easier to modify copies of existing Web pages, when practical, than to create new ones. The following process for creating a test Web site for a class library is similar to that described in the section "Add Multiple DataTables to an Existing Web Site," earlier in this chapter:

1. Create a new Web site and, for this example, add the LinkedGridView.aspx and LinkedDetailsView .aspx pages from the \VB2005DB\Chapter08\NWOrdersTDS Web site. Delete the Default.aspx page, and set LinkedGridView.aspx as the start page.

The NWOrdersTDS Web site uses the prebuilt NwindDAL.dll class library from the \VB2005DB\ Chapter08\NwindDAL folder.

2. Choose Web Site ⇨ Add Reference, click the Browse tab, navigate to the location of the DALC class library DLL you created in the preceding section (\VB2005DB\Chapter08\NwindDALC\ debug\bin), and double-click the DLL (NwindDALC.dll) to add the .dll, .pdb, and .xml files to the new Web site's ...\bin folder.

3. Open the Configure Data Source dialog for each ObjectDataSource from copied pages or add new ObjectDataSources to the pages. For this example, select NwindDALC .NorthwindDataSetTableAdapters.OrdersTableAdapter as the name of the odsOrders and odsOrdersLinked business objects, and verify or set the Update, Insert, and Delete methods.

Don't refresh the GridView or DetailsView when you change the data source.

4. Repeat Step 3 for the odsOrderDetailsLinked data source, but select NwindDALC .NorthwindDataSetTableAdapters.Orders_DetailsTableAdapter as the business object name.

5. Build, run, and add a new Web.config file, and test the project for Orders and Order Details updates and new Order Details entries.

If you update the class library, remove the related files from the ...\bin folder and repeat Step 2 to refresh the local copies.

ObjectDataSources from Custom Business Objects

Custom business objects free you from the relational data constraints of typed DataSets and DataTables at the expense of increased code complexity. Best practices dictate business object classes with public properties that have accessors and mutators (getters and setters). However, ObjectDataSources disregard public properties or fields and use reflection to invoke Select, Update, Insert, and Delete methods. This means you must add wrapper functions to your class that return or modify objects or object collections. Object collections to fill GridViews or DetailsViews must implement the IEnumerable interface; ArrayList, Hashtable, List, and most generic lists implement IEnumerable. GridViews you create from lists — rather than DataSets — don't support sorting, caching, or filtering.

Partial classes for wrapper methods maintain your original class definition files and let you repurpose the methods for other implementations, such as Web services or remoting. The object definition and wrapper method classes must be designated Public Partial ClassName. If you omit Partial from the object definition class declaration, the class name won't appear in the object name list of the first Configure Data Source Wizard's first dialog. (You must clear the Show Only Data Components checkbox to make custom business objects visible in the list.) The Select method determines the type returned to ObjectDataSource. The Select method examples of this chapter return ArrayLists of one or more items.

Most production business objects persist their data in relational database tables. Often, the business object is an intermediary whose purpose is to abstract the relational metadata into an object hierarchy, which can be serialized to an XML stream or file. The following sections show you how to create and manipulate objects that emulate a single DataTable, which is the recommended design for ObjectDataSources. Order and OrderDetail objects are populated by and saved to rows of the Northwind Orders and Order

Details tables. `Select` methods define `ArrayLists` of `Order` and `OrderDetail` objects to populate a read-only GridView, and read-write DetailsViews. `OrderDetail` `Update` and `Insert` methods instantiate objects; `Delete` methods operate on the tables directly.

The NWOrdersBE Web site in the \VB2005DB\Chapter08\NWOrdersBE folder is based on the LinkedGridView.aspx and LinkedDetailsView.aspx pages described in the preceding sections. The OrdersBE.vb file contains the definitions for the `Order`, `OrderDetail`, *and* `OrderDetails` *objects. OrdersBEMethods.vb contains the* `Select`, `Update`, `Insert`, *and* `Delete` *methods for the ObjectDataSources.*

Define the Business Objects

For simplicity, the `Order` and `OrderDetail` objects represent their source tables. Following is an abbreviated definition of the `OrdersBE` class's `Order` class:

```
Public Class Order
    Private orderIDField As Integer
    Private customerIDField As String
    Private employeeIDField As Integer
    Private orderDateField As Date
    Private requiredDateField As Date
    Private shippedDateField As Nullable(Of Date)
    Private shipViaField As Integer
    Private freightField As Decimal
    Private shipNameField As String
    Private shipAddressField As String
    Private shipCityField As String
    Private shipRegionField As String
    Private shipPostalCodeField As String
    Private shipCountryField As String

    Public Property OrderID() As Integer
        Get
            Return Me.orderIDField
        End Get
        Set(ByVal value As Integer)
            Me.orderIDField = value
        End Set
    End Property

    ...

    Public Property ShippedDate() As Nullable(Of Date)
        Get
            Return Me.shippedDateField
        End Get
        Set(ByVal value As Nullable(Of Date))
            'Convert default null date value to null
            If value.HasValue Then
                If value.ToString = "1/1/0001 12:00:00 AM" Then
                    Me.shippedDateField = Nothing
                Else
                    Me.shippedDateField = value
                End If
```

```
          Else
              Me.shippedDateField = value
          End If
      End Set
  End Property

...

  Public Property ShipCountry() As String
      Get
          Return Me.shipCountryField
      End Get
      Set(ByVal value As String)
          Me.shipCountryField = value
      End Set
  End Property
End Class
```

The `GetOrders` method, which the section "Match Method Signatures and Parameter Lists" later in this chapter describes, casts single or multiple `Order` instances to an `ArrayList`.

The `shippedDateField`'s business logic is required to handle null date values expressed as `1/1/0001 12:00:00` AM.

Here's the full definition of the `OrderDetail` object:

```
Public Class OrderDetail
    Private orderIDField As Integer
    Private productIDField As Integer
    Private unitPriceField As Decimal
    Private quantityField As Short
    Private discountField As Decimal

    Public Property OrderID() As Integer
        Get
            Return Me.orderIDField
        End Get
        Set(ByVal value As Integer)
            Me.orderIDField = value
        End Set
    End Property

    Public Property ProductID() As Integer
        Get
            Return Me.productIDField
        End Get
        Set(ByVal value As Integer)
            Me.productIDField = value
        End Set
    End Property

    Public Property UnitPrice() As Decimal
        Get
            Return Me.unitPriceField
```

```
            End Get
            Set(ByVal value As Decimal)
                Me.unitPriceField = value
            End Set
        End Property

        Public Property Quantity() As Short
            Get
                Return Me.quantityField
            End Get
            Set(ByVal value As Short)
                Me.quantityField = value
            End Set
        End Property

        Public Property Discount() As Decimal
            Get
                Return Me.discountField
            End Get
            Set(ByVal value As Decimal)
                Me.discountField = value
            End Set
        End Property
    End Class
```

The OrderDetails object is an array of OrderDetail objects, which the GetDetails method casts to an ArrayList.

Repurpose Pages to Display Business Objects

Preceding ObjectDataSource examples use copies of GridView and DetailsView pages created from SqlDataSources; page copies reduce design effort greatly. Basing new GridViews and DetailsViews on ObjectDataSources bound to custom business objects requires autogenerating columns or fields. Autogeneration results in a random column or field sequence because reflection doesn't respect the order of the object's public properties. Reordering the columns or fields requires opening the Fields dialog, clearing the Autogenerate Fields checkbox, adding a default BoundField for each object field, typing the HeaderText and DataField property values, and setting optional property values, such as DataFormatString. (Reflection doesn't populate the DataField list.) The TestGridViewBE.aspx page of this section's sample project is a partially completed version of this tedious process. TestDetailsViewBE.aspx is an example of a DetailsView with autogenerated fields.

You have the following two choices when you add an existing page with a GridView or DetailsView and then add or reconfigure an ObjectDataSource to a custom business object:

❑ **Refresh the fields and keys for the control.** This choice preserves GridView and DetailsView formatting, but autogenerates fields and deletes all templates and validator controls. You must re-create or copy and paste the templates and validator controls you added.

❑ **Preserve the original control, templates, and validators.** If your added GridView or DetailsView includes a DataKeyNames property value, which most do, the page designer displays an error placeholder instead of the design view of the control. To display the control in Design mode, you must clear the DataKeyNames text box.

Although the designer won't display the control, read-only bound controls — such as the GridView of the LinkedGridView.aspx page — render and operate as expected. Read-only controls don't require DataKeyNames to identify primary key field(s).

> **Clearing the** `DataKeyNames` **property value prevents parameterized GridViews and DetailsViews from returning** `original_FieldName` **parameters. If you clear the values, retype them before performing the following procedures.**

To test a templated DetailsView that has validator controls with a custom business object, do the following:

1. Add the ValidatedDetailsView.aspx page to the NWOrdersBE project.

2. Add an ObjectDataSource from the toolbox adjacent to the dsNWOrdersDetails SqlDataSource control, set the object name to OrdersBE, the SELECT method to GetAllOrders(), the UPDATE method to UpdateOrder(), and the INSERT method to InsertOrder().

3. Click No in the message box that opens when you click Finish.

4. Change the ObjectDataSource's ID property value to odsNWOrders, and set dvOrders' DataSource to odsNWOrders.

5. Set ValidatedDetailsView.aspx as the start page.

6. Build and run the project, and then edit and add a few new orders.

The page's behavior is identical to that for the SqlDataSource, except that adding a new order also adds a default OrderDetails item.

Add an ObjectDataSource adjacent to the dsNWOrderDetailsFiltered SqlDataSource, and repeat the preceding process, except as follows: Select GetDetailsByOrderID() as the Select method, UpdateDetail() as the Update method, and DeleteDetail() as the Delete method. Set the OrderID parameter to dvOrders.SelectedValue, change the two DataSources to odsNWOrderDetailsFiltered, and enable deletions. Edits work as expected, but deletions throw an error similar to that described in the preceding note.

Finally, repeat the preceding process for dvOrderDetails, but add InsertDetails() as the Insert method, and change the DataSource to odsNWOrderDetails. In this case, only the Insert method works as expected. Updates and deletions fail with mismatched method signatures.

The two GridViews on the LinkedDetailsViewBE.aspx page have the fixes described in the following sections applied.

Match Method Signatures and Parameter Lists

Read-write GridViews with Update and Delete methods, and DetailsViews with Update, Insert, and Delete methods usually require at least one modification to prevent errors from mismatched parameters and method signatures. The following sections describe how to fix the errors described in the preceding section and problems you might encounter when assigning parameter values from objects with fields of the Nullable(Of TypeName) data type.

Solve the Order and OrderDetail Deletion Errors

Following is the code for the `DeleteOrder` function, which has a simple `original_OrderID Integer` value as its signature:

```
Public Function DeleteOrder(ByVal original_OrderID As Integer) As Integer
    'Delete the records directly
    Dim cnNwind As New SqlConnection(strConn)
    Dim cmOrder As SqlCommand = Nothing
    Try
        'Delete Order Details and Orders records
        Dim strSQL As String = "DELETE FROM [Order Details] " + _
        "WHERE OrderID = " + original_OrderID.ToString + _
        "; DELETE FROM Orders WHERE OrderID = " + original_OrderID.ToString
        cmOrder = New SqlCommand(strSQL, cnNwind)
        cnNwind.Open()
        Return cmOrder.ExecuteNonQuery()
    Catch exc As Exception
        'Client handles the exception
        Throw exc
    Finally
        cnNwind.Close()
        cmOrder.Dispose()
        cnNwind.Dispose()
    End Try
End Function
```

You could alter the signature to match the `original_original_OrderID` *and* `original_OrderID` *parameters, but doing this isn't productive and probably would confuse anyone examining your code.*

GridViews and DetailsViews that have `DataKeyNames` property values automatically generate an `original_DataKeyName` parameter for each primary key field name when these controls invoke `Update` and `Delete` methods. The extra `original_original_OrderID` parameter is an artifact generated from the `original_OrderID` parameter of the `DeleteOrders` function. To solve the mismatch, open the `odsNWOrders'` properties window, click the `DeleteParameters` property builder button, and delete the `original_OrderID` parameter. Deletions then behave as expected.

The `DeleteDetail` function's signature is:

```
Public Function DeleteDetail(ByVal original_OrderID As Integer, _
  ByVal original_ProductID As Integer) As Integer
```

Thus, deleting the `original_OrderID` and `original_ProductID` parameters from the `DeleteParameters` collections of `odsNWOrderDetailsFiltered` and `odsNWOrderDetailsView` solves the OrderDetail deletion problem of both controls.

Fix the OrderDetail Update Errors

The `UpdateDetail` function's signature is:

```
Public Function UpdateDetail( _
  ByVal OrderID As Integer, ByVal ProductID As Integer, _
  ByVal UnitPrice As Decimal, ByVal Quantity As Short, _
  ByVal Discount As Decimal, ByVal original_OrderID As Integer, _
  ByVal original_ProductID As Integer) As Integer
```

Making the same change to the GridView's `UpdateParameters` collection works as expected, but doing the same for the DetailsView's `UpdateParameters` collection throws an "ObjectDataSource 'odsNWOrderDetailsView' could not find a method 'UpdateDetail' that has parameters: UnitPrice, Quantity, Discount, ProductID, original_OrderID, original_ProductID" error.

Fields included in the DetailsView's `UpdateParameters` collection and the `DataKeyNames` property value don't return values if the fields' `ReadOnly` property value is `True` — the default for primary-key members. To work around this issue, which is specific to DetailsViews with composite primary keys, you must set each primary key field's `ReadOnly` property value to `False`. Doing this permits users to change the `OrderID` value when performing an update, but you can add a custom exception for this case to your `Update` wrapper method.

Following is the final source code for the `dvDetails` DetailsView's ObjectDataSource:

```
<asp:ObjectDataSource ID="odsNWOrderDetailsView" Runat="server" TypeName="OrdersBE"
    SelectMethod="GetDetailsByOrderID" DeleteMethod="DeleteDetail"
    InsertMethod="InsertDetail" UpdateMethod="UpdateDetail">
    <UpdateParameters>
        <asp:Parameter Type="Int32" Name="OrderID"></asp:Parameter>
        <asp:Parameter Type="Int32" Name="ProductID"></asp:Parameter>
        <asp:Parameter Type="Decimal" Name="UnitPrice"></asp:Parameter>
        <asp:Parameter Type="Int16" Name="Quantity"></asp:Parameter>
        <asp:Parameter Type="Decimal" Name="Discount"></asp:Parameter>
    </UpdateParameters>
    <SelectParameters>
        <asp:ControlParameter Name="OrderID" Type="Int32" ControlID="dvOrders"
            PropertyName="SelectedValue"></asp:ControlParameter>
    </SelectParameters>
    <InsertParameters>
        <asp:Parameter Type="Int32" Name="OrderID"></asp:Parameter>
        <asp:Parameter Type="Int32" Name="ProductID"></asp:Parameter>
        <asp:Parameter Type="Decimal" Name="UnitPrice"></asp:Parameter>
        <asp:Parameter Type="Int16" Name="Quantity"></asp:Parameter>
        <asp:Parameter Type="Decimal" Name="Discount"></asp:Parameter>
    </InsertParameters>
</asp:ObjectDataSource>
```

All pages of this chapter's examples that include OrderDetail DetailsViews have ProductID fields with the `ReadOnly` property value set to False, which permits users to change the ProductID value in an update operation. The alternative is to require users to delete and then add a new OrderDetail item with a different ProductID, which is a more common business practice.

Explore the Select, Update, Insert, and Delete Wrapper Functions

The OrdersBEMethods.vb file's four wrapper functions for each object consist of 640 lines of code and are far too lengthy to reprint here in their entirety. The `Get...` functions emulate several `GetOrder(s)` and `GetDetails` overloads that return `ArrayLists` of all, `TOP n`, or a specific customer's `Order` and `OrderDetail` objects or a particular `Order` and its `OrderDetail` objects. The `UpdateOrder` and `InsertOrder` functions implement parameterized or dynamically generated SQL statements. `UpdateDetails` and `InsertDetails` use parameterized SQL statements. The parameterized SQL statements simplify the conversion of the project's production version to stored procedures.

The Order object's ShippedDate field — shown in the section "Define the Business Objects," earlier in this chapter — has a `Nullable(Of Date)` data type to accommodate null ShippedDate values. Setting a parameter value from a `Nullable(Of DataType)` property requires casting to the value data type, as shown in the following snippet from the `InsertOrder` and `InsertDetail` functions:

```
prmUpdate = New SqlParameter("@ShippedDate", SqlDbType.DateTime)
If ordUpdate.ShippedDate.HasValue Then
    prmUpdate.Value = CType(ordUpdate.ShippedDate, Date)
Else
    prmUpdate.Value = Convert.DBNull
End If
.Add(prmUpdate)
```

If you don't cast to the value data type — Date for this example — assigning a `Nullable(Of Date)` value to the parameter throws "Failed to convert parameter value from a Nullable`1 to a DateTime" and "Object must implement IConvertible" exceptions.

Don't assign `Nullable(Of DataType)` *types to* `Update` *or* `Insert` *method arguments. Doing this causes the ObjectDataSource's method calls to fail.*

Read XML Files with the XmlDataSource

The XmlDataSource control enables one-way databinding to tabular or hierarchical XML document files or strings. You can bind element-centric or attribute-centric tabular documents to templated DataGrid, DataList, DetailsView, and Repeater controls by substituting `XPath("ColumnPath")` for `Bind("ColumnName")` as the binding code. The most common control for displaying hierarchical documents is the TreeView control. TreeViews require documents whose elements include an attribute to display element values. XmlDataSources let you specify a custom XSLT file to transform conventional element-centric documents to the special TreeView format.

The NWOrdersXML Web site in the \VB2005DB\Chapter08\NWOrdersXML *folder has pages that demonstrate populating DataGrid, Repeater, and TreeView controls from sample XML documents.*

Create XmlDataSources from XML Documents

The following sections' examples use two XML source documents in the NWOrderXML Web site's App_Data folder—Orders.xml and OrdersAttrib.xml.

Orders.xml is based on Chapter 5's Output.xml examples and has the following structure for 18 Orders groups:

```xml
<?xml version="1.0" standalone="yes"?>
<Northwind>
  <Orders>
    <OrderID>11077</OrderID>
    <CustomerID>RATTC</CustomerID>
    <EmployeeID>2</EmployeeID>
    <OrderDate>1998-05-06</OrderDate>
    <RequiredDate>1998-06-03</RequiredDate>
    <ShippedDate>1998-05-15</ShippedDate>
    <ShipVia>1</ShipVia>
    <Freight>88.53</Freight>
    <ShipName>Rattlesnake Canyon Grocery</ShipName>
    <ShipAddress>2817 Milton Dr.</ShipAddress>
    <ShipCity>Albuquerque</ShipCity>
    <ShipRegion>NM</ShipRegion>
    <ShipPostalCode>87110</ShipPostalCode>
    <ShipCountry>USA</ShipCountry>
  </Orders>
  ...
</Northwind>
```

To create an XmlDataSource from the Orders.xml file, drag a GridView, DetailsView, DataList, or Repeater control to the page, select New Data Source to open the Data Source Configuration dialog, select XML File, assign the data source an appropriate ID property value, and click OK to open the Configure Data Source dialog. Alternatively, drag an XmlDataSource from the Toolbox, and click Configure Data Source.

Type the path and file name for the source XML document in the Data File text box, or click Browse and select the document. If you have a schema for the source document, you can specify it in the Schema File text box, but the XmlDataSource control ignores it. Specify the path and file name of the XSLT file, if you need one, in the Transform File text box. You can reduce the length of XPath binding statements or filter the source document by typing the appropriate XPath expression in the last text box. As an example, specifying Northwind/Orders returns all Orders elements of Orders.xml (see Figure 8-14).

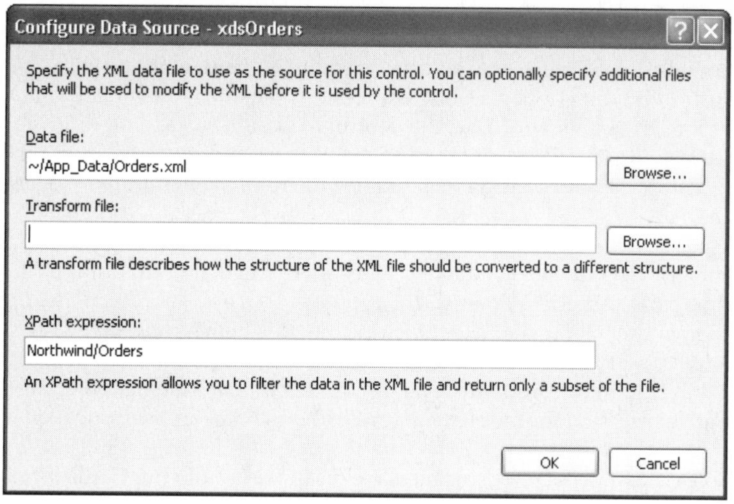

Figure 8-14

Following is the structure of the OrdersAttrib.xml source document for populating a TreeView control with 18 Order nodes:

```xml
<?xml version="1.0" standalone="yes"?>
<Orders>
  <Order>
    <OrderID id="11077" />
    <CustomerID id="RATTC" />
    <EmployeeID id="2" />
    <OrderDate date="1998-05-06T00:00:00.0000000-07:00" />
    <RequiredDate date="1998-06-03T00:00:00.0000000-07:00" />
    <ShippedDate date="1998-06-03T00:00:00.0000000-07:00" />
    <ShipVia id="1" />
    <Freight amount="88.5300" />
    <ShipName value="Rattlesnake Canyon Grocery" />
    <ShipAddress value="2817 Milton Dr." />
    <ShipCity value="Albuquerque" />
    <ShipRegion value="NM" />
    <ShipPostalCode value="87110" />
    <ShipCountry value="USA" />
  </Order>
</Orders>
```

Configuring an XmlDataSource control with OrdersAttrib.xml as the source document is similar to the preceding example. In this case, specify `Orders/Order` as the XPath Expression.

Although XmlDataSources are inherently read-only, you can gain access to the underlying XML document by assigning it to an XmlDocument object with the GetXmlDocument method in the Load event handler for the XmlDataSource. You must write code to alter the in-memory document's structure or data values, and then save the modified document to another XML file.

Populate a GridView with Orders.xml

Complex databound controls, such as GridViews, require an ItemTemplate for each column to permit changing the Custom Binding option's Code Expression. When you assign an XmlDataSource to a templated GridView, DetailsView, or DataList control in Design mode, you receive this or a similar error message: "The data source for GridView with id 'GridView1' did not have any properties or attributes from which to generate columns." The exception results from an attempt to autogenerate columns with `Bind` expressions.

To solve this problem, open the Fields dialog, clear the Autogenerate Columns checkbox, and, for each column you want to display, add a BoundField, type `HeaderText` and `DataField` property values, and convert the field to an ItemTemplate field. Open each field's ItemTemplate and its *LabelID* Binding dialog, and change `Bind` to `XPath`, if you specified in the Configure Data Source dialog the XPath expression that points to the appropriate level in your document's element hierarchy. If not, you must type the full XPath expression for the element (or attribute) name in the Code Expression text box.

When you complete the process, the error message disappears and your GridView appears as expected in Design mode and in IE when you build and run the page (see Figure 8-15). GridViews and DetailsViews support selection only; server-side paging and editing aren't supported.

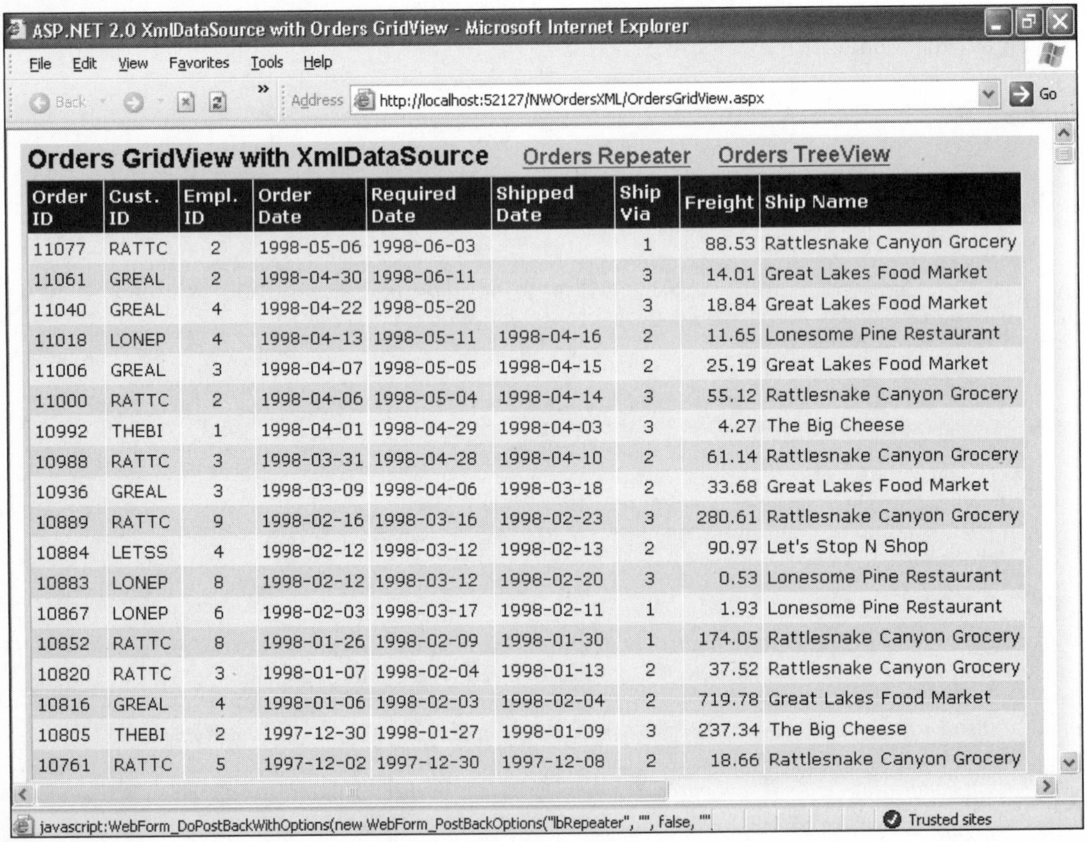

Order ID	Cust. ID	Empl. ID	Order Date	Required Date	Shipped Date	Ship Via	Freight	Ship Name
11077	RATTC	2	1998-05-06	1998-06-03		1	88.53	Rattlesnake Canyon Grocery
11061	GREAL	2	1998-04-30	1998-06-11		3	14.01	Great Lakes Food Market
11040	GREAL	4	1998-04-22	1998-05-20		3	18.84	Great Lakes Food Market
11018	LONEP	4	1998-04-13	1998-05-11	1998-04-16	2	11.65	Lonesome Pine Restaurant
11006	GREAL	3	1998-04-07	1998-05-05	1998-04-15	2	25.19	Great Lakes Food Market
11000	RATTC	2	1998-04-06	1998-05-04	1998-04-14	3	55.12	Rattlesnake Canyon Grocery
10992	THEBI	1	1998-04-01	1998-04-29	1998-04-03	3	4.27	The Big Cheese
10988	RATTC	3	1998-03-31	1998-04-28	1998-04-10	2	61.14	Rattlesnake Canyon Grocery
10936	GREAL	3	1998-03-09	1998-04-06	1998-03-18	2	33.68	Great Lakes Food Market
10889	RATTC	9	1998-02-16	1998-03-16	1998-02-23	3	280.61	Rattlesnake Canyon Grocery
10884	LETSS	4	1998-02-12	1998-03-12	1998-02-13	2	90.97	Let's Stop N Shop
10883	LONEP	8	1998-02-12	1998-03-12	1998-02-20	3	0.53	Lonesome Pine Restaurant
10867	LONEP	6	1998-02-03	1998-03-17	1998-02-11	1	1.93	Lonesome Pine Restaurant
10852	RATTC	8	1998-01-26	1998-02-09	1998-01-30	1	174.05	Rattlesnake Canyon Grocery
10820	RATTC	3	1998-01-07	1998-02-04	1998-01-13	2	37.52	Rattlesnake Canyon Grocery
10816	GREAL	4	1998-01-06	1998-02-03	1998-02-04	2	719.78	Great Lakes Food Market
10805	THEBI	2	1997-12-30	1998-01-27	1998-01-09	3	237.34	The Big Cheese
10761	RATTC	5	1997-12-02	1997-12-30	1997-12-08	2	18.66	Rattlesnake Canyon Grocery

Figure 8-15

Design a Repeater Control with an XmlDataSource

Repeater controls don't have a designer, so you must add the code for child controls and their databinding in Source mode. Repeaters offer the advantage of flexible display formatting but don't enable paging. The following code creates a repeating two-column table that displays all Orders.xml elements:

```
<asp:Repeater ID="rptOrders" Runat="server" DataSourceID="xdsOrders">
<HeaderTemplate>
  <table cellpadding="1" cellspacing="3" border="0">
</HeaderTemplate>
<ItemTemplate>
  <tr>
     <td>OrderID:</td><td><b><%#XPath("OrderID")%></td>
     <td>CustomerID:</td><td><b><%#XPath("CustomerID")%></td>
  </tr>
  <tr>
     <td>EmployeeID:</td><td><b><%#XPath("EmployeeID")%></td>
     <td>OrderDate:</td><td><b><%#XPath("OrderDate")%></b></td>
  </tr>
  <tr>
     <td>RequiredDate:</td><td><b><%#XPath("RequiredDate")%></b></td>
     <td>ShippedDate:</td><td><b><%#XPath("ShippedDate")%></b></td>
  </tr>
  <tr>
     <td>ShipVia:</td><td><b><%#XPath("ShipVia")%></b></td>
     <td>Freight:</td><td><b><%$XPath("Freight")%></b></td>
  </tr>
  <tr>
     <td>ShipName:</td><td><b><%#XPath("ShipName")%></b></td>
     <td>ShipAddress:</td><td><b><%#XPath("ShipAddress")%></b></td>
  </tr>
  <tr>
     <td>ShipCity:</td><td><b><%#XPath("ShipCity")%></b></td>
     <td>ShipRegion:</td><td><b><%#XPath("ShipRegion")%></b></td>
  </tr>
  <tr>
     <td>ShipPostalCode:</td><td><b><%#XPath("ShipPostalCode")%></b></td>
     <td>ShipCountry:</td><td><b><%#XPath("ShipCountry")%></b></td>
  </tr>
</ItemTemplate>
<SeparatorTemplate>
  <td height="1" bgcolor="black"><td height="1" bgcolor="black">
  <td height="1" bgcolor="black"><td height="1" bgcolor="black">
</SeparatorTemplate>
<FooterTemplate>
  </table>
</FooterTemplate>
</asp:Repeater>
<asp:XmlDataSource ID="xdsOrders" Runat="server" DataFile="~/App_Data/Orders.xml"
  SchemaFile="~/Data/Orders.xsd" XPath="Northwind/Orders">
</asp:XmlDataSource>
```

Configuring the XmlDataSource control adds the emphasized code in the preceding listing.

Figure 8-16 shows the Repeater control generated by the preceding source code.

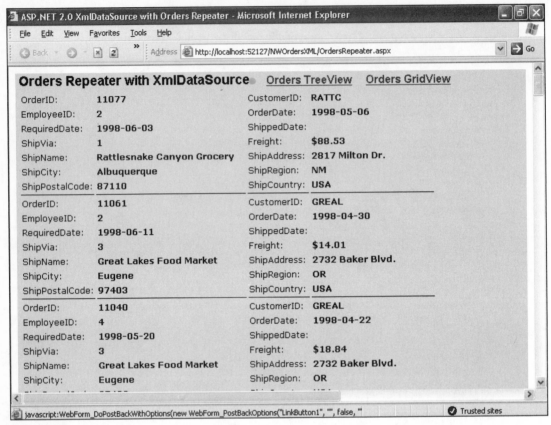

Figure 8-16

Fill a TreeView with Tabular Data

TreeViews provide a TreeView DataBindings Editor for XmlDataSources that have source documents with the appropriate structure. When you specify the XmlDataSource for a TreeView control with autogenerated nodes, element names, rather than values, appear in Design mode and when you run the page. You use the TreeView DataBindings Editor to specify the attribute name that replaces the element's name with the value. Open the Editor by right-clicking the TreeView and choosing Edit TreeView Databindings.

You must add each element (column) to the Selected Data Bindings list and select the associated attribute name from the TextField dropdown list to provide the value. Optionally, add a prefix to the value with a FormatString (see Figure 8-17).

> *Unfortunately, the TreeView's* FormatString *property doesn't support standard formats, such as* {0:d} *for dates and* {0:c2} *for currency.*

Figure 8-17

Here's the source code for the TreeView with the databindings shown in Figure 8-17:

```
<asp:TreeView ID="tvOrders" Runat="server" Font-Names="Verdana"
    DataSourceID="xdsOrdersTV"
    Font-Size="10pt" AutoGenerateDataBindings="False" ExpandDepth="0"
    Width="346px" Height="367px" BorderStyle="Solid" BorderWidth="1px">
    <DataBindings>
        <asp:TreeNodeBinding DataMember="Order" Value="Order" Text="Order">
        </asp:TreeNodeBinding>
        <asp:TreeNodeBinding TextField="id" DataMember="OrderID">
            FormatString="Order ID: {0}"</asp:TreeNodeBinding>
        <asp:TreeNodeBinding TextField="id" DataMember="CustomerID">
            FormatString="Customer ID: {0}"</asp:TreeNodeBinding>
        <asp:TreeNodeBinding TextField="id" DataMember="EmployeeID">
            FormatString="Employee ID: {0}"</asp:TreeNodeBinding>
        <asp:TreeNodeBinding TextField="date" DataMember="OrderDate">
            FormatString="Order Date: {0:d}"</asp:TreeNodeBinding>
        <asp:TreeNodeBinding TextField="date" DataMember="RequiredDate">
            FormatString="Required Date: {0:d }"</asp:TreeNodeBinding>
        <asp:TreeNodeBinding TextField="date" DataMember="ShippedDate">
            FormatString="Shipped Date: {0:d }"</asp:TreeNodeBinding>
        <asp:TreeNodeBinding TextField="id" DataMember="ShipVia">
            FormatString="Ship Via: {0}"</asp:TreeNodeBinding>
        <asp:TreeNodeBinding TextField="amount" DataMember="Freight">
            FormatString="Freight: {0:c2}"</asp:TreeNodeBinding>
        <asp:TreeNodeBinding TextField="value" DataMember="ShipName">
            FormatString="Ship Name: {0}"</asp:TreeNodeBinding>
        <asp:TreeNodeBinding TextField="value" DataMember="ShipAddress">
            FormatString="Ship Address: {0}"</asp:TreeNodeBinding>
        <asp:TreeNodeBinding TextField="value" DataMember="ShipCity">
            FormatString="Ship City: {0}"</asp:TreeNodeBinding>
```

```
            <asp:TreeNodeBinding TextField="value" DataMember="ShipRegion">
                FormatString="Ship Region: {0}"></asp:TreeNodeBinding>
            <asp:TreeNodeBinding TextField="value" DataMember="ShipPostalCode">
                FormatString="Ship Postal Code: {0}"></asp:TreeNodeBinding>
            <asp:TreeNodeBinding TextField="value" DataMember="ShipCountry">
                FormatString="Ship Country: {0}"></asp:TreeNodeBinding>
        </DataBindings>
        <LeafNodeStyle ForeColor="Black"></LeafNodeStyle>
        <HoverNodeStyle ForeColor="Red"></HoverNodeStyle>
    </asp:TreeView>
    <asp:XmlDataSource ID="xdsOrdersTV" Runat="server"
        DataFile="~/App_Data/OrdersAttrib.xml" XPath="/Orders/Order">
    </asp:XmlDataSource></td>
```

Figure 8-18 shows the TreeView generated by the preceding code with one node expanded.

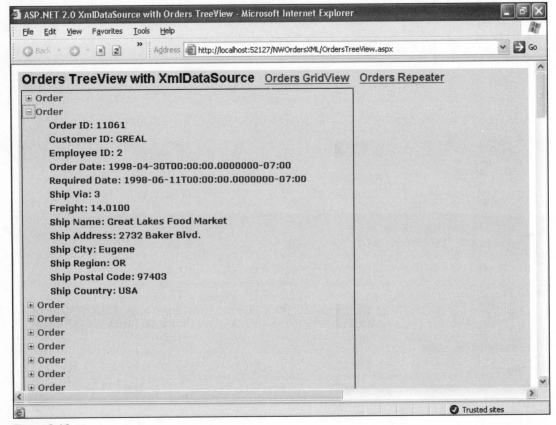

Figure 8-18

Clicking a leaf node performs a postback with the name of the control and the value, including the `FormatString` *prefix, as the* `__doPostBack` *function argument. For example, clicking the OrderID node returns* `__doPostBack('tvOrders','sOrder','Order ID: 11077')`.

Trace Web Pages to Compare DataSource Performance

The OrdersTreeView.aspx page described in the preceding section takes about 0.75 second to display the entire page in IE when you run it for the first time on a fast machine with the built-in Web server. The delay occurs in the PreRender and Render events. The OrdersGridView.aspx and OrdersRepeater.aspx pages display almost instantaneously. An `<%@ OutputCache Duration="60" VaryByParam="none" %>` directive ensures that the built-in Web server caches the three pages.

> *Your results probably will differ, depending on computer performance and system configuration. This section's data is based on a 2.33 GHz Pentium 4 computer with 1GB RAM running Windows Server 2003. The delay is an artifact of running the project in debugging mode. You can eliminate the delay by pressing Ctrl+F5 to run the project without debugging.*

If you want to find the reason for the TreeView's debugging performance hit, enable ASP.NET tracing of the page by adding `Trace="True" TraceMode="SortByTime"` to the `<%@ Page...` directive. Page-level tracing is enabled for the three pages of the NWOrdersXML Web site. The most important trace sections for performance analysis are Trace Information and Control Tree. Trace Information's End Render item reports the total time required by the Web server to deliver the cached page, which is about 50 milliseconds. Thus the initial `<span>` section appears immediately. Control Tree reports the number of bytes required to render the page and its controls. The total size of the page is 210,170 bytes, of which the TreeView form contributes 209,599 bytes, including the control's viewstate (see Figure 8-19).

aspx.page	Begin PreRender	0.0354505949778533	0.000051
aspx.page	End PreRender	0.363687563642865	0.328237
aspx.page	Begin PreRenderComplete	0.36397530971115	0.000288
aspx.page	End PreRenderComplete	0.364362789125434	0.000387
aspx.page	Begin SaveState	0.399394615796142	0.035032
aspx.page	End SaveState	0.440007878096238	0.040613
aspx.page	Begin SaveStateComplete	0.440088614614427	0.000081
aspx.page	End SaveStateComplete	0.440517440065707	0.000429
aspx.page	Begin Render	0.440569681342182	0.000052
aspx.page	End Render	0.700584850867918	0.260015

Control Tree

Control UniqueIDType		Render Size Bytes (including children)	ViewState Size Bytes (excluding children)	ControlState Size Bytes (excluding children)
__Page	ASP._OrdersTreeView_aspx	210170	0	0
ctl02	System.Web.UI.LiteralControl	151	0	0
ctl00	System.Web.UI.HtmlControls.HtmlHead	326	0	0
ctl01	System.Web.UI.HtmlControls.HtmlTitle	66	0	0
ctl03	System.Web.UI.LiteralControl	68	0	0
frmTreeView	System.Web.UI.HtmlControls.HtmlForm	209599	0	0
ctl04	System.Web.UI.LiteralControl	201	0	0
LinkButton1	System.Web.UI.WebControls.LinkButton	246	0	0
ctl05	System.Web.UI.LiteralControl	19	0	0
lbRepeater	System.Web.UI.WebControls.LinkButton	244	0	0
ctl06	System.Web.UI.LiteralControl	172	0	0
tvOrders	System.Web.UI.WebControls.TreeView	171528	33812	0
ctl07	System.Web.UI.LiteralControl	73	0	0

Figure 8-19

Compare the render size of the TreeView control with that of the GridView (9,256 bytes) and the Repeater (24,533 bytes). The comparison indicates that the extraordinary size of the TreeView control is responsible for the performance hit when debugging.

> *You can reduce the size of the TreeView by about 30KB and improve performance a bit by removing the* `<HoverNodeStyle ForeColor="Red"></HoverNodeStyle>`*setting. Setting HoverStyleNode property values adds* `onmouseover="TreeView_HoverNode(tvOrders_Data, this, '', 'none')"` `onmouseout="TreeView_UnhoverNode(this)"><a class="aspnet_s1 aspnet_s2 " href="javascript:__doPostBack('tvOrders','sOrder')" onclick="TreeView_ SelectNode(tvOrders_Data, this, 'tvOrderst0');"` *to each of the TreeView's 270 rows.*

If you want to save multiple traces for all your application's pages, add the following line to the `<system.web>` section of your Web.config file:

```
<trace enabled="true" traceMode="SortByTime" requestLimit="20"
    mostRecent="true" localOnly="true" pageOutput="true"/>
```

To view the saved traces with the Web server's built-in trace viewer, replace the URL's `PageName.aspx` with `Trace.axd`, as shown in Figure 8-20. Click a View Details link to display a trace page similar to Figure 8-19.

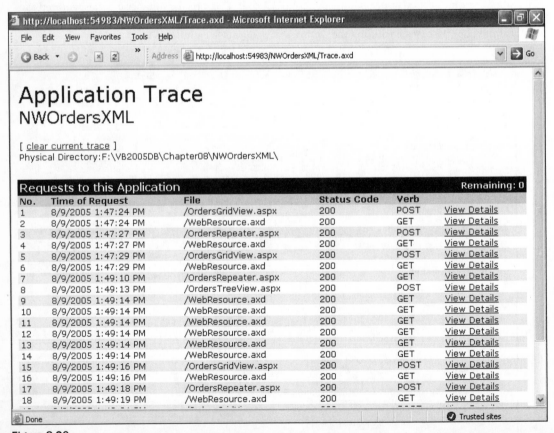

Figure 8-20

WebResource.axd is a new ASP.NET 2.0 handler for resources that are embedded in an assembly. The `Page.GetWebResourceUrl(Type, strResourceId)` *method returns the resource's URL.*

Deploy Completed Web Sites to IIS

After you complete the design and testing of a production VS 2005 Web site with the built-in Web server, you must deploy the application to an IIS 5 or 6 virtual directory to make it accessible to users. The Website and Build menus offer two deployment choices — Website ⇨ Copy Web Site and Build ⇨ Publish *WebsitePath*. Copy Web Site simply copies all files from your development folder to the folder designated for the virtual directory. Publish *WebsitePath* precompiles the Web site's pages and copies files other than page source files to the virtual directory. Precompiling the source code eliminates the compilation delay experienced by the first user who opens a page. Publishing the site also removes the source code, which improves application security.

If your production project includes a class library with a debug symbol file (ClassName.pdb), compile the class library in Release configuration before deploying your application. Remove the class library files from the \bin folder and add a reference to the Release version of the class library DLL. Configuration Manager doesn't offer a Release configuration option for Web sites.

Create a Virtual Directory for Your Site

To create an IIS virtual directory on your development computer, do the following:

1. Create a folder to store the virtual directory's files. For this example, create a subfolder of \Inetpub\wwwroot named NWOrdersXMLCopy.

2. Open the Internet Information Services (IIS) Manager, expand the *COMPUTER-NAME* (Local Computer) and Web Sites node, right-click the Default Web Site node, and choose New ⇨ Virtual Directory to start the Virtual Directory Creation Wizard. Click Next.

3. Specify the name of the virtual directory — NWOrdersXMLCopy for this example — in the Alias text box, and click Next.

4. Click Browse, navigate to the folder you created in Step 1, and click Next.

5. Accept the default Read permission, mark the Run Scripts permission checkbox, and click Next and Finish to dismiss the wizard.

6. If your Web site doesn't have a Default.aspx page, right-click the site's node, choose Properties, click the SiteName Properties dialog's Documents tab, and remove the existing entries from the list box.

7. Click Add to open the Add Content Page dialog; type the default page file name — OrdersGridView.aspx for this example — in the text box, and click OK twice.

If you've enabled page tracing and leave the existing default entries in the Documents list box, a tracing page opens if you don't include the initial page's file name in the site's URL.

Accepting the default values for the virtual directory enables Windows authentication. If anonymous access is enabled for the Default Web site, anonymous access is enabled for all virtual directories under the node.

Copy a Web Site to a Virtual Directory Folder

Copying the Web site to a virtual directory lets you open and modify the deployed project in VS 2005. To copy a completed Web site to the virtual directory that you created in the preceding section, do this:

1. Choose Website ⇨ Copy Web Site to open the Copy Web *ProjectDirectoryPath* window, which displays your current Web site files in the Source Web Site list.

2. Click the Connect button to open the Open Web Site dialog. Then click the Local IIS button, select the virtual directory you added in the preceding section, and click Open.

3. Select all files and folders in the Source Web Site list, and click the button with the right-pointing arrow to copy all project source files to the virtual directory (see Figure 8-21).

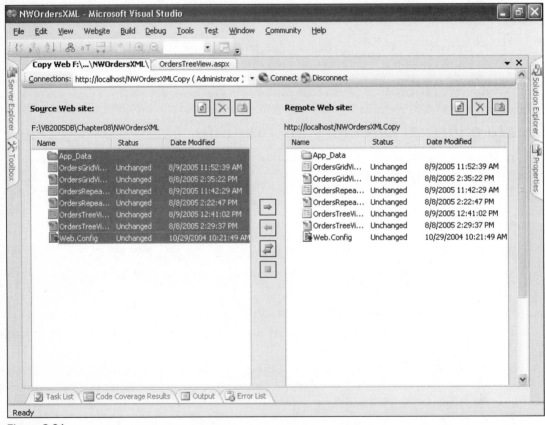

Figure 8-21

4. Open IE and type `http://localhost/virtualdirectory name/` or `http://computername /virtualdirectory name/` to display the default page. For this example, type **http:// localhost/NWOrdersXMLCopy/**.

5. Choose File ⇨ Open Web Site to open the dialog of the same name. Click the Local IIS button, and double-click the virtual directory name to open the Web site from the virtual directory folder. Solution Explorer's project name node now displays the virtual server URL.

6. Open the Web.config file, and change `<compilation debug="true"/>` to `<compilation debug="false"/>`, which removes the debugging symbols from the temporary files and improves performance slightly.

7. Open each page and change `Trace="True"` to `Trace="False"` so page-level tracing information doesn't appear. If you've enabled application-level tracing, change `pageOutput="true"` in Web.config to `pageOutput="false"`. The `localOnly="true"` attribute prevents users from opening Trace.axd.

8. Build and run the project under IIS, which replaces the built-in Web server. Select the Run without Debugging option in the Debugging Not Enabled dialog, and click OK.

9. Repeat Step 4 and try to determine the difference in performance without debugging.

You can copy a Web site to any remote IIS server virtual directory for which you have write permissions. Alternatively, you can use FTP to upload the Web site to a hosting provider that supports ASP.NET 2.0 sites.

Publish Precompiled Web Sites

As mentioned earlier, precompiling a Web site substitutes compiled source code files for *PageName*.aspx files. To publish the NWOrdersXML Web site to IIS 5 or 6, do the following:

1. Create an \Inetpub\wwwroot subfolder named `NWOrdersXML` and a virtual directory of the same name that points to the subfolder. Set OrdersGridView.aspx as the only default page.

2. Open the \VB2005DB\Chapter08\NWOrdersXML Web site, and, if you specified page-level or application-level tracing, make the changes to the pages and Web.config file that are described in the preceding section's Step 7.

3. Choose Build ⇨ Publish Web Site to open the Publish Web Site dialog. Type in the text box the URL of the virtual directory you created in Step 1, `http://localhost/NWOrdersXML`, and accept the remaining defaults (see Figure 8-22).

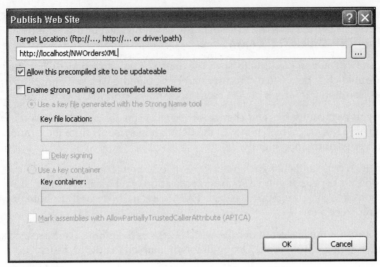

Figure 8-22

4. Click OK. The Build window displays a series of Found Schema messages, followed by Publish Web Site Beginning and Publish Web Site Complete.

5. Choose File ⇨ Open Web Site, and navigate to the virtual directory folder. Disable debugging in the Web.config file, and open one of the *PageName*.aspx files to display the placeholder text message.

6. Open the \bin subfolder to view the list of precompiled files. The *Random*.dll is the compiled assembly; *.compiled files are XML documents that contain references to the original *PageFile*.aspx files.

7. Launch IE and open the virtual directory to confirm your default page setting.

8. If you enabled application-level tracing, add `trace.xsd` to the virtual directory, and verify that tracing is operational for users on the computer hosting IIS.

Copied or precompiled Web sites play an important role in ASP.NET 2.0 Web services, which is the subject of the next chapter.

Summary

Client-side data entry validation is critical to the performance and scalability of production Web sites. Validating all user entries — to the extent possible — before submitting them to the Web server minimizes server roundtrips and, for databound controls, database server exceptions. ASP.NET validator controls aren't as elegant as the validation techniques available for Windows forms, but they are likely to suffice for simple data-intensive Web sites. If you need finer-grained or more complex client-side validation, add CustomValidator controls with JScript or — for IE-only organizations — VBScript validation functions.

SqlDataSources, like their Windows-form SqlClient or OracleClient counterparts, implement conventional client/server application architecture. ObjectDataSources based on objects other than data components enable *n*-tier architecture with middle-tier business logic for data-intensive Web pages. You can create middle-tier DALCs that deliver typed DataTables to Web clients, but adding business logic to typed DataSets can involve complex code. Alternatively, you can gain table metadata independence with custom business objects that you define in project class files or compiled class libraries. Custom business objects let you implement business rules in the object class definition; `Update`, `Insert`, and `Delete` wrapper functions; or any combination of these locations.

XmlDataSources rely on XML source documents or strings and are inherently read-only. Complex databound controls, such as templated GridViews and DetailsViews, don't support editing operations when bound to XmlDataSources. Thus, XmlDataSources probably won't be as widely used as SqlDataSources and ObjectDataSources.

ASP.NET 2.0 tracing features haven't changed substantially from those offered by ASP.NET 1.*x*. However, tracing Web server activity and analyzing control rendering is critical to page debugging and site debottlenecking.

Adoption of a new ASP.NET 2.0 UI and built-in Web server required VS 2005 to enable updated Web site deployment techniques. The automated Copy Web Site and Publish *WebsitePath* commands make moving a site from the development or staging computer's file system to a remote IIS 5 or 6 instance a point-and-click process. The ability to quickly copy or publish ASP.NET 2.0 Web services to production servers is an important feature, as you'll discover in the next chapter.

Publishing Data-Driven Web Services

The February 13, 2002, release of Visual Studio .NET coincided with a remarkable surge in press coverage of Web services as the latest "big thing" for the IT industry. Press releases, such as "Microsoft Launches XML Web Services Revolution with Visual Studio .NET and .NET Framework" and "Microsoft Extends XML Web Services Support in .NET Enterprise Servers Through Visual Studio .NET," led many readers to believe that VS 2002 (then VS .NET) was a new toolkit for creating Web services only. Simple Object Access Protocol (SOAP) 1.1, which is the foundation for the majority of today's Web services, was—and still is—a W3C Note dated May 8, 2000. Another W3C Note, Web Services Description Language (WSDL) 1.1, arrived on March 15, 2001. Industry pundits predicted a multi-billion-dollar hardware, software, and consulting market for Web services. Research firm IDC predicted in 2002 that this market would grow from $1.6 billion in 2004 to $21 billion in North America by 2007, with worldwide revenues over ten years reaching $184 billion.

As the Web services "bubble" deflated in the succeeding three years, Microsoft dropped the .NET suffix from its server products and Visual Studio, and is in the process of abandoning the XML prefix for ASP.NET Web services. Analysts reduced their Web service market estimates in reports typified by IDC's June 1, 2004, "Worldwide Web Services Software Forecast, 2004–2008: Cautious Adoption Continues." SOAP 1.2 became a W3C Recommendation on June 24, 2003. WSDL 2.0 was a second-edition W3C Working Draft when this book was written. The advance of SOAP and WSDL specifications from W3C Note to Recommendation and near-final Working Draft status removes the "proprietary" stigma from the early Web service standards. Stable industry-wide standards promise interoperability of Web services created with an increasing variety of development tools. There's no question that Web services will become the predominate enterprise application integration (EAI) technology by 2007—or sooner.

ASP.NET 2.0 Web services support SOAP 1.1 and 1.2 with WSDL 1.1. VS 2005's Add Web Reference designer, built-in Web server, and copy or publish deployment simplify basic Web service development and debugging. These features ensure that VS 2005 will enhance Visual Studio's reputation as the most rapid Web service development tool in the industry. WS-Security, an OASIS standard, and the proliferation of other proposed WS-* specifications address industry concerns about the suitability of Web services for enterprise-scale projects. Microsoft's Web Service Enhancements (WSE) 3.0 address — but don't overcome — the complexity of encrypting and adding digital signatures to SOAP payloads. WSE 3.0 also supports WS-Policy, WS-SecurityPolicy, WS-Trust, WS-ReliableMessaging, WS-SecureConversation, and WS-Addressing. Adding WSE 3.0 extensions to Web services and client consumers is beyond the scope of this book.

VS 2005 requires WSE 3.0 and doesn't support WSE 2.0. You can install WSE 3.0 side-by-side with WSE 2.0.

This chapter assumes you have a basic understanding of SOAP 1.1 messaging and WSDL 1.1 documents. The sample Web services and clients perform CRUD operations on database tables, either directly or through an intermediary typed DataSet object that serves as a data access layer component (DALC). When this book was written, DataSets weren't interoperable with non-Microsoft Web service consumers (clients), so the examples include a generic business object (business entity) Web service and client.

Sample projects in the \VB2005DB\Chapter09 folder are based on the ObjectDataSources you created in Chapter 8's "Replace SqlDataSources with ObjectDataSources" section and have the same Northwind database prerequisites.

Web Service Development Strategies

ASP.NET Web services are the simplest method for implementing the middle tier of a three-tiered, distributed data access architecture. Wrapping an existing DALC as a basic Web service usually involves only a few hours of development and initial test time. You add a `<WebMethod>` attribute to the existing functions that return, update, insert, or delete base table records. Exception handlers throw a `SoapException`, instead of an `SqlException` or other .NET exception type. Simplicity, however, has its drawbacks; Web services don't match the performance of DCOM or .NET remoting with binary formatting over a TCP channel on a private intranet. On the other hand, the stateless and loosely coupled nature of Web services enables data transport with the HTTP or HTTPS protocol over private intranets and the public Internet.

Transactions

Statelessness and loose-coupling often preclude conventional single-database or distributed transactions. Transactions may involve interaction with multiple Web services, some of which might be operated by third parties, exhibit variable response times, and have less than 100 percent uptime. Such operations are called *long-running transactions*. If an update requires multiple SOAP messages and one or more messages fail, you must undo the work performed by the messages that succeeded by performing a *compensating transaction*. Compensating transactions are very difficult to implement and require transaction state management on the Web service — not the database — server. If you require updates to multiple related tables, your Web service should execute the set of updates with a single SOAP request message and report the transaction commit or rollback status in the SOAP response message.

DataSets

DataSets make it easy to create Web services that update multiple tables with a single request response message. The Web service returns a multi-table DataSet and accepts a diffgram of client edits to update the base tables. Bound controls let Windows form clients update many base table records with a single SOAP request and response message. You can implement transactions with `SqlConnection.Transaction` or `System.Transaction` objects and DataAdapters. Alternatively, implement the techniques described in Chapter 6 in the section "Apply Transactions to Base-Table Updates."

The downside of DataSets is that they're a .NET-specific data type. As mentioned previously, today's Java Web service toolkits don't create client proxies to support these .NET objects. ADO.NET 2.0 typed and untyped DataSets don't include their schema in the WSDL document, as you'll see in the later "Create and Deploy a Simple Web Service" section. Thus, Web service client toolkits would need to obtain the DataSet schema from a WebMethod that returns `DataSet.GetXmlSchema` or at runtime from the schema embedded in a SOAP response message. When this book was written, only InfoPath SP-1 and VS 2005 supported runtime DataSet schemas to enable Design mode data sources.

> *Web services that publish or consume DataSets violate the "share schema and contract, not class" tenet of Microsoft's "Service-Oriented Integration" patterns & practices white paper. Schemas define SOAP message structure, and contracts (WSDL documents) define service behavior.*

Embedding a typed DataSet schema for the Northwind Orders and OrderDetails tables adds up to 14,302 bytes (including whitespace) to the 1,226-byte SOAP response message for a single order. If your Web service client doesn't need handlers for the typed DataSet schema's `TableNameRowChange`, `FieldNameChanging`, and `FieldNameChanged` events, you can save substantial message overhead by defining an untyped DataSet. The size of the untyped DataSet for the same SOAP response message is about 3,317 bytes.

> *Gzip compression reduces the size of SOAP response messages at the expense of CPU resource consumption to compress the messages on the server and client. For more information about enabling Gzip compression, see the section "Compress SOAP Response Messages," later in this chapter.*

Custom Business Objects

Custom business objects embed their schema in the WSDL file, which enables Web service client toolkits to autogenerate operable Web service proxies for most programming languages and operating systems. SOAP request and response messages don't include a schema, so message size is much smaller than that for a corresponding DataSet. Combining Windows forms' Web Service and Object data sources lets you autogenerate bound DataGridViews and details views with bound text boxes. You can update multiple tables by passing objects or arrays of objects to multiple WebMethod parameters. If multiple tables populate a hierarchical business object, you can pass a single object or an array of objects to a single input parameter. All commercial Web service toolkits support object arrays as WebMethod input parameters and return values.

Custom business objects with fields of primitive types or arrays of primitive types let you implement the "share schema and contract, not class" best practice for Web services. Business objects provide independence from the metadata of the underlying base tables. Design classes to represent business entities that meet your current and short-term future requirements. Standards-based business entities, such as purchase orders and invoices based on Universal Business Language (UBL) 1.0 schemas, are far too complex for most organizations. Simple schemas that avoid `<include...>` and `<import...>` elements simplify Web service implementation and aid interoperability.

Multiple WebMethods and Versioning

VS 2005's documentation emphasizes simple Web services that execute a single trivial WebMethod, such as adding two integers. Production Web services that are deployed on the Internet or corporate intranets usually involve multiple, related WebMethods. As an example, Microsoft Research's public ASP.NET TerraService at `http://terraserver-usa.com/TerraService.asmx` publishes 16 WebMethods for retrieving worldwide satellite and aerial images or U.S. Geological Survey topographic maps of the U.S. TerraService clients must consume several WebMethods to retrieve and combine specific 200-pixel by 200-pixel bitmaps (called *tiles*) to display an image of the appropriate geographic location and scale.

> *You can download an upgradable .NET 1.1 Windows form TerraService Web service client at* `http://www.ftponline.com/vsm/2004_08/magazine/features/rjennings/default.aspx`. *The project also consumes Microsoft's MapPoint Web service, which requires at least an evaluation account. Go to* `http://msdn.microsoft.com/mappoint/mappointweb/` *for more details.*

A data-intensive Web service should expose multiple WebMethods that support common data access and update scenarios. For example, a service that delivers multiple business entities — such as sales orders or invoices — should provide the ability to return entity collections based on attributes. This service type should at least implement TOP n queries in reverse-date or primary-key order and single entity response messages by primary-key values. This chapter's Web service examples include WebMethods that return Northwind Orders records by CustomerID or OrderID and require only a few lines of additional code to add WebMethods with other WHERE clause criteria, such as EmployeeID or starting and ending dates.

> *Don't expose WebMethods that accept SQL statements as a* String *parameter. Enabling ad hoc queries makes your Web service and its database subject to malicious SQL injection attacks.*

Most Web services evolve over time, so version control is an important issue. WebMethods — like COM interfaces — are immutable. You must not define a new version of a current WebMethod and assign it the same public function name. You can modify the internal code for a WebMethod, if the modifications don't alter the WSDL document or the schema of DataSets. For example, substitution of stored procedures for SQL batch statements don't affect WSDL documents or schemas. You can make changes to the data source for a business object if you don't alter the object's structure or data type.

You can add new WebMethods to a service, which adds elements to the dynamic WSDL document. .NET Web service clients maintain a static file copy of the original WSDL document. Updating the source code's Web Reference incorporates the added elements, but doesn't break code that invokes the original WebMethods.

Moving a Web service to a different server, domain, or both requires clients to change the URL for the service. Adding a Web Reference inserts an `<add key="ProxyClassName" value="URL">` element into the app.config or Web.config file's `<appSettings>` group. The Web service proxy class constructor reads this value prior to invoking the WebMethod, so you can alter the URL with a text editor instead of rebuilding and redeploying the client application when the URL changes.

> *You can add alternative URLs to a Windows form's* `<applicationSettings>` *node on the ProjectName Properties windows Settings page. If the client incurs an "Unable to connect to remote server" exception when invoking the WebMethod, you can add code to try the alternative URLs.*

Web Service Security

Integrated Windows authentication usually provides sufficient security for accessing private intranet Web services whose messages don't incorporate confidential information. The simplest approach to securing Web services that are accessible from the public Internet is to require the Secure Sockets Layer (SSL or HTTPS) protocol and X.509 client certificates to connect to the Web service's IIS 5 or 6 virtual directory. HTTPS encrypts the SOAP messages and you can map client certificates to Windows user accounts for Windows authentication. If you're not ready to implement client certificates, you can enable basic authentication for users in the same or a trusted domain; HTTPS encrypts usernames and passwords. In either case, you can authorize users to invoke specific WebMethods by Windows group membership or a database table of authenticated users and the WebMethods for which each user role has execute permissions.

HTTPS is a transport protocol, so it's suitable for securing point-to-point messages only. If you need to route messages securely, the WS-Security standard is your best bet. WS-Security enables encrypting the SOAP request and response messages independently of the transport protocol. WS-Security also enables digital signatures for request and response messages. Digital signatures implement non-repudiation by ensuring that messages aren't modified at any point in the routing process. Implementing WS-Security for Web services and Web service clients is a complex process because it requires installing and configuring WSE 3.0 on both Web servers and client machines. If your Windows Web services expose custom business objects to clients running under other operating systems or other programming languages, these clients will need a Web service proxy toolkit that supports WS-Security.

If your Web service messages are point-to-point and non-repudiation isn't a requirement, HTTPS with client certificates or basic authentication probably will satisfy your basic security requirements.

ASP.NET 2.0 Web Service Programming

The process of creating ASP.NET 2.0 Web services is similar to that for conventional ASP.NET 2.0 Web Sites. The most obvious difference is lack of a Design mode window for adding controls; Web services don't support UI elements.

> *ASP.NET 2.0's built-in Web server eliminates earlier versions' requirement that you create an IIS virtual directory for the service prior to creating the project. Otherwise, the process is identical for all ASP.NET versions.*

Here's an overview of the steps to create and publish a simple Web service:

1. Create a new Web service Web site, which adds Service.asmx to the Web Site folder and Service.vb to the Application_Code folder. Service.asmx contains a compile directive only. Service.vb has Imports statements for the `System.Web`, `System.Web.Services`, and `System.Web.Services .Protocols` namespaces. Service.vb also includes code to implement a simple Web service with a WebMethod that returns "Hello World."

2. Rename the Service.asmx file to complete the service's URL for the built-in Web server: `http://localhost:TCPPort/WebSiteName/ServiceFileName.aspx`.

3. Optionally, rename the Service.vb file and its default `Service` class. Conform the .asmx file's compiler directive to the renamed .vb file and its Web service class. If you rename the `Service` class and don't modify the compiler directive, building the service throws an error.

4. Replace `Namespace:="http://tempuri.org"` with `Namespace:="AnyUniqueURLorURN"` and add an optional `Description:="DescriptionOfService"` attribute to the default `<WebService()>` class attribute. If you don't change the namespace, you receive a suggestion to do so when you run the project.

The following illustrates a typical modified compiler directive and initial Web service code:

```
<%@ WebService Language="vb" CodeBehind="~/App_Code/DCOrdersWS.vb" _
Class="DCOrdersWS" %>

Imports System.Web
Imports System.Web.Services
Imports System.Web.Services.Protocols

<WebService(Namespace:="http://whatever.com/webservices/examples", _
 Description:="The starting point for Chapter 9's examples.")> _
 <WebServiceBinding(ConformsTo:=WsiProfiles.BasicProfile1_1)> _
Public Class DCOrdersWS
    Inherits System.Web.Services.WebService

    <WebMethod()> _
    Public Function HelloWorld() As String
      Return "Hello World"
    End Function
End Class
```

The `<WebServiceBinding(ConformsTo:=WsiProfiles.BasicProfile1_1)>` *attribute asserts that the Web service complies with the Web Services Interoperability Organization (WS-I.org) Basic Provide 1.1. For more information on WS-I.org and Web service profiles, see Chapter 3's "Ensure Fully Interoperable Web Services" section.*

The Web Service Help Page and WSDL Document

Most Java Web service toolkits generate a static *ServiceName*.wsdl file on the Web service application server. ASP.NET Web services generate dynamic WSDL documents. Opening the *ServiceName*.aspx file opens a standard ASP.NET Web service help page with links to execute WebMethods and display the WSDL document.

The following steps describe how to use the Web service help page to execute a simple WebMethod and display the WSDL document in IE:

1. Press F5 to build and run the service with the built-in Web server. Click OK with the Add a New Web.config file with Debugging Enabled radio button selected to enable Web service debugging and display the Web service help page, as shown in Figure 9-1.

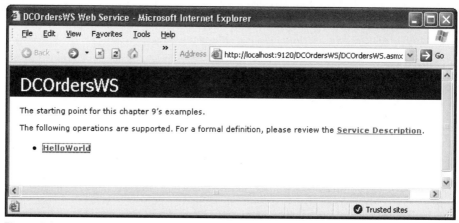

Figure 9-1

> If running the Web service displays a directory listing instead of the Web service help page, close IE and set *ServiceName*.aspx as the start page.

2. Click the WebMethod link — HelloWorld for this example — to open the page that lets you invoke the WebMethod (see Figure 9-2).

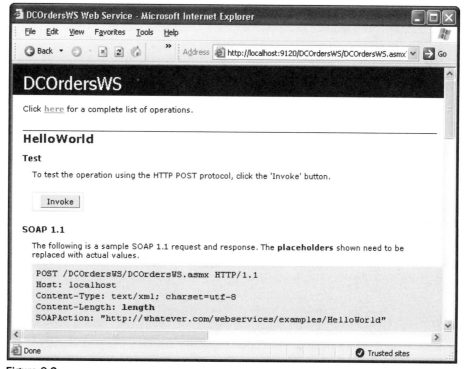

Figure 9-2

You can invoke a WebMethod that doesn't require parameters or has parameters that are simple (primitive) types, such as `Integer` *or* `String`, *or arrays of primitive types. The invoke page doesn't support parameters with complex types, such as a DataSet or business object, or invocations of Web methods of services on remote servers.*

3. Click Invoke to display the WebMethod's return value in IE (see Figure 9-3).

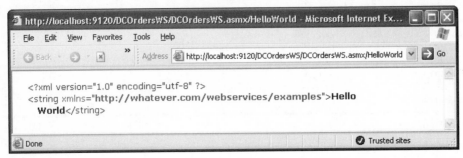

Figure 9-3

4. Close IE and click the `here` link to return to the initial help page, and click the Service Description link to open the WSDL document in IE (see Figure 9-4).

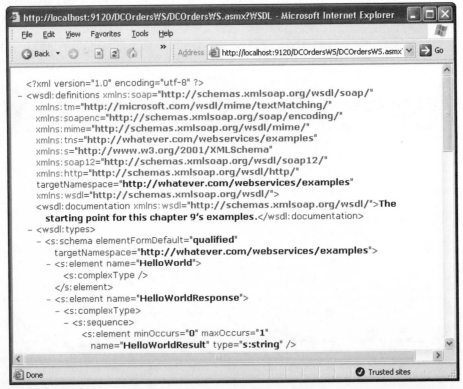

Figure 9-4

Displaying the WSDL document requires adding a ?WSDL or ?wsdl query string to the Service.asmx file's URL.

Following is the complete WSDL document for the sample DCOrdersWS Web service and its `HelloWorld` WebMethod:

```xml
<?xml version="1.0" encoding="utf-8"?>
<wsdl:definitions xmlns:soap="http://schemas.xmlsoap.org/wsdl/soap/"
  xmlns:tm="http://microsoft.com/wsdl/mime/textMatching/"
  xmlns:soapenc="http://schemas.xmlsoap.org/soap/encoding/"
  xmlns:mime="http://schemas.xmlsoap.org/wsdl/mime/"
  xmlns:tns="http://whatever.com/webservices/examples"
  xmlns:s="http://www.w3.org/2001/XMLSchema"
  xmlns:soap12="http://schemas.xmlsoap.org/wsdl/soap12/"
  xmlns:http="http://schemas.xmlsoap.org/wsdl/http/"
  targetNamespace="http://whatever.com/webservices/examples"
  xmlns:wsdl="http://schemas.xmlsoap.org/wsdl/">
  <wsdl:documentation xmlns:wsdl="http://schemas.xmlsoap.org/wsdl/">
   The starting point for Chapter 9's examples.</wsdl:documentation>
  <wsdl:types>
   <s:schema elementFormDefault="qualified"
     targetNamespace="http://whatever.com/webservices/examples">
     <s:element name="HelloWorld">
      <s:complexType />
     </s:element>
     <s:element name="HelloWorldResponse">
      <s:complexType>
        <s:sequence>
         <s:element minOccurs="0" maxOccurs="1" name="HelloWorldResult"
           type="s:string" />
        </s:sequence>
      </s:complexType>
     </s:element>
   </s:schema>
  </wsdl:types>
  <wsdl:message name="HelloWorldSoapIn">
   <wsdl:part name="parameters" element="tns:HelloWorld" />
  </wsdl:message>
  <wsdl:message name="HelloWorldSoapOut">
   <wsdl:part name="parameters" element="tns:HelloWorldResponse" />
  </wsdl:message>
  <wsdl:portType name="DCOrdersWSSoap">
   <wsdl:operation name="HelloWorld">
     <wsdl:input message="tns:HelloWorldSoapIn" />
     <wsdl:output message="tns:HelloWorldSoapOut" />
   </wsdl:operation>
  </wsdl:portType>
  <wsdl:binding name="DCOrdersWSSoap" type="tns:DCOrdersWSSoap">
   <soap:binding transport="http://schemas.xmlsoap.org/soap/http"
     style="document" />
   <wsdl:operation name="HelloWorld">
     <soap:operation
      soapAction="http://whatever.com/webservices/examples/HelloWorld"
      style="document" />
     <wsdl:input>
      <soap:body use="literal" />
```

```
      </wsdl:input>
      <wsdl:output>
       <soap:body use="literal" />
      </wsdl:output>
    </wsdl:operation>
  </wsdl:binding>
  <wsdl:binding name="DCOrdersWSSoap12" type="tns:DCOrdersWSSoap">
   <soap12:binding transport="http://schemas.xmlsoap.org/soap/http"
     style="document" />
   <wsdl:operation name="HelloWorld">
     <soap12:operation
      soapAction="http://whatever.com/webservices/examples/HelloWorld"
      style="document" />
     <wsdl:input>
      <soap12:body use="literal" />
     </wsdl:input>
     <wsdl:output>
      <soap12:body use="literal" />
     </wsdl:output>
   </wsdl:operation>
  </wsdl:binding>
  <wsdl:service name="DCOrdersWS">
   <wsdl:documentation xmlns:wsdl="http://schemas.xmlsoap.org/wsdl/">
     The starting point for this chapter's examples.</wsdl:documentation>
   <wsdl:port name="DCOrdersWSSoap" binding="tns:DCOrdersWSSoap">
     <soap:address
      location="http://localhost:9120/DCOrdersWS/DCOrdersWS.asmx" />
   </wsdl:port>
   <wsdl:port name="DCOrdersWSSoap12" binding="tns:DCOrdersWSSoap12">
     <soap12:address
      location="http://localhost:9120/DCOrdersWS/DCOrdersWS.asmx" />
   </wsdl:port>
  </wsdl:service>
</wsdl:definitions>
```

The random TCP port number (9120) in the service's URL doesn't appear when you publish the Web service to an IIS virtual directory. The Web service doesn't use the four highlighted namespaces near the beginning of the document. Unlike common URL namespace declarations, which return HTTP 404 errors, most `http://schemas.xmlsoap.org/...` *URLs open schema documents and* `http://www.w3.org/...` *URLs open pages with links to related pages.*

The preceding example is the simplest WSDL document that fully describes a document/literal (doc/lit) Web service that supports both SOAP 1.1 and SOAP 1.2 clients. By default, ASP.NET 2.0 Web service clients send SOAP 1.1 request messages.

Here's the SOAP request message generated by the client's Web service proxy class:

```
<?xml version="1.0" encoding="utf-8"?>
<soap:Envelope xmlns:soap="http://schemas.xmlsoap.org/soap/envelope/"
xmlns:xsi="http://www.w3.org/2001/XMLSchema-instance"
xmlns:xsd="http://www.w3.org/2001/XMLSchema">
  <soap:Body>
   <HelloWorld xmlns="http://whatever.com/webservices/examples" />
  </soap:Body>
</soap:Envelope>
```

The Web service's SOAP response message with its HTTP headers is:

```
ResponseCode: 200 (OK)
Server:Microsoft VisualStudio .NET WebServer/8.0.1200.0
Date:Tue, 09 Nov 2004 18:42:38 GMT
X-AspNet-Version:2.0.50215
Cache-Control:private, max-age=0
Content-Type:text/xml; charset=utf-8
Content-Length:384
Connection:Close

<?xml version="1.0" encoding="utf-8"?>
<soap:Envelope xmlns:soap="http://schemas.xmlsoap.org/soap/envelope/"
xmlns:xsi="http://www.w3.org/2001/XMLSchema-instance"
xmlns:xsd="http://www.w3.org/2001/XMLSchema">
  <soap:Body>
    <HelloWorldResponse xmlns="http://whatever.com/webservices/examples">
      <HelloWorldResult>Hello World</HelloWorldResult>
    </HelloWorldResponse>
  </soap:Body>
</soap:Envelope>
```

Web Service Deployment

You must deploy the Web service to an IIS 5 or 6 virtual directory to enable access by production Windows or Web forms clients. The process of deploying a Web service Web site to IIS is identical to that described for ASP.NET Web forms in the section "Deploy Completed Web Sites to IIS" in Chapter 8.

A Web service client that specifies the current TCP port in the service's URL can access a Web service that's running in the built-in Web server, as you'll see in the next section. In this case, the URL is valid only for the current running instance of the server. Running a Web service on a TCP port other than 80 (HTTP) or 443 (HTTPS) is an uncommon practice.

If you want the capability to debug your Web service by stepping through the WebMethod invocation in your Web service client, copy the Web Site folder to the virtual directory. Source code and the symbols file — ...\bin*ServiceName*.pdb — must be present to enable Web service debugging.

If you receive an "Unrecognized attribute 'xmlns'" server error, open the Properties dialog for the service's IIS virtual directory, click the ASP.NET tab, and change the version number from 1.1.BuildNumber to 2.0.BuildNumber.

After you test your Web service thoroughly, you can improve its performance by setting `<compilation debug="true"/>` to `<compilation debug="false"/>` in the Web.config file and publishing the Web site to the virtual directory. Publishing the Web site overwrites all source code files with stub files.

Web Service Clients and Proxies

Windows and Web forms clients require a Web service proxy class to consume Web services. You must add code to an event handler to instantiate the proxy class and execute a WebMethod.

Add a Web Service Proxy Class

You create the proxy class by adding a Web reference to the service. Here's how:

1. Create a new Windows form client. In Solution Explorer, right-click the project and choose Add Web Reference to open the Add Web Reference dialog.

2. If you created and deployed the DCOrdersWS Web service in the preceding sections, you can create proxy for the service by typing the URL for the *ServiceName*.asmx file in the text box. Alternatively, click the Web Sources on the Local Machine list, and double-click the link to the deployed service to display its help file.

3. If you didn't deploy the Web service to IIS, build and run the Web service, copy the URL from IE's Address text box to the Clipboard, paste the URL to the Add Web Reference dialog's text box, and click the Go button to display the help file.

4. Replace the default `localhost` Web Reference Name with a more descriptive name — usually the service name — as shown in Figure 9-5.

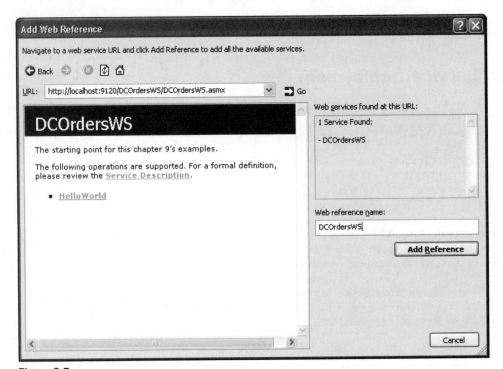

Figure 9-5

5. Click Add Reference to add the Web reference under Solution Explorer's Web References node, choose Project ➪ View All Files, and expand the added nodes.

A Web reference consists of *ReferenceName*.disco (discovery), *ReferenceName*.wsdl, *Reference*.map (discovery), and Reference.vb files. *ReferenceName*.wsdl is a local copy of the service's WSDL document and Reference.vb is the proxy class file. The two discovery-related files enable a proprietary — and obsolescent — mechanism for populating the Web Services on Local Machine list.

> *BEA Systems, Canon, Intel, and Microsoft proposed in October 2004 a WS-Discovery specification* (`http://msdn.microsoft.com/library/en-us/dnglobspec/html/ws-discovery.pdf`) *that's considerably more complex than the proprietary disco approach. WS-Discovery depends on another pending specification — WS-Addressing* (`http://www.w3.org/Submission/2004/SUBM-ws-addressing-20040810/`). *The prospect for widespread adoption of the WS-Discovery specifications is dubious, at best.*

Instantiate the Proxy Class and Invoke a WebMethod

A Web service proxy class's namespace is the name you assign to a Web reference — DCOrdersWS for the "Hello World" example. The proxy's Partial Public Class WebServiceName, which contains synchronous and asynchronous methods that mirror each WebMethod, inherits from the SoapHttpClientProtocol class. Thus the fully qualified name of the Web service proxy class is WebReferenceName.WebServiceName or DCOrdersWS.DCOrdersWS for this example.

The following table lists the commonly used properties and methods of the SoapHttpClientProtocol class.

Property or Method	Data Type	Description	Default Value
Credentials	System.Net .ICredentials	Supplies the user's credentials for authentication	Nothing
Enable- Decompression	Boolean	Enables Gzip decompression of the SOAP response message	False
Proxy	System.Net .IWebProxy	Gets or sets proxy settings for a firewall	Nothing
SoapVersion	SoapProtocol Version	Sets or gets the request message's SOAP version (1.1 or 1.2)	SoapProtocolVersion .Default (SOAP 1.1)
Timeout	Integer	Gets or sets the WebMethod timeout in milliseconds	100000
Url	String	Gets or sets the Web service URL	From <appSettings> group
UserAgent	String	Gets or sets the User-Agent HTTP header for the request message	Mozilla/4.0 (compatible; MSIE 6.0; MS Web Services Client Protocol 2.0.50215.44)

The code to instantiate the Web service proxy class and invoke a WebMethod is simple. Here's the generic version:

```
Dim wsProxy as New WebReferenceName.ServiceName
'Authentication code if required
Dim varResult as DataType = wsProxy.WebMethodName([ByVal Parameter(s)])
```

Here's the code snippet to return "Hello World" to a text box:

```
Try
    Dim wsOrders As New DCOrdersWS.DCOrdersWS
    wsOrder.UseDefaultCredentials = True
    'Invoke the HelloWorld WebMethod
    txtResult.Text = wsOrders.HelloWorld
Catch exc As Exception
    MsgBox(exc.Message, MsgBoxStyle.Exclamation, "Error Invoking WebMethod")
End Try
```

> *The* wsOrder.UseDefaultCredentials = True *statement is required to authenticate the client's request with the user's Windows account. User credentials aren't required if the Web service's virtual directory has anonymous access enabled.*

Alternatively, you can drag the *ServiceName* tool from the Toolbox's *ProjectName* section to add a named instance of the proxy class in a Windows form's tray and set the SoapHttpClientProtocol object's property values in its Properties window. For this example, the default instance name is DcOrdersWS1. You invoke the HelloWorld WebMethod with a DcOrdersWS1.HelloWorld instruction.

Add User Credentials for Web Service Authentication

The built-in Web server accepts Windows authentication only. When you deploy a Web service to an IIS virtual directory that has anonymous access disabled, you must provide credentials for Windows, Basic, or Digest authentication, depending on the Authentication and Access Control settings you establish. Windows authentication is the best choice for intranet access.

Digest authentication requires IIS running on Windows Server 2003 and users to have Windows 2000 or later Active Directory accounts in the Web server's domain or a domain that's trusted by the Web server. Domain Security Policy's Windows Settings/Security Settings/Account Policies/Password Policy/Store Password Using Reversible Encryption must be enabled. IIS sends a hash of the password, which works across proxy servers and firewalls.

> **Enabling reversible encryption reduces password security. You should not enable reversible encryption unless Digest authentication is absolutely critical to the success of your Web service. It's improbable that any member of an organization's DomainAdmins group would permit enabling reversible encryption.**

Authenticating Web service access over the public Internet requires Basic authentication, which sends usernames and passwords in clear text. Thus, the virtual directory must use Secure Sockets Layer (SSL) or Transport Layer Security (TLS) and TCP port 443 to prevent interception of authentication data.

If you enable HTTPS for the virtual directory, you can authenticate clients with their X.509 certificates. Certificate-based authentication is beyond the scope of this chapter.

Windows Credentials

Supplying Windows credentials of the client's user is the simplest of the three alternatives: Here's the generic code:

```
Dim wsProxy as New WebReferenceName.ServiceName
wsProxy.Credentials = System.Net.CredentialCache.DefaultCredentials
Dim varResult as DataType = wsProxy.WebMethodName([ByVal Parameter(s)])
```

As mentioned earlier, an alternative for Windows authentication is to set the proxy's UseDefaultCredentials *property value to* True*.*

Basic and Digest Credentials

Providing Basic or Digest credentials requires creating a new CredentialsCache instance and adding NetworkCredentials objects to it. The following generic code enables Basic authentication for the Windows user account specified by UserName, Domain, and Password:

```
Dim wsCredCache As New CredentialCache
Dim wsCred As New NetworkCredential
wsCred.UserName = txtUserName.Text
wsCred.Domain = txtDomain.Text
wsCred.Password = txtPassword.Text
wsCredCache.Add(New Uri(wsOrders.Url), "Basic", wsCred)
wsProxy.Credentials = wsCredCache
```

Specifying the user's domain is optional for Basic authentication. Substitute "Digest" *for* "Basic" *to enable Digest authentication.*

The DCOrdersWSClient.sln Windows form project in the \VB2005DB\Chapter09\DCOrdersWSClient folder lets you specify the Web service proxy's Url, Timeout, UserAgent, Credentials, UseDecompression, SoapVersion, and properties (see Figure 9-6). You must copy or publish the DCOrdersWS Web service to an IIS virtual directory, modify the default URL, if necessary, and disable Anonymous access to test Windows, Basic, or Digest authentication.

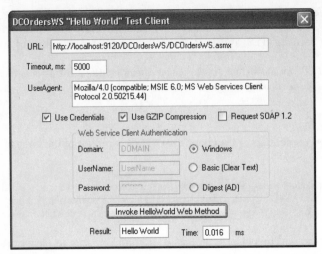

Figure 9-6

Compress SOAP Response Messages

As mentioned in the section "DataSets" earlier in this chapter, ASP.NET 2.0 adds an
`EnableDecompression` property to the `SoapHttpClientProtocol` class. Set this property value to
`True` with the following code:

```
wsProxy.EnableDecompression = True
```

Enabling client-side decompression adds `gzip` (GNU zip compression) as an `accept-encoding` argument value to the request message's HTTP header. Compression reduces the size of large SOAP response
messages to 25 to 65 percent of their uncompressed size.

> *IIS 6.0 supports HTTP compression by default. To enable compression with IIS 5.x, run the configura-
> tion scripts from Microsoft Knowledge Base article Q-322603, "HOW TO: Enable ASPX Compression
> in IIS."*

Debug Web Services

The ASP.NET 1.0 Web services and Windows or Web form client applications you create run in debug
mode by default. The debugging process is similar to that for referenced class libraries. You can
debug a Web service by setting a breakpoint on the line that invokes a WebMethod and stepping into
the WebMethod's code. After a few-second delay, a window opens with the code behind the
WebService.asmx file, as shown in Figure 9-7.

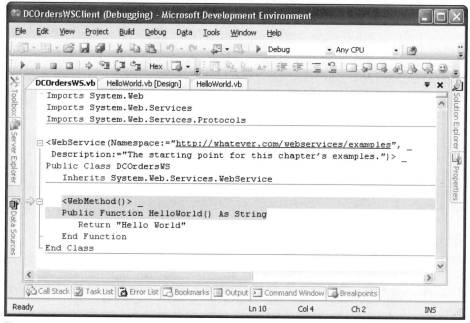

Figure 9-7

Attempting to step into a WebMethod of a published Web service displays a message box with an "Unable to automatically step into server. Unable to determine a stepping location" message, because source code and symbols are missing. Copy the service Web site to the IIS virtual directory to enable debugging with the client's default URL.

Changes you make to WebMethod code don't take effect until you save the *WebService*.vb file and execute the WebMethod again.

Create and Deploy a Simple Data Web Service

The two-table data component you created in the section "ObjectDataSources from Typed DataSet DALCs" in Chapter 8 is a good candidate for creating a basic Web service from an existing ASP.NET 2.0 project. The following example is based on the DCOrdersWS Web service that's described in the preceding sections.

You can use the DCOrdersWS Web site in the \VB2005DB\Chapter09\DCOrdersWS folder as the starting point for this section's example.

Open DCOrdersWS, right-click the App_Code node, choose Add Existing Item, navigate to the GridAndDetailsView Web site you created in Chapter 8, or in the \VB2005DB\Chapter08\GridAndDetailsView folder, select the OrderComponent.xsd and DataComponent.settings files in the ...\App_Code folder, and click Add. This step adds the runtime typed DataSet and its connection string to your Web service.

Web Service Connection Strings

Web services that require a database connection commonly use SQL Server authentication with a login ID and password for a user account. SQL Server authentication enables anonymous users to consume the Web services, which is acceptable during the development process but usually isn't for production services. For SQL Server databases, the Web service user account must be assigned to the db_datareader and, for updates, db_datawriter roles, and have execute permission for stored procedures. The generic connection string is:

```
Server=ServerName[/InstanceName];User ID=LoginID;Password=Password;
Database=DatabaseName;Persist Security Info=True"
```

Your SQL Server instance must be installed in Mixed Mode, which enables integrated Windows and SQL Server authentication to use the preceding connection string. If you installed your local instance of SQL Server with the default Windows Authentication Mode, the preceding connection string won't work.

Connection Strings for Data Components

ASP.NET 2.0 data components store their connection string in the Web.config file's <ConnectionStrings> group, which you edit in the Settings Designer window. Data components use this connection string when executing TableAdapter Fill, FillBy, GetData, and GetDataBy methods, and update operations.

Data components don't expose their runtime TableAdapters to Web service code. The TableAdapter class is a member of the System.Web.UI.WebControls.Adapters namespace, and Web services don't have a UI. Thus, you must use a DataAdapter to fill and update the data component's DataSet tables. You can add code to obtain the data component's connection string for the SqlDataAdapter .SqlConnection.ConnectionString property value, but it's a better practice to add the connection string to the Web.config file's <configuration> section with the following generic <connectionStrings> group:

```
<connectionStrings>
 <add name="ConnectionName" connectionString="Server=ServerName;
    User ID=LoginID;Password=Password;Database=DatabaseName;
    Persist Security Info=True" providerName="System.Data.SqlClient" />
</connectionStrings>
```

The connectionString *attribute value must be on a single line.*

You obtain the connection string in ASP.NET 2.0 projects with the following instruction:

```
Dim strConn As String = _
 ConfigurationManager.ConnectionStrings("ConnectionStringName").ConnectionString
```

The new .NET 2.0 ConfigurationManager *class requires adding a project reference to System.Configuration.dll.*

This chapter's Web service examples include the following default connection string in their Web .config files:

```
Server=localhost;User ID=sa;Password=whidbey;Database=Northwind;
Persist Security Info=True"
```

The preceding whidbey *password doesn't comply with good security practices. The* sa *and all other SQL Server user passwords should be at least eight characters in length and include uppercase and lowercase letters, numerals, and punctuation characters. Create a special Web service login ID for production Web services.*

You must edit the example connection strings' Password and, optionally, User ID elements to connect to the default SQL Server instance. Add /InstanceName to the Server element if you're using SQL Server 2005 Express (/SQLEXPRESS) or another named instance of SQL Server 2000, 2005, or MSDE.

Web Services and Windows Authentication Mode

If you installed your SQL Server instance in Windows Authentication Mode and can't or don't want to change to Mixed Mode, your Web service must use the following generic connection string for Windows authentication:

```
Server=ServerName;Integrated Security=True;Database=DatabaseName
```

You receive a "Login failed for user 'NT AUTHORITY\NETWORK SERVICE'" error message when a Web service client invokes a WebMethod from the copied or published version. The easiest way to enable an SQL Server connection for anonymous Web service users with Windows authentication is to add the following *<identity>* section to the Web.config file's *<system.web>* group

```
<system.web>
  <identity impersonate="true" userName="WindowsUserName" password="Password" />
  ...
</system.web>
```

In this case, you must add an SQL Server login, and database and stored procedure permissions for the Windows user account you specify as WindowsUserName. You can specify your Administrator account and password as a shortcut during development, but the production Web service must use a Windows account with much more restricted privileges. Even with restricted privileges, impersonating a user with credentials stored as plain text in the Web.config file invites security breaches.

If you disable anonymous access and enable Windows authentication, Basic authentication, or both, you can omit the userName *and* password *attributes if you set the* WebServiceProxy.Credentials *property value, as described in the section "Add User Credentials for Web Service Authentication," earlier in this chapter. An* <identity impersonate="true" /> *element returns a "Login failed for user 'SERVERNAME\IUSR_SERVERNAME'" message if you don't provide credentials or the credentials aren't valid.*

Add a General-Purpose Procedure to Return a Typed DataSet

All Web services that connect to databases commonly add Imports System.Data and an Imports statement for the data source type — usually System.Data.SqlClient or System.Data.OleDb — to eliminate the need to type these prefixes. All remaining examples assume Imports System.Data and Imports System.Data.SqlClient are present.

The following function accepts individual SQL SELECT statements to populate the DataSet's Orders and Order Details tables with DataAdapters:

```
Private Function GetOrders(ByVal strOrdersSql As String, _
 ByVal strDetailsSql As String) As DataSet
    'Create the DataSet from the DataComponent
    Dim dsOrders As DataSet = New OrdersComponent
    'Replace tempuri.org
    dsOrders.Namespace = _
       "http://whatever.com/webservices/northwind/orders/ordersdc"
    'Set up the connection
    Dim cnNwind As New SqlConnection
    Dim strConn As String = ConfigurationManager.ConnectionStrings( + _
       "NorthwindConnectionString").ConnectionString
    cnNwind.ConnectionString = strConn

    'Define SqlCommands and SqlDataAdapters
    Dim cmOrders As SqlCommand = Nothing
    Dim cmDetails As SqlCommand = Nothing
    Dim daOrders As SqlDataAdapter = Nothing
    Dim daDetails As SqlDataAdapter = Nothing

    If strOrdersSql.Length > 0 Then
       'Create the Orders command and data adapter
       cmOrders = cnNwind.CreateCommand
       cmOrders.CommandText = strOrdersSql
       daOrders = New SqlDataAdapter
       daOrders.SelectCommand = cmOrders
    End If

    If strDetailsSql.Length > 0 Then
       'Create the Order Details command and data adapter
       cmDetails = cnNwind.CreateCommand
       cmDetails.CommandText = strDetailsSql
       daDetails = New SqlDataAdapter
       daDetails.SelectCommand = cmDetails
    End If

    Dim strDetailsTable As String = dsOrders.Tables(1).TableName
    'Name is "[Order Details]"
    Try
       'Open the connection and fill either or both tables
       cnNwind.Open()
       If daOrders IsNot Nothing Then
          daOrders.Fill(dsOrders, "Orders")
       End If
       If daDetails IsNot Nothing Then
          daDetails.Fill(dsOrders, strDetailsTable)
       End If
       cnNwind.Close()
       Return dsOrders
    Catch exc As Exception
       Dim excSoap As New _
         SoapException(exc.Message, SoapException.ClientFaultCode, _
```

```
        Context.Request.Url.AbsoluteUri)
        Throw excSoap
    Finally
        cnNwind.Close()
        cnNwind.Dispose()
        dsOrders.Dispose()
        If daOrders IsNot Nothing Then
            daOrders.Dispose()
        End If
        If daDetails IsNot Nothing Then
            daDetails.Dispose()
        End If
    End Try
End Function
```

ConfigurationManager is the preferred .NET 2.0 class for managing ASP.NET Web.config files. As mentioned earlier, using ConfigurationManager requires adding a project reference to System.Configuration.dll.

The preceding function is "vanilla" `SqlConnection`, `SqlCommand`, and `SqlDataAdapter` code, except for the highlighted error handler that returns a SOAP exception to the Web service client. ASP.NET will convert any Web service exception to a SOAP exception with a `ServerFaultCode`. If you want to customize the exception, such as specifying a `ClientFaultCode` to indicate that the client made an invalid request, you should create and throw a `SoapException`.

Three of this chapter's sample Web services — WSOrdersDC, WSOrdersDS, and WSOrdersTDS — include minor variations of this function.

Add a WebMethod to Define and Return the DataSet

The following WebMethod supplies the two SQL `SELECT` statements, invokes the `GetOrders` function, and returns a serialized, typed DataSet to the Web service client:

```
<WebMethod(Description:="Returns the TOP n Orders and Order Details records.")> _
  Public Function GetTopOrdersAndDetails(ByVal Number As Integer) As DataSet
    Dim strSQL1 As String = "SELECT TOP " + Number.ToString + _
        " * FROM Orders ORDER BY OrderID DESC"
    Dim strSQL2 As String = "SELECT * FROM [Order Details] " + _
    " WHERE OrderID IN (SELECT TOP " + Number.ToString + _
    " OrderID FROM Orders ORDER BY OrderID DESC)"
    Return GetOrders(strSQL1, strSQL2)
End Function
```

The preceding WebMethod is only one of many `Get...` and `Fill...` methods that the three sample DataSet-based Web services provide.

Running the service with the built-in Web browser requires invoking the WebMethod with an appropriate `Number` parameter value. Figure 9-8 shows part of the 11-KB SOAP response message for a single order.

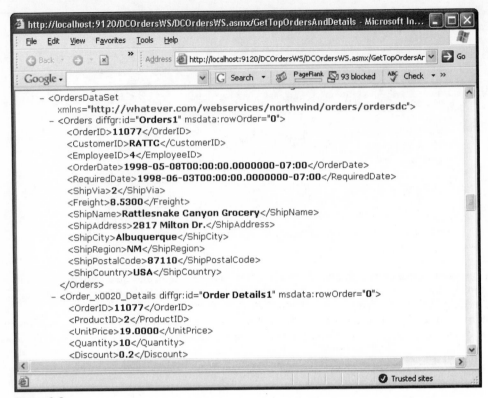

Figure 9-8

Add DataGridViews to the Web Service Client

If you created the HelloWorld Web service client in the section "Web Service Clients and Proxies," earlier in this chapter, you can use it as the starting point for a Web service client that displays Orders and Order details in DataGridViews. Otherwise, use the sample DCOrdersWSClient.sln project in the \VB2005DB\Chapter09\DCOrdersWSClient folder. You must deploy your version of DCOrdersWS with the GetTopOrdersAndDetails WebMethod or the sample Web site in \VB2005DB\Chapter09\DCOrdersWS by copying it to the subdirectory to which http://localhost/dcordersws points. Right-click the client's DCOrdersWS Web Reference node and choose Update Web Reference to refresh Reference.vb, which adds the new WebMethod.

If you receive an error message because your Web Reference points to a version with a random TCP port, delete the existing Web Reference and recreate it as DCOrdersWS.

Here's the fastest method to add DataGridViews that bind to the DataSet returned by the DCOrdersWS Web service:

1. Add a new form to the project and set it as the startup form in the ProjectName Properties window.

2. Drag an instance of the DCOrdersWS proxy from the top *ProjectName* section of the Toolbox to the tray. Accept the default `DcOrdersWS1` instance name.

3. Add a new Database data source with the same connection as the Web service. Do *not* save the connection string to app.config. Add the Orders table's 14 original columns and the Order Details table to the data source.

4. Drag the Orders table node from the Data Sources window to the top of the form to add an `OrdersDataGridView` and `OrdersBindingNavigator`.

5. Expand the Orders table node, drag its Order Details table subnode below the `OrdersDataGridView`, and build and run the project.

6. Optionally, delete the OrdersTableAdapter and Order_DetailsTableAdapter items from the tray.

7. Add a Load Grids button (`btnLoadGrids`), Number (`txtTopN`) text box, and optional label.

8. Add an `Imports System.Data` instruction to the code behind the form and `Private dsOrders As DataSet` to the declarations section.

9. Delete the code in the `Form_Load` event handler, and add the following code to the Load Grids button's event handler, which changes the `DataSource` and `DataMember` property values of the two BindingSources to the Web service's DataSet and DataTables:

```
Private Sub btnLoadGrids_Click(ByVal sender As System.Object, _
  ByVal e As System.EventArgs) Handles btnLoadGrids.Click
    With DcOrdersWS1
        .UseDefaultCredentials = True
        .Timeout = 10000 'milliseconds
        dsOrders = .GetTopOrdersAndDetails(CInt(txtTopN.Text))
    End With
    OrdersBindingSource.DataSource = dsOrders
    'Remaining BindingSource properties are correct
End Sub
```

The values assigned to the `OrdersBindingSource.DataMember`, `Order_DetailsBindingSource.DataSource`, and `Order_DetailsBindingSource.DataMember` properties from the DataSources nodes are valid for the DataSet returned by the Web service. Build and run the project, type **25** in the text box, and click the button to display the payload of the Web service's SOAP response message in the DataGridViews (see Figure 9-9).

> *This project is an example of the rapid application development (RAD) techniques that DataSet-based Web services enable. However, this client includes 2,136 lines of unused code in the NorthwindDataSet .Designer.vb file and instantiates an empty `NorthwindDataSet` object on startup. Thus, defining untyped DataSets and binding them to customized databound controls is a better practice for production projects.*

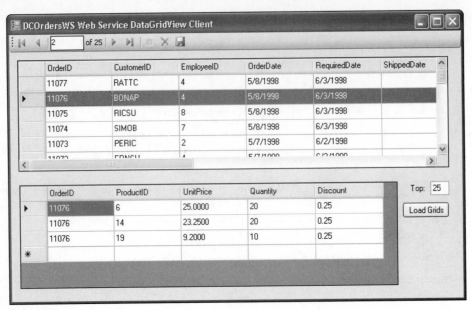

Figure 9-9

Update the Web Service DataSet

Code for a WebMethod with a DataSet parameter that updates the Web service's DataSet and its under-lying base tables is simple if you use a `CommandBuilder` object to generate the required UPDATE, INSERT, and DELETE SQL statements or stored procedure calls. The downside of CommandBuilders is the added server roundtrips to obtain the required table metadata.

Production Web services should use custom parameterized stored procedures for all updates and trans-actions for multi-table updates. Like the preceding example, using CommandBuilder objects is a RAD technique that's suitable for development but not production projects.

Add the following WebMethod code to the DCOrdersWS Web service to enable updates to the Orders and Order Details tables:

```
<WebMethod(Description:="Updates the Orders and Order Details tables.")> _
Public Function UpdateDataSet(ByVal dsUpdate As DataSet) As Integer
    Dim strDetailsTable As String = dsUpdate.Tables(1).TableName
    Dim strConn As String = ConfigurationManager.ConnectionStrings( + _
        "NorthwindConnectionString").ConnectionString
    Dim cnNwind As New SqlConnection(strConn)
    Dim daOrders As New SqlDataAdapter("SELECT * FROM Orders", cnNwind)
    Dim cbOrders As New SqlCommandBuilder(daOrders)
    Dim daDetails As New SqlDataAdapter("SELECT * FROM [Order Details]", cnNwind)
    Dim cbDetails As New SqlCommandBuilder(daDetails)
    Try
        cnNwind.Open()
```

```
            'Invoke the Update method of both DataAdapters
            Dim intUpdates As Integer = daOrders.Update(dsUpdate, "Orders")
            intUpdates += daDetails.Update(dsUpdate, strDetailsTable)
            cnNwind.Close()
            Return intUpdates
        Catch excSql As SqlException
            Dim excSoap As New SoapException("SQLException: " + excSql.Message, _
                SoapException.ClientFaultCode, Context.Request.Url.AbsoluteUri)
            Throw excSoap
        Catch excSys As System.Exception
            Dim excSoap As New SoapException("SystemException: " + excSys.Message, _
                SoapException.ClientFaultCode, Context.Request.Url.AbsoluteUri)
            Throw excSoap
        Finally
            cnNwind.Close()
            cnNwind.Dispose()
            dsUpdate.Dispose()
            daOrders.Dispose()
            cbOrders.Dispose()
            daDetails.Dispose()
            cbDetails.Dispose()
        End Try
End Function
```

You can't test WebMethods that use complex parameter types, such as DataSet, *with the Web service help page.*

Copy the updated Web service to its IIS virtual directory folder and do the following to test updates with the "Five-Minute Client" you created in the preceding section:

1. Update the DCOrdersWS Web Reference to add the UpdateDataSet WebMethod.

2. Add an Imports System.Web.Services.Protocols statement to enable SoapExceptions.

3. Replace or create a BindingNavigatorSaveItem_Click event handler, and add the following code to it:

```
Private Sub BindingNavigatorSaveItem_Click(ByVal sender As System.Object, _
    ByVal e As System.EventArgs) Handles BindingNavigatorSaveItem.Click
    'Send updategram of DataSet updates, if any
    OrdersBindingSource.EndEdit()
    Order_DetailsBindingSource.EndEdit()
    Dim strMsg As String = Nothing
    If dsOrders.HasChanges Then
        Try
            Dim dsUpdate As DataSet = dsOrders.GetChanges
            Dim intUpdates As Integer
            Dim lngTicks As Long = Now.Ticks
            intUpdates = DcOrdersWS1.UpdateDataSet(dsUpdate)
            If intUpdates > 0 Then
                lngTicks = Now.Ticks - lngTicks
                strMsg = "Updated " + intUpdates.ToString + " record(s) in " + _
                Format(lngTicks / 10000000, "0.000") + " secs." + vbCrLf + vbCrLf + _
                "Click Load Grids to verify the changes and enable updates."
            Else
```

```
                    strMsg = "Updates failed."
               End If
          Catch excSoap As SoapException
               MsgBox(excSoap.Message, MsgBoxStyle.Exclamation, _
                  "SOAP Exception Updating DataSet")
               Return
          Catch excOther As Exception
               MsgBox(excOther.Message, MsgBoxStyle.Exclamation, _
                  "General Exception Updating DataSet")
               Return
          End Try
     Else
          strMsg = "There are no DataSet updates to process."
     End If
     MsgBox(strMsg, MsgBoxStyle.Information, "Updating Base Tables")
End Sub
```

4. Build and run the client and verify that updates, insertions, and deletions behave as expected.

Substitute Custom Business Objects for DataSets

The section "Custom Business Objects," earlier in this chapter, describes the operating system and programming language interoperability benefits of platform-independent Web services. However, ensuring interoperability requires Web service developers to add a substantial amount of code to Web services and their client applications. Web services for business objects whose field values are persisted in relational database tables can't take advantage of VS 2005's data sources and typed DataSet designers. CommandBuilders to generate parameters for stored procedures or SQL statements aren't applicable to business objects. Plan on writing most or all code to implement a Web service that manipulates custom business objects.

You can copy starting code for SQL statements and SqlParameter *objects from the* InitDeleteCommand, InitInsertCommand, *and* InitUpdateCommand *procedures of the* DataSetName.Designer.vb *file. If you need to implement optimistic concurrency, start with code from the* InitAdapter *procedure. You'll need to make extensive use of the Find and Replace tool to adapt the copied code to update business objects.*

Windows form clients for business object Web services can take advantage of the Object Data Source designer to generate forms with BindingSources, a BindingNavigator, and DataGridViews or text boxes to display and update their associated objects. TableAdapters and DataAdapters don't work with business objects, so you must add the code to populate BindingSources with object instances. You must process individual updates, insertions, and deletions for parent tables; object arrays handle operations on multiple related records of child tables. Updates, deletions, and insertion of multiple child records require deleting all existing records and re-inserting all child records, unless you add code to emulate the `DataSet.GetChanges` method.

Web form clients that include GridView or DetailsView controls can use WebMethods that accept the same `ObjectData.Source.UpdateMethod`, `InsertMethod`, and `DeleteMethod` signatures and `Parameters` collections as SqlDataSources.

Explore a Business Object Web Service

The WSOrdersBE Web service in the \VB2005DB\Chapter09\WSOrdersBE folder exposes 32 WebMethods for two business objects and one business entity. The Northwind Orders and Order Details tables persist the objects' field values. The OrdersBE.vb partial class file incorporates the `Order` and `OrderDetail` classes imported from Chapter 8's OrdersBE_DAL.sln project. Individual WebMethods return arrays of `Order` or `OrderDetail` objects populated by `SqlDataReader` objects. Version 1.0 update operations require passing object field parameter values in the SOAP request message to parameterized SQL statements that update the Orders and Order Details base tables. These WebMethods are compatible with ASP.NET 2.0's table-oriented GridView and DetailsView controls.

The WSOrdersBE Web service demonstrates code reuse for successive updates that don't break backward compatibility. Version 1.1's WSOrders11.vb partial class adds WebMethods that accept an `Order` object and `OrderDetail` arrays as SOAP request method parameters, which the methods pass to version 1.0's private `Execute...` methods. Object input parameters simplify Windows form Web service clients that have BindingSources, DataGridViews, and Details views, which you generate by adding an Object Data Source to the form. The `OrderDetail` array enables users to update multiple `OrderDetail` objects with a single WebMethod invocation.

Independent `Order` and `Detail` classes don't fit the common definition of a business entity, such as a sales order, invoice, packing list, bill of lading, or other business transaction document. Thus, WSOrdersBE Version 1.2 adds a SalesOrder.vb partial class file that includes a definition and WebMethods for a `SalesOrder` object. The hierarchical `SalesOrder` object has an `OrderDetails` field — an array of `OrderDetail` objects that represent line items. WebMethods return arrays of `SalesOrder` objects, and update an individual `Order` object and its `OrderDetails` field with a single Web service call. Update WebMethods also invoke version 1.0's `Execute...` methods. Figure 9-10 is a diagram of the relationships between WSOrdersBE's public WebMethods and private functions.

> Common private `Execute...` methods minimize code modifications when database or table metadata changes, and don't require clients to update their Web References.

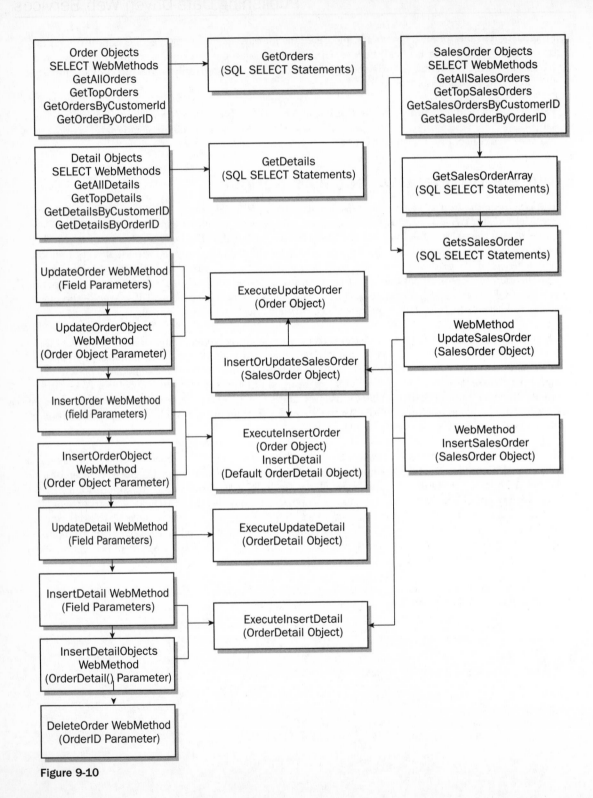

Figure 9-10

Hierarchical Objects and Relational Data

Object-relational mapping (O-RM) is a hot topic among .NET developers. Microsoft's .NET ObjectSpaces framework, which made its debut as a technology preview at the 2001 Professional Developer's Conference, was included in early (alpha) versions of VS 2005. ObjectSpaces uses a three-part mapping schema to define an object-persistence model. Microsoft announced in 2004 that .NET ObjectSpaces was postponed to the next Windows version (then Longhorn, now Windows Vista), and subsequently postponed the ObjectSpaces implementation to some time after Windows Vista's release.

There's no shortage of third-party O-RM class libraries for .NET; some have open-source (GPL or LGPL) licenses. Typically, the libraries map objects to a new or existing database schema and most support transacted updates. The multitude of similar O-RM offerings presents a choice crisis to developers, and evaluating the third-party products requires more persistence and dedication than most developers possess. An LPGL open-source O-RM example is the ATOMS Framework, which is written in VB.NET and includes VB.NET sample projects. The ATOMS Framework supports SQL Server, Jet, MySQL, and other databases.

> *You can download the source code and binary files for the ATOMS Framework 2.0 for the .NET Framework 1.1 from* `http://jcframework.sourceforge.net/`. *You can upgrade the source code to .NET 2.0 without errors, but you'll see many warnings in the Errors window.*

Populate Hierarchical Objects with SqlDataReaders

Classes that have a 1:1 relationship with a corresponding table's rows, such as the `Order` class and Orders table, and the `OrderDetail` class and Order Details table, are easy to implement without an O-RM application. Classes with a 1:*n* relationship to an underlying table's rows, such as the `SalesOrder` object and the Order Details table are a bit more difficult. Using an `SqlDataReader` object to generate an array of 1:*n* objects is cumbersome because you must retrieve each parent object and its child objects individually, as illustrated by Figure 9-11's `GetSalesOrderArray` method. `GetSalesOrderArray` calls the `GetSalesOrder` method, which requires a database server roundtrip for each array member you add.

Here's the code for the `GetSalesOrderArray` function:

```
Private Function GetSalesOrdersArray(ByVal strSQL As String) As SalesOrder()
    'This process is inefficient because code executes GetSalesOrder for each order
    Dim strConn As String = ConfigurationManager.ConnectionStrings( + _
        "NorthwindConnectionString").ConnectionString
    Dim cnNwind As New SqlConnection(strConn)
    Dim cmOrders As New SqlCommand(strSQL, cnNwind)
    Dim drOrders As SqlDataReader = Nothing
    Try
        cnNwind.Open()
        drOrders = cmOrders.ExecuteReader()
        Dim SalesOrders As New ArrayList
        With drOrders
            If .HasRows Then
                'Get the OrderIDs to process
                Dim OrderIDs As New ArrayList
                While .Read
                    OrderIDs.Add(.GetInt32(0))
                End While
                .Close()
                cnNwind.Close()
```

```
                Dim intItem As Integer
                For intItem = 0 To OrderIDs.Count - 1
                    Dim objOrder As New SalesOrder
                    If intItem = OrderIDs.Count - 1 Then
                        'Close the connection
                        objOrder = GetSalesOrder(CType(OrderIDs.Item(intItem), Integer), _
                         False, True)
                    Else
                        If intItem = 0 Then
                            'Open but don't close the connection
                            objOrder = GetSalesOrder(CType(OrderIDs.Item(intItem), _
                             Integer), True, False)
                        Else
                            'Don't open or close the connection
                            objOrder = GetSalesOrder(CType(OrderIDs.Item(intItem), _
                             Integer), False, False)
                        End If
                    End If
                    SalesOrders.Add(objOrder)
                Next
                Return CType(SalesOrders.ToArray(GetType(SalesOrder)), SalesOrder())
            Else
                Dim strMsg As String = "Orders for parameter supplied not found."
                Dim excSoap As New SoapException(strMsg, _
                 SoapException.ClientFaultCode, Context.Request.Url.AbsoluteUri)
                Throw excSoap
            End If
        End With
    Catch excSql As SqlException
        Dim excSoap As New SoapException("SQLException: " + excSql.Message, _
         SoapException.ClientFaultCode, Context.Request.Url.AbsoluteUri)
        Throw excSoap
    Catch excSys As System.Exception
        Dim excSoap As New SoapException("SystemException: " + excSys.Message, _
         SoapException.ClientFaultCode, Context.Request.Url.AbsoluteUri)
        Throw excSoap
    Finally
        drOrders.Close()
        cnNwind.Close()
        drOrders.Dispose()
        cmOrders.Dispose()
        cnNwind.Dispose()
    End Try
End Function
```

Following is the GetSalesOrder function:

```
Private Function GetSalesOrder(ByVal intOrderID As Integer, _
 By Val blnOpenConnection As Boolean, ByVal blnCloseConnection As Boolean) _
 As SalesOrder
    'Populates an SalesOrder object with a single order
    Dim strSQL As String = "SELECT * FROM Orders WHERE OrderID = @OrderID " + _
     "; SELECT * FROM [Order Details] WHERE OrderID = @OrderID"
    Dim strConn As String = ConfigurationManager.ConnectionStrings( + _
        "NorthwindConnectionString").ConnectionString
```

```
Static cnNwind As SqlConnection
If blnOpenConnection Then
    cnNwind = New SqlConnection(strConn)
End If
Dim cmOrder As New SqlCommand(strSQL, cnNwind)

'Parameterize SELECT query
Dim prmSelect As SqlParameter
prmSelect = New SqlParameter("@OrderID", SqlDbType.Int)
prmSelect.Value = intOrderID
cmOrder.Parameters.Add(prmSelect)

Dim drOrder As SqlDataReader = Nothing
Try
    If blnOpenConnection Then
        cnNwind.Open()
    End If
    drOrder = cmOrder.ExecuteReader()
    With drOrder
        If .HasRows Then
            Dim objOrder As New SalesOrder
            .Read()
            objOrder.OrderID = .GetInt32(0)
            objOrder.CustomerID = .GetString(1)
            objOrder.EmployeeID = .GetInt32(2)
            objOrder.OrderDate = .GetDateTime(3)
            If Not IsDBNull(.Item(4)) Then
                objOrder.RequiredDate = .GetDateTime(4)
            Else
                objOrder.RequiredDate = #12:00:00 AM#
            End If
            If Not IsDBNull(.Item(5)) Then
                objOrder.ShippedDate = .GetDateTime(5)
            Else
                objOrder.ShippedDate = #12:00:00 AM#
            End If
            objOrder.ShipVia = .GetInt32(6)
            If Not IsDBNull(.Item(7)) Then
                objOrder.Freight = .GetDecimal(7)
            Else
                objOrder.Freight = 0D
            End If
            objOrder.ShipName = .GetString(8)
            objOrder.ShipAddress = .GetString(9)
            objOrder.ShipCity = .GetString(10)
            If Not IsDBNull(.Item(11)) Then
                objOrder.ShipRegion = .GetString(11)
            End If
            If Not IsDBNull(.Item(12)) Then
                objOrder.ShipPostalCode = .GetString(12)
            End If
            objOrder.ShipCountry = .GetString(13)

            'Add the OrderDetails array of OrderDetail objects
            Dim Details As New ArrayList
```

```
                Dim objDetail As OrderDetail = Nothing
            If .NextResult Then
                While .Read
                    objDetail = New OrderDetail
                    objDetail.OrderID = .GetInt32(0)
                    objDetail.ProductID = .GetInt32(1)
                    objDetail.UnitPrice = .GetDecimal(2)
                    objDetail.Quantity = .GetInt16(3)
                    objDetail.Discount = CType(.Item(4), Decimal)
                    Details.Add(objDetail)
                End While
                .Close()
                If blnCloseConnection Then
                    cnNwind.Close()
                End If
            Else
                'Business rule: All orders must have at least one Order detail
                Dim strMsg As String = "OrderDetails for " + _
                 intOrderID.ToString + " not found."
                Dim excSoap As New SoapException(strMsg, _
                 SoapException.ClientFaultCode, Context.Request.Url.AbsoluteUri)
                Throw excSoap
            End If
            'Add the array of OrderDetails
            objOrder.OrderDetails = _
             CType(Details.ToArray(GetType(OrderDetail)), OrderDetail())
            Return objOrder
        Else
            Dim strMsg As String = "Order " + intOrderID.ToString + " not found."
            Dim excSoap As New SoapException(strMsg, _
             SoapException.ClientFaultCode, Context.Request.Url.AbsoluteUri)
            Throw excSoap
        End If
    End With
Catch excSql As SqlException
    Dim excSoap As New SoapException("SQLException: " + excSql.Message, _
     SoapException.ClientFaultCode, Context.Request.Url.AbsoluteUri)
    Throw excSoap
Catch excSys As System.Exception
    Dim excSoap As New SoapException("SystemException: " + excSys.Message, _
     SoapException.ClientFaultCode, _
     Context.Request.Url.AbsoluteUri)
    Throw excSoap
Finally
    If blnCloseConnection Then
        cnNwind.Close()
        cnNwind.Dispose()
    End If
    drOrder.Close()
    drOrder.Dispose()
    cmOrder.Dispose()
End Try
End Function
```

Tests with the WSOrdersBE Web service show that this approach for `SalesOrder` objects takes about twice as long as returning the same number of `Order` and `OrderDetail` objects independently. Alternative approaches are to employ an O-RM application or fill a typed or untyped DataSet and populate the `SalesOrder` objects from the DataSet's `Orders` table and related records from its `Order_Details` table.

Neither alternative approach is likely to improve object-array data retrieval performance substantially. The performance hit can be minimized by limiting the number of SalesOrder objects returned to a Web service client.

Bind Object Arrays to DataGridViews

Windows form Web service clients let you bind DataGridViews and Details view text boxes to custom business objects, including objects returned by Web services, by adding an Object Data Source. The process is a bit trickier when you bind DataGridViews to array fields of hierarchical objects. The WinOrdersBEClient.sln project in the \VB2005DB\Chapter09\WinOrdersBEClient folder has two forms, both of which display `Order` and `OrderDetail` objects in DataGridViews. The OrdersBE.vb form retrieves and updates `Order` objects and arrays of `OrderDetail` objects individually by calling the `InsertOrderAndOrderDetails` or `UpdateOrderAndOrderDetails` WebMethod. SalesOrdersBE.vb retrieves and updates `SalesOrder` objects.

The WinOrdersBEClient project includes a SoapSnoop.vb class file that copies SOAP request and response messages to the Windows Clipboard for analysis and debugging. The code for this class is the original C# version from SQL Server 2005's Books Online's "Adding SOAP Trace Support to Client Applications" topic converted to VB 2005. To activate the SoapSnoop feature, open the Reference.vb Web Reference class file and prefix the WebMethod of interest's <System.Web.Services .Protocols.SoapDocumentMethodAttribute() _ attribute with <SnoopAttribute> _. As an example, see the sample project's Reference.vb file before you invoke the Update Web Reference command. Refreshing the Web reference removes the added <SnoopAttribute> _ decorations.

Windows form Web service clients can generate the `SalesOrder` object by combining a row from a DataGridView or Details view text box values for `Order` objects and similar controls for an `ArrayList` or `BindingList(Of OrderDetail)`. This technique minimizes Web service client modifications when you change the service's object structure.

Create Object Data Sources and DataGridViews from Web Services

Adding a Web Reference to a Windows form client automatically adds data sources for each object that's defined by the Web service's classes. An *ObjectName*.datasource file specifies the `TypeInfo` property of a `GenericObjectDataSource` for each data source. The `TypeInfo` value is `ProjectName .WebReferenceName.ClassName`. For example, adding a Web Reference to the WSOrdersBE Web service adds Order.datasource, OrderDetail.datasource, and SalesOrder.datasource files to the Web Reference's Reference.map node.

Objects must have private fields and public properties (accessors) to enable complex databinding and autogenerate Design-mode components. If your Web service's objects don't meet this requirement, you won't see the fields when you expand the data source's object node.

Drag an object node—Order for this example—to the form, which generates an OrderBindingSource and OrderBindingNavigator in the tray, and OrderDataGridView and BindingNavigator controls on the form. Repeat the process for the related object node—in this case OrderDetail—to add an OrderDetailBindingSource and an OrderDataGridView control. Reflection adds the DataGridView columns, so they appear in random order.

Optionally, add an instance of your Web service proxy to the tray by dragging the Web service component from the Toolbox's ProjectName section to the tray. For this example, the default instance name is WsOrdersBE1.

Object data sources don't have Fill... methods, so you must add code to the Form1_Load or a button event handler. Here's the code to fill the two DataGridViews from the Order and OrderDetail object arrays by invoking the appropriate WebMethods:

```
Private Sub btnLoadGrids_Click(ByVal sender As System.Object, _
  ByVal e As System.EventArgs) Handles btnLoadGrids.Click
    Dim objOrders As Order() = WsOrdersBE1.GetTopOrders(25)
    Dim objDetails As OrderDetail() = WsOrdersBE1.GetTopDetails(25)
    With OrderBindingSource
        .Clear()
        .DataSource = objOrders
    End With
    With OrderDetailBindingSource
        .Clear()
        .DataSource = objDetails
    End With
End Sub
```

Build and run the project, and load the DataGridViews. The grids are read-only when you replace their Design-time BindingSource.DataSource property values—WSOrdersBE.Order and WSOrdersBE .OrderDetail—with the corresponding object arrays. If your Web service client doesn't need to update the objects, the preceding code is adequate (and fast).

You must add the object array elements individually to the BindingSources to enable editing, updating, and deleting objects and their underlying base table rows with code that's similar to the following:

```
Private Sub btnLoadGrids_Click(ByVal sender As System.Object, _
  ByVal e As System.EventArgs) Handles btnLoadGrids.Click
    Dim wsOrders As New WSOrdersBE
    Dim objOrders As Order() = wsOrders.GetTopOrders(25)
    Dim objDetails As OrderDetail() = wsOrders.GetTopDetails(25)
    Dim intRow As Integer
    With OrderBindingSource
        .Clear()
        For intRow = 0 To objOrders.Length - 1
```

```
            .Add(objOrders(intRow))
      Next
   End With
   With OrderDetailBindingSource
      .Clear()
      For intRow = 0 To objDetails.Length - 1
         .Add(objDetails(intRow))
      Next
   End With
End Sub
```

The emphasized instruction of the preceding code creates a new instance of the WSOrdersBE Web service proxy if you don't add a designer instance to the tray.

Use the `DataGridView.Columns` collection to reorder and format the columns. You can't sort DataGridViews or filter BindingSources whose `DataSource` property value is an array or a generic `BindingList(Of ObjectType)`, so set the columns' `SortMode` property to `NotSortable`. If you need sortable and filterable data sources, you must derive a class from `BindingList(Of ObjectType)` and override the appropriate base class methods and properties. This section's Web service client design principles apply to any Web service that returns objects or arrays of objects, not just ASP.NET Web services.

The WinOrdersBEClient.sln project in the \VB2005DB\Chapter09\WinOrdersBEClient folder is a full-featured Web service client that displays, updates, inserts, and deletes `Order`, `OrderDetail`, *and* `SalesOrder` *objects. The OrdersBE.vb form includes an enhanced version of the preceding code.*

Bind DataGrids to Hierarchical Business Objects

You can add the BindingSource, BindingNavigator, and DataGridView or Details text boxes for the parent and child object(s) of a hierarchical business object to the form. The data source designer lets you drag the SalesOrders data source's `OrderDetails` field — an array of `OrderDetail` objects — to the form to generate an `OrderDetailsBindingSource` and `OrderDetailsDataGridView`.

For this example, rename the `OrderDetailsBindingSource` to `SalesOrderDetailsBindingSource`, and verify that its `DataSource` property value is `SalesOrderBindingSource` and its `DataMember` property value is `OrderDetails`. Verify that the child DataGridView's `DataSource` property value is `SalesOrderDetailsBindingSource`. Your form appears as shown in Figure 9-11.

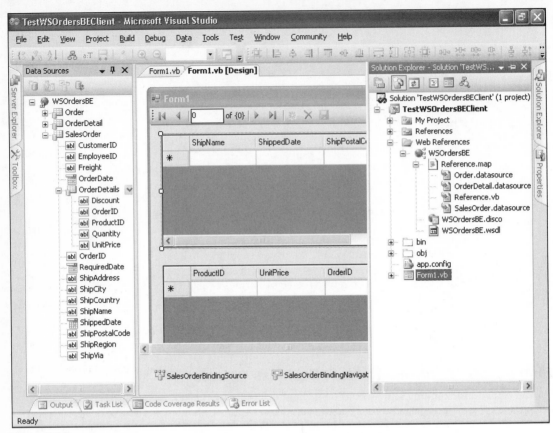

Figure 9-11

Populating the BindingSources and DataGridViews with parent and child object arrays requires processing each parent object individually to add its child objects to the BindingSource. If you generate a generic `BindingList(Of ChildObject)`, you can set the child object BindingSource's `DataSource` to the BindingList and obtain an updatable DataGridView. Creating a generic BindingList requires adding the following `Imports` statement to your class:

```
Imports System.ComponentModel
```

Here's the code to load the two DataGridViews with the `SalesOrder` object array and a `BindingList(Of OrderDetail)`:

```
Private Sub btnLoadGrids_Click(ByVal sender As System.Object, _
  ByVal e As System.EventArgs) Handles btnLoadGrids.Click
    Dim objOrders() As SalesOrder
    objOrders = WsOrdersBE1.GetTopSalesOrders(25)
    With SalesOrderBindingSource
        Dim lstDetails As New BindingList(Of OrderDetail)
        Dim intRow As Integer
        For intRow = 0 To objOrders.Length - 1
            'Add the SalesOrder object
            .Add(objOrders(intRow))
            'Add the OrderDetails objects to lstDetails
            Dim objDtls As OrderDetail()
            objDtls = objOrders(intRow).OrderDetails
            Dim intItem As Integer
            For intItem = 0 To objDtls.Length - 1
                lstDetails.Add(objOrders(intRow).OrderDetails(intItem))
            Next
        Next
        With SalesOrderDetailsBindingSource
            'Set the DataSource to the OrderDetails BindingList
            .DataMember = ""
            .DataSource = lstDetails
        End With
    End With
End Sub
```

The WinOrdersBEClient.sln project's SalesOrdersBE.vb form includes the production version of the preceding code.

Update, Insert, and Delete Objects

The basic code for updating Order, OrderDetail, and SalesOrder objects is brief. The Web service deletes and then adds all OrderDetail items when you update an Order or SalesOrder object. Unlike DataSets, GenericObjectDataSources don't store original and current values, so there's no simple method to determine OrderDetail edits, insertions, and deletions individually. Thus, you must restrict the contents of the OrderDetailBindingSource or the SalesOrderDetailBindingSource to the OrderDetail items for the selected Order. The quick and easy approach is to repopulate the OrderDetailBindingSource by invoking the GetDetailsByOrderID WebMethod when the user selects an Order to update.

Invoking a WebMethod each time the user selects an order violates the "chunky, not chatty" Web service best practice. Executing WebMethods is a much more resource-intensive process than executing an SQL statement or stored procedure over an intranet. Thus, a single WebMethod invocation should return or update one or more complete objects, not individual fields of objects. A more efficient approach is to create a copy of the OrderDetail array as a BindingList(Of OrderDetail) object, scan the copy for OrderDetail objects with matching OrderID values, and add matching objects to the BindingSource's DataSource.

The WinOrdersBEClient.sln's OrdersBE.vb form takes the WebMethod approach in the
`SalesOrderDataGridView_SelectionChanged` *event-handler code. The SalesOrdersBE.vb's*
version scans the `BindingList(Of OrderDetail)` *object, which is faster.*

Following is the basic code for inserting or updating a `SalesOrder` object with the
`BindingNavigatorSaveItem_Click` event handler:

```
Private Sub BindingNavigatorSaveItem_Click(ByVal sender As Object, _
  ByVal e As System.EventArgs) Handles BindingNavigatorSaveItem.Click
    With SalesOrderBindingSource
        'Update or insert a SalesOrder
        Dim objSalesOrder As SalesOrder = CType(.Current, SalesOrder)
        If objSalesOrder.OrderID = 0 Then
            .EndNew(.Position)
            WsOrdersBE1.InsertSalesOrder(objSalesOrder)
        Else
            'Create an ArrayList of OrderDetails
            .EndEdit()
            Dim objDetails As New ArrayList
            With SalesOrderDetailsBindingSource
                Dim intRow As Integer
                For intRow = 0 To .Count - 1
                    objDetails.Add(.Item(intRow))
                Next
            End With
            'Create a strongly typed array and set the OrderDetails field
            objSalesOrder.OrderDetails = _
              CType(objDetails.ToArray(GetType(OrderDetail)), OrderDetail())
            WsOrdersBE1.UpdateSalesOrder(objSalesOrder)
        End If
    End With
End Sub
```

Deleting a SalesOrder and its OrderDetails items invokes WSOrdersBE version 1.0's `DeleteOrder`
WebMethod, which deletes related Order Details rows and the Order row from the base tables.

Figure 9-12 shows the WinOrdersBEClient.sln's SalesOrderBE.vb form after updating an order. The two
forms let you compare the performance of the two object models by varying the number of orders.
Obtaining the data is faster for WSOrdersBE versions 1.*x* than version 2.0, but the grids fill faster with
`SalesOrder` objects.

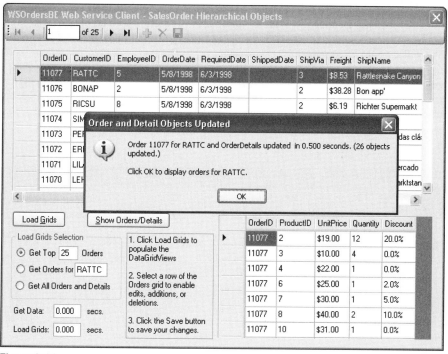

Figure 9-12

Create an ASP.NET Business Objects Web Services Client

The procedure for creating an ASP.NET client for a Web service that returns generic business objects is similar to that for services that return DataSets. Add a Web reference to the service, specify the service's object class as the Object Data Source, and use the Configure Data Source Wizard to set the appropriate WebMethods as the `SelectMethod`, `InsertMethod`, `UpdateMethod`, and `DeleteMethod`. Unlike DataSets, business objects don't have primary keys defined, so all field values are updatable by default in GridViews and DetailsViews. The WebOrdersBEClient Web site in the \VB2005DB\Chapter09\ WebOrdersBEClient folder is a modification of the Web form clients described in the section "Replace SqlDataSources with ObjectDataSources" in Chapter 8. For this example, the Business Object (`TypeName` property value) is `WSOrdersBE.WSOrdersBE` Web service class for the LinkedGridView and LinkedDetailsView pages. Assigning the `GetAllOrders()`, returns `Orders[]` WebMethod as the SELECT Data Method loads the LinkedGridView.

Publish the WSOrdersBE Web Site to a WSOrdersBE virtual directory (`http://localhost/ WSOrdersBE`) and enable anonymous access to the Web service to eliminate the need to enable Windows authentication of the client.

The `GetOrderByOrderID(Int32 OrderID), returns Order[]` WebMethod loads the LinkedDetailsView page's dvOrdersLinked DetailsView with the data for the OrderID specified on the LinkedGridView page. `GetDetailsByOrderID(Int32 OrderID, returns OrderDetail[])` loads the dvDetailsLinked DetailsView. The `UpdateOrder(String CustomerID, Int32 EmployeeID, DateTime OrderDate, DateTime RequiredDate, DateTime ShippedDate, Int32 ShipVia, Decimal Freight, String ShipName, String ShipAddress, String ShipCity, String ShipRegion, String ShipPostalCode, String ShipCountry, Int32 original_OrderID), returns Int32` WebMethod updates the selected Order object. A similar `InsertOrder()` Web method adds new orders, and `DeleteOrder(Int32 original_OrderID), returns Int32` deletes them. Figure 9-13 shows a sample order in the editing process.

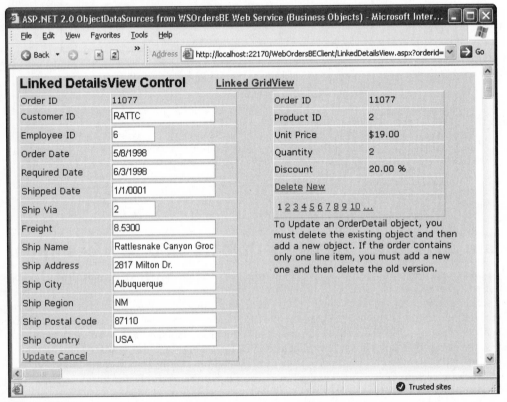

Figure 9-13

To prevent SOAP exceptions when executing the `SelectMethod` after deleting an `Order` object, add a `Private blnDeleted as Boolean` variable declaration and the following event handlers:

```
Private Sub dvOrdersLinked_ItemDeleting(ByVal sender As Object, _
  ByVal e As System.Web.UI.WebControls.DetailsViewDeleteEventArgs) _
  Handles dvOrdersLinked.ItemDeleting
    blnDeleted = True
End Sub

Private Sub odsOrderQueryString_Selecting(ByVal sender As Object, _
  ByVal e As System.Web.UI.WebControls.ObjectDataSourceSelectingEventArgs) _
  Handles odsOrderQueryString.Selecting
```

```
    'An exception occurs when deleting an order if you don't redirect
    If blnDeleted Then
        Response.Buffer = True
        Response.Redirect("LinkedGridView.aspx")
        blnDeleted = False
    End If
End Sub
```

Summary

Following an initial surge of IT-industry enthusiasm, Web services are finally emerging as a practical method for implementing a standards-based service-oriented architecture. ASP.NET 2.0 Web services broaden the reach of .NET applications by making data easily available to clients in other domains. The capability to pass SOAP 1.1 or 1.2 messages through firewalls enables data-intensive operations over the public Internet.

Before you embark on a production Web service project, you need to understand the many issues that have impeded the wide-spread adoption of Web services. The two most important Web service design considerations are interoperability and security. If potential consumers of your Web services use operating systems other than Windows or programming tools other than Visual Studio, substitute generic business objects for DataSets. SSL or TLS provides adequate transport security for most Web service message content. Implementing WS-Security for transport-independent encryption and digital signatures isn't a piece of cake and imposes interoperability challenges.

ASP.NET 2.0 doesn't change the basic process of creating Web services and client Web service proxies. VS 2005's built-in Web server makes it easier to test Web services that have WebMethods with primitive datatype parameters. Copy or publish deployment of completed Web services to IIS virtual directories is quick and easy. Improvements to the Windows and Web forms' Add Web Reference dialog enable new Web service search methods and simplify the form design process for services that return and update DataSets or custom business objects. ASP.NET 2.0's ObjectDataSource controls minimizes the code required to create, update, or delete custom business objects.

Web services that expose hierarchical object structures to represent business entities — such as purchase orders, sales orders, or invoices — involve object-relational mapping. Unless you're willing to adopt a third-party mapping library, you must write Web service code to generate the required object structure. You also must add a substantial amount of code to your Web service clients to display and edit hierarchical objects with databound controls.

Part IV

SQL Server 2005 and ADO.NET 2.0

10

Upgrading from SQL Server 2000 to 2005

Five years is an unusually long interval between versions of a relational database management system. SQL Server 2000 released to manufacturing on August 8, 2000. By 2004, according to Gartner Group, SQL Server had gained 20 percent of the total relational database management systems (RDBMS) market, with traditional market leader Oracle taking 33.7 percent and IBM holding the top spot with 34.1 percent. Most industry analysts attribute SQL Server 2000's increasing market share to easy installation and management, relatively low licensing costs, bundled online analytical processing (OLAP) capabilities, and free add-ons — such as Reporting Services, SQLXML 3.0, and SQL Server Accelerator for Business Intelligence. Upgrades from the freely distributable SQL Server 2000 Desktop Engine (MSDE) undoubtedly are a significant contributor to SQL Server revenues.

> Go to http://www.eweek.com/article2/0,1759,1820629,00.asp for an eWeek article that provides more details behind the Gartner market share numbers.

SQL Server 2000's continuing success in the RDBMS market gave Microsoft's developers the breathing room required to ensure that SQL Server 2005's security, performance, and enhanced feature set will continue to take Windows and UNIX market shares from Oracle and IBM. SQL Server 2005 Express Edition — the replacement for MSDE — will fend off the threat from open-source RDBMSs, such as MySQL, PostgreSQL, and, more recently, a semi-open-source version of the venerable Ingres database from Computer Associates. MSDE offered no built-in graphical management tools; SQL Express Manager provides a simple GUI to author T-SQL queries and manage SQL 2005 Express Edition and higher instances.

This chapter briefly describes the differences between SQL Server 2005 editions and their most important new features, provides sample scripts that illustrate new T-SQL features, and explains the design of and code behind sample Windows form clients for query notifications, Database Mail (formerly SQLiMail), and SQL Server native Web services. Chapters 11, "Creating SQL Server Projects," and 12, "Exploring the xml Datatype," supplement this chapter's introductions to these topics.

SQL Server 2005 Editions

SQL Server 2005 comes in six editions, each of which has a corresponding SQL Server 2000 edition. The following sections describe the similarities and differences between the SQL Server 2005 editions and their SQL Server 2000 counterparts.

Express Edition

Express Edition is a freely distributable version of the SQL Server 2005 database engine that's intended to replace MSDE 2000. All 32-bit VS 2005 editions, including the Express versions, install SQL Server 2005 Express as a named instance (SQLEXPRESS) by default. Here's a brief comparison of the Express Edition's and MSDE 2000's features and specifications:

❑   Express Edition requires installing .NET Framework 2.0 before running the setup program; MSDE installs MDAC 2.6 during setup.

❑   Express Edition has a maximum database size of 4GB versus MSDE 2000's 2GB limit.

❑   Express Edition doesn't have a workload governor. MSDE supports a maximum of five simultaneously executing queries and queues additional queries for execution.

❑   Express Edition supports one CPU, 1GB RAM, and up to 50 named instances on a single computer. MSDE 2000 supports 2 CPUs, 2GB RAM, and up to 16 local named instances.

❑   Express Edition installs from a 37MB self-extracting executable or Windows installer file, which doesn't include a sample database. MSDE 2000 Release A (MSDE2000A.exe) is 43MB without online help but it includes the Northwind sample database.

❑   Express Edition doesn't install an MDAC stack; MSDE 2000 Release A installs MDAC 2.6.

❑   Express Edition doesn't install SQL Server Agent; MSDE does. Scheduling services requires Remote Management Objects (RMO) programming.

❑   Express Edition doesn't support replication publishing; MSDE 2000 supports merge and snapshot replication publishing. Both products handle transactional, merge, and snapshot replication subscriptions. Replication synchronization requires RMO programming, an on-demand add-on to SQL Express Manager, or scheduling synchronization with Windows Sync Manager.

❑   Express Edition supports .NET CLR integration, and acts as a Service Broker client and database mirroring witness instance; MSDE 2000 doesn't.

❑   Express Edition performs a system configuration check during installation and hides advanced installation options unless the user marks Show Advanced Configuration Options. Advanced options include the ability to rename the instance, enable SQL Server authentication with mixed mode, and choose a non-standard collation.

❑   Express Edition installs SQL Server Configuration Manager, a Microsoft Management Console (MMC) snap-in, which replaces MSDE 2000's SQL Server Service Manager, and the SQL Server 2005 Surface Area Configuration tool, which enables services and features.

❑   Express Edition installs with only the Shared Memory Provider enabled; network access isn't enabled by default. Use SCM to enable TCP/IP, NamedPipes (optional), and the SQL Browser service for TCP/IP network connectivity.

❑   Express Edition will gain a reduced-functionality version of SQL Server Management studio during the first half of 2006. MSDE 2000 has no graphical management tools.

❑ Express Edition offers minimal (SqlExpressBOL.msi, 230KB) and abridged (SqlAbridgedBOL.msi, 33MB) versions of SQL Server Books Online as separate downloads. MSDE 2000 users must download the complete SQL Server 2000 Books Online installer (SqlBOLSetup.msi, 33 MB).

❑ Express Edition supports SQL Server 2005 Reporting Services locally. MSDE databases can supply data to Reporting Services but MSDE instances can't store the Report Server Database.

❑ Express Edition provides XCopy application and database deployment with the relative or absolute path of a Database.mdf file as the value of the connection string's `AttachDBFileName` argument. By default, applications automatically attach and detach the *Database*.mdf and *Database*.ldf files on opening and closing, but detaching is subject to an 8-minute delay for cleaning up pooled connections. MSDE doesn't offer this feature.

Following is a list of SQL Server 2005 Developer Edition and higher features that SQL Express doesn't install or support:

❑ SQL Server Analysis Services and business intelligence (BI) services, such as data mining.

❑ SQL Server Management Studio, SQL Profiler, Business Intelligence Studio.

❑ Replication publishing.

❑ Full-text search.

❑ Integration Services (formerly Data Transformation Services, DTS)

❑ HTTP services, including SQL Server native Web services.

❑ High-availability services, such as database mirroring and the administrative SQL Command prompt.

❑ Service Broker communication with the same or other SQL Express database instances. Service Broker messages must pass through a Developer Edition or higher version to communicate with another SQL Express instance.

SQL Express's Server Broker limitations and lack of HTTP services prevent users from running the T-SQL batch commands in the section "Service Broker," later in this chapter, and the SqlNativeWebServices.sln sample project.

Developer Edition

SQL Server 2005 Developer Edition consists of all Standard Edition features except a license for production use. Developer Edition, which is licensed for development purposes only, is included with VS 2005 Professional and Team Services editions, and Visual Studio Tools for Office (VSTO).

Workgroup Edition

SQL Server 2005 Workgroup Edition is a scaled-down version of SQL Server Standard Edition that's intended for production use by small and medium-sized businesses (SMBs). The estimated retail price (ERP) of a Workgroup Edition license is US$3,899 per processor. Per-processor SQL Server 2005 licenses for all editions (except Express) treat a multicore processor as a single CPU; Oracle and IBM licenses count each core as a CPU.

Workgroup Edition has no limit on database size, but has the following restrictions:

❑ Supports a maximum of 3GB of RAM; RAM support in Standard and Enterprise editions is determined by the Windows operating system.

❑ Supports one or two CPUs; Standard Edition supports a maximum of four CPUs.

❑ Doesn't support Standard Edition's database mirroring, two-node clustering, replication publishing, data warehousing, Analysis Services, data mining, or native XML Web services (HTTP endpoints).

❑ SQL Server Business Intelligence Development Studio is limited to Reporting Services projects.

❑ Doesn't include Notification Services or Integration Services.

Standard Edition

SQL Server 2005 Standard Edition incorporates all mainstream SQL Server features: Analysis, Integration, Notification and Reporting Services, Report Builder, Service Broker, query notifications, BI, data mining, full-text search, and upgraded management tools. The Standard Edition license ERP is US$5,999 per processor. For a summary of new SQL Server 2005 features, follow the link to the "SQL Server 2005 Overview" document at http://www.microsoft.com/sql/2005/.

SQL Server 2005 Developer, Standard, or Enterprise Edition is required to execute all sample VS 2005 projects for this chapter.

Enterprise Edition

SQL Server 2005 Enterprise Edition has no restrictions on the number of CPUs, and adds partitioning for large tables, high-performance database mirroring, online indexing, online page and file restoration, advanced transforms for Integration Services, and advanced business analytics. Enterprise Edition usually runs under Windows Server 2003 Enterprise or DataCenter Edition. The ERP for an Enterprise Edition license is US$24,999 per processor.

Mobile Edition

SQL Server Mobile Edition is the successor to the Windows CE Edition (SQL Server CE). Integration with SQL Server 2005 enables developers to use Management Studio with Mobile Edition databases on desktop computers or devices, including Tablet PCs, take advantage of Integration Services, and create and synchronize databases with a new Subscription Wizard. Mobile Edition supports bulk copy program (BCP) table loading, partitioned articles, and column-level tracking. Column-level tracking replicates changes to individual column values within a row, instead of replacing the entire row.

New SQL Server 2005 Features in Brief

The following sections highlight the new features of SQL Server 2005 and SQL Server 2005 Express in these categories:

❑ Management tools, including System Management Objects (SMO) and RMO

❑ SQL Server Reporting Services

❑ CLR integration

❑ The xml datatype and XQuery

❑ SQL Native Client

❑ Multiple Active Result Sets (MARS)

❑ Data availability and reliability

These topics have T-SQL script examples, sample Windows form applications, or both:

❑ T-SQL and relational engine enhancements

❑ Service Broker messaging

❑ Query notifications

❑ Database Mail

❑ Native SOAP Web services

SQL Server Books Online provides tutorials for many of the topics that this chapter covers. Online tutorials use the AdventureWorks or AdventureWorksDW databases. The chapter's T-SQL scripts and sample applications use the Northwind database.

New or Updated Management Tools

SQL Server 2005 adds new Configuration Management and SQL Express Manager tools. SQL Server Management Studio and Business Intelligence Development Studio are major upgrades to their SQL Server 2000 predecessors. Integration Services is the new name for Data Transformation Services (DTS). SQL Profiler and Database Tuning Advisor (formerly the Index Tuning Wizard) get a minor facelift and a few new features.

SQL Server Configuration Manager

SQL Server 2005 and SQL Express install SQL Server Configuration Manager (SSCM). SSCM combines SQL Server 2000's Server Network Utility, Client Network Utility, and Services Manager into a single MMC snap-in. The SSCM snap-in integrates with My Computer's Management snap-in by adding an SQL Server Configuration Manager subnode under Services and Applications. You also can run SSCM from the Programs\Microsoft SQL Server 2005\Configuration Tools\SQL Server Configuration Manager menu command.

SSCM configures SQL Server 2005's shared memory (Sm), named pipes (Np), TCP/IP (Tcp), and Virtual Interface Architecture (VIA) network libraries for servers and clients. VIA is a high-speed interconnect that replaces TCP/IP for connecting multiple servers in a system area network (SAN). You can enable or disable each network library for server and client, and set priorities for local client connections by selecting the Client Network Configuration node (see Figure 10-1). Shared Memory's priority is fixed at 1, but you can alter the priorities of TCP/IP, Named Pipes, or VIA.

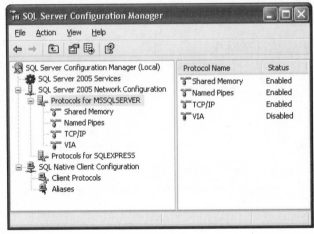

Figure 10-1

SQL Express users must enable TCP/IP network libraries for the server to enable remote clients to connect to the SQL Express instance. Similarly, client-side TCP/IP must be enabled for clients to connect to remote SQL Express instances. TCP/IP is enabled by default for other SQL Server 2005 editions.

SQL Server Surface Area Configuration Tool

The SQL Server 2005 Surface Area Configuration Tool (SACT) is intended to increase SQL Server 2005 security by disabling unused services, remote connections, and features. You open SACT from the Programs\Microsoft SQL Server 2005\Configuration Tools\SQL Server Surface Area Configuration menu command, and then click the Services and Connections or Features link. The Surface Area Configuration for Services and Connections dialog duplicates most capabilities of SSCM's SQL Server 2005 Services node.

The Surface Area Configuration for Features dialog lets you enable SQL Server 2005 features that are disabled by default, such as CLR integration (see Figure 10-2). You also can start or stop individual HTTP Endpoints that define Native Web services.

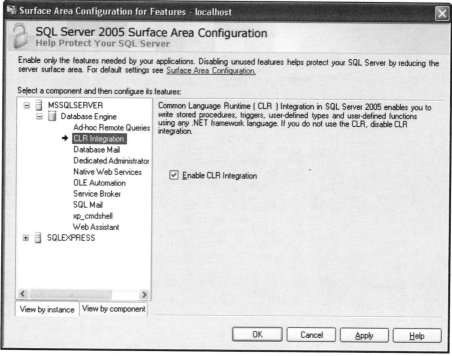

Figure 10-2

SQL Server Management Studio

SQL Server Management Studio (SSMS) combines SQL Server 2000's individual Enterprise Manager, Query Analyzer, Analysis Manager, Report Manager, and Notification Services tools into a unified UI that's based on the VS 2005 IDE. You can manage SQL Server 2005, earlier SQL Server versions, and SQL Server Mobile Edition, Notification Services, replication, and Reporting Services in a single UI. SMSS lets you create and save solutions containing projects that incorporate connection, query, and related miscellaneous files.

Query Editor replaces Query Analyzer and lets you write T-SQL scripts without a database connection. Template Explorer lets you select one of more than 100 predefined T-SQL queries. You also can write SQL Mobile, Multidimensional Expressions (MDX), XML for Analysis (XML/A), and Data Mining Extensions (DMX) scripts. Query Editor includes an XML editor for resultsets that return XML documents and a graphical execution plan tool for SQL Server and SQL Server Mobile Edition. Figure 10-3 shows an SSMS project with Object Explorer, Query Editor, and Template Explorer windows open.

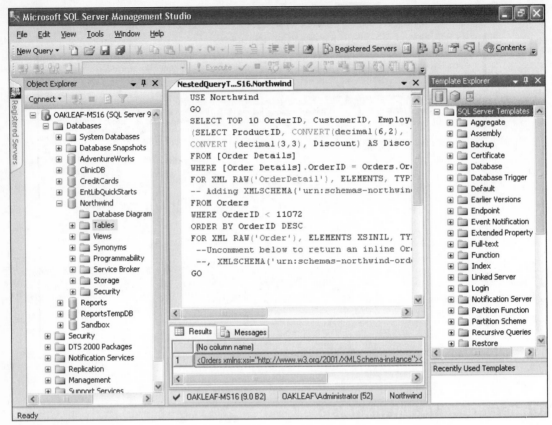

Figure 10-3

A new SQLCMD mode lets Query Editor scripts execute operating system instructions with SMO. The sqlcmd.exe utility supplements osql.exe; sqlcmd.exe uses SMO and an OLE DB–based connection. You can continue to use osql.exe, if you don't want or need SMO's additional capabilities.

The section "SQL Management Objects," later in this chapter, provides a brief description of SMO and RMO objects.

Business Intelligence Development Studio

Business Intelligence Development Studio (BIDS) replaces and extends the capabilities of SQL Server 2000's Analysis Manager. BIDS lets you design and edit data source views, cubes, dimensions, mining models, reports, and Integration Services packages in a BI solution. A BI solution is a VS 2005–style container that can contain multiple Reporting Services, Analysis Services, and data mining projects. Figure 10-4 shows BIDS with the sample AdventureWorksDW database's AdventureWorks cube open.

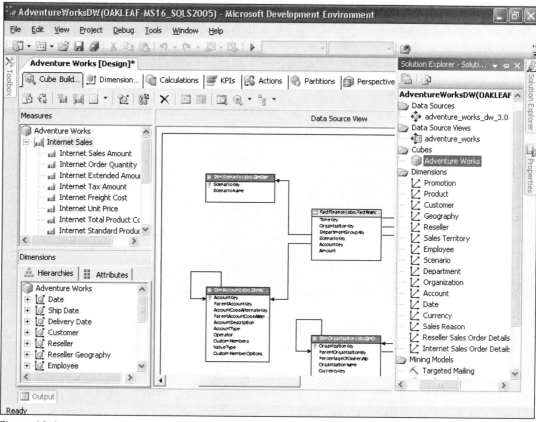

Figure 10-4

Integration Services

SQL Server Integration Services (SSIS) is SQL Server 2005's enhanced version of Data Transformation Services. The graphical Integration Services Designer can extend packages created by the upgraded SSIS Import and Export Wizard, which provides improved support for flat-file import. You can customize column widths and data types, then preview the result to make sure data isn't truncated. The wizard also lets you specify creation of a new database, a new table, or new columns in an existing table.

SQL Management Objects

SQL Management Objects (SMO) and Replication Management Objects (RMO) replace SQL Distributed Management Objects (SQL-DMO). SMO and RMO are .NET 2.0 assemblies that provide the `Microsoft .SqlServer.Management` and `Microsoft.SqlServer.Replication` namespaces. Both objects deliver improved performance, support new SQL Server 2005 features, and are compatible with SQL Server 2000 and 7.0. SMO eases your transition to the new managed-code version by using SQL-DMO terminology where possible.

You program SMO and DMO operations with VS 2005 by adding .NET references to `Microsoft .SqlServer.Smo` and `MicrosoftSqlServer.Rmo`. Add the references to a sample project and explore the classes with Object Browser to learn more about using managed code to automate SMO or RMO tasks.

SQL Profiler

SQL Server 2005 Profiler is a substantial upgrade to the SQL Server 2000 version. The new Profiler works with Analysis Services, correlates with Performance Monitor, saves Showplans as XML files that you can import into Query Editor, and you can save XML-formatted trace result files to open for replay.

Database Tuning Advisor

The Database Tuning Advisor replaces SQL Server 2000's Index Tuning Wizard, correlates partitioning, and adds the capability to save and import XML files.

Reporting Services

SQL Server 2005 installs SQL Server Reporting Services during the setup process and adds ReportServer and ReportServerTempDB databases to a local or remote SQL Server instance. SQL Express requires you to specify the addition of Reporting Services during the setup process. You create basic reports in Business Intelligence Development Studio by opening a new project and selecting Report Project Wizard from the templates list. Add a data source, select the report type and style, and design a query. For a matrix (crosstab) report, specify query fields as page, row, or column headers and detail items. Figure 10-5 shows a preview of a wizard-generated matrix report based on the OrdersByProduct1997 rollup table that you create in the section "Explore the PIVOT and UNPIVOT Operators," later in this chapter.

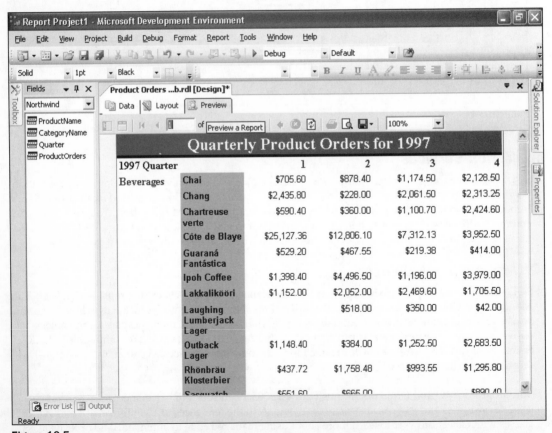

Figure 10-5

BIDS' Report Builder is a graphical design tool that enables end users to design ad hoc reports. In this case, "end users" refers to business managers who want to modify reports but aren't conversant with SQL syntax. Report Builder is based on ActiveViews, a third-party product that Microsoft purchased in early 2004.

CLR Integration

Microsoft cites CLR integration as one of the primary incentives for migrating or upgrading to SQL Server 2005. CLR integration is much more likely to appeal to VS 2005 developers than to DBAs and IT management. Whether production databases will run in-process .NET 2.0 assemblies on a routine basis remains an open question. Acceptance depends on the justification for moving managed code from the middle tier to the database engine to "get closer to the data."

CLR integration isn't enabled by default. Executing SELECT * FROM sys.sysconfigures in the master database and scrolling to config variable 1562 shows a value of 0 after installation. EXECUTE sp_configure returns 0 for config_value and run_value. To enable and verify CLR integration with T-SQL, execute the following statements:

```
EXECUTE sp_configure 'clr enabled', 1
RECONFIGURE
EXECUTE sp_configure
```

VS 2005 lets you write stored procedures, user-defined functions (UDFs), triggers, user-defined types (UDTs), and user-defined aggregates (UDAs) by choosing the SQL Server Project template for a new project and selecting or creating a connection to the target SQL Server 2005 database. SQL Server projects add references to sqlaccess, System, System.Data, and System.Xml namespaces. The Add New Item dialog includes Stored Procedure, User-Defined Type, Aggregate, User-Defined Function, Trigger, and Class Diagram templates. Choosing a template — other than Class Diagram — adds a Public Class or Partial Public Class with Imports statements and stub code for the selected object type. Imports System.Data.SqlServer replaces Imports System.Data.SqlClient for SQL Server classes.

After you've written the code for the classes you want to implement, press F5 to build and deploy the objects to the target database. The objects appear under the appropriate nodes in VS 2005's Server Explorer and SSMS's Object Explorer. Object Explorer's Assemblies node gains an *SqlServerProjectName* item.

As mentioned earlier, Chapter 11 is devoted to creating and deploying SQL Server projects.

The xml Data Type and XQuery Implementation

SQL Server 2005 and earlier versions let you store XML documents in text columns; varchar(max) and nvarchar(max) are SQL Server 2005's preferred data types for long ANSI or Unicode strings. Storing an exact copy of the XML document preserves document hierarchy, element order, and recursive structures. However, the client application must retrieve the entire document to one of .NET 2.0's XML objects — such as XmlReader, XmlDocument, or XPathDocument — to extract individual elements or element groups. If the client application edits the document, the UPDATE operation replaces the entire original version.

An alternative approach is to map the XML document's structure to columns of one or more relational tables from which you obtain an XML view of the data. SQLXML 3.0 or later defines annotated XML schemas (AXSD) for mapping. XPath queries against the XML view return specific XML content. Updategrams, which are similar to the DataSet updategram format, enable INSERT, UPDATE, and DELETE operations on the mapped tables. However, XML views don't preserve element order and don't support recursive schemas, which might be issues for some applications.

SQL Server 2005's new xml data type overcomes the limitations of XML document copies and XML views by providing a native representation of XML documents or fragments, but not both, in a single column. The XML content must be well-formed, but schemas are optional. Assigning a schema to the xml column enables document validation and strong data typing. Adding a primary XML index, which indexes all tags, values, and paths, improves query performance and enables adding secondary indexes on paths, properties, and values. A full-text search on xml columns disregards XML markup, which includes tags and attribute values.

> Chapter 12, "Exploring the xml Data Type," shows you how to load, index, and retrieve data from xml columns.

You can retrieve data from xml columns with T-SQL's implementation of XQuery, such as the following:

```
SELECT Order.value ('(/OrderID)[1]', 'nvarchar(8)'),
    Order.value ('(/CustomerID[1]', 'nvarchar(5)'),
    Orders.value ('(/EmployeeID[1]', 'nvarchar(1)')
FROM Orders
```

The preceding query returns scalar OrderID, CustomerID, and EmployeeID values from Order column documents in all rows of the Orders table. Alternatively, you can use XQuery's FLWOR (for, let, where, orderby, return) syntax, which resembles SQL. SQL Server 2005's XQuery engine doesn't process the let operator, which enables defining variables. The W3C's XQuery 1.0 recommendation doesn't support updates, so Microsoft added proprietary XQuery extensions (XML DML) to enable updating data in xml columns.

Chapter 12 also introduces you to SQL Server 2005's XQuery syntax.SQL Native Client

The SQL Native Client—commonly referred to by the acronym *SNAC*—replaces SQL Server's OLE DB (SQLOLEDB.dll) and ODBC (SQLSRV32.dll) data providers with a single DLL (Sqlncli.dll). SNAC's objective is to eliminate the need to update the MDAC stack to accommodate new SQL Server 2005 features. Sqlncli.dll doesn't require clients to install MDAC 2.8 or 2.9; MDAC 2.5 SP3 or later is sufficient. You can upgrade Windows 2000 and later clients with the redistributable Windows Installer version (Sqlncli.msi), which is included on the SQL Server 2005 installation CD-ROM and available for download from MSDN.

> Managed data providers don't use SNAC, which is intended for downlevel applications only.

SNAC enables ActiveX Data Objects (classic ADO) applications to handle new SQL Server 2005 objects and data types, such as user-defined types (UDTs) and xml, varchar(max), nvarchar(max), and varbinary(max) columns. It also lets Microsoft Office applications that rely on ODBC, such as Access (for importing data from or linking SQL Server tables to Jet databases), substitute SQL Native Client for the aging SQL Server ODBC provider. SQL Native Client appears above SQL Server in the Create New Data Source dialog's list of ODBC drivers. Selecting SNAC substitutes `DRIVER={SQL Native Client}` for `DRIVER={SQL Server}` in the ODBC connection string. Figure 10-6 shows the last step in the process of linking SQL Server 2005 AdventureWorks tables to an Access 2003 Jet database with SNAC.

Figure 10-6

Access 2003 displays values from linked tables' xml *and* datatype(max) *columns as Text fields with a maximum length of 255 characters. You receive an error message when you attempt to update a linked table that contains an* xml *column. You can create an Access data project from an existing SQL Server 2005 database, but you can't use Design view to modify table structures. The next Access version might support new SQL Server 2005 data types correctly, but managing the* xml *datatype will be a challenge.*

Multiple Active Result Sets (MARS)

SQL Server 2005's new MARS feature lets you execute multiple SqlDataReaders on a single connection. MARS appears to be more of a marketing than a developer feature; Oracle databases have offered a MARS equivalent in the last several versions. MARS also lets you open one or more SqlDataReaders from SqlCommands and execute UPDATE, INSERT, or DELETE statements from separate SqlCommands. In this case, your code can update tables while the SqlDataReader iterates them.

You enable MARS by adding `;MultipleActiveResultSets=True` to the end of your current connection string. Similarly, disable MARS explicitly with a `;MultipleActiveResultSets=False` name-value pair. MARS prevents "There is already an open DataReader ..." messages when you execute multiple SqlCommands simultaneously.

Microsoft's Angel Saenz-Badillos MARS is concerned that "this feature is going to be misused" by .NET developers (`http://blogs.msdn.com/angelsb/archive/2004/09/07/226597.aspx`). MARS improves performance compared with multiple pooled connections only in a very limited range of scenarios. Otherwise, MARS is likely to exact a performance penalty. Saenz-Badillos also casts a jaundiced eye on session pooling_the technique used to implement MARS_in a related blog post (http://blogs .msdn.com/angelsb/archive/2005/01/13/352718.aspx). The general consensus of Microsoft and independent developers is: Unless you *must* process simultaneous commands on a single connection, don't use MARS in production projects.

> The "Multiple Active Result Set (MARS) in SQL Server 2005" white paper (`http://msdn .microsoft.com/library/en-us/dnsql90/html/MARSinSQL05.asp`) provides a detailed description of data access with MARS and the SQL Server native provider.

Data Availability and Reliability Enhancements

It's a common practice to partition tables of very large databases. For example, many DBAs divide transactional databases into active (current month) and historical (prior months) partitions. SQL Server 2005's new approach to table partitioning places all partitions in a single table with specific filegroups that correspond to the partitioning key value. This approach simplifies partition and query design, reduces partition maintenance, and improves query performance. T-SQL's CREATE PARTITION FUNCTION statement establishes the number and domain of the partitions of a partitioned table or index. CREATE PARTITION SCHEME statement maps a partitioned table's partitions or index to the filegroups you specify.

Database mirroring lets you create hot-standby database servers that can substitute for failover clusters and are much easier to manage. You can mirror databases to a remote location for disaster recovery. You also can combine failover clusters and database mirroring to achieve super-high availability. To configure a database for mirroring, open the database's Properties dialog and select the Mirroring page. You can select Synchronous with Automatic Failover, Asynchronous, or Synchronous mirroring modes. Asynchronous mirroring improves update performance at the expense of full data integrity when substituting the mirror for the principal instance. Automatic Failover requires an SQL Server 2005 witness instance to monitor the status of the principal and mirror instances and control the failover.

Members of the sysadmins role can use a dedicated Admin connection when the target server won't accept new connections. To open a dedicated Admin connection from SSMS, type **ADMIN:**_ServerName_ as the Server Name value in the Connect to Server dialog.

T-SQL and Database Engine Enhancements

SQL Server 2005 implements most ANSI SQL-99 elements and a few ANSI SQL-2003 elements, such as the bigint data type, windowed functions (RANK() OVER, DENSE_RANK() OVER, and ROW_NUMBER() OVER), and TABLESAMPLE. SQL Server 2005 continues to use proprietary features rather than ANSI SQL-2003 elements, such as SQL/XML. SQL/XML has nothing in common with Microsoft SQLXML 3.0 or the new xml data type.

The following sections provide brief descriptions and generic syntax examples of SQL Server 2005's new T-SQL and related database engine features. Later sections include working examples of the more important SQL Server 2005 T-SQL additions with sample SQL scripts and Windows form clients.

The following and later sections' sample queries require attaching the Northwind database to your SQL Server 2005 instance. You can download the scripts to create the Northwind and pubs sample databases from a link on the http://www.microsoft.com/sql/downloads/ *page. The* \VB2005DB\ *Chapter10\T-SQLEnhancements folder contains the sample T-SQL scripts. For more extensive coverage of SQL Server 2005's T-SQL enhancements, see "Take Advantage of New T-SQL Features"* (http://www.ftponline.com/vsm/2005_09/magazine/columns/databasedesign/).

TRY . . . CATCH Exception Handling

Structured BEGIN TRY...END TRY and BEGIN CATCH and END CATCH blocks replace traditional T-SQL IF @@ERROR <> 0 tests. CATCH blocks can use any or all of these new system functions: ERROR_MESSAGE, ERROR_NUMBER, ERROR_SEVERITY, and ERROR_STATE. These functions return NULL if executed outside a CATCH block. The BEGIN CATCH statement must be on the line following the END TRY statement, as shown here:

```
BEGIN TRY
    -- Batch statements
END TRY
BEGIN CATCH
    -- Error handling statements, typically
    SELECT ERROR_NUMBER() AS ErrorNumber,
        ERROR_LINE() AS ErrorLine,
        PROCEDURE() As ProcedureName,
        ERROR_SEVERITY() AS ErrorSeverity,
        ERROR_STATE() as ErrorState,
        ERROR_MESSAGE() as ErrorMessage;
END CATCH
```

You can nest TRY...CATCH blocks with the following generic T-SQL statement:

```
BEGIN TRY
    -- Outer level statements
END TRY
BEGIN CATCH
    -- Outer level error handling statements
    BEGIN TRY
    -- Inner level statements
    END TRY
    BEGIN CATCH
    -- Inner level error handling statements
    END CATCH
END CATCH
```

Following is an example of a simple DELETE query (TryCatchBlocks.sql) with a TRY...CATCH block:

```
USE Northwind;
GO
BEGIN TRAN;
GO
```

```
BEGIN TRY
    -- Causes a constraint violation on the Order Details table.
    DELETE FROM Products WHERE ProductID = 15;
END TRY
BEGIN CATCH
    SELECT ERROR_NUMBER() AS ErrorNumber,
        ERROR_SEVERITY() AS ErrorSeverity,
        ERROR_STATE() as ErrorState,
        ERROR_MESSAGE() as ErrorMessage;
END CATCH
GO
ROLLBACK TRAN;
GO
```

The preceding query returns a rowset with 547 as ErrorNumber, 16 as ErrorSeverity, 0 as ErrorState, and `DELETE statement conflicted with REFERENCE constraint 'FK_Order_Details_Products'.` `The conflict occurred in database 'Northwind', table 'Order Details', column` `'ProductID'.` as ErrorMessage column values.

> *The* CATCH *block doesn't trap warnings or errors with a severity level greater than 20, which usually terminate the connection.*

PIVOT and UNPIVOT Operators

The PIVOT operator rotates a table's columns and rows to generate summary crosstab reports. PIVOT adds columns that you specify by an IN predicate list. The IN predicate matches — and usually aggregates — unique values of the column specified by the FOR operator in columns added to the SELECT statement. The resulting rowset is identical to that produced by an Access crosstab query and is similar to a static Excel PivotTable.

Here's the generalized syntax of the PIVOT and FOR operators:

```
SELECT RowHeader1, RowHeader2, ... ColValue1 AS ColHeader1,
    ColValue2 AS ColHeader2, ColValue3 AS ColHeader3, ...
FROM TableName
PIVOT (Aggregate(ValueColName) FOR ValueSourceColName
    IN(ColValue1, ColValue2, ColValue3, ...))
```

The PIVOT operator replaces the complex SQL statements required by earlier SQL Server versions to generate crosstab tables. Unlike Access crosstabs, which can generate the added columns from an expression, PIVOT operators require a specified set of column header names.

> *The section "Explore the PIVOT and UNPIVOT Operators," later in this chapter, has examples for creating a crosstab table and normalizing the crosstab table by converting the repeating columns to rows.*

SNAPSHOT Transaction Isolation

SQL 2005 introduces a new SNAPSHOT transaction isolation level, which implements an optimistic concurrency error detection method that isn't in the ANSI SQL-99 specification. Each SNAPSHOT transaction behaves as if it has received a copy of the data that was committed when the first statement after BEGIN TRANSACTION executes. SNAPSHOT isolation doesn't request read locks during execution, so it increases data availability when compared to SQL Server's default READ COMMITTED isolation. READ COMMITTED isolation holds locks on all data read by the transaction for its duration and implements pessimistic concurrency.

> *Pessimistic concurrency with READ COMMITTED isolation doesn't apply to DataSet updates with optimistic concurrency specified for DELETE, INSERT, and UPDATE commands. In this case, stored procedures or SQL statements manage concurrency conflicts.*

SNAPSHOT is the only isolation level that implements optimistic concurrency by row versioning and isn't subject to dirty or non-repeatable reads, or phantom rows. A SNAPSHOT transaction won't commit if a second transaction on another connection modifies the same data after the first transaction starts and before it completes.

> *For detailed information on row versioning, see Books Online's "Isolation Levels in the Database Engine" and "Choosing Row Versioning" topics.*

Enabling SNAPSHOT transactions within a database requires executing an ALTER DATABASE Name SET ALLOW_SNAPSHOT_ISOLATION ON statement, which enables row versioning. You issue a T-SQL SET TRANSACTION_LEVEL SNAPSHOT statement or execute ADO.NET 2.0's SqlConnection .BeginTransaction(IsolationLevel.Snapshot) instruction to create a snapshot transaction object.

You can force READ COMMITTED isolation to use row versioning by issuing a T-SQL SET READ_COMMITTED _SNAPSHOT ON statement, which changes READ COMMITTED isolation to optimistic concurrency, but permits non-repeatable reads and phantom rows.

Row versioning is best suited to scenarios where read operations predominate over transacted updates and the probability of concurrency conflicts is low. Row versioning consumes additional resources and adds 14 bytes to each row header. The tempdb database stores row versions, so I/O operations between the user database and tempdb might affect transaction performance.

TOP n and TABLESAMPLE Operators

The TOP operator now supports a numeric variable value, in addition to an explicit number for TOP (n) rows or TOP (n) PERCENT. The parentheses are required if you specify a variable, which SQL Server 2005 converts to bigint for TOP (n) or float for TOP (n) PERCENT. You can pass the variable as a parameter to SQL queries or stored procedures, which eliminates the need for dynamic SQL or individual SELECT statements in stored procedures to support multiple values.

The FROM clause's TABLESAMPLE operator resembles the TOP operator but returns a random sampling of rows from a query. SELECT * FROM TableName TABLESAMPLE SYSTEM (10 ROWS) [REPEATABLE (n)] returns a representative set of about ten rows. SELECT * FROM TableName TABLESAMPLE SYSTEM (25 PERCENT) [REPEATABLE (n)] returns all rows from 25 percent of the pages. Thus, the number of rows is approximately 25 percent. The TABLESAMPLE operator is useful for quickly estimating aggregate values from tables with a very large number of records.

As an example, the following T-SQL expression (OrdersTablesample.sql returns two resultsets from the 840-row Orders table:

```
USE Northwind;
GO
SELECT * FROM Orders TABLESAMPLE SYSTEM (10 PERCENT) REPEATABLE (1);
GO
SELECT * FROM Orders TABLESAMPLE SYSTEM (84 ROWS) REPEATABLE (2);
GO
```

Tests show the first resultset has 79 rows and the second has 83 rows; you're likely to receive different numbers of rows when you execute the preceding query.

Rank and Windowed Table Functions

Rank and windowed table functions return row number values. The following query (ProductsRank.sql) generates RANK(), DENSE_RANK(), and ROW_NUMBER() values for the Northwind Products table's UnitPrice column:

```
USE Northwind
GO
SELECT ProductID, ProductName, UnitPrice,
RANK() OVER (ORDER BY UnitPrice DESC) AS Rank,
DENSE_RANK() OVER (ORDER BY UnitPrice DESC) AS DenseRank,
ROW_NUMBER() OVER (ORDER BY UnitPrice DESC) AS RowNumber
FROM Products
GO
```

This table represents a subset of the preceding query's resultset that demonstrates the difference between RANK() and DENSE_RANK().

ProductID	ProductName	UnitPrice	Rank	DenseRank	RowNumber
43	Ipoh Coffee	46.00	9	9	9
28	Rössle Sauerkraut	45.60	10	10	10
27	Schoggi Schokolade	43.90	11	11	11
63	Vegie-spread	43.90	11	11	12
8	Northwoods Cranberry Sauce	40.00	13	12	13
17	Alice Mutton	39.00	14	13	14
12	Queso Manchego La Pastora	38.00	15	14	15
56	Gnocchi di nonna Alice	38.00	15	14	16
69	Gudbrandsdalsost	36.00	17	15	17

RANK() and DENSE_RANK() designate ties with the same value, as illustrated by row numbers 11 and 12, and 15 and 16. RANK() values have gaps in the ranking after encountering ties; DENSE_RANK() generates sequential values (no gaps) following ties.

You can add the PARTITION ColumnName operator to window (group) rankings and row numbers into groups based on unique values in *ColumnName*. Ranking and row numbers start over for each new partition. The following query (ProductsPartition.sql) partitions the preceding resultset by CategoryID values:

```
USE Northwind
GO
SELECT CategoryID, ProductID, ProductName, UnitPrice,
RANK() OVER (PARTITION BY CategoryID ORDER BY UnitPrice DESC) AS Rank,
DENSE_RANK() OVER (PARTITION BY CategoryID ORDER BY UnitPrice DESC) AS DenseRank,
ROW_NUMBER() OVER (PARTITION BY CategoryID ORDER BY UnitPrice DESC) AS RowNumber
FROM Products
GO
```

The following subset of the preceding query's resultset illustrates the effect of adding PARTITION BY CategoryID to the query.

	ProductID	ProductName	UnitPrice	Rank	DenseRank	RowNumber
1	70	Outback Lager	15.00	8	5	8
1	67	Laughing Lumberjack Lager	14.00	9	6	9
1	34	Sasquatch Ale	14.00	9	6	10
1	75	Rhönbräu Klosterbier	7.75	11	7	11
1	24	Guaraná Fantástica	4.50	12	8	12
2	63	Vegie-spread	43.90	1	1	1
2	8	Northwoods Cranberry Sauce	40.00	2	2	2
2	61	Sirop d'érable	28.50	3	3	3
2	6	Grandma's Boysenberry Spread	25.00	4	4	4
2	4	Chef Anton's Cajun Seasoning	22.00	5	5	5

You can further subdivide partitions into n groups (buckets) of approximately the same number of rows by adding an NTILE(n) OVER (...) expression, which returns the consecutive group number 1...n. Aggregate expressions in the SELECT list preclude use of the ORDER BY clause.

Common Table Expressions and Recursive Queries

Common table expressions (CTEs) are temporary, in-memory table objects that can reference themselves. Recursive CTEs enable recursive queries, which typically return tables containing hierarchical data. A recursive query has a minimum of two SELECT statements; the first creates the anchor member, and the second defines the recursive member. Recursion terminates when no more records are added by the recursive member.

You create a CTE by executing WITH CTEName (ColumnList) AS (SELECT statement) to return the anchor member row(s). Recursive CTE's add UNION ALL and a second SELECT statement to return the recursive rows. The following recursive query (EmployeeDirectReportsCTE.sql) returns Northwind employee FirstName and LastName, EmployeeID, and ReportsTo ID values:

```
USE Northwind
GO
WITH DirectReports (Name, EmployeeID, ReportsTo) AS
--Anchor member
(SELECT FirstName + ' ' + LastName, EmployeeID, ReportsTo
FROM Employees
WHERE ReportsTo IS NULL
UNION ALL
--Recursive member
SELECT emp.FirstName + ' ' + emp.LastName, emp.EmployeeID, emp.ReportsTo
FROM Employees emp INNER JOIN DirectReports dr
ON emp.ReportsTo = dr.EmployeeID)

SELECT * FROM DirectReports;
GO
```

The section "Replace the Source Table with a Common Table Expression," later in this chapter, illustrates use of a CTE with the new PIVOT operator.

FOR XML Enhancements

The most significant new FOR XML feature is the capability to generate nested queries with the TYPE directive, which returns an xml type for inner, outer, or both queries. Adding the TYPE directive to both queries lets you populate xml columns with individual fragments of the structure that you define by the FOR XML AUTO clause.

As an example, the following query (NestedQueryType.sql) returns a nested structure of element-centric Orders fragments as an xml type:

```
USE Northwind
GO
SELECT TOP 10 OrderID, CustomerID, EmployeeID, OrderDate,
   (SELECT ProductID, CONVERT(decimal(6,2), UnitPrice) as UnitPrice, Quantity,
    CONVERT (decimal(3,3), Discount) As Discount
    FROM [Order Details] AS OrderDetail
    WHERE OrderDetail.OrderID = Orders.OrderID
    FOR XML AUTO, ELEMENTS, TYPE)
FROM Orders
ORDER BY OrderID DESC
FOR XML AUTO, ELEMENTS, TYPE
GO
```

Following is a subset of the Orders fragments (NestedQueryType.xml) returned by the preceding query:

```
<Orders>
  <OrderID>11076</OrderID>
  <CustomerID>BONAP</CustomerID>
  <EmployeeID>4</EmployeeID>
  <OrderDate>1998-05-06T00:00:00</OrderDate>
  <OrderDetail>
    <ProductID>6</ProductID>
    <UnitPrice>25.00</UnitPrice>
    <Quantity>20</Quantity>
    <Discount>0.250</Discount>
```

```
      </OrderDetail>
      <OrderDetail>
        <ProductID>14</ProductID>
        <UnitPrice>23.25</UnitPrice>
        <Quantity>20</Quantity>
        <Discount>0.250</Discount>
      </OrderDetail>
      <OrderDetail>
        <ProductID>19</ProductID>
        <UnitPrice>9.20</UnitPrice>
        <Quantity>10</Quantity>
        <Discount>0.250</Discount>
      </OrderDetail>
    </Orders>
    <Orders>
      <OrderID>11075</OrderID>
      <CustomerID>RICSU</CustomerID>
      <EmployeeID>8</EmployeeID>
      <OrderDate>1998-05-06T00:00:00</OrderDate>
      <OrderDetail>
        <ProductID>2</ProductID>
        <UnitPrice>19.00</UnitPrice>
        <Quantity>10</Quantity>
        <Discount>0.150</Discount>
      </OrderDetail>
      <OrderDetail>
        <ProductID>46</ProductID>
        <UnitPrice>12.00</UnitPrice>
        <Quantity>30</Quantity>
        <Discount>0.150</Discount>
      </OrderDetail>
      <OrderDetail>
        <ProductID>76</ProductID>
        <UnitPrice>18.00</UnitPrice>
        <Quantity>2</Quantity>
        <Discount>0.150</Discount>
      </OrderDetail>
    </Orders>
```

Some sample XML document files in the \VB2005DB\Chapter10\T-SQLEnhacements folder have a top level <addedRoot> *element to enable viewing the documents in IE.*

You can combine an element-centric representation of the outer query with an attribute-centric inner query by omitting the ELEMENTS directive from the inner query. Here's the same subset (NestedQueryMixed.xml) returned by NestedQueryMixed.sql:

```
<Orders>
  <OrderID>11076</OrderID>
  <CustomerID>BONAP</CustomerID>
  <EmployeeID>4</EmployeeID>
  <OrderDate>1998-05-06T00:00:00</OrderDate>
  <OrderDetail ProductID="6" UnitPrice="25.00" Quantity="20" Discount="0.25" />
  <OrderDetail ProductID="14" UnitPrice="23.25" Quantity="20" Discount="0.25" />
  <OrderDetail ProductID="19" UnitPrice="9.20" Quantity="10" Discount="0.25" />
</Orders>
```

```
<Orders>
  <OrderID>11075</OrderID>
  <CustomerID>RICSU</CustomerID>
  <EmployeeID>8</EmployeeID>
  <OrderDate>1998-05-06T00:00:00</OrderDate>
  <OrderDetail ProductID="2" UnitPrice="19.00" Quantity="10" Discount="0.15" />
  <OrderDetail ProductID="46" UnitPrice="12.00" Quantity="30" Discount="0.15" />
  <OrderDetail ProductID="76" UnitPrice="18.00" Quantity="2" Discount="0.15" />
</Orders>
```

If you don't add a `TYPE` *directive to the inner query,* `FOR XML AUTO` *escapes (entitizes) the inner query's tag brackets, which creates well-formed but useless fragments (NestedQueryElements.xml). Thus, the* `TYPE` *directive is essential for at least the inner query of nested queries.*

Other new `FOR XML` features include the ability to add an inline XML schema with an optional namespace by adding an `XMLSCHEMA('namespace')` directive, specify a root element name for inner and outer queries with `ROOT('elementName')`, and use the `ELEMENT` directive's `XSINIL` parameter to replace missing `NULL`-valued elements with `<elementName xsi:nil="true" />` elements. The new `FOR XML` `PATH` mode lets you designate individual query columns as elements or attributes.

The `XMLSCHEMA` *directive is limited to* `FOR XML AUTO` *and* `FOR XML RAW` *modes. The* `ROOT` *directive applies only to* `FOR XML RAW` *and* `FOR XML PATH` *queries.*

The later "Customize FOR XML Queries" section shows you how to take advantage of these new features and describes some of their limitations.

DDL Triggers

New Data Definition Language (DDL) triggers fire on execution of `CREATE`, `ALTER`, or `DROP` statements. DDL triggers give admins precise control over users' DDL permissions for specific objects or generate detailed audit events for object creation, modification, or deletion.

Data Encryption with Symmetric or Asymmetric Keys

SQL Server 2005 Developer Edition and higher provides column-level and cell-based data encryption to enable conformance with government-mandated security regulations, such as the federal Health Insurance Portability and Accountability Act (HIPAA). Data encryption also exempts organizations from the provisions of California's Information Practices Act (SB 1386). Hierarchical encryption and key management services rely on a Service Master Key for an SQL Server instance and a Database Master Key for each database that contains encrypted data. Installing SQL Server creates the master system database's Service Master Key automatically.

You must execute `CREATE MASTER KEY ENCRYPTION BY PASSWORD = 'strong_password'` to create a TRIPLE_DES-encrypted Database Master Key. You can encrypt specific cleartext data as varbinary ciphertext with an asymmetric key, an X.509v3 certificate, or a symmetric key. Symmetric key encryption with a strong password offers the best performance; asymmetric keys and certificates aren't recommended for encrypting or decrypting data in table columns.

Data encryption is beyond the scope of this chapter. Search Books Online for encrypt *with SQL Server Database Engine as the Technology filter for a complete list of encryption-related T-SQL topics. You can read the online article, "Encrypt and Decrypt Data in Yukon," about SQL Server 2005 encryption and download a sample VB 2005 encryption project at* http://www.ftponline.com/ vsm/2005_08/magazine/features/rjennings/.

Service Broker

Service Broker is a new feature that provides reliable asynchronous transactional messaging between local or remote databases. Databases persist sets of related messages, called *conversations*, which ensure that messages survive restarts or failovers and are preserved in backups. Messages between two databases (one-to-one messages) are called *dialogs*. Service Broker and Microsoft Message Queue (MSMQ) have similar architectures. MSMQ supports messaging between Windows applications; Service broker supports messaging within and between instances of SQL Server. Service Broker is especially efficient for managing interactions between stored procedures and handling asynchronous interactions within a database, such as asynchronous triggers. Several other new SQL Server 2005 features, such as query notification services and Database Mail, depend on the Service Broker infrastructure.

SQL Server 2005 Express can receive Service Broker messages from and send messages to SQL Server 2005 Developer Edition or higher instances but can't use Service Broker to communicate with other SQL Server 2005 Express instances.

Set Up a Northwind Service Broker

Creating a simple, one-way Service Broker for the Northwind database involves the following steps:

1. Enable Service Broker in the database by executing an ALTER DATABASE Northwind SET ENABLE_BROKER statement.

2. Define an XML MESSAGE TYPE with a CREATE MESSAGE TYPE NwindXmlMessage VALIDATION = WELL_FORMED_XML; statement.

3. Define a one-way CONTRACT with a CREATE CONTRACT NwindContract (NwindXmlMessage SENT BY INITIATOR); statement.

4. Create a QUEUE for the INITIATOR of the message with a CREATE QUEUE dbo .NwindInitiatorQueue; statement.

5. Specify a SERVICE for the INITIATOR by executing a CREATE SERVICE NwindInitiatorService ON QUEUE dbo.NwindInitiatorQueue; statement.

6. Specify a QUEUE for the message destination with a CREATE QUEUE dbo.NwindTargetQueue; statement.

7. Specify a SERVICE for the destination by executing a CREATE SERVICE NwindTargetService ON QUEUE dbo.NwindTargetQueue (NwindContract); statement.

Here's the T-SQL batch statement:

```
USE Northwind;
GO
ALTER DATABASE Northwind SET ENABLE_BROKER;
GO
CREATE MESSAGE TYPE NwindXmlMessage VALIDATION = WELL_FORMED_XML;
GO
CREATE CONTRACT NwindContract (NwindXmlMessage SENT BY INITIATOR);
GO
CREATE QUEUE dbo.NwindInitiatorQueue;
GO
CREATE SERVICE NwindInitiatorService ON QUEUE dbo.NwindInitiatorQueue;
GO
CREATE QUEUE dbo.NwindTargetQueue;
GO
CREATE SERVICE NwindTargetService ON QUEUE dbo.NwindTargetQueue (NwindContract);
```

The preceding batch query is ServiceBrokerSetup.sql in the \VB2005DB\Chapter10\ServiceBroker folder. This folder contains the batch queries listed in this and the following sections.

Send an XML Message

After you create the required Service Broker elements with the ServiceBrokerSetup.sql batch, run the following batch (ServiceBrokerSendMessage.sql) to start a transaction and send a well-formed XML message to its destination queue when the transaction commits:

```
USE Northwind;
GO
BEGIN TRANSACTION;
GO
DECLARE @MessageXML XML;
SET @MessageXML = N'<messageXml>Message from the Northwind database</messageXml>';
DECLARE @conversationGUID UNIQUEIDENTIFIER;
BEGIN DIALOG CONVERSATION @conversationGUID
    FROM SERVICE NwindInitiatorService
    TO SERVICE 'NwindTargetService'
    ON CONTRACT NwindContract;
SEND ON CONVERSATION @conversationGUID MESSAGE TYPE NwindXmlMessage(@MessageXML);
END CONVERSATION @conversationGUID;
GO
COMMIT TRANSACTION;
GO
SELECT * FROM dbo.NwindTargetQueue;
GO
```

Figure 10-7 shows SSMS displaying the preceding query and the queue grid after sending the preceding message. The second message contains an empty schema for the XML message.

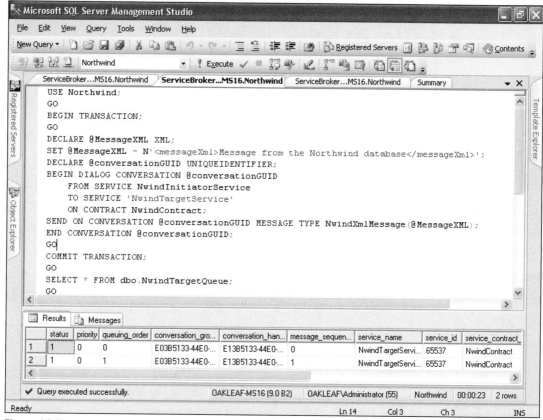

Figure 10-7

Retrieve the Message from the Queue

Run the following batch (ServiceBrokerReceiveMessages.sql) to receive the message you created with
ServiceBrokerSendMessage.sql:

```
USE Northwind;
GO
WHILE (1 = 1)
BEGIN
    DECLARE @conversation_handle UNIQUEIDENTIFIER,
            @conversation_group_id UNIQUEIDENTIFIER,
            @message_body XML,
            @message_type_name NVARCHAR(128);
    BEGIN TRANSACTION;
    WAITFOR(GET CONVERSATION GROUP @conversation_group_id
        FROM dbo.NwindTargetQueue), TIMEOUT 500;
    IF @conversation_group_id IS NULL
        BEGIN
            ROLLBACK TRANSACTION;
            BREAK;
        END;
    WHILE (1 = 1)
    BEGIN
```

```
        RECEIVE TOP(1)
            @conversation_handle = conversation_handle,
            @message_type_name = message_type_name,
            @message_body = CAST(message_body AS XML)
        FROM dbo.NwindTargetQueue
        WHERE conversation_group_id = @conversation_group_id;
        IF @@ROWCOUNT = 0 OR @@ERROR <> 0 BREAK;
        SELECT 'Conversation Group Id' = @conversation_group_id,
               'Conversation Handle' = @conversation_handle,
               'Message Type Name' = @message_type_name,
               'Message Body' = @message_body;
        IF @message_type_name =
                'http://schemas.microsoft.com/SQL/ServiceBroker/EndDialog'
            OR @message_type_name =
                'http://schemas.microsoft.com/SQL/ServiceBroker/Error'
        BEGIN
            END CONVERSATION @conversation_handle;
        END;
    END;
    COMMIT TRANSACTION;
END;
```

Figure 10-8 shows part of the preceding query and the grid after receiving the message.

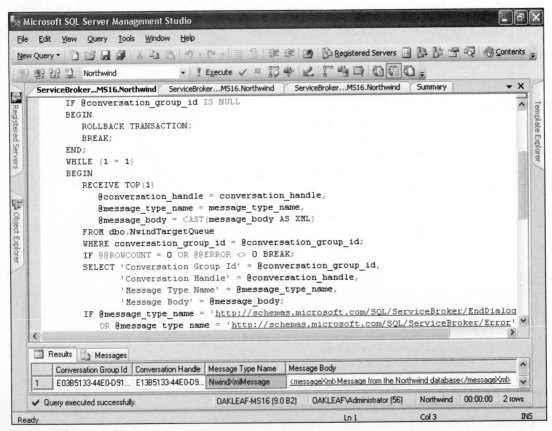

Figure 10-8

The Database Engine Samples' ServiceBroker group includes three sample Service Broker applications. The preceding examples are derived from the HelloWorld SQL Server Management Studio project (HelloWorld.ssmssln), which includes detailed comments for most statements of the similar ServiceBroker... .sql queries.

> *To install the Database Engine Samples from their .msi files, choose Microsoft SQL Server 2005 ⇨ Install Samples ⇨ SQL Server Database Engine Samples. The \Program Files\Microsoft SQL Server\ 90\Tools\Samples\1033\Engine\Service Broker folder contains subfolders with the sample files.*

> *To remove the Nwind... Service Broker objects that you created, execute the DropServiceBrokerObjects .sql query.*

Event Notifications

SQL Server 2005 event notifications create one or more Service Broker conversations between the SQL Server 2005 instance and a service you specify. Event notifications can log or review database changes or other activities and can perform a specified action in response to a particular event. For example, you can create an event notification that's an asynchronous equivalent to a DDL trigger. You also can perform asynchronous operations in response to SQL Trace events. Event notification programming is beyond the scope of this chapter.

Notification Services

Notification Services integrate SQL Server 2000 Notification Services 2.0 components into an enhanced native service that's included with SQL Server 2005 Developer Edition or higher. If you're familiar with Notification Services 2.0, native Notification Services programming methodology and basic architecture are similar.

> *Programming Notification Services is beyond the scope of this chapter. The SQL Server 2005 Database Engine Samples include several Notification Services sample projects with C# and VB versions. The \Program Files\Microsoft SQL Server\90\Tools\Samples\1033\Engine\Notification Services folder contains four subfolders with the sample project files.*

Query Notifications

SQL Server 2005 query notifications aren't related to Notification Service's event notifications, other than by common use of the Service Broker. Query notifications enable client applications to request notifications when table updates result in a change to the resultset of a specified query or indexed view. Thus query notifications are related to event notifications.

Query notifications eliminate unnecessary roundtrips to maintain lookup table and catalog data currency. The primary application for query notifications is invalidating ASP.NET 2.0's SqlCacheDependency objects that you add to the Response object. Prior to SQL Server 2005 and .NET 2.0, invalidating the cache required triggers or timers.

You also can use query notifications to trigger a Fill operation on a TableAdapter or execute an SqlDataReader object that repopulates a DataTable. The database stores notification subscriptions when a client program executes an ADO.NET 2.0 SqlCommand bound to an SqlDependency object with a handler for its OnChange event. Data modifications that affect the query you specified as the

`SqlCommand.CommandText` property value cause SQL Server 2005 to place a message in a previously defined queue, which fires the `SqlDependency.OnChange` event. Alternatively, you can program the client to poll periodically for an `SqlNotificationRequest`.

The section "Process Query Notifications," later in this chapter, describes a Windows form that processes notifications of changes to one or more of three Northwind Products table columns.

Database Mail

SQL Server 2000 mail options—SQLMail and AgentMail—use the Extended Messaging API (MAPI), which doesn't have a 64-bit version. AgentMail supports 64-bit Simple MAPI, but both require Exchange Server. SQLMail requires Outlook 2000 or later on the server and won't run on a cluster. SQLMail and AgentMail are deprecated, and might not be included in SQL Server versions beyond 2005.

Database Mail overcomes the MAPI issues by replacing the `xp_sendmail` extended stored procedure with `sendimail_sp`, which has a similar parameter set. Database Mail requires you to use the Database Mail Setup Wizard to establish a mail host database for the SQL Sever 2005 instance and a profile with at least one designated SMTP e-mail account. When you execute `sendmail_sp` it adds the message to a Service Broker queue; Service Broker then runs an instance of DatabaseMail90.exe to send the message and archives it in the `dbo.sysmail_mailitems` database. Multiple DatabaseMail90.exe instances run outside the SQL Server process, which greatly improves messaging scalability. However, there's no Database Mail equivalent to SQLMail's `xp_readmail` extended stored procedure in SQL Server 2005. Microsoft promises `readimail_sp` or its equivalent in a later SQL Server version.

The section "Automate Reorder Processing with Database Mail," near the end of the chapter, describes a Database Mail implementation within a query notifications demonstration project.

SQL Server Native SOAP Web Services

SQL Server 2000 and earlier rely on the Tabular Data Stream (TDS) protocol to communicate with clients. TDS requires Windows clients to have an MDAC stack installed; other operating systems require a JDBC or ODBC driver. SQL Server 2005 adds native SOAP Web services. This feature, like the SQLXML 3.0 SOAP Web services you create with the IIS Virtual Directory Management for SQL Server snap-in, eliminates the need for MDAC but requires clients to implement a Web service proxy. Native SOAP Web services substitute the kernel-mode HTTP.sys driver for IIS, which limits service deployment to machines running Windows XP SP2 or Windows Server 2003. Unlike SQLXML 3.0 or ASP.NET Web services, native SOAP Web services don't support anonymous access; all requests must be authenticated. SQL Server 2005 supports integrated Windows or WS-Security authentication. WS-Security authentication requires installing the Web Service Enhancements (WSE) 3.0 runtime on machines running VS2005 Windows form clients.

Native SOAP Web services are based on SQL Server 2005 endpoints, which support SOAP, database mirroring, Service Broker, and T-SQL payloads with HTTP and TCP protocols. It's likely SOAP payloads over the HTTP protocol will represent at least 90 percent of all production SQL Server endpoints.

To learn more about WSE 3.0 and WS-Security, go to `http://msdn.microsoft.com/webservices/building/wse/`.

Native SOAP Web services let clients execute T-SQL or CLR stored procedures, UDFs that return scalar values, or ad hoc SQL queries with or without parameters. The default format for a SELECT statement's SOAP response messages is an `<SqlRowSet>` element in diffgram format, which VS interprets as a

DataSet; adding the DataSet's inline schema is optional. SELECT...FOR XML queries return <SqlXml> elements and add as inline schema if you include the XMLSCHEMA modifier in the FOR XML clause.

The CREATE ENDPOINT command registers one or more HTTP URL namespaces, such as http://servername/servicename with HTTP.sys. You specify servername as the SITE parameter and /servicename with the PATH parameter. By default, HTTP.sys listens for and receives requests on TCP ports 80 and 443, but you can specify custom port numbers with the CLEAR_PORT = number and CLEAR_PORT = number parameters. You can specify BASIC, DIGEST, INTEGRATED, or a comma-separated combination, as the transport AUTHENTICATION parameter; INTEGRATED is the simplest method for Windows clients. Add COMPRESSION = ENABLED to use gzip encoding if the client's SOAP request specifies gzip in its accept-encoding HTTP header and SESSIONS = ENABLED to maintain session state between multiple SOAP message pairs.

Specify WebMethods by adding FOR SOAP (WEBMETHOD...) clauses for stored procedures and scalar UDFs; WEBMETHODs don't support table-returning UDFs. The following T-SQL batch creates a SOAP HTTP endpoint with methods for four of the Northwind database's stored procedures and enables ad hoc batch queries:

```
CREATE ENDPOINT NorthwindEP
STATE = STARTED
AS HTTP(
    PATH = '/wsnwindep',
    AUTHENTICATION = (INTEGRATED),
    PORTS = (CLEAR),
    SITE = 'localhost',
    COMPRESSION = ENABLED
    )
FOR SOAP (
    WEBMETHOD 'TenMostExpensiveProducts'
        (NAME = 'Northwind.dbo.[Ten Most Expensive Products]',
         FORMAT = ROWSETS_ONLY, SCHEMA = STANDARD),
    WEBMETHOD 'SalesByCategory'
        (NAME='Northwind.dbo.SalesByCategory',
         FORMAT = ROWSETS_ONLY, SCHEMA = STANDARD),
    WEBMETHOD 'EmployeeSalesByCountry'
        (NAME='Northwind.dbo.[Employee Sales by Country]',
         FORMAT = ROWSETS_ONLY, SCHEMA = STANDARD),
    WEBMETHOD 'CustomerOrderHistory'
        (NAME='Northwind.dbo.CustOrderHist',
         FORMAT = ROWSETS_ONLY, SCHEMA = STANDARD),
    BATCHES = ENABLED,
    WSDL = DEFAULT,
    DATABASE = 'Northwind',
    NAMESPACE = 'http://oakleaf.ws/webservices/northwindep'
    )
GO
```

CREATE ENDPOINT *can substitute* TCP *for* HTTP *as the transport protocol and the* FOR *clause also supports* TSQL, SERVICE_BROKER, *and* DATABASE_MIRRORING.

Stored procedures and UDFs require three-part (database.owner.object) names. You access the WSDL document with the conventional http://SITEvalue/PATHvalue?wsdl URL. The 706-line WSDL document for the preceding endpoint incorporates an XML schema that correlates SQL Server and XSD datatypes. The schema also includes eight instances of a 1,400-character Microsoft disclaimer (weasel clause). You can substitute a custom-written WSDL document for the default version if the default WSDL document isn't interoperable with SOAP toolkits for other programming languages, operating systems, or both.

> *You must run the preceding query (CreateNwindEndpoint.sql in the \VB2005DB\Chapter10\ SqlNativeWebServices folder) before you run the SqlNativeWebServices.sln client project that's described in the section "Consume SQL Server Native Web Services," near the end of the chapter.*

To enable users other than sysadmins members and the endpoint's owner to execute the WEBMETHODs with Windows authentication, you must grant them permission with the following statement:

```
GRANT CONNECT ON HTTP ENDPOINT::endpointname TO [domain/][username]
```

Users also must have appropriate permissions for stored procedures, UDFs, and objects involved in ad hoc batch queries.

Optional SQL Server authentication requires WS-Security headers for username/password credentials, a LOGIN_TYPE = MIXED parameter for each WEBMETHOD, and encrypted HTTPS transport. Basic transport authentication, which probably will be the most common encryption method for clients on other platforms, also requires SSL.

> *SQL Server native Web services are likely to be a controversial topic among DBAs. Serializing SOAP messages consumes substantially more server CPU and memory resources than TDS and increases data-related network traffic by an order of magnitude or more. If your servers' network adapters don't have hardware-based SSL encryption/decryption capability, basic and SQL Server authentication add more CPU load. ASP.NET (ASMX) Web services enable three-tier architecture and can scale-out with Web gardens and farms, probably at a lower cost than scaling up the database server hardware to handle the additional load.*

Customize FOR XML Queries

FOR XML AUTO mode determines the structure (shape) of the query's XML document by comparing column values in adjacent rows. You have no control over the document's shape and content, other than adding the ELEMENTS directive and its optional XSINIL parameter, and nested FOR XML queries that include the TYPE directive. You can't add a root-element tag to documents that contain multiple top-level elements.

FOR XML RAW and FOR XML EXPLICIT modes give you added control over the XML document's shape. FOR XML EXPLICIT mode gives you total control of the shape and content but requires very complex queries. Books Online describes FOR XML EXPLICIT mode syntax as "cumbersome," which is an understatement at best; a better description is "Query from Hell." The new FOR XML PATH mode lets you define the document structure with a much simpler, XPath-like syntax. The following two sections show you how to take advantage of the new features of FOR XML RAW and FOR XML EXPLICIT modes.

> *The \VB2005DB\Chapter10\T-SQLEnhancements folder contains the SQL queries for the examples of the following sections.*

Add Root Elements and Embed XML Schemas with FOR XML RAW Queries

The FOR XML RAW mode lets you add a named document root node and wrap nested nodes with a named element. Like the FOR XML AUTO mode, you can add XML schemas for the outer query's elements but not those of the inner query.

The following nested FOR XML RAW query (NestedQueryTypeRaw.sql) includes XML schemas for an added <Orders> root element, replaces the <Orders> fragment tags with <Order>, wraps <OrderDetail> elements within an <OrderDetails> group, and adds elements for NULL values:

```
USE Northwind
GO
SELECT TOP 10 OrderID, CustomerID, EmployeeID, OrderDate, ShippedDate,
   (SELECT ProductID, CONVERT(decimal(6,2), UnitPrice) as UnitPrice, Quantity,
       CONVERT (decimal(3,2), Discount) As Discount
    FROM [Order Details] AS OrderDetail
    WHERE OrderDetail.OrderID = Orders.OrderID
    FOR XML RAW('OrderDetail'), ELEMENTS, TYPE, ROOT('OrderDetails'))
    -- , XMLSCHEMA('urn:schemas-northwind-order') generates a schema for
    -- every OrderDetails group
FROM Orders
ORDER BY OrderID DESC
FOR XML RAW('Order'), ELEMENTS XSINIL, TYPE, ROOT('Orders')
    -- Comment below to remove inline schema
    , XMLSCHEMA('urn:schemas-northwind-order')
GO
```

The RAW parameters ('Order' and 'OrderDetail') replace the default <row> element name with <Order> and <OrderDetail>. The ROOT parameters ('Orders' and 'OrderDetails') replace <root> with <Orders> and <OrderDetails>.

The XMLSCHEMA directive specifies a namespace for the <Order> element and adds the following inline schemas to the <Orders> root element (NestedQueryTypeRawSchema.xml):

```
<xsd:schema xmlns:xsd="http://www.w3.org/2001/XMLSchema"
   targetNamespace="http://schemas.microsoft.com/sqlserver/2004/sqltypes">
   <xsd:simpleType name="int">
     <xsd:restriction base="xsd:int" />
   </xsd:simpleType>
   <xsd:simpleType name="nchar">
     <xsd:restriction base="xsd:string" />
   </xsd:simpleType>
   <xsd:simpleType name="datetime">
     <xsd:restriction base="xsd:dateTime">
       <xsd:pattern value="((000[1-9])|(00[1-9][0-9])|(0[1-9][0-9]{2})|([1-9]
         [0-9]{3}))-((0[1-9])|(1[0,1,2]))-((0[1-9])|([1,2][0-9])|(3[0,1]))
         T(([0,1][0-9])|(2[0-3]))(:[0-5][0-9]){2}(\.[0-9]{2}[0,3,7])?" />
       <xsd:minInclusive value="1753-01-01T00:00:00.000" />
       <xsd:maxInclusive value="9999-12-31T23:59:59.997" />
     </xsd:restriction>
   </xsd:simpleType>
   <xsd:complexType name="xml">
     <xsd:complexContent mixed="true">
```

```
          <xsd:restriction base="xsd:anyType">
            <xsd:sequence>
              <xsd:any processContents="skip" minOccurs="0" maxOccurs="unbounded" />
            </xsd:sequence>
          </xsd:restriction>
        </xsd:complexContent>
      </xsd:complexType>
  </xsd:schema>
  <xsd:schema xmlns:xsd="http://www.w3.org/2001/XMLSchema"
    xmlns:sqltypes="http://schemas.microsoft.com/sqlserver/2004/sqltypes"
    targetNamespace="urn:schemas-northwind-order" elementFormDefault="qualified">
    <xsd:import namespace="http://schemas.microsoft.com/sqlserver/2004/sqltypes" />
    <xsd:element name="Order">
      <xsd:complexType>
        <xsd:sequence>
          <xsd:element name="OrderID" type="sqltypes:int" nillable="1" />
          <xsd:element name="CustomerID" nillable="1">
            <xsd:simpleType>
              <xsd:restriction base="sqltypes:nchar" sqltypes:localeId="1033"
                  sqltypes:sqlCompareOptions="IgnoreCase IgnoreKanaType IgnoreWidth"
                  sqltypes:sqlSortId="52">
                <xsd:maxLength value="5" />
              </xsd:restriction>
            </xsd:simpleType>
          </xsd:element>
          <xsd:element name="EmployeeID" type="sqltypes:int" nillable="1" />
          <xsd:element name="OrderDate" type="sqltypes:datetime" nillable="1" />
          <xsd:element name="ShippedDate" type="sqltypes:datetime" nillable="1" />
          <xsd:element name="" type="sqltypes:xml" nillable="1" />
        </xsd:sequence>
      </xsd:complexType>
    </xsd:element>
  </xsd:schema>
```

The first schema defines SQL Server `sqltypes` for the outer query's elements but ignores the inner query's elements with the `<xsd:any processContents="skip" minOccurs="0" maxOccurs="unbounded" />` instruction. The second schema imports the first schema and types the elements with `sqltypes:int`, `.sqltypes:datetime`, or `sqltypes:nchar`. The schema validates the `<Order>` element and its subelements, except `<OrderDetails>` and its subelements. If you need a basic schema for a nested document, the better approach is to use SQL Server Management Studio's XML Editor to infer the schema and then edit it as necessary.

Adding a schema is the only method for namespace-qualifying the top-level element. Adding any other namespace qualifier requires FOR XML EXPLICIT *mode.*

Following is a subset of the `<Orders>` document with an `<Order>` element that contains `<OrderDetails>` subelements and doesn't contain an inline schema (NestedQueryTypeRaw.xml):

```
<Orders xmlns:xsi="http://www.w3.org/2001/XMLSchema-instance">
  <Order>
    <OrderID>11071</OrderID>
    <CustomerID>LILAS</CustomerID>
    <EmployeeID>1</EmployeeID>
    <OrderDate>1998-05-05T00:00:00</OrderDate>
    <ShippedDate xsi:nil="true" />
```

```
          <OrderDetails>
            <OrderDetail>
              <ProductID>7</ProductID>
              <UnitPrice>30.00</UnitPrice>
              <Quantity>15</Quantity>
              <Discount>0.05</Discount>
            </OrderDetail>
            <OrderDetail>
              <ProductID>13</ProductID>
              <UnitPrice>6.00</UnitPrice>
              <Quantity>10</Quantity>
              <Discount>0.05</Discount>
            </OrderDetail>
          </OrderDetails>
        </Order>
        ...
    </Orders>
```

The structure of the preceding XML document corresponds approximately to a serialized `SalesOrders` *object, as described in the section "Explore a Business Object Web Service" in Chapter 9.*

Fine-Tune Document Structure with FOR XML PATH

FOR XML PATH mode lets you specify by the column alias name whether column values should appear as element or attribute values, create group subelements, and add subelements to groups. Column alias names use XPath syntax to specify column values as attributes of the outer query's top element with AS @AttributeName, subelements of the top element with AS ElementName, or members of subgroups you specify with AS SubgroupName/ElementName. Attribute declarations must precede element declarations.

Add Attributes to Top-Level Elements

For example, a column list for the Northwind Orders table that contains OrderID AS [@OrderID], CustomerID AS [@CustomerID], EmployeeID AS [@EmployeeID], CompanyName AS [Customer/Name] returns the following XML fragment:

```
<Orders OrderID="11077" CustomerID="RATTC" EmployeeID="2" />
  <Customer>
    <Name>Rattlesnake Canyon Grocery</Name>
  </Customer>
</Orders>
```

Specify Group and Element Names

You also can specify group and element names for nested queries. This nested query (OrdersPathSample1.sql) creates a <LineItems> group element with <LineItem> subelements:

```
SELECT TOP 10 OrderID AS [@OrderID], CustomerID AS [@CustomerID],
 EmployeeID AS [@EmployeeID], OrderDate, ShippedDate, ShipRegion,
 (SELECT Quantity AS [LineItem/Quantity], Products.ProductID AS [LineItem/SKU],
 ProductName AS [LineItem/Product], QuantityPerUnit AS [LineItem/Package],
 [Order Details].UnitPrice AS [LineItem/ListPrice], Discount AS [LineItem/Discount]
 FROM [Order Details], Products
 WHERE [Order Details].OrderID = Orders.OrderID AND
 Products.ProductID = [Order Details].ProductID
 FOR XML PATH(''), TYPE) AS LineItems
```

```
FROM Orders WHERE OrderID < 11077 ORDER BY OrderID DESC
FOR XML PATH('Order'), ELEMENTS XSINIL, TYPE, ROOT('Orders')
```

Adding the highlighted ELEMENTS *directive with the* XSINIL *parameter doesn't preclude specifying attributes of the top-level element. The nested query's empty PATH parameter prevents adding attributes to the* <LineItem> *element.*

Here's a subset of the document (OrdersPathSample1.xml) returned by the preceding query:

```
<Orders xmlns:xsi="http://www.w3.org/2001/XMLSchema-instance">
  ...
  <Order OrderID="11073" CustomerID="PERIC" EmployeeID="2">
    <OrderDate>1998-05-05T00:00:00</OrderDate>
    <ShippedDate xsi:nil="true" />
    <ShipRegion xsi:nil="true" />
    <LineItems>
      <LineItem>
        <Quantity>10</Quantity>
        <SKU>11</SKU>
        <Product>Queso Cabrales</Product>
        <Package>1 kg pkg.</Package>
        <ListPrice>21.0000</ListPrice>
        <Discount>0.0000000e+000</Discount>
      </LineItem>
      <LineItem>
        <Quantity>20</Quantity>
        <SKU>24</SKU>
        <Product>Guaraná Fantástica</Product>
        <Package>12 - 355 ml cans</Package>
        <ListPrice>4.5000</ListPrice>
        <Discount>0.0000000e+000</Discount>
      </LineItem>
    </LineItems>
  </Order>
  ...
</Orders>
```

The <Discount> *element has a floating point format because the Discount column has the* real *data type as a result of importing the original version of the table from an early version of Microsoft Access.*

Add Attributes to Nested Query Elements

The following query (OrdersPathSample2.sql), which returns an identical document (OrdersPathSample2.xml), specifies the <LineItems> and <LineItem> elements in the subquery's highlighted FOR XML PATH and ROOT parameters, which simplifies the syntax and enables you to add attributes to the <LineItem> elements:

```
SELECT TOP 10 OrderID AS [@OrderID], CustomerID AS [@CustomerID],
EmployeeID AS [@EmployeeID], OrderDate, ShippedDate,
(SELECT Quantity, Products.ProductID AS SKU,
   ProductName AS Product, QuantityPerUnit AS Package,
   [Order Details].UnitPrice AS ListPrice, Discount
   FROM [Order Details], Products
   WHERE [Order Details].OrderID = Orders.OrderID AND
      Products.ProductID = [Order Details].ProductID
   FOR XML PATH('LineItem'), TYPE, ROOT('LineItems'))
```

```
FROM Orders WHERE OrderID < 11077 ORDER BY OrderID DESC
FOR XML PATH('Order'), ELEMENTS XSINIL, TYPE, ROOT('Orders')
```

Generate a Complex Invoice Document

FOR XML PATH mode enables you to generate XML documents with proprietary or standards-based structures. The most important limitation for standards-based structures—such as Universal Business Language (UBL) 1.0—is FOR XML PATH mode's inability to namespace-qualify elements for validation by published XML schemas. Post-processing documents to add XML namespace declarations and qualifiers requires complex XSL transforms or procedural code. On the other hand, "bare-bones" documents with a default namespace are much easier for human recipients to read, and they simplify transforms to HTML or other XML structures.

This query (InvoicesPathXML.sql), which might contend for the "Query from Hell" title, generates a structured XML representation of a typical business invoice that has formatted numeric values, extended <LineItem> amounts, and a <Summary> section with <Subtotal>, <Freight>, and <Total> elements:

```
DECLARE @Top int, @Country nvarchar(15)
SELECT @Top = 10 SELECT @Country = 'USA'
--Invoice groups
SELECT TOP(@Top) Orders.OrderID AS [@OrderID], Orders.CustomerID AS [@CustomerID],
Orders.EmployeeID AS [@EmployeeID], '1' AS [@PaymentID], '1' AS [@CurrencyID],
'1' AS [@FobID], Orders.ShipVia AS [@ShipperID],
Orders.OrderID + 210017 AS InvoiceNumber, Orders.ShippedDate AS InvoiceDate,
--Terms group
'Net 30 Days' AS [Terms/Payment], 'US$' AS [Terms/Currency],
--Shipment group
'Redmond, WA' AS [Shipment/FOB],
Shippers.CompanyName AS [Shipment/Shipper],
CONVERT(decimal(6,2), Orders.Freight) AS [Shipment/PrepaidFreight],
--BillTo group
Customers.CompanyName AS [BillTo/Name], Customers.Address AS [BillTo/Address],
Customers.City AS [BillTo/City], Customers.Region AS [BillTo/Region],
Customers.PostalCode AS [BillTo/PostalCode], Customers.Country AS [BillTo/Country],
--Buyer group
Customers.ContactName AS [BillTo/Buyer/Name],
Customers.ContactTitle AS [BillTo/Buyer/Title],
Customers.Phone AS [BillTo/Buyer/Phone], REPLACE(Customers.ContactName, ' ', '_') +
    '@mail.msn.com' AS [BillTo/Buyer/EMail],
SUBSTRING(Customers.CustomerID, 1, 1) + SUBSTRING(Customers.CustomerID, 5, 1) +
STR(Orders.OrderID + 12345, 5, 0) AS [BillTo/Buyer/PurchaseOrder],
--SalesContact group
Employees.FirstName + ' ' + Employees.LastName AS [SalesContact/Name],
Employees.Title AS [SalesContact/Title], '(925) 555-8081 X' +
    Employees.Extension AS [SalesContact/Phone],
LOWER(SUBSTRING(Employees.FirstName, 1, 1) + Employees.LastName) +
    '@northwind.com' AS [SalesContact/EMail],
--OrderDates group
Orders.OrderDate AS [OrderDates/Ordered],
Orders.RequiredDate AS [OrderDates/Required],
Orders.ShippedDate AS [OrderDates/Shipped],
--ShipTo group
Orders.ShipName AS [ShipTo/Name], Orders.ShipAddress AS [ShipTo/Address],
Orders.ShipCity AS [ShipTo/City], Orders.ShipRegion AS [ShipTo/Region],
Orders.ShipPostalCode AS [ShipTo/PostalCode],
```

```
Orders.ShipCountry AS [ShipTo/Country],
--LineItems group inner query
(SELECT [Order Details].OrderID AS [@OrderID], [Order Details].ProductID AS
[@ProductID], ROW_NUMBER() OVER (ORDER BY [Order Details].ProductID) AS [@ItemID],
[Order Details].Quantity AS Quantity, Products.ProductID AS SKU,
Products.ProductName AS Product, Products.QuantityPerUnit AS Package,
CONVERT(decimal(6,2), [Order Details].UnitPrice) AS ListPrice,
CONVERT(decimal(3,1), [Order Details].Discount * 100) AS Discount,
CONVERT(decimal(8,2), [Order Details].Quantity * [Order Details].UnitPrice *
    (1 - [Order Details].Discount)) AS Extended
FROM [Order Details], Products
WHERE [Order Details].OrderID = Orders.OrderID AND
    Products.ProductID = [Order Details].ProductID
FOR XML PATH('LineItem'), TYPE, ROOT('LineItems')),
--Summary group
(SELECT SUM(Quantity) FROM [Order Details]
WHERE [Order Details].OrderID = Orders.OrderID) AS [Summary/NumberOfItems],
(SELECT CONVERT(decimal(8,2), SUM(Quantity * UnitPrice * (1 - Discount)))
FROM [Order Details]
WHERE [Order Details].OrderID = Orders.OrderID) AS [Summary/Subtotal],
CONVERT(decimal(6,2), Freight) AS [Summary/Freight],
(SELECT CONVERT(decimal(8,2), SUM(Quantity * UnitPrice * (1 - Discount)) + Freight)
FROM [Order Details]
WHERE [Order Details].OrderID = Orders.OrderID) AS [Summary/InvoiceTotal]
--Invoice groups and Invoices wrapper
FROM Customers, Orders, Employees, Shippers
WHERE Customers.CustomerID = Orders.CustomerID AND
Employees.EmployeeID = Orders.EmployeeID AND
Shippers.ShipperID = Orders.ShipVia AND Orders.ShipCountry = @Country AND
    Orders.ShippedDate IS NOT NULL
ORDER BY Orders.OrderID DESC
FOR XML PATH('Invoice'), ELEMENTS XSINIL, ROOT('Invoices')
```

The Northwind tables lack many columns for values that are required to generate a representative invoice. Thus, the preceding query simulates values, such as e-mail addresses, and creates arbitrary invoice and purchase order numbers. A similar query creates the SalesOder2 XML documents for Chapter 12's xml datatype examples.

Here's one of the <Invoice> elements returned by the preceding query:

```
<Invoices xmlns:xsi="http://www.w3.org/2001/XMLSchema-instance">
  ...
  <Invoice OrderID="11006" CustomerID="GREAL" EmployeeID="3" PaymentID="1"
    CurrencyID="1" FobID="1" ShipperID="2">
    <InvoiceNumber>221023</InvoiceNumber>
    <InvoiceDate>1998-04-15T00:00:00</InvoiceDate>
    <Terms>
      <Payment>Net 30 Days</Payment>
      <Currency>US$</Currency>
    </Terms>
    <Shipment>
      <FOB>Redmond, WA</FOB>
      <Shipper>United Package</Shipper>
      <PrepaidFreight>25.19</PrepaidFreight>
    </Shipment>
```

```xml
    <BillTo>
      <Name>Great Lakes Food Market</Name>
      <Address>2732 Baker Blvd.</Address>
      <City>Eugene</City>
      <Region>OR</Region>
      <PostalCode>97403</PostalCode>
      <Country>USA</Country>
      <Buyer>
        <Name>Howard Snyder</Name>
        <Title>Marketing Manager</Title>
        <Phone>(503) 555-7555</Phone>
        <EMail>Howard_Snyder@mail.msn.com</EMail>
        <PurchaseOrder>GL23351</PurchaseOrder>
      </Buyer>
    </BillTo>
    <SalesContact>
      <Name>Janet Leverling</Name>
      <Title>Sales Representative</Title>
      <Phone>(925) 555-8081 X3355</Phone>
      <EMail>jleverling@northwind.com</EMail>
    </SalesContact>
    <OrderDates>
      <Ordered>1998-04-07T00:00:00</Ordered>
      <Required>1998-05-05T00:00:00</Required>
      <Shipped>1998-04-15T00:00:00</Shipped>
    </OrderDates>
    <ShipTo>
      <Name>Great Lakes Food Market</Name>
      <Address>2732 Baker Blvd.</Address>
      <City>Eugene</City>
      <Region>OR</Region>
      <PostalCode>97403</PostalCode>
      <Country>USA</Country>
    </ShipTo>
    <LineItems>
      <LineItem OrderID="11006" ProductID="1" ItemID="1">
        <Quantity>8</Quantity>
        <SKU>1</SKU>
        <Product>Chai</Product>
        <Package>10 boxes x 20 bags</Package>
        <ListPrice>18.00</ListPrice>
        <Discount>0.0</Discount>
        <Extended>144.00</Extended>
      </LineItem>
      <LineItem OrderID="11006" ProductID="29" ItemID="2">
        <Quantity>2</Quantity>
        <SKU>29</SKU>
        <Product>Thüringer Rostbratwurst</Product>
        <Package>50 bags x 30 sausgs.</Package>
        <ListPrice>123.79</ListPrice>
        <Discount>25.0</Discount>
        <Extended>185.68</Extended>
      </LineItem>
    </LineItems>
    <Summary>
      <NumberOfItems>10</NumberOfItems>
```

```
      <Subtotal>329.68</Subtotal>
      <Freight>25.19</Freight>
      <InvoiceTotal>354.87</InvoiceTotal>
    </Summary>
  </Invoice>
  ...
</Invoices>
```

Minor modifications to the query can create related documents — such as purchase orders, packing lists, and receiving reports.

Explore the PIVOT and UNPIVOT Operators

Microsoft Access 1.0 popularized crosstab queries with a Crosstab Wizard that simplified the generation of summary reports — especially time-series reports. The inability of later Access versions' Upsizing Wizard to export crosstab queries to SQL Server 7.0 and later was a major impediment to upgrading Jet databases to MSDE and other SQL Server editions. SQL Server 2005's PIVOT operator doesn't solve the Jet crosstab query upgrading problem because T-SQL doesn't support Jet expressions. But the PIVOT operator does reduce the complexity of the T-SQL statements you write to generate comparable crosstab reports.

Create the Source Table

You can generate crosstab queries directly from OLTP tables, but it's a more common practice to create intermediate summary tables or views — commonly called *rollups*. The following batch (OrdersByProduct1997.sql) creates a source table that aggregates the values of orders received by Northwind Traders during each quarter of 1997 for products by name and category:

```
USE Northwind
GO
IF OBJECT_ID (N'OrdersByProduct1997', N'U') IS NOT NULL
DROP TABLE dbo.OrdersByProduct1997
GO
CREATE TABLE dbo.OrdersByProduct1997 (ProductName nvarchar(40),
CategoryName nvarchar(20), Quarter int, ProductOrders money)
GO
INSERT OrdersByProduct1997(ProductName, CategoryName, Quarter, ProductOrders)
SELECT ProductName, CategoryName, DatePart(quarter, OrderDate) AS Quarter,
  CONVERT(money, SUM([Order Details].UnitPrice * Quantity * (1-Discount)))
  AS ProductOrders
FROM Categories INNER JOIN (Products INNER JOIN (Orders INNER JOIN [Order Details]
   ON Orders.OrderID = [Order Details].OrderID)
   ON Products.ProductID = [Order Details].ProductID)
   ON Categories.CategoryID = Products.CategoryID
WHERE OrderDate BETWEEN '1/1/1997' And '12/31/1997'
GROUP BY ProductName, CategoryName, DatePart(quarter, OrderDate)
ORDER BY CategoryName, ProductName, Quarter
GO
SELECT * FROM dbo.OrdersByProduct1997
GO
```

Following are the first 8 of the 286 rows of the OrdersByProduct1997 table:

ProductName	CategoryName	Quarter	ProductOrders
Chai	Beverages	1	705.60
Chai	Beverages	2	878.40
Chai	Beverages	3	1174.50
Chai	Beverages	4	2128.50
Chang	Beverages	1	2435.80
Chang	Beverages	2	228.00
Chang	Beverages	3	2061.50
Chang	Beverages	4	2313.25

Apply the PIVOT Operator

The following batch (OrdersByProduct1997Pivot.sql) uses the highlighted PIVOT query to create an OrdersByProduct1997Pivot table to demonstrate the use of the UNPIVOT operator in the next section:

```
USE Northwind
GO
IF OBJECT_ID (N'OrdersByProduct1997Pivot', N'U') IS NOT NULL
DROP TABLE dbo.OrdersByProduct1997Pivot
GO
CREATE TABLE dbo.OrdersByProduct1997Pivot (Category nvarchar(20),
    Product nvarchar(40), Y1997Q1 money, Y1997Q2 money, Y1997Q3 money,
    Y1997Q4 money, Y1997Totals money)
GO
INSERT dbo.OrdersByProduct1997Pivot(Category, Product,
    Y1997Q1, Y1997Q2, Y1997Q3, Y1997Q4)
    SELECT CategoryName AS Category, ProductName AS Product,
        [1] AS Y1997Q1, [2] AS Y1997Q2, [3] AS Y1997Q3, [4] AS Y1997Q4
    FROM dbo.OrdersByProduct1997
    PIVOT (SUM(ProductOrders) FOR Quarter IN([1], [2], [3], [4])) AS QuarterlyOrders
    ORDER BY CategoryName, ProductName
GO
--The following returns 308 rows with UNPIVOT (NULL Quarter values replaced with 0)
--UPDATE dbo.OrdersByProduct1997Pivot SET Y1997Q1 = ISNULL(Y1997Q1, 0),
    Y1997Q2 = ISNULL(Y1997Q2, 0), Y1997Q3 = ISNULL(Y1997Q3, 0),
    Y1997Q4 = ISNULL(Y1997Q4, 0)
--UPDATE dbo.OrdersByProduct1997Pivot SET Y1997Totals = Y1997Q1 + Y1997Q2 +
    Y1997Q3 + Y1997Q4
--The following returns the original 286 rows with UNPIVOT (NULL values skipped)
UPDATE dbo.OrdersByProduct1997Pivot SET Y1997Totals = ISNULL(Y1997Q1, 0) +
    ISNULL(Y1997Q2, 0) + ISNULL(Y1997Q3, 0) + ISNULL(Y1997Q4, 0)
GO
SELECT * FROM dbo.OrdersByProduct1997Pivot
```

The OrdersByProduct1997's ProductName and CategoryName columns create the crosstab report's row headers. Quarter numbers transform to aliased column names and ProductOrders supplies the added columns' values. The query's UPDATE statements replace NULL values with 0, which enables the calculation of the Y1997Totals column values.

Here are 8 representative rows of the 77-row OrdersByProduct1997Pivot table with NULL values replaced by 0.00:

Category	Product	Y1997Q1	Y1997Q2	Y1997Q3	Y1997Q4	Y1997Totals
Beverages	Outback Lager	1148.40	384.00	1252.50	2683.50	5468.40
Beverages	Rhönbräu Klosterbier	437.72	1758.475	993.55	1295.80	4485.545
Beverages	Sasquatch Ale	551.60	665.00	0.00	890.40	2107.00
Beverages	Steeleye Stout	1310.40	1368.00	1323.00	1273.50	5274.90
Condiments	Aniseed Syrup	544.00	600.00	140.00	440.00	1724.00
Condiments	Chef Anton's Cajun Seasoning	225.28	2970.00 5214.88	1337.60	682.00	
Condiments	Chef Anton's Gumbo Mix	0.00	0.00	288.225	85.40	373.625
Condiments	Genen Shouyu	0.00	331.70	1143.125	0.00	1474.825

Replace the Source Table with a Common Table Expression

You can replace persistent tables or views with temporary tables, table-valued functions, or variables of the table data type. Another option is to replace the rollup table with a common table expression.

The following query (OrdersByProduct1997PivotCTE.sql) produces a basic crosstab report with a CTE:

```
USE Northwind
GO
WITH cteRollup (ProductName, CategoryName, Quarter, ProductOrders) AS
   (SELECT ProductName, CategoryName, DatePart(quarter, OrderDate) AS Quarter,
       CONVERT(money, SUM([Order Details].UnitPrice * Quantity * (1-Discount)))
       AS ProductOrders
     FROM Categories INNER JOIN (Products INNER JOIN (Orders INNER JOIN
       [Order Details] ON Orders.OrderID = [Order Details].OrderID) ON
       Products.ProductID = [Order Details].ProductID) ON
       Categories.CategoryID = Products.CategoryID
     WHERE OrderDate BETWEEN '1/1/1997' And '12/31/1997'
     GROUP BY ProductName, CategoryName, DatePart(quarter, OrderDate))

SELECT CategoryName AS Category, ProductName AS Product,
   [1] AS Y1997Q1, [2] AS Y1997Q2, [3] AS Y1997Q3, [4] AS Y1997Q4
FROM cteRollup
PIVOT (SUM(ProductOrders) FOR Quarter IN([1], [2], [3], [4])) AS QuarterlyOrders
ORDER BY CategoryName, ProductName
```

The cteRollup CTE's column list is optional because the SELECT statement supplies the column names. A SELECT, UPDATE, INSERT, or DELETE statement must follow the CTE's SELECT statement, which removes the CTE from memory.

Add the following statement to generate a well-formed XML document:

```
FOR XML RAW('Crosstab'), ELEMENTS XSINIL, ROOT('OrdersByProduct1997')
```

If you created the OrdersByProduct1997Pivot table in the preceding section, you can populate it with the following batch (OrdersByProduct1997PivotCTEInsert.sql):

```
USE Northwind
GO
TRUNCATE TABLE OrdersByProduct1997Pivot
GO
WITH cteRollup (ProductName, CategoryName, Quarter, ProductOrders) AS
    (SELECT ProductName, CategoryName, DatePart(quarter, OrderDate) AS Quarter,
        CONVERT(money, SUM([Order Details].UnitPrice * Quantity * (1-Discount)))
        AS ProductOrders
    FROM Categories INNER JOIN (Products INNER JOIN (Orders INNER JOIN
        [Order Details] ON Orders.OrderID = [Order Details].OrderID) ON
        Products.ProductID = [Order Details].ProductID) ON
        Categories.CategoryID = Products.CategoryID
    WHERE OrderDate BETWEEN '1/1/1997' And '12/31/1997'
    GROUP BY ProductName, CategoryName, DatePart(quarter, OrderDate))

INSERT dbo.OrdersByProduct1997Pivot(Category, Product,
    Y1997Q1, Y1997Q2, Y1997Q3, Y1997Q4)
    SELECT CategoryName AS Category, ProductName AS Product,
        [1] AS Y1997Q1, [2] AS Y1997Q2, [3] AS Y1997Q3, [4] AS Y1997Q4
    FROM cteRollup
    PIVOT (SUM(ProductOrders) FOR Quarter IN([1], [2], [3], [4])) AS QuarterlyOrders
    ORDER BY CategoryName, ProductName
GO
SELECT * FROM OrdersByProduct1997Pivot
GO
```

UNPIVOT the Crosstab Report

The UNPIVOT operator reverses the PIVOT operator's operation and recreates the original table if the crosstab report contains NULL values. If you replace NULL values with 0, the resultset also contains these rows.

The following query (OrdersByProduct1997Unpivot.sql) regenerates the rows of the original OrdersByProduct1997 table:

```
SELECT Product AS ProductName, Category AS CategoryName, Quarter, ProductOrders
FROM (SELECT Category, Product, Y1997Q1 AS [1], Y1997Q2 AS [2],
    Y1997Q3 AS [3], Y1997Q4 AS [4]
    FROM dbo.OrdersByProduct1997Pivot) AS P1
UNPIVOT (ProductOrders FOR Quarter IN([1], [2], [3], [4])) AS QuarterlyOrders
GO
```

Compare the preceding query with the original PIVOT query:

```
SELECT CategoryName AS Category, ProductName AS Product,
    [1] AS Y1997Q1, [2] AS Y1997Q2, [3] AS Y1997Q3, [4] AS Y1997Q4
FROM dbo.OrdersByProduct1997
PIVOT (SUM(ProductOrders) FOR Quarter IN([1], [2], [3], [4])) AS QuarterlyOrders
ORDER BY CategoryName, ProductName
```

The UNPIVOT query's sub-SELECT statement is the same as the PIVOT query's SELECT clause with the crosstab column names and aliases reversed. The PIVOT and UNPIVOT clauses are identical, except the PIVOT clause aggregates the added crosstab column values.

Process Query Notifications

DML triggers are the traditional method for enabling client applications to determine changes to data tables. A typical trigger-based example is notification of impending inventory shortages. The Northwind Products table has UnitsInStock, UnitsOnOrder, and ReorderLevel columns. If UnitsInStock + UnitsOnOrder – ReorderLevel <= 0, the trigger adds a row to a Reorder table. Users' applications scan the table periodically and process reorders. Each reorder operation adds the quantity to the UnitsOnOrder value and deletes the corresponding record from the Reorder table. This approach is satisfactory when shortages are infrequent, but trigger overhead can limit scalability as transaction volume increases.

SQL Server 2005 query notifications eliminate the trigger overhead but don't provide the identity of the row that changed to generate the notification. The notification message indicates only that data has changed and supplies the first change's type — updated, inserted, or deleted. This information is adequate to invalidate an ASP.NET 2.0 page cache or refresh a Windows form's locally persisted lookup DataTable with the Fill method. If your application must identify the row that changed, add code to inspect the refreshed data or a custom validation handler.

The QueryNotifications.sln project in the \VB2005DB\Chapter10\QueryNotifications folder demonstrates the following two methods for updating locally stored data for a Windows form application:

❑ Add an SqlDependency.Notification object to an SqlCommand object and a delegated handler for the SqlDependency_OnChanged event. In this case, out-of-band TDS packets initiate an SqlNotificationRequest on the server and register a query notification automatically. Any change to the table values that results in a change to the query specified as the SqlCommand.Text property value sends an out-of-band message, which fires the OnChanged event. Clients must have an active network connection to receive notification messages but don't require an open SqlConnection object.

❑ Add Service Broker QUEUE and SERVICE objects to the database, create an SqlNotificationRequest object, and add it as the SqlCommand object's Notification property value. Any change to the table values that results in a change to the query specified as the SqlCommand.Text property value adds a message to the queue. You must poll the queue with a T-SQL RECEIVE instruction to retrieve a message, if any are present. The server persists the message queues, so client applications usually poll for notifications on startup.

You don't need to specify a Service Broker MESSAGE_TYPE *because query notifications use the built-in*
`http://schemas.microsoft.com/SQL/Notifications/PostQueryNotification`
message type.

Both notification methods require that you execute a SELECT query or EXECUTE command with an
SqlDataReader object to register a sequentially numbered QUERY NOTIFICATION SUBSCRIPTION in the
current database. The subscription exists for the number of seconds you specify as the SqlCommand
.Notification.Timeout or SqlNotificationRequest.Timeout property value or, for SqlDependency
.Notification objects, until the server produces the notification message. Omitting the Timeout
property value of an SqlCommand.Notification object results in the default timeout of 432,000 seconds.

Query notifications share the notification engine for indexed views, so the SELECT query or stored
procedure requires an explicit column list and two-part names for local tables. You can't include TOP(n)
or UNION operators in the query. All query notifications with the same SELECT statement share a single
notification object identified by an ObjectId value.

SQL Server 2005 Books Online's "Creating a Query for Notification" topic lists all requirements for
SELECT *statements to register a query notification. If these requirements aren't met, you receive an*
immediate error notification.

The QueryNotifications project populates Products and Suppliers DataTables from diffgram files.
Clicking the Refresh button updates the diffgram files. Figure 10-9 shows the QueryNotifications
project's form after clicking the Refresh Data button and dismissing the message that lists low-inventory
products, which are indicated by a yellow highlight in the DataGridView.

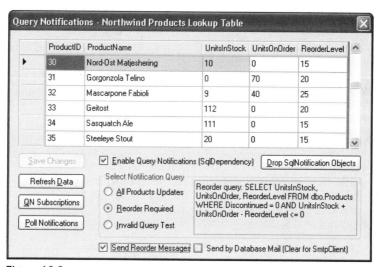

Figure 10-9

Marking the form's Enable Query Notifications checkbox enables the three radio buttons and generates a default `SqlDependency.Notification` object. Clicking Add SqlNotification Objects generates the Service Broker `QUEUE`, `SERVICE`, and optional `ROUTE` objects and creates a persistent `SqlNotificationRequest` subscription.

> *As mentioned in the section "Set Up a Northwind Service Broker," earlier in this chapter, you must enable Service Broker in the Northwind database by executing an* ALTER DATABASE Northwind SET ENABLE_BROKER *statement. If you're using SQL Express or your SQL Server 2005 instance isn't* localhost, *change the* NorthwindConnection *string in App.config.*

Add SqlDependency Notifications

Adding `SqlDependency` notifications requires enabling Service Broker in the current database but no other T-SQL batch statements. The following sections show that the client code to add a notification and subscription, and handle notification events, is minimal.

Create a New Notification and Subscription

The following code from the QueryNotifications project's Notifications.vb file removes an existing event handler and notification, and optionally creates a new notification and subscription:

```
Private Sub AddOrRemoveNotification(ByVal blnAdd As Boolean)
    'depProds, cmdProds, and strSql are Private variables
    If depProds IsNot Nothing Then
        'Remove previous handler
        RemoveHandler depProds.OnChanged, AddressOf SqlDependency_OnChanged
    End If
    If cmdProds IsNot Nothing Then
        'Remove previous notification
        cmdProds.Notification = Nothing
    End If
    If blnAdd Then
        'Create the notification and subscription
        strSQL = "SELECT UnitsInStock, UnitsOnOrder, ReorderLevel FROM dbo.Products"
        Try
            If cnNwind Is Nothing Then
                cnNwind = New SqlConnection(My.Settings.NorthwindConnection)
            End If
            cmdProds = New SqlCommand(strSQL, cnNwind)

            'Add an SqlDependency for the connection
            depProds = New SqlDependency(cmdProds)

            'Add a delegated handler for the OnChanged event
            AddHandler depProds.OnChanged, _
              New OnChangedEventHandler(AddressOf SqlDependency_OnChanged)

            'Execute the command to establish the notification
            cnNwind.Open()
            Dim sdrDep As SqlDataReader = cmdProds.ExecuteReader
```

```
            sdrDep.Close()
            cnNwind.Close()
        Catch exc As Exception
            MsgBox(exc.Message, MsgBoxStyle.Exclamation, _
                "Create Dependency Operation Failed")
        End Try
    End If
End Sub
```

Add a Notification Event Handler

A handler for the SqlDependency object's OnChange event is optional, but your application will ignore notifications if you don't add one. Here's the abbreviated code for the sample project's SqlDependency _OnChange event handler:

```
Private Sub SqlDependency_OnChange(ByVal sender As Object, _
  ByVal args As SqlNotificationEventArgs)
    'Open a message box with query notification details (omitted for brevity)
    'This event-handler runs on its own thread

    Dim strMsg As String = "Click Refresh Data to update the Products lookup table."
    MsgBox(strMsg, MsgBoxStyle.Information, "Query Notification Received")

    'Recreate the notification
    AddOrRemoveNotification(True)
End Sub
```

An SqlDependency query notification subscription produces a single event message. Your application must generate another notification after receiving an SqlDependency_OnChange event.

SqlNotificationEventArgs has the following three properties:

❏ Type returns Changed for table data changes or Subscribe for notification errors, which usually result from an invalid query.

❏ Source returns one of eight SqlNotificationSource enumerations to indicate the source of the notification, such as Data for table data changes or Object, which indicates a change to the table structure.

❏ Info returns one of 12 SqlNotificationInfo enumerations, which provide details about the Source property. For example, if the SqlNotificationSource is Data, Info returns Alter, Delete, or Update.

Generate a Notification with the Sample QueryNotifications Project

To generate an SqlDependency query notification, mark the Enable Query Notifications checkbox, change a value in one of the three updatable columns, and click Save Changes. Figure 10-10 shows the detailed message generated from an update to the grid's UnitsInStock column with the default All Products Updates notification selected.

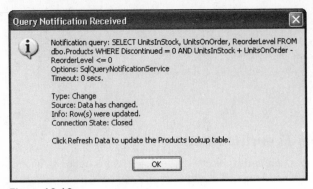

Figure 10-10

The default `SqlDependency` query generates a notification whenever any inventory-related value changes. To emulate the more selective DDL trigger example mentioned at the beginning of this topic, select the Reorder Required query. Select a row with a UnitsOnOrder value of 0, set the UnitsOnHand value to less than or equal to ReorderLevel value, and click Save Changes.

Selecting the Invalid Query option results in an immediate error message because the TOP operator isn't permitted and the table name is one-part, not two-part.

Create SqlNotificationRequest Objects and Subscriptions

Creating an `SqlNotificationRequest` requires substantially more code than an `SqlDependency` object, regardless of whether you create the required QUEUE and SERVICE Service Broker objects with individual T-SQL query executions or by VB code.

Create QUEUE, SERVICE, and Optional ROUTE Objects

Here's the abbreviated code in the Notifications.vb form's `CreateQueue` function to add the required and optional Service Broker objects:

```
Private Function CreateQueue(ByVal blnSilent As Boolean) As Boolean
    'Create a QUEUE
    Dim strQueueSQL As String = "CREATE QUEUE ProductsQnQueue; "

    'Create a SERVICE with a PostQueryNotification MESSAGE TYPE
    strQueueSQL += "CREATE SERVICE ProductsQnService ON QUEUE ProductsQnQueue" + _
      "([http://schemas.microsoft.com/SQL/Notifications/PostQueryNotification]); "

    'Add an optional ROUTE to the local SQL Server instance
    strQueueSQL += "CREATE ROUTE ProductsQnRoute WITH SERVICE_NAME = " + _
      "'ProductsQnService', ADDRESS = 'LOCAL'; "

    Dim cmdQueues As New SqlCommand(strQueueSQL, cnNwind)
```

```
        Dim strMsg As String
        Try
            cnNwind.Open()
            cmdQueues.ExecuteNonQuery()
            cnNwind.Close()
            'Add an SqlNotificationRequest
            AddSqlNotificationRequest()
            Return True
        Catch exc As Exception
            'Handle the exception
        Finally
            cmdQueues.Dispose()
            cnNwind.Close()
        End Try
    End Function
```

You don't need to create a Service Broker MESSAGE_TYPE *or* CONTRACT *because query notifications use the built-in* http://schemas.microsoft.com/SQL/Notifications/ PostQueryNotification *message type and its contract.*

The CREATE ROUTE *statement is optional unless you want the message to be delivered to the* ADDRESS *of an SQL Server 2005 instance other than the default (*LOCAL*). Routing is a complex subject, as you'll discover in Books Online's "Service Broker Routing" topic.*

Add an SqlNotificationRequest

The following code in the AddSqlNotificationRequest procedure adds and registers the SqlNotificationRequest:

```
Private Sub AddSqlNotificationRequest()
    Dim strRequestSQL As String = "SELECT UnitsInStock, UnitsOnOrder, " + _
    "ReorderLevel FROM dbo.Products"
    cmdRequest = New SqlCommand(strRequestSQL, cnNwind)
    'Create an SqlNotification request with the maximum timeout (Int32.MaxValue)
    snsProds = New SqlNotificationRequest(Guid.NewGuid().ToString, _
        "ProductsQnService", Int32.MaxValue)
    'Attach the notification to the command
    cmdRequest.Notification = snsProds
    Try
        'Register the notification
        cnNwind.Open()
        Dim rdrProds As SqlDataReader = cmdRequest.ExecuteReader
        rdrProds.Close()
        cnNwind.Close()
    Catch exc As Exception
        MsgBox(exc.Message, MsgBoxStyle.Exclamation, _
        "Error Creating SqlNotificationRequest")
    Finally
        cnNwind.Close()
    End Try
End Sub
```

The highlighted lines in the preceding code illustrate the differences between instructions for creating SqlNotificationRequest *and* SqlDependency *objects.*

449

Remove Service Broker Objects and Subscriptions

To remove the Service Broker objects and all notification subscriptions, execute code like the following from the `CreateQueue` function:

```
Private Function CreateQueue(ByVal blnSilent As Boolean) As Boolean
    ...
    Try
        cnNwind.Open()
        Dim strDropSQL As String = "DROP SERVICE ProductsQnService; "
        strDropSQL += "DROP ROUTE ProductsQnRoute; "
        strDropSQL += "DROP QUEUE dbo.ProductsQnQueue; "
        strDropSQL += "KILL QUERY NOTIFICATION SUBSCRIPTION ALL; "
        cmdQueues.CommandText = strDropSQL
        cmdQueues.ExecuteNonQuery()
        cnNwind.Close()
        btnCreateQueues.Text = "&Add SqlNotification Objects"
    Catch ex As Exception
        MsgBox(ex.Message, MsgBoxStyle.Exclamation, _
          "Error Dropping Queue and Service")
    Finally
        cnNwind.Close()
    End Try
    ...
End Function
```

Poll the Queue for Data Change Notifications

Unlike the `SqlDependency` approach, you must poll the queue with a `RECEIVE` instruction to test for pending notifications. The following code from the `PollNotifications` function returns `1` if notifications are present, `0` if not, and `-1` if Service Broker objects are missing:

```
Private Function PollNotifications(ByVal blnSilent As Boolean) As Integer
    'Poll the ProductsQnQueue for changes
    Dim intRetValue As Integer
    Dim strPollSQL As String = "RECEIVE CAST(message_body AS XML) AS " + _
      "ProductsQnMessage FROM ProductsQnQueue; "
    Dim strProdsMessage As String = Nothing
    Dim strMsg As String = Nothing
    Dim cmdPoll As New SqlCommand(strPollSQL, cnNwind)
    Try
        cnNwind.Open()
        Dim rdrPoll As SqlDataReader = cmdPoll.ExecuteReader
        If rdrPoll.HasRows Then
            'Queue has a message
            strMsg = "ProductsQnQueue has changes. " + _
              "Click Refresh Data to update the Products lookup table." + _
              vbCrLf + vbCrLf + Replace(strProdsMessage, "><", ">" + vbCrLf + "<")
            cnNwind.Close()
            If Not ListSubscriptions(True) Then
                'Don't add duplicate notification requests
                AddSqlNotificationRequest()
            End If
            intRetValue = 1 'Message present
            MsgBox(strMsg, MsgBoxStyle.Information, "Polling ProductsQnQueue")
```

```
            Else
                intRetValue = 0 'No message present
                strMsg = "ProductsQnQueue is empty, or notification has expired " + _
                    "or was deleted."
                MsgBox(strMsg, MsgBoxStyle.Information, "Polling ProductsQnQueue")
            End If
            cnNwind.Close()
            Return intRetValue
        Catch exc As Exception
            strMsg = exc.Message
            If exc.Message.Contains("Invalid object") Then
                strMsg += vbCrLf + vbCrLf + _
                    "Click Add SqlNotification Objects to create the queue and service."
            End If
            MsgBox(strMsg, MsgBoxStyle.Exclamation, "Error Polling ProductsQnQueue")
            Return -1 'Error
        Finally
            cnNwind.Close()
            cmdPoll.Dispose()
        End Try
    End Function
```

The single-row resultset that's returned by executing the RECEIVE query has 15 columns, but the only column of immediate significance is message_body, which has the xml data type. Figure 10-11 shows the reformatted message_body text, which includes type, source, info, and other attribute values.

To view all columns of the RECEIVE query resultset, change a value in the DataGridView, click Save Changes, and use SSMS to execute an external RECEIVE * FROM ProductsQnQueue query.

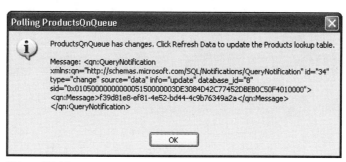

Figure 10-11

Test SqlNotificationRequests with the Sample Project

The QueryNotifications project doesn't add Service Broker objects and an SqlNotificationRequest by default. Run the project and click Add SqlNotification Objects to create them. The notification request's query is the same as the All Products Updates, so change a value, click Save Changes, and then click Poll Notifications to open a message box similar to that of Figure 10-11.

The project's Form_OnLoad event handler tests for pending notification messages when the project starts, which justifies the effort required to add an SqlNotificationRequest. To verify that the messages are persistent, change a value, click Save changes, and close the application. On restart, the Polling ProductQnQueue message box opens. Stopping and restarting the server generates a similar message.

Automate Reorder Processing with Database Mail

Supply-chain management (SCM) projects usually interact with Web services, but you can emulate the first phase of a simple e-mail SCM application with SQL Server 2005's new Database Mail feature. As mentioned in the section "Database Mail," earlier in this chapter, Database Mail capability isn't installed by default. You must use SQL Server Management Studio to set up a mail host database, install Database Mail profiles and accounts, and add the sendimail_sp stored procedure. Thus, Database Mail isn't available to SQL Server 2005 Express users.

The QueryNotifications project's RefreshProducts procedure generates reorder messages and sends them with Database Mail, if you have a profile named NorthwindSuppliers with a default SMTP account. To install the profile and account, open Management Studio, and connect to the SQL Server 2005 localhost instance. Expand the instance's Management node, right-click the Database Mail item, and choose Configure Database Mail to start the Database Mail Configuration Wizard. Click Next, accept the default Set Up Database Mail by Performing the Following Tasks option, select the Northwind database, and create an e-mail profile named NorthwindSuppliers. Click Add to specify the mail server parameters for a valid Exchange Server or other SMTP e-mail account. Finally, change the RefreshOrders procedure's strToEmail value to the destination e-mail address.

Mark the Send Reorder Message and Send by Database Mail checkboxes, and click the Refresh Data button. Click Yes when asked if you want to send the reorder messages by Database Mail. Figure 10-12 shows a sample test message open in Outlook Express.

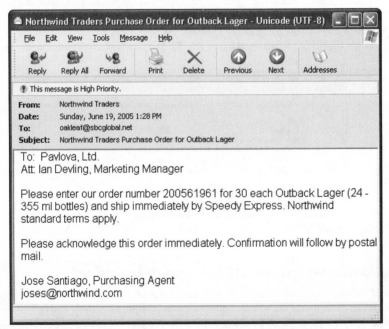

Figure 10-12

If you're running SQL Express or don't want to set up Database Mail, clear the Send by Database Mail checkbox to send messages with the new SmtpClient class. You must replace the SendReordersBySMTP procedure's strHost, strFromEmail, and strPassword placeholders with the values required by your e-mail provider. Find `somewhere` *in the Notifications.vb file to locate the placeholders.*

The Books Online topic for `sp_send_dbmail` indicates that all parameters are optional, but the automated Database Mail reorder process generates a statement similar to the following:

```
EXECUTE dbo.sp_send_dbmail
@profile_name = 'NorthwindSuppliers',
@recipients = 'recipient@email.somewhere.com',
@subject = 'Northwind Traders Purchase Order for Uncle Bobs Organic Dried Pears',
@body = 'To:  Grandma Kellys Homestead...',
@body_format = 'TEXT',
@importance = 'HIGH'
```

The `@subject`, `@body_format`, *and* `@importance` *parameters are optional;* `@body_format` *defaults to* `TEXT` *and* `@importance` *defaults to* `NORMAL`.

Code in the `SendReordersBySMTP` procedure queries the `dbo.sysmail_mailitems` table for duplicate messages. This table contains 27 columns of message information, including all message fields, status, and date/time sent to the e-mail server, if the sent_status value is 1 (sent). When you send a recipient two messages on the same day, a message box similar to that shown in Figure 10-13 opens.

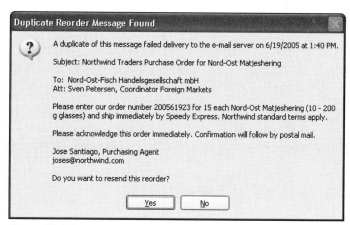

Figure 10-13

Database Mail is more complex than necessary for simple Windows form messaging applications. If you need to send basic text messages and enclosures through your ISP, consider using the new `SmtpClient` *class.*

Consume SQL Server Native Web Services

The earlier "Consume SQL Server Native Web Services" section describes how to add Web service endpoints and WebMethods to databases with an example T-SQL script for the sample stored procedures in the Northwind database. This section describes how code for .NET client applications that consume SQL Server native Web services differs from code for their ASP.NET counterparts.

The SqlNativeWebServices.sln project in the \VB2005DB\Chapter10\SqlNativeWebServices folder is a test harness for four Northwind Web services and ad hoc queries. You must execute the CreateNwindEndpoint .sql script from the same folder before you run the project to create the NorthwindEP endpoint. Figure 10-14 shows the project's Client.vb form. Select one of the WebMethods to display the results in the DataGridView, or select Ad Hoc Batch Query, edit the SQL statement, and click Execute.

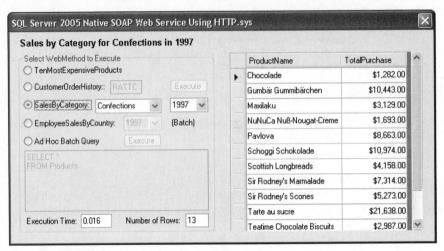

Figure 10-14

Enabling users to execute ad hoc queries with T-SQL statements in SOAP request messages is a potential security threat and should not be used in Web methods for production Web services.

Adding a Web Reference to a native Web service requires that you type the URL (http://sitename/ pathname?wsdl) in the Add Web Reference dialog's URL text box. You won't find the service in the list generated by clicking the Web Services on the Local Machine link because native Web services don't have a corresponding *ServiceName*.disco file. You must type the sitename URL element exactly as it appears in the assignment to the HOST parameter of the AS HTTP clause; substituting localhost when HOST = 'servername' results in an HTTP 404 error.

Expanding the Web Reference nodes shows an added file named SqlParameter.datasource. SQL Server native Web services require parameters passed to stored procedures or UDFs to have SQL Server — rather than native .NET — data types. As an example, passing datetime parameters to the EmployeeSalesByCountry WebMethod requires the following code:

```
Private wsNwind As New WSNwindEP.NorthwindEP
Private dsNwind As DataSet
...
Dim datBegDate As New SqlDateTime(1997, 1, 1)
Dim datEndDate As New SqlDateTime(1997, 12, 31)
dsNwind = wsNwind.EmployeeSalesByCountry(datBegDate, datEndDate)
```

It's not necessary to create structures for other common data types, such as SqlString, SqlInt32, or SqlMoney, so you can pass the value.

The project saves DataSets as WebMethodName.xml files in the ...\bin folder. WebMethodName_app1.xml and WebMethodName_app2.xml files contain the DataSets' imported schemas.

The functions of the `WSNwindEP.NorthwindEP` proxy class cast the SOAP response message payload for resultsets to the `DataSet` type. Scalar values from UDFs and XML documents from `FOR XML` ad hoc queries or stored procedures have the default `Object` array data type. The first array member contains the data or, in the case of an error, an `SqlMessage` object. For resultsets, the second member contains an `SqlRowCount` object. Cast XML document payloads to the `System.Xml.XmlElement` data type and invoke the `OuterXml` method to return a `String` with code such as this:

```
Dim objResult() As Object = Nothing
...
objResult = wsNwind.sqlbatch(strSQL, Nothing)
Dim xmlResult As XmlElement = CType(objResult(0), XmlElement)
Dim strResult As String = xmlResult.ToString
If objResult.Length > 1 Then
   Dim srcCount As WSNwindEP.SqlRowCount = _
     CType(objResult(1), WSNwindEP.SqlRowCount)
   Dim intRowCount As Integer = srcCount.Count
End If
```

Enabling ad hoc queries exposes your server to the potential security risk of SQL injection attacks. Few, if any, DBAs permit ad hoc queries against production databases.

Figure 10-15 shows the Client.vb form after executing a `FOR XML AUTO` query.

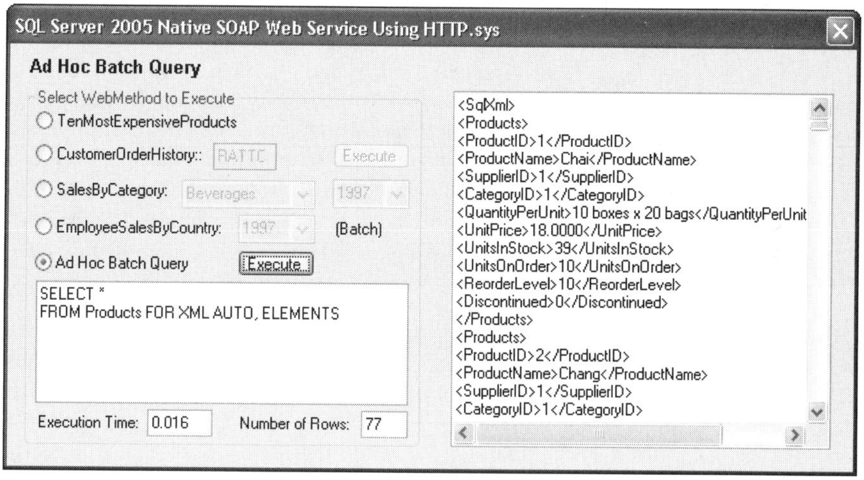

Figure 10-15

Executing `sp_executesql` to avoid recompiling the execution plan for parameter value changes allows you to pass a `ParamArray` of `SqlParameter` objects as the second `sqlbatch` WebMethod argument, which is `Nothing` in the preceding code snippet.

Summary

SQL Server 2005's six editions correspond to those of SQL Server 2000 editions. SQL Server 2005 Express Edition replaces MSDE 2000 and adds significant benefits, such as a 4GB maximum database size and no query throttling. SQL Express has a few limitations, such as the inability to act as a replication publisher. SQL Express Manager provides a simple GUI for managing SQL Express databases and executing queries. All SQL Server 2005 editions install SQL Computer Manager, which combines SQL Server 2000's Server Network Utility, Client Network Utility, and Services Manager into a single MMC snap-in.

SQL Server Management Studio replaces SQL Server 2000's Enterprise Manager and integrates Query Analyzer in a VS 2005-base IDE. You can execute T-SQL, MDX, DMX, and XMLA queries against Analysis Server databases, and write SQL Mobile queries. Business Intelligence Developer Studio integrates Analysis Manager features and Reporting Services design/deployment capabilities, and lets you extend Integration Services scripts. SQL Profiler and Database Tuning Advisor (formerly the Index Tuning Wizard) get minor enhancements. Sqlcmd.exe replaces osql.exe and uses an SQL Native Client OLE DB connection. SMO and RMO replace SQL-DMO for automating server management chores. New data availability and reliability features include enhanced table partitioning, database mirroring, and an Sqlcmd.exe enhancement that enables DBAs to run commands when the server won't accept new connections.

CLR integration enables you to create stored procedures, UDFs, triggers, UDTs, and UDAs with managed code that runs in the SQL Server process. VS 2005's SQL Server projects include stubs for each of the five object types, and automatically deploy assemblies to the target database when you build and run the project.

New Large Data types—nvarchar(max), varchar(max), and varbinary(max)—store up to 2^31-1 bytes of data and replace the ntext, text, and image data types, which remain for backward compatibility only. The new xml scalar data type can be used for table columns and as a T-SQL variable, stored procedure or UDF parameters, and UDF return values. T-SQL gains many new enhancements, including nested FOR XML queries, structured exception handling, common table expressions and recursive queries, PIVOT and UNPIVOT operators, SNAPSHOT Transaction Isolation, TOP n and TABLESAMPLE operators, ranking table functions (RANK() OVER, DENSE_RANK() OVER, and ROW_NUMBER() OVER), TABLESAMPLE, DDL triggers, and cell-scoped or column-scoped data encryption with certificates stored in the database.

Service Broker provides reliable asynchronous transactional messaging between local or remote databases, enhances Notification Services, and enables query notifications. Query notifications occur when DML or DDL operations affect the resultset of a specified query. Database Mail replaces SQLMail's extended stored procedures, and SQL native SOAP Web services use HTTP.sys to emulate SQLXML 3.0 Web services without a requirement for setting up IIS virtual directories. Native Web services also enable ad hoc queries.

11

Creating SQL Server Projects

Visual Studio 2005 and SQL Server 2005 introduce SQL Server projects, which let you substitute .NET Framework 2.0 assemblies for T-SQL stored procedures, scalar and table-returning functions, and triggers. You also can create custom user-defined data types and user-defined aggregates, which isn't possible with T-SQL. This chapter calls the objects defined within SQL Server project assemblies *SQL/CLR objects*.

The capability to substitute assemblies, which can define one or more SQL/CLR objects of the six types, for tried-and-true T-SQL objects doesn't mean that .NET developers should abandon T-SQL for VB or C# 2005 to define stored procedures, user-defined functions, and triggers. T-SQL remains the better language choice for creating conventional SQL Server objects that operate on sets of tabular data. Moving code from Data Access Logic Components (DALC) in a middle tier to a production database server's engine requires business justification, thorough planning, expert coding, exhaustive testing, and a willing DBA. As is the case for SQL Server–hosted Web services, you can expect DBAs to be very reluctant to add SQL/CLR objects to "their" production databases.

Consider using SQL/CLR objects when T-SQL queries and commands require procedural code, complex string manipulation or calculations, temporary tables, or cursors to meet your data access or update requirements. T-SQL procedural code, such as WHILE, CASE, and data-dependent IF...ELSE blocks, is interpreted. SQL/CLR objects are compiled, so performance is likely to be better. SQL/CLR objects enable array processing, which T-SQL doesn't support. Data-intensive applications, such as sales and production forecasting, that require performing calculations on many records to return a small amount of data are logical candidates for SQL/CLR objects; so are operations that perform processing on individual rows returned by a forward-only (firehose) cursor.

Most sample code for SQL/CLR objects in SQL Server Books Online and on the Internet is trivial, can be implemented with T-SQL easily, and doesn't meet the test of the preceding use cases. The beginning of this chapter offers a few such simplified examples to illustrate SQL/CLR object coding and deployment methods. Later sections concentrate on more complex examples of stored procedures and user-defined types that might justify adding .NET assemblies and SQL/CLR objects to a production database.

An Introduction to SQL Server Projects

VS 2005 SQL Server projects generate assemblies that SQL Server 2005 executes with an instance of the .NET Framework 2.0 runtime that's hosted by the database engine. Thus, these projects run within the SQL Server process and share its memory space. The database engine, not the .NET Framework, handles SQL/CLR object memory management, garbage collection, and threading. By default, SQL Server project assemblies can't access external system resources or execute unmanaged code, which preserves the server's security and reliability. However, substituting complex managed code for conventional T-SQL stored procedures, functions, user-defined data types, triggers, and native aggregate functions can affect server performance.

Commands to Enable CLR Integration

As mentioned in the section "CLR Integration" in Chapter 10, SQL Server 2005 or SQL Express CLR integration isn't enabled by default. In most cases, you enable CLR integration on the SQL Server 2005 Surface Area Configuration Tool's Surface Area Configuration page. To enable and verify CLR integration with T-SQL, execute the following batch in SQL Server Management Studio (SMSS):

```
EXEC[UTE] sp_configure 'clr enabled', 1
RECONFIGURE
[EC[UTE] sp_configure]
```

Include EXEC[UTE] sp_configure to confirm clr enabled = 1.

Attribute Decorations for SQL Server Projects

The following five attribute decorations identify classes and structures as SQL/CLR objects:

❑ <SqlProcedure()> specifies a CLR stored procedure (CSP) and is used for VS 2005 deployment only.

❑ <SqlUserDefinedFunction()> specifies a CLR scalar or table-valued user-defined function (CFS or CFT) and is used for deployment and at runtime. This book considers scalar and table-valued functions to be individual SQL/CLR object types because there are substantial differences in their implementation.

❑ <SqlUserDefinedType()> specifies a CLR user-defined type (UDT), which is an extended version of SQL Server's user-defined data type (UDDT) and is used for deployment and at runtime.

❑ <SqlUserDefinedAggregate()> specifies a CLR user-defined aggregate (UDA), which extends SQL Server's native aggregation functions, such as COUNT and SUM and is used for deployment and at runtime.

❑ <SqlTrigger> specifies a CLR trigger (CTR) for INSERT, UPDATE, or DELETE operations and is used for deployment only.

The UDT and UDA abbreviations are commonly used by SQL/CLR developers. The CSP, CFS, CFT, and CTR abbreviations identify objects that are user-defined by definition — stored procedures and triggers — and distinguish a CLR scalar or table-valued functions from a T-SQL user-defined function (UDF). This book uses the abbreviations as prefixes or suffixes to identify SQL/CLR object types (other than UDTs).

A method within a UDT project's `Public Class` or `Public Structure` requires an `<SqlMethod (DataAccess:=DataAccessKind.Read)>` attribute to gain access to tables in the current or another database.

Visual Studio 2005 SQL Server Project Templates

Creating a complex user-defined object, such as a UDT or UDA, is a daunting task for the uninitiated developer. Thus, VS 2005 Developer Edition and higher include `Class` and `Structure` templates for an SQL Server project. You add the templates by choosing them from the Project menu or the Solution Explorer *ProjectName* node's Add context menu.

Following are brief descriptions of the five `Class` and `Structure` templates:

❑ **Stored Procedure** has skeleton code for `Public Partial Class StoredProcedures` with an empty `Public Public Shared Sub StoredProcedure1` that's decorated with the required `<[Microsoft.SqlServer.Server].SqlProcedure()>` attribute. The class can contain multiple CSPs defined as `Public Subs` or `Functions`.

❑ **User-Defined Function** is a stub for `Partial Public Class UserDefinedFunctions` with a sample `<[Microsoft.SqlServer.Server].SqlFunction()>Public Shared Function Function1() As SqlString` method that returns "Hello" without "World". Like stored procedures, you can define multiple CFSs and CFTs in a single Class file.

❑ **User-Defined Type** is a stub for `Public Structure Type1` with `<Serializable()><[Microsoft.SqlServer.Server].SqlUserDefinedType(Format .Native)>` attributes and required (but mostly empty) methods, properties, and a `var1` field member. Each UDT requires its own `Structure` or `Class`, which names the UDT.

❑ **Aggregate** is a stub for `Public Class Aggregate1` with `<Serializable()><[Microsoft .SqlServer.Server].SqlUserDefinedAggregate(Format.Native)>` attributes and empty `Init`, `Accumulate`, `Merge`, and `Terminate` methods. Each UDA requires its own `Class`, which names the UDA.

❑ **Trigger** is a stub for `Public Class Triggers` with an empty `Public Shared Sub Trigger1` and a commented `<[Microsoft.SqlServer.Server].SqlTrigger(Name:="Trigger1", Target:="Table1", Event:="FOR UPDATE")>` attribute.

All templates include `Imports System`, `Imports System.Data`, `Imports System.Data.Sql`, `Imports System.Data.SqlTypes`, and `Imports Microsoft.SqlServer.Server`. Thus, the `Microsoft .SqlServer.Server` prefix for attribute names is optional. You must add `Imports System.Data .SqlClient` to create an ADO.NET 2.0 SqlConnection to the SQL Server instance that hosts the assembly (called a *context connection*) or a conventional SqlConnection to the local or another SQL Server instance.

Visual Basic 2005 Express Edition doesn't include an SQL Server Project template, so you must create SQL Server projects as class libraries and add class files to implement user-defined SQL Server CLR objects. All editions of SQL Server 2005, including SQL Server Express, have the same support for SQL Server projects.

The SqlServerProjectCLR Sample Project

You can build an SQL Server project by adding the five default `Class` and `Structure` templates and deploy the project by pressing F5 or choosing Build ➪ Deploy Solution in VS 2005. However, the only functional class is the user-defined function, which returns Hello. The SqlServerProjectCLR.sln project in the \VB2005DB\Chapter11\SqlServerProjectCLR folder provides examples of five simple but operational CLR object types that you can deploy to the Northwind database with VS 2005's automatic post-build deployment process.

The sample project's connection string specifies `localhost` as the SQL Server 2005 instance that includes the Northwind database. If you receive a message similar to Figure 11-1 when you open the project in VS 2005, click Yes. Open the project's Properties window's Database page and click the builder button at the right of the Connection String text box to open the Add Database Reference dialog (see Figure 11-2). If you've defined a connection to the instance, select it and click OK. Otherwise click Add New Reference and create the appropriate connection.

Figure 11-1

Figure 11-2

Code for SQL Server Objects

SqlServerProjectCLR's objective is to create simple, deployable examples of the five basic SQL/CLR object types. The code for the sample objects is trivial and, with the exception of the `SampleUDT` `Structure` and `SampleUDA Class`, the objects are better suited to implementation with T-SQL than managed code.

The SampleCSP Stored Procedure Class

The `SampleCSP Class`'s `csp_OrdersByCustomerID` stored procedure introduces the `SqlContext` and `SqlPipe` objects from the `Microsoft.SqlServer.Server` namespace that's provided by the reference to System.Data.dll. Following are brief descriptions of the `SqlContext` object's two commonly used methods:

❑ `Pipe` returns the `SqlPipe` object, which has an overloaded `Send` method and related methods. You use the `Send` method to send an `ISqlReader` (`SqlDataReader`), `SqlError`, or a message (`SqlString`) to the calling application.

❑ `TriggerContext` returns the `SqlTriggerContext` object that's used in the `SampleCTR` class.

Creating a context connection to the SQL Server instance running the SQL/CLR stored procedure requires a special `"context connection=true"` connection string. Context connections and SqlCommands within the SQL/CLR context are identical to those in ordinary Windows and Web form contexts.

The following SQL/CLR stored procedure code returns Orders rows for the specified `CustomerID` parameter value:

```
Imports System
Imports System.Data
Imports System.Data.Sql
Imports System.Data.SqlTypes
Imports Microsoft.SqlServer.Server

'Added
Imports System.Data.SqlClient

Partial Public Class StoredProcedures
<SqlProcedure()> _
Public Shared Sub csp_OrdersByCustomerID(ByVal CustomerID As SqlString)
    Using cnNwind As New SqlConnection("context connection=true")
        Dim strSQL As String = "SELECT * FROM Orders WHERE CustomerID = '" + _
        CustomerID.ToString + "' ORDER BY OrderID DESC"
        Dim cmOrders As New SqlCommand(strSQL, cnNwind)
        cmOrders.CommandType = CommandType.Text
        cnNwind.Open()
        SqlContext.Pipe.ExecuteAndSend(cmOrders)
        cnNwind.Close()
    End Using
End Sub
End Class
```

The `SqlPipe.ExecuteAndSend(SqlCommand)` method enables you to send the resultset directly, rather than by creating and executing an `SqlDataReader`.

If you want to add a return value to your CSP, change `Public Shared Sub` *to* `Public Shared Function` *and add a* `Return Value` *instruction. For the preceding example, a useful return value is the number of rows in the resultset.*

Run the following command from SMSS with Northwind as the current database to test the procedure:

```
EXEC [dbo.]csp_OrdersByCustomerID 'ALFKI'
```

The SampleCFS Scalar User-Defined Function Class

The following `cfs_OrderCountByCustomerID` scalar function returns the number of orders placed by the customer with the `CustomerID` parameter value:

```
Imports System
Imports System.Data
Imports System.Data.Sql
Imports System.Data.SqlTypes
Imports Microsoft.SqlServer.Server

'Added
Imports System.Data.SqlClient

Partial Public Class UserDefinedFunctions
<SqlFunction(DataAccess:=DataAccessKind.Read)> _
Public Shared Function cfs_OrderCountByCustomerID(ByVal CustomerID As SqlString)
  As SqlInt32
    Using cnNwind As New SqlConnection("context connection=true")
        Dim strSQL As String = "SELECT COUNT(OrderID) " + _
          "FROM Orders WHERE CustomerID = '" + CustomerID.ToString + "'"
        Dim cmOrders As New SqlCommand(strSQL, cnNwind)
        cmOrders.CommandType = CommandType.Text
        cnNwind.Open()
        Dim intCount As SqlInt32 = CType(CInt(cmOrders.ExecuteScalar), SqlInt32)
        cnNwind.Close()
        Return intCount
    End Using
End Function
End Class
```

The `SqlFunction` requires the `DataAccess:=DataAccessKind.Read` member to read values from database objects. If the member is missing or `DataAccess:=DataAccessKind.None`, you incur an exception when you execute a function that invokes an SqlCommand.

Run the following command from SMSS with Northwind as the current database to test the function:

```
SELECT dbo.cfs_OrderCountByCustomerID('RATTC')
```

The SampleUDT User-Defined Type Structure

The `SampleUDT Structure` for the `PointUDT` type is an abbreviated version of code for the `Point` UDT, which the section "A Simple Value-Type UDT," later in this chapter, describes in depth. The `PointUDT` type doesn't implement the `Point` type's `DistanceTo` method.

The SampleUDA User-Defined Aggregate

The `SampleUDA` Class's CSVStringUDA aggregate returns a comma-separated-value (CSV) formatted string for all values in the column of the table that you specify as the UDA's argument. For example, executing `SELECT dbo.CSVStringUDA(CompanyName) AS CSVString FROM Customers` returns `"Alfreds Futterkiste","Ana Trujillo Emparedados y helados", ... "Wilman Kala","Wolski Zajazd"`.

```
Imports System
Imports System.Data
Imports System.Data.Sql
Imports System.Data.SqlTypes
Imports Microsoft.SqlServer.Server

'Added
Imports System.Text
Imports System.IO

<Serializable()> _
<SqlUserDefinedAggregate(Format.UserDefined, IsInvariantToDuplicates:=False, _
 IsInvariantToNulls:=True, IsInvariantToOrder:=False, IsNullIfEmpty:=True,
 MaxByteSize:=8000)> _
Public Class CSVStringUDA
Implements IBinarySerialize

Private sbCSV As StringBuilder

Public Sub Init()
    'Initialize with an opening "
    sbCSV = New StringBuilder()
    sbCSV.Append(ControlChars.Quote)
End Sub

Public Sub Accumulate(ByVal sqlString As SqlString)
    If (sqlString.IsNull) Then
        Return
    Else
        'Append the separator (",")
        sbCSV.Append(sqlString.Value).Append(""",""")
    End If
End Sub

Public Sub Merge(ByVal csvString As CSVStringUDA)
    'Merge the current instance with the another thread's instance, if present
    sbCSV.Append(csvString.sbCSV)
End Sub

Public Function Terminate() As SqlString
    'Return the string from the StringBuilder or an empty string
```

```
        If sbCSV.Length > 0 Then
            sbCSV.Append(vbCrLf)
            Return New SqlString(sbCSV.ToString(0, sbCSV.Length - 4))
        Else
            Return New SqlString("")
        End If
End Function

Public Sub Read(ByVal brCSV As System.IO.BinaryReader) _
  Implements IBinarySerialize.Read
        'Format.UserDefined, so a BinaryReader is required
        sbCSV = New StringBuilder(brCSV.ReadString())
End Sub

Public Sub Write(ByVal bwCSV As System.IO.BinaryWriter) _
  Implements IBinarySerialize.Write
        'Format.UserDefined, so a BinaryWriter is required
        bwCSV.Write(sbCSV.ToString())
End Sub
End Class
```

The `Format.UserDefined` attribute requires that you implement the `IBinarySerialize` interface and its `Read` and `Write` methods. The section "UserDefined-Format UDT Class Code," later in this chapter, illustrates a more complex implementation of this interface.

The `CSVStringUDA` aggregate isn't limited to `SqlString` fields. As an example, you can return CSVs for the Products table's UnitPrice (`money`), QuantityOnHand (`smallint`), and Discontinued (`bit`) columns. The preceding code doesn't include protection against generating strings longer than 8,000 bytes (4,000 Unicode characters), which is specified by the `MaxByteSize:=8000` attribute and is the maximum permissible value. If you execute `SELECT dbo.CSVStringUDA(OrderDate) AS CSVString FROM Orders`, you receive an exception that states: "The buffer is insufficient. Read or write operation failed." You can limit the length of the return value by adding `GROUP BY` clauses to the `SELECT` statement.

The SampleCTR Trigger

The `SampleCTR Class`'s `ctr_Products` method returns a message when an application updates the Products table. The code uses the `SqlTriggerContext` object to determine the update type and send the appropriate message with the `SqlPipe.Send` method's `String` overload.

```
Imports System
Imports System.Data
Imports System.Data.Sql
Imports System.Data.SqlTypes
Imports Microsoft.SqlServer.Server

Partial Public Class SampleCTRs
<SqlTrigger(Name:="ctr_Products", Target:="Products", _
  Event:="FOR INSERT, UPDATE, DELETE")> _
  Public Shared Sub ctr_Products()
    Dim ctxTrigger As SqlTriggerContext
    Dim spPipe As SqlPipe = SqlContext.Pipe
    ctxTrigger = SqlContext.TriggerContext()
```

```
Select Case ctxTrigger.TriggerAction

    Dim intCol As Integer
    Dim strCols As String = Nothing
    For intCol = 0 To ctxTrigger.ColumnCount - 1
        If ctxTrigger.IsUpdatedColumn(intCol) Then
            Select Case intCol
                Case 6
                    strCols += "UnitsInStock, "
                Case 7
                    strCols += "UnitsOnOrder, "
                Case 8
                    strCols += "ReorderLevel, "
            End Select
        End If
    Next
    If strCols Is Nothing Then
        spPipe.Send("Products table row updated.")
    Else
        strCols = strCols.Substring(0, strCols.Length - 2)
        strCols = "Products table " + strCols
        If strCols.IndexOf(", ") > 0 Then
            strCols += " columns updated."
        Else
            strCols += " column updated."
        End If
        spPipe.Send(strCols)
    End If
End Select
End Sub
End Class
```

The `SqlTriggerContext.IsUpdatedColumn()` property returns a `Boolean True` value for an updated column. The preceding code sends a "Products table UnitsInStock, UnitsOnOrder, ReorderLevel columns updated" message if the three column values are updated.

DDL triggers return an `SqlTriggerContext.EventData` XML document that describes the DDL operation.

You can trace VS 2005's automatic deployment commands by selecting SQL Profiler's T-SQL template and pressing F5 to build and deploy the project.

Test Scripts

A Test.sql script in the project's Test Scripts folder enables you to debug the code for each object. VS 2005's post-build process for SQL Server projects reads and executes the test script as the last step in the build-and-run process. The script's return values appear in the Output window when you select the Debug item in the Show Output From list. The default Test.sql script is a placeholder. The SqlServerProjectCLR project includes a Test.sql script with instructions to execute each of the sample SQL/CLR objects. Figure 11-3 shows the Database output from Test.sql. The first value (6) is generated by csf_OrderCountByCustomerID; `PointUDT` outputs the following three numeric rows. The remaining sections represent the output from csp_OrdersByCustomer, ctr_Products, and CSVStringUDA. The sequence represents completion of execution, not the order of the Test.sql script's command.

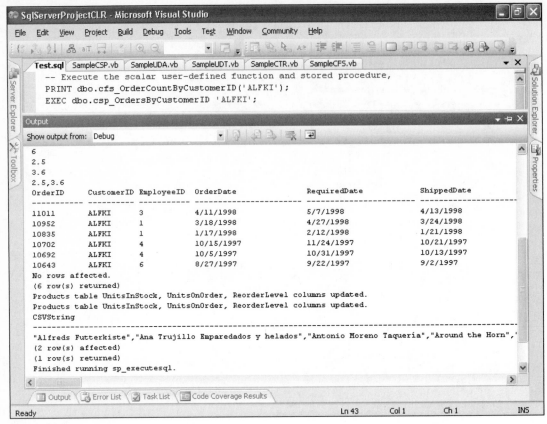

Figure 11-3

If you receive a "Cannot deduce the default test script" message, expand the Test Scripts node, right-click Test.sql, and choose Set as Default Debug Script.

To add an empty Test1.sql script to a new SQL Server project, right-click the ProjectName node, and choose Add Test Script to create the TestScripts folder and file. Change the file name, if you want, and then set it as the Default Debug Script.

The section "Debug SQL Server Projects," later in this chapter, describes alternative debugging methods for VS 2005 and VB Express.

The CREATE ASSEMBLY Instruction

VS 2005's post-build T-SQL script installs assemblies automatically. If you're using VB Express or your project includes a reference to another assembly, you must install the assembly in SQL Server manually. The following T-SQL instruction adds an SQL Server project assembly and its related files to the current database:

```
CREATE ASSEMBLY assembly_name
[ AUTHORIZATION owner_name ]
FROM { <client_assembly_specifier> | <assembly_bits> [,...n] }
[ WITH PERMISSION_SET = { SAFE | EXTERNAL_ACCESS | UNSAFE } ]
```

where:

❏ assembly_name is the symbolic name of the assembly, such as StoredProceduresCLR, which must be unique within the database. The value normally is the assembly name without the .dll extension, but can be any value that's valid for SQL Server symbolic names.

❏ owner_name is the name of a role that's valid for the current user. Omitting AUTHORIZATION owner_name assigns ownership to the current user.

❏ <client_assembly_specifier> is the well-formed path to the assembly DLL, such as C:\SQLServerProjects\bin\StoredProceduresCLR.dll. You also can specify a UNC path. Dependent assemblies are added automatically and must be located in the same folder. The alternative <assembly_bits> is the binary representation of an assembly and its dependent assemblies, if any. VS 2005 post-build deployment uses <assembly_bits> instead of the assembly's path and file name.

❏ SAFE is the default permission set and prohibits access to external resources, such as the file system, registry, network, and environment variables. SAFE assemblies have execute permissions only and can't compromise the server's security or reliability.

❏ EXTERNAL_ACCESS permission extends SAFE permission to enable access to external resources, such as the network or local file system.

❏ UNSAFE permission enables running wrapped COM objects, PInvoke, and unmanaged code in the server process. Only members of the sysadmin role can register UNSAFE assemblies, which, like COM-based extended stored procedures, *can* compromise the server's security *and* reliability.

The following instruction installs the SqlServerProjectCLR assembly from the specified local file:

```
CREATE ASSEMBLY SqlServerProjectCLR FROM
'D:\WROX\Projects\Chapter11\SqlServerProjectCLR\bin\SqlServerProjectCLR.dll'
```

with the default SAFE permission set. You must be logged into the SQL Server 2005 instance with Windows authentication to execute the CREATE ASSEMBLY command.

The CreateAllObjects.sql script in the \VB2005DB\Chapter11\SqlServerProjectCLR\bin folder includes the preceding CREATE ASSEMBLY instruction and the CREATE ObjectType instructions that the following sections describe. You must edit the file path to conform to your sample files installation. A DropAllObjects.sql script enables recreating the SQL/CLR objects.

The server tests the assembly for type-safeness and conformance to the PERMISSION_SET value, which eliminates the need for the JIT compiler's test on initial loading. If the assembly is conformant, the assemblies are cataloged in the target database's sys.assemblies and sys.assembly_files system tables. Entries in the sys.assembly_types, sys.assembly_modules, and sys.assembly_references tables occur when required by a specific assembly.

To specify a PERMISSION_SET value other than SAFE, open the ProjectName Properties window, select the Database page, and select the value from the Permission Level list. You must be a member of the sysadmin role to specify UNSAFE.

The assembly you add appears under the *DatabaseName*\Assemblies node of the VS 2005 Server Explorer and under the *DatabaseName*\Programmability\Assemblies node of SMSS's Object Explorer. Expanding Server Explorer's *AssemblyName* node displays links to source code files and object items.

Create ObjectType Instructions

After you catalog the assembly in the database, you must execute a CREATE ObjectType instruction for each SQL Server object you define in a Class or Structure. The instructions follow conventional T-SQL syntax for creating stored procedures, user-defined functions, and triggers. You substitute EXTERNAL NAME for the T-SQL code that ordinarily follows the AS predicate. The EXTERNAL NAME syntax for stored procedures, functions, and triggers, whose classes can contain multiple objects, is:

```
[CatalogName].[AssemblyName.ClassName].[ProcedureOrFunctionName]
```

UDTs and UDAs, which don't have T-SQL implementations, contain a single object per Structure or Class, and require the following syntax:

```
[CatalogName].[AssemblyName.TypeOrAggregateName]
```

The following instructions create the five basic SQL/CLR object types from the SqlServerProjectCLR assembly added in the preceding section, and typical batch commands to return values. The assembly doesn't implement a table-valued function because of the complexity of implementing the required ISqlReader, ISqlRecord, and ISqlTypeData interfaces, which require writing more than 60 methods and properties.

The batch commands are variations on instructions provided earlier in the chapter.

Stored Procedures

The following command adds the csp_OrdersByCustomerID stored procedure to the Northwind database:

```
CREATE PROCEDURE [csp_OrdersByCustomerID] @CustomerID nvarchar(MAX)
AS EXTERNAL NAME
[SqlServerProjectCLR].[SqlServerProjectCLR.SampleCSP].[csp_OrdersByCustomerID]
```

Execute the following instruction to return 18 rows of Orders data:

```
EXEC dbo.csp_OrdersByCustomerID 'RATTC'
```

The Test.sql script includes the execution instructions in this and the following sections.

Scalar Functions

The following command adds the cfs_OrderCountByCustomerID scalar user-defined function:

```
CREATE FUNCTION [cfs_OrderCountByCustomerID](@CustomerID nvarchar(MAX))
RETURNS [int]
AS EXTERNAL NAME
[SqlServerProjectCLR].[SqlServerProjectCLR.SampleCFS].[cfs_OrderCountByCustomerID]
```

Execute the following instruction to return 18:

```
PRINT dbo.cfs_OrderCountByCustomerID('RATTC')
```

Table-Valued Functions

As mentioned earlier, the sample project doesn't include an SQL/CLR table-valued function. If you create a cft_OrdersByCustomerID TVF that returns Orders table rows, the following instruction would install it:

```
CREATE FUNCTION [cft_OrdersByCustomerID(@CustomerID nvarchar(5))
RETURNS @Orders TABLE
(OrderID int, CustomerID nchar(5), EmployeeID int, OrderDate datetime,
 RequiredDate datetime, ShippedDate datetime, ShipVia int, Freight money,
 ShipName nvarchar(40), ShipAddress nvarchar(60), ShipCity nvarchar(15),
 ShipRegion nvarchar(15), ShipPostalCode nvarchar(10),
 ShipCountry nvarchar(15))
AS EXTERNAL NAME
[SqlServerProjectCLR].[SqlServerProjectCLR.SampleCFT].[cft_OrdersByCustomerID]
```

and the following command would return a table with 18 rows:

```
SELECT * FROM cft_OrdersByCustomerID('RATTC')
```

User-Defined Types

The following command adds a user-defined PointUDT type to the current database:

```
CREATE TYPE PointUDT
EXTERNAL NAME SqlServerProjectCLR.[SqlServerProjectCLR.PointUDT]
```

and these commands test the UDT by creating an instance of the point and printing its values:

```
DECLARE @pt PointUDT
SET @pt = CONVERT(PointUDT, '2.5,3.6');
PRINT @pt.X;
PRINT @pt.Y;
PRINT @pt.ToString();
```

The section "Test the Point UDT with T-SQL Instructions," later in this chapter, describes UDT test instructions.

User-Defined Aggregates

The following instruction creates the CSVStringUDA aggregate and its argument and returns data types:

```
CREATE AGGREGATE CSVStringUDA(@sqlString nvarchar(MAX))
RETURNS nvarchar(MAX)
EXTERNAL NAME SqlServerProjectCLR.[SqlServerProjectCLR.CSVStringUDA]
```

This command returns a comma-separated-value string of CompanyNames:

```
SELECT dbo.CSVStringUDA(CompanyName) AS CSVString FROM Customers
```

This UDA can return CSV strings from columns of any native or user-defined data type. As an example, the following command returns a CSV string from the PointUDT column of the PointsUDT table that you create later in the chapter:

```
SELECT dbo.CSVStringUDA(PointUDT.ToString()) AS CSVString FROM PointsUDT
```

Triggers

Execute the following instruction to create a trigger that fires on any Products table value modification:

```
CREATE TRIGGER [ctr_Products] ON Products
FOR INSERT, UPDATE, DELETE
AS EXTERNAL NAME
    [SqlServerProjectCLR].[SqlServerProjectCLR.SampleCTRs].[ctr_Products]
```

These commands fire the trigger and return the column value to its initial state:

```
UPDATE Products SET UnitsInStock = UnitsInStock + 1 WHERE ProductID = 1;
UPDATE Products SET UnitsInStock = UnitsInStock - 1 WHERE ProductID = 1;
```

Drop SQL/CLR Objects

The DropAllObjects.sql script in the sample project's Test Scripts folder illustrates the T-SQL commands for dropping each type of SQL/CLR object. You can use IF OBJECT_ID('ObjectName') IS NOT NULL tests for all but UDTs and assemblies, which require queries against the sys.types and sys.assemblies system views. Following is the script to drop the SQL/CLR objects created in the preceding sections:

```
USE Northwind;
GO
IF OBJECT_ID('csp_OrdersByCustomerID') IS NOT NULL
DROP PROCEDURE [csp_OrdersByCustomerID];
GO
IF OBJECT_ID('cfs_OrderCountByCustomerID') IS NOT NULL
DROP FUNCTION [cfs_OrderCountByCustomerID];
GO
IF OBJECT_ID('CSVStringUDA') IS NOT NULL
DROP AGGREGATE [CSVStringUDA];
GO
IF EXISTS(SELECT name FROM sys.types WHERE name = 'PointUDT')
DROP TYPE [PointUDT];
GO
IF OBJECT_ID('ctr_Products') IS NOT NULL
DROP TRIGGER [ctr_Products];
GO
IF EXISTS(SELECT name FROM sys.assemblies WHERE name = 'SqlServerProjectCLR')
DROP ASSEMBLY [SqlServerProjectCLR];
GO
```

You must drop all objects created by the assembly before you can drop the assembly.

Debug SQL Server Projects

VS 2005's Test.sql script lets you debug SQL/CLR objects automatically during the build-and-deploy process. This debugging technique commonly is called *F-5 debugging*. If you're using VS 2005 and don't want to write a Test.sql script or are running VB Express, you must use the Attach to Process method to debug the object. The following sections describe these two debugging methods.

> *Debugging an SQL/CLR database object disables execution of all other SQL/CLR objects of the SQL Server instance. Thus, it's not a good troubleshooting practice to debug SQL/CLR objects on production servers.*

Automatic Debugging with VS 2005 and Test.sql

If you replace VS 2005's Test.sql's default instructions with the execution commands from the preceding sections, you can debug the CLR objects after post-build deployment. Debugging with Test.sql commands requires the following procedure:

1. Add the appropriate instructions to the Test.sql script in the TestScripts folder and specify Test.sql as the default test script. (You can choose a different file name, if you want.)

2. Mark the Enable SQL Server Debugging checkbox on the Debugging page of the *ProjectName* Properties window. (This checkbox is marked by default.)

3. Right-click Server Explorer's current database node, choose Allow SQL/CLR Debugging, and acknowledge the warning message about stopping managed threads on the server.

4. Add a breakpoint at an appropriate location in your code.

When you build and deploy the project, execution halts at the breakpoint. The project remains in the Running state, so you must press Shift+F5 to halt the debugging process. Allow SQL/CLR Debugging is a toggle, so you must choose Allow SQL/CLR Debugging again to return to normal build-and-deploy mode.

Manual Debugging with VS 2005 or VB Express

Manual debugging uses the Attach to Process method and T-SQL commands executed with SMSS to debug your code. Manual debugging requires the following steps:

1. If you specified Allow SQL/CLR Debugging in VS 2005, choose Allow SQL/CLR Debugging again to toggle the setting off.

2. Choose Debug ⇨ Attach to Process to open the dialog of the same name, select sqlservr.exe (see Figure 11-4), and click Attach to close the dialog to place your project in Running mode.

3. Add a breakpoint at an appropriate location in the code to debug (SampleCSP's `csp_OrdersByCustomerID` method for this example).

4. Open SMSS, and type a T-SQL command to execute the method (`EXEC dbo.csp_OrdersByCustomerID 'RATTC'` for this example).

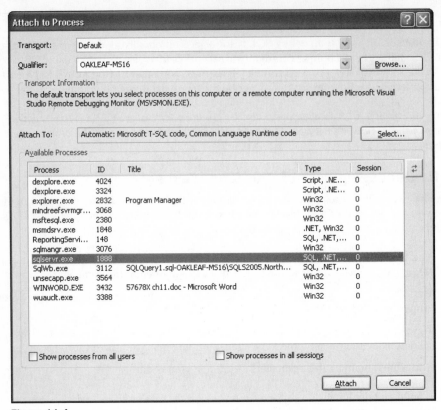

Figure 11-4

When you execute the T-SQL command, execution stops at the breakpoint. Choose Debug ➪ Detach All to return from Running to editing mode.

Design SQL/CLR Stored Procedures

SQL/CLR stored procedures are best suited to methods that return custom resultsets, create specialized data structures, manipulate strings or date/time values, access local or network resources, or perform complex calculations. The following sections illustrate SQL/CLR stored procedures that perform more complex operations than the preceding introductory examples.

The StoredProceduresCLR.sln project in the \VB2005DB\Chapter11\StoredProceduresCLR folder contains code for the three SQL/CLR stored procedures that are the subjects of the sections that follow. The project's ...\Test Scripts folder contains CreateAllObjects.sql and DropAllObjects.sql scripts for manual installation and deletion of the procedures.

The StoredProceduresClient.sln project in the \VB2005DB\Chapter11\StoredProceduresClient folder is a test harness for the SQL/CLR procedures. You must run the StoredProceduresClient project to create one or two user stored procedures for the csp_LinearRegression procedure before you run StoredProceduresCLR.

Return Content-Dependent SqlDataRecords

The csp_CustomerDataRecord procedure illustrates the delivery of a customized SQLDataRecord object whose metadata is partly determined by the value of the Customers table's Country column. The metadata changes original CompanyName, ContactName, ContactTitle, and Address fields to Name, Buyer, Title, and Street. For USA values, the procedure changes the Region column name to State, PostalCode to ZIPCode, and returns a NULL Country value. Other countries return the original two column names with NULL values for Region and PostalCode, depending on the Customers row's values.

This procedure introduces the SqlMetaData object, which defines the structure of a custom SqlDataRecord column. You specify the number of columns by the size of the array of SqlMetaData objects, and add column metadata with the following generic instruction:

```
mdName(intColIndex) = New SqlMetaData(strColumnName, SqlDbType.Type [, intMaxSize])
```

The intMaxSize *argument is required for character data and is optional for the* SqlDecimal *data type. For the* SqlDecimal *data type you substitute* intPrecision, intScale *for* intMaxSize.

Then you create a new SqlDataRecord object and assign column values with the following generic instructions:

```
Dim sdrName As New SqlRecord(mdName)
sdrName.SetDataType(intColIndex, typColValue)
...
```

The application-specific versions of the preceding instructions are highlighted in the following code for the csp_CustomerDataRecord function:

```
<SqlProcedure()> _
    Public Shared Function csp_CustomerDataRecord(ByVal CustomerID As SqlString) _
As Integer
'Define the metadata for an SqlDataRecord (default for USA)
Dim mdCust(8) As SqlMetaData
mdCust(0) = New SqlMetaData("ID", SqlDbType.NVarChar, 5)
mdCust(1) = New SqlMetaData("Company", SqlDbType.NVarChar, 40)
mdCust(2) = New SqlMetaData("Buyer", SqlDbType.NVarChar, 30)
mdCust(3) = New SqlMetaData("Title", SqlDbType.NVarChar, 30)
mdCust(4) = New SqlMetaData("Street", SqlDbType.NVarChar, 60)
mdCust(5) = New SqlMetaData("City", SqlDbType.NVarChar, 15)
mdCust(6) = New SqlMetaData("State", SqlDbType.NVarChar, 15)
mdCust(7) = New SqlMetaData("ZIPCode", SqlDbType.NVarChar, 10)
mdCust(8) = New SqlMetaData("Country", SqlDbType.NVarChar, 15)

Dim spCust As SqlPipe = SqlContext.Pipe
Dim cnNwind As New SqlConnection("context connection=true")
Dim cmCust As New SqlCommand
With cmCust
    .Connection = cnNwind
    .CommandType = CommandType.Text
    .Parameters.Clear()
    .Parameters.AddWithValue("@CustomerID", CustomerID)
    .CommandText = "SELECT CustomerID, CompanyName, ContactName, " + _
        "ContactTitle, Address, City, Region, PostalCode, Country " + _
```

```
                "FROM Customers WHERE CustomerID = @CustomerID;"
        End With
        Try
            Dim sdrCustOrig As SqlDataReader = cmCust.ExecuteReader
            If sdrCustOrig.HasRows Then
                sdrCustOrig.Read()
            Else
                Throw New Exception("CustomerID '" + CustomerID.ToString + "' not found.")
                sdrCustOrig.Close()
                cnNwind.Close()
                Return 1
            End If
            Dim intIsUSA As Integer
            If sdrCustOrig(8).ToString = "USA" Then
                intIsUSA = -1
            Else
                'Use international field names
                mdCust(6) = New SqlMetaData("Region", SqlDbType.NVarChar, 15)
                mdCust(7) = New SqlMetaData("PostalCode", SqlDbType.NVarChar, 10)
            End If
            Dim sdrCust As New SqlDataRecord(mdCust)
            Dim intCtr As Integer
            For intCtr = 0 To 8
                If intIsUSA = -1 Then
                    If intCtr = 8 Then
                        'NULL country
                        Exit For
                    End If
                End If
                If sdrCustOrig(intCtr).ToString = "" Then
                    'NULL Region or PostalCode
                Else
                    sdrCust.SetString(intCtr, sdrCustOrig(intCtr).ToString)
                End If
            Next intCtr
            sdrCustOrig.Close()
            cnNwind.Close()
            spCust.Send(sdrCust)
            Return intIsUSA
        Catch exc As Exception
            cnNwind.Close()
            Throw New Exception(exc.Message)
            Return 1
        End Try
    End Function
```

If you want to send a return value, change Public Shared Sub *to* Public Shared Function *and specify the return value, as illustrated near the end of the preceding listing.*

Figure 11-5 shows the StoredProceduresClient project's startup form displaying SqlDataRecord column names and values for a U.S. customer. The client also generates mailing label text.

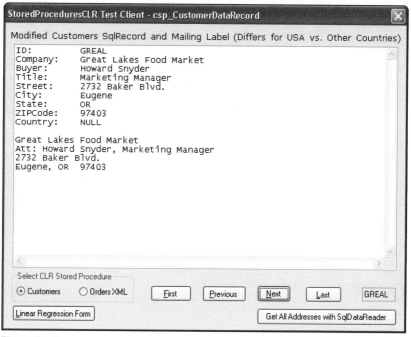

Figure 11-5

The StoredProceduresCLR project includes a `csp_CustomerDataStream` function that delivers all Customers table rows as `SqlDataRecord` objects. This approach eliminates the need to implement the `IDataReader` interface, which requires implementing several required and many provider-specific members. The sample code executes an initial `SqlPipe.SendResultsStart(SqlDataRecord, False)` instruction, followed by an `SqlPipe.SendResultsRow(SqlDataRecord)` for each row, and a terminating `SqlPipe.SendResultsEnd()` instruction. The client reads the rows into an `SqlDataReader` object with an `SqlCommand.ExecuteReader` instruction. The CLR stored procedure can interleave `SqlDataReader.Read` and `SqlPipe.SendResultsRow(SqlDataRecord)` instructions without implementing Multiple Active Result Sets (MARS). However, streaming the data disables country-based changes to the metadata, which is determined by the initial `SqlPipe.SendResultsStart(SqlDataRecord)` instruction.

> *Clicking the client's Get All Addresses with SqlDataReader button demonstrates fixed metadata, which is required for resultsets that the `ExecuteReader` method returns to an `SqlDataReader`.*

Generate XML Documents with an XmlWriter

Chapter 10's "Generate a Complex Invoice Document" section describes the T-SQL required to generate an invoice XML document with a 70-line T-SQL FOR XML PATH query. The StoredProceduresCLR project's `csp_SalesOrderXML` procedure uses an `XmlWriter` object to generate a similar sales order document, save it as a file in the project's ...\Test Scripts folder, and send the contents to the client. The following chapter, which covers SQL Server 2005's `xml` data type, uses similar sample documents to emulate real-world business processes.

The .NET Framework 2.0's XmlWriter *object, which you instantiate with the static* XmlWriter
.Create *method, replaces the earlier* XmlTextWriter, *which is a concrete implementation of the*
XmlWriter *class.*

It requires about 200 lines of code to create a document that's similar to the FOR XML PATH version.
Generating documents with an XmlWriter lets you format the content with indentation and line breaks;
the FOR XML PATH query returns an unformatted character stream. An XmlWriter also enables you to
insert the XML document prefix, and add namespace prefixes and xmlns attributes to subelements,
which FOR XML PATH queries don't support. Adding WITH PERMISSION_SET = EXTENAL_ACCESS to the
CREATE ASSEMBLY instruction or setting the Permission Level to External on the *ProjectName* Properties
window's Database page lets you save the XML document to a file for further processing.

You can pass the path to the folder for the XML document files as a stored procedure parameter. This
example stores the files in the project's ...\Test Scripts folder by querying the SqlAssemblyProjectRoot
extended property with the highlighted code at the beginning of the csp_SalesOrderXML procedure
listing. If you install the assembly manually, you must add the following instruction after CREATE
ASSEMBLY to add the extended property:

```
EXEC sp_addextendedproperty 'SqlAssemblyProjectRoot',
N'd:\path\Chapter11\StoredProceduresCLR',
'ASSEMBLY',N'StoredProceduresCLR';
```

where d:\path is the installation path.

Following is the code for the csp_SalesOrderXML stored procedure with the code to return the assembly
folder (near the start of the procedure) highlighted:

```
<SqlProcedure()> _
Public Shared Sub csp_SalesOrderXML(ByVal OrderID As SqlInt32)
    'Save an XML representation of a SalesOrder object as a local file
    'and send the XML document string with a pipe
    'This requires the assembly to be deployed with External Permission Level
    Dim spOrder As SqlPipe = SqlContext.Pipe
    Dim cnNwind As New SqlConnection("context connection=true")
    Dim cmNwind As New SqlCommand
    Dim sdrOrder As SqlDataReader = Nothing
    'Get the directory for the SQL Server project (extended property)
    Dim strDir As String = Nothing
    Dim strSQL As String = "SELECT value FROM " + _
      "fn_listextendedproperty('SqlAssemblyProjectRoot', " + _
      "'ASSEMBLY', default, default, default, default, default) " + _
      "WHERE objname = 'StoredProceduresCLR'"
    Try
        cnNwind.Open()
        With cmNwind
            .Connection = cnNwind
            .CommandText = strSQL
            .CommandType = CommandType.Text
            strDir = CStr(.ExecuteScalar)
        End With
    Catch exc As Exception
        cnNwind.Close()
        Throw New Exception("Exception getting folder location.")
```

```
        Return
    End Try
    If strDir = Nothing Then
        cnNwind.Close()
        Throw New Exception("No folder location returned by query.")
    End If

    strDir += "\Test Scripts\"

    strSQL = "SELECT o.OrderID, o.CustomerID, c.CompanyName, c.ContactName, " + _
        "c.ContactTitle, c.Address, c.City, c.Region, c.PostalCode, c.Country, " + _
        "c.Phone, o.EmployeeID, e.FirstName, e.LastName, e.Title, e.Extension, " + _
        "o.OrderDate, o.RequiredDate, o.ShippedDate, o.ShipVia, s.CompanyName, " + _
        "o.Freight, o.ShipName, o.ShipAddress, o.ShipCity, o.ShipRegion, " + _
        "o.ShipPostalCode, o.ShipCountry " + _
        "FROM Orders AS o, Customers AS c, Employees AS e, Shippers AS s " + _
        "WHERE o.OrderID = " + OrderID.ToString + _
        "AND c.CustomerID = o.CustomerID AND e.EmployeeID = o.EmployeeID " + _
        "AND s.ShipperID = o.ShipVia"
    Try
        With cmNwind
            .CommandText = strSQL
            sdrOrder = .ExecuteReader
        End With
        If sdrOrder.HasRows Then
            sdrOrder.Read()
        Else
            sdrOrder.Close()
            cnNwind.Close()
            Throw New Exception("Order " + OrderID.ToString + " is missing.")
            Return
        End If
    Catch exc As Exception
        sdrOrder.Close()
        cnNwind.Close()
        Throw New Exception("Exception executing order body query.")
        Return
    End Try
    If sdrOrder Is Nothing Then
        cnNwind.Close()
        Throw New Exception("Order body query returned nothing.")
        Return
    End If
    'OrderID = 0, CustomerID = 1, CompanyName = 2, ContactName = 3 ContactTitle = 4
    'Address = 5, City = 6, Region = 7, PostalCode = 8, Country = 9, Phone = 10
    'EmployeeID = 11, FirstName = 12, LastName = 13, Title = 14, Extension = 15
    'OrderDate = 16, RequiredDate = 17, ShippedDate = 18, ShipVia = 19,
    'ShipCompanyName = 20, Freight = 21 'ShipName = 22, ShipAddress = 23,
    'ShipCity = 24, ShipRegion = 25, ShipPostalCode = 26, ShipCountry = 27
    Dim intOrderID As Integer = sdrOrder.GetInt32(0)

    Dim strFile As String = strDir + "SO" + intOrderID.ToString() + ".xml"
    Dim xwSettings As New XmlWriterSettings
    With xwSettings
        .Encoding = Encoding.UTF8
```

```vb
        .Indent = True
        .IndentChars = ("  ")
        .OmitXmlDeclaration = False
        .ConformanceLevel = ConformanceLevel.Document
    End With
    Dim xwOrder As XmlWriter = XmlWriter.Create(strFile, xwSettings)
    With xwOrder
        .WriteStartElement("SalesOrder", _
         "http://www.northwind.com/schemas/SalesOrder")
        .WriteAttributeString("OrderID", sdrOrder.GetInt32(0).ToString)
        .WriteAttributeString("OrderDate", sdrOrder.GetDateTime(16).ToString("s"))
        .WriteAttributeString("CustomerID", sdrOrder.GetString(1))
        .WriteAttributeString("EmployeeID", sdrOrder.GetInt32(11).ToString)
        .WriteAttributeString("PaymentID", "1")
        .WriteAttributeString("CurrencyID", "1")
        .WriteAttributeString("FobID", "1")
        .WriteAttributeString("ShipperID", sdrOrder.GetInt32(19).ToString)
        .WriteElementString("SalesOrderNumber", sdrOrder.GetInt32(0).ToString)
        .WriteElementString("SalesOrderDate", sdrOrder.GetDateTime(16).ToString("s"))
        .WriteStartElement("Terms")
        .WriteElementString("Payment", "Net 30 Days")
        .WriteElementString("Currency", "US$")
        .WriteEndElement() 'Terms
        .WriteStartElement("Shipment")
        .WriteElementString("FOB", "Redmond, WA")
        .WriteElementString("Shipper", sdrOrder.GetString(20))
        .WriteElementString("EstimatedFreight",
         sdrOrder.GetDecimal(21).ToString("#0.00"))
        .WriteEndElement() 'Shipment
        .WriteStartElement("BillTo")
        .WriteElementString("Name", sdrOrder.GetString(2))
        .WriteElementString("Address", sdrOrder.GetString(5))
        .WriteElementString("City", sdrOrder.GetString(6))
        If sdrOrder.IsDBNull(7) Then
            .WriteElementString("Region", "")
        Else
            .WriteElementString("Region", sdrOrder.GetString(7))
        End If
        If sdrOrder.IsDBNull(8) Then
            .WriteElementString("PostalCode", "")
        Else
            .WriteElementString("PostalCode", sdrOrder.GetString(8))
        End If
        .WriteElementString("Country", sdrOrder.GetString(9))
        .WriteStartElement("Buyer")
        .WriteElementString("Name", sdrOrder.GetString(3))
        .WriteElementString("Title", sdrOrder.GetString(4))
        .WriteElementString("Phone", sdrOrder.GetString(10))
        Dim strEmail As String = sdrOrder.GetString(3)
        strEmail = Replace(strEmail, " ", "_") + "@mail.msn.com"
        .WriteElementString("EMail", strEmail)
        Dim strPurch As String = Now.Ticks.ToString.Substring(12)
        .WriteElementString("PurchaseOrder", strPurch)
        .WriteEndElement() 'Buyer
        .WriteEndElement() 'BillTo
```

```
            .WriteStartElement("SalesContact")
            Dim strEmplName As String = sdrOrder.GetString(12) + _
             " " + sdrOrder.GetString(13).ToString
            .WriteElementString("Name", strEmplName)
            .WriteElementString("Title", sdrOrder.GetString(14))
            Dim strEmpPhone As String = "(925) 555-8081 X" + sdrOrder.GetString(15)
            .WriteElementString("Phone", strEmpPhone)
            strEmail = sdrOrder.GetString(12).ToString.Substring(0, 1).ToLower
            strEmail += sdrOrder.GetString(13).ToLower + "@northwind.com"
            .WriteElementString("EMail", strEmail)
            .WriteEndElement() 'SalesContact
            .WriteStartElement("OrderDates")
            .WriteElementString("OrderDate", sdrOrder.GetDateTime(16).ToString("s"))
            .WriteElementString("RequiredDate", sdrOrder.GetDateTime(17).ToString("s"))
            .WriteEndElement() 'OrderDates
            .WriteStartElement("ShipTo")
            .WriteElementString("Name", sdrOrder.GetString(22))
            .WriteElementString("Address", sdrOrder.GetString(23))
            .WriteElementString("City", sdrOrder.GetString(24))
            If sdrOrder.IsDBNull(25) Then
               .WriteElementString("Region", "")
            Else
               .WriteElementString("Region", sdrOrder.GetString(25))
            End If
            If sdrOrder.IsDBNull(26) Then
               .WriteElementString("PostalCode", "")
            Else
               .WriteElementString("PostalCode", sdrOrder.GetString(26))
            End If
            .WriteElementString("Country", sdrOrder.GetString(27))
            .WriteEndElement() 'ShipTo
            .WriteStartElement("LineItems")
        End With
        'Save estimated freight
        Dim decFreight As Decimal = sdrOrder.GetDecimal(21)
        sdrOrder.Close()

        'Add line items with full product descriptions
        Dim intItem As Integer
        Dim intItems As Integer
        Dim decAmount As Decimal
        strSQL = "SELECT d.ProductID, p.ProductName, p.QuantityPerUnit, " + _
         "d.Quantity, d.UnitPrice, d.Discount " + _
         "FROM [Order Details] AS d, Products AS p " + _
         "WHERE d.OrderID = " + intOrderID.ToString + _
         " AND p.ProductID = d.ProductID"
        Dim sdrItem As SqlDataReader = Nothing
        Try
            With cmNwind
                'Use current connection
                .CommandText = strSQL
                sdrItem = .ExecuteReader
            End With
        Catch exc As Exception
            cnNwind.Close()
```

```
            Throw New Exception("Exception executing line item query.")
            Return
    End Try
    With sdrItem
        If .HasRows Then
            While .Read
                intItem += 1
                xwOrder.WriteStartElement("LineItem")
                xwOrder.WriteAttributeString("OrderID", intOrderID.ToString)
                xwOrder.WriteAttributeString("ProductID", .GetInt32(0).ToString)
                xwOrder.WriteAttributeString("ItemID", intItem.ToString)
                xwOrder.WriteElementString("ItemNumber", intItem.ToString)
                xwOrder.WriteElementString("Ordered", .GetInt16(3).ToString)
                xwOrder.WriteElementString("SKU", .GetInt32(0).ToString)
                xwOrder.WriteElementString("Product", .GetString(1))
                xwOrder.WriteElementString("Package", .GetString(2))
                xwOrder.WriteElementString("ListPrice", _
                  .GetDecimal(4).ToString("#0.00"))
                'Following accommodates real and decimal data types
                Dim decDisc As Decimal = CDec(.GetValue(5))
                xwOrder.WriteElementString("Discount", (100 * _
                  CDec(.GetValue(5))).ToString("#0.0"))
                Dim decExt As Decimal = .GetInt16(3) * .GetDecimal(4) * (1 - decDisc)
                xwOrder.WriteElementString("Extended", (decExt.ToString("0.00")))
                xwOrder.WriteEndElement() 'LineItem
                intItems += CInt(.GetInt16(3))
                decAmount += decExt
            End While
            .Close()
            cnNwind.Close()
        Else
            .Close()
            cnNwind.Close()
            Throw New Exception("No rows returned by line item query.")
            Return
        End If
    End With
    With xwOrder
        .WriteEndElement() 'LineItems
        .WriteStartElement("Summary")
        .WriteElementString("ItemsOrdered", intItems.ToString)
        .WriteElementString("Subtotal", decAmount.ToString("0.00"))
        .WriteElementString("EstimatedFreight", decFreight.ToString("0.00"))
        Dim decTotal As Decimal = decAmount + decFreight
        .WriteElementString("Total", decTotal.ToString("0.00"))
        .WriteEndElement() 'Summary
        .WriteEndElement() 'SalesOrder
        .Flush()
        .Close()
    End With

    Dim strOrderXML As String = Nothing
```

```
        If File.Exists(strFile) Then
            strOrderXML = File.ReadAllText(strFile, Encoding.Unicode)
            Dim intCols As Integer = (strOrderXML.Length \ 4000)
            Dim intCol As Integer
            Dim strColName As String = "SalesOrderXML"
            Try
                'spOrder.Send(strOrderXML) doesn't work, because order 11077
                'is 10,487 chars and SqlPipe is limited to 4,000 chars
                'Create multiple 4,000-char columns when necessary
                Dim mdCust(intCols) As SqlMetaData
                For intCol = 0 To intCols
                    mdCust(intCol) = New SqlMetaData(strColName + intCol.ToString, _
                        SqlDbType.NVarChar, 4000)
                Next intCol
                Dim sdrCust As New SqlDataRecord(mdCust)
                For intCol = 0 To intCols
                    If strOrderXML.Length <= 4000 Then
                        sdrCust.SetString(intCol, strOrderXML)
                    Else
                        sdrCust.SetString(intCol, strOrderXML.Substring(0, 4000))
                        strOrderXML = strOrderXML.Substring(4000)
                    End If
                Next intCol
                spOrder.Send(sdrCust)
            Catch exc As Exception
                Throw New Exception(exc.Message)
            End Try
        Else
            Throw New Exception("Failed to create '" + strFile + "' file.")
        End If
    End Sub
```

The `SqlPipe.Send` method is limited to 8,000 bytes or 4,000 Unicode characters. The highlighted code at the end of the preceding listing breaks documents that are longer than 4,000 characters — such as that for OrderID 11077 — into multiple, sequentially numbered `SqlDataRecord` columns. The StoredProcedureClient project's `GetSalesOrderXML` procedure concatenates the characters from multiple columns.

Figure 11-6 shows the StoredProcedureClient's startup form displaying part of the 10,503-character XML document generated by OrderID 11077, which requires three `SqlDataRecord` columns. Generating most SalesOrderXML documents with a fast (2.66 GHz) computer requires 16 milliseconds or less, which includes the time required to save and read the file.

Performance of SQL/CLR objects depends on available RAM, CPU speed, and disk I/O performance. If you don't have enough RAM to avoid paging when creating and saving the XML document, performance deteriorates dramatically.

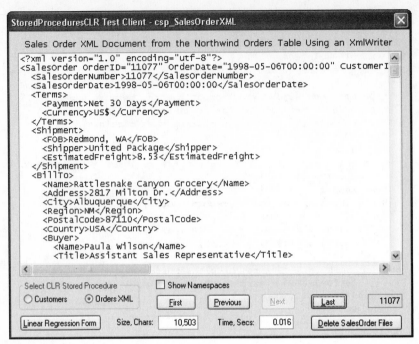

Figure 11-6

Following is the complete XML document for the first Northwind order:

```
<?xml version="1.0" encoding="utf-8"?>
<SalesOrder OrderID="10248" OrderDate="1996-07-04T00:00:00" CustomerID="VINET"
EmployeeID="5" PaymentID="1" CurrencyID="1" FobID="1" ShipperID="3"
xmlns="http://www.northwind.com/schemas/SalesOrder">
  <SalesOrderNumber>10248</SalesOrderNumber>
  <SalesOrderDate>1996-07-04T00:00:00</SalesOrderDate>
  <Terms>
<Payment>Net 30 Days</Payment>
<Currency>US$</Currency>
  </Terms>
  <Shipment>
<FOB>Redmond, WA</FOB>
<Shipper>Federal Shipping</Shipper>
<EstimatedFreight>32.38</EstimatedFreight>
  </Shipment>
  <BillTo>
<Name>Vins et alcools Chevalier</Name>
<Address>59 rue de l'Abbaye</Address>
<City>Reims</City>
<Region />
<PostalCode>51100</PostalCode>
<Country>France</Country>
<Buyer>
  <Name>Paul Henriot</Name>
  <Title>Accounting Manager</Title>
```

```xml
    <Phone>26.47.15.10</Phone>
    <EMail>Paul_Henriot@mail.msn.com</EMail>
    <PurchaseOrder>517098</PurchaseOrder>
  </Buyer>
 </BillTo>
 <SalesContact>
<Name>Steven Buchanan</Name>
<Title>Sales Manager</Title>
<Phone>(925) 555-8081 X3453</Phone>
<EMail>sbuchanan@northwind.com</EMail>
 </SalesContact>
 <OrderDates>
<OrderDate>1996-07-04T00:00:00</OrderDate>
<RequiredDate>1996-08-01T00:00:00</RequiredDate>
 </OrderDates>
 <ShipTo>
<Name>Vins et alcools Chevalier</Name>
<Address>59 rue de l'Abbaye</Address>
<City>Reims</City>
<Region />
<PostalCode>51100</PostalCode>
<Country>France</Country>
 </ShipTo>
 <LineItems>
<LineItem OrderID="10248" ProductID="11" ItemID="1">
  <ItemNumber>1</ItemNumber>
  <Ordered>12</Ordered>
  <SKU>11</SKU>
  <Product>Queso Cabrales</Product>
  <Package>1 kg pkg.</Package>
  <ListPrice>14.00</ListPrice>
  <Discount>0.0</Discount>
  <Extended>168.00</Extended>
</LineItem>
<LineItem OrderID="10248" ProductID="42" ItemID="2">
  <ItemNumber>2</ItemNumber>
  <Ordered>10</Ordered>
  <SKU>42</SKU>
  <Product>Singaporean Hokkien Fried Mee</Product>
  <Package>32 - 1 kg pkgs.</Package>
  <ListPrice>9.80</ListPrice>
  <Discount>0.0</Discount>
  <Extended>98.00</Extended>
</LineItem>
<LineItem OrderID="10248" ProductID="72" ItemID="3">
  <ItemNumber>3</ItemNumber>
  <Ordered>5</Ordered>
  <SKU>72</SKU>
  <Product>Mozzarella di Giovanni</Product>
  <Package>24 - 200 g pkgs.</Package>
  <ListPrice>34.80</ListPrice>
  <Discount>0.0</Discount>
  <Extended>174.00</Extended>
</LineItem>
 </LineItems>
```

```
  <Summary>
 <ItemsOrdered>27</ItemsOrdered>
 <Subtotal>440.00</Subtotal>
 <EstimatedFreight>32.38</EstimatedFreight>
 <Total>472.38</Total>
  </Summary>
 </SalesOrder>
```

The StoredProceduresCLR project includes a SalesOrdersXML_NS procedure to demonstrate the XmlWriter's namespace assignment capabilities. Marking the client application's Show Namespaces checkbox displays attributes and subelements that are qualified with namespace prefixes and local xmlns attributes, such as xmlns:nwbt="http://www.northwind.com/schemas/BillTo, as shown in Figure 11-7.

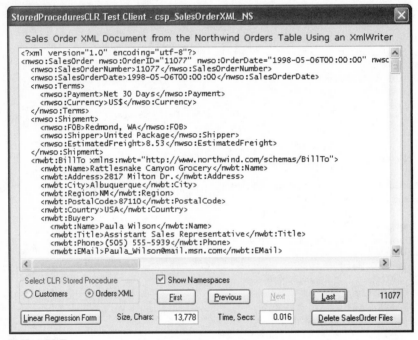

Figure 11-7

Project Product Sales with Linear Regression Analysis

Linear regression analysis is a statistical method to determine the coordinates of a straight line that best fits the values of a set of data points. Analysts use linear regression and related, more complex non-linear techniques to generate projections that are based on historical data. The StoredProceduresCLR project's csp_LinearRegression procedure accepts ProductID, LastMonth, Months, and UseSalesOrders parameters to return an 11-column SqlDataRecord. The columns provide the intercept (a) and slope (b) of the regression line, and additional statistical data, such as the correlation coefficient (r), significance (t), and confidence interval (c). Additional columns provide average unit and dollar sales for the selected product.

The csp_LinearRegression procedure illustrates use of date/time calculations, arrays, and complex calculations in SQL/CLR stored procedures. If a middle-tier or client application was to perform the linear regression calculations, many rows would be returned for a real-world application. Thus, this procedure is well suited to SQL/CLR implementation.

> *If you're not familiar with linear regression statistics techniques, see "Correlation and Regression Analysis" at* http://home.millsaps.edu/~lawrecn/f04/plsc2550/lectures/schacht-10-web.pdf. *For a more detailed analysis of significance tests and confidence intervals, go to* http://psych.rice.edu/online_stat/chapter11/inferential.html.

A significant problem with aggregate queries that supply the historical sales data is handling periods — usually months — with no sales for the specified product. A data point for the specified product is required for each period, including periods with no sales. (Many Northwind products have several months with no sales.) One solution is to create a temporary pivot table, replace NULL values with 0, and then unpivot the table, as described in the section "Explore the PIVOT and UNPIVOT Operators" in Chapter 10. An alternative approach, which demonstrates the use of arrays in SQL Server projects, requires these steps:

1. Create a multi-dimension array with elements for each historical period. Elements contain the period ordinals (year and month), an optional sequential month number, and empty values for unit and dollar sales for the period.

2. Execute a conventional aggregate query or stored procedure to populate an array of the same structure that has values for unit and dollar sales, but has no elements for periods without sales.

3. Replace the empty unit and dollar sales values of the first array with values from the second array by matching period ordinals.

4. Iterate the second array and perform calculations to generate regression line coordinates, correlation coefficient, statistical significance, and confidence interval data.

5. Return the statistical and related data to the client as an SqlDataRecord.

The T-SQL statement for the aggregate stored procedure (usp_GetOrdersAggregates or usp_GetSalesOrdersAggregates) is:

```
CREATE PROCEDURE usp_GetOrdersAggregates (@ProductID int, @StartDate datetime,
@EndDate datetime) AS
SELECT @ProductID AS ProductID,
DATEPART(year, OrderDate) AS Year, DATEPART(month, OrderDate) AS Month,
ROW_NUMBER() OVER(ORDER BY DATEPART(year, OrderDate),
DATEPART(month, OrderDate)) AS MonthNum,
SUM(Quantity) AS TotalUnits,
CONVERT(int, SUM([Order Details].UnitPrice * Quantity * (1 - Discount))) AS
TotalSales , ProductName
FROM Orders, [Order Details], Products
WHERE Orders.OrderID = [Order Details].OrderID
AND [Order Details].ProductID = @ProductID
AND Products.ProductID = @ProductID
AND OrderDate BETWEEN @StartDate AND @EndDate
GROUP BY DATEPART(year, OrderDate), DATEPART(month, OrderDate), ProductName
ORDER BY DATEPART(year, OrderDate) DESC, DATEPART(month, OrderDate) DESC;
```

The @EndDate parameter value is the last day of the month that precedes the latest month with sales of any product. The @StartDate value is the date of the first day of the month that begins the historical period.

The usp_GetSalesOrderAggregates stored procedure substitutes potentially very large SalesOrders and SalesOrderItems tables for the original Northwind Orders and Order Details tables. The SalesOrders table contains a SalesOrderXML column of the xml datatype for use in the next chapter's examples. See the section "Create and Fill the SalesOrders and SalesOrderItems Tables" in Chapter 12 for instructions on how to add these two tables to your Northwind database and populate them with randomized data.

Following is the code for the csp_LinearRegression procedure, with highlighted comments that correspond to the steps described in the earlier list:

```
<SqlProcedure()> _
Public Shared Sub csp_LinearRegression(ByVal ProductID As SqlInt32, _
    ByVal LastMonth As SqlDateTime, ByVal Months As SqlByte, _
    ByVal UseSalesOrders As SqlByte)

    Dim cnNwind As New SqlConnection("context connection=true")
    Dim cmNwind As New SqlCommand
    Dim strSQL As String = Nothing
    Dim strProductName As String = Nothing
    Dim intMonths As Integer = CInt(Months)
    Dim datLastMonth As DateTime = CDate(LastMonth)
    Dim blnUseSalesOrders As Boolean
    If CByte(UseSalesOrders) <> 0 Then
        blnUseSalesOrders = True
    End If

    'Calculate the starting and ending date parameters
    Dim datStartParam As DateTime = datLastMonth.AddMonths(-intMonths)
    'End date is the last day of the month preceding the date of the last order
    Dim datEndParam As DateTime = datLastMonth.AddDays(-1)

    'Create an array of months in ascending date sequence
    Dim intMonth As Integer
    Dim datMonth As DateTime = datLastMonth.AddMonths(-1)
    Dim astrFinal(intMonths - 1, 5) As String
    For intMonth = intMonths To 1 Step -1
        astrFinal(intMonth - 1, 0) = ProductID.ToString
        astrFinal(intMonth - 1, 1) = datMonth.Year.ToString
        astrFinal(intMonth - 1, 2) = datMonth.Month.ToString
        astrFinal(intMonth - 1, 3) = intMonth.ToString
        astrFinal(intMonth - 1, 4) = "0"
        astrFinal(intMonth - 1, 5) = "0"
        datMonth = datMonth.AddMonths(-1)
    Next intMonth

    'Execute the appropriate stored procedure
    If blnUseSalesOrders Then
        strSQL = "usp_GetSalesOrdersAggregates"
    Else
        strSQL = "usp_GetOrdersAggregates"
    End If
```

```
Try
    cnNwind.Open()
    With cmNwind
        .Connection = cnNwind
        .Parameters.Clear()
        .CommandText = strSQL
        .Parameters.AddWithValue("@ProductID", ProductID)
        .Parameters.AddWithValue("@StartDate", datStartParam)
        .Parameters.AddWithValue("@EndDate", datEndParam)
        .CommandType = CommandType.StoredProcedure
    End With
    Dim rdrData As SqlDataReader = cmNwind.ExecuteReader

    'Create the array for months with sales
    Dim intRow As Integer
    Dim astrData(intMonths - 1, 5) As String
    With rdrData
        If .HasRows Then
            While .Read
                astrData(intRow, 0) = .GetInt32(0).ToString    'Product ID
                astrData(intRow, 1) = .GetInt32(1).ToString    'Year
                astrData(intRow, 2) = .GetInt32(2).ToString    'Month
                astrData(intRow, 3) = .GetInt64(3).ToString    'MonthNum (x)
                astrData(intRow, 4) = .GetInt32(4).ToString    'TotalUnits (y)
                astrData(intRow, 5) = .GetInt32(5).ToString    'TotalSales
                If intRow = 0 Then
                    strProductName = .GetString(6)
                End If
                intRow += 1
            End While
            .Close()
            cnNwind.Close()
        Else
            .Close
            cnNwind.Close()
            Throw New Exception("No rows returned by stored procedure")
            Return
        End If
    End With

    'Fill the astrFinal array with matching astrData sales values
    Dim intMax As Integer = intRow
    For intRow = 0 To intMax - 1
        For intMonth = 0 To intMonths - 1
            If astrData(intRow, 1) = astrFinal(intMonth, 1) And _
               astrData(intRow, 2) = astrFinal(intMonth, 2) Then
                astrFinal(intMonth, 4) = astrData(intRow, 4)
                astrFinal(intMonth, 5) = astrData(intRow, 5)
                Exit For
            End If
        Next
    Next

    'Linear Regression variables
    Dim SumX As Long, SumY As Long, SumXY As Long, SumX2 As Long
```

```vb
Dim SumY2 As Long, SumSales As Decimal, N As Integer, b As Double
Dim a As Double, r As Double, t As Double, t95 As Boolean, t99 As Boolean

'Aggregate the datapoints for the regression line
Dim intRows As Integer
For intRow = 0 To intMonths - 1
   SumX += CLng(astrFinal(intRow, 3))
   SumY += CLng(astrFinal(intRow, 4))
   SumXY += CLng(astrFinal(intRow, 3)) * CLng(astrFinal(intRow, 4))
   SumX2 += CLng(astrFinal(intRow, 3)) * CLng(astrFinal(intRow, 3))
   SumY2 += CLng(astrFinal(intRow, 4)) * CLng(astrFinal(intRow, 4))
   SumSales += CLng(astrFinal(intRow, 5))
   intRows += 1
Next intRow
N = intMonths
b = (SumXY - (SumX * SumY) / N) / (SumX2 - (SumX * SumX) / N) 'Slope
a = SumY / N - (b * SumX / N) 'Intercept

'Correlation coefficient
r = Abs(SumXY - (SumX * SumY) / N) / + _
 (Sqrt(SumX2 - ((SumX * SumX) / N)) * Sqrt(SumY2 - ((SumY * SumY) / N)))

'Significance test (Student's t)
t = r * Sqrt((N - 2) / (1 - (r * r)))

'Confidence intervals - 95% and 99%
If N > 3 Then
   Dim df As Integer = N - 2
   Dim tCrit95 As Double
   Select Case df
      Case Is >= 20
         tCrit95 = 2.086
      Case Is >= 10
         tCrit95 = 2.228
      Case Is >= 8
         tCrit95 = 2.306
      Case Is >= 5
         tCrit95 = 2.571
      Case Is >= 4
         tCrit95 = 2.776
      Case Is >= 3
         tCrit95 = 3.182
      Case Is >= 2
         tCrit95 = 4.303
   End Select
   If t >= tCrit95 Then
      t95 = True
   End If

   Dim tCrit99 As Double
   Select Case df
      Case Is >= 20
         tCrit99 = 2.845
      Case Is >= 10
         tCrit99 = 3.169
```

```
                    Case Is >= 8
                        tCrit99 = 3.554
                    Case Is >= 5
                        tCrit99 = 4.032
                    Case Is >= 4
                        tCrit99 = 4.604
                    Case Is >= 3
                        tCrit99 = 5.841
                    Case Is >= 2
                        tCrit99 = 9.925
                End Select
                If t >= tCrit99 Then
                    t99 = True
                End If
            End If
            Dim dblAverageUnits As Double = SumY / N
            Dim decAverageSales As Decimal = CDec(SumSales / N)

            'Define and populate the SqlDataRecord
            Dim mdRegr(10) As SqlMetaData
            mdRegr(0) = New SqlMetaData("ProductID", SqlDbType.Int)
            mdRegr(1) = New SqlMetaData("ProductName", SqlDbType.NVarChar, 40)
            mdRegr(2) = New SqlMetaData("StartDate", SqlDbType.DateTime)
            mdRegr(3) = New SqlMetaData("Months", SqlDbType.TinyInt)
            mdRegr(4) = New SqlMetaData("Intercept", SqlDbType.Decimal, 16, 6)
            mdRegr(5) = New SqlMetaData("Slope", SqlDbType.Decimal, 12, 6)
            mdRegr(6) = New SqlMetaData("Correlation", SqlDbType.Decimal, 7, 6)
            mdRegr(7) = New SqlMetaData("Significance", SqlDbType.Decimal, 10, 6)
            mdRegr(8) = New SqlMetaData("Confidence", SqlDbType.TinyInt)
            mdRegr(9) = New SqlMetaData("AverageUnits", SqlDbType.Int)
            mdRegr(10) = New SqlMetaData("AverageSales", SqlDbType.Money)
            Dim sdrRegr As New SqlDataRecord(mdRegr)
            sdrRegr.SetSqlInt32(0, ProductID)
            If strProductName IsNot Nothing Then
                sdrRegr.SetSqlString(1, strProductName)
            End If
            sdrRegr.SetSqlDateTime(2, datStartParam)
            sdrRegr.SetSqlByte(3, CByte(Months))
            sdrRegr.SetSqlDecimal(4, CDec(a))
            sdrRegr.SetSqlDecimal(5, CDec(b))
            sdrRegr.SetSqlDecimal(6, CDec(r))
            sdrRegr.SetSqlDecimal(7, CDec(t))
            If t95 Then
                sdrRegr.SetSqlByte(8, CByte(95))
            End If
            If t99 Then
                sdrRegr.SetSqlByte(8, CByte(99))
            End If
            sdrRegr.SetSqlInt32(9, CInt(dblAverageUnits))
            sdrRegr.SetSqlMoney(10, decAverageSales)

            'Send the LinearRegression record
            Dim spRegr As SqlPipe = SqlContext.GetPipe
            spRegr.Send(sdrRegr)
        Catch exc As Exception
```

```
    Throw New Exception(exc.Message)
  End Try
  End Sub
```

The StoredProceduresClient project's CSPRegression.vb form determines the date of the last order for any product, and then executes the appropriate user stored procedure to populate the list box, which provides data that you can use to test the reasonableness of the regression data. Code then executes csp_LinearRegression to populate the Intercept (a), Slope (b), Correlation (r), Significance (t), Confidence (c), Average Units, and Average Sales text boxes. The client calculates values for This Month, Three Months, (average) Unit Price, Average Discount, Inventory Units, and (inventory) Days text boxes. Figure 11-8 shows the data for Chai, whose regression line has a 99 percent confidence interval.

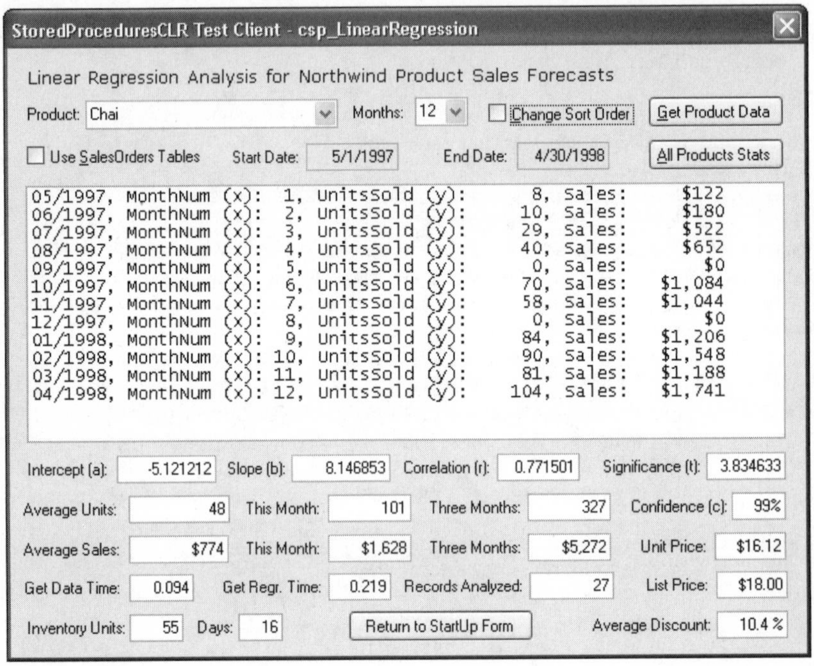

Figure 11-8

It's surprising to find several products with regression lines that have confidence intervals of 95 percent or more, when you consider the small sample size of the Northwind Order Details table. A confidence interval of 95 percent or more indicates that the regression data is reasonably trustworthy for projecting future sales (This Month and Three Months). You can shorten or lengthen the historical period by selecting other values from the Months combo box to gain better insight into sales trends over time.

Clicking the All Products Stats button fills the list box with items representing statistical data for all Northwind products. Clicking an item displays a tooltip with all data for the row. Double-clicking an item populates the text boxes for the selected ProductID, as shown in Figure 11-9.

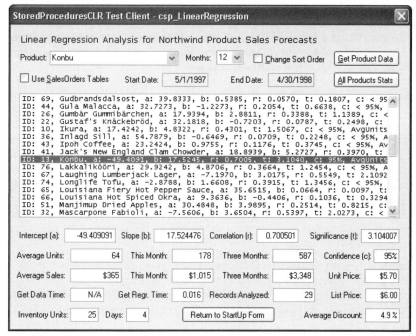

Figure 11-9

The csp_LinearRegression procedure's execution time with the computer used to write this book is less than 16 milliseconds for a 12-month analysis of a single product and about 0.75 second for all products, which scans a total of 1,369 Order Details records. As you'd expect, scans of large OLTP tables take longer. For example, with a SalesOrders table with 500,000 rows and about 2 million SalesOrderItems rows, the average execution time for a single product with an average of 14,000 records is about 6 seconds. Returning data for all products in the period (940,000 SalesOrderItems records) takes about 7 minutes. In a real-world scenario, statistical calculations usually query tables or OLAP cubes of pre-aggregated data. SQL Server Analysis Services and data mining features provide several built-in time series algorithms.

Create User-Defined Types

User-defined types (UDTs) let you design and implement custom data types of arbitrary complexity. All recent SQL Server versions enable the creation of user-defined data types (UDDTs). UDDTs — also called *alias data types* — return SQL Server native data types and can incorporate a single RULE to specify acceptable values. UDDTs are most useful for ensuring data-type consistency among columns in multiple tables of one or more databases. Nullability, precision, and scale of decimal or numeric data types, and RULE-based value restrictions are typical consistency constraints. UDTs extend the scope of UDDTs by eliminating the native data-type restriction and enabling more sophisticated value constraints. UDTs also support custom instance methods that can return different representations of the data, execute comparisons, or perform calculations.

Creating a UDDT or UDT in the model database adds the UDDT or UDT and its assembly to new databases. According to Books Online's "CREATE RULE" topic, future SQL Server versions won't include the CREATE RULE instruction and will rely on table-based CHECK constraints for restricting values. Thus, UDDTs will lose one of their primary features. To ensure future-version compatibility, write and deploy a CLR UDT to emulate a UDDT with a RULE.

You specify a UDT's type by the following Format enum members:

❑ Format.Native is the simplest UDT type, and you can implement the UDT with a Structure or Class. Native serialization restricts field data types to fixed-length value types — specifically Boolean, Byte, SByte, Short, UShort, Int, UInt, Long, ULong, Float, Double, SqlByte, SqlInt16, SqlInt32, SqlInt64, SqlDateTime, SqlSingle, SqlDouble, SqlMoney, and SqlBoolean. (Notice that Decimal and SqlDecimal types are missing from the list because precision specifies the data type's length.) Serialization to and deserialization from byte-ordered format is automatic. The database engine saves the storage size requirement as UDT metadata. The later section, "A Simple Value-Type UDT," describes the code required to implement a Native-format UDT.

❑ Format.UserDefined lets you include reference types — String and SqlString — and Decimal and SqlDecimal as field data types. Reference and Decimal types require adding serialization and deserialization code by implementing the IBinarySerialize interface with Public Overridable Read and Write procedures that handle interaction between T-SQL and managed code. You must implement the UserDefined type as a Class and add a default constructor.

All UDTs must implement the INullable interface to support required IsNull and Null read-only properties for compatibility with NULL column values. The required Parse and ToString functions enable T-SQL statements to handle writing and reading character-based representations of property values. You can index UDT columns of Native types; indexing UserDefined types requires that you add the IsByteOrdered:=True attribute. You also can specify an indexable UDT column as the table's primary key.

Like CLR stored procedures and user-defined functions, pressing F5 in VS 2005 Standard Edition and higher builds and deploys UDTs to the database of the connection you assign when you start the SQL Server Project.

Native-Format UDT Code for Structures and Classes

Following is the skeleton code for a Native-format UDT implemented as a Structure:

```
Imports System
Imports System.Data.Sql
Imports System.Data.SqlTypes        'Provides INullable
Imports Microsoft.SqlServer.Server  'Provides SqlUserDefinedTypeAttribute

<Serializable(), SqlUserDefinedType(Format.Native)> _
Public Structure UDTName
Implements INullable

Private blnIsNull As Boolean
'Private field definitions
Private fieldName as ValueDataType
```

```
'...

Public ReadOnly Property IsNull() As Boolean _
    Implements INullable.IsNull
    Get
        Return blnIsNull
    End Get
End Property

Public Shared ReadOnly Property Null() As UDTName
    Get
        Dim udtNew As [New] UDTName
        udtNew.blnIsNull = True
        Return udtNew
    End Get
End Property

Public Overrides Function ToString() As String
    If Me.IsNull Then
        Return "Null" 'Or "NULL" or "null"
    Else
        'Code to create string representation
    End If
End Function

Public Shared Function Parse(ByVal sqlString As SqlString) As UDTName
    'Creates a Point by splitting an input string at the separator character
    If sqlString.IsNull Then
        Return Nothing
    Else
        Dim udtNew As [New] UDTName
        Dim strNew As String = sqlString.ToString
        Dim astrNew() As String = strNew.Split("?"c)
        'Code to populate array by parsing string representation at ?
        fieldName = astrNew(0)
        'Remaining field assignments
        Return udtNew
    End If
End Function


Public Property prpName As ValueDataType
    'For each field
    Get
        Return Me.fieldName
    End Get
    Set(ByVal Value As ValueDataType)
        Me.fieldName = Value
        blnIsNull = False
    End Set
End Property

Public Function optFunction As ValueDataType
    'Optional function(s) that perform calculations or other operations
End Function
End Structure
```

To implement the UDT as a `Class`, you must add a `StructLayout(LayoutKind.Sequential)` attribute from the `System.Runtime.InteropServices` namespace and a default constructor by making the following emphasized modifications to the `Structure` code:

```
Imports System
Imports System.Data.Sql
Imports System.Data.SqlTypes
Imports Microsoft.SqlServer.Server
Imports System.Runtime.InteropServices 'Provides StructLayout()

<Serializable(), SqlUserDefinedType(Format.Native), _
 StructLayout(LayoutKind.Sequential)> _
Public Class UDTClass
Implements INullable

Private blnIsNull As Boolean
'Private field definitions
Private fieldName As ValueDataType
'...

Public Sub New()
   'Default constructor required for class
   Me.blnIsNull = True
   Me.fieldName = 0
   'Additional private fields
End Sub

'Same properties, procedures, and functions as Structure version

End Class
```

The `New` keyword, which is optional (and disregarded) in the `Structure` code example, is required for the `Class` implementation.

> *It's up to you whether to use a* `Structure` *or* `Class` *to implement value-type UDTs;* `Structures` *are simpler to implement. The default skeleton code that VS 2005 Standard Edition and higher creates by choosing Project ⇨ New User-Defined Type is a* `Structure`.

UserDefined-Format UDT Class Code

Following is the skeleton code for the additions and modifications — shown emphasized — required for a `Native`-format class to create a `UserDefined` UDT with `String` or `Decimal` field data types:

```
Imports System
Imports System.Data.Sql
Imports System.Data.SqlTypes
Imports Microsoft.SqlServer.Server
Imports System.IO 'Provides IBinarySerialize

<Serializable(), SqlUserDefinedType(Format.UserDefined, IsByteOrdered:=True, _
[IsFixedLength:=False], MaxByteSize:=200)> _
```

```
Public Class UDTName
   Implements INullable, IBinarySerialize

Private blnIsNull As Boolean
'Private field definitions
Private fieldName As String
'...

'Same constructor, IsNull and Null procedures, ToString and Parse functions,
'Properties and optional functions as Native Class version.

Public Overridable Sub Write(ByVal binWriter As BinaryWriter) _
 Implements IBinarySerialize.Write
   Dim bytHeader As Byte
   If Me.IsNull Then
      bytHeader = 0
   Else
      bytHeader = 1
   End If
   With binWriter
      .Write(bytHeader)
      If bytHeader = 0 Then
         Return
      End If
      .Write(Me.fieldName)
      '...
   End With
End Sub

Public Sub Read(ByVal binReader As BinaryReader) _
 Implements IBinarySerialize.Read
   Dim bytHeader As Byte = binReader.ReadByte()
   If bytHeader = 0 Then
      Me.blnIsNull = True
      Return
   End If

   Me.blnIsNull = False
   With binReader
      Me.fieldName = .ReadString()
      '...
   End With
End Sub
EndClass
```

The `IsByteOrdered:= True` attribute specifies that the UDT members can be used in WHERE constraints with T-SQL comparison operators, and ORDER BY, GROUP BY, and PARTITION clauses. The section "Test the Address UDT with WHERE Constraints and ORDER BY Clauses," later in this chapter, describes T-SQL WHERE, ORDER BY, and GROUP BY syntax for tables that include a `UserDefined`-format UDT column. The `MaxByteSize:=Number` attribute determines the UDT's storage space; `Number` must be greater than the maximum number of bytes contained in a serialized instance.

A Simple Value-Type UDT

The Point type, which requires two numeric (Double or Integer) coordinates, is the archetypical example of a simple value-type UDT, but few sample implementations have identical code. The following code implements a Point Structure with Point.X and Point.Y properties and an optional DistanceTo function that computes and returns the distance between the current Point instance and a second ptTest instance:

```
Imports System
Imports System.Data.Sql
Imports System.Data.SqlTypes
Imports Microsoft.SqlServer.Server
Imports System.Math

<Serializable(), SqlUserDefinedType(Format.Native, MaxByteSize:=512)> _
Public Structure Point
Implements INullable

Private blnIsNull As Boolean
'Coordinates
Private dblX As Double
Private dblY As Double

Public ReadOnly Property IsNull() As Boolean _
   Implements INullable.IsNull
    'Required
    Get
        Return blnIsNull
    End Get
End Property

Public Shared ReadOnly Property Null() As Point
    'Required
    Get
        Dim ptNew As Point
        ptNew.blnIsNull = True
        Return ptNew
    End Get
End Property

Public Overrides Function ToString() As String
    'Return the comma-separated values
    If Me.IsNull Then
        Return "Null"
    Else
        Return Me.dblX.ToString + "," + Me.dblY.ToString
    End If
End Function

Public Shared Function Parse(ByVal sqlString As SqlString) As Point
    'Creates a Point by splitting an input string at the separator character
    If sqlString.IsNull Then
        Return Nothing
    Else
        Dim ptNew As Point
```

```
            Dim strNew As String = sqlString.ToString
            Dim astrXY() As String = strNew.Split(",",c)
            ptNew.X = CType(astrXY(0), Double)
            ptNew.Y = CType(astrXY(1), Double)
            Return ptNew
        End If
    End Function

    Public Property X() As Double
        'X-coordinate
        Get
            Return Me.dblX
        End Get
        Set(ByVal Value As Double)
            Me.dblX = Value
            blnIsNull = False
        End Set
    End Property

    Public Property Y() As Double
        'Y-coordinate
        Get
            Return Me.dblY
        End Get
        Set(ByVal Value As Double)
            Me.dblY = Value
            blnIsNull = False
        End Set
    End Property

    Public Function DistanceTo(ByVal ptTest As Point) As Double
        'Optional function: Calculate the distance from Me to ptTest
        Return Sqrt((Me.X - ptTest.X) * (Me.X - ptTest.X) + _
          (Me.Y - ptTest.Y) * (Me.Y - ptTest.Y))
    End Function
End Structure
```

The string representation of a `Point` instance is `'X, Y'` for input (`Parse()`) and output (`ToString()`), where `X` and `Y` are literal values within the range of the `Double` data type.

> *The sample UserDefinedTypesCLR.sln project in the \VB2005DB\Chapter11\UserDefinedTypesCLR folder includes* `Point` *and* `PointClass` *UDTs that you can deploy to the Northwind database. Like other SQL Server projects, the project's Properties window contains a Database page with a Connection String text box for* `localhost` *as the default instance. Edit the Connection String, if necessary, to specify your SQL Server 2005 instance with the Northwind sample database.*

Deploy the UDT with the CREATE TYPE Instruction

Visual Studio 2005 Express Editions don't deploy UDTs automatically. Use the following batch to deploy the `Point` UDT with the T-SQL `CREATE ASSEMBLY` and `CREATE TYPE` instructions:

```
CREATE ASSEMBLY UserDefinedTypesCLR FROM '\Path\bin\UserDefinedTypesCLR.dll';
CREATE TYPE Point EXTERNAL NAME UserDefinedTypesCLR.UserDefinedTypesCLR.Point;
```

`Path` is the well-formed path to the \VB2005DB\Chapter11\UserDefinedTypesCLR folder.

To redeploy a revised version of the `Point` UDT, add the following commands before the preceding instructions: If you've added an instance of a Point type as a table column, you must drop the table before dropping the UDT.

```
DROP TYPE Point;
DROP ASSEMBLY UserDefinedTypesCLR;
```

The CreateUDT.sql script in the \VB2005DB\Chapter11\UserDefinedTypesCLR\Test Scripts folder creates the ASSEMBLY *and the project's four* TYPES — Point, PointClass, Address, *and* AddressBasic. *Commented instructions drop the* TYPES *and then the* ASSEMBLY. *You must edit the file paths to point to your sample files installation folder.*

Test the Point UDT with T-SQL Instructions

It's a good practice to verify the behavior of your UDT before creating a table with a UDT field. After you assign the UDT to a table column, you can't redeploy assembly revisions. You must drop all tables that include the UDT column and then redeploy the UDT assembly to the database.

Connect to the database in SMSS and type instructions like the following to test the `Point` UDT:

```
DECLARE @pt Point
SET @pt = CONVERT(Point, '0,0')
SET @pt.X = 1
SET @pt.Y = 2
PRINT @pt.ToString()
--Returns 1,2

SET @pt = CONVERT(Point, '2.5,3.6')
PRINT @pt.X
PRINT @pt.Y
PRINT @pt.ToString()
--Returns 2.5,3.6

SET @pt.X = 2
SET @pt.Y = 2
PRINT @pt.ToString()
--Returns 2,2

PRINT @pt.DistanceTo(CONVERT(Point, '1,1'))
--Returns 1.41421...
```

The UserDefinedTypesCLR project's Test.sql script includes the preceding commands. The UserDefinedTypesClient.sln project in the \VB2005DB\Chapter11\UserDefinedTypesClient folder executes a T-SQL script (Point.sql in the ...\bin\Debug folder) that tests the Point *UDT.*

Add a UDT Column to a Table

The process for creating a table with a UDT column is identical to that for columns of native data types. UDTs that you add to a database appear at the end of the Data Type list when you right-click Server Explorer's Northwind Tables node and choose Add New Table. Add PointID `int` and PointUDT `dbo.Point` columns, as shown in Figure 11-10. Right-click the PointID column, select Set Primary Key, and save the table as `PointUDT`.

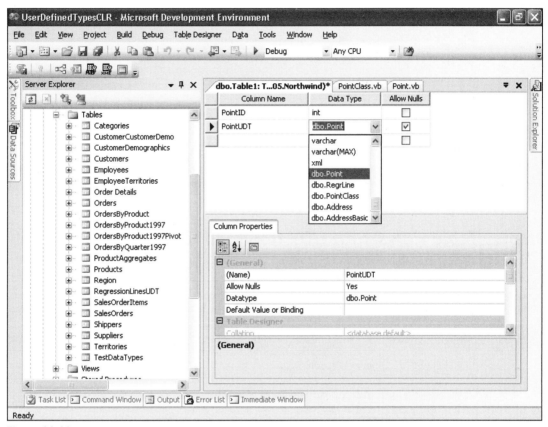

Figure 11-10

To add `Point` instances to the table rows, right-click the PointsUDT table and choose Show Table Data. Type a few PointID values and PointUDT coordinates (X, Y), as shown in Figure 11-11.

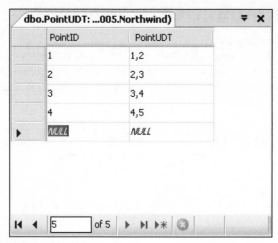

Figure 11-11

Typing an invalid PointUDT value, such as a space after the comma separator, displays a validation error icon, which you can remove by correcting the error. You must correct the error, and then close and reopen the grid.

Display Table Rows with UDT Columns

Executing SELECT * FROM PointsUDT in the SMSS query editor returns "An error occurred while uting batch. Error message is: File or assembly name 'UserDefinedTypesCLR, Version=1.0.1822.31408, Culture=neutral, PublicKeyToken=null', or one of its dependencies, was not found" error message. The message occurs because neither application is aware of the assembly. If you add the assembly with a strong name to the GAC, the query succeeds. The query returns the PointID value followed by the binary representation of the PointUDT instance, similar to this:

```
1  0x00000000000000f03f00000000000022c0
```

*SQLCMD.exe returns the preceding binary representation of the UDT when you execute a SELECT * FROM PointsUDT query from an input batch file with a Visual Basic Shell instruction.*

The query editors require you to invoke the ToString() method to return string values. Executing SELECT PointID, PointUDT.ToString() FROM PointsUDT solves the problem and returns the rows you added.

UDT column names aren't case-sensitive, but method names are case-sensitive and the parenthesis pair is required. If you type PointUDT.tostring() instead of PointUDT.ToString() you receive a "Could not find method 'tostring' for type 'UserDefinedTypesCLR.Point' in assembly 'UserDefinedTypesCLR'" error message. Typing PointUDT.ToString returns a similar message.

The UserDefinedTypesClient project displays data from the PointsUDT and AddressesUDT tables in several formats. Later sections describe the UserDefined-format Address UDT and the AddressesUDT table.

Use an SqlDataReader to Return UDT Values

The following snippet is extracted from the UserDefinedTypesClient project's `btnPopulate_Click` event handler behind the UDTTables.vb form. This simplified code retrieves from the PointsUDT table the `PointID`, `PointUDT`, and `DistanceTo` a fixed (10, 0) Point object:

```
...
strSQL = "SELECT PointID, PointUDT.ToString(), " + _
 "PointUDT.DistanceTo(CONVERT(Point, '10,0')) FROM PointsUDT"
cmNwind = New SqlCommand(strSQL, cnNwind)
cnNwind.Open()
Dim rdrData As SqlDataReader = cmNwind.ExecuteReader
With rdrData
    If .HasRows Then
        While .Read
            strRow = "ID: " + .GetInt32(0).ToString
            strRow += " UDT: " + .GetString(1)
            strRow += " Distance from 10,1: " + .GetDouble(2).ToString
        End While
        .Close()
    End If
End With
cnNwind.Close()
...
```

Figure 11-12 shows the UDTTables.vb form with values generated by the full version of the preceding code.

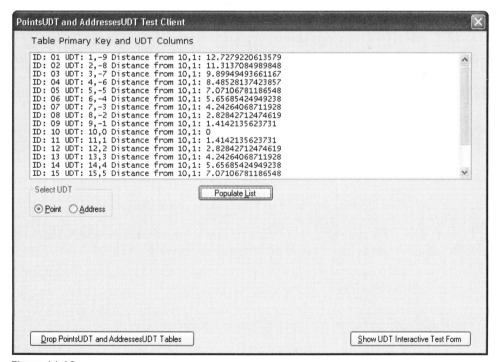

Figure 11-12

The PointsUDT table is a version of the PointUDT table that's generated by the `CreateUDTTables` *procedure behind the UserDefinedTypesClient project's UDTInteractive.vb form. You must drop the PointUDT table manually before redeploying the* `Point` *UDT from the UserDefinedTypesCLR project.*

The Drop PointsUDT and AddressesUDT Tables button that's shown in Figure 11-14 enables you to redeploy the `Point` *and* `Address` *UDTs after you delete the PointUDT table.*

Work with a Complex UserDefined-Format UDT

The UserDefinedTypesCLR project creates two UserDesigned-format UDTs — `Address` and `AddressBasic` — that are based on the six address columns of the Northwind Customers table. UDT best practices dictate that developers withstand the temptation to create UDTs to represent objects whose public fields are values from what ordinarily would be table columns. The ability to represent objects with UDTs doesn't — or at least shouldn't — imply that SQL Server 2005 is an object-oriented or object-relational database management system. Operations other than value comparison require the database engine to deserialize the UDT prior to invoking a method. Deserializing large objects consumes substantial resources and impacts performance.

Object-relational transformations ordinarily belong in a middle tier. The purpose of this section's UDTs is to demonstrate the flexibility of optional methods and illustrate incorporation of UserDefined-format UDT property (field) values in T-SQL `WHERE` constraints, and `ORDER BY` and `GROUP BY` clauses. The `Address` UDT also contains data-access methods that generate XML fragments and execute `SELECT` statements. Don't interpret the `Address` UDT examples as a recommendation to model complex business objects in production UDTs.

UDT examples similar to `AddressBasic` *appear in several Microsoft blogs and the "Managed UDTs Let You Extend the SQL Server Type System" MSDN article* (`http://msdn.microsoft.com/msdnmag/issues/04/02/UDTsinYukon/`).

The `Address` UDT includes code to validate the presence and length of required Name, Address, City, and Country values, and optional Region and PostalCode values. Required column zero-length string or excessive-length values throw an `ArgumentException` with an explanation of the error. Exceeding the `nvarchar(length)` constraint returns an SQL Server error message, but a zero-length string in a required column doesn't.

The `Address` UDT adds the following methods to the AddressBasic UDT:

❑ `MailingLabel()` and `MailingListCSV()` generate formatted, plain-text mailing labels and strings of address data in standard comma-separated-value (CSV) format.

❑ `MailingListHeaderCSV()` demonstrates a function to return a `String` constant that doesn't rely on a `Not IsNull` UDT instance.

❑ `AddressXML()` uses an `XmlTextWriter` to return address data as well-formed XML fragments and demonstrates how to add a `SELECT` query to a method.

❑ `OrderCountByCustomerID` and `CustomerOrderCount` use aggregate queries to return the number of orders for a customer specified by a `CustomerID` argument or the instance's `Me.Name` property value.

❑ IsEqualTo() returns 1 if the String representations of the current and a test Address object are identical; otherwise the function returns 0.

❑ GetHashCode() returns the Integer value of the hash code for the String representation.

Code in the CreateUDTTables procedure behind the UserDefinedTypesClient project's UDTInteractive.vb form generates the AddressesUDT table and populates it from the Northwind Customers table. Handling NULL values in UDTs requires complex code, so the code that generates the AddressesUDT table replaces NULL Region and PostalCode values with String.Empty.

The AddressBasic UDT

Address UDT contains 400 lines of code and is too lengthy to reproduce here, so following is the bare-bones code of the AddressBasic UDT:

```
Imports System
Imports System.Data.SqlTypes
Imports System.Data.Sql
Imports Microsoft.SqlServer.Server
Imports System.IO

<Serializable(), SqlUserDefinedType(Format.UserDefined, _
 IsByteOrdered:=True, IsFixedLength:=False, MaxByteSize:=500)> _
Public Class AddressBasic
'The AddressBasic UDT expects zero-length strings instead of nulls
'for Region and PostalCode fields
Implements INullable, IBinarySerialize

Private blnIsNull As Boolean
Private strName As String
Private strAddress As String
Private strCity As String
Private strRegion As String
Private strPostalCode As String
Private strCountry As String

Public Sub New()
    'Default constructor (required for a class)
    Me.blnIsNull = True
    Me.strName = ""
    Me.strAddress = ""
    Me.strCity = ""
    Me.strRegion = ""
    Me.strPostalCode = ""
    Me.strCountry = ""
End Sub

Public ReadOnly Property IsNull() As Boolean _
 Implements INullable.IsNull
    'IsNull property is required for all UDTs
    Get
       Return blnIsNull
    End Get
```

```vb
   End Property

Public Shared ReadOnly Property Null() As AddressBasic
   Get
      Dim objAddr As New AddressBasic()
      objAddr.blnIsNull = True
      Return objAddr
   End Get
End Property

Public Shared Function Parse(ByVal sqlAddr As SqlString) As AddressBasic
   If sqlAddr.IsNull Then
      Return Nothing
   Else
      Dim objAddr As New AddressBasic
      Dim str As String = sqlAddr.ToString
      Dim astrAddr As String() = str.Split(";"c)
      objAddr.strName = astrAddr(0)
      objAddr.strAddress = astrAddr(1)
      objAddr.strCity = astrAddr(2)
      objAddr.strRegion = astrAddr(3)
      objAddr.strCountry = astrAddr(5)
      objAddr.blnIsNull = False
      Return objAddr
   End If
End Function

Public Overrides Function ToString() As String
   If Me.IsNull Then
      Return "Null"
   Else
      Dim strDelimeter As String = ";"
      Return Me.strName + strDelimeter + Me.strAddress + strDelimeter + _
       Me.strCity + strDelimeter + Me.strRegion + strDelimeter + _
       Me.strPostalCode + strDelimeter + Me.strCountry
   End If
End Function

'Fields
Public Property Name() As String
   Get
      Return Me.strName
   End Get
   Set(ByVal value As String)
      Me.strName = value
      Me.blnIsNull = False
   End Set
End Property

Public Property Address() As String
   Get
      Return Me.strAddress
   End Get
   Set(ByVal value As String)
      Me.strAddress = value
```

```
      Me.blnIsNull = False
   End Set
End Property

Public Property City() As String
   Get
      Return Me.strCity
   End Get
   Set(ByVal value As String)
      Me.strCity = value
      Me.blnIsNull = False
   End Set
End Property

Public Property Region() As String
   Get
      Return Me.strRegion
   End Get
   Set(ByVal value As String)
      Me.strRegion = value
      Me.blnIsNull = False
   End Set
End Property

Public Property PostalCode() As String
   Get
      Return Me.strPostalCode
   End Get
   Set(ByVal value As String)
      Me.strPostalCode = value
      Me.blnIsNull = False
   End Set
End Property

Public Property Country() As String
   Get
      Return Me.strCountry
   End Get
   Set(ByVal value As String)
      Me.strCountry = value
      Me.blnIsNull = False
   End Set
End Property

'Required serializer and deserializer
Public Overridable Sub Write(ByVal binWriter As BinaryWriter) _
 Implements IBinarySerialize.Write
   Dim bytHeader As Byte
   If Me.IsNull Then
      bytHeader = 0
   Else
      bytHeader = 1
   End If
   With binWriter
      .Write(bytHeader)
```

```
        If bytHeader = 0 Then
            Return
        End If
        .Write(Me.Name)
        .Write(Me.Address)
        .Write(Me.City)
        .Write(Me.Region)
        .Write(Me.PostalCode)
        .Write(Me.Country)
    End With
End Sub

Public Sub Read(ByVal binReader As BinaryReader) _
 Implements IBinarySerialize.Read
    'Required for Format.UserDefined, not Format.Native
    Dim bytHeader As Byte = binReader.ReadByte()
    If bytHeader = 0 Then
        Me.blnIsNull = True
        Return
    End If
    Me.blnIsNull = False
    With binReader
        Me.strName = .ReadString()
        Me.strAddress = .ReadString()
        Me.strCity = .ReadString()
        Me.strRegion = .ReadString()
        Me.strPostalCode = .ReadString()
        Me.strCountry = .ReadString()
    End With
End Sub
End Class
```

The maximum allowable length of the six nvarchar *(Unicode)* String *fields is 310 bytes (155 characters) so the* MaxByteSize:=500 *attribute value is adequate. The maximum size of values from the Customers table is about 200 bytes.*

Verify the Address UDT Methods

Running the following batch in the SMSS query editor verifies that the Address UDT's basic functions execute as expected:

```
DECLARE @Addr Address
SET @Addr = CONVERT(Address, ' ; ; ; ; ; ')
SET @Addr.Name = 'Rattlesnake Canyon Grocery'
SET @Addr.Address = '2817 Milton Dr.'
SET @Addr.City = 'Albuquerque'
SET @Addr.Region = 'NM'
```

```
SET @Addr.PostalCode = '87110-5455'
SET @Addr.Country = 'USA'
PRINT @Addr.ToString()
PRINT @Addr.MailingLabel()
PRINT @Addr.MailingListHeaderCSV()
PRINT @Addr.MailingListCSV()
DECLARE @Addr1 Address
SET @Addr1 = CONVERT(Address, 'Rattlesnake Canyon Grocery;2817 Milton
Dr.;Albuquerque;NM;94610-5708;USA')
PRINT @Addr1.MailingLabel()
```

The SET @Addr1 *instruction must be a single line to prevent generating a mailing label with a two-line address.*

The preceding batch returns the following output:

```
Rattlesnake Canyon Grocery;2817 Milton Dr.;Albuquerque;NM;87110-5455;USA
Rattlesnake Canyon Grocery
2817 Milton Dr.
Albuquerque, NM  87110-5455
"Name","Address","City","Region","PostalCode","Country"
"Rattlesnake Canyon Grocery","2817 Milton Dr.","Albuquerque","NM",
"87110-5455","USA"
Rattlesnake Canyon Grocery
2817 Milton Dr.
Albuquerque, NM  94610-5708
```

The UserDefinedTypesCLR project's Test.sql script includes the preceding commands. Selecting the UDTInteractive.vb form's Address radio button loads the upper text box with the Address.sql script, which also contains the preceding batch instructions.

Test the Address UDT with WHERE Constraints and ORDER BY Clauses

The following query tests UDT value comparison and returns Address strings for customers in Germany in descending PostalCode order:

```
SELECT CustomerID, AddressUDT.ToString() AS AddressUDT FROM AddressesUDT
WHERE AddressUDT.Country = 'Germany'
ORDER BY AddressUDT.PostalCode DESC
```

This query returns the 11 rows shown in Figure 11-13. Adding AND AddressUDT.PostalCode < 50000 to the WHERE clause returns 4 rows.

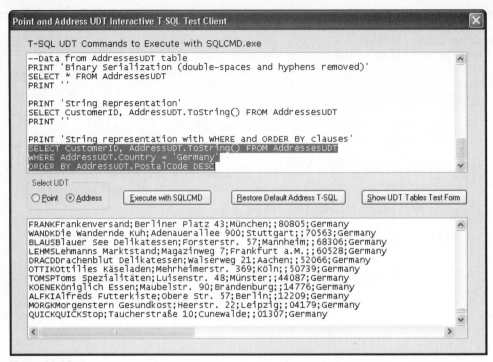

Figure 11-13

You also can specify fields for use in GROUP BY clauses. The following aggregate query returns the expected resultset of 21 rows:

```
SELECT AddressUDT.Country, COUNT(*) AS [Count] FROM AddressesUDT
GROUP BY AddressUDT.Country
ORDER BY AddressUDT.Country
```

As mentioned earlier, the UserDefinedTypesClient project's UDTInteractive.vb form uses the Shell instruction to execute T-SQL scripts with SQLCMD.exe. Following is the Shell instruction's Path argument to run the Address.sql script from the project's bin folder:

```
sqlcmd -S localhost -d Northwind
-i "\InstallPath\Chapter11\UserDefinedTypesClient\bin\Address.sql"
-o "\InstallPath\Chapter11\UserDefinedTypesClient\bin\Address.txt" -y 0 -u
```

The preceding command stores SQLCMD's output in the Address.txt file, which populates the lower text box of Figure 11-15. The -S[erver] argument is obtained from the Server=localhost; element of the project's connection string. The -y 0 argument ensures that UDT field values aren't truncated. The -u argument specifies Unicode (UTF-16) encoding of the output text in the Address.txt file. If you don't include the -u argument, Latin-1 characters with diacritical marks, such as ü, don't appear in the output text box.

Access Data from Other Fields or Tables with UDT Queries

Adding the `<SqlMethod(DataAccess:=DataAccessKind.Read)>` attribute to a UDT method enables you to execute queries against other fields in the table that contains the UDT column or a table in the same or another database. This attribute lets you create an `SqlCommand` object with the `SqlContext.GetConnection.CreateCommand()` instruction that's used with CLR functions and stored procedures.

The `Address` UDT doesn't include a `CustomerID` field because the Address type might be used as AddressUDT columns of vendors, contacts, or other tables. If you want to provide a method that returns the number of orders for the current Address instance, you can query the Customers table to return the CustomerID for a CompanyName value supplied by the `Me.Name` property. Then you execute an aggregate query against the Orders table to return the number of orders for the customer.

The following `CustomerOrderCount()` method illustrates external data access by a UDT:

```
<SqlMethod(DataAccess:=DataAccessKind.Read)> _
Public Function CustomerOrderCount() As Integer
   'Return the number of orders from the current-instance customer
   If Me.IsNull Then
      Return 0
   End If
   Dim cmNwind As SqlCommand = SqlContext.GetConnection.CreateCommand()
   With cmNwind
      .CommandText = "SELECT COUNT(OrderID) FROM Orders " + _
       "WHERE CustomerID IN (SELECT CustomerID FROM Customers WHERE " + _
       "CompanyName = N'" + Replace(Me.Name, "'", "''") + "')"
      .CommandType = CommandType.Text
      Return CInt(.ExecuteScalar())
   End With
End Function
```

Escaping single quote characters with `Replace(Me.Name, "'", "''")` *is critical for fields that might contain them, such as* Name, Address, *and* City.

Execute the following query to test the `CustomerOrderCount()` method:

```
DECLARE @Addr1 Address
SET @Addr1 = CONVERT(Address, 'Rattlesnake Canyon Grocery;2817 Milton
Dr.;Albuquerque;NM;94610-5708;USA')
PRINT @Addr1.CustomerOrderCount()
```

The method returns 18 if you haven't added or deleted RATTC orders.

Generate Well-Formed XML with an XmlTextWriter

If users need an XML representation of the UDT type, you can use an `XmlWriter` or `XmlTextWriter` object to create a serialized version of an `Address` instance with the following method:

```
<SqlMethod(DataAccess:=DataAccessKind.Read)> _
Public Function AddressXML() As String
'Return the XML representation of an address
```

```
        If Me.IsNull Then
            Return Nothing
        End If
        'Get the CustomerID for the attribute value
        Dim strCustomerID As String = Nothing
        Dim cmNwind As SqlCommand = SqlContext.GetConnection.CreateCommand()
        With cmNwind
            .CommandText = "SELECT CustomerID FROM Customers WHERE " + _
            "CompanyName = N'" + Replace(Me.Name, "'", "''") + "'"
            .CommandType = CommandType.Text
            strCustomerID = .ExecuteScalar.ToString
        End With

        Dim msAddr As New MemoryStream()
        Dim xtwAddr As New XmlTextWriter(msAddr, Encoding.UTF8)
        With xtwAddr
            .Formatting = Formatting.Indented
            .Indentation = 2
            .WriteStartElement("Address")
            If strCustomerID IsNot Nothing Then
                .WriteAttributeString("CustomerID", strCustomerID)
            End If
            .WriteElementString("Name", Me.Name)
            .WriteElementString("Street", Me.Address)
            .WriteElementString("City", Me.City)
            .WriteElementString("Region", Me.Region)
            .WriteElementString("PostalCode", Me.PostalCode)
            .WriteElementString("Country", Me.Country)
            .WriteEndElement()
            .Flush()
            .Close()
        End With
        'Return the MemoryStream buffer's Byte array as a UTF-8 string
        Dim strAddrXML As String = Encoding.UTF8.GetString(msAddr.GetBuffer())
        msAddr.Close()
        'The buffer has extra characters at the end
        Dim intLength As Integer = strAddrXML.IndexOf("</Address>") + 9
        strAddrXML = strAddrXML.Substring(1, intLength)
        Return strAddrXML
    End Function
```

The preceding method requires that you add `Imports System.Xml` and `Imports System.Text` directives.

Test the method with the following batch:

```
DECLARE @Addr1 Address
SET @Addr1 = CONVERT(Address, 'Rattlesnake Canyon Grocery;2817 Milton
Dr.;Albuquerque;NM;94610-5708;USA')
PRINT @Addr1.AddressXML()
```

which returns:

```
<Address CustomerID="RATTC">
  <Name>Rattlesnake Canyon Grocery</Name>
  <Street>2817 Milton Dr.</Street>
  <City>Albuquerque</City>
  <Region>NM</Region>
  <PostalCode>94610-5708</PostalCode>
  <Country>USA</Country>
</Address>
```

The UserDefinedTypesCLR project's Test.sql script includes the preceding commands and the resulting XML document.

Figure 11-14 shows the UDTTables.vb form displaying an `AddressXML()` instance with extended characters ó and é, which proves that the `Encoding.UTF8.GetString(msAddr.GetBuffer())` instruction behaves as expected.

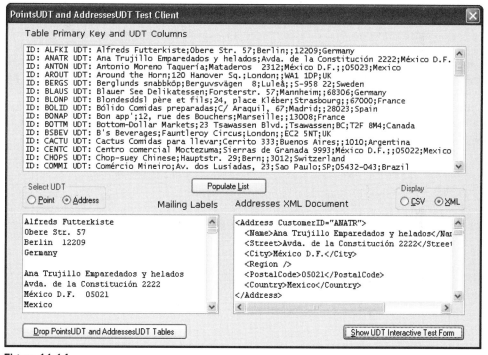

Figure 11-14

Data-access methods in UDTs encroach on the realm of CLR functions and stored procedures, but UDTs offer a single object that can incorporate a multitude of type-specific optional functions. The obvious downside of complex UDTs is the need to drop all tables that contain the UDT before redeploying assemblies with bug fixes or modifications, such as added methods. Thus, each production UDT you develop should have its own assembly.

Summary

The capability to write CLR stored procedures, user-defined functions, triggers, UDTs, and UDAs and quickly deploy them for execution within the SQL Server 2005 database engine's process is a major accomplishment of the .NET and SQL Server development teams. VS 2005's SQL Server Project templates ease the development process and simplify testing and deployment. Conservative DBAs and IT management will be reluctant to deploy SQL/CLR objects in production databases. You must be ready to demonstrate short-term and long-term returns on the investment required to prove the security, reliability, and performance of SQL/CLR objects that replace or supplement conventional T-SQL–based objects.

The greatest return on development investments will come from SQL/CLR objects that process data with methods that T-SQL doesn't support, such as array processing, complex mathematics, or convoluted string manipulation. Lesser returns result from replacing T-SQL procedural code and cursors with .NET counterparts. Avoid the temptation to substitute SQL/CLR objects for T-SQL stored procedures, user-defined functions, and triggers that operate on conventional sets of relational data. UDTs and UDAs bring new functionality to SQL Server 2005, but UDTs, in particular, are subject to misuse by enthusiastic developers. Best practices dictate that UDTs not be used to represent objects whose fields consist of values that are suited to table columns.

This chapter provides an initial set of trivial SQL/CLR sample objects, which is intended to demonstrate basic coding and deployment techniques. More complex examples of SQL/CLR stored procedures and UDTs perform functions that are difficult or impossible to achieve with T-SQL objects. With the exception of the csp_SalesOrdersXML_NS and csp_LinearRegression stored procedures, the complex examples are contrived. Don't consider their presence in this chapter as a recommendation to implement similar SQL/CLR objects in real-world database projects.

12

Exploring the XML Data Type

SQL Server 2000 XML document management methods often involved storing the full text as Unicode (UTF-16) XML documents or fragments in `nvarchar` or `ntext` columns. Creating effective columnar indexes for text-based XML in content was difficult, and full-text indexes seldom returned useful results from complex documents. Alternative generation and retrieval methods included dynamic XML document generation with `FOR XML` queries, preparing documents and retrieving rowsets with `OPENXML`, shredding element and attribute values into relational columns, and retrieving documents with annotated XML schemas and XML views. XML-to-relational and relational-to-XML mapping techniques were complex and involved substantial development and testing time.

SQL Server 2005's new native `xml` data type and XQuery 1.0 implementation simplifies and adds flexibility to XML document storage, retrieval, and management. The native `xml` data type lets you store a representation of the original document or fragment in a variant of an `nvarbinary(max)` field, ensure the content is well-formed, use the XPath 2.0 and XQuery 1.0 languages to perform `SELECT`-style queries, and speed query performance with specialized XML indexes. If you associate one or more XML schemas with the `xml` column, validation occurs when content is added or updated, and values become strongly typed. Full-text search on `xml` columns examines element values only.

The XQuery 1.0 specification doesn't include methods for updating content, so the SQL Server team added a `modify` method to add or remove optional elements and alter element or attribute values. Microsoft calls modify expressions *XML DDL*. The `sql:column` and `sql:variable` extended functions support incorporating relational data in XQuery expressions. Microsoft calls such expressions *cross-domain queries* because they bridge the hierarchical (XML) and relational (SQL) domains.

> W3C's set of XQuery 1.0 and XPath 2.0 recommendations were in the Working Draft stage when this book was written (mid-2005). SQL Server 2005's XQuery and XPath implementations are based on Working Drafts in effect as of the XQuery 1.0 and XPath 2.0 Data Model draft of November 2003 at `http://www.w3.org/TR/2004/WD-xpath-datamodel-20040723/`.

Part 14 of the ANSI SQL specification, which also is a work in progress, is based on the forthcoming W3C XQuery 1.0 and XPath 2.0 recommendations. According to an article by Bob Beauchemin in MSDN Magazine, the "new XML features in SQL Server follow the standard closely." You can read the entire article at http://msdn.microsoft.com/msdnmag/issues/04/02/XMLinYukon/.

This chapter covers the essential features of the SQL Server 2005 native xml data type, simple and complex XmlSchemaCollections and XML namespaces, XML indexes, and basic XPath and XQuery expressions for retrieving and modifying xml column content. With the exception of one section, which uses the AdventureWorks database, the sample documents are contained in pairs of xml columns you add to the Northwind database's Customers and Orders tables.

To get the most out of this chapter, you should have the following sample VB 2005 projects available on your development machine:

❑ The NWxmlColumns.sln project in the \VB2005DB\Chapter12\NWxmlColumns folder, which automates adding two temporary xml columns to the Northwind Customers and Orders tables, generating and associating XmlSchemaCollections, and adding XML indexes to the columns. This project offers sample XQuery expressions that you can edit to gain experience with XQuery syntax. This project demonstrates the effect of document size, XML indexes, and schema validation on xml column UPDATE performance and XQuery response time.

❑ The xmlColumnExplorer.sln project in the \VB2005DB \Chapter12\xmlColumnExplorer folder, which lets you view all columns of the native xml data type in the AdventureWorks and Northwind databases, display the content of selected documents, and read the XmlSchemaCollections of typed xml columns.

❑ The FillSalesOrdersTables.sln project in the \VB2005DB \Chapter12\FillSalesOrdersTables folder, which lets you clone the Orders and Order Details tables with automatically generated SalesOrders and SalesOrderItems tables. The tables can contain a number of rows that's limited only by your patience and available disk space. The rows consist of simulated orders with random CustomerID and ProductID values, as well as a specified average number of line items per order. Creating these tables is optional, but they are useful for determining the effect of XML indexes on XQuery response time. The XQuery performance test data near the end of this chapter is based on a SalesOrders table with 10,000 rows and two xml columns.

An understanding of basic XPath 1.0 expression syntax is required and some familiarity with XQuery 1.0 and XPath 2.0 concepts is helpful for executing XQuery expressions against xml column content. The NWxmlColumns project's relatively simple XQuery expressions can serve as a starting point for adapting your SQL authoring skills to more complex XQuery equivalents. Making the transition from T-SQL to XPath 2.0 and XQuery syntax is similar to that for learning to write and debug Multidimensional Expressions (MDX). The familiar SQL SELECT, FROM, and WHERE keywords are supported, but what follows them differs greatly.

Like all other sample projects in this book, the default SQL Server instance is localhost. *Edit the app.config file's* connectionString *attribute value to suit your SQL Server 2005 or SQL Express instance.*

Select the Appropriate XML Data Model

Governmental regulations or business policies often dictate storing original or archival copies of XML documents in `nvarchar(max)` columns. If full-text search or `WHERE ColumnName LIKE '%SomeElementOrAttributeAndValue%'` queries don't return the results you need, you must add columns to contain key values for conventional `SELECT` queries. Shredding complex XML instances into relational columns isn't a simple task, but indexing the added columns improves query performance.

If document structure variation or indexing requirements exceed your ability to create an adequate set of key columns, consider importing the original document into an `xml` column. However, inserting XML content into an `xml` column might not return an exact duplicate of the original document. The process removes whitespace to minimize storage requirements and might not preserve element order with recursive document structures. If you don't require absolute identity between the source and retrieved documents, `xml` columns enable execution of XQuery-based `SELECT` and `UPDATE` expressions on the XML content. The following sections describe options for `xml` column content management, validation, and indexing.

SQL Server 2005 Books Online contains help topics for `xml` columns and XQuery expressions.

Untyped XML Columns

Native `xml` columns are untyped by default and don't require associated XML schemas. Use the following syntax to add an untyped `xml` column to a new or existing table:

```
CREATE TABLE TableName(KeyColumnName data_type PRIMARY KEY, xmlColumnName XML
[NULL][, ...]);
ALTER TABLE TableName ADD xmlColumnName XML [NULL];
```

You can't specify an `xml` column as the table's primary key or a foreign key; you receive an error message if you try. However, you can add a primary *XML index* to an `xml` column, as described in the section "Indexed xml Columns," later in this chapter. You can't apply a `UNIQUE` constraint or add a `COLLATE` modifier to an `xml` column.

Launch the NWxmlColumns project and, with the default Customers Table tab active, click the Drop xml Columns button and then click Add xml Columns to execute typical `ALTER TABLE` statements to drop and add two `xml` columns.

Populate an XML Column

Populating an `xml` column requires an `INSERT` or `UPDATE` operation with the following syntax:

```
INSERT TableName(xmlColumnName) VALUES(N'well_formed_xml_content');
UPDATE TableName SET xmlColumnName = N'well_formed_xml_content';
```

The content must be UTF-16-encoded and either a well-formed document or document fragment(s).

The following batch adds CustomersXML1 and CustomersXML2 columns to the Customers table and updates the CustomersXML1 column with content that's generated by a parameterized `FOR XML AUTO TYPE` query against the Customers table:

```
ALTER TABLE dbo.Customers ADD CustomerXML1 xml NULL, CustomerXML2 xml NULL;
DECLARE @CustomerXML xml SET @CustomerXML = (SELECT CustomerID, ContactName,
   ContactTitle, CompanyName, Address, City, Region, PostalCode, Country, Phone, Fax
FROM Customers AS Customer
WHERE CustomerID = @CustomerID FOR XML AUTO, ELEMENTS, TYPE)
UPDATE Customers SET CustomerXML1 = @CustomerXML WHERE CustomerID = @CustomerID;
```

The highlighted TYPE modifier causes FOR XML AUTO to return a stream of the highlighted xml type.

Figure 12-1 shows the NWxmlColumns project's Customers Table tab page displaying the first CustomerXML1 column content created from a FOR XML AUTO query.

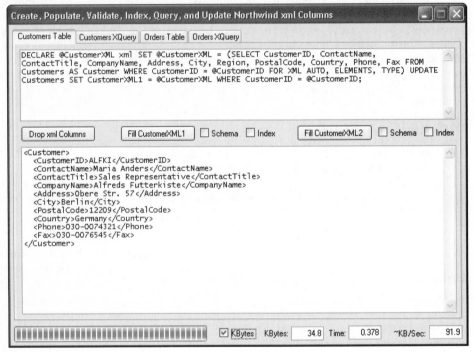

Figure 12-1

If you can generate the document structure you need with a FOR XML AUTO query, consider the tradeoffs between creating the document dynamically or storing it in an xml column. Generating large documents on demand consumes substantial CPU resources, but inserting them in xml columns — especially indexed xml columns — is resource- and I/O-intensive, and can consume substantial storage resources.

Alternatively, you can pass the XML content as a string, as shown in the following example for the CustomersXML2 column:

```
SELECT CustomerID, CompanyName, ContactName, ContactTitle, Address,
   City, Region, PostalCode, Country, Phone, Fax
FROM Customers WHERE CustomerID = 'ALFKI';
UPDATE Customers SET CustomerXML2 = N'<?xml version="1.0" encoding="utf-16"?>
<nwc:Customer xmlns:nwc="http://www.northwind.com/schemas/Customer">
```

```
                <nwc:CustomerID>ALFKI</nwc:CustomerID>
                <nwc:CompanyName>Alfreds Futterkiste</nwc:CompanyName>
                <nwc:ContactName>Maria Anders</nwc:ContactName>
                <nwc:ContactTitle>Sales Representative</nwc:ContactTitle>
                <nwc:Address>Obere Str. 57</nwc:Address>
                <nwc:City>Berlin</nwc:City>
                <nwc:PostalCode>12209</nwc:PostalCode>
                <nwc:Country>Germany</nwc:Country>
                <nwc:Phone>030-0074321</nwc:Phone>
                <nwc:Fax>030-0076545</nwc:Fax>
            </nwc:Customer>' WHERE CustomerID = 'ALFKI';
```

Notice that the string must be formatted as UTF-16, as illustrated by the highlighted encoding attribute. The XML declaration is optional, but UTF-16 encoding with N' isn't. Each character requires 2 bytes of storage space.

Click Fill CustomerXML1 and Fill CustomerXML2 to execute the two preceding batches for all Customers table rows. The SQL batch statement appears in the upper text box and the lower text box shows the first row data.

You also can declare a variable of the xml data type, CAST or CONVERT a string to the xml type, assign the xml value, and then substitute the variable for the literal content string with the following generic instructions:

```
DECLARE @XmlVar xml;
SET @XmlVar = CONVERT(xml, 'well_formed_xml_content');
UPDATE TableName SET xmlColumnName = @XmlVar;
```

This approach is useful when you populate xml columns with XML documents stored in the file system or delivered as a stream.

Retrieve and Reformat Data from an XML Column

The SqlCommand.ExecuteXmlReader method returns a single row's xml column content — usually to an XmlReader. In this respect, the ExecuteXmlReader method is similar to the ExecuteScalar method for relational data types. The highlighted lines of the following snippet illustrate retrieval by an XmlReader and formatting by an XmlTextWriter:

```
...
cmNwind.CommandText = "SELECT CustomerXML1 FROM Customers"
cnNwind.Open()
Dim xrData As XmlReader = cmNwind.ExecuteXmlReader
'Use an XmlTextWriter for simplicity
Dim xtwData As New XmlTextWriter(strXmlFile, Encoding.Unicode)
xtwData.Formatting = Formatting.Indented
xrData.MoveToContent()
xtwData.WriteNode(xrData, False)
xtwData.Flush()
xtwData.Close()
xrData.Close()
cnNwind.Close()
Dim strXML As String = File.ReadAll(strXmlFile)
...
```

The preceding snippet is from the sample NWxmlColumns project's SaveAndDisplayData *function in the NwXmlCols.vb file.*

You use an SqlDataReader and the SqlXml SqlDataType to return multiple rows of typed data to an XmlReader for formatting and, optionally, appending to a StringBuilder with an XmlWriter, as shown in the following (condensed) GetXQueryResult function:

```
Private Function GetXQueryResult(ByVal strXQL As String)
 ByVal strRootName As String, ByVal As String
    Dim xrResult As XmlReader
    Dim xwSettings As XmlWriterSettings
    Dim xwResult As XmlWriter = Nothing
    Dim sbXML As New StringBuilder()
    xwSettings = New XmlWriterSettings
    With xwSettings
        .Encoding = Encoding.Unicode
        .Indent = True
        .IndentChars = ("  ")
        .OmitXmlDeclaration = False
        .ConformanceLevel = ConformanceLevel.Document
    End With
    'Create an XmlWriter to format the result
    xwResult = XmlWriter.Create(sbXML, xwSettings)
    cmNwind.CommandText = strXQL
    cnNwind.Open()
    Dim sdrData As SqlDataReader
    sdrData = cmNwind.ExecuteReader
    With sdrData
        If .HasRows Then
            Dim xmlData As SqlXml
            xwResult.WriteStartElement("Customer")
            While .Read
                xmlData = .GetSqlXml(0)
                'Add child elements to the XmlWriter
                xrResult = xmlData.CreateReader
                xrResult.MoveToContent()
                xwResult.WriteNode(xrResult, False)
            End While
            'Add the end element
            xwResult.WriteEndElement()
            xwResult.Flush()
            xwResult.Close()
        Else
            sbXML.Append("XQuery expression returned no rows. ")
        End If
        .Close()
    End With
    cnNwind.Close()
    Return sbXML.ToString
End Function
```

The full version of the preceding function is in the NWxmlColumns project's NwXmlCols.vb file. The XmlWriter *has many more overloads than the* XmlTextWriter, *including the* StringBuilder *target object.*

Typed XML Columns

Applying strong typing to an xml column by associating an XmlSchemaCollection provides the following benefits:

- ❑ The schema validates the inserted or updated content. The database engine returns an immediate error message if the content fails validation.

- ❑ Static types eliminate the need to perform explicit casts in some cases, such as from an XQuery string to a double value.

- ❑ XQuery operations on atomic types (values) are more precise. For example, an XQuery order by clause on an xs:int often is more precise than with an xs:string.

- ❑ The column stores atomic values as types, which saves storage space and can improve XQuery performance in some cases.

- ❑ You can perform indexed range scans. You can't perform indexed range scans with the XQuery comparison operators, such as > or <, on untyped values. Indexed range scans increase SELECT query performance markedly, as you'll see in the later sections that discuss the benefits and drawbacks of XML indexes.

Create XMLSchemaCollections

An XmlSchemaCollection contains one or more schemas for each document namespace. You create a member of an XmlSchemaCollection and associate it with an xml column by executing the following generic syntax:

```
CREATE XML SCHEMA COLLECTION SchemaCollectionName AS
N'<xs:schema>PrimarySchema</xs:schema>[<xs:schema>ImportedSchema1</xs:schema>]
[<xs:schema>ImportedSchema2</xs:schema> ...]';
ALTER TABLE TableName ADD XmlColumnName xml([DOCUMENT] SchemaCollectionName)
[NULL];
```

You also can create an XmlSchemaCollection from a primary schema that includes the <xs:import namespace="ValidUri" /> directive. The imported schemas' content, which is highlighted in the preceding batch commands, follow that of the primary schema.

XML schemas that you produce with VS 2005's XML editor's schema inference engine from XML source documents are adequate for simple to moderately complex documents, including documents that contain multiple namespaces. As noted in earlier chapters, you must edit the schema(s) to correct inferred XSD datatypes for numeric, date/time, and other non-string elements and attributes. You also must add minOccurs="0" attributes for optional elements and, in some cases, add element definitions for those elements that are missing in the initial source document.

> *The \VB2005DB\Chapter12\NWxmlColumns\bin folder holds *.xsd files that contain the sample schemas and use the column names as file names. An exception is the set of four SalesOrder*.xsd files that provide the source for the OrderXML2 columns' primary and imported XmlSchemaCollections. These schema files were created and edited with the VS 2005 XML editor.*

If the ALTER TABLE instruction doesn't include the highlighted DOCUMENT directive, which requires that the column's documents have a single root node, the default CONTENT directive applies and document fragments are valid.

You must drop an existing untyped `xml` column before associating it with an `XmlSchemaCollection`. The following batch drops the OrderXML1 column, creates an `OrderXML1SchemaColl` collection, and associates the collection with the re-created column:

```
ALTER TABLE dbo.Orders DROP COLUMN OrderXML1;
CREATE XML SCHEMA COLLECTION OrderXML1SchemaColl
AS N'<?xml version="1.0" encoding="utf-16"?>
<xs:schema attributeFormDefault="unqualified" elementFormDefault="qualified"
xmlns:xs="http://www.w3.org/2001/XMLSchema">
  <xs:element name="Order">
    <xs:complexType>
      <xs:sequence>
        <xs:element name="OrderID" type="xs:int" />
        <xs:element name="EmployeeID" type="xs:int" />
        <xs:element name="OrderDate" type="xs:dateTime" />
        <xs:element name="RequiredDate" type="xs:dateTime" />
        <xs:element name="ShippedDate" type="xs:dateTime" minOccurs="0"/>
        <xs:element name="ShipVia" type="xs:int" />
        <xs:element name="Freight" type="xs:decimal" />
        <xs:element name="ShipName" type="xs:string" />
        <xs:element name="ShipAddress" type="xs:string" />
        <xs:element name="ShipCity" type="xs:string" />
        <xs:element name="ShipRegion" type="xs:string" minOccurs ="0"/>
        <xs:element name="ShipPostalCode" type="xs:string" minOccurs ="0"/>
        <xs:element name="ShipCountry" type="xs:string" />
      </xs:sequence>
    </xs:complexType>
  </xs:element>
</xs:schema>';
ALTER TABLE dbo.Orders ADD OrderXML1 xml (DOCUMENT OrderXML1SchemaColl) NULL;
```

To execute the preceding batch with the NWxmlColumns project, select the Orders Table tab and mark the Schema checkbox adjacent to the Fill OrderXML1 button. The `CreateXmlSchemaCollection` *function in the NwXmlCols.vb file contains the code that generates the* `XmlSchemaCollection`. *OrderXML2 document instances are based on the SalesOrders XML document of Chapter 11's "Generate XML Documents with an XmlWriter" section.*

After you've created the column and associated the `XmlSchemaCollection`, you can add new namespaces or element(s) with the following generic syntax:

```
ALTER XML SCHEMA COLLECTION SchemaCollectionName ADD 'SchemaComponent'
```

`XmlSchemaCollections` have database-level scope. You can't remove namespaces, elements, or attributes with the `ALTER XML SCHEMA COLLECTION` instruction. These modifications require recreating the column and its `XmlSchemaCollection`.

Read XMLSchemaCollections

SQL Server 2005 shreds the `XmlSchemaCollections` you create into components that are optimized for document validation. Shredding removes whitespace and comments, and substitutes abbreviations for namespace prefixes. As an example, following are the root and `xs:import` elements of the schema for the SalesOrder documents of the Orders table's OrderXML2 column, with the namespaces highlighted for comparison:

```
<xs:schema xmlns:nwst="http://www.northwind.com/schemas/ShipTo"
  xmlns:nwsc="http://www.northwind.com/schemas/SalesContact"
  xmlns:nwbt="http://www.northwind.com/schemas/BillTo"
  xmlns:nwso="http://www.northwind.com/schemas/SalesOrder"
  attributeFormDefault="unqualified" elementFormDefault="qualified"
  targetNamespace="http://www.northwind.com/schemas/SalesOrder"
  xmlns:xs="http://www.w3.org/2001/XMLSchema">
<xs:import namespace="http://www.northwind.com/schemas/BillTo" />
<xs:import namespace="http://www.northwind.com/schemas/SalesContact" />
<xs:import namespace="http://www.northwind.com/schemas/ShipTo" /> ...
```

Here's the reconstructed version of the preceding elements in the XmlSchemaCollection:

```
<xsd:schema xmlns:xsd="http://www.w3.org/2001/XMLSchema"
  xmlns:ns3="http://www.northwind.com/schemas/ShipTo"
  xmlns:ns2="http://www.northwind.com/schemas/SalesContact"
  xmlns:ns1="http://www.northwind.com/schemas/BillTo"
  xmlns:t="http://www.northwind.com/schemas/SalesOrder"
  targetNamespace="http://www.northwind.com/schemas/SalesOrder"
  elementFormDefault="qualified">
<xsd:import namespace="http://www.northwind.com/schemas/ShipTo"
  schemaLocation="urn:schemas-microsoft-com:sql:database" />
<xsd:import namespace="http://www.northwind.com/schemas/SalesContact"
  schemaLocation="urn:schemas-microsoft-com:sql:database" />
<xsd:import namespace="http://www.northwind.com/schemas/BillTo"
  schemaLocation="urn:schemas-microsoft-com:sql:database" /> ...
```

Shredding replaces the primary schema's nwso namespace prefix with t, and the imported nwbt, nwsc, and nwst namespaces with ns1, ns2, and ns3, respectively, as highlighted in the preceding schema fragment. The highlighted schemaLocation attribute values specify that the imported schemas are stored in the XmlSchemaCollection.

> *Shredding XML schemas makes substantial changes to their content, so it's a good practice to archive the original schemas in individual SchemaName.xsd files or an* nvarchar(max) *table column.*

Shredded schemas aren't readable directly, so you must execute the xml_schema_namespace system function to return their content for review as xml data. As an example, the following instruction returns the complete schema for the OrderXML2 column:

```
SELECT xml_schema_namespace(N'dbo',N'OrderXML2SchemaColl'). _
query('/xs:schema[@targetNamespace="http://www.northwind.com/schemas/SalesOrder"]')
```

If you don't include the XQuery query method to specify the SalesOrder (nwso) namespace, the preceding instruction returns only schemas for the three imported namespaces. Later sections describe XQuery method syntax. Figure 12-2 shows the NWxmlColumns sample project displaying part of the batch command and the reformatted XmlSchemaCollection.

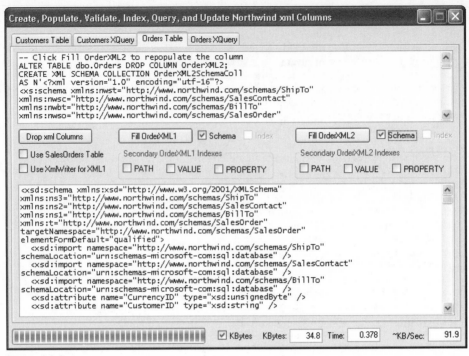

Figure 12-2

To display the batch commands and reconstructed content of the four schemas, select the Orders Table tab and mark the Schema checkbox adjacent to the Fill OrderXML2 button. The ReadXmlSchemaCollection *function in the NwXmlCols.vb file contains the code that executes the* xml_schema_namespace *system function.*

Indexed XML Columns

XML indexes on xml columns improve the performance of XQuery SELECT queries. The performance improvement is most effective for queries that include WHERE constraints based on atomic values of an xml column's content. The table must contain a conventional (relational) primary key column to add an XML index, and you can't create composite or clustered indexes on xml columns.

Following are the four types of XML indexes you can apply to xml columns:

❑   PRIMARY is an XML index that relates xml column nodes to the relational primary key column. A PRIMARY index assists the query processor when optimizing the execution plan. Ad hoc XQuery SELECT and UPDATE...WHERE statements take advantage of PRIMARY XML indexes, which are required to add any of the following three secondary XML indexes. According to Microsoft's Michael Rys, "The primary index is basically like a materialized view on a table-valued function. As such, it is a node table and a b-tree."

❑   PATH is a secondary XML index that speeds execution of XQuery path expressions, especially those with extended paths, such as \nwso:SalesOrder\nwbt:BillTo\nwbt:Buyer\ nwbt:Name.

❑   VALUE indexes all atomic element and attribute values and speeds searches for specific values or ranges of values.

❑   PROPERTY indexes are intended to improve query performance for simple XML document hierarchies that represent primarily name-value pairs.

If you don't create a PRIMARY index on an xml column, XPath queries generate the node table dynamically, which causes a performance hit — especially with large documents. After you create a PRIMARY index, you can add any or all three secondary index(es).

Add and Drop XML Indexes

You add XML primary and secondary indexes to xml columns with the following generic syntax:

```
CREATE [PRIMARY] XML INDEX PrimaryIndexName ON TableName (xmlColumnName);
CREATE XML INDEX SecondaryIndexName ON TableName (xmlColumnName)
   USING XML INDEX PrimaryXmlIndexName FOR {PATH|VALUE|PROPERTY};
```

For example, the following batch commands add a PRIMARY and three secondary indexes to the Customers table's CustomerXML1 column:

```
CREATE PRIMARY XML INDEX pidx_CustomerXML1 ON Customers (CustomerXML1);
CREATE XML INDEX sidx_path_CustomerXML1 ON Customers (CustomerXML1)
   USING XML INDEX pidx_CustomerXML1 FOR PATH;
CREATE XML INDEX sidx_value_CustomerXML1 ON Customers (CustomerXML1)
   USING XML INDEX pidx_CustomerXML1 FOR VALUE;
CREATE XML INDEX sidx_prop_CustomerXML1 ON Customers (CustomerXML1)
   USING XML INDEX pidx_CustomerXML1 FOR PROPERTY;
```

The syntax for dropping an XML index is identical to that for relational indexes:

```
DROP INDEX XmlIndexName ON TableName
```

You must drop all secondary indexes before you drop the PRIMARY index.

To execute the preceding instruction sets, mark and clear the sample project's Customers Table page's Index checkbox adjacent to the Fill CustomersXML1 button.

Figure 12-3 shows the report returned from the sys.dm_db_index_physical_stats system data management function with the following query:

```
SELECT ix.name, dm.index_type_desc, dm.page_count, dm.avg_fragmentation_in_percent
FROM sys.dm_db_index_physical_stats (DB_ID(), @objID , NULL, NULL, 'LIMITED') AS dm
INNER JOIN sys.indexes ix
ON dm.object_id = ix.object_id AND dm.index_id = ix.index_id ORDER BY ix.index_id;
```

where @objID is the sys.object.object_id (int) of the Orders table.

The four XML indexes added by the GetXMLIndexStats function after marking the Index checkbox adjacent to the Fill CustomersXML2 button are highlighted in Figure 12-3.

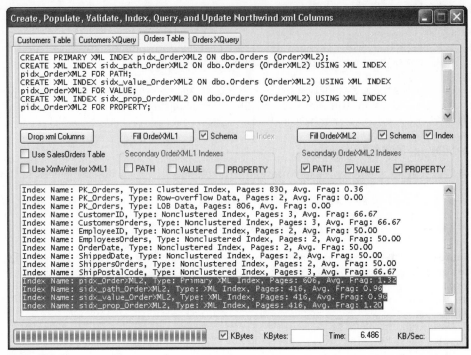

Figure 12-3

The sys.dm_db_index_physical_stats *data management function replaces the* DBCC SHOWCONTIG *command, which is deprecated. You can use the data management function to verify the existence of indexes on* xml *columns, estimate their size in pages, and display their fragmentation percentage.*

Promote xml Atomic Values to Table Columns

As mentioned earlier, XML indexes slow INSERT, UPDATE, and DELETE modify function execution on xml columns. Each secondary index type you add contributes to the performance hit. The reduction in modify function performance can be dramatic, as demonstrated with the NWxmlColumns project in later sections. Corresponding indexes on relational columns usually have a much lesser effect on the performance of modify operations.

You probably can improve query method performance by adding a computed column that you populate with atomic (scalar) values extracted from the xml column. This process is called *property promotion*. Improvements to the modify method result from elimination of all XML indexes or a reduction of the number of secondary indexes required for query optimization. You write a user-defined function to extract the values from the xml column and populate a computed column, and then add an index to the column, with SQL statements similar to the following example:

```
CREATE FUNCTION udf_xmlCountry (@xmlCountry xml) RETURNS varchar(15)
    WITH SCHEMABINDING
BEGIN
    RETURN @xmlCountry.value('/Order[1]/ShipCountry', 'varchar(15)')
```

```
END;

ALTER TABLE Orders ADD c_ShipCountry AS dbo.udf_xmlCountry(OrderXML1);

CREATE INDEX idx_c_ShipCountry ON Orders(c_ShipCountry);
```

You use the c_ShipCountry column as needed in SELECT lists, WHERE constraints, and ORDER BY clauses.

The section "Execute XPath and XQuery Expressions," later in this chapter, explains the syntax of the RETURN *XQuery expression.*

The Customers and Orders tables with added xml columns emulate a table in which all or, in the case of the Orders.OrderXML2 column, most properties have been promoted to computed columns.

Explore the AdventureWorks xml Columns

The AdventureWorks sample database has tables with seven xml columns, six of which are typed. The untyped column (Production.Illustration.Diagram) contains scalable vector graphics (SVG) content. You can list all columns of the xml data type in a database by executing the following query against the sys.schemas, sys.tables, and sys.columns system views:

```
SELECT sys.schemas.name AS SchemaName, sys.tables.name AS TableName,
   sys.columns.name AS ColumnName
FROM sys.schemas, sys.tables, sys.columns
WHERE sys.tables.schema_id = sys.schemas.schema_id
   AND sys.tables.object_id = sys.columns.object_id
   AND sys.columns.system_type_id = 241
ORDER BY SchemaName, TableName, ColumnName;
```

The xmlColumnExplorer.sln sample project lets you explore xml columns and members of XmlSchemaCollections in the AdventureWorks database or those that you add to the Northwind database. All SQL Server 2005 Books Online examples for operations on xml columns use the AdventureWorks database, so you'll probably find this project to be of assistance when executing the sample code. By default, the first tab page displays all xml columns in the AdventureWorks database by executing the preceding query when loading.

The following query returns rows that include the xml_schema_collections.name and xml_namespace.name values for typed xml columns:

```
SELECT sys.schemas.name AS SchemaName, sys.tables.name AS TableName,
   sys.columns.name AS ColumnName, sys.xml_schema_collections.name AS XmlSchemaName,
   sys.xml_namespaces.name AS XmlNamespace
FROM sys.schemas, sys.tables, sys.columns, sys.xml_schema_collections,
   sys.xml_namespaces
WHERE sys.tables.schema_id = sys.schemas.schema_id
   AND sys.tables.object_id = sys.columns.object_id
   AND sys.xml_schema_collections.schema_id = sys.schemas.schema_id
   AND sys.xml_namespaces.xml_collection_id =
     sys.xml_schema_collections.xml_collection_id
   AND sys.columns.system_type_id = 241
ORDER BY SchemaName, TableName, ColumnName
```

The sys.columns.system_type_id *value of* 241 *represents a column of the* xml *data type.*

Clicking the sample project's Get Typed xml Columns button executes the preceding query and displays a DataGridViewRow for each XmlSchemaCollection namespace on the Tables with Typed xml Columns tab page, as shown in Figure 12-4. If you've added typed xml columns to the Northwind database with the NWxmlColumns project, clicking the Northwind (toggle) button displays them.

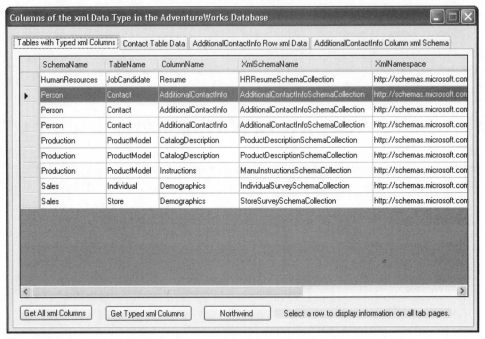

Figure 12-4

Selecting a row and the second tab page displays, by default, only the rows that contain content in the selected xml column, as shown in Figure 12-5.

Selecting a row that contains XML data displays the content in the third tab page, as shown in Figure 12-6. The AdditionalContactInfo column contains mixed content, which is highlighted in the figure. This proves that typed xml columns can handle mixed content, which causes problems for some XML-based applications — such as InfoPath 2003.

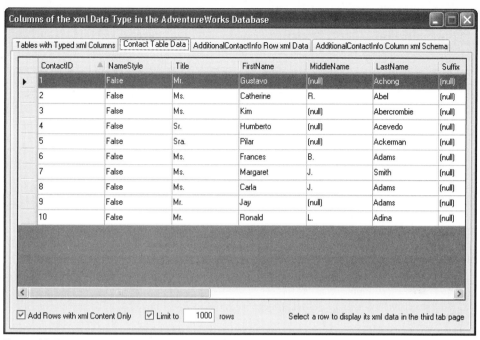

Figure 12-5

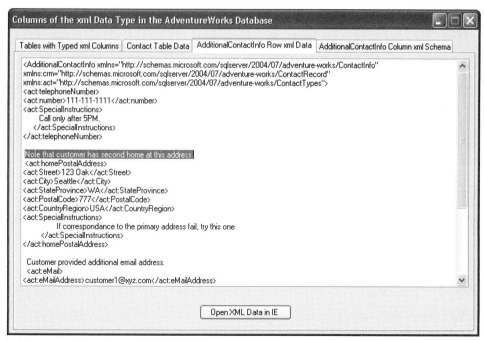

Figure 12-6

The fourth tab page displays the schema for the namespace you specify on the first tab page. Figure 12-7 shows the AdditionalContactInfo column's simple schema with one of the mixed content specifiers highlighted.

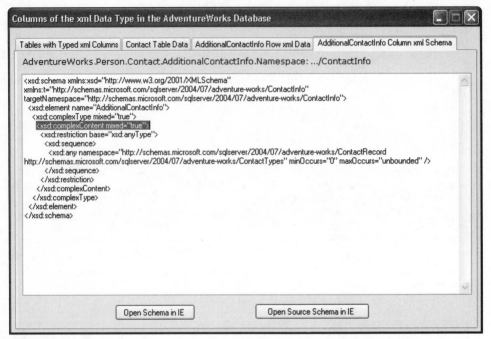

Figure 12-7

Execute XQuery Expressions

A thorough exposition of XQuery 1.0 and XPath 2.0 query syntax is beyond the scope of this book, but expressions specific to SQL Server 2005's XQuery implementation for xml columns deserve simple examples and a brief explanation.

The W3C XML Query Use Cases Working Draft at http://www.w3.org/TR/xquery-use-cases/ provides examples of abbreviated-syntax XQuery expressions that return values from individual documents. As an example, the following expressions return all author names from a bib.xml document:

```
doc("http://bstore1.example.com/bib.xml")//author
doc("C:\usecases\bib.xml")//author
```

The basic syntax for executing XQuery methods on xml columns is:

```
SELECT xmlColumn.XQueryMethod(XQueryExpressionString) FROM TableName
    [WHERE Criteria]

UPDATE xmlColumn.modify(XML_DDLExpressionString) FROM TableName
    [WHERE Criteria]
```

This statement returns all `Customer` documents from the CustomerXML1 column:

```
SELECT CustomerXML1.query('/Customer') FROM Customers;
```

The following statement uses an XML DDL expression to insert a `<Fax>` element into a specific `Customer` document specified by a `WHERE` constraint on a relational column:

```
UPDATE Customers SET CustomerXML1.modify('insert <Fax>(5) 555-3933 (Inserted)</Fax>
    as last into (/Customer)[1]') WHERE CustomerID = 'ANTON';
```

The `as last` modifier specifies that the `<Fax>` element is the last child of the `Customer` document. Other modifiers are `as first` (NodeExpression), `before` (NodeExpression), and `after` (NodeExpression).

This modified expression specifies the row to update without reference to a relational column as a `WHERE` constraint:

```
UPDATE Customers SET CustomerXML1.modify('insert <Fax>(5) 555-3933 (Inserted)</Fax>
    as last into (/Customer)[/Customer/CustomerID="ANTON"]');
```

> *`INSERT` and `DELETE` statements apply at the row level, so they aren't applicable to operations on `xml` column content.*

The sections that follow describe the XQuery methods and offer simple, abbreviated-syntax XQuery expressions that you can execute against the `xml` columns of the Customers and Orders tables. Most expressions are based on examples provided by the NWxmlColumns project's Customers XQuery and Orders XQuery tab pages.

XQuery Methods for xml Columns

Following are the five methods that the SQL Server 2005 XQuery engine supports for `xml` columns:

❑ `xmlColumn.query('expression')` returns a document, document node(s), or atomic value(s), depending on the XQuery `expression` string's value. The `query` method corresponds to a simple SQL `SELECT` statement that substitutes the result of executing `expression` for the column list.

❑ `xmlColumn.value('expression', 'SqlDataType')` returns a single atomic (scalar) value with the SQL Server data type that you specify as the `SqlDataType` argument value. The value method corresponds to a `SELECT 'expression'` statement executed by the `SqlCommand` `.ExcuteScalar` method. If `'expression'` returns a non-scalar value, more than one value, or the value can't be cast to the specified `SqlDataType`, the XQuery processor returns an error message.

❑ `xmlColumn.exist('expression')` returns 1 (true) if the item specified by `expression` exists or 0 (false) if the item doesn't exist (is null). The `exist` method is most useful for establishing `WHERE` clause constraints.

❑ `xmlColumn.nodes('expression')` returns an unnamed rowset that contains logical copies of the document instances contained in the specified `xml` column; `'expression'` specifies the context node. Invoking `value` methods on the rowset to return multiple scalar values lets you shred document instances into a relational table format.

❑ `xmlColumn.modify('expression')` executes one of three SQL Server 2005 XML DDL extensions — `insert`, `replace [value of]`, and `delete`, which usually operate on a single node or specified group of nodes.

Namespace Declarations and Case-Sensitivity

XQuery expressions consist of a prolog and body, which are separated by a semicolon. Documents that have element or attribute namespace prefixes require an XQuery prolog that includes the `declare namespace prefix="ValidUri";` instruction. Here's a modification of the earlier Customers query for the CustomerXML2 column, which has an `nwc` namespace prefix:

```
SELECT CustomerXML2.query('declare namespace
   nwc="http://www.northwind.com/schemas/Customer";
   /nwc:Customer') FROM Customers;
```

The default collation for SQL Server 2005 and its recent predecessors is case-insensitive for comparisons. XQuery expressions, however, are case-sensitive. Thus, namespace declarations must match the text *and* case of their document and schema counterparts. XQuery keywords and node names are case-sensitive also.

You specify multiple namespace prefixes by adding `declare namespace` instructions followed by a semicolon prolog terminator. Whitespace between multiple instructions is optional. Following is a more complex expression that returns `BillTo` nodes for all OrdersXML2 instances:

```
SELECT OrderXML2.query('declare namespace
   nwso="http://www.northwind.com/schemas/SalesOrder";
   declare namespace nwbt="http://www.northwind.com/schemas/BillTo";
   /nwso:SalesOrder/nwbt:BillTo') FROM Orders;
```

Alternatively, you can specify a default namespace for the returned node(s) with a `declare default namespace "AnyUri"` instruction.

Sample query Expressions

The simplest XQuery expression that you can execute is the following:

```
SELECT OrderXML1.query('/') FROM Orders
```

which returns all `Customer` document instances.

The following query returns the `Customer` instance for a `CustomerID` value of `WOLZA`:

```
SELECT CustomerXML1.query('(/Customer[/Customer/CustomerID="WOLZA"])')
   FROM Customers;
```

The highlighted expression (within brackets) is called a *predicate*, which returns a `boolean` *predicate truth value* that filters child nodes.

This query returns an `Order` instance for the specified (`integer`) `OrderID` element value:

```
SELECT OrderXML1.query('(/Order[/Order/OrderID=11076])') FROM Orders;
```

Replacing `[/Order/OrderID=11076]` with `[//OrderID=11076]` achieves the same result because there's only one instance of an `OrderID` element within the document.

You can substitute the other XQuery general comparison operators (`<`, `<=`, `!=`, `>=`, and `>`) for = in predicates. These operators can compare node sequences. Value comparison operators (`lt`, `le`, `eq`, `ne`, `ge`, and `gt`) compare atomic values of the same XML datatypes. XQuery also has the common numeric operators (`+`, `-`, `*`, and `/`).

`OrderID` is an attribute in `OrderXML2` instances, so you add an at-symbol (`@`) to specify an attribute value, as highlighted in this example:

```
SELECT OrderXML2.query('declare namespace
    nwso="http://www.northwind.com/schemas/SalesOrder";
    (/nwso:SalesOrder[/nwso:SalesOrder/@nwso:OrderID=11076])') FROM Orders;
```

The `@nwso:OrderID` and `11076` operands are atomic values, but the attribute value is `xs:untypedAny` in an untyped `xml` column and the 11076 literal is `xs:int`. The following expression with the highlighted value comparison returns an error with an untyped column; a typed column returns the expected node set:

```
SELECT OrderXML2.query('declare namespace
    nwso="http://www.northwind.com/schemas/SalesOrder";
    (/nwso:SalesOrder[/nwso:SalesOrder/@nwso:OrderID eq 11076])') FROM Orders;
```

XQuery offers numeric functions — `ceiling`, `floor`, and `round` — and aggregate functions — `count`, `sum`, `avg`, `max`, and `min`. String functions include `concat`, `contains`, `substring`, and `string-length`.

The following sections provide examples of `query` method expressions that are executed in combination with other method types, and use of several numeric, aggregate, and string functions.

Sample value Expressions

The following query returns `Wolski Zajazd` with a WHERE constraint that accepts an SQL Server `nvarchar(5)` value:

```
SELECT CompanyName FROM Customers WHERE
    CustomerXML1.value('(/Customer/CustomerID)[1]', 'nvarchar(5)') = 'WOLZA'
```

The `[1]` numeric predicate specifies a singleton (first) element from the document instance, which is required for most `value` expressions. The numeric predicate also assists the query optimizer in preparing the most efficient execution plan. If you omit the predicate and the expression returns more than one value, you receive an error message.

This variation with the OrdersXML2 column returns `Rattlesnake Canyon Grocery` with a WHERE constraint that accepts an `int` value:

```
SELECT ShipName FROM Orders
WHERE OrderXML2.value('declare namespace
    nwso="http://www.northwind.com/schemas/SalesOrder";
    /nwso:SalesOrder[1]/@nwso:OrderID[1]', 'int') = 11077;
```

The numeric predicates are optional in this case also, but they illustrate an alternative syntax that would retrieve the first `OrderID` value from the first `SalesOrder` node, if there were more than one of each.

Sample exist Expressions

The `exist` method is a logical operator that's usable as a `WHERE` constraint, as in the following example, which returns `Order` instances for shipment to U.S. addresses:

```
SELECT OrderXML1.query('/Order') FROM Orders
WHERE OrderXML1.exist('/Order[data(ShipCountry)="USA"]') = 1
```

The `data` function returns the typed value of the `ShipCountry` node if the `xml` column has an `XmlSchemaCollection`. ShipCountry is a `string`, so you can substitute the `string` function for the `data` function and achieve the same result.

This expression returns a singleton `Order` instance:

```
SELECT OrderXML1.query('/Order') FROM Orders
WHERE OrderXML1.exist('/Order[data(OrderID)=10262]') = 1
```

Substituting the `string` for the `data` function with a typed column results in an error message.

Here's a more complex variation that returns `BillTo` nodes for U.S. orders:

```
SELECT OrderXML2.query('declare namespace
    nwso="http://www.northwind.com/schemas/SalesOrder";
    declare namespace nwbt="http://www.northwind.com/schemas/BillTo";
    /nwso:SalesOrder/nwbt:BillTo') FROM Orders
WHERE OrderXML2.exist('declare namespace
    nwso="http://www.northwind.com/schemas/SalesOrder"; declare namespace
    nwbt="http://www.northwind.com/schemas/BillTo";
    /nwso:SalesOrder/nwbt:BillTo[data(nwbt:Country)="USA"]') = 1
```

You must add namespace declarations to the `exist` *expression for each namespace prefix it contains.*

The following query highlights the syntax for casting string literals to the `xs:dateTime` datatype for use with XQuery comparison operators to return `Order` instances for a range of dates:

```
SELECT OrderXML1.query('/Order') FROM Orders
    WHERE OrderXML1.exist('/Order[data(OrderDate) >=
        xs:dateTime("1996-07-10T00:00:00Z")]') = 1
    AND OrderXML1.exist('/Order[data(OrderDate) <=
        xs:dateTime("1997-07-10T00:00:00Z")]') = 1;
```

This alternative syntax uses the dot (.) selector to return the `OrderDate` context node's value:

```
SELECT OrderXML1.query('/Order') FROM Orders
    WHERE OrderXML1.exist('/Order/OrderDate[. >=
        xs:dateTime("1996-07-10T00:00:00Z")]') = 1
    AND OrderXML1.exist('/OrderOrderDate[. <=
        xs:dateTime("1997-07-10T00:00:00Z")]') = 1;
```

Multiple `exist` methods exact a performance penalty. Combining the two `OrderDate` expressions as emphasized in the following query reduces by about half the execution time of the preceding expression:

```
SELECT OrderXML1.query('/Order') FROM Orders
    WHERE OrderXML1.exist('/Order/OrderDate[. >=
      xs:dateTime("1996-07-10T00:00:00Z") and
      . <= xs:dateTime("1997-07-10T00:00:00Z")]') = 1
```

The performance improvement is about 15 to 20 percent with PRIMARY and PROPERTY XML indexes on the OrderXML1 column.

Sample nodes Expressions

The `nodes` method returns a rowset that consists of logical copies of the document instances that you specify with the following generic expression:

```
xmlColumn.nodes(/ContextNode) AS RowSet(Columns)
```

You can't execute a SELECT XQuery expression against the node copies directly because the copies aren't materialized. You must use the new T-SQL CROSS APPLY operator to expose the node copies to an XQuery SELECT expression. The CROSS APPLY operator lets you invoke a table-valued function (TVF) on each row returned by a query. The `xmlColumn.nodes(/ContextNode)` expression serves as the TVF. Alternatively, you can substitute the OUTER APPLY operator, which returns NULL values for missing instances. CROSS APPLY returns NULL values for elements that are missing in an instance.

One of the most useful features of the `nodes` method is its capability to return multiple atomic (scalar) values as columns of a relational rowset. You shred the instances with a SELECT statement whose column list consists of comma-separated `Columns.value('NodeName', 'data type') AS ColumnName` expressions.

The following query returns a relational resultset from OrdersXML1 column instances for Rattlesnake Canyon Grocery (RATTC):

```
SELECT Columns.value('./OrderID', 'int') AS OrderID,
    Columns.value('./EmployeeID', 'int') AS EmployeeID,
    CONVERT(datetime, Columns.value('./OrderDate', 'varchar(19)'), 126)
        AS OrderDate,
    CONVERT(datetime, Columns.value('./RequiredDate', 'varchar(19)'), 126)
        AS RequiredDate,
    CONVERT(datetime, Columns.value('./ShippedDate', 'varchar(19)'), 126)
        AS ShippedDate,
    Columns.value('./ShipVia', 'int') AS ShipVia,
    Columns.value('./Freight', 'money') AS Freight,
    -- Ship... elements omitted for brevity
FROM Orders
CROSS APPLY OrderXML1.nodes('/Order') AS RowSet(Columns)
WHERE OrderXML1.exist('/Order[data(CustomerID)="RATTC"]') = 1
ORDER BY OrderXML1.value('/Order[1]/OrderID[1]', 'int') DESC;
```

The CONVERT *operator and truncation of* xs:datetime *string values is required for the* datetime *data type because SQL Server's ISO-8601 date format (*126*) won't accept the trailing* z *(Zulu or UTC) indicator or time-zone offsets. The* '/Order' *node name is required in the nodes expression; using* '.' *returns an error message.*

You can execute the preceding query from the NWxmlColumns project's Orders XQuery page by selecting the Nodes (Shred) option and clicking Execute XQuery. A DataGridView displays the resulting rowset, as shown in Figure 12-8.

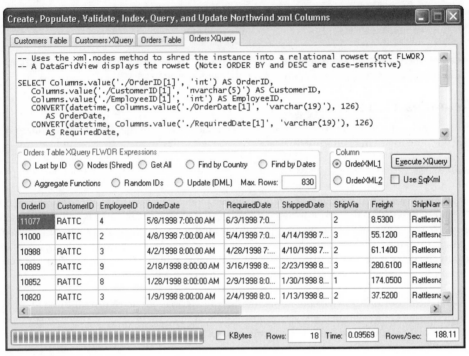

Figure 12-8

Sample modify Expressions

The following three statements and expressions add, modify the value of, and delete a `<Fax>` element for a `Customer` instance:

```
UPDATE Customers SET CustomerXML1.modify('insert <Fax>(5) 555-3933 (Inserted)</Fax>
as last into (/Customer)[1]') WHERE CustomerID = 'ANTON';
UPDATE Customers SET CustomerXML1.modify('replace value of
(/Customer/Fax[1])[1] with "(5) 555-3934 (Modified)"') WHERE CustomerID = 'ANTON';
UPDATE Customers SET CustomerXML1.modify('delete /Customer[1]/Fax')
WHERE CustomerID = 'ANTON';
```

Even a minor update to an `xml` document instance requires you to extract the entire instance, modify the instance, and reinsert it in the column. Thus, increasing document size reduces the performance of modify operations. XML indexes also impose a performance toll on the `modify` method.

The first statement appeared in the section "Execute XPath and XQuery Expressions" section, but is repeated here for completeness.

This statement and expression updates the `ShipperID` attribute value to 1 in all `OrdersXML2` instances for U.S. customers:

```
UPDATE Orders SET OrderXML2.modify('declare namespace
  nwso="http://www.northwind.com/schemas/SalesOrder";
  replace value of (/nwso:SalesOrder/@nwso:ShipperID)[1] with xs:unsignedByte(1)')
WHERE ShipCountry = 'USA';
```

You can edit the preceding statement to compare UPDATE performance with WHERE constraints that use `exist` method expressions. The execution time difference is negligible.

FLWOR XQuery Expressions

Section 3.8, "FLWOR Expressions," of W3C's "XQuery 1.0: An XML Query Language" specification defines an SQL-like syntax to add support for node iteration, intermediate variable binding, joins between documents, element or attribute construction, and ordering of results. The FLWOR acronym, pronounced "flower" as you'd expect, derives from the syntax's basic keywords — for, let, order by, where, and return. SQL Server 2005's FLWOR implementation doesn't support the let keyword, which is an alternative to the for clause, and is missing a few minor modifier keywords. However, these omissions aren't likely to impair your ability to emulate basic SQL SELECT statements and XSLT-like features.

The following table compares T-SQL and basic FLWOR clauses for SELECT operations.

SQL Clause	FLWOR Clause
`SELECT table1.xmlColA, table1 .xmlColB, table2.xmlColC`	`return $varA (! $varB or $varC)`
`FROM table1, table2`	`for $varA in /path1 (! for $varB in /path1 or for $varA in /path2)`
`WHERE`	`where`
`ORDER BY`	`order by`

Unlike XQuery expressions for conventional document instances, you can't create joins between instances in two xml columns. SQL Server 2005 XQuery methods are limited to operations on a single xml column. Thus you can't set the value of $varB from xmlColB or $varC from xmlColC, which is in a different table. However, you can use the sql:column function to include values from relational columns from the same or another table in the query result document instance, as described in the section "The sql:column Function, Joins, and Conditional Expressions," later in this chapter.

Following is the simplest XQuery expression you can write:

```
SELECT CustomerXML1.query('for $Result in /Customer return $Result')
FROM Customers;
```

which returns all Customer instances. Unlike the earlier simplest query method example, the path must contain at least the root node name; a / without a node name returns an error message.

Selecting Get All (FLWOR) and clicking Execute XQuery on the NWxmlColumns project's Customers XQuery tab page project executes the preceding query.

Adding a `where` constraint returns those instances that comply with the `where` expression. As an example, the following two expressions return orders for Alfreds Futterkiste:

```
SELECT OrderXML1.query('for $Result in /Order
where /Order/CustomerID="ALFKI" return $Result') FROM Orders;

SELECT OrderXML1.query('for $Result in /Order
where $Result/CustomerID="ALFKI" return $Result') FROM Orders;
```

The preceding FLWOR expression eliminates the need for a separate WHERE `OrderXML1.value('/Order[1]/CustomerID[1]', 'nvarchar(5)') = 'ALFKI'` constraint. However, the query performs a full table scan and returns empty (zero-length string) instances for orders that don't match the ALFKI criterion.

The following expression substitutes a `where` expression for the sample `OrderXML1.exist(...)` method expression for a date range and returns the resulting instances in descending OrderID order.

```
SELECT OrderXML1.query('for $Result in /Order
where $Result/OrderDate >= xs:dateTime("1996-07-10T00:00:00Z") and
$Result/OrderDate <= xs:dateTime("1997-07-10T00:00:00Z") return $Result')
FROM Orders ORDER BY OrderXML1.value('/Order[1]/OrderID[1]', 'int') DESC;
```

The ORDER BY expression must use the `OrderXML1.value(...)` method because an `order by` expression within the FLWOR query operates on the current instance, not the collection of instances returned by the SELECT statement. This statement returns empty instances for out-of-range OrderDate values.

To test the preceding expressions that contain `where` constraints, select the Get All query on the Orders XQuery tab page, edit the default expression, and click Execute XQuery. Notice that the Rows text box displays 830 for any `where` constraint. (The Rows value will differ if you've added or deleted Orders table rows.) Compare the number of rows returned by the last query with the 303 rows returned by executing the Find by Dates query.

Element and Attribute Constructors

XQuery includes *XML constructors*, which let you emulate XSLT transformations of XML documents. Constructors generate document, element, attribute, text, comment, and processing instruction nodes. A *direct element constructor* uses constants for element names and supports expressions, which must be enclosed by French braces, for element values.

Following is an example of a direct element and attribute constructor expression that generates instances with renamed Customer elements:

```
SELECT CustomerXML1.query('for $Result in /Customer return
<USCustomer CustomerID="{data($Result/CustomerID[1])}">
  <Name>{data($Result/CompanyName)}</Name>
  <Contact>{concat("Attn: ", data($Result/ContactName[1]), ", ",
    data($Result/ContactTitle[1]))}</Contact>
  <Street>{data($Result/Address)}</Street>
  <City>{data($Result/City)}</City>
  <State>{data($Result/Region)}</State>
```

```
    <ZIPCode>{data($Result/PostalCode)}</ZIPCode>
  </USCustomer>')
FROM Customers WHERE Country = 'USA';
```

Figure 12-9 shows part of the preceding query and the first instance produced by the preceding query, which also demonstrates use of the concat function.

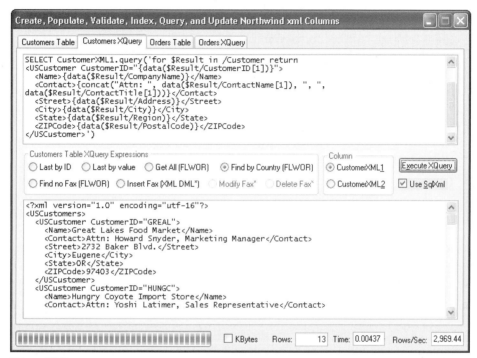

Figure 12-9

Selecting Find by Country (FLWOR) and clicking Execute XQuery on the Customers XQuery tab page executes the preceding query.

Element constructors are especially useful when creating instances with elements whose values are returned by XQuery aggregate functions. The following query demonstrates use of count, sum, and average aggregate functions, plus round and string functions, with SalesOrder instances:

```
SELECT OrderXML2.query('declare namespace
nwso="http://www.northwind.com/schemas/SalesOrder";
for $Result in /nwso:SalesOrder return
<SalesOrder>
  <SalesOrderNum>{data($Result/@nwso:OrderID)}</SalesOrderNum>
  <SalesOrderDate>{data($Result/@nwso:OrderDate)}</SalesOrderDate>
  <LineItemsCount>{count($Result/nwso:LineItems/nwso:LineItem)}</LineItemsCount>
  <LineItemsValue>{concat("$", xs:string(round(sum($Result/nwso:LineItems/
    nwso:LineItem/nwso:Extended))))}</LineItemsValue>
  <LineItemsAverage>{concat("$", xs:string(round(avg($Result/nwso:LineItems/
    nwso:LineItem/nwso:Extended))))}</LineItemsAverage>
</SalesOrder>') FROM SalesOrders;
```

You must use the `string` *function to concatenate string constants or variables with numeric values. The pairs of lines split at* `nwso:LineItems/` *for the book's line-length limitation must be single lines to execute correctly.*

Here's the first instance returned by the preceding query:

```
<SalesOrder>
  <SalesOrderNum>10248</SalesOrderNum>
  <SalesOrderDate>1996-07-04T00:00:00</SalesOrderDate>
  <LineItemsCount>3</LineItemsCount>
  <LineItemsValue>$440</LineItemsValue>
  <LineItemsAverage>$147</LineItemsAverage>
</SalesOrder>
```

Selecting Aggregate Functions and clicking Execute XQuery on the Orders XQuery tab page executes the preceding query, which runs against the OrderXML2 column only.

The sql:column Function, Joins, and Conditional Expressions

As mentioned earlier, you can use the `sql:column` function to supply relational values to direct element or attribute constructors. The generic syntax of this function is:

```
sql:column("[SchemaName.][TableName.]ColumnName")
```

If the column is in another table, you must specify a join between the other table's column and a value expression from the document instance, if you haven't promoted a calculated column for the property.

FLWOR also has keywords for `if`, `then`, and `else` conditional expressions, whose counterparts are available only in T-SQL stored procedures.

This FLWOR query demonstrates the use of a conditional expression with an `sql:column` function and a join of the Customers.CustomerID column with the value of the `Order` instance's `CustomerID` element:

```
SELECT OrderXML1.query('for $Result in /Order return
<Order>
  <OrderDate>{data($Result/OrderDate)}</OrderDate>
  <OrderID>{data($Result/OrderID)}</OrderID>
  <ShipName>{data($Result/ShipName)}</ShipName>
  <ShipPhone>{sql:column("Customers.Phone")}</ShipPhone>
  {if (not(empty(sql:column("Customers.Fax")))) then
    <ShipFax>{sql:column("Customers.Fax")}</ShipFax>
  else ()}
</Order>')
FROM Orders, Customers WHERE
  OrderXML1.exist('/Order/OrderDate[. >=
    xs:dateTime("1996-07-10T00:00:00Z") and
    . <= xs:dateTime("1997-07-10T00:00:00Z")]') = 1 AND
  Customers.CustomerID = OrderXML1.value('(/Order/CustomerID)[1]', 'nvarchar(5)');
```

The preceding FLWOR expression also illustrates use of the XQuery `not` and `empty` logical functions. Figure 12-10 shows the sample project's Orders XQuery tab page displaying part of the preceding query and the first result instances.

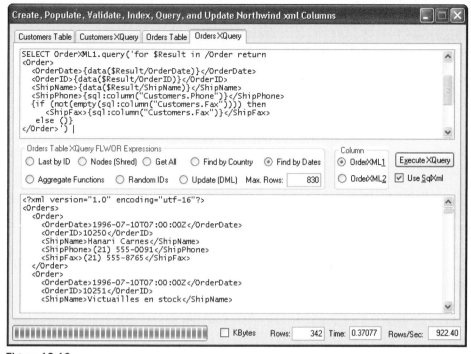

Figure 12-10

Here's the full version of the first two instances returned by the preceding query:

```
<Order>
  <OrderDate>1996-07-10T00:00:00</OrderDate>
  <OrderID>10253</OrderID>
  <ShipName>Hanari Carnes</ShipName>
  <ShipPhone>(21) 555-0091</ShipPhone>
  <ShipFax>(21) 555-8765</ShipFax>
</Order>
<Order>
  <OrderDate>1996-07-11T00:00:00</OrderDate>
  <OrderID>10254</OrderID>
  <ShipName>Chop-suey Chinese</ShipName>
  <ShipPhone>0452-076545</ShipPhone>
</Order>
```

The second instance omits the `ShipFax` element as a result of the conditional `if (not(empty...))` `then` test. The `else` keyword with parenthesis is required, regardless of whether you supply an `else` expression.

> *Selecting Find By Country and clicking Execute XQuery on the Orders XQuery tab page executes the preceding query.*

The SQL Server XQuery engine also supports `some`, `every`, and `satisfies` keywords for quantified expressions, which are beyond the scope of this chapter.

Execute XQuery Expressions with Code

The CustomersXQuery.vb and OrdersXQuery.vb files start with the code that generates the sample XQuery expressions. Most expression code uses the `Replace` function to modify the basic CustomerXML1 and OrderXML1 expressions to accommodate the more complex CustomerXML2 and OrderXML2 instances.

Many of the sample project's XQuery expression examples return multiple document instances, in which case the single-instance `SqlCommand.ExecuteXmlReader` method isn't applicable. Instead, invoking the `SqlCommand.ExecuteReader` method creates an `SqlDataReader` that iterates and returns the instances as `SqlXml` objects by invoking the `SqlDataReader.GetSqlXml(0)` method. Alternatively, you can return untyped `Objects` by invoking the `SqlDataReader.GetValue(0)` method.

The following abbreviated version of the NwXmlCols.vb file's `GetXQueryResult` function executes the XQuery expression (`strXQuery`) and returns a formatted string of one or more instances enclosed within a `<Root>` element:

```
Private Function GetXQueryResultShort(ByVal strXQuery As String,
  ByVal strRoot As String) As String
    Dim xrResult As XmlReader
    Dim xwSettings As XmlWriterSettings
    Dim xwResult As XmlWriter = Nothing
    sbXML = New StringBuilder()    'Private-scope variable
    xwSettings = New XmlWriterSettings
    With xwSettings
        .Encoding = Encoding.Unicode
        .Indent = True
        .IndentChars = ("  ")
        .OmitXmlDeclaration = False
        .ConformanceLevel = ConformanceLevel.Document
    End With
    'Create an XmlWriter to format the result
    xwResult = XmlWriter.Create(sbXML, xwSettings)
    cmNwind.CommandText = strXQuery
    cnNwind.Open()
    Dim sdrData As SqlDataReader
    sdrData = cmNwind.ExecuteReader
    With sdrData
        If .HasRows Then
            Dim xmlData As SqlXml
            xwResult.WriteStartElement(strRoot)
            While .Read
                xmlData = .GetSqlXml(0)
                xrResult = xmlData.CreateReader
                xrResult.MoveToContent()
                'Add the instances to the StringBuilder
                xwResult.WriteNode(xrResult, False)
            End While
            'Add the end element
            xwResult.WriteEndElement()
            xwResult.Flush()
            xwResult.Close()
        End If
```

```
      End With
      Return sbXML.ToString
   End Function
```

SqlXml objects outperform untyped Objects by about 15 percent for documents that have an average size of 560 bytes (OrderXML1) to 3.7KB (OrderXML2), despite the overhead of formatting the instances with an XmlWriter. Thus, the project uses SqlXml as the default, except for XQuery examples that return scalar values and the Random IDs query.

Clicking the Execute XML button's event handler invokes the GetXQueryResult function to return and display the resulting instance(s) in the lower text box. Alastair Dallas's Stopwatch class (http://www.codeproject.com/vb/net/vbnetstopwatch.asp) uses the QueryPerformanceCounter API to provide microsecond-resolution interval measurement for query execution. Writing the instance content from the XmlWriter's StringBuilder to the text box isn't included in the elapsed-time value.

The following simplified example, which is based on the ReadXmlSchemaCollection function, illustrates code to execute the XQuery expression by invoking the ExecuteXmlReader method and save the result to a file with an XmlTextWriter:

```
Private Sub SaveSingleInstance(ByVal strXQuery As String,
  ByVal strXmlFile As String)
    'Execute strXQuery and save result to a file with an XmlTextWriter
    cmNwind.CommandText = strXQuery
    cnNwind.Open()
    Dim xrXQuery As XmlReader = cmNwind.ExecuteXmlReader
    cnNwind.Close()
    Dim xtwXQuery As New XmlTextWriter(strXmlFile, Encoding.Unicode)
    xtwXQuery.Formatting = Formatting.Indented
    xrXQuery.MoveToContent()
    With xtwXQuery
        .WriteNode(xrXQuery, False)
        .Flush()
        .Close()
    End With
    xrXQuery.Close()
End Sub
```

Evaluate Performance Effects of Data Model Choices

Obviously, the verbosity of xml columns' document instances negatively affects query and update performance. Dire warnings abound in the computer press about network overloads caused by moving bloated XML documents instead of the compact binary representation of relational data. Script-laden HTML pages — especially pages containing images — display similar bloat, although the increasing use of gzip HTTP 1.1 compression ameliorates this issue except for bitmapped graphics. You can minimize storage requirements by applying lossless compression algorithms to original XML documents that you store in varbinary(max) columns, but you lose text search capability and consume substantial CPU resources to compress and decompress the content.

Performance and resource consumption are vital issues for developers who face the requirement to generate, validate, store, modify, and transport XML documents. As mentioned earlier in the chapter, indexing xml columns speeds most XQuery query, value, and exists operations at the expense of SQL Server UPDATE and XQuery modify operations. At this early point in SQL Server 2005's lifecycle, it's difficult — perhaps impossible — to anticipate the XML index combinations that strike the right balance between these competing factors, and the structure and volatility of xml column content.

> *The "Performance Optimizations for the XML Data Type" white paper at* http://msdn.microsoft
> .com/library/en-us/dnsql90/html/sqloptxml.asp *states, "Analysis of the query workload
> is required to determine whether one or more of the secondary XML indexes are helpful. Index mainte-
> nance cost should be taken into account in measuring the overall benefit of indexing the XML data."*

You can accurately predict the effect of XML indexes on xml column population with UPDATE operations only by running a test regimen on production hardware with document instances that reflect the size, complexity, and diversity of production versions. This rule also is true for testing how XML indexes affect the performance of query, value, exists, and modify methods. Finally, tests should run against tables having row counts that are representative of the production environment.

A reasonably complete index performance test suite, using the SalesOrders table as an example, consists of the following activities:

1. Populate the untyped OrderXML1 and OrderXML2 xml columns with randomized XML document instances. The average size of randomly generated OrderXML1 instances is 511 characters with whitespace and 449 characters without whitespace. OrderXML2 documents average 4,315 characters with whitespace and 3,648 characters without whitespace. Elapsed times include generating the document instance and updating the xml columns.

2. Obtain the elapsed time to generate the documents without performing the UPDATE operation. Subtract the value from the elapsed times to fill the xml columns. You need the net elapsed time to compare the effects of indexes on UPDATE operations accurately.

3. Repopulate the OrderXML1 and OrderXML2 columns with typed columns, PRIMARY-only, PRIMARY and PATH, PRIMARY and VALUE, PRIMARY and PROPERTY, and PRIMARY, PATH, and PROPERTY indexes. These tests predict the performance hit of indexes on column population.

4. Execute a suite of typical XQuery query, value, exists, and modify methods to predict the performance improvement gained by indexes on the first three methods and the penalty imposed on the modify method.

5. Optionally, analyze Showplan query optimization data to uncover XQuery expressions that demonstrate abnormally high I/O and CPU resource consumption. For more accurate data, substitute SET STATISTICS [XML] ON for SET SHOWPLAN[_XML] ON. STATISTICS XML and SHOWPLAN_XML are new SQL Server 2005 options.

> *To obtain representative performance comparisons, you should test your fixed disks for fragmentation. If
> the analyzer recommends it, defragment the volume on which you run SQL Server 2005 before or after
> creating the SalesOrders and SalesOrderItems tables. Running the tests with the four sample index
> configurations requires about 300MB of free disk space.*

The following sections describe a typical xml column and index performance test scenario with an autogenerated, 10,000-row SalesOrders table running under SQL Server 2005 Standard Edition on a single-CPU Dell server with Windows 2003 Server Standard Edition. The section "Hardware Used to

Create and Run the Sample Projects" in the Introduction describes the test hardware in detail. The sample FillSalesOrders and NWxmlColumns projects let you perform similar tests with any Windows 2000 or later operating system and a hardware configuration that meets Microsoft's recommendations — not minimum requirements — for VS 2005 and SQL Server or SQL Express 2005.

The \VB2005DB\Chapter12 folder contains a ShortFormInstructions.txt file that provides an abbreviated version of the next two sections' instructions.

Create and Fill the SalesOrders and SalesOrderItems Tables

The sample FillSalesOrders.sln project lets you create an up-to-date clone of the Northwind Orders and Order Details tables as SalesOrders and SalesOrderItems tables in the Northwind database.

When you first run FillSalesOrders from VS 2005 or start FillSalesOrders.exe, a message box asks if you want to create the two tables. Click Yes to execute the CreateSalesOrdersFromProject.sql script from the ...\bin folder, and click OK to acknowledge the message box that confirms the process.

If you've added the SalesOrders and SalesOrderItems tables previously, click the Truncate Tables button to open a message box that lets you choose whether to truncate or drop the tables. Click No to drop the tables and start over with an initial OrderID of 100001.

The initial form defaults create 10,000 SalesOrders records having OrderDate values that end with the system date. The OrderDate values start at an earlier date that's calculated from the Orders per Day values. Accept 50 Orders per Day as the Start value, set 50 as the End value to maintain a constant number of orders per month, and click Recalculate to estimate the ending date. To deliver a consistent number of records with the Find by Dates query, the End Date should be the last day of a recent month. Adjust the Start Date as necessary and click Recalculate to set an appropriate End Date, as shown in Figure 12-11.

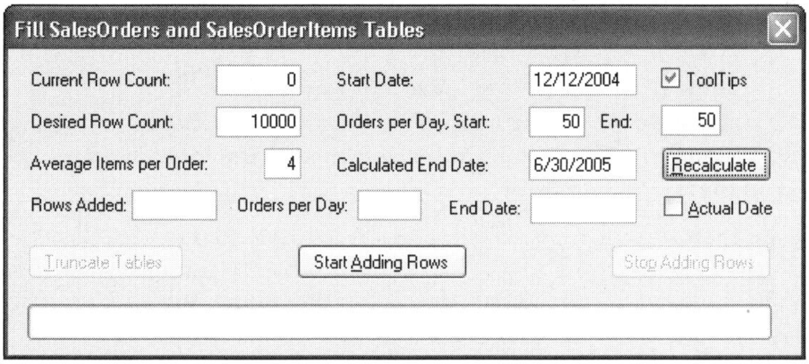

Figure 12-11

Optionally, mark the Actual Date checkbox and click Recalculate to run a test that determines the actual end date. Then clear the checkbox to enable the Start Adding Rows button. For this example, the two values match within a day or two.

Accept the remaining default values, and click the Start Adding Rows button to fill the tables with 10,000 Sales Orders records and approximately 41,000 SalesOrderItems records. Figure 12-12 shows the form as the project adds rows.

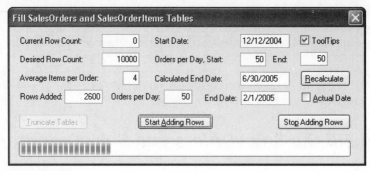

Figure 12-12

When addition completes, which usually takes less than a minute, the form expands to display the last SalesOrder and SalesOrderItems added, as shown in Figure 12-13. CustomerID, EmployeeID, ShipperID, and Freight values are random. The number of SalesOrderItems per SalesOrder varies randomly from 2 to 8 with an average of about 4. ProductID and Quantity values also are random. A table based on Quantity assigns Discount percentages.

Fill SalesOrders and SalesOrderItems Tables

Current Row Count:	10000
Desired Row Count:	10000
Average Items per Order:	4
Rows Added:	10000

Start Date: 6/30/2005   ☑ ToolTips
Orders per Day, Start: 52   End: 102
Calculated End Date: 6/30/2005   Recalculate
Orders per Day: 50   End Date: 6/29/2005   ☐ Actual Date

Truncate Tables   Start Adding Rows   Stop Adding Rows

OrderID:	110000	ShipName:	Piccolo und mehr
CustomerID:	PICCO	ShipAddress:	Geislweg 14
EmployeeID:	1	ShipCity:	Salzburg
OrderDate:	6/29/2005	ShipRegion:	
RequiredDate:	7/10/2005	ShipPostalCode:	5020
ShippedDate:	7/3/2005	ShipCountry:	Austria
ShipVia:	2	Freight:	$46.64

OrderID	ProductID	UnitPrice	Quantity	Discount
110000	50	$16.25	3	0.0%
110000	55	$24.00	23	20.0%
110000	56	$38.00	9	5.0%

|◄ ◄ 1 of 100 ► ►|

Figure 12-13

You can add more than 10,000 orders to start, if you have the patience and disk space. The two projects let you automatically add rows and populate xml *columns incrementally, so you can perform tests with more rows at any time.*

You now have the records that are required for generating XML documents to populate the SalesOrder table's OrdersXML1 and OrdersXML2 columns, so close the project to conserve resources.

Populate the SalesOrders Table's OrdersXML1 and OrdersXML2 Columns

Close all open applications, start NWxmlColumns.exe, and click OK to close the message box that lets you choose whether to use the SalesOrders table. After an initial delay induced by executing the DBCC CLEAN TABLE command, the form opens. Populate the default Customers columns by clicking Fill CustomerXML1 and Fill CustomerXML2. Open the Orders Table page, fill both Orders columns, and then mark the Use SalesOrders checkbox, which is enabled when the SalesOrders table is present. Accept 10000 in the Set Number of SalesOrders Rows to Update input box, and click OK.

Running NWxmlColumns.exe — rather than NWxmlColumns.sln — makes additional RAM resources available to SQL Server.

With the default Schema and Index selections, click Fill OrderXML1 to populate the untyped column; note the elapsed time. Click Fill OrderXML2 and again note the elapsed time. Figure 12-14 shows the SalesOrders Table page after filling the OrderXML2 column.

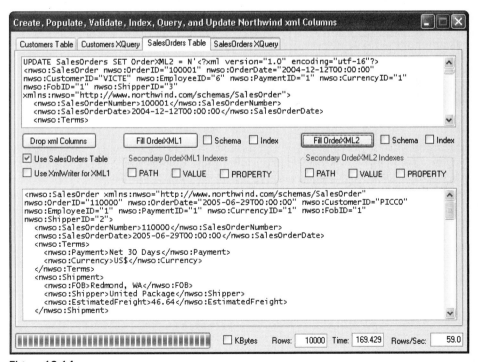

Figure 12-14

Obtain Baseline Times for Document Generation

One of the objectives of the test scenario is to isolate the elapsed time of bulk UPDATE operations from the effect of document generation, which is substantial for the XmlWriter used to populate the OrderXML2 column. The project includes an UpdateColumns application-level setting that you set as False to generate document instances without updating the columns.

> *The Orders/SalesOrders tab page has a Use XmlWriter for XML1 checkbox that lets you compare the performance of FOR XML AUTO, ELEMENTS, TYPE queries with an XmlWriter that uses the table's relational columns to generate the OrderXML1 document instance. The XmlWriter method is about ten times slower than the FOR XML AUTO query with no XML indexes.*

Close NWxmlColumns.exe, open the app.config file, locate the `<setting name="UpdateColumns" ...>` element, and change its `<value>` element value from True to False. Reopen NWxmlColumns.exe, and click Yes to dismiss the startup message. Repeat the preceding section's two fill operations, and note the completion times. Close the application, reset the UpdateColumns attribute to its original True value, and start a new session.

> *The baseline values are 4.023 seconds for OrderXML1 and 75.244 seconds for OrderXML2 with the hardware used to write this book. All time values in this chapter are based on VS 2005 release candidate and SQL Server 2005 September CTP, so you might find some differences with the release versions. However, the test suite's performance comparisons are relative — not absolute — so comparisons aren't likely to change dramatically.*

Re-create and Repopulate Typed Columns with Indexes

The SalesOrder tab page lets you add or drop the XmlSchemaCollection and PRIMARY XML indexes with or without secondary XML indexes of both xml columns. As mentioned earlier in the chapter, adding or dropping an XmlSchemaCollection requires dropping XML indexes, dropping the column, and then recreating and repopulating the column.

Adding or dropping XML indexes doesn't affect the column contents or XmlSchemaCollection, but you must mark the secondary index checkbox(es) you want to add before marking the associated Index checkbox. Clearing the Index checkbox drops all XML indexes on the column.

Determining the effect of XML indexes on xml column population time requires dropping, recreating, and repopulating the columns with the new index combination. Simply dropping and recreating the index(es) is much faster but doesn't yield useful performance measurements. The fastest method for starting over is to clear and mark the Schema checkbox. Adding an XmlSchemaCollection to both xml columns increases population time by about 40 percent and adds about 5 percent to the size of the sample database.

> *When you drop an XmlSchemaCollection, a message box lets you defer recreating previous indexes. If you're not testing population time with indexes, click Yes to prevent adding the previous indexes, repopulate the column, and then regenerate the index.*

Evaluate the Effect of XML Indexes on UPDATEs

As mentioned earlier in the chapter, adding XML indexes to xml columns has a profound effect on the performance of UPDATE and INSERT operations. If your application requires real-time addition of a large number of document instances to a table, such as when archiving Web services SOAP messages, adding indexes might reduce overall system scalability. Running the tests in the following two sections provides the initial data required for analyzing tradeoffs between update and query execution speed.

Populate xml Columns with New Instances

The following table compares the net elapsed time (total population time reduced by document generation time) to update 10,000 rows of empty OrderXML1 and OrderXML2 columns with randomized document instances. SQL Server Management Studio's *TableName* Properties dialog provides the Table Data Size. Index size is calculated from the number of pages reported by SMSS's *IndexName* Properties dialog after rebuilding the indexes to minimize fragmentation. All indexed data is based on typed xml columns.

Population Time, and Table and Index Size for 10,000 Rows	Net Order Population Time, Secs.		Table Data Size, MB	Index Size, MB (Defragmented)	
Columns and Indexes	**XML1**	**XML2**	**Both**	**XML1**	**XML2**
Untyped with No Indexes	8.52	64.63	78.13	N/A	N/A
Typed with No Indexes	11.69	90.43	84.84	N/A	N/A
PRIMARY Index	114.47	255.09	84.60	9.16	71.13
PRIMARY and PATH Indexes	166.28	513.49	84.84	15.30	120.87
PRIMARY and VALUE Indexes	130.30	339.49	84.79	15.29	120.83
PRIMARY and PROPERTY Indexes	131.15	322.56	84.62	15.2	98.39

The size of the SalesOrders table before adding the xml columns was 1.906MB with 0.964MB of relational indexes. The 10,000 OrderXML1 instances contain about 4,960,000 characters and OrderXML2 instances contain about 36,240,000 characters without whitespace. Multiplying by 2 for UTF-16 storage corresponds approximately to the 78.13MB data size for untyped columns with no indexes.

It's clear from the preceding table that PRIMARY XML indexes are heavyweight database objects — about the same size as the table data without secondary indexes and about 60 percent larger than the table data with a PATH or VALUE secondary index. Adding a primary index slows column updates by a factor of 10 for small (0.5MB) instances and about 2.5 for moderate-size (3.6MB) instances. Of the three secondary index options, a PROPERTY index adds the least index maintenance overhead and database growth. XML index size, not table data size, is the most important factor when planning storage resources for tables with xml columns.

Add XML Indexes to Populated xml Columns

It's obvious that you would bulk-populate xml columns by the NWxmlColumns project's techniques or BCP without XML indexes. Adding indexes after bulk operations is faster by at least an order of magnitude than for bulk UPDATE operations with XML indexes. The following table compares the times to add XML indexes to prepopulated typed XML columns.

Index Regeneration Times for 10,000 SalesOrders Rows	Regenerate Index, Seconds	
Column	OrderXML1	OrderXML2
PRIMARY Index	2.440	17.494
PRIMARY and PATH Indexes	6.261	41.511
PRIMARY and VALUE Indexes	8.131	45.535
PRIMARY and PROPERTY Indexes	3.534	27.318
PRIMARY, PATH, and PROPERTY	7.747	60.245

As was the case for column repopulation, the PROPERTY index has the least impact of the three secondary index types on index regeneration time. Adding more than one secondary index has the expected effect.

Analyze Improvement of XQuery Performance

The sole objective of XML indexes is to improve the performance of XQuery methods other than the modify function. In addition to demonstrating XQuery syntax, the sample SELECT queries of the SalesOrders XQuery tab page are designed to test the effect of XML indexes on all XQuery methods other than nodes. The following sections describe the sample queries and compare their performance with combinations of XML indexes. Elapsed time values—except for the Random IDs query—don't include the time to open the SqlConnection or the SqlDataReader, or the time to copy the data to the lower text box. The timer starts when SqlDataReader.HasRows returns True and stops after the instance appends to the StringBuilder. The Last by ID and Last by Value queries aren't included in the following analysis because these queries execute in less than a millisecond with or without indexes.

> *The execution times reported in the following sections are the least of three trials, which were executed without caching. When set to True, the ClearQueryCache configuration setting sends a DBCC FREEPROCCACHE instruction before executing the XQuery expression. You can monitor cache state by setting CheckCacheState to true. In this case, the program queries the sys.syscacheobjects system table and reports cache reference counts, use counts, and pages used after the expression executes.*

Return SHOWPLAN_XML or STATISTICS XML Data

Analyzing Showplan data is useful for determining queries' CPU and I/O resource consumption. Showplan reports query optimizer data for individual operations, such as row scans, joins, nested loops, table spools, and clustered index updates of optimized queries. The following generic batch returns a Showplan report as an XML document:

```
SET {SHOWPLAN_XML | STATISTICS XML} ON
GO
{SELECT | UPDATE} xmlColumn.method.XQueryExpression FROM TableName
    [WHERE {xmlColumn.exist.XQueryExpression | RelationalConstraint}]
GO
SET {SHOWPLAN_XML | STATISTICS XML} OFF
GO
```

SHOWPLAN_XML prepares an execution plan but doesn't execute the query. STATISTICS XML executes the query to provide actual compilation and execution costs.

You can save the instances returned by the preceding batch in an `xml` column of a dedicated Showplan table or as individual *ShowPlan*.xml files. XQuery expressions can return individual or aggregated `EstimateIO`, `EstimateCPU`, and `EstimatedTotalSubtreeCosts` attribute values for physical and logical operations (`PhysicalOp` and `LogicalOp`). Setting `STATISTICS XML ON` adds `<RunTimeInformation>` nodes with `ActualRows`, `ActualRebinds`, and `ActualRewinds` attribute values. In this case, the Showplan document appears in a second rowset that follows the query rowset.

Optimization of queries against `xml` columns is a much more complex process than that for queries against relational columns only. As an example, the Showplan document for the sample Find by Dates query against the OrdersXML2 column with three secondary indexes is 120KB without whitespace. A similar relational query generates a 5KB document. Much of the Showplan content consists of `<OutputList>` elements with mysterious `<ColumnReference Column="Expr1133" />` or similar child elements, which refer to elements or attributes of the `xml` column's instance.

The 60KB Showplanxml.xsd schema file for Showplan documents is in the \Program Files\Microsoft SQL Server\90\Tools\Binn\schemas\sqlserver\2003\03\showplan\ folder. The file contains minimal documentation.

The NWxmlColumns project's NwXmlCols.vb file includes a `ShowPlanXML` function, which executes `SHOWPLAN_XML` or `STATISTICS XML` for the sample query you select in the group box and displays the instance in the lower text box, as shown for the Find by Dates query in Figure 12-15.

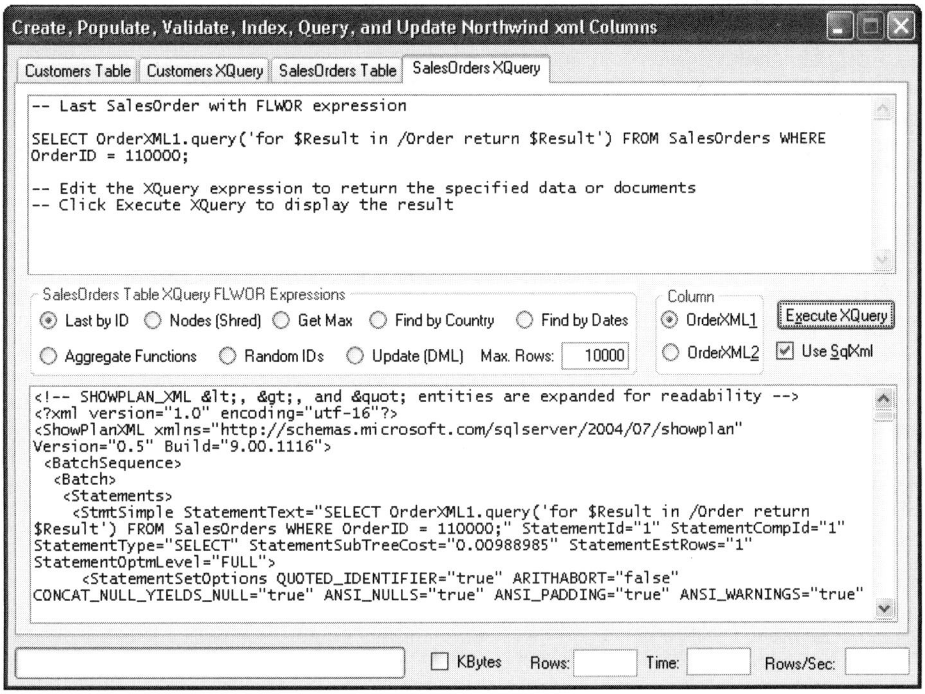

Figure 12-15

The `DisplayShowplanXML`, `DisplayStatisticsXML`, `ExpandShowplanEntities`, and `ShowplanInGrid` application-level settings, which are `False` by default, control if and how `ShowPlanXML` executes. Set `DisplayShowplanXML` to `True` to enable the function. Setting `DisplayStatisticsXML` to `True` executes the query before returning the content, which is time-consuming on slower machines. Setting `ExpandShowplanEntities` to `True` translates `&lt;`, `&gt;`, and `&quot;` to <, >, and " to improve readability but results in a malformed instance.

Setting `ShowplanInGrid` to `True` executes `SHOWPLAN_ALL` instead of `SHOWPLAN_XML` and displays the resultset in a `DataGridView` control. The grid makes it easier to compare `EstimateRows`, `EstimateIO`, `EstimateCPU`, `AverageRowSize`, and `TotalSubtreeCost` values for the sample queries, as shown for the Find by Dates query in Figure 12-16.

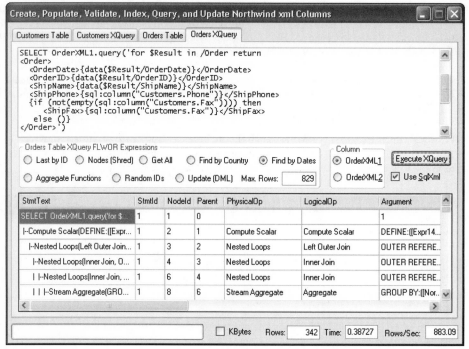

Figure 12-16

The code retrieves Showplan data prior to query execution, so edits you make to the query aren't reflected in the XML elements or grid columns. The grid doesn't appear if you specify `SHOWPLAN_XML` data.

Get Max

The Get Max FLWOR query returns the number of instances specified in the Max. Rows text box and displays the first million characters in the lower text box.

```
SELECT OrderXML1.query('for $Result in /Order return $Result')
FROM SalesOrders WHERE OrderXML1 IS NOT NULL;
```

The following table shows the time in seconds to execute the preceding expression against the OrderXML1 and OrdersXML2 columns.

Get Max (10,000 Rows)	OrderXML1	OrderXML2
No Indexes	4.882	26.571
PRIMARY XML Index	4.109	24.874
PRIMARY and PATH Indexes	4.124	25.484
PRIMARY and VALUE Indexes	4.149	25.364
PRIMARY and PROPERTY Indexes	4.170	25.269

The query performs a row scan in primary key order, so adding a PRIMARY XML index doesn't provide a significant performance improvement. Adding a secondary index slows execution slightly.

The query's WHERE constraint prevents you from testing rows without OrderXML1 content, which isn't applicable to the test examples. If you omit the WHERE xmlColumn IS NOT NULL constraint, the query optimizer adds it.

Find by Country

The Find by Country query returns an average of about 1,415 Order instances. The query's WHERE constraint uses the exist method, which benefits from XML indexing.

```
SELECT OrderXML1.query('for $Result in /Order return $Result')
FROM SalesOrders WHERE OrderXML1.exist('/Order[data(ShipCountry)="USA"]') = 1
```

The following table shows the time in seconds to return 1,417 Orders and SalesOrders instances.

Find by Country (1,417 Rows)	OrderXML1	OrderXML2
No Indexes	2.132	4.299
PRIMARY XML Index	1.155	2.198
PRIMARY and PATH Indexes	1.071	1.367
PRIMARY and VALUE Indexes	1.086	1.468
PRIMARY and PROPERTY Indexes	0.979	1.158
PRIMARY, PROPERTY, and PATH Indexes	0.986	1.200

In this case, adding a PRIMARY index provides a substantial performance boost, and any secondary XML index delivers an incremental improvement. Adding a PROPERTY index provides better query performance than a VALUE index. Adding PROPERTY and PATH indexes doesn't improve performance.

You can compare the performance of XML and relational indexes by replacing the original WHERE constraint with WHERE ShipCountry = 'USA', which emulates adding an indexed promoted column. The Orders and SalesOrders tables have a non-clustered index (IDX_ShipCountry) on the ShipCountry field. Executing the query with the modified constraint requires 0.647 seconds for OrdersXML1 and 1.634 seconds for OrdersXML2. This unexpected result for OrdersXML2 indicates that XML indexes optimize the response time of larger document instances.

Find by Dates

The Find by Dates FLWOR query returns a transformation of Orders and SalesOrders instances with a cross-domain join to the Customers table. The Customers table supplies the `<ShipPhone>` and, if present, the `<ShipFax>` element values. Here's the query for the OrdersXML1 column:

```
SELECT OrderXML1.query('for $Result in /Order return
<Order>
  <OrderDate>{data($Result/OrderDate)}</OrderDate>
  <OrderID>{data($Result/OrderID)}</OrderID>
  <ShipName>{data($Result/ShipName)}</ShipName>
  <ShipPhone>{sql:column("Customers.Phone")}</ShipPhone>
  {if (not(empty(sql:column("Customers.Fax")))) then
     <ShipFax>{sql:column("Customers.Fax")}</ShipFax>
   else ()}
</Order>')
FROM SalesOrders, Customers WHERE
OrderXML1.exist('/Order/OrderDate[.>= xs:dateTime("2004-12-12T00:00:00Z") and
   .<= xs:dateTime("2005-01-11T00:00:00Z")]') = 1 AND
Customers.CustomerID = OrderXML1.value('(/Order/CustomerID)[1]', 'nvarchar(5)');
```

The following table lists the time in seconds to execute the preceding FLWOR query.

Find by Dates (One exist Method, 1,666 Rows)	OrderXML1	OrderXML2
No Indexes	1.580	3.731
PRIMARY XML Index	1.188	2.531
PRIMARY and PATH Indexes	1.103	2.145
PRIMARY and VALUE Indexes	1.109	2.275
PRIMARY and PROPERTY Indexes	1.171	2.403
PRIMARY, PROPERTY, and PATH Indexes	1.117	2.248

The section "Sample exist Expressions," earlier in this chapter, mentioned that using multiple `exist` methods for OrderDate tests, as in the following query, exacts a performance penalty:

```
SELECT OrderXML1.query('for $Result in /Order return
<Order>
  <OrderDate>{data($Result/OrderDate)}</OrderDate>
  <OrderID>{data($Result/OrderID)}</OrderID>
  <ShipName>{data($Result/ShipName)}</ShipName>
  <ShipPhone>{sql:column("Customers.Phone")}</ShipPhone>
  {if (not(empty(sql:column("Customers.Fax")))) then
     <ShipFax>{sql:column("Customers.Fax")}</ShipFax>
   else ()}
</Order>')
FROM SalesOrders, Customers WHERE
OrderXML1.exist('/Order[data(OrderDate) >=
```

```
    xs:dateTime("2004-12-12T00:00:00Z")]') = 1 AND
OrderXML1.exist('/Order[data(OrderDate) <=
    xs:dateTime("2005-01-11T00:00:00Z")]') = 1 AND
Customers.CustomerID = OrderXML1.value('(/Order/CustomerID)[1]', 'nvarchar(5)');
```

This table reports the time in seconds to execute the preceding query.

Find by Dates (Two exist Methods, 1,666 Rows)	OrderXML1	OrderXML2
No Indexes	4.488	8.563
PRIMARY XML Index	1.921	3.574
PRIMARY and PATH Indexes	2.035	3.333
PRIMARY and VALUE Indexes	1.972	3.387
PRIMARY and PROPERTY Indexes	1.726	2.774
PRIMARY, PROPERTY, and PATH Indexes	1.733	2.786

In this case, the PRIMARY and PROPERTY indexes, rather than the PRIMARY and PATH indexes, provide better performance. The example also demonstrates that XML indexes can mask the full performance impact of non-optimized FLWOR queries.

Aggregate Functions

The following Aggregate Functions FLWOR query returns the counts, sums, and averages of <LineItems> child elements for all OrderXML2 column instances:

```
SELECT OrderXML2.query('declare namespace
    nwso="http://www.northwind.com/schemas/SalesOrder";
  for $Result in /nwso:SalesOrder return
<SalesOrder>
  <SalesOrderNum>{data($Result/@nwso:OrderID)}</SalesOrderNum>
  <SalesOrderDate>{data($Result/@nwso:OrderDate)}</SalesOrderDate>
  <LineItemsCount>{count($Result/nwso:LineItems/nwso:LineItem)}</LineItemsCount>
  <LineItemsValue>
    {concat("$",
xs:string(round(sum($Result/nwso:LineItems/nwso:LineItem/nwso:Extended))))}
  </LineItemsValue>
  <LineItemsAverage>
    {concat("$",
xs:string(round(avg($Result/nwso:LineItems/nwso:LineItem/nwso:Extended))))}
  </LineItemsAverage>
</SalesOrder>') FROM SalesOrders;
```

The following table reports execution time in seconds for the OrderXML2 column only because the OrderXML1 column doesn't have element values that can be aggregated.

Aggregate Functions (10,000 Rows)	OrderXML2
No Indexes	23.732
PRIMARY XML Index	21.922
PRIMARY and PATH Indexes	21.415
PRIMARY and VALUE Indexes	22.068
PRIMARY and PROPERTY Indexes	15.360
PRIMARY, PROPERTY, and PATH Indexes	15.601

In contrast to most previous examples, a PRIMARY XML index delivers little performance improvement. In this case, a PROPERTY secondary index is required to optimize query performance.

Random IDs

The following Random IDs FLWOR query returns the number of rows specified by the Max. Rows text box value with a constraint on the OrderID value:

```
SELECT OrderXML1.query('for $Result in /Order return $Result')
FROM SalesOrders
WHERE OrderXML1.exist('/Order/OrderID[.> 109990 and .<= 110000]') = 1;
```

Code in the sample application's btnExecuteOrders event handler in the OrdersXQuery.vb file executes the preceding expression the number of times specified in the Max. Rows text box. Thus, the default 10 Max. Rows value returns 100 rows. Starting OrderID values are random, which prevents caching the multiple query expressions.

The RandomIDs query uses the SqlDataReader.GetValues(0) method, which is slower than the GetSqlXml(0) method, but this query doesn't require an XmlReader and XmlWriter to return content for all instances. The sample project displays the first ten query expressions and the last instance of the query in the lower text box, as shown in Figure 12-17.

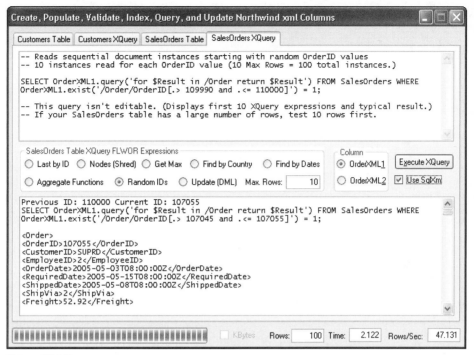

Figure 12-17

Following are the execution times in seconds for the Random IDs query with 100 as the Max. Rows value.

Random IDs (100 Repetitions, 10,000 Instances)	OrderXML1	OrderXML2
No Indexes	50.094	216.507
PRIMARY XML Index	18.381	89.012
PRIMARY and PATH Indexes	9.571	33.805
PRIMARY and VALUE Indexes	10.210	36.793
PRIMARY and PROPERTY Indexes	14.868	64.688
PRIMARY, PATH, and VALUE Indexes	9.986	35.041

The preceding query is another example of substantial performance improvement by adding any secondary XML index. In this case, the PATH secondary index delivers the optimum result, followed by the PATH index.

Executing this simpler XQuery expression instead of the preceding FLWOR query produces unexpected results:

```
SELECT OrderXML1.query('(/Order[./OrderID > 109990 and ./OrderID <= 110000])')
FROM SalesOrders;
```

The `SqlDataReader` executed by the `GetXQueryResults` procedure in the NwXmlCols.vb file returns an average of about 5,000 empty (zero-length, not NULL) `SqlXml` instances before returning the `xml` column content for each random starting OrderID value. The empty instances indicate that the XQuery engine doesn't treat the starting OrderID value as the equivalent of a `WHERE` clause criterion. Returning empty rows causes severe performance degradation, regardless of the XML index(es) in use.

You can test the preceding XQuery expression by setting the `UseFLWORForRandomIDs` configuration setting value to `False`. In this case, the lower text box reports the total number of `SqlXml` instances returned, as illustrated by Figure 12-18.

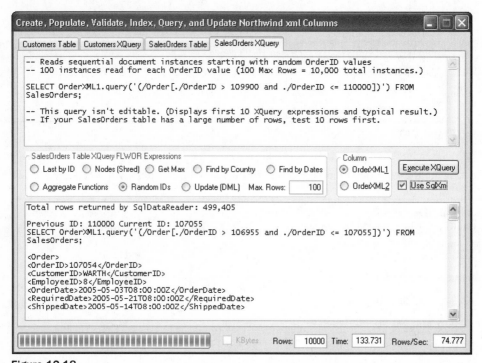

Figure 12-18

Update (DDL)

This XML DDL instruction demonstrates the effect of one or more indexes on a simple update to the `ShipVia` element value of the OrderXML1 column:

```
UPDATE SalesOrders SET OrderXML1.modify('replace value of
   (/Order/ShipVia/text())[1] with "1"')
WHERE ShipCountry = 'USA' AND OrderXML1 IS NOT NULL;
```

Updating an instance requires the XQuery engine to extract the instance, perform the update, reinsert the modified instance into the row, and update the column's index(es). Updates to multiple nodes or atomic values require a `modify` operation for each update. The following table demonstrates the effect of indexes on the `modify` method.

Update (DDL) (1,417 Rows)	OrderXML1	OrderXML2
No Indexes	2.188	4.345
PRIMARY XML Index	5.037	36.492
PRIMARY and PATH Indexes	6.458	52.408
PRIMARY and VALUE Indexes	7.072	56.532
PRIMARY and PROPERTY Indexes	7.218	46.145
PRIMARY, PROPERTY, and PATH Indexes	8.764	76.541

The preceding data corresponds approximately to comparisons of the effect of PRIMARY and secondary indexes on bulk updates in the section "Re-create and Repopulate Typed Columns with Indexes," earlier in this chapter. If your application needs to make frequent modifications to document instances, index maintenance might become the critical bottleneck.

Conclusions

It's clear from the elapsed times reported in the preceding tables that PRIMARY indexes deliver the greatest performance boost for queries other than simple table scans, such as the Get Max query. However, predicting the most effective secondary index for a particular XQuery expression isn't easy. A PROPERTY index provides the greatest performance increase for the sample queries other than Get by Dates and Random IDs. This index also has the least impact on UPDATE operations, including indexed column population time, and its size for the more complex OrderXML2 column is about 20 percent smaller than the other two choices. If a PRIMARY index doesn't satisfy your performance requirements, try adding a PROPERTY index first.

Summary

The native `xml` data type is one of the most important additions to SQL Server 2005. The `xml` data type enables you to store related document instances in special-purpose `varchar(max)` columns. Optional `XmlSchemaCollections` apply strong-typing and validate instances on content insertion or modification. XQuery expressions return the instances, subnodes, or values you specify, and FLWOR queries let you customize the structure of the returned instance. Optional PRIMARY and three types of secondary XML indexes — PATH, VALUE, and PROPERTY — improve performance of most SELECT queries but slow instance insertions and modifications.

SQL Server 2005 SELECT statements support four XQuery methods: `query`, `exist`, `value`, and `nodes`. The `query` method returns the result of an XPath 2.0 expression or FLWOR query. Invoking the `SqlCommand.ExecuteXmlReader` method returns the query result from the first document instance to an `XmlWriter` for processing. Queries that return data from multiple rows require an `SqlDataReader`, which returns nodes as instances of the `SqlXml` type that you process with an `XmlReader` and `XmlWriter`. The `exist` and `value` methods most commonly supply values for `WHERE` clauses and joins. The `exist` method returns `1` if the node specified in the XQuery expression exists or an atomic value specified matches that of the corresponding node in an instance. Otherwise the method returns `0`. The `value` method requires an expression that returns a single atomic value, which you cast to an SQL Server data type, such as `int`. The sample NWxmlColumns.sln project has XQuery expression examples for each `SELECT` query method except `nodes`, which most commonly shreds instances to return relational resultsets.

The XQuery 1.0 specification doesn't include data manipulation keywords that are equivalent to SQL's `INSERT`, `UPDATE`, and `DELETE` keywords. The editors of the specification intended XQuery 1.0 to be limited to returning — not modifying — data. Microsoft's proprietary XML DML extension to the XQuery `modify` method enables you to execute `insert`, `replace value of`, and `delete` expressions. The sample project's XQuery expressions also illustrate use of all XML DML keywords.

Adding optional XML `PRIMARY` and secondary `PATH`, `VALUE`, or `PROPERTY` indexes increases execution speed of most XQuery `query`, `exist`, and `value` expressions. The SQL Server 2005 query optimizer references XML indexes when generating execution plans. An index performance test regimen shows that XML indexes slow `xml` column population and content updates with the `modify` method. The impact of XML indexes on update operations is substantially greater than that of corresponding relational indexes. Comparing the execution time of the NWxmlColumns project's sample XQuery expressions aids in selecting the optimum secondary index for typical queries.

Index

Index

powered by
books24x7

Take your library wherever you go

Now you can access more than 70 complete Wrox books online, wherever you happen to be! Every diagram, description, screen capture, and code sample is available with your subscription to the **Wrox Reference Library**. For answers when and where you need them, go to wrox.books24x7.com and subscribe today!

Find books on
- ASP.NET
- C#/C++
- Database
- General
- Java
- Mac
- Microsoft Office
- .NET
- Open Source
- PHP/MySQL
- SQL Server
- Visual Basic
- Web
- XML

www.wrox.com